T0133371

Digitizing Medieval and
Early Modern Material Culture

New Technologies in Medieval and Renaissance Studies
Volume 3

Series edited by
William R. Bowen and Raymond G. Siemens

ITER

MEDIEVAL AND RENAISSANCE TEXTS AND STUDIES
VOLUME 426

Digitizing Medieval and Early Modern Material Culture

Edited by
Brent Nelson, University of Saskatchewan
Melissa Terras, University College London

Iter: Gateway to the Middle Ages and Renaissance
Toronto, Ontario
in collaboration with
ACMRS
(Arizona Center for Medieval and Renaissance Studies)
Tempe, Arizona
2012

The publication of this volume has been greatly assisted by a grant from the University of Saskatchewan.

Published by Iter, Inc., Toronto, Ontario and
ACMRS (Arizona Center for Medieval and Renaissance Studies)
Tempe, Arizona

Library of Congress Cataloging-in-Publication Data

Digitizing medieval and early modern material culture / edited by Brent Nelson, University of Saskatchewan; Melissa Terras, University College London.
        pages cm. -- (New technologies in medieval and Renaissance studies ; volume 3) (Medieval and Renaissance texts and studies ; volume 426)
    Includes bibliographical references.
    ISBN 978-0-86698-474-4 (alk. paper)
1. Humanities--Research--Methodology. 2. Material culture--Research--Methodology. 3. Learning and scholarship--Technological innovations.
4. Communication in learning and scholarship--Technological innovations.
5. Library materials--Digitization. 6. Archival materials--Digitization.
7. Manuscripts--Digitization. 8. Document markup languages. 9. Humanities--Digital libraries. 10. Information storage and retrieval systems--Humanities.
I. Nelson, Brent, 1966- II. Terras, Melissa M.
    AZ186.D54 2012
    025.8'4--dc23

                                                              2012010561

ISBN 978-0-86698-499-7 (online)

∞
This book is made to last. It was typeset in SIL Gentium, smyth-sewn and printed on acid-free paper to library specifications. Printed in the United States of America

For the boys:
Elias and Jesse
Anthony, Edward, and Fergusson

Contents

Introduction*

Brent Nelson
University of Saskatchewan
brent.nelson@usask.ca

Melissa Terras
University College London
m.terras@ucl.ac.uk

As much as digital media have enabled new and innovative approaches to the study of medieval and early modern texts, these same media hold perhaps even more potential for investigating and representing the material cultures of these remote periods. In the last two decades there has been a decided turn to materiality in medieval and early modern studies. Medieval studies have long recognized that material artefacts are as important a source of cultural information as are documentary records. Similarly, scholars of the early modern period have begun to recognize "the importance of physical things in shaping early modern history and culture" (Swann 2001, 6). Citing two influential collections of essays on materiality—De Grazia, Quilligan, and Stallybrass's *Subject and Object in Renaissance Culture* (1996) and Fumerton and Hunt's *Renaissance Culture and the Everyday* (1999)—Jonathan Gil Harris notes that "Renaissance historicism has witnessed something of a sea change in recent years," from "the new historicism of the 1980s [that] was preoccupied primarily with the fashioning of early modern *subjects*" to "the growing tendency at the millennium, evidenced in the recent turn to 'material culture,' ... to engage with *objects*" (2001, 479).[1] This turn has been felt in object-based disciplines, such as archaeology, as well as in the text-centred humanities.

With studies in material culture now proliferating and embracing a wide range of the object-world, it seems a good time to consider what digital humanities might have to offer humanities-based approaches to the study

* Publication of this collection of essays was significantly enabled by the generous support of the University of Saskatchewan's aid to publication fund and by a grant from the Social Sciences and Humanities Research Council of Canada for CaSTA 2008 New Directions in Text Analysis (https://ocs.usask.ca/ocs/index.php/casta/casta08/index).

[1] In his 2009 book Jonathan Gil Harris similarly notes the shift in New Historicism from subject to object with an emphasis on "thing-ness." This is part of a more general trend in historical studies (Bynum 2009, 77–80). See also Peterson (1997, 262–64) and Lubar and Kingery (1993, i–xvii).

of materiality. This collection of essays builds on the accomplishments of material culture studies by bringing together innovative scholarship on the theory and praxis of digitizing materials of the premodern era. For our purposes, "material culture" (or "material history" as it is sometimes called in the Canadian context, or "social history" in the U.K.)[2] is understood in the broad, inclusive sense in which it is now commonly used across a number of disciplines as pertaining not only to portable, material objects but, in the definition of James Deetz, to "[t]hat section of our physical environment that we modify through culturally determined behaviour" (1977, 24). In the context of this book, this includes coins, jewellery, books, architectural space, and the medieval village, to name a few.[3] But while the physical world has a prominent place in the study of material culture, it is culture that is the ultimate object of study. Ian Woodward's textbook description of this kind of study is wonderfully inclusive in this respect: the objective is

> [to] understand social life through the application of structural and hermeneutic approaches to capture discourses, narratives, codes and symbols which situate objects, along with their interpretation, symbolic manipulation and individual performance within a variety of social contexts (2007, vi–vii).

Given this breadth of scope, it is not surprising that scholars of material culture recognize the need for a multidisciplinary framework. Calling for "a rapprochement between the disciplines" John Moreland asserts the need for an approach that can combine text- and object-focused methodologies and transcend corresponding disciplinary boundaries, as between archaeology and history, for example (2006, 135–36, 142). Digital humanities must be factored into the multidisciplinary approach that Carl Knappett similarly prescribes to meet the "complex and daunting" demands of studying material culture (2005, 1). It is not just the sheer amount of data, but also the often recalcitrant nature of the materials under investigation. Relevant materials are sometimes scattered, geographically remote, or even entirely absent, remaining only in textual traces. Often they are damaged or simply misunderstood, having been removed from their context. Digital tools and methods can be effective in mitigating the difficulties posed by such materials.

---

[2] See Schlereth (1989, 11) and Pearce (1989, 1) respectively.

[3] On the use of the narrower definition in museum studies, see Pearce (1989, 1–2), and in the field of anthropology, Reynolds and Stott (1987, 3, 155).

A central principle in studies of material culture is the complementary relationship between object- and text-based evidence.[4] This relationship is inherent in the objects themselves. Very often the objects in question bear some
explicit element of textuality: most obviously, a coin typically contains text,
while a book is an objective manifestation of a text. Implicitly, all cultural
objects have a symbolic function that can be read and understood by the
people involved with them. There was a long iconographic tradition continuing through the Middle Ages into the early modern period of communicating
ideas through the imagery of objects. In the nascent empiricism of the early
modern period, the rapidly expanding world of objects gained new significance as visual signs by which one could come to interpret—i.e., "read"—the
nature of things, both natural and artificial. Correspondingly, the recent
turn to materiality in academic discourse has brought with it new attention
to objects as evidence and new ways of understanding that are respectful of
the signifying properties of medieval and early modern cultural materials
(see Hood 2009, 177–78). John Moreland finds in this emphasis on the object
a corrective to a prior bias in favour of what he calls the "linguistic turn,"
resulting in a recalibration of the balance between artefactual and textual
source in history-based research (2001). The digital medium has encouraged
this reconsideration, even in textual studies. The advent of digital editing
has placed a greater emphasis on the complementary relationship between
object and text, between visual and verbal means of representation. This relationship runs right through the centre of digital humanities. Among the
most exciting applications of digital methods is in the use of textual evidence
to build visual simulations of historical objects and spaces using AR (Augmented Reality) and VR (Virtual Reality) technologies. Interestingly, many
other expressions of the digital humanities are moving somewhat in the
other direction in the text-image relationship, emphasizing the importance
of marrying rich metadata to digital images (Jespersen and Jespersen 2004;
Anderson et al. 2006; Polfreman et al. 2006). And in recent years, ontologies
have gained importance in a mediating role between real-world objects and
their verbal and visual representation. Thus, the consideration of words,
whether as structured data and metadata or free-form description, in relation to visual forms of representation, is as integral to digital humanities as
it is to the study of material culture.

The use of digital tools to enable and enhance access to material objects has
potential to expose further some of the fault lines in the study of material

---

[4] Regarding the complementary relationship between documentary and archaeological evidence, see Deetz (1977, 8) and Moreland (2006, 142).

culture, as between object and social context. For Douglas Bruster, the turn
to the "thingness of the thing" (in Hood's formulation) has led to a "critical
fetishism" that "threatens to restrict the new materialism's usefulness as social and historical explanation" (2001, 237). Bruster specifically laments the
erosion of the Marxist grounding on which the study of material culture was
based in the "cultural materialism" of Raymond Williams. While the study
of material culture has diversified in its theoretical orientations, an emphasis on the social meaning of objects in their political and historical context
remains central to the project. It regards cultural objects as instruments
and catalysts for social reactions and interactions (Edwards et al. 2006, 1–3).
It is concerned not only with physical properties and qualities of objects,
but also with their provenance and their place in the social networks that
created, circulated, and received them, what Stephen Harold Riggins calls
the "socialness of things." From this perspective, the purpose of studying
cultural artefacts is "to call attention to the integration of objects in the social fabric of everyday life," building on the "blurring of the human-object
boundary" in material culture studies to emphasize the agency of things in
shaping individuals and society (1994, 1–2).[5] For others, close attention to
the material objects of culture provides the essential grounding that can
keep theory accountable to the "discipline of empirical context" (Grassby
2005, 600). Maureen Quilligan, for example, looks to the object world of the
particular moment to provide a critical context that can dislocate the search
for the "early modern subject" from the entelechial pull of modernity (2002,
427). Reconstitution of an object within its historical moment thus enables
a critique of scholarly perspective and provides a reference point for a better understanding of the subject-object relationship, and perhaps, then, a
reconsideration of the premodern subject.

Richard Grassby frames this consideration of object-and-context in terms of
method, making a helpful distinction between *etic* analysis, which attends to

---

[5] Daniel Miller similarly answers the charge of fetishism with an essentially ethno-
graphic approach that asks "which things matter to whom and why?": "through
dwelling upon the more mundane sensual and material qualities of the object, we
are able to unpick the more subtle connections with cultural lives and values that
are objectified through these forms, in part, because of the particular qualities they
possess" (1998, 15, 9). See DeMarrais et al. (2004) for a recent collection of essays
on the social meaning of material objects, and also Bynum (2009, 80) and Moreland
(2006, 139). In a similar vein, several theorists see physical space as not just a product
of but also constitutive of culture, concretizing social relations to create "affective
geographies" (Sullivan 1998, 197).

the material object itself and its attributes, and *emic* analysis, which studies the significance of the object to the humans who interacted with it in its social context (Grassby 2005, 592). It is probably best to understand these modes of analysis as emphases on a continuum of analysis rather than discrete approaches. Writing from the perspective of art history, Jules David Prown sets out a method of object analysis that we might take as an example of an approach that moves from etic to emic:

> The analysis proceeds from *description*, recording the internal evidence of the object itself; to *deduction*, interpreting the interaction between the object and the perceiver; to *speculation*, framing hypotheses and questions which lead out from the object to external evidence for testing and resolution (2001, 79).

This has been the trajectory of bibliography and book history in recent decades, beginning with a new attention to the material object and its productiveness in the New Bibliography of the early twentieth century and leading to a broader concern for the sociology of books in recent decades.

Many of the computational methods represented here are particularly adept at placing material evidence in relational contexts. Databases are the most obvious instances of a tool that identifies and visualizes relationships between things. GIS mapping makes similar connections spatially, while visual modeling techniques can be used to reconstruct objects in their human context. While the details that can be revealed in a high-quality digital image of a medieval manuscript might for some evoke a fetishizing impulse, in the hands of an adept palaeographer they can resituate that object in the socio-political world of the people who interacted with it and tell us much about the human world it inhabited. Yet the computer has the potential to exacerbate the concerns of fetishism expressed by Bruster (2001), or its near cousin "detailism," which Julia Flanders defines (and historicizes) as "the concreteness, the scientism, the certainties and empiricism of quantifiable method" leading to a close attention to "reductionist detail" of the particular in resistance to the generalizing impulse to create a cohesive picture of a totalizing whole (2005, 44). Conscious of the potential charge of what Flanders articulates as detailism, Lynette Hunter avers that "there is nothing in computer use which necessarily leads to the decontextualized or reductive logic of quantification. Indeed the use of computers can sharply foreground those contexts and contribute to the construction of valid actions and assessments of action that the humanities pursue" (1990, 49). Notwithstanding the potential pitfalls, in the study of material culture, as in textual studies, it is in the accumulation of particulars and granular detail that relationships and patterns begin to emerge. The database can be a particularly good tool to aid in revealing such relationships to build a context for understanding the qualities of things as they relate to the social world in which they circulated. Similarly, much of the pioneering work on the use of digital tools for the study of other kinds of material objects involves *editioning*, creating digital surrogates that remediate the object to present it in its materiality—not only to repair or restore something that was lost in the passage of time, but also to enable new ways of seeing it and analysing its physical qualities (Bolter and Grusin 2000). But once digitization of the object begins, and its metadata is collected, its relationships to other objects and to the people who experienced it—its place and meaning in the social world—become accessible in ways that they were not before.

It should be noted that the application of computational methods to history-based research is not new. Scholars in the humanities have been using these methods to aid them in their research tasks since the first digital machines became available. As early as the 1940s, historians were embracing the affordances of the new technology to help sort and analyse complex mathematical data and construct multidimensional databases which would allow novel insight into existing historical records (Owsley 1949). This first phase of quantitative history then moved towards the social sciences and social history in the 1960s, where computational methods were used to find patterns in large-scale datasets that were emerging from governmental structures, allowing access to historical data on county elections, census data, congressional roll call votes, and other miscellaneous political files (Swierenga 1974). The focus on databases, quantitative methodologies, and access to mainframe computers to allow analysis changed with the emergence of the home computing market in the 1980s and the development of the World Wide Web in the 1990s (Greenstein 1994). Towards the close of the twentieth century, large-scale digitization efforts were being undertaken in all types of memory institutions, providing remote and virtual access to primary historical and literary source material and large-scale datasets (Terras 2008). Techniques were developed for presentation and analysis of digital texts, opening up opportunities for scholarly editing and for querying the resulting digital representation of texts (Finneran 1996; Hockey 2000; Sinclair 1991; Stubbs 1996; Popping 2000). Additionally, the lowering costs of computational equipment allowed any scholar who was interested to use relatively advanced tools and techniques to address their research questions. As a result, computational techniques have had a profound impact on the way scholars in the humanities understand and undertake their research, "opening the historical imagination to new questions and forms of presentation" (Thomas 2004). It is therefore necessary to reflect upon which digital techniques are appropriate—or can be imaginatively appropriated—for humanities-based research, and where emergent technologies can aid in particular applications of the study of distinct areas, in this case the study of material culture.

In his mapping of the intellectual landscape of humanities computing, Willard McCarty posits two main branches of computation processes for the study of material culture: imaging and database design (2003, 1235, fig. 1). The electronic database is one of the most powerful tools for gathering and ultimately modeling materiality in historical context. In stating that studies of material culture take "artifacts as a primary database," Thomas Schlereth implies not only a certain *quality*, but also (as is often the case) a *quantity* of data that calls for a computational treatment (1989, 13). Imaging and visualization—from scanning to image analysis to full-scale virtual reality modeling—similarly enable access that would otherwise be impossible in cases where the object is remote, no longer extant, or in some way damaged, making apparent those arresting details and information that might otherwise remain obscure. They also enable new ways of experiencing the material more deeply and closely by means of a well-wrought digital facsimile of a medieval manuscript, for example, or by immersive interaction, as in a 3D model of an early modern site. Using image analysis and recognition techniques, these images and objects can even be searched and analysed comparatively within a corpus of objects. Collections of related objects can be virtually reunited, allowing scholars greater facility for cross-corpus analysis. In a database, text description in the form of data and metadata adds further search and analysis potential. Through concentration on a single object, a mixture of imaging and database technology can enable etic analysis; when applied to a defined corpus, particularly in combination with a database of primary and secondary textual material, the potential for emic analysis grows exponentially, affording multiple views of a complex of data. Emergent technologies such as augmented reality can further enhance the user experience of data sets. This digital interactivity allows new insights into the relationship between materials and their historical contexts. Spatial-relationship modeling techniques, such as GIS, allow the rendering of historic information in geographic form, providing possibilities for integrated and networked locative and temporal analysis. From this multiplicity of views emerge new theoretical perspectives, new ways of seeing.

The practical possibilities of digital media for the study of material culture are compelling, both for the kind of work they enable, but even more so for the intellectual and theoretical questions they provoke. It has become a truism that digital media draw attention to the fact of mediation in all forms of cultural expression and communication, inviting a certain self-consciousness of perspective. The very act of translating an object from its native form into digital form "alters one's view of the original material" (McGann 2001, 82). Although much digital remediation is done with the idea of recovering the past, once the material is digitized it is open to endless possibilities of manipulation and reformulation, what Jerome McGann calls "deformation," where all forms are transforms that dispel the notion of transcendent form while forcing the dislocation of the viewer from his/her accustomed vantage point (2001, 101–2; see also McCarty 2005, 22). Thus, in digital humanities, praxis very often is theory. In an inverse formulation of this relationship, McGann talks in terms of the "the pragmatics of theory" in digital humanities, where *poiesis* (the concrete act of imagining) is privileged over *gnosis* (conceptual undertakings) (2001, 83). With a similar emphasis on *poiesis*, McCarty insists that *modeling* is the core function of humanities computing. In this context, modeling is "the heuristic process of constructing and manipulating models," where a model is understood as "a representation of something for the purposes of study, or a design for realizing something new" (2005, 24). McCarty's choice of the gerund (modeling) over the noun (model) emphasizes process over product, so that computational models are "*temporary states in a process of coming to know* rather than fixed structures of knowledge" (2005, 27). There is a speculative quality to this kind of modeling or editioning. Rather than trying to achieve some kind of empirical recovery of the past (product, leading to detailism), a digital surrogate of any form provides a new and reflective medium for examining the past (process).

Modeling is implicit in the study of material culture. Moreland cites Thomas Huxley on the need in various disciplines (history, archaeology, geology, physical astronomy, etc.) "to reconstruct complex realities that cannot be experienced directly" (2006, 136). Reconstruction of the materiality of a culture serves a mediating and immediating function in bringing the thoughts and actions of an earlier time into closer contact (Grassby 2005, 592–93 and 601). But the materials of culture are themselves often inaccessible in some aspect. The computer can be a powerful tool for reconstruction, gathering the fragments and scattered remains of materiality, both textual and artefactual, to model how these pieces fit together in the material and social world, or to build surrogates that give a sense of immediacy to what was once remote. Again, digital methodology alerts us to certain tendencies in this orientation towards materiality. Daniel Miller observes the paradox of the "extreme visibility and invisibility of objects," that their sense of presence and impression on the senses works profoundly upon the subconscious on a symbolic level (1987, 108). This leads to Riggins's contention that "the materiality of objects gives the false impression of rendering their meaning more visible than those of linguistic statements" (1994, 3); even more so when materiality is digitally rendered. Martin Foys cautions against a "potent version of hyperreality" that is potential in the digital medium and the ease with which one can convince oneself that a well-wrought digital surrogate is, in the words of Edward Christie, "more authentic than the original" (2007, 39; 2003, 146).[6] There is, in short, the potential for digital media to encourage a fallacy of presence, but there is also a counter possibility in what Bolter and Grusin term *hypermediacy*, which is "[a] style of visual representation whose goal is to remind the viewer of the medium" (2000, 272). The often dazzling effect of immediacy created by a digital surrogate, whether a high-quality image or an object in VR or AR, could lead to intellectual fetishism; but done well, it can force a recognition of the distance between viewing subject and historical object in its context. Digital modeling creates a space for a new kind of access to a remote culture in an artificial environment that is itself a reminder that the model is a theoretical construct.

Despite this attention to material culture in medieval and early modern studies, there has not been a dedicated focus on the computational tools and techniques that can be applied to further research in this area. We are therefore at an appropriate juncture to ask what particular applications and methods in the digital humanities—and indeed, in computer science—can be successfully appropriated for the study of premodern material culture. The essays that we present in this collection aim to give an overview of both the range of humanities research that necessitates computational approaches and the va-

---

[6] David Arnold similarly warns against the totalizing effect of digital objects, reminding us that "a digital representation of an artefact is a representation of certain relevant characteristics of the artefact. It is not the original and complete artefact, nor even a metonymy or *simulacrum* of the complete artefact. It is only a representation of some 'relevant characteristics'" (2008, 159). Foys's book is a good example of the potential of digital humanities as theoretical praxis; see especially his epilogue (2007, 189–201). Bolter and Grusin provide the foundational discussion of the danger of "transparent immediacy," which they define as "[a] style of visual representation whose goal is to make the viewer forget the presence of the medium … and believe that he is in the presence of the objects of representation" (2000, 272).

riety of computational methods that can be successfully applied to the study of medieval and early modern culture. By doing so, we wish to present both practical issues and the theoretical concerns of employing digital methods to the study of medieval material culture, while discussing in detail individual research applications and approaches that have necessitated the technological approach taken. We present in this collection a full spectrum of digital material scholarship—from innovative textual approaches to image-based methods—dealing with a wide variety of objects, starting with manuscripts, printed books, and related text-based systems, and moving on to other kinds of objects that require more than transcription and markup. In the humanities, much of the groundbreaking work on material culture has focused on the book and manuscript as physical object. Given that books (including manuscripts) comprise a significant portion of the material remains of the historic past, it is not surprising that an early anticipation of this turn to materiality occurred in textual studies with the so-called New Bibliography and the close attention given to the means of production and the material form of the book in its historical context. The subsequent movement towards the "unediting" of the text—of representing texts in their original instantiations—has flourished in the digital environment, where multiple witnesses in high-quality digital images,[7] alongside machine-readable transcriptions, give the reader access to individual instantiations of a text in its original material form (McLeod 1982; Kiernan 1981; Shillingsburg 2006). Yet despite so much work on the use of digital media to represent the materiality of historical and literary texts, Andrew Prescott in a seminar on "Imaging of Historical Documents" presented in 2006 laments that digital editing is still marked by a preference for searchability rather than close attention to the material document. The opening set of essays in this volume emphasizes the necessity of and the benefit to be gained from a deeper digital engagement with the textual artefact.

Beginning the volume is a chapter by Alan Galey, Richard Cunningham, Brent Nelson, Ray Siemens, and Paul Werstine, which considers the role of textual studies in the digital age, stressing that efforts to reinvent the book's future cannot afford to neglect its past. This chapter describes the theoretical and

---

[7] The issue of quality in digital imaging is dependent on a variety of factors, including capturing at high resolution, the following of digitization guidelines related to capture environment, formats, and documentation (such as those provided by the Library of Congress 2007), and the benchmarking of digital image surrogates to ensure that they are as close a representation of the original as possible given the current technologies.

interdisciplinary contexts of a research project to design new digital environments to support reading and research in the humanities and beyond. It asks how the act of reading has changed since the rise of digital media and suggests that the history of textual practices can inform the future in helping us to rethink what the book can become in a digital environment, providing examples from early modern texts to illustrate some of the considerations involved in the transition from paper to a digital support. James Cummings's chapter follows with a primer on the most common text-based technology for the translation of medieval and early modern manuscripts into digital form: the Text Encoding Initiative's (TEI) markup language (TEI Consortium 2010). Cummings's chapter illustrates the analytical function of markup and the necessity of understanding and interpreting the object in every detail in order to be able to describe it adequately in XML (eXtensible Markup Language). Marking up a text is not only an act of interpretation, but also an expression of a relationship between materially extant texts and the linguistic or intellectual concepts contained within them. Cummings introduces the TEI's recommendations for manuscript description, focusing especially on those aspects relating to the materiality of the physical manuscript, while negotiating the tensions between individual adaptation of the TEI guidelines and the necessary requirements for interoperability of texts and corpora.

These are followed by chapters that explore aspects of materiality, digitization, markup, and analysis of particular textual materials. Judith Siefring and Pip Willcox detail the work of the *Shakespeare Quartos Archive* in bringing together text and physical object in a pilot of a single digital edition of *Hamlet* that emphasizes the physicality of the quartos. The chapter focuses on issues related to the representation of the book as printed, as well as postprint additions. It outlines decisions, rationales, and areas of debate that arose when attempting to represent manuscript annotations and damage, as well as information about stamps, marks of ownership, and bindings, in building individual digital editions of each of the five extant pre-1642 editions of *Hamlet*. Angus Vine and Sebastiaan Verweij's chapter provides a complementary discussion of the representation of non-linear features of manuscript material within digital editions. Manuscripts do not always document a chronological, historical, or scribal progression from the first leaf to the last, and Vine and Verweij investigate how best to convey in standardized markup language the textual sense of a non-linear manuscript, while also preserving its physical integrity. Concentrating on one particular kind of non-linear material—a reversed manuscript—they explore the technological possibilities and challenges of digitizing non-linear documents.

The focus of the next two chapters turns to the handwriting found on manuscript material. The field of palaeography is one that has been much affected
by developments in technology, and recent advances in digitization raise
new opportunities and challenges with the construction of "virtual libraries"
of manuscripts. Peter Stokes examines some of the ways in which palaeography has changed owing to the development of digital methodologies. Stokes
highlights both theoretical and practical difficulties to be overcome in the
future application of digital tools to this subject, such as access, copyright
and reproduction rights, searching and nomenclature, and how to use digital
images better to codify and understand handwriting. This is followed by a
chapter that uses digital methods to investigate a particular palaeographic
problem: how to determine the number of exemplars drawn upon in the production of a manuscript copy of a literary work in a single scribal hand. Jacob
Thaisen demonstrates that probabilistic modeling methods can be applied
in the stylometric analysis of Middle English documents, in this case a copy
of Geoffrey Chaucer's unfinished composition, the *Canterbury Tales.* Thaisen
uses this digital method to identify different orthographies (stretches of text
that are orthographically distinct from other stretches of text) and provides
evidence that multiple textual fragments came together to form just two exemplars within a provincial area within a generation after Chaucer's death.

The book as material object occupies the following two chapters. Athanasios
Velios and Nicholas Pickwoad report on the digitization of book bindings:
a major component of the physical book and one which often reflects the
status of the owner and the intended or actual use of the book. Their chapter summarizes recent work done on the digitization of medieval and early
modern bookbindings from the library of St. Catherine's Monastery in Sinai,
Egypt, a process that involves producing an extensive set of metadata for
a binding, based on specified guidelines. Velios and Pickwoad explain the
importance of bookbinding to historical study, demonstrating that the digitization of bindings is a critical element for understanding the social history
of publishing, libraries, and archives. Paul Dyck, Ryan Rempel, and Stuart
Williams return to the issue of the non-linear text, while keeping a central
focus on the material object of study as they discuss their digitization of the
Little Gidding "harmonies"—cut-up and reassembled biblical texts and images handmade by the extended Ferrar family at Little Gidding in the 1630s.
It is necessary, then, to study not only the harmonies as complete objects,
but also the extensive range of material sources that comprise these books,
and to digitize these in such a way as to allow as full an exploration as possible of the activities of the Little Gidding workshop as a remarkable site of

early modern book compilation and production. The authors demonstrate that these composite documents supply the model for their own digitization, displaying a kind of markup that informs their development of an XML interface as a working tool both for constructing the edition and for modeling the original material process of production.

Our focus then moves from text to consideration of the characteristics and requirements of image-based resources. Patricia Fumerton, Carl Stahmer, Kris McAbee, and Megan Palmer Browne draw attention to the study of early modern ephemera, particularly black-letter, seventeenth-century broadside ballads printed in English. Their chapter describes the development of the *English Broadside Ballad Archive* and its aim to make these ballads fully accessible as cultural records of text, song, and visual art of the period. Highlighting the impermanent and changing nature of the ephemeral artefact, this chapter examines various challenges and their solutions in documenting and cataloguing woodcut illustrations, while exploring new possibilities for expanding access to popular cultures of the past. Stephen Pigney and Katherine Hunt similarly stress the importance of prints as examples of early modern visual and material culture, reporting on the development of a digital library of sixteenth- and seventeenth-century British prints: *British Printed Images to 1700*. Their chapter details the considerations required in constructing a database structure that will allow for the rational presentation of multiple objects to enable a fuller understanding of prints and their production. Instrumental to this database is a subject thesaurus facilitating sophisticated iconographic and historical research. Their approach to the organization, classification, indexing, and presentation of prints demonstrates the necessity of careful planning and development in creating a digital resource that will be useful to non-specialists, while simultaneously facilitating specialist research. Christine McWebb and Diane Jakacki's chapter looks at how integrated text-image annotation tools can contribute to the study of materiality, using a dataset of *Roman de la rose* manuscripts to prototype a tool that will provide manual and semi-automated ways of enriching images and text in an integrated fashion. Their suite of "Rose Tools" aims to provide the scholarly community with an infrastructure for comparative analysis of hitherto disparate texts and image datasets, and they demonstrate its applicability with a discussion of how it will undoubtedly lead to the revision of many commonplace notions in *Roman de la rose* scholarship.

Digital methods for representing geopolitical space offer powerful means for visual mapping of material cultures. Wouter Bracke, Gérard Bouvin, and Benoît Pigeon discuss digital research methods in the field of antique maps, and in particular the development of their Digmap tool, which allows the overlaying, linking, and manipulation of geographic information to facilitate historical research. Their vision of a pan-European virtual library of cartographic documents proposes a system for geolocalized digital libraries of early maps and related documents to provide a resource for scholars undertaking detailed geohistorical research. In a similar vein, Paul Vetch, Catherine Clarke, and Keith Lilley detail a project that brings together scholars from the fields of literary studies, historical geography, and digital humanities to explore the ways in which material and imagined urban landscapes construct and convey a sense of place-identity. Their Mapping Medieval Chester project uses both cartographic and textual sources to extend our understanding of how place-identities were forged in the medieval city, indicating the potential for medieval studies in enabling users to consult literary and cartographic sources in digital media and, more generally, in fostering transferable methodologies and working models for integrating geographical and textual data.

Visualization technologies, such as virtual reality and its emergent counterpart, augmented reality (AR), present some of the most spectacular and groundbreaking applications of digital humanities. Lisa Snyder provides an overview of how virtual reality (VR) is challenging the dominance of two-dimensional drawings and static images in research and teaching methods related to architectural and urban form, focusing on the application of this technology in historical study. Her chapter is framed by case studies of the construction of VR models of the Temple Mount in Jerusalem and of Santiago de Compostela in Spain, demonstrating that academically-generated virtual reality projects are uniquely suited to the study of built environments.

David Humphrey represents very well what can be learned by close attention to the material object *in situ* through the use of computer simulation and modeling, demonstrating the ways in which a cultural artefact can reflect attitudes, individual motivation, the psychology of taste, and the inseparableness of the meaning of any object from its conditions of desirability. While the study of jewellery in the medieval and early modern periods has traditionally relied on textual sources, Humphrey demonstrates that digital, three-dimensional simulation and visualization of jewellery and jewels, together with their background and settings, can model their material characteristics so that when they are juxtaposed, they interact as they would if made of real materials. The digital tools described here act as agents of interpretation, opening up our understanding of historical objects in their material and social contexts. The final paper in this volume—Jonathan Jarrett, Reinhold

Huber-Mörk, Sebastian Zambanini, and Achille Felicetti's description of the Combat Online Illegal Numismatic Sales, or COINS, project—demonstrates that a combination of web technologies, image processing, and digitized resources can advance our understanding of a particular class of object—in this case, coins—while potentially enabling the protection and policing of their lawful circulation. Jarrett describes the development of a connected set of software tools that were first conceived to help stop the trade in stolen or illegally obtained coins by harvesting images from the Web, identifying coins from those images, and then comparing those coins against a reference database, allowing curators and numismatists to assemble and also contribute datasets that would benefit both law enforcement and historical scholarship. This interdisciplinary project demonstrates the potential reach and application of digital tools in preserving and understanding our material cultural heritage.

The papers in this volume come together to explore and demonstrate the potential of digital humanities technologies for the study of medieval and early modern material culture and the importance of identifying and adapting emergent tools and techniques to enable research that would otherwise prove impossible or impractical. We hope they will inspire scholars in the humanities to imagine new ways of engaging and representing their materials of study—both the objects themselves and their historical contexts—to produce new ways of seeing and understanding.

WORKS CITED

Anderson, Sheila, Mike Pringle, Mick Eadie, Tony Austin, Andrew Wilson, and Malcolm Polfreman. 2006. *Digital Images Archiving Study*. JISC Archiving Study Final Report. Arts and Humanities Data Service (AHDS). http://www.jisc.ac.uk/media/documents/programmes/preservation/finaldraftimagesarchivingstudy.pdf.

Arnold, David. 2008. "Digital Artifacts: Possibilities and Purpose." In *The Virtual Representation of the Past*, edited by Mark Greengrass and Lorna Hughes, 159–70. Farnham: Ashgate.

Bolter, J. David, and Richard Grusin. 2000. *Remediation: Understanding New Media*. Cambridge, MA: MIT Press.

Bruster, Douglas. 2001. "New Materialism in Renaissance Studies." In *Material Culture and Cultural Materialism in the Middle Ages and Renaissance*, edited by Curtis Perry, 225–35. Amsterdam: Brepols.

Bynum, Caroline W. 2009. "Perspectives, Connections and Objects: What's Happening in History Now." *Daedalus* 138 (1): 71–87.

Christie, Edward. 2003. "The Image of the Letter: From the Anglo-Saxons to the *Electronic Beowulf.*" *Culture, Theory & Critique* 44 (2): 129–50.

Deetz, James. 1977. *In Small Things Forgotten: The Archaeology of Early American Life*. Garden City, NY: Anchor Press/Doubleday.

De Grazia, Margreta, Maureen Quilligan, and Peter Stallybrass. 1996. *Subject and Object in Renaissance Culture*. Cambridge: Cambridge University Press.

DeMarrais, Elizabeth, Colin Renfrew, and Chris Gosden, eds. 2004. *Rethinking Materiality: The Engagement of Mind with the Material World*. Cambridge: McDonald Institute for Archaeological Research, University of Cambridge.

Edwards, Elizabeth, Chris Gosden, and Ruth B. Phillips, eds. 2006. *Sensible Objects: Colonialism, Museums, and Material Culture*. Oxford: Berg.

Finneran, Richard J., ed. 1996. *The Literary Text in the Digital Age*. Ann Arbor: University of Michigan Press.

Flanders, Julia. 2005. "Detailism, Digital Texts, and the Problem of Pedantry." *Text Technology* 14 (2): 41–70.

Foys, Martin K. 2007. *Virtually Anglo-Saxon: Old Media, New Media, and Early Medieval Studies in the Late Age of Print*. Gainesville: University of Florida Press.

Fumerton, Patricia, and Simon Hunt, eds. 1999. *Renaissance Culture and the Everyday*. Philadelphia: University of Pennsylvania Press.

Grassby, Richard. 2005. "Material Culture and Cultural History." *Journal of Interdisciplinary History* 35 (4): 591–603.

Greenstein, Daniel I. 1994. *A Historian's Guide to Computing*. Oxford: Oxford University Press.

Harris, Jonathan Gil. 2001. "Shakespeare's Hair: Staging the Object of Material Culture." *Shakespeare Quarterly* 52 (4): 479–91.

_____ 2009. *Untimely Matter in the Time of Shakespeare.* Philadelphia: University of Pennsylvania Press.

Hockey, Susan. 2000. *Electronic Texts in the Humanities: Principles and Practice.* Oxford: Oxford University Press.

Hood, Adrienne D. 2009. "Material Culture: The Object." In *History Beyond the Text: A Student's Guide to Approaching Alternative Sources,* edited by Sarah Barber and Corinna Peniston-Bird, 176–98. London: Routledge.

Hunter, Lynette. 1990. "Fact–Information–Data–Knowledge: Databases as a Way of Organizing Knowledge." *Literary and Linguistic Computing* 5 (1): 49–57.

Jespersen, Heather P., and John Kresten Jespersen. 2004. "The Problem of Subject Access to Visual Materials." *Journal of Educational Media and Library Sciences* 42 (1): 37–48.

Kiernan, Kevin S. 1981. *Beowulf and the Beowulf Manuscript.* New Brunswick, NJ: Rutgers University Press.

Knappett, Carl. 2005. *Thinking Through Material Culture: An Interdisciplinary Perspective.* Philadelphia: University of Pennsylvania Press.

Library of Congress. 2007. "Technical Standards for Digital Conversion of Text and Graphic Materials." http://memory.loc.gov/ammem/about/techStandards.pdf.

Lubar, Steven D., and W. David Kingery, eds. 1993. *History from Things: Essays on Material Culture.* Washington, DC: Smithsonian Institution Press.

McCarty, Willard. 2003. "Humanities Computing." In *Encyclopedia of Library and Information Science,* edited by Miriam A. Drake, 1224–35. New York: Marcel Dekker.

_____ 2005. *Humanities Computing.* Basingstoke, UK; New York: Palgrave Macmillan.

McGann, Jerome J. 2001. *Radiant Textuality: Literature After the World Wide Web.* New York: Palgrave.

McLeod, Randall. 1982. "UN editing Shak-Speare." *Sub-Stance* 10 (33–34): 26–55.

Miller, Daniel. 1987. *Material Culture and Mass Consumption.* Oxford and New York: Basil Blackwell.

_____ 1998. *Material Cultures: Why Some Things Matter.* London: UCL Press; Chicago: University of Chicago Press.

Moreland, John. 2001. *Archaeology and Text.* London: Duckworth.

_____ 2006. "Archaeology and Texts: Subservience or Enlightenment." *Annual Review of Anthropology* 35:135–51.

Owsley, Frank L. 1949. *Plain Folk of the Old South.* Baton Rouge: Louisiana State University Press.

Pearce, Susan M. 1989. "Museum Studies in Material Culture." In *Museum Studies in Material Culture,* edited by Susan M. Pearce, 1–10. London: Leicester University Press.

Peterson, Thomas V. 1997. "Introduction: Cultural and Historical Interpretation Through Nontextual Material." *Historical Reflections* 23 (3): 259–67.

Polfreman, M., V. Broughton, and A. Wilson. 2006. *Metadata Generation for Resource Discovery: Final Report.* Arts and Humanities Data Service. http://www.ahds.ac.uk/about/projects/metadata-generation/index.htm.

Popping, Roel. 2000. *Computer-Assisted Text Analysis.* London: Sage Publications.

Prescott, Andrew. 2006. "Imaging of Historical Documents." Presented at the Methods Network Expert Seminar on History and Archaeology, University of Sheffield, April 19–21. Audio recording. http://www.arts-humanities.net/audio/andrew_prescott_imaging_historical_documents.

Prown, Jules David. 2001. *Art as Evidence: Writing on Art and Material Culture.* New Haven, CT: Yale University Press.

Quilligan, Maureen. 2002. "Renaissance Materialities: Introduction." *Journal of Medieval and Early Modern Studies* 32 (3): 427–31.

Reynolds, Barrie, and Margaret A. Stott. 1987. *Material Anthropology: Contemporary Approaches to Material Culture.* Lanham, MD: University Press of America.

Riggins, Stephen Harold. 1994. *The Socialness of Things: Essays on the Socio-Semiotics of Objects.* Berlin: Mouton de Gruyter.

Schlereth, Thomas J. 1989. "Material Culture Research and North American Social History." In *Museum Studies in Material Culture,* edited by Susan M. Pearce, 11–26. London: Leicester University Press.

Shillingsburg, Peter L. 2006. *From Gutenberg to Google: Electronic Representations of Literary Texts.* Cambridge: Cambridge University Press.

Sinclair, John. 1991. *Corpus, Concordance, Collocation.* Oxford: Oxford University Press.

Stubbs, Michael. 1996. *Text and Corpus Analysis: Computer-Assisted Studies of Language and Culture.* Oxford: Blackwell.

Sullivan, Garrett A. 1998. *The Drama of Landscape: Land, Property, and Social Relations on the Early Modern Stage.* Stanford, CA: Stanford University Press.

Swann, Marjorie. 2001. *Curiosities and Texts: The Culture of Collecting in Early Modern England.* Philadelphia: University of Pennsylvania Press.

Swierenga, Robert P. 1974. "Computers and American History: The Impact of the 'New' Generation." *Journal of American History* 60 (4): 1045–220.

TEI Consortium, eds. 2010. *TEI P5: Guidelines for Electronic Text Encoding and Interchange.* Version 1.6.0. TEI Consortium. Accessed 23 October 2009. http://www.tei-c.org/release/doc/tei-p5-doc/en/html/.

Terras, Melissa. 2008. *Digital Images for the Information Professional.* Farnham: Ashgate.

Thomas, William G. 2004. "Computing and the Historical Imagination." In *A Companion to Digital Humanities,* edited by Susan Schreibman, Ray Siemens, and John Unsworth. Oxford: Blackwell. http://www.digitalhumanities.org/companion/view?docId=blackwell/9781405103213/9781405103213.xml&chunk.id=ss1-2-5&toc.depth=1&toc.id=ss1-2-5&brand=9781405103213_brand.

Woodward, Ian. 2007. *Understanding Material Culture.* Los Angeles: Sage
    Publications.

Beyond Remediation: The Role of Textual Studies in Implementing New Knowledge Environments[1]

Alan Galey
University of Toronto
alan.galey@utoronto.ca

Richard Cunningham
Acadia University
richard.cunningham@acadiau.ca

Brent Nelson
University of Saskatchewan
brent.nelson@usask.ca

Ray Siemens
University of Victoria
siemens@uvic.ca

Paul Werstine
King's University College, University of Western Ontario
werstine@uwo.ca

The INKE Team[2]

Introduction

To claim to digitize premodern material culture is to speak in paradoxes. We cannot literally digitize an artefact from the past, in the sense of rearranging its molecules to make it transmissible in digital media. For now, at least, all we can do is create digital surrogates for artefacts and hope those surrogates

---

[1] This essay expands upon the brief description of INKE's Textual Studies team published in Siemens et al. (2009). The authors wish to thank audiences at gatherings of NT2: Nouvelles Technologies/Nouvelles Textualités, the Society for Digital Humanities/Société pour l'étude des médias interactifs, and the Alliance of Digital Humanities Organizations for their comments on early versions of this article, and gratefully acknowledge the support of the Social Sciences and Humanities Research Council of Canada. We are also grateful to Peter Gorman and Rebecca Niles for editorial assistance, and to the staff of the Folger Shakespeare Library and the Thomas Fisher Rare Book Library.

[2] A complete list of INKE team members and partners may be found at http://inke.ca/, accessed 23 October 2009.

ISBN 978-0-86698-499-7 (online)   ISBN 978-0-86698-474-4 (print)
New Technologies in Medieval and Renaissance Studies 3 (2012) 21–48

measure up to expectations, even as second-order representations. However, to digitize something successfully in this sense is to move a step beyond representation and remediation, and to create a model: an implemented representation that is tractable and manipulable according to structured inquiry (McCarty 2005, 20–72 and *passim*). A model should be capable of answering questions its creator did not conceive; conversely, successful *modeling*, to invoke the difference the verb makes, should prompt the discovery of new questions in one's material. Merely celebrating the power of computers as modeling environments, however, is not enough; as Willard McCarty points out, there is no escaping paradoxes: "On the one hand, modelling cultural artifacts treats them as something like the empirical objects of nature; on the other hand, paradoxically modelling anything is just as clearly an imaginative act" (2005, 72). To claim to digitize material *culture*, then, requires us to think beyond the conservative notions that Ronald Day associates with traditional forms of computing and information science, which hold that "history is the transmission of the past to receivers in subsequent generations (cultural heritage)" (2000, 810). Culture is not a transmissible thing, to be passed on like old taxidermy whether the next generation wants it or not, but a network of imaginative investments that cannot be contained within material artefacts, yet cannot be understood without them. With McCarty's paradox in mind, we can understand digitizing material culture not in terms of new digital technologies acting upon passive written records, but as the imaginative investments of the past meeting those of the present. To paraphrase Hamlet, "[t]his was sometime a paradox, but now the time gives it proof" (3.1.113–14).

Textual scholars have served both as chroniclers of how humans interact with written records of material culture, and as agents in some of the ways those interactions have changed. This chapter describes the rationale and initial goals of a particular group of digital textual scholars, the Textual Studies team within the Implementing New Knowledge Environments project (INKE.ca), but also considers the role of textual studies generally in a digital world. How has reading changed since the rise of digital media, and how can the history of textual practices inform the future? Pursuing that primary research question within a project like INKE requires that textual scholarship be anything but the hermetic, antiquarian discipline some still mistake it for. INKE's Textual Studies team works in an interdisciplinary context alongside other teams in User Experience, Interface Design, and Information Management, as well as with many public- and private-sector partners. We do so within a project framework built on the idea of strategic prototyping, as opposed to building a single mega-resource, as a key to understanding how reading can change with developments in digital media. INKE's purpose is to rethink what the book can become in a digital environment, to pursue that thinking in a broadly interdisciplinary intellectual commons supported by partnerships with the knowledge industries, and—crucially—to implement that thinking in prototypes to be shared on an open-source basis with the public.

This essay describes theoretical and interdisciplinary contexts for the work of INKE's Textual Studies team in particular, and advances the argument, made by other textual scholars before us, that efforts to reinvent the book's future cannot afford to neglect its history (Chartier 1995; McKenzie 1999; McGann 2001; Kirschenbaum 2008; Darnton 2009). Our team's seven-year research plan connects the study of print and digital environments in order to develop a technical vocabulary for describing the salient features of electronic artefacts based on research into the history of book design, print production, and bibliography. This aspect of our work will develop the multimedia focus inherent to *digital* textual scholarship by bringing together traditional bibliographic methods and new forms of digital narrative, such as electronic literature and video games. The resulting technical vocabulary will inform the prototyping activities of INKE's other teams, who will take into account the material transmission (manuscript, print, and electronic) of texts. To document the complexity of past and present textual forms, INKE's Textual Studies team plans to compile an online, open-access knowledge base of textual features (titled *Architectures of the Book*) which illustrates technologies and human practices of transmitting knowledge in textual form. The repository will provide a set of facsimile exemplars of samples of type, columns, marginalia, tables, charts, volvelles, indexes, pictures, title pages, and error-control mechanisms. All of these are elements of the pre-digital information architecture of books which digital implementations must reconfigure.

INKE takes textual scholarship as one of its priorities for several reasons, all of which depend on the idea that what's past is prologue. Textual scholars study not only the past, in the form of writing technologies and the reading practices that humans have developed over centuries, but also the past in the present, in the form of new scholarly editions and studies of the transmission of texts and artefacts over time. Although past practices do not necessarily determine the future, the study of new technologies in historical context can reveal patterns of cultural use and meaning that connect past and future knowledge environments on the same continuum. The orientation of the Textual Studies team is therefore aligned with the recent turn away from determinism (i.e., oversimplifications of cause and effect, such as "print caused the Reformation" [Kingdon 1980, 140]), narratives of revolutionary change, and rigid divisions between periods in the history of technology (generally associated with the work of Marshall McLuhan [1962] and Elizabeth Eisenstein [1979], as well as much of the hypertext and new media theory dominant in the late nineties).[3] Textual studies, book history, literary studies, and other humanities disciplines have recently moved toward approaches that examine long-term continuities and discontinuities, overlap between new and old technologies, and the multiplicity of social and cultural effects that result.[4]

In addition to offering alternatives to outdated successionist models of technology and society, the Textual Studies team also furnishes INKE's research program with a vocabulary and set of methods for studying the particular. Many of the dominant accounts of new media repeat McLuhan's and Eisenstein's neglect of primary materials (such as print and manuscript books) from the periods about which they generalize, and thus have not done justice to the often idiosyncratic and even intractable particularity of human artefacts.[5] As a discipline that links mechanical and craft processes such as book-making with interpretive modes such as literary studies and cultural history, textual scholarship is inescapably qualitative in its methods. This orientation enables INKE to study human activities like reading and meaning-making in methodological terms not available to disciplines for whom quantification and generalization define the horizon of knowledge: one book is not like another in the same way that one carbon atom is like another. We need digital tools that recognize this particularity. Finally, according to Greetham, "Textual scholars study *process* (the historical stages in the production, transmission, and reception of texts), not just *product* (the text resulting from such production, transmission, and reception)" (1994, 2; emphasis in original). This attention to process enables textual studies naturally to extend its methods to digital texts, and, along with a corresponding

---

[3] For the most influential examples, see McLuhan (1962), Eisenstein (1979), and Landow (1992).

[4] This critical turn is well described in the introduction to Thorburn and Jenkins (2003); other examples may be found in Joseph Dane (2003), Lisa Gitelman (2006), N. Katharine Hayles (2005), Adrian Johns (1998), and Matthew G. Kirschenbaum (2008), to name a few. See also the debate between Johns and Eisenstein in *American Historical Review* (Grafton, Eisenstein, and Johns 2002).

[5] For a critique of Eisenstein, in particular on her decision to use only secondary sources, see Johns (1998) and his contributions to the debate with Eisenstein in Grafton, Eisenstein, and Johns (2002).

attention to context, represents a fundamental methodological link among all of INKE's teams.

The following discussion will turn first to historical and disciplinary contexts for digital textual scholarship, and then to the questioning of remediation as a dominant theoretical model for the future of the book. At stake in these contextualizing accounts is a question faced not only by INKE, but also by researchers undertaking similar work in the present: what does it mean to study the book at this particular historical moment, and how have we arrived at that moment? It seems inevitable that medieval and early modern studies should be one of the principal contexts where we answer this question. This is partly due to persistent interest in these overlapping periods as an analogue to our own present (Rhodes and Sawday 2000), and partly to these fields being important proving-grounds for relevant theoretical approaches such as New Historicism and its discontents (Patterson 1987; Veeser 1989; Gallagher and Greenblatt 2000), and more recently, presentism (Hawkes 2002; Fernie 2005). Another part of the answer must be that studying the history of the book helps us to see digital technology with new eyes. Hand-press books, like manuscript books, remind us that the cheap machine-made paperbacks of the twentieth century are not the essential form of the book; indeed, the book may have survived so long only because its essence is multiple and protean. In that spirit, this chapter turns to aspects of book design such as content orientation and *mise-en-page* as examples of the early modern book's own construction of information architectures.

Textual studies and digital media in transition

To a textual scholar, a book is not an inert object left behind by the passage of time. Rather, a book is a nexus of physical materials, metaphors, human relationships, cultural preconceptions, and readerly interventions. Textual scholarship at its best is therefore a synthesis of disciplinary approaches and methods (Greetham 1999). Over the twentieth century, however, the study of the material transmission of texts, and of human interactions with them, has been subject to the same specializing impulse that segmented much of the academy in general, especially in North America (Howsam 2006; Moran 2002; Liu 2004). By the end of the twentieth century, this tendency had resulted in a number of possible approaches to the study of books and communication, many of which ironically did not themselves communicate or even acknowledge the others' existence.[6] Leslie Howsam, looking at the kinds of textual

---

[6] For example, McLuhan's *Gutenberg Galaxy* (1962) does not cite a single bibliographer, even though the New Bibliography was actively theorizing about early print at the

scholarship that have relatively recently come together under the banner of book history, schematizes the primary disciplinary divisions as: 1) *history*, which focuses on "agency, power, and experience" in relation to books, reading, and publishing; 2) *literature*, which focuses on the text as an object for interpretation, and takes the material and historical instantiations of texts to be partly constitutive of their meaning; and 3) *bibliography*, whose primary focus is on books and documents as artefacts that reflect the details of their manufacture (2006, 3–15).

Another scheme we could use to explain the evolution of the study of the book is national. The French *histoire du livre* tradition developed out of the mid-twentieth-century *Annales* school of historiography, and brought a social-history focus to the study of books and publishing, placing these activities in a broad social context, and preferring as evidence quantifiable data about large social groups (Febvre and Martin 1958; Darnton 1979; Chartier 1995). If traditional *histoire du livre* sometimes gave insufficient attention to the material complexities of books themselves, then its Anglo-American counterpart, the New Bibliography, may be accused of excesses in the opposite direction. Following the lead of A.W. Pollard, W.W. Greg, R.B. McKerrow, and later Fredson Bowers and G. Thomas Tanselle, Anglo-American bibliography was resolutely empirical, and narrowed the understanding of books to describing their physical form, reconstructing their manufacture, and hypothesizing the manuscripts used as copy for printed books. This latter pursuit, the most contentious for recent critics, often happened in service of an idealized notion of authorial composition, allegedly recoverable through the New Bibliography's arguably less rigorous editorial theory.[7]

The division between these approaches impoverished all of them. For example, bibliography is by nature a highly specialized discipline which requires years of training and hours of painstaking labour to produce knowledge that often applies only to highly specified contexts. Although that knowledge can radically change our understanding of the nature of a cultural artefact—the Shakespeare First Folio, for example (Hinman 1963)—bibliography often

---

time, nor does Landow (1992 and subsequent editions). On the textual studies side, see the gaps in the tables of contents of the Routledge *Book History Reader* (Finkelstein and McCleery 2006) and the Blackwell *Companion to the History of the Book* (Eliot and Rose 2007) in the areas of project-based research on e-books and other forms of digital textuality.

[7] There are many contesting accounts of this history; representative overviews may be found in Wilson (1970) and Maguire (1996).

has difficulty with outreach to non-specialists. By contrast, other fields like media studies and intellectual history advance highly accessible narratives about the history of technology. Marshall McLuhan, for example, was interviewed by *Playboy* and makes a cameo appearance in Woody Allen's *Annie Hall*; one struggles to imagine a bibliographer achieving comparable status as a public intellectual. However, the kinds of accessible narratives for which McLuhan was known generally lack a technically rigorous vocabulary for describing their putative materials, often treating a term like *the book* as what computer scientists call a "black box" that conceals complexity. In a critique that would apply to McLuhan and his followers, such as Elizabeth Eisenstein and Bruno Latour, Adrian Johns has argued that "cultural historians' appreciation of print has too frequently stopped short of the doors of the printing house" (1998, 42); conversely, Johns also notes that bibliographers "have often been too modest in their historiographical objectives" (1998, 42n66). Given the raised stakes that digital technologies bring to the study of textual forms, and the temptation to exaggerate the explanatory power of single technologies in understanding those stakes, the study of new knowledge environments must balance attention to big pictures with respect for arresting details.[8]

As textual scholarship began to overlap with what are now called the digital humanities, the study of the history of textuality became linked with the practice of making new editions using digital media (Hockey 2000; Smith 2004; Shillingsburg 2006; Price 2007). Even before the inception of the World Wide Web, the capacity of computing to alter the direction of textual studies has been a topic of controversy. First hypertext and then the Web have been celebrated for their liberation of texts from the linearity of print (Bolter 2001; Landow 1992; McKnight, Dillon, and Richardson 1991) or from the hierarchy that characterizes traditional editing (Smith 2004), especially the copy-text editing of the Greg-Bowers school, with its privileging of final authorial intention. It has been particularly tempting to marry electronic editing to certain versions of poststructuralism (Landow 1992; Marcus 1996; Ross 1996); however, several experts in humanities computing and textual studies demur from rhetorics of revolution in favour of more nuanced positions (McGann 1997, 2001, and elsewhere; Kirschenbaum 2002; Greetham 2004, 2006; Shillingsburg 2006; Hockey 2004 and elsewhere; Bryant 2008; O'Donnell 2008; Eggert 2009), and G. Thomas

---

[8] As Bolter points out, drawing on Raymond Williams, social and economic determinisms are no less dangerous than the technological kind (2001, 19–20).

Tanselle, the most able advocate of the Greg-Bowers tradition, denies that the electronic medium can fundamentally alter his field.[9]

Tanselle focuses on the difference between what he terms the *work* and the *document, witness, reproduction,* or *copy* of that work: "One must be able to distinguish the work itself from attempts to reproduce it. A work, at each point in its life, is an ineluctable entity, which one can admire or deplore but cannot alter without becoming a collaborator with its creator (or creators); a reproduction is an approximation, forever open to question and always tempting one to remedial action" (1989, 13–14). For Tanselle, a change in the medium of the work's reproduction from book to screen makes no difference to his foundational distinction (2001, 2006); however, what Tanselle does not allow is that our conception of works as ineluctable entities may depend at least in part on an effect of the still dominant medium for reproducing these works, namely the fixity of print that emerged only a little more than a century ago (McLuhan 1962; Eisenstein 1979; Kernan 1987; Johns 1998). If so, the boundary between the metaphysical *work* and the material *reproduction* has been porous. Reproduction can also be altered by the medium, this time the computer: "[I]t is technically possible for the same bitstream [the form in which a reproduction of a work is stored in a computer] to generate a different perceived object [the reproduction itself], depending on hardware and software configurations, and plausible that different bitstreams could generate the same perceived object" (Barwell 2005, 422). Tanselle aside, many of those who have reservations about the doctrine of liberation through computing nonetheless respect the achievements either they or others have created in the electronic medium: "[C]reative cybernauts have long since created marvels that place online readers in hypertextual experiences that constitute new genres of representation and reading" (Bryant 2008, 92)—included among these marvels might be the *Blake Archive,* the *Perseus Digital Library,* the *Rossetti Archive,* the *Women Writers Project,* and the *Walt Whitman Archive,* as well as the next generation of Web 2.0 projects now emerging.[10]

Beyond being available for revision, the electronic archive or edition has been credited with exceeding the codex in many other ways. Martha Nell

---

[9] In particular, see Tanselle's ambivalent foreword to the recent volume *Electronic Textual Editing* (2006), and Greetham's discussion of that ambivalence in his review (2007).

[10] See http://www.blakearchive.org, http://www.perseus.tufts.edu, http://www.rossettiarchive.org, http://www.wwp.brown.edu, http://www.whitmanarchive.org (all accessed 20 September 2011).

Smith offers an impressive list of advantages in the digital edition: "images of all primary documents (1) [often unique or rare and dispersed among libraries and museums, with severely limited access] ... including, where applicable, sound and even video reproductions"; networking and communication (2) among editors and readers; (3) critical feedback from readers (2004, 308); (4) "demotic," rather than "hieratic," editions (2004, 316); (5) broadly collaborative "teams of editors, rather than a solitary master with her assistants" (2004, 319). Smith's reader, though, is hard pressed to identify which of these advantages constitute "ontological differences between electronic and bibliographic scholarly editions" (2004, 312), as we can demonstrate by looking closely at each of Smith's five points. There are bibliographic editions containing (1) images of all primary documents, like Michael Warren's The Complete King Lear, 1608-1623 (1989), which provides facsimiles not only of all three of the earliest printed versions of the play, but also of their formes in every known state of correction—on loose leaves for combination by the reader. And, as Smith notices, associated sound and video can be put on a CD slipped inside the cover of a book edition. However, it is true, as Stephen Reimer observes (2006), that (2) networking, communication, and collaboration (5), although hardly coeval with the electronic medium, have been enormously facilitated by it, first by email, then by wikis, blogs, writeboards, and other software. Critical feedback from readers (3) also did not await the coming of the computer; the Folger Library edition of Shakespeare, a reading edition collaboratively edited by Barbara A. Mowat and Paul Werstine, records the genesis of its structure in such feedback, first through "the Folger Institute's Center for Shakespeare Studies' ... fortuitous sponsorship of a workshop on 'Shakespeare's Texts for Students and Teachers' ..., from which we learned an enormous amount about what is wanted by college and high-school teachers" and then from "Shakespeare teachers and students ... who used our texts in manuscript in their classrooms" (1992, x–xi). Nonetheless, in favour of Smith's argument it must be granted that in the electronic medium reader feedback is dynamic and ongoing, not, as in the bibliographic, only pre-publication. Finally, though, as Smith is keenly aware, it is hard to fashion the electronic edition as ontologically demotic, rather than hieratic (4), when such an edition must be encoded in TEI-conformant XML, a system of tagging that originates in the representation of the hierarchal structure of books. And, as Daniel O'Donnell points out, there is nothing in the ontology of the electronic edition that forbids a single editor from imposing on a text a well-informed but individual conception of its textual history in an edition of the traditional bibliographic kind that offers only a single perspective on a work or its reproduction (to revert, appropriately in this context, to Tanselle's distinction) (O'Donnell 2009).

What distinguishes the electronic edition from the bibliographic one may not then be any of the former's single features, but instead its capacity simultaneously to be more than one kind of edition. As Jerome McGann writes, "[O]ne can build editorial machines capable of generating on demand multiple textual formations—eclectic, facsimile, reading, genetic" (2006, 57).[11] Finally, then, for textual critics, what may distinguish the electronic edition from its predecessors is its provision of both editions and the resources to lay bare the decisions of editors in these editions, reambiguating the editorial process with reference to a comprehensive array of primary documents (Smith and McGann's facsimiles). After all, as Randall McLeod's brilliant unediting attacks on editors continue, they threaten to break the bounds of the codex and cry out for digitization (McLeod 2004).

Re-opening the book

Thus far the history of digitizing books has focused on *re*presenting and re-purposing. Digital facsimiles reproduce the book in spectacular visual detail, while encoded texts endeavour to represent historic artefacts analytically, with potential for diplomatic facsimile rendering. Once rendered into machine-readable text, a book becomes malleable into infinite forms for any number of purposes. Some instances of representation and re-purposing are more valuable than others. A large portion of Google Books's literary corpus, for example, comprises little more than recycled books from the dusty recesses of the library stacks: outdated and otherwise unused public domain editions unsuitable for detailed, text-sensitive scholarly work, *re*presented as OCR-scanned PDF images that are now machine-searchable, but only with the simplest of word-string queries. The best digital editions take fuller advantage of the digital medium to provide a clean, edited text that is enriched in ways that are impossible in print, supporting complex searches and visualization tools (Lavagnino 1995; Siemens 1998, 1999, 2005; Werstine 2008; Galey 2009). In almost all cases, from bald representation to multifunctional re-purposing, the end result is explicitly anchored—either representationally or notionally—to the historical print artefact.

The heuristic possibilities—and limitations—of re-examining the book in light of the digital age are evoked in Bolter and Grusin's notion of reme-

---

[11] See also Peter Shillingsburg's proposal for "an electronic infrastructure for representing script acts" (2006, 80–125).

diation, which arises from the recognition that so-called new media technology has intensified a cultural tendency to repackage and recombine old media content in new forms (2000).[12] As an analytical term, "remediation" therefore "offers us a means of interpreting the work of earlier media" (55). This relationship between old and new media is reciprocal. To begin with, remediation and a host of ancillary terms are understood with reference to the anterior medium: each new medium in a *re*flexive manner, to *re*spond to, *re*deploy, *re*form, *re*fashion, or *re*habilitate the original (55–56). There is a good deal of ambivalence and ambiguity encoded in these reflexive relationships. In one sense, the terms imply a reliance and respect for the anterior form. The imprint of the book upon the digital medium can be seen at every turn on the Web. Currently available e-books are not only books in the more abstract sense of ideational content (ideas encoded in language), but in the more concrete sense of their instantiated form (the codex). The most common form of the e-book is a simple PDF or EPUB file of a printed book. Even the electronic edition of Bolter and Grusin's *Remediation: Understanding New Media* is bound up in the old print medium: although it is displayed in a browser in HTML, it is still partitioned into pages which correspond to the printed artefact. The digital-born book is yet to be established as publishing staple, and it is far from erasing its immense indebtedness to a reading technology that is now many centuries old.

Despite the new medium's reliance on the old, the term "remediation" also implies the need to fix something that is broken, or to restore it to some ideal or imagined form.[13] But the book—more precisely, the codex—is not exactly broken, as its cultural persistence in the digital age attests: it is a remarkably refined and effective technology. To be sure, not all reading technologies have survived. The scroll superseded wax and clay tablets; the codex superseded the scroll.[14] And yet the printed book has survived as our primary

---

[12] Scholars and students of the Middle Ages and Renaissance will recognize echoes of what Ong calls the "rhapsodic method" of composition (1965, 148–50; cf. Bolter and Grusin 2000, 11, 21).

[13] Bolter and Grusin acknowledge the implied "euphemism for restoring what is damaged, from the Latin *remederi*—'to heal, to restore to health.'" They also note the connotations of social reform (2000, 59–60).

[14] While the scroll is no longer used, it should be noted that epigraphy does persist in such applications as the cornerstones of public buildings, gravestones, and even concrete sidewalks. For example, a version of one of bpNichol's concrete poems exists as an inscription in the laneway next to Coach House Press at the University of Toronto ("a / lake / a / lane / a / line / a / lone"; cf. bpNichol 1981, n.p.).

reading tool for some 550 years. That said, there have been features of codex technology that never caught on. Its history is one of remarkable innovation and success mixed in (as innovations are) with failures. Often these failures are as interesting and instructive as the successes. Another implication of this notion of remediation as a restoration to an ideal form is the imperative to retrain the codex form, to improve or enhance it.

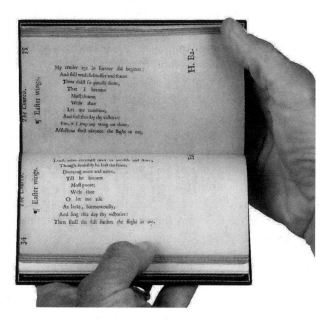

Figure 1. George Herbert's "Easter Wings," as printed in the 1633 edition of *The Temple* (reproduced by permission of the Folger Shakespeare Library)

The book is only an incidental consideration in Bolter and Grusin's theory of remediation, which is chiefly concerned with non-textual media. Yet the book presents a slightly different case precisely because of its double status as content and form, which are in a sense distinct but not easily separated. The intellectual content—the form that the written language takes in the book—has been conditioned by the material form, even as the material form was at first shaped by its content. Take, for example, one of the most famous of seventeenth-century English poems, George Herbert's "Easter Wings," as printed in the 1633 edition of *The Temple*.[15] The poem resists typical reading

---

[15] For a representative literary interpretation see Leah S. Marcus's *Unediting the Renaissance* (1996, 257 ff. and fn.).

in its early printed form in that one has to change the orientation of the page in order to either read the poem or see two sets of wings. Random Cloud describes the cumulative effect of this and other ambiguities: "As the printed shape-poem is inherently an object of both reading and gazing, it cannot exist wholly in a single spatiality and temporality. In our performative processing of this poem-that-is-a-picture, we cannot be in all modalities at once" (1994, 72).[16] Looking closer, one also notices that each ten-line stanza represents a decline and an elevation, with the decline emphasized in the shortening of the poetic lines, which move towards the unifying phrase "With thee" in the middle of each stanza; the rise is indicated by increasing line lengths from the centre of each stanza to its end. Interpretations of the poem often work toward the notion expressed in the second-to-last line of page 35—"if I imp my wing on thine"—and treat it as a plea of the speaker, who presents the poem as a prayer for his own rise with the ascension of Christ. In Leah Marcus's reading, "The shaped poem and the duodecimo volume it microcosmically recapitulates are both 'fall' and means of recovery, 'most thin' and 'most poor' in their material-ity, yet a means for spiritual flight" (1996, 182). This instance of text-as-image (or image-as-text, depending—literally—on one's orientation) cannot be re-duced to remediation: the process of meaning-making at work here depends not upon a linear progression of one medium (printed text) subsuming another (illustration), but rather upon poetic effects made possible by different orders of information, thought, and experience all co-present within the same print artefact.

When we imagine this seventeenth-century devotional poem as a distinctly bookish artefact within the hands of an embodied reader, some important as-pects of the reading process become apparent. The reading process requires holding the book; it is necessary to turn the volume such that the poem(s) can be read, thus requiring both hands on the volume, one on each page and cover. After reading, the book may be returned to its usual alignment and then, with two hands still on the pages and bindings, the volume closed. It is the closure of the text that brings the greatest formal significance, for in closing the book, two very important things happen: one is that the two sets of wings on opposite pages—one belonging to man and the other to God— are "imped," (1.9) or brought together, in the way called for by the poet's prayer; the other is that the most natural position of the closed hands on the volume as the book is closed is that of prayer. "Easter Wings" thus provides

---

[16] Related to this discussion is the unavoidable question, explored in Cloud's biblio-graphic tour de force, of whether "Easter Wings" is one or two poems; if one poem, which stanza comes first?

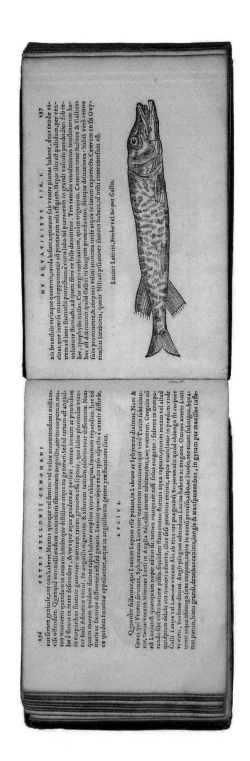

Figure 2. Pierre Belon's *De aquatilibus*, 1553 (reproduced by permission of the Folger Shakespeare Library)

an example of the richness of understanding that can flow from an informed appreciation of how the material form of the text influences, shapes, and may even on occasion determine its intellectual content.

Content orientation of the kind on display in "Easter Wings" was an important consideration in the development of print technology. This is an aspect of book history that is clearly relevant to the development of electronic reading technologies as diverse sizes and configurations of screen surfaces proliferate, even as the shape and form of the electronic document continues to change and adapt to new means of delivery. The case of the oblong book is a telling example of the early modern printed book whose interface responded and adapted to the special nature of the material being presented. In 1553, when the illustrious Estienne publishing house set out to print Pierre Belon's *De aquatilibus*, which contains illustrations interspersed with text, they elected to print the book in an oblong octavo format, in recognition of the type of material they were dealing with. The decision to print in octavo was in part a reflection of the amount of material that was involved. It was certainly not enough to print in folio, but it certainly *could* have been printed in quarto: in octavo the book is some 450 pages, which makes for a rather thick octavo. The decision to print in this format, it seems, was also dictated by the material shape of the subject matter: most fish are by nature long and thin, and so is an octavo (a quarto, in contrast, is more squat). This means that the illustrations could be nicely and easily formatted on the page. The text commentary could, of course, be easily adapted to any set of dimensions. But in the normal printing process, each page would have been oriented in the forme, printed, and then folded in such a way as to facilitate sewing and binding along the length of the page. This would have resulted in an unnatural reading interface where the fishes would appear standing on their heads or their tails. In recognition of the natural orientation of a fish in the water, the printer (perhaps at the urging of the author) elected to set the pages in an unusual format that would enable the book to be sewn along the width of the page, so that the book would present the reader with a very wide opening that would allow a fish to fill out a large portion of the page, or even an entire page, with the added benefit that the reader would not have to turn the book to view the fish in its normative, horizontal position. This oblong orientation was by no means common, and would have required the printer to set the pages in a completely different orientation in the forme than was usual, making the printer's task much more difficult.[17]

Here is a case where an early modern printer responded to two very important considerations in his design of the reading surface: the size of the surface in relation to the structure and amount of information required for a single view of a coherent and complete set of data; and the configuration and orientation of the reading surface in consideration of the intrinsic form of the material.[18]

The importance of the opening as a coherent grouping of information is emphasized in another instance of an oblong printing, in this case a quarto: Otto van Veen's *Amorvm emblemata* (1608). There were three distinct polyglot versions of this book issued in the same year: a Latin-Dutch-French version; a Latin-Italian-French version; and a Latin-English-Italian version. In all cases, the desire to provide the text portion of the emblem in three languages posed a challenge. For emblem books, keeping the picture and the accompanying text together is even more essential than it was for Belon: indeed, the picture and the text of an emblem comprise an integral unit. It was therefore advantageous that the complete emblem—text and picture—be visible at once to the reader. Nonetheless, in many cases, emblem books in quarto spilled their content beyond two pages, so that one emblem might stretch across two openings. One solution to this problem of containment was to print in folio, as in the case of George Wither's *A Collection of Emblemes* (1635), which enabled him to present a generously sized picture together with thirty lines of verse: one complete emblem per page, two per opening. Because Wither had ample material (two hundred emblems), a folio edition was viable. Otto van Veen, however, had only 124 emblems with only twelve lines of verse per emblem. A quarto was the right size of container for this amount of material, but a single page would have allowed only enough room for a small picture. The solution was to print the book in oblong quarto, placing the text on one side of the opening and the picture on the other, so that each turn of the page would reveal a complete emblem. The quarto format meant that there would be less difference between the length and the width of the page than is the case with an octavo, resulting in a more square surface that fit the sonnet-like dimensions of the text

---

[17] In the British Library's *English Short Title Catalogue*, of the 24,705 octavo catalogued books printed between 1500 and 1700, only 55 are classified as oblong; of 44,404 quartos, 125 are oblong; and of 10,172 folios, 52 are oblong.

[18] Cf. Cloud's discussion of the factors bearing on the decision to impose the 1633 "Easter Wings" text(s) vertically (1994, 83–85).

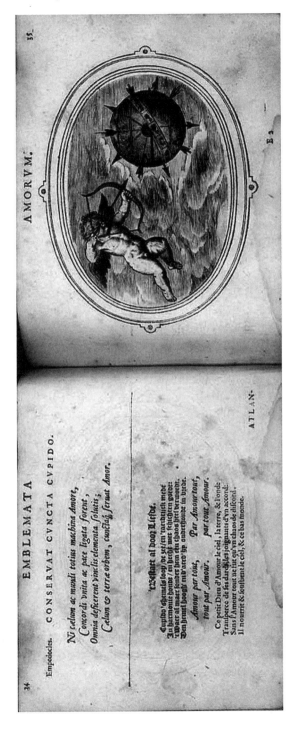

Figure 3. Otto van Veen's *Amorum emblemata*, 1608 (reproduced by permission of the Thomas Fisher Rare Book Library, University of Toronto)

quite nicely: a horizontal line through the middle of the page adds a sense of width to balance the whole composition in relation to the edges of the page. More importantly, these dimensions enabled maximum sizing of Cornelis Bol's engravings, which are in an oblong format that suits perfectly the landscaped scenes in which he places his Cupid figure, the key element in each emblem.

Print technology was relatively quick to respond to the special needs of such material and their users. It is not surprising that music publication was the first to introduce this innovation of oblong publication (as early as 1527), given that the musical staff has a long horizontal dimension and that such publications were often printed with multiple parts to enable sharing of songbooks.[19] Electronic reading technology, however, has not been as quick to come to the aid of readers. For the first decades of commercially available computers, the landscape-oriented screen has been the most common reading surface (though exceptions did exist, such as monitors scaled to legal paper). The landscape orientation works well for creators and users of databases and spreadsheets, but it is an unnatural orientation for writers and readers of documents, which typically conform to the 8.5 x 11″ or A4 standards of paper—the modern equivalent to the golden section often used in ruling the medieval manuscript page.[20] It took a surprisingly long time for portrait screen orientations to become available to non-specialist computer users, and the most common methods seen today result from accident as much as design: with the increased size of monitors and the easy availability of dual-monitor display, writers and readers of documents can now display a full page on a horizontal monitor, and indeed more than one side by side; alternately, the combination of flat-panel monitors and articulated monitor arms make it easy to rotate a single screen on the fly depending on content, requiring only slightly more effort than it takes to rotate "Easter Wings." We have seen much more rapid accommodation in the development of portable devices such as the iPhone, iPad, and Kindle DX, whose screen display responds immediately to the way the device is held. These adjustments (or

---

[19] A catalogue printed anonymously at the end of the eighteenth century cites an oblong quarto printed by Pierre Attaingnant in 1527 with the title *Chansons nouvelles en musique a quatre parties* (Levron 1948, 26). Attaingnant was a pioneer in music printing, and the first to use single-impression printing of music using movable type (Perkins 1999, 93–95). *Chansons nouvelles*, Attaingnant's second publication, was issued in 1528, although it is imprinted 1527 (Taruskin 2005, 692). Longeon's *Catalogue des incunables et des ouvrages imprimés au XVIe siècle conservés a la bibliothèque municipale de Saint-Étienne* (1973) cites Jehan Divry, *Scrinium medicine* (1519) (28).

[20] See Jan Tschichold (1991, 36–63).

lack of adjustment) to the reading surface, however, have not always followed from a conscious and thoughtful recognition of the requirements of
the document and the needs of the reader. In this respect, those seeking to
implement new knowledge environments have much to learn from the history of the book.

Conclusion

The fact that a project like INKE can happen today owes as much to intellectual
and cultural changes as to technological developments. When we assess what
it means to pursue textual scholarship at the end of the first decade of the
twenty-first century, we can identify three recent developments that make
a project like INKE possible. First, the field has moved on from the debate
about the death of the book, or that of *the computer* versus *the book*—which
means that we can recognize the opposed extremes of hypertext enthusiasts
like George Landow and radical traditionalists like Sven Birkerts as the distractions they always were. The narrative in which one technology drives out
another (for better or worse) no longer holds much force in contemporary
textual studies; rather, book historians like Roger Chartier (1995), Peter Stallybrass (2002), and Adrian Johns (1998; and in Grafton, Eisenstein, and Johns
2002), and media historians like Lisa Gitelman (2006), have prompted us to
consider how writing technologies overlap and change each other, and how
those technologies are implicated in reading practices that have their own
histories. Second, the proliferation of reading devices and mobile computing
means that serious scholars can no longer float vague generalizations or es-
sentialist claims about "the computer" as though there was only one kind. As
McCarty has argued, following Michael Mahoney, "Computing appears to us
in a myriad of forms, changing and proliferating as it progresses. ... [T]here is
not one but many computings" (2005, 14). The tendency among scholars and
the popular media to essentialize computing in terms of workplace-oriented
desktop devices is becoming less easy to sustain—a positive change that
prompts us to appreciate the rich diversity of computing practices, just as
textual scholars have long been doing with the rich metonymy of a term like
the book. Finally, speculation about the future of the book is now in a more
healthy balance with practical design work than it was even a decade ago.
INKE, in the best tradition of the digital humanities (borrowed in turn from
design), embodies the philosophy of thinking through making, and helps
textual scholars regain their historical position as the makers of new textual
technologies, not merely users or observers of them.

These are enabling conditions, a few among many, but we also recognize the in-between position of the present historical moment, in which the book is no longer what it once was, and in which computing's possible future is still a moving target. Scholars of premodern forms of textuality are especially well positioned to appreciate these changes because the period they study is a technological threshold-space, where we can see multiple, competing futures for the book in formation. Like the early modern period, our transitory present provides a fleeting opportunity to see the book's past and future with a kind of double vision. Bolter and Grusin assert that "[t]o believe that with digital technology we have passed beyond mediation is also to assert the uniqueness of our present technological moment" (2000, 24). At the same time they recognize that the persistence of remediation is not an a priori truth, "but rather ... that at this extended historical moment, all current media function as remediators and that remediation offers us a means of interpreting the work of earlier media as well" (55). INKE rests on the crux of this paradox, on the one hand insisting that current and future developments of the digital reading environment must learn from the successes and failures of the remarkable technologies they seek to replace; and on the other, insisting with equal force that these new reading environments must make an attempt to move beyond remediation, to move beyond the paradigm of the printed book and take advantage of the unique affordances of the digital medium. The latter point is no small challenge, for in the very term *book* there is a persistent identification of a certain kind of content (the ideational book, and extended discourse on a particular topic) with a particular container for that content (the physical book, or *codex*). *The computer* and *the book*—two terms whose meaning we are still discovering—may not be such irreconcilable forms after all, so long as we look beyond them both as mere containers.

The future of books and computers has been a matter of much speculation. Predicting the future, however, is usually easier than working to influence it. Although our discussion here has not offered predictions about what forms e-books will take, we believe that those who build them must look beyond the twentieth-century book and understand premodern forms of textuality. The closest connections between the past and future are not always the most proximate ones, and digitization requires us to exercise the kind of historical imagination that can reconcile vast differences without effacing them. "Easter Wings," in its original form as a print artefact, similarly calls upon its embodied readers to reconcile two seemingly incommensurable orders of experience, image and text. In our readerly attempts, the book we hold becomes a new and strange artefact as we rotate it, and the symbolic potential of the poem's imping of one set of wings on another becomes fulfilled only when the book is closed, and the text unreadable to human eyes. While a divine perspective might see all modalities as one, and while an ideal text might be all things to all readers, the poem ineluctably casts us back into the human scale of reading. In its historical moment, a project like INKE is not so much an ideal perspective as an attempt, while the book is still turning, to see with different eyes the changing object in our hands.

WORKS CITED

Andersen, Jennifer, and Elizabeth Sauer, eds. 2002. *Books and Readers in Early Modern England: Material Studies.* Philadelphia: University of Pennsylvania Press.

Attaingnant, Pierre, Clément Janequin, and Claudin de Sermisy. 1527. *Chansons nouvelles en musique a quatre parties.* Paris: Attaingnant.

Barwell, Graham. 2005. "Original, Authentic, Copy: Conceptual Issues in Digital Texts." *Literary and Linguistic Computing* 20 (4): 415–24.

Belon, Pierre. 1553. *Petri Bellonii Cenomani De aquatilibus, libri duo.* Paris: Apud Carolum Stephanum.

_____ 1555. *La nature & diuersité des poissons, auec leurs pourtraicts, representez au plus pres du naturel.* Paris: Chez Charles Estienne.

Bolter, Jay David. 2001. *Writing Space: Computers, Hypertext, and the Remediation of Print.* 2nd ed. Mahwah, NJ: Lawrence Erlbaum.

Bolter, Jay David, and Richard Grusin. 2000. *Remediation: Understanding New Media.* Cambridge, MA: MIT Press.

Bryant, John. 2008. "Studying Textual Studies: Problems and Agendas." *Textual Cultures* 3 (2): 90–112.

Chartier, Roger. 1995. *Forms and Meanings: Texts, Performances, and Audiences from Codex to Computer.* Philadelphia: University of Pennsylvania Press.

Cloud, Random. 1994. "FIAT fLUX." In *Crisis in Editing: Texts of the English Renaissance,* edited by Randall McLeod, 61–172. New York: AMS Press.

Dane, Joseph. 2003. "The Myth of Print Culture." In *The Myth of Print Culture: Essays on Evidence, Textuality, and Bibliographical Method*, 10–31. Toronto: University of Toronto Press.

Darnton, Robert. 1979. *The Business of Enlightenment: A Publishing History of the Encyclopédie, 1775–1800*. Cambridge, MA: Harvard University Press.

——————— 2009. *The Case for Books: Past, Present, and Future*. New York: PublicAffairs.

Day, Ronald E. 2000. "The 'Conduit Metaphor' and the Nature and Politics of Information Studies." *Journal of the American Society for Information Science* 51 (9): 805–11.

Divry, Jehan. 1519. *Scrinium medicine authore Joanne Diurio Bellovaco*. [Paris?].

Eggert, Paul. 2009. *Securing the Past: Conservation in Art, Architecture, and Literature*. Cambridge: Cambridge University Press.

Eisenstein, Elizabeth. 1979. *The Printing Press as an Agent of Change: Communications and Cultural Transformations in Early-Modern Europe*. 2 vols. Cambridge: Cambridge University Press.

Eliot, Simon, and Jonathan Rose, eds. 2007. *A Companion to the History of the Book*. Oxford: Blackwell.

Febvre, Lucien, and Henri-Jean Martin. 1958. *The Coming of the Book: The Impact of Printing, 1450–1800*. London: Verso.

Fernie, Ewan. 2005. "The Last Act: Presentism, Spirituality, and the Politics of *Hamlet*." In *Spiritual Shakespeares*, edited by Ewan Fernie, 186–211. London: Routledge.

Finkelstein, David, and Alistair McCleery. 2006. *The Book History Reader*. 2nd ed. London: Routledge.

Galey, Alan. 2009. "Signal to Noise: Designing a Digital Edition of *The Taming of a Shrew* (1594)." *College Literature* 36 (1): 40–66.

Gallagher, Catharine, and Stephen Greenblatt. 2000. *Practicing New Historicism*. Chicago: University of Chicago Press.

Gitleman, Lisa. 2006. *Always Already New: Media, History, and the Data of Culture*. Cambridge, MA: MIT Press.

Grafton, Anthony, Elizabeth L. Eisenstein, and Adrian Johns. 2002. "AHR Forum: How Revolutionary Was the Print Revolution?" *American Historical Review* 107 (1): 84–128.

Greetham, David. 1994. *Textual Scholarship: An Introduction.* New York: Garland.

_____ 1999. *Theories of the Text.* London: Oxford University Press.

_____ 2004. "The Function of [Textual Criticism] at the Present Time." In *Voice, Text, Hypertext: Emerging Practices in Textual Studies,* edited by Raimonda Modiano, Leroy F. Searle, and Peter Shillingsburg, 22–53. Seattle: University of Washington Press.

_____ 2006. "Against Millennialism: First and Last Words from the Cross." *Text* 16:1–32.

_____ 2007. "Review of *Electronic Textual Editing,* eds. Lou Burnard, Katherine O'Brien O'Keeffe, and John Unsworth." *Textual Cultures* 2 (2): 133–36.

Hayles, N. Katharine. 2005. "Translating Media." In *My Mother was a Computer: Digital Subjects and Literary Texts,* 89–116. Chicago: University of Chicago Press.

Hawkes, Terrence. 2002. *Shakespeare in the Present.* London: Routledge.

Herbert, George. 1633. *The Temple: Sacred Poems and Private Ejaculations.* Cambridge: Thomas Buck and Roger Daniel.

Hinman, Charlton. 1963. *The Printing and Proof-Reading of the First Folio of Shakespeare.* 2 vols. Oxford: Clarendon Press.

Hockey, Susan. 2000. *Electronic Texts in the Humanities: Principles and Practice.* Oxford: Oxford University Press.

_____ 2004. "The Reality of Electronic Editors." In Modiano, Searle, and Shillingsburg, eds. 2004, 361–77.

Howsam, Leslie. 2006. *Old Books and New Histories: An Orientation to Studies in Book and Print Culture.* Toronto: University of Toronto Press.

Johns, Adrian. 1998. *The Nature of the Book: Print and Knowledge in the Making.* Chicago: University of Chicago Press.

Kernan, Alvin. 1987. *Printing Technology, Letters, and Samuel Johnson.* Princeton, NJ: Princeton University Press.

Kingdon, Robert M. 1980. "Review of *The Printing Press as an Agent of Change: Communications and Cultural Transformations in Early-Modern Europe*, by Elizabeth Eisenstein." *Library Quarterly* 50 (1): 139–41.

Kirschenbaum, Matthew G. 2002. "Editing the Interface: Textual Studies and First Generation Electronic Objects." *TEXT: An Interdisciplinary Annual of Textual Studies* 14:15–51.

———. 2008. *Mechanisms: New Media and the Forensic Imagination.* Cambridge, MA: MIT Press.

Landow, George P. 1992. *Hypertext: The Convergence of Contemporary Critical Theory and Technology.* Baltimore: Johns Hopkins University Press.

Latour, Bruno. 1986. "Visualization and Cognition: Thinking with Eyes and Hands." *Knowledge and Society: Studies in the Sociology of Culture Past and Present* 6:1–40.

Lavagnino, John. 1995. "Reading, Scholarship, and Hypertext Editions." *TEXT: Transactions of the Society for Textual Scholarship* 8:109–24.

Levron, Jacques. 1948. *Clément Janequin, musicien de la Renaissance.* Grenoble: B. Arthaud.

Liu, Alan. 2004. *The Laws of Cool: Knowledge Work and the Culture of Information.* Chicago: University of Chicago Press.

Longeon, Claude. 1973. *Catalogue des incunables et des ouvrages imprimés au XVIe siècle conservés à la bibliothèque municipale de Saint-Étienne.* Saint-Etienne: Bibliothèque municipale, Centre d'études foréziennes.

Maguire, Laurie E. 1996. *Shakespearean Suspect Texts: The "Bad" Quartos and Their Contexts.* Cambridge: Cambridge University Press.

Marcus, Leah S. 1996. *Unediting the Renaissance: Shakespeare, Marlowe, Milton.* London: Routledge.

McGann, Jerome. 1997. "The Rationale of Hypertext." In *Electronic Text: Investigations in Method and Theory*, edited by Kathryn Sutherland, 19–46. Oxford: Clarendon Press.

_____ 2001. *Radiant Textuality: Literature After the World Wide Web.* New York: Palgrave Macmillan.

_____ 2006. "From Text to Work: Digital Tools and the Emergence of the Social Text." *TEXT: An Interdisciplinary Annual of Textual Studies* 16:49–62.

McCarty, Willard. 2005. *Humanities Computing.* Basingstoke, UK; New York: Palgrave Macmillan.

McKenzie, D.F. 1999. *Bibliography and the Sociology of Texts.* Cambridge: Cambridge University Press.

McKerrow, R.B. 1927. *An Introduction to Bibliography for Literary Students.* Oxford: Oxford University Press.

McKnight, Cliff, Andrew Dillon, and John Richardson. 1991. *Hypertext in Context.* Cambridge: Cambridge University Press.

McLeod, Randall. 2004. "Gerard Hopkins and the Shapes of His Sonnets." In Modiano, Searle, and Shillingsburg, eds. 2004, 177–297 [*sic*].

McLuhan, Marshall. 1962. *The Gutenberg Galaxy: The Making of Typographic Man.* Toronto: University of Toronto Press.

Moran, Joe. 2002. *Interdisciplinarity.* London: Routledge.

Mowat, Barbara A., and Paul Werstine, eds. 1992. *Hamlet.* The Folger Library Shakespeare. New York: Washington Square Press.

Nichol, bp. 1981. *Extreme Positions.* Edmonton, AB: Longspoon Press.

O'Donnell, Daniel Paul. 2008. "Resisting the Tyranny of the Screen; or, Must a Digital Edition be Electronic?" *The Heroic Age: a Journal of Early Medieval Northwestern Europe* 11: http://www.mun.ca/mst/heroicage/issues/11/em.php.

_____ 2009. "Back to the Future: What Digital Editors Can Learn From Print Editorial Practice." *Literary and Linguistic Computing* 24:113–25.

Ong, Walter J. 1965. "Oral Residue in Tudor Prose Style." *PMLA* 80:145–54.

Patterson, Lee. 1987. *Negotiating the Past: The Historical Understanding of Medieval Literature.* Madison: University of Wisconsin Press.

Perkins, Leeman L. 1999. *Music in the Age of the Renaissance.* New York: W.W. Norton.

Price, Kenneth. 2007. "Electronic Scholarly Editions." In *A Companion to Digital Literary Studies,* edited by Ray Siemens and Susan Schreibman, 434–50. Oxford: Blackwell.

Reimer, Stephen R. 2006. "A Perspective on Humanities Computing and Textual Studies." In *Mind Technologies: Humanities Computing and the Canadian Academic Community,* edited by Raymond Siemens and David Moorman, 57–62. Calgary: University of Calgary Press.

Rhodes, Neil, and Jonathan Sawday, eds. 2000. *The Renaissance Computer: Knowledge Technology in the First Age of Print.* London: Routledge.

Ross, Charles L. 1996. "The Electronic Text and the Death of the Critical Edition." In *The Literary Text in the Digital Age,* edited by Richard J. Finneran, 225–32. Ann Arbor: University of Michigan Press.

Shakespeare, William. 2006. *Hamlet.* Edited by Ann Thompson and Neil Taylor. London: Arden Shakespeare.

Shillingsburg, Peter L. 2006. *From Gutenberg to Google: Electronic Representations of Literary Texts.* Cambridge: Cambridge University Press.

Siemens, Ray. 1998. "Disparate Structures, Electronic and Otherwise: Conceptions of Textual Organisation in the Electronic Medium, with Reference to Electronic Editions of Shakespeare and the Internet." *Early Modern Literary Studies* 3 (3) / Special Issue 2: 6.1–29. http://purl. oclc.org/emls/03-3/siemshak.html.

_____ 2002. "Shakespearean Apparatus? Explicit Textual Structures and the Implicit Navigation of Accumulated Knowledge." *TEXT: An Interdisciplinary Annual of Textual Studies* 14:209–40.

_____ 2005. "Text Analysis and the Dynamic Edition? Some Concerns With an Algorithmic Approach in the Electronic Scholarly Edition." Working papers from the first and second Canadian Symposium on Text Analysis Research (CaSTA). Joint Special Issue: *Computing in the Humanities Working Papers* (A.37) and *Text Technology* 14 (1): 91–98.

Siemens, Ray, Claire Warwick, Richard Cunningham, Teresa Dobson, Alan Galey, Stan Ruecker, Susan Schreibman, and the INKE Team. 2009.

"Codex Ultor: Toward a Conceptual and Theoretical Foundation for New Research on Books and Knowledge Environments." *Digital Studies / Le champ numérique* 1 (2): http://www.digitalstudies.org/ojs/index. php/digital_studies/article/view/177/220.

Smith, Martha Nell. 2004. "Electronic Scholarly Editing." In *A Companion to Digital Humanities*, edited by Susan Schreibman, Ray Siemens, and John Unsworth, 306–21. Oxford: Blackwell.

Stallybrass, Peter. 2002. "Books and Scrolls: Navigating the Bible." In Andersen and Sauer 2002, 42–79.

Tanselle, G. Thomas. 1989. *A Rationale of Textual Criticism.* Philadelphia: University of Pennsylvania Press.

_____ 2001. "Thoughts on the Authenticity of Electronic Texts." *Studies in Bibliography* 54:133–36.

_____ 2006. "Foreword." In *Electronic Textual Editing*, edited by Lou Burnard, Katherine O'Brien O'Keeffe, and John Unsworth, 1–6. New York: Modern Language Association.

Taruskin, Richard. 2005. *The Oxford History of Western Music.* Vol. 1. Oxford: Oxford University Press.

Thorburn, David, and Henry Jenkins, eds. 2003. *Rethinking Media Change: The Aesthetics of Transition.* Cambridge, MA: MIT Press.

Tschichold, Jan. 1991. *The Form of the Book: Essays on the Morality of Good Design.* Translated by Hajo Hadeler. Edited by Robert Bringhurst. Vancouver: Hartley & Marks.

Veen, Otto van. 1608. *Amorum emblemata: figuris aeneis incise.* Antwerp: Venalia apud auctorem.

Veeser, H. Aram, ed. 1989. *The New Historicism.* New York: Routledge.

Warren, Michael, ed. 1989. *The Complete King Lear 1608-1623.* Berkeley: University of California Press.

Werstine, Paul. 2008. "Past is Prologue: Electronic New Variorum Shakespeares." *Shakespeare* 4:224–36.

Wilson, F.P. 1970. *Shakespeare and the New Bibliography.* Revised and edited by Helen Gardner. Oxford: Clarendon Press.

The Materiality of Markup and the Text Encoding Initiative[1]

James Cummings
University of Oxford
james.cummings@oucs.ox.ac.uk

Introduction

The application of markup to a text is not only an act of interpretation but also an expression of a relationship between materially extant acts and the linguistic or intellectual concepts they embody. We recognize that some portion of written text in a manuscript is a different size, hand, or location, and from that are able to interpret its meaning as, for example, a marginal note or a rubric. These forms of material difference are significantly distinct from those where in a textual string of characters we are able to recognize a name or some particular linguistic or semantic feature. Textual phenomena that have a physical rather than intellectual basis for distinction from the surrounding text are, of course, those that are most readily visible to us. It is the correspondence between markup as deriving from or expressing the materiality of the object and the intellectual understanding of what it represents textually that this chapter will examine below while surveying some of the aspects of the Text Encoding Initiative (TEI) P5 Guidelines most useful to those working with historical manuscript materials.[2]

In order to take advantage of modern tools for digitally assisted research into historical materials we must continue to embrace new technology. Indeed, along with classicists, those researching the Middle Ages and Renaissance have often been at the forefront of digital resource creation and use. These communities have also led digital humanities in creating self-defined groups

---

[1] This chapter is indebted to the TEI Consortium's guidelines (2010) and much of the TEI community as a whole for their constant pushing of the boundaries of text encoding but also certainly my TEI@Oxford colleagues Lou Burnard and Sebastian Rahtz.

[2] See TEI Consortium, TEI: Text Encoding Initiative, 2010 or http://www.tei-c.org/ for more information about the Text Encoding Initiative.

ISBN 978-0-86698-499-7 (online)   ISBN 978-0-86698-474-4 (print)
New Technologies in Medieval and Renaissance Studies 3 (2012) 49–81

to share best practices and experiences in these areas. For example, Digital Medievalist is a community run by elected volunteers revolving around an email list, an open access peer-reviewed online journal, and sponsored conference sessions.[3] In providing an introduction to some of the TEI's recommendations for dealing with manuscript materials, this chapter hopes to continue this tradition by encouraging more scholars to examine the nature of digital technology with regard to the research they undertake.

It is not the place of this chapter to attempt to instruct readers in XML, the overall framework of the TEI, or its applicability to literary studies: a variety of material already exists to aid readers in those areas.[4] Rather, this chapter introduces the TEI's recommendations for manuscript description, focusing especially on those aspects relating to the materiality of the physical manuscript. Following on from this, there is a brief examination of some of the methods for representing editorial choices in transcriptions of text, the TEI's methods for documenting non-standard characters, TEI recommendations for creating digital facsimiles of objects, and the benefits of tailoring the overall TEI scheme to the needs of one's particular project. The chapter concludes with a consideration of one of the major problems inhibiting the interoperability of many resources.

Description of manuscripts

The TEI module for the description of manuscripts is especially of interest to any scholar working with handwritten materials.[5] Manuscripts (here the term is being used very loosely to encompass any document created by hand rather than a typescript or mechanically printed document) are of interest not only because of their texts but also because the physical method of their production, the creation of their material form, is necessarily that of producing a unique cultural artefact. As much as a scribe may copy an exemplar document, the result will always be itself unique. That is not to say that two

---

[3] See Digital Medievalist, accessed 23 October 2009, http://www.digitalmedievalist. org/, for more information. As an example of cooperation between such groups, in 2008 Digital Medievalist published a journal issue containing Digital Classicist research that would be of interest to medievalists as well. See also O'Donnell (2008) and Robinson (2005).

[4] See, for example, Cummings (2008) and TEI Consortium (2010, sec. v), also "Learn the TEI."

[5] See TEI Consortium (2010, sec. 10); this includes, of course, modern letters, cf. Vanhoutte and Van den Branden (2009).

documents printed one after another on a laser printer are not also unique individual objects, but because the nature of the differences is usually less pronounced than any object created by hand, we tend to classify them as instantiations of the same object, for example, using abstract bibliographic references to the text rather than to that specific physical object.

While those editing manuscript texts often put aside the more bibliographic aspects, no edition of a manuscript text should be considered scholarly without at least some basic description of its source. There are those for whom a manuscript description is simply a bibliographic record, and for others it is an additional source of data which, when combined with many other manuscript descriptions, opens up new and interesting fields of research. Most manuscript descriptions, however, are not created in the context of scholarly editions (electronic or print) but as items in a larger catalogue in manuscript libraries and archives. In its continual attempt to be general in application, the TEI caters to all of these desires in its module on manuscript description.

Manuscript description and retrospective conversion

One of the requirements of encoding manuscript descriptions is that the format be flexible enough to cope with the wide range of forms of data found in existing legacy catalogues of manuscript descriptions. The recommendations of the TEI for manuscript description are highly flexible, and this is a result of the history of its development out of other collaboratively agreed standards (Driscoll 2006). This means that for a TEI <msDesc> one could equally provide an extremely limited manuscript description with only a required section on identification and optional prose as shown in Figure 1, or a highly structured description.

```
<msDesc xml:lang="en" xml:id="AM08-169">
  <msIdentifier n="KK2381">
    <country>Danmark</country>
    <settlement>København</settlement>
    <repository>Det Arnamagnæanske Institut</repository>
    <idno>AM 169 8vo</idno>
  </msIdentifier>
  <p>Calendarium latinum, Denmark, 1490. Latin. The manuscript once belonged to
    AM 10 8vo. ff. 1r-7r: Calendarium Latinum Parchment codex. 7. f. 7v is
    blank. 144x107. Bound in a vellum leaf taken from a double columned
    liturgical manuscript in Latin. On the AM-slip Árni Magnússon has written
    the following: "Þetta Calendarium er teked framan af Jutskre Logbok sem
    P[er] Terkilse[n] till i Føwling hefur lated rita 1490. og ritad hefur
    Johannes Nicolai." Written in Denmark in 1490. Catalogued 12.04.2000 by
    EW-J. Parsed 10.07.2000. Photographed in 1960. Lent out to Record Office
    for the use of Erik Kroman 02.03.1964-26.05.1964. See also: microfilm
    (master) Gneg.221 1960; microfilm (archive) Gpos.256 1960; b/w prints AM
    169 8vo March 1979</p>
</msDesc>
```

Figure 1: A prose <msDesc> element[6]

This description, while more useful than a similarly printed one, is limited because the majority of the information is not structured. As existing legacy catalogues may contain more or less degrees of structure, the flexibility of the <msDesc> element allows the most scope for the wide variety of retrospective conversion projects possible. The organization of descriptive information into minimally agreed categories of data is more useful for future interoperability than rigorous adherence to any single approach of cataloguing or an agreed level of encoding granularity. In converting legacy data one might separate the existing record into individual paragraphs of general categories, for example, one for the intellectual content, another for

---

[6] This example and the following ones are derived from the ENRICH project; ENRICH was a COST eContent+ funded EU project attempting to standardize medieval manuscript metadata across Europe. It had, predictably, variable degrees of success. This example is based on an excerpt chosen almost at random from a test bed on a previous ENRICH web location, accessed 23 October 2009, http://tei.oucs.ox.ac.uk/ENRICH/. The test bed was converted from MASTER encoding to the TEI P5 ENRICH specification as part of the ENRICH project's testing of XSLT-based migration routes for MASTER documents. For more information about the ENRICH project's transformation of MASTER records, see the deliverable reports (especially D 3.3) at the current site at TEI@Oxford, accessed 23 October 2009, http://projects.oucs.ox.ac.uk/ENRICH/. See also the case studies on migration to the ENRICH specification, which include samples and conversion scripts.

its physical description, another for the manuscript's provenance, and a final one for administrative metadata (cf. Cummings 2006).

```
<msDesc xml:lang="en" xml:id="AM08-169">
  <msIdentifier n="KK2381">
    <country>Danmark</country>
    <settlement>København</settlement>
    <repository>Det Arnamagnæanske Institut</repository>
    <idno>AM 169 8vo</idno>
  </msIdentifier>
  <p>Calendarium latinum, Denmark, 1490. Latin. The manuscript once belonged to
    AM 10 8vo.</p>
  <p>ff. 1r-7r: Calendarium Latinum </p>
  <p>Parchment codex. 7. f. 7v is blank. 144x107. Bound in a vellum leaf taken
    from a double columned liturgical manuscript in Latin. On the AM-slip Árni
    Magnússon has written the following: "Þetta Calendarium er teked framan af
    Jutskre Logbok sem P[er] Terkilse[n] till i Føwling hefur lated rita 1490.
    og ritad hefur Johannes Nicolai." </p>
  <p>Written in Denmark in 1490.</p>
  <p>Catalogued 12.04.2000 by EW-J. Parsed 10.07.2000. Photographed in 1960.
    Lent out to Record Office for the use of Erik Kroman
    02.03.1964-26.05.1964. </p>
  <p>See also: microfilm (master) Gneg.221 1960; microfilm (archive) Gpos.256
    1960; b/w prints AM 169 8vo March 1979</p>
</msDesc>
```

Figure 2: A very slightly better <msDesc> element

Splitting the description into separate paragraph elements begins to allow greater scope for resource discovery since (if done consistently across a collection) it enables the possibility of user-querying of limited subsets. A format such as this is certainly acceptable as a first pass when automatically converting legacy data that is not available at a finer level of granularity; however, even such a basic manuscript description would need some form of checking or human interaction to ensure the paragraphs group appropriate information together. Indeed, if the resources do exist to create such a basic record, then it is a very short step to adding even a small amount more structure that would give the potential for a much richer resource.

```
<msDesc xml:lang="en" xml:id="AM08-169">
  <msIdentifier n="KK2381">
    <country>Danmark</country>
    <settlement>København</settlement>
    <repository>Det Arnamagnæanske Institut</repository>
    <idno>AM 169 8vo</idno>
  </msIdentifier>
  <head n="msHeading">Calendarium latinum, Denmark, 1490. Latin. The manuscript
    once belonged to AM 10 8vo.</head>
  <msContents><p>ff. 1r-7r: Calendarium Latinum </p></msContents>
  <physDesc><p>Parchment codex. 7. f. 7v is blank. 144x107. Bound in a vellum leaf
    taken from a double columned liturgical manuscript in Latin. On the
    AM-slip Árni Magnússon has written the following: "Þetta Calendarium
    er teked framan af Jutskre Logbok sem P[er] Terkilse[n] till i Føwling
    hefur lated rita 1490. og ritad hefur Johannes Nicolai." </p></physDesc>
  <history><p>Written in Denmark in 1490.</p></history>
  <additional>
    <adminInfo>
      <note>Catalogued 12.04.2000 by EW-J. Parsed 10.07.2000. Photographed
        in 1960. Lent out to Record Office for the use of Erik Kroman
        02.03.1964-26.05.1964. </note>
    </adminInfo>
    <listBibl><bibl> microfilm (master) Gneg.221 1960 </bibl>
      <bibl> microfilm (archive) Gpos.256 1960 </bibl>
      <bibl> b/w prints AM 169 8vo March 1979 </bibl></listBibl>
  </additional>
</msDesc>
```

Figure 3: A slightly structured <msDesc> element

All of this is fairly straightforward and the point at which many retrospective conversion projects might stop; however, the TEI provides a highly flexible vocabulary for the description of manuscripts which can be used to build data structures of many varying degrees of detail or meet a range of resource discovery or retrospective conversion needs.[7] If one creates a manuscript description from scratch in TEI, then a much more structured record is likely to be more suitable. Some of the available elements for creating this structure are surveyed below.

Identification and heading

Every manuscript description in the TEI (and, one could argue, in any sensible catalogue of manuscripts of any form) needs to provide for each manuscript identifying information of some sort. This can range from information about the object's physical location (e.g., <settlement> or <country>), its political

---

[7] One example of this is the updated version of the original M-Tool created for the ENRICH project, see Manuscriptorium, accessed 23 October 2009, http://www.manuscriptorium.com/apps/m-tool/m-tool.php#itemDesc.

location or controls (e.g., <repository> or <institution>), or some identifying designation (e.g., <idno>). Place-related information might include metadata such as the country, city, or region where the manuscript is located. The political information might include the name of the institution which holds it, which of its repositories it is located in, and of which collection it is a part. Finally, the identifying designation might simply be some identification number such as a classmark or a name by which the manuscript is known.

```xml
<msDesc xml:lang="en" xml:id="AM08-169">
  <msIdentifier n="KK2381">
    <country>Danmark</country>
    <settlement>København</settlement>
    <repository>Det Arnamagnæanske Institut</repository>
    <idno>AM 169 8vo</idno>
  </msIdentifier>
  <head type="msHeading">
    <title xml:lang="LAT">Calendarium latinum</title>
    <origPlace>Denmark</origPlace>
    <origDate cert="high" evidence="external">1490</origDate>
    <seg type="textLang" subtype="LAT">Latin</seg>
    <note>The manuscript once belonged to <ref>AM 10 8vo</ref>.</note>
  </head>

  <!-- more here -->

</msDesc>
```

Figure 4: The start of a manuscript description

It should be noted that in this example the record also gives the description itself a unique identifier through the use of the @xml:id attribute on <ms-Desc>. Similarly, the @xml:lang attribute indicates the language of the description itself (not the language of manuscript). The <head> element inside an <msDesc> is sometimes employed to give a more formal summary of the most important aspects of the description for convenience of later output.

Intellectual contents

After recording the information useful in identifying the object, manuscript descriptions catalogue the intellectual contents of the manuscript, meaning the textual items the manuscript contains and any information known about them. Descriptions of the manuscript contents (<msContents> element) can contain one or more manuscript item item (<msItem>) elements which refer to the discrete intellectual units inside the physical object. In this case, there is only a single <msItem> element:

```
<msContents>
  <textLang mainLang="lat">Latin</textLang>
  <msItem>
    <locus from="1r" to="7r">ff. 1r-7r</locus>
    <title xml:lang="LAT">Calendarium Latinum</title>
  </msItem>
</msContents>
```

Figure 5: An <msContents> element

An optional <textLang> element can be used to indicate the language(s) in which the text of the manuscript is written. If it is used, it must be placed within the <msContents> element and must be placed before any <msItem> element. This has the benefit of providing a single straightforward location where later systems processing the text can retrieve both an ISO standard code for the language and a human-readable description of the language (or languages) that are found in the document.

Physical description

In many ways the physical description of a manuscript (<physDesc> element) is one of the most important aspects of the description. It is often the material details of the manuscript which set it apart from mass-printed non-manuscript materials. While many of the elements presented here are also useful for very rare or unique printed texts (such as incunabula) or other text-bearing objects (such as inscriptions), modern mass-market printed volumes benefit less from such in-depth physical description. The TEI, in recognizing this use of manuscript description elements for special classes of non-manuscript materials, also includes a <typeDesc> element.[8]

The <physDesc> element can be further subdivided into more or less structural categories including the following:

  ★ <additions>: any significant additions, such as marginalia or other annotations
  ★ <bindingDesc>: the present and former bindings of the manuscript
  ★ <decoDesc>: the decoration of a manuscript
  ★ <handDesc>: the kinds of hands and writing forms used
  ★ <musicNotation>: the nature of any musical notation
  ★ <objectDesc>: the physical components making up the object

---

[8] Manuscripts can be bound with printed materials, and thus using a <typeDesc> for manuscript materials is not inconceivable. Moreover, <msDesc> has sometimes been used for incunabula.

★ <sealDesc>: the seals or other external items attached to a manuscript

★ <typeDesc>: the typefaces or other aspects of the printing of an incu-
nable or other printed source

★ <accMat>: closely associated accompanying matter

A very complete <physDesc> element could contain all of these categories:

```
<physDesc>
  <objectDesc><!-- physical components --></objectDesc>
  <handDesc><!-- hands --></handDesc>
  <typeDesc><!-- typefaces --></typeDesc>
  <musicNotation><!-- musical notation --></musicNotation>
  <decoDesc><!-- decoration --></decoDesc>
  <additions><!-- additions --></additions>
  <bindingDesc><!-- bindings --></bindingDesc>
  <sealDesc><!-- seals --></sealDesc>
  <accMat><!-- accompanying matter --></accMat>
</physDesc>
```

Figure 6: The structure of a <physDesc>

In most cases, however, manuscript descriptions do not use all of these categories, and in reality most manuscripts do not contain each of these aspects.
The manuscript being described earlier might have a <physDesc> such as the
following:

```
<physDesc>
  <objectDesc form="codex">
    <supportDesc material="perg">
      <support>Parchment.</support>
      <extent>7. f. 7v is blank. <dimensions type="leaf" scope="all">
          <height>144</height>
          <width>107</width>
        </dimensions>
      </extent>
    </supportDesc>
  </objectDesc>
  <bindingDesc>
    <binding contemporary="unknown">
      <p>Bound in a vellum leaf taken from a double columned liturgical
        manuscript in Latin.</p>
    </binding>
  </bindingDesc>
  <accMat>
    <p>On the AM-slip <name type="person" key="ArnMag01">Árni Magnússon</name>
      has written the following: <quote xml:lang="ISL">Þetta Calendarium er
      teked framan af Jutskre Logbok sem <name type="person"
      key="PerTer01">P<expan>er</expan> Terkilse<expan>n</expan>
      </name> till i <name type="place">Føwling</name> hefur lated rita
      <date>1490</date>. og ritad hefur <name type="person"
      key="JenNil01">Johannes Nicolai</name>.</quote></p>
  </accMat>
</physDesc>
```

Figure 7: A <physDesc> element

History

One of the prime concerns in describing a manuscript is its provenance, from its creation to the acquisition by the modern resource-holding institution where it resides. The <history> element allows either unstructured paragraphs or an optional <summary> element followed by an optional <origin> element to contain any information known about the manuscript's original creation. This can optionally be followed by any number of <provenance> elements detailing the life of the manuscript up to an <acquisition> element, which records the information concerning the acquisition of the manuscript by its current owner or institution. All aspects of the <history> element are optional, so it can contain as much or as little information as is available concerning the history of the manuscript:

```
<history>
  <origin notBefore="1490" notAfter="1490" cert="high">
    <p>Written in <origPlace>Denmark</origPlace> in <origDate
      evidence="external" cert="high">1490</origDate>.</p>
  </origin>
  <!-- followed by optional <provenance> elements and an <acquisition> element -->
</history>
```

Figure 8: A <history> element

Additional

In manuscript descriptions there is sometimes a need to record additional information grouped together inside an <additional> element: for example, bibliographic information about the manuscript, itemization of surrogate copies (such as photographic or digital facsimiles), and curatorial or administrative information. Inside this, the <adminInfo> element can contain information concerning the manuscript's custodial history, including the history of the manuscript description itself. Also grouped together under <additional> is bibliographic information about facsimiles of the manuscript contained in a <surrogates> element and, optionally, other bibliographic information enclosed in a <listBibl> element.

```
<additional>
  <adminInfo>
    <recordHist>
      <source><p>Catalogued <date>12.04.2000</date> by EW-J. Parsed
        <date>10.07.2000</date>.</p></source>
    </recordHist>
    <custodialHist>
      <custEvent type="photography"><p>Photographed in
        <date>1960</date></p></custEvent>
      <custEvent type="loan">
        <p>Lent out to Record Office for the use of <name type="person"
          key="EriKro01">Erik Kroman</name>
          <date>02.03.1964-26.05.1964</date></p>
      </custEvent>
    </custodialHist>
  </adminInfo>
  <surrogates>
    <listBibl>
      <bibl><title type="gmd">microfilm (master)</title>
        <idno>Gneg.221</idno><date>1960</date></bibl>
      <bibl>
        <title type="gmd">microfilm (archive)</title>
        <idno>Gpos.256</idno><date>1960</date></bibl>
      <bibl>
        <title type="gmd">b/w prints</title>
        <idno>AM 169 8vo</idno><date>March 1979</date></bibl>
    </listBibl></surrogates>
</additional>
```

Figure 9: An <additional> element

Composite manuscripts

In cases where a manuscript was formed from several originally distinct manuscripts, a description may contain multiple <msPart> elements to provide information for each of the distinct manuscript parts. In general this structure might look like the following:

```
<msDesc xml:id="ms007">
  <msIdentifier>
    <!-- General identifying information -->
  </msIdentifier>
  <!-- other elements here as applicable-->
  <msPart>
    <altIdentifier>
      <idno>MS 007 Part 1</idno>
    </altIdentifier>
    <!-- other information specific to this part here -->
  </msPart>
  <msPart>
    <altIdentifier>
      <idno>MS 84</idno>
    </altIdentifier>
    <!-- other information specific to this part here -->
  </msPart>
  <!-- other msParts here -->
</msDesc>
```

Figure 10: The structure of a composite manuscript

The <msPart> element can include an <altIdentifier> element to cope with those cases where parts of a composite manuscript are identified or catalogued independently.

The possibilities of quantitative codicology

It is valid to ask why one might want to invest resources in creating digital catalogues that are based on highly structured records rather than just free-text paragraphs. There are many possible answers to this, but the prime motivation is for more sophisticated forms of resource discovery; however, this is simply the beginning of the research potential of a large corpus of detailed manuscript descriptions.[9] Once a sample of manuscripts is large enough to be considered representative of the determining aspect (e.g., location, country, script), then forms of quantitative codicology, where aspects

---

[9] It should be remembered that "manuscripts" here may also include modern letters. See, for example, the work of Vanhoutte and Van den Branden (2009).

of one individual manuscript (or a smaller sample) are studied with respect to a larger sample of similar manuscripts, is increasingly possible. This kind of research can help to discover patterns in manuscript production and codicological clusters of activity that might go unnoticed if such research were not computer-assisted.[10]

Textual transcriptions

The TEI aims to provide all the elements one might need for recording the common phenomena encountered in transcribing a text.[11] One of the ways in which it does this is by generalizing our understanding of textual phenomena, so the damage which makes part of the text on a clay tablet illegible is an instance of the same type of phenomenon as an ink blot that obscures some words in a manuscript, or some damage caused by a woodworm in the text of a printed work. In all such cases an unintended physical change to the object has interrupted the textual stream by making the text illegible on account of some form of damage. That the two instances of damage have different agents does not stop it being the same textual phenomenon documented in the TEI with the <damage> element. The TEI provides numerous elements for representing physical obstructions of the textual stream that are usually noted in any scholarly edition. It provides elements such as <add>, <del>, <subst>, <supplied>, <unclear>, and <gap> among many others. The use of these tags to represent what is seen on the physical object being transcribed is fairly straightforward, and so I will not discuss them here;[12] however, one set of transcriptional elements does warrant further explanation, partly because it yokes together what can be seen on the physical object with an interpretation which necessarily is not manifest in the document. These interpretations are nested inside a <choice> element to provide an alternative between a set of elements for particular textual phenomena. For example, it enables editors to mark both apparent errors and their corrections, or to note a reading following the original rather than its editorial regularization, or an abbreviation and its corresponding expansion. In each of these cases only one side of this so-called "Janus" pairing appears in the material object, and the other of these is an interpretation by the editor. The <choice> ele-

---

[10] See for example Bart (2006) for codicological experimentation using TEI; or Bozzolo and Ornato (1980) for an early work on quantitative codicology. See also Stokes (2007) for similar concepts applied to palaeography.

[11] See TEI Consortium (2010, sec. 11).

[12] Some of these elements are discussed in the TEI guidelines (TEI Consortium 2010, sec. 3.4.3).

ment enables an editor to encode a text without having to choose, at that stage, between a diplomatic or normalized representation of the text. In an original document one can have a segment of text which one later regularizes, an apparent error one later corrects, or an abbreviation or expansion which one later then either contracts or expands. In each of these instances one can see that the desired rendering might call for either of these to be available in the output. If a manuscript says "angues" instead of "augens,"[13] the apparent error can be grouped together with its correction:

```
<ab>
  Nos autem iam ostendimus quod nutrimentum et
  <choice>
    <sic>angues</sic>
    <corr>augens</corr>
  </choice>.
</ab>
```

Figure 11: A <choice> element with a correction[14]

Or it might be that the editor desires that an original reading be regularized.

```
<l>But this will be a
  <choice>
    <orig>meere</orig>
    <reg>mere</reg>
  </choice> confusion</l>
<l>And hardly shall we all be
  <choice>
    <orig>vnderstoode</orig>
    <reg>understood</reg>
  </choice>
</l>
```

Figure 12: A <choice> element with a regularization[15]

In both of these cases it is quite unlikely that the original will have contained the other alternative. While copy-texts do have corrections, these are not in-

---

[13] "Angues" from "anguis" meaning "a serpent, snake," versus "augens" from "augeo," meaning "to increase, augment, enlarge, spread, extend."

[14] This example is derived from the TEI guidelines. See TEI Consortium, "P5: Guidelines for Electronic Text Encoding and Interchange," 2010, at http://www.tei-c.org/release/doc/tei-p5-doc/en/html/PH.html#PHCC.

[15] This example is derived from the TEI guidelines. See TEI Consortium, "P5: Guidelines for Electronic Text Encoding and Interchange," 2010, at http://www.tei-c.org/release/doc/tei-p5-doc/en/html/ref-orig.html.

terventions by the current editor. Corrections made within the manuscript by one of the scribes are encoded with elements such as <del> and <add>, possibly grouped together by a <subst> element to indicate they are a single act of substitution present on the physical object. Scribal convention in many early manuscripts is to abbreviate words where possible, whereas modern editing convention is to provide these in expanded form. Below, the <abbr> and <expan> elements are used to indicate the abbreviated and expanded form respectively, with the <g> element being used to reference a fuller description of the non-standard abbreviation glyph (with optional text content).

```
<choice>
  <abbr>ev<g ref="#ab-er"/>y</abbr>
  <expan>every</expan>
</choice>
<choice>
  <abbr><g ref="#ab-per"/>sone</abbr>
  <expan>persone</expan>
</choice>
```

Figure 13: A <choice> element with an expansion[16]

However, abbreviations, as all those working with highly abbreviated manuscripts will know, are special.[17] While an editorial correction of an apparent error is a generally unitary act (either you agree with the suggested correction, or you disagree) the same is not necessarily true of an expanded abbreviation. You may agree with part of an expansion of an abbreviation, or indeed agree that this is one of the possible options for the expansion but that others are possible. In a hypothetical example with regard to the figure above, if a reader believes the editor misread the "v" instead of an "n," and thus the nature of the abbreviation, then he or she might suspect that this word should be expanded as "enemy" instead of "every." To cope with this, <abbr> and <expan> have specialized elements allowed inside them to indicate the original abbreviation marker with the <am> (abbreviation marker) element or the expansion inside an <ex> (editorial expansion) element containing the corresponding sequence of letters added by the editor in expanding an abbreviation.

---

[16] This example and the following three are derived from the TEIguidelines. See TEI Consortium, "P5: Guidelines for Electronic Text Encoding and Interchange," 2010, at http://www.tei-c.org/release/doc/tei-p5-doc/en/html/PH.html#PHAB.

[17] See, for example, the attempts at categorization by Parkinson and Emiliano (2002).

```
<choice>
  <abbr>ev<am><g ref="#ab-er"/></am>y</abbr>
  <expan>ev<ex>er</ex>y</expan>
</choice>
<choice>
  <abbr><g ref="#ab-per"/>sone</abbr>
  <expan><ex>per</ex>sone</expan>
</choice>
```

Figure 14: Demonstrating <am> and <ex>

This allows for alternative rendering of the expanded characters, such as italics, which gives a proper scholarly indication of which characters were present in a manuscript folio and which have been supplied, with all good intentions, by the editor (Cummings 2009). Each of these alternatives is repeatable multiple times inside the <choice> element. Additionally, the <choice> element itself can self-nest, allowing choices between sets of choices, for example, in the following hypothetical case:

```
<choice>
  <choice>
    <abbr>ev<am cert="high"><g ref="#ab-er"/></am>y</abbr>
    <expan resp="#JC">ev<ex cert="high">er</ex>y</expan>
  </choice>
  <choice>
    <abbr>en<am cert="low"><g ref="#ab-em"/></am>y</abbr>
    <expan resp="#LB">en<ex cert="low">em</ex>y</expan>
  </choice>
</choice>
<choice>
  <choice>
    <abbr><am cert="high"><g ref="#ab-per"/></am>sone</abbr>
    <expan><ex cert="high" resp="#JC">per</ex>sone</expan>
  </choice>
  <choice>
    <abbr><am cert="low"><g ref="#ab-pri"/></am>sons</abbr>
    <expan><ex cert="low" resp="#LB">pri</ex>sons</expan>
  </choice>
</choice>
```

Figure 15: Nested <choice>

Above we are offering a choice between two nested alternatives, one which claims that the abbreviated text physically present on the manuscript is meant to be interpreted by the reader as "every persone" and another which believes it should be understood as "enemy prisons." The encoding here hinges on how the respective editors interpreted the two minims that make up the "v" or "n" and the single abbreviation mark which could be either "per" or "pri." Our certainty concerning the nature of the abbreviation marks and their expansions has been characterized as "low" or "high," and the editor responsible has been recorded. There are more detailed methods for recording certainty should a project require it, but in most cases simply the indication of the editor's degree of certainty is a sufficient distinction for scholarly editing. The <choice> element is thus a powerful mechanism that allows the relation of an editor's perception of the abbreviation marks on a manuscript to be given in parallel to their interpretation about what these marks might mean.

One of the reasons for the invention of the <choice> element is that earlier ways to encode such information involved storing the alternative reading in an attribute value. Thus one of the elements would be used depending on the priority of the editor (either to present a diplomatic or an editorial version) and the other would be consigned to the lesser status of an attribute.

```
<abbr expan="every">ev&ab-er;ry</abbr>
```

Figure 16: A TEI P4 expansion

This was removed in TEI P5 because it is impossible to include further XML markup inside an attribute value that is storing textual content. In the example above, there would have been no way to indicate which letters were expanded, because attribute values cannot contain markup. This is an identical problem to that caused by the need for an element-based (rather than attribute-based) solution to problematic issues concerning the internationalization of texts, specifically cases where there was a need to use or describe a non-Unicode character. This might include characters which were not yet included in the Unicode standard or those specialized forms of glyphs that for research purposes the creator of the text was interested in recording.[18] Organizations such the Medieval Unicode Font Initiative (MUFI) have been extremely successful in introducing new characters into the Unicode standard for the community they represent. MUFI is a non-profit group of scholars and font designers working towards improving the encoding and display of special characters in medieval texts.[19]

---

[18] For a more detailed introduction to the TEI recommendations for the representation of non-standard characters and glyphs, see TEI Consortium, "P5: Guidelines for Electronic Text Encoding and Interchange," 2010, at http://www.tei-c.org/release/doc/tei-p5-doc/en/html/WD.html.

[19] See the Medieval Unicode Font Initiative, accessed 23 October 2009, http://www.

While getting characters accepted by the Unicode standard and well represented in mainstream fonts is the ideal, in cases where characters do not yet exist in Unicode, additional markup is required. This markup could not be contained in an attribute value as discussed above but required an additional element <g> (glyph) which would refer back to the <teiHeader> for documentation of the character. The need for these <g> elements may appear in almost any location where free text attributes were allowed, and since markup is not allowed in attributes, any TEI P4 attributes whose values could not be expressed by more controlled schema-based datatypes were changed into child elements. This is one of the reasons that the TEI P4 version of the <abbr> element above needed to be changed to a <choice> structure: once you are forced to represent an expansion with an <expan> element, you need something to contain these two elements as alternatives.

The TEI developed a system whereby one could document any non-Unicode character (or specialized glyph) and refer to metadata about it stored in the <teiHeader>. This was the invention of the <g> element which could point to a variety of metadata elements to store information about this glyph.

```
<char xml:id="f161">
  <desc>F161</desc>
  <charProp>
    <localName>entity</localName>
    <value>punctelev</value>
  </charProp>
  <mapping type="MUFI" subtype="Unicode">ⸯ </mapping>
  <mapping type="MUFI" subtype="PUA">U+F161</mapping>
  <graphic url="images/f161.png"/>
</char>

<!-- elsewhere in the document -->
<ab>Praeoccupemus faciem domini in confessione<g ref="#f161"/></ab>
```

Figure 17: Pointing from the text to a <char>[20]

---

mufi.info/. There are a number of fonts implementing MUFI proposals in the Private Use Area. Andron Scriptor Web is the only one with full compatability, but Junicode is also commonly used. These are available from The MUFI Font Page, accessed 23 October 2009, http://www.mufi.info/fonts/.

[20] This example and the next couple combine text from the CURSUS project (*CURSUS: An Online Resource of Medieval Liturgical Texts*, edited by David Chadd and James Cummings, University of East Anglia website, accessed 23 October 2009) with a <char> element created by the ENRICH project (European Network Resources and Information Concerning Cultural Heritage: Towards a European digital library of manuscripts,

In addition to being able to distinguish properly between a series of medieval abbreviation marks that organizations such as MUFI have not yet managed to get into Unicode, one of the great benefits of this for those working with early manuscript materials is the enabling of in-depth palaeographic study which, among other things, is leading to scribal identification based on the characteristics of a manuscript's glyphs. Using a URI (Uniform Resource Identifier) as an @ref attribute to point to a <char> also means one can point into external documents, or a URL (Uniform Resource Locator) elsewhere on the Web. A project might more usefully store all of their character descriptions in a separate file and point to that.

```
<ab>Praeoccupemus faciem domini in confessione<g ref="chars/punc.xml#f161"/></ab>
```

Figure 18: Pointing to an external file

However, in a growing networked economy of international research projects, it probably makes more sense for large projects or academic subdisciplines to arrange their own simple web services to allow reference to a larger pool of agreed non-Unicode character definitions. The ENRICH project created such a repository for its own use, also making it publicly available, but it has no scope for maintenance or updating of such a repository since funding has ceased. The difficulties in establishing such repositories primarily consist in the participants' agreements on the definition of characters, and the maintenance of such a repository of <char> elements added by individual participants in the project or subdiscipline.

```
<ab>Praeoccupemus faciem domini in confessione<g
        ref="http://www.example.com/chars/punc.xml#f161"/></ab>
```

Figure 19: Pointing to a remote URL[21]

TEI@Oxford, accessed 23 October 2009, http://projects.oucs.ox.ac.uk/ENRICH/) based on the work of the Medieval Unicode Font Initiative, accessed 23 October 2009, http://www.mufi.info/.

[21] Such a bank of <char> declarations is provided as an output of the ENRICH project; see the ENRICH site at TEI@Oxford, accessed 23 October 2009, http://projects.oucs. ox.ac.uk/ENRICH/.

Digital facsimile surrogates

In any modern digital edition of a medieval or Renaissance manuscript, one of the most desirable aspects is a set of digital images of the original object. Indeed, there are some for whom the raison d'etre of digitization projects is primarily the creation and dissemination of high-resolution images of one or more works rather than full-text editions of them. In any field's study of material culture, the more such resources are made available, of course, the better. To create a scholarly edition, however, one must also provide a carefully edited full text accompanied, it is hoped, by such images. In such cases the images are useful as arbitrators of editorial practice. If you are not convinced of the editor's decision you can then check the provided digital surrogate to make your own informed decision. The increasingly common practice of including digital images in electronic scholarly editions is an often-overlooked revolution in editorial practice which democratizes many of the individual editorial acts undertaken in producing the edition.[22] While, obviously, this happened previously with the print publication of accompanying or facing-page facsimile images, it has now become much more common in the digital research environment.[23]

For creating digital editions which include page facsimiles, the TEI P5 guidelines provide a sophisticated method for referencing single page images, multiple images of the same page, and zones within these images.[24] The <facsimile> element is an optional sibling to the TEI's <text> element, only one of which is strictly required. This could be useful for creating a digital facsimile of a material object, but it is much more common for the <facsimile> element to be used alongside a textual transcription to link sections of the text with images of the artefact they represent. Inside the <facsimile> element one can provide either individual <graphic> elements or embed these inside a <sur-

---

[22] See, for example, McLeod (1982), especially on the "un-editing" of texts; however, the democratization of making textual editing decisions available for inspection (if desired) by the reader should not be confused with the publishing of material without analysis or interpretation, rightly derided by some (cf. Robinson 2009 and Shillingsburg 2009).

[23] Indeed, the technologies and interfaces for viewing images are becoming increasingly sophisticated; cf. Ainsworth and Meredith (2009) or Martin Holmes, The UVic Image Markup Tool Project, University of Victoria, accessed 23 October 2009, http://www.tapor.uvic.ca/~mholmes/image_markup/.

[24] See TEI Consortium (2010, sec. 11), specifically http://www.tei-c.org/release/doc/tei-p5-doc/en/html/PH.html#PHFAX, for more information on digital facsimiles.

face> element to group multiple images of the same physical written surface. This allows one to group references to different images of a single folio: for example, high/low resolution surrogates, ultraviolet scans, or detailed sections.

```
<facsimile>
  <graphic url="page1.png"/>
  <surface>
    <graphic url="page2-highRes.png"/>
    <graphic url="page2-lowRes.png"/>
  </surface>
  <graphic url="page3.png"/>
  <graphic url="page4.png"/>
</facsimile>
```

Figure 20: A <facsimile> element

One can also define rectangular zones inside any surface, for example to highlight a particular detail or area of interest on the physical object. Moreover, since such zones (as is true with <surface> and <graphic> elements) can be referred to from the body of the text, this functionality can be used to provide a direct linkage between particular textual phenomena and their material manifestation evinced in the surrogate image.

```
<surface ulx="0" uly="0" lrx="1357" lry="2965" xml:id="stPaul-f37r">
  <desc>Folio 37r of MS Digby 133</desc>
  <graphic url="f37r.jpg"/>
  <zone ulx="1036" uly="25" lrx="1142" lry="115" xml:id="stPaul-f37r-signature">
    <desc>Myles Blomefylde's signature</desc>
  </zone>
</surface>
```

Figure 21: A <zone> element

The attributes in <zone> refer to the upper-left and lower-right sets of x/y coordinates in a rectangular coordinate space. These coordinates, it should be emphasized, are in an abstract two-dimensional coordinate space which may or may not have any relation to pixels of a digital image, millimetres of the original object, or any other material object. The attribute @facs used in the textual transcription can contain a URI pointing back to the @xml:id attribute of a <zone>, <surface>, or <graphic> element in the header. This enables editors to highlight specific features of the document and/or display these in any number of forms. A particular editor might be quite interested in paratextual features on the document, such as signatures, and so point from their transcription to the <zone> with the coordinates containing this feature.

```
<add place="right" facs="#stPaul-f37r-signature">
  <w xml:id="w1">Myles</w>
  <w xml:id="w2">Blomefylde</w>
</add>
```

Figure 22: Using the @facs attribute

Originally there were limitations inherent to the way <zone> was used because its provision of only four coordinate attributes meant that one could only mark rectilinear sections of images, and some features might require more complex polygons. However, the TEI guidelines are an evolving community-based standard, and after much discussion in the community the TEI guidelines now include an @points attribute on <zone> and <surface> which identifies a (possibly) non-rectangular area as a series of coordinates. There remain limitations to this approach, and for certain use-cases some projects may prefer to embed Scalable Vector Graphics (SVG) and XML vocabulary recommended by the World Wide Web Consortium. The SVG standard provides more robust methods of defining polygonal shapes, and the TEI does mention potential uses for SVG in the TEI guidelines.[25] Others might use SVG to record not the general location of the textual area, but the boundaries of the very glyphs themselves, possibly enabling highlighting down to an individual glyph level if desired (Cayless 2008).

While the creation of facsimile images for digital editions is nothing new, their use in research is still in its infancy. The tools that have been created to take advantage of the TEI <facsimile> structure do so to add value to the reader's experience. For example, Martin Holmes's Image Markup Tool, which allows easy annotation of particular zones of an image, stores the annotation as TEI XML.[26] Some pedagogic uses for such markup are instantly recognizable to those teaching palaeography. Students learn much quicker with high-resolution, zoomable images with transcription pop-ups when you hover over a particular inscrutable portion of a document. However, it is not just the ability to access images or the highlighting of image and/or text that

---

[25] See TEI Consortium (2010, sec. 16), especially http://www.tei-c.org/release/doc/tei-p5-doc/en/html/SA.html#SACSXA.

[26] See Martin Holmes, The UVic Image Markup Tool Project, University of Victoria, accessed 23 October 2009, http://www.tapor.uvic.ca/~mholmes/image_markup/.

are useful. Having discrete textual locations (say on a word-level granularity) marked and related to a digital surrogate enables different methodologies that are only starting to be exploited. Optical Character Recognition (OCR) on handwritten manuscripts is notoriously unproductive. While some research is promising, it is far from generally applicable given the wide variety of human scripts. However, the combination of trainable OCR engines and digital-assisted palaeographic recognition for use in transcription is a viable and developing area (Ciula 2005). One can imagine a transcription application where, when suggested characters were corrected, the editor could then opt for a selection of other, as-yet-unviewed glyphs from images that potentially match the same correction. The transcriber's job would be to mark these as definitely the same, possibly the same, definitely not the same, or unknown. In such a system, by the time the end of the text was being transcribed, the transcriber would in fact have already agreed to the meaning of the glyphs and would be proofreading his/her own earlier decisions. Attempts at such (and indeed more advanced) systems have been made for individual projects, but as of yet no widely popular application has been created that has been adopted by medieval digitization projects as a de facto standard. The relation of textual transcription to facsimile images of the physical object can only be seen as a positive step (however tentative) in our desire to understand our historical material documents. While the storing of digital facsimile information is a new area for TEI-based editions, it is one that is certainly already starting to be explored and capitalized upon by the digital humanities community.

Customization of the TEI

In order to use the TEI guidelines properly, one should customize them. The TEI recommends well over five hundred elements to record various textual phenomena and metadata concerning encoded text.[27] This is more than any individual encoding project will ever need, and so in order to provide those doing the encoding less choice (and thus less chance for errors) most projects constrain the TEI to include just those elements they need. The TEI provides some example customizations such as a slimmed-down version called TEI Lite. However, just using these unmodified is almost certainly a mistake because they still include many elements that any given project will not need, or might exclude something useful to it. It is always better to constrain the TEI as much possible, or to start with a highly constrained schema such as

---

[27] See http://www.tei-c.org/release/doc/tei-p5-doc/en/html/REF-ELEMENTS.html, accessed 23 October 2009.

the "TEI Absolutely Bare" minimal schema and then see what textual phenomena one encounters that are not able to be marked up. Having a schema
which adequately reflects a project's encoding needs is important in maintaining consistency through validation of your documents.

Part of the problem with any guidelines for encoding digital text is that of
interoperability when there is such a wide range of terminology and methodology. One solution to variance in practice is, of course, to agree mutually to
acceptable encoding guidelines that are far more tightly constrained than the
fairly loose TEI recommendations. An example of this is the ENRICH project,
which in virtually aggregating manuscript descriptions across Europe was
able to agree to a slightly more restrictive subset of the TEI guidelines.[28] This
includes restrictions such as requiring attributes that are usually optional in
TEI and constraining the attribute value lists to a closed set of possibilities.
Thus, for example, the usually optional @form attribute on the <objectDesc>
element is required and allows only the values of "codex," "scroll," "leaf,"
or "other." While this limits the freedom of participants, the benefits of
conformity are immeasurably preferable when attempting to build a search
interface on top of this.

However, one of the major problems with the ENRICH customization, or any
similar endeavour, is that unless you are cataloguing manuscripts afresh,
rather than converting existing records, the levels of granularity of information provided between two archives can be significantly different. And so,
while <objectDesc> must have an @form attribute, there is no requirement
that <objectDesc> itself must be present. Because of the flexibility between
structured and unstructured data that the ENRICH schema has inherited
from the TEI guidelines, a manuscript description may instead use only a
set of paragraphs inside the enclosing <physDesc> element. This is not to say
that ENRICH or another project could not constrain the TEI even further,
to require all sorts of elements, but this would necessarily reduce potential
partners in such a project because many archives' existing records either
do not have the required data or do not have it in a form that can be readily
converted to the required format. Any project striving for such a kind of
interoperability is then forced to tread a middle ground between too much
laxity to be useful and too rigorous a schema to meet the needs and abilities
of their partners. In this manner, nonetheless, projects that provide custom-

---

[28] See ENRICH, accessed 23 October 2009, http://enrich.manuscriptorium.eu/; for
the technical aspects, see the ENRICH site at TEI@Oxford, accessed October 23 2009,
http://projects.oucs.ox.ac.uk/ENRICH/.

ized schemas like ENRICH are a model for groups of researchers, archives, or projects that can agree on coordinated levels of encoding and controlled vocabularies to follow.

Documenting TEI customizations

The TEI provides an internal mechanism for customization of the TEI scheme using elements specifically for the documentation and specification of schemas. A TEI document which includes such schema documentation is referred to as a TEI ODD.[29] "ODD" in this context means "One Document Does-it-all," because the file not only stores a meta-schema and documentation for long-term preservation, but is itself the source of generated schemas (DTD, Relax NG, W3C Schema) and documentation in various formats (such as HTML and PDF). As the file records when a project has deleted a specific element (or module or class) that it has no use for, this enables the documentation to be specific to that project and does not contain reference material for those elements that have been removed. Moreover, because there are translations available of element descriptions in a number of foreign languages, this documentation could be generated in any one of those languages.

The modular structure of the TEI

The TEI defines many modules (sets of tags) which can be swapped in and out prior to generating a schema (and/or project-specific internationalized documentation).[30]

Module Name	Description
analysis	Simple analytic mechanisms
certainty	Certainty and uncertainty
core	Elements common to all TEI documents
corpus	Corpus texts
dictionaries	Dictionaries
drama	Performance texts

[29] See TEI Consortium, "Getting Started with P5 ODDS."

[30] See TEI Consortium (2010, sec. 1). Some of these are more or less useful to any individual project depending on its encoding needs. These modules are defined by individual chapters of the TEI guidelines; however, there are chapters of the TEI guidelines which do not define modules, such as TEI Consortium (2010, sec. 23).

figures	Tables, formulæ, and figures
gaiji	Character and glyph documentation
header	The TEI Header
iso-fs	Feature structures
linking	Linking, segmentation, and alignment
msdescription	Manuscript Description
namesdates	Names and dates
nets	Graphs, networks, and trees
spoken	Transcribed Speech
tagdocs	Documentation of TEI modules
textcrit	Critical Apparatus
textstructure	Default text structure
transcr	Transcription of primary sources
verse	Verse structures

For example, if a project is not transcribing spoken audio texts, then it would be unnecessary for it to include the "spoken" module; the elements this module provides will be of no use, and their existence might potentially lead to error or confusion of those working on the project. Almost all projects need to include the "core," "header," and "textstructure" modules. Most projects undertaking scholarly editions of textual documents will need to include the "transcr" module (transcription of primary sources), and if there are multiple witnesses for a text, the "textcrit" module provides the necessary elements to create an *apparatus criticus*. The "msdescription" module is, obviously, for those who wish to provide in-depth manuscript descriptions as discussed earlier. In some cases the choice of additional modules might be determined by the genre of the text (is it verse, a drama, or even a verse drama?) or the intended analysis or publication infrastructure of the text (e.g., "analysis," "certainty," or "linking"). In most textual editions, after marking up structural aspects, one of the most frequent desires is to record information about names and the people, places, or organizations that they refer to, or in some cases record processable metadata about the dates in the text; the elements in the "namesdates" module helps to enable doing this.

What may seem less obvious at first glance is how useful some of the other seemingly more specialized modules are in the creation of a rigorous electronic edition. In any scholarly edition it is not simply the editing of the text that is important, especially in a pedagogic context, but the inclusion of secondary information which makes that text accessible. This means that any number of modules might possibly be of interest. One common example might be the inclusion of a glossary or word-list defining or glossing difficult words. In this case the "dictionaries" module might be a useful way to store the information about each of these words in as little or much detail as needed.

The problem of fragmentation and solutions for interoperability

The use of the TEI as a format for textual interchange or interoperability is one of the long-sought goals for the TEI. The TEI's greatest strength—its flexibility and generalistic nature—is also one of its greatest weaknesses. Many standards insist that there is only one way to do things and that you must follow its method. The TEI on the other hand is far more flexible in its requirements, often allowing multiple methods to achieve the same goal, reflecting multiple schools of thought. Rather than forcing people to "do what I do," the TEI recommends that you "do what you need to do, but describe what you do in a manner that I can understand." One of the inherent problems with providing a customization mechanism alongside a set of recommendations is that it necessarily undermines the cohesiveness that using a shared encoding model promotes. Use of a variety of TEI customizations, which not only constrain the TEI but extend it into areas the TEI does not cover, leads to a real problem with the fragmentation of the underlying data model. Just because two projects are both using the TEI does not make them automatically interoperable: that would require the precise same use of the TEI. As the TEI develops over time, the fragmentation of increasingly divergent TEI-based schemas in successive versions problematizes future attempts at interoperability between such resources. Extension of the TEI model is a necessary evil departing from easy interoperability; but it is comforting to know that since this divergence should be documented, if a TEI ODD file has been created, the fragmentation is not irreparable, it is just not necessarily easy. Some projects group together to create a single TEI extension, perhaps with a controlled vocabulary or set of required elements, in order that their data might be mutually interoperable within their community. A good example of this is the EpiDoc guidelines and the collaboration surrounding them. In this case many separate projects are using the EpiDoc guidelines for encoding epigraphs; these guidelines are based on the TEI guidelines, and in their latest form are a pure TEI P5 subset (Bodard 2008). EpiDoc members have made feature requests on the TEI's SourceForge site to encourage development in line with the needs of epigraphers. That the EpiDoc customization is now a TEI P5 subset means that those using EpiDoc also benefit from any tools and resources created to assist other TEI users, and the TEI community is enriched by the experience of the editing of many more texts (Cayless et al. 2009). If a particular text encoding extension remains marginalized, it is probably because its efficacy and applicability to the TEI community at large have not been demonstrated; if it does become generalized in adoption by the TEI, then we all benefit from the increased richness of the TEI (Cummings 2008).

Many in the field of digital humanities have long desired greater interoperability between resources, and this is unachievable without greater openness and transparency in those resources that are available. As resources provide a rendered version of the data online one might expect that providing the underlying TEI XML would be straightforward and commonplace, but this is rarely the case. Reasons for this range from concerns about intellectual property rights, through models of sustainability that are predicated on commercial partnerships, to simple academic insecurity over perceived sloppy encoding in the underlying data. Whatever the validity of these concerns, it is more beneficial to the future of the digital humanities field as a whole to have unfettered access to such research data. It is a truism often quoted that "[t]he coolest thing to do with your data will be thought of by someone else" (Walsh and Pollock 2007). It is even useful to see sloppy encoding or abuse of the semantics of TEI elements, because it is from issues such as these that the TEI community learns where and how the TEI guidelines need to be improved to reflect real world encoding needs (Cummings 2009).

In imagining the digital future for epigraphers, Cayless et al. envision seamless access to multiple repositories of inscriptional evidence that is then able to be repurposed for use in many tools and published as a new dataset alongside academic publications (2009). But to do this, they realize that the tools themselves need to change alongside the slowly developing digital publication models.

> What we hope will change and improve by 2017 are the tools available for gathering information and analyzing it as well as the forms and venues for publishing the results of scholarly inquiry. None of this will be possible unless information is published in such a way that it is not concealed behind an interface, but is in addition retrievable in bulk (Cayless et al. 2009).

This statement strikes at the core of the problems with current attempts at interoperability of digital resources. The creation of resources that are dependent upon bespoke interfaces of other resources cannot be stable or scalable. Instead, resources need to adhere to well-documented and internationally agreed standards (such as the TEI, RDF, etc.) and make their material easily available and freely prelicensed for reuse, integration, and republication as parts of new datasets.

Conclusion

In briefly looking at the TEI's recommendations for manuscript description, transcription, representation of non-standard characters, digital facsimiles, and schema customization, I have tried to emphasize the benefits that TEI markup can bring to research into historical materials in manuscript form. I have attempted to highlight those aspects of the TEI where there is a correspondence between the markup as an interpretation of the physical manuscript and the markup of its textual or intellectual content. The TEI provides a free, community-developed, open format which underlies much digital humanities research. The main benefit of materials encoded in TEI is the structuring of knowledge concerning our cultural artefacts and the future availability of these resources. This structured data, if openly available, can be richly mined for analysis and research in ways we might not yet be able to predict. In any scholarly environment, but especially in academic projects funded with public money, it should become not only standard to release information in such a free manner but also considered shamefully unprofessional not to do so. In another field, such as medical sciences, not to openly release one's underlying data so that it can be poked, prodded, retested, extracted, remixed, republished (with citation), and reused would signal alarm bells of possible methodological flaws, unscientific hoaxes, or commercial corruption. The glorious futures that digital humanities envision are severely compromised by its own projects' reluctance to make their data easily available. We should not be afraid that someone else might make use of our work, as the most interesting things to be done with it, we must hope, are yet to happen and could very well be done by someone else.

WORKS CITED

Ainsworth, Peter, and Michael Meredith. 2009. "e-Science for Medievalists: Options, Challenges, Solutions and Opportunities." *Digital Humanities Quarterly* 3 (4): http://digitalhumanities.org/dhq/vol/3/4/000071/000071.html.

Bart, Patricia R. 2006. "Experimental Markup in a TEI-Conformant Setting." *Digital Medievalist* 2 (1): http://www.digitalmedievalist.org/journal/2.1/bart/.

Bodard, Gabriel. 2008. "The *Inscriptions of Aphrodisias* as Electronic Publication: A User's Perspective and a Proposed Paradigm." *Digital Medievalist* 4: http://www.digitalmedievalist.org/journal/4/bodard/.

Bozzolo, Carla, and Ezio Ornato. 1980. *Pour une histoire du livre manuscrit au moyen âge: Trois essais de codicologie quantitative.* Paris: CNRS.

Cayless, Hugh. 2008. "Linking Page Images to Transcriptions with SVG." Presented at Balisage, 13 August 2008. http://www.unc.edu/~hcayless/img2xml/presentation.html.

Cayless, Hugh, Charlotte Roueché, Tom Elliott, and Gabriel Bodard. 2009. "Epigraphy in 2017." *Digital Humanities Quarterly* 3 (1): http://digitalhumanities.org/dhq/vol/3/1/000030/000030.html.

Ciula, Arianna. 2005. "Digital Palaeography: Using the Digital Representation of Medieval Script to Support Palaeographic Analysis." *Digital Medievalist* 1 (1): http://www.digitalmedievalist.org/journal/1.1/ciula/.

Cummings, James. 2006. "Liturgy, Drama, and the Archive: Three Conversions from Legacy Formats to TEI XML." *Digital Medievalist* 2 (1): http://www.digitalmedievalist.org/journal/2.1/cummings/.

_____ 2008. "The Text Encoding Initiative and the Study of Literature." In *A Companion to Digital Literary Studies,* edited by Susan Schreibman and Ray Siemens, 451–76. Oxford: Blackwell. http://www.digitalhumanities.org/companion/view?docId=blackwell/9781405148641/9781405148641.xml&chunk.id=ss1-6-6&toc.depth=1&toc.id=ss1-6-6&brand=9781405148641_brand or http://snipurl.com/dlstei.

_____ 2009. "Converting Saint Paul: A New TEI P5 Edition of *The Conversion of Saint Paul* Using Stand-Off Methodology." *Literary and Linguistic Computing* 24 (3): http://llc.oxfordjournals.org/cgi/content/abstract/fqp019.

Driscoll, M. J. 2006. "P5-MS: A General Purpose Tagset for Manuscript Description." *Digital Medievalist* 2 (1): http://www.digitalmedievalist.org/journal/2.1/driscoll/.

McLeod, Randall. 1982. "UN editing Shak-Speare." *Sub-Stance* 10 (33/34): 26–55.

O'Donnell, Daniel Paul. 2008. "Disciplinary Impact and Technological Obsolescence in Digital Medieval Studies." In Schreibman and Siemens, eds. 2008, 65–81. Oxford: Blackwell. http://www.digitalhumanities.org/companion/view?docId=blackwell/9781405148641/9781405148641.xml&chunk.id=ss1-4-2&toc.id=0&brand=9781405148641_brand or http://snipurl.com/dlsdpod.

Parkinson, Stephen R., and António H. A. Emiliano. 2002. "Encoding Medieval Abbreviations for Computer Analysis (from Latin–Portuguese and Portuguese Non-Literary Sources)." *Literary and Linguistic Computing* 17 (3): 345–60. Abstract: http://llc.oxfordjournals.org/content/17/3/345.abstract. DOI:10.1093/llc/17.3.345.

Robinson, Peter. 2005. "Current Issues in Making Digital Editions of Medieval Texts—or, Do Electronic Scholarly Editions Have a Future?" *Digital Medievalist* 1 (1): http://www.digitalmedievalist.org/journal/1.1/robinson/.

_____ 2009. "The Ends of Editing." *Digital Humanities Quarterly* 3 (3): http://www.digitalhumanities.org/dhq/vol/3/3/000051/000051.html.

Shillingsburg, Peter. 2009. "How Literary Works Exist: Convenient Scholarly Editions." *Digital Humanities Quarterly* 3 (3): http://www.digitalhumanities.org/dhq/vol/3/3/000054/000054.html.

Stokes, Peter. 2007. "Palaeography and Image-Processing: Some Solutions and Problems." *Digital Medievalist* 3: http://www.digitalmedievalist.org/journal/3/stokes/.

TEI Consortium, eds. 2010. *TEI P5: Guidelines for Electronic Text Encoding and Interchange.* Version 1.6.0. TEI Consortium. http://www.tei-c.org/Guidelines/P5/.

_____ 2010. "v. A Gentle Introduction to XML." *TEI P5: Guidelines for Electronic Text Encoding and Interchange.* TEI Consortium. http://www.tei-c.org/release/doc/tei-p5-doc/en/html/SG.html.

_____ 2010. "1. The TEI Infrastructure." *TEI P5: Guidelines for Electronic Text Encoding and Interchange.* TEI Consortium. http://www.tei-c.org/release/doc/tei-p5-doc/en/html/ST.html.

_____ 2010. "3.4.3 Additions, Deletions, Omissions." *TEI P5: Guidelines for Electronic Text Encoding and Interchange.* TEI Consortium. http://www.tei-c.org/release/doc/tei-p5-doc/en/html/CO.html#COEDADD.

_____ 2010. "10. Manuscript Description." *TEI P5: Guidelines for Electronic Text Encoding and Interchange.* TEI Consortium. http://www.tei-c.org/release/doc/tei-p5-doc/en/html/MS.html.

_____ 2010. "11. Representation of Primary Sources." *TEI P5: Guidelines for Electronic Text Encoding and Interchange.* TEI Consortium. http://www.tei-c.org/release/doc/tei-p5-doc/en/html/PH.html.

_____ 2010. "16. Linking, Segmentation, and Alignment." *TEI P5: Guidelines for Electronic Text Encoding and Interchange.* TEI Consortium. http://www.tei-c.org/release/doc/tei-p5-doc/en/html/SA.html.

_____ 2010. "23. Using the TEI." *TEI P5: Guidelines for Electronic Text Encoding and Interchange.* TEI Consortium. http://www.tei-c.org/release/doc/tei-p5-doc/en/html/USE.html.

_____ 2010. "Learn the TEI." TEI Consortium. http://www.tei-c.org/Support/Learn/.

_____ 2010. "Getting Started with P5 ODDs." TEI Consortium. http://www.tei-c.org/Support/Learn/odds.xml.

Unsworth, John. 2000. "Scholarly Primitives: What Methods do Humanities Researchers Have in Common, and How Might Our Tools Reflect This?" Presented at the Humanities Computing: Formal Methods, Experimental Practice Symposium, King's College, London, 13

May   2000.   http://www3.isrl.illinois.edu/~unsworth/Kings.5-00/
primitives.html.

Vanhoutte, Edward, and Ron Van den Branden. 2009. "Describing,
Transcribing, Encoding, and Editing Modern Correspondence Material:
A Textbase Approach." *Literary and Linguistic Computing* 24 (1): 77–98.
http://llc.oxfordjournals.org/cgi/content/abstract/24/1/77.

Walsh, Jo, and Rufus Pollock. 2007. "Open Data and Componentization."
Presented at XTech 2007 Conference. http://m.okfn.org/files/talks/
xtech_2007/.

More than was Dreamt of in Our Philosophy: Encoding *Hamlet* for the *Shakespeare Quartos Archive*[1]

Judith Siefring
Oxford Digital Library
Bodleian Library
Oxford University
judith.siefring@bodleian.ox.ac.uk

Pip Willcox
Oxford Digital Library
Bodleian Library
Oxford University
pip.willcox@bodleian.ox.ac.uk

Our philosophy

The *Shakespeare Quartos Archive* (SQA) is an online resource co-owned by participating libraries holding copies of the quartos, based on high-quality digital images, most of which were taken by Octavo, an imaging company no longer in business.[2] A pilot encoding of *Hamlet* seemed the perfect opportunity to bring together the text and the physical objects in single digital editions. Octavo's images were, unusually, of double-page spreads. Immediately this view gives the impression of physical closeness, of holding the book in your hands and turning the pages. Our aim throughout the project was to emphasize the physicality of the quartos. With this in mind, we made a point of including the quartos' cover boards and fly-leaves in their image sets and of recording other physical features, such as the paste-ins, marks of

---

[1] The authors' particular thanks go Jim Kuhn of the Folger Shakespeare Library and Doug Reside of the Maryland Institute for Technology in the Humanities for their unflagging interest and generosity in sharing their expertise for this chapter. There were numerous contributors to the *Shakespeare Quartos Archive* project, details of whom can be found on the website, http://quartos.org/ (accessed 23 December 2009). Institutional members include the Bodleian Library, British Library, Folger Shakespeare Library, Huntington Library, Maryland Institute for Technology in the Humanities, National Library of Scotland, Shakespeare Institute of the University of Birmingham, and the University of Edinburgh. The authors would also like to thank Brent Nelson and Melissa Terras for their expert help in shaping the final version of this chapter.

[2] Early printed book and manuscript digitization by Octavo can be found at *The Rare Bookroom*, accessed 14 October 2009, http://www.rarebookroom.org/.

ISBN 978-0-86698-499-7 (online)   ISBN 978-0-86698-474-4 (print)
New Technologies in Medieval and Renaissance Studies 3 (2012) 83–111

ownership, and manuscript annotations which make each copy unique, in the encoded texts.

Rather than creating a collated edition of all quartos of *Hamlet,* or of each of the five pre-1642 editions, we built the project on individual copies and made an edition of each—that is, we encoded each copy of each of the five editions as a stand-alone text, amounting to thirty-two texts of *Hamlet.* In these editions, printed texts are transcribed as they stand, with their manuscript annotations and damage, and information supplied about stamps, marks of ownership, and bindings. This approach was approved by librarians and academics, but as the project proceeded we faced questions about where to stop: we had a clearly defined project in terms of budget and schedule and a piece of work that could be extended seemingly indefinitely.

This chapter outlines the practice of our decisions and rationales, highlighting some areas of debate. Our theoretical approach to the project is discussed elsewhere (Kuhn, forthcoming). The complexities, philosophical or otherwise, only become fully apparent in the midst of a piece of work. Here we will focus on issues related to representation of the book as printed, and of postprint additions—issues that, in a perfect world, we would have explored *before* starting to dream.

Project background

In March 2008, the Bodleian Library at Oxford and the Folger Shakespeare Library in Washington, D.C. received funding from the National Endowment for the Humanities (NEH) and the Joint Information Systems Committee (JISC), under a Joint Transatlantic Digitization Collaboration Grant, for Phase One of the Shakespeare Quartos Archive project. Phase One aimed to expand the British Library's *Shakespeare in Quarto* website[3] to create a complete, digital collection which brings together at least one copy of each of the seventy-five extant pre-1642 quarto editions of Shakespeare's plays into a single online collection. The British Library provided the bulk of the required digital images, and the others were supplied by the Bodleian Library, the Folger Shakespeare Library, the Huntington Library, the National Library of Scotland, and the University of Edinburgh Library.

---

[3] *Shakespeare in Quarto,* British Library, accessed 14 October 2009, http://www.bl.uk/treasures/shakespeare/homepage.html.

Additionally, Phase One was to include creation of a prototype for the multi-institutional *Shakespeare Quartos Archive* (SQA),[4] whose pilot would focus on a single play, *Hamlet*. This proof of concept aimed to encode the thirty-two pre-1642 copies from participating institutions of the five quarto editions of *Hamlet*, making them available together with digital images of those copies. *Hamlet* was chosen for four reasons: its canonical status means it is widely performed and taught at all levels; it has wide cultural reach; textually, it is one of the most complex of the quartos, with major differences between the first and later editions; and finally, the choice of this play celebrates the collaborative nature of the SQA, with each partner library contributing at least one copy of *Hamlet*. The encoding, on which this chapter will concentrate, was carried out by the Oxford Digital Library (ODL), part of the Bodleian Library, and was done within a strict one-year timeline: April 2008 to April 2009.

The SQA image collection and the *Hamlet* full-text resource have been brought together in a single user interface and digital toolset prototype, designed and developed by the Maryland Institute for Technology in the Humanities (MITH).[5] Research and teaching functions of the interface include the ability to overlay images, compare images side by side, search across full-text transcriptions, and mark up images with user annotations.

The project was structured so that partner institutions with different areas of expertise took responsibility for different tasks. Shakespeare specialists at the Folger and the British Library provided expertise on issues related to textual history and transmission. Digital editors at the Oxford Digital Library were responsible for the transcription and encoding of texts. MITH, a leading interdisciplinary centre for developing and enriching digital tools for humanities scholars, advised on and developed the technical infrastructure. Professionally facilitated evaluations were carried out at the British Library, the Folger, and the Shakespeare Institute of the University of Birmingham.[6] Feedback from these sessions was used to refine the prototype interface.

Our aim and philosophy was to draw on the expertise of partners to create an innovative resource allowing free access to otherwise highly restricted material. The combination of image and text in the prototype interface en-

---

[4] *The Shakespeare Quartos Archive*, accessed 14 October 2009, http://www.quartos.org (accessed October 14 2009).

[5] MITH: Maryland Institute for Technology in the Humanities, accessed 14 October 2009, http://mith.umd.edu/.

[6] The Shakespeare Institute, University of Birmingham, accessed 14 October 2009, http://www.shakespeare.bham.ac.uk/.

ables Shakespeare enthusiasts, whether schoolchildren, academics, actors, or bibliophiles, to engage with the quartos in new and exciting ways.[7] From the outset the site was conceived as a resource which could meet the needs of these diverse users, whether the desired access point was through the electronic text (through one particular copy, or one character's speeches, for example) or through material copy details revealed through digital images. While there are many ways to encode a text (for example, as a linguistic corpus, or for meter and rhyme), we decided, on advice from specialists in various fields, to concentrate on making the quartos as easy to search and as open to interpretation as possible.[8] This decision was consistent with our stated aims, but it was also expedient. Had we but world enough and time, we could have encoded the quartos to reflect any number of different approaches and analyses. With limited funding and time, a pragmatic decision had to be taken. The happy conjunction of our concentration on the textual and material aspects of the quartos means that, for example, the same encoding that allows a scholar to narrow a search to text contained in stage directions also allows the display of the electronic text to reflect the layout of the original books, useful for people less experienced in reading early modern texts. Bringing multiple copies of each edition together, perhaps for the first time since leaving the printing house, simplifies the identification of small differences in their texts and also brings to light how differently the books have fared in their lifetimes: some appear near pristine, given their age; others, whether through love and frequent reading, or disregard and neglect, bear the marks of harder lives; some have been rebound in fine leather; others, seemingly prized for their content alone, have been disbound, mounted, and bound with other plays. Where it is possible to trace the names of binders, annotators or owners, these are included in the transcriptions. All of these

---

[7] The resource was evaluated, with professional facilitation, while the project was in development. No part of the funding was allocated to investigate its usage. Our knowledge of its use is therefore necessarily partial and anecdotal. The resource was demonstrated to teachers at the Folger Shakespeare Library summer school in 2010. At the University of Oxford it has been used to introduce first-year undergraduates to the idea of multiple versions of a text and to editing. The project has been well received in the academic community. For example, Whitney Anne Trettien (2010) reviewed it favourably for the *Shakespeare Quarterly* and on the HASTAC blog (2009). On the SHAKSPER listserv Hardy M. Cook described the resource as "the highest quality facsimile site I have ever viewed [...]. This is one impressive web site," 10 January 2011.

[8] For more discussion on our editorial approach and the SQA's Advisory Forum, see below.

features, and many others, can act as starting points to search the *Archive*. Access to a fully searchable electronic text allows users to grapple directly with the early modern text; the richness of the encoding allows them to chart the quartos' progress through the intervening centuries.

XML encoding

The SQA project chose to adopt the Text Encoding Initiative (TEI P5) as its encoding standard.[9] Adopting a widely accepted standard allows encoders to benefit from the experience of others in the field, facilitates interoperability, and enables users of the new resource to understand the principles on which it is based. TEI guidelines are widely applied in the humanities and social sciences for full-text digital projects because of their flexibility and breadth.[10] TEI is used by other projects to encode early printed books, including Early English Books Online–Text Creation Partnership (EEBO-TCP),[11] and the Women Writers Project (WWP).[12] Such projects must decide on the balance they wish to achieve between the textual and the material aspects of the books, and the TEI scheme makes provision for both these aspects. The WWP texts, for example, prioritize the textual or linguistic aspects of the texts, but do include certain aspects of the physical books, such as catchwords, signatures, and some handwritten additions.[13] EEBO-TCP excludes almost all non-textual information and all handwritten material. For the SQA, we wanted to combine as far as possible the textual and the material aspects of the individual quartos.[14] To that end we used the TEI manuscript description module <msDesc> for the purpose of describing early printed books.

---

[9] See TEI Consortium, "P5: Guidelines for Electronic Text Encoding and Interchange," accessed 21 May 2009, http://www.tei-c.org/Guidelines/P5/.

[10] The TEI provides a list of selected projects that use its encoding scheme at http://www.tei-c.org/Activities/Projects/ (accessed 21 May 2009).

[11] EEBO-TCP, University of Michigan, accessed 12 October 2009, http://www.lib.umich.edu/tcp/eebo/.

[12] Women Writer's Project, Brown University, accessed 12 October 2009, http://www.wwp.brown.edu/.

[13] A discussion of the editorial principles of the Women Writers Project can be found at "Methodology for Transcription and Editing," WWP, accessed 26 May 2009, http://www.wwp.brown.edu/texts/help/editorial_principles.html. Handwritten annotations are only included if they are deemed to be near contemporary to the original text.

[14] At the time of our project, there were no TEI guidelines for treating printed books as individual objects, as manuscripts are routinely treated. James Cummings of Oxford University Computing Services has kindly drawn our attention to plans the TEI

While there is crossover between manuscript and early print materials in some of the types of information that we wished to include, many aspects of the printed text do not fit comfortably within manuscript description. Dot Porter discusses the difficulties of using the manuscript description module for the description of printed books in an article written for the 2008 TEI members meeting. In it she recommends a systematic investigation into ways in which the TEI guidelines can better support the descriptions of printed books.[15] If such work does indeed go ahead, the resulting guidelines would be invaluable for projects such as ours. How we adapted aspects of the TEI guidelines relating to manuscripts for the SQA falls broadly into two parts: the use of the manuscript description module to include copy-specific information; and the encoding we used to describe annotations. Both are detailed later in this chapter. By encoding the printed books using the manuscript description module we were electing to treat them as artefacts in their own right, focusing on individual copies rather than treating them as exemplars of their respective literary works.[16] Challenges in transforming library catalogue records into manuscript description form included fitting the former more "data-centric" (to use Porter's term) information into a tagging scheme designed for a more narrative approach.[17]

Our approach of focusing on individual copies, exemplified by our use of the manuscript description module, is one feature distinguishing the SQA from other online Shakespeare resources. Editions of Shakespeare's plays proliferate on the Web. In many cases, texts have been standardized: spelling and punctuation have been modernized and character names regularized. Fewer resources offer a critical apparatus to explain the collation of the text. Of these, the excellent *Internet Shakespeare Editions* (ISE)[18] is perhaps best known. The ISE site's methodology differs significantly from ours. ISE's critical edi-

---

Consortium has to revise the manuscript description module to cope better with early printed books.

[15] See Porter (2008).

[16] For clarification of this use of <msDesc>, and other discussion, we are indebted to Lou Burnard and Sebastian Rahtz, both of Oxford University Computing Services and TEI Advisory Board Members.

[17] We are grateful to colleagues at all the partner institutions for their advice and help in dealing with these issues, and particularly to Sarah Wheale, one of the Bodleian Library's curators of rare books, for prioritizing the recataloguing of all the Bodleian's copies of *Hamlet*.

[18] Internet Shakespeare Editions, University of Victoria, accessed 12 October 2009, http://internetshakespeare.uvic.ca.

tions present a collated version of each play, whereas the SQA pilot presents an edition of each of the thirty-two copies of five editions of one play. The resources also differ in some features not immediately apparent to users. ISE has chosen to transcribe every ligature, swash letter, and long *s* (visible in the XML, rather than in the display version), typographical features that we chose to omit in the SQA texts. Not only would such detailed work take more time than was available to us, but the complications of dubious readings of such type by non-specialist readers would outweigh their usefulness to the small number of typographically motivated readers. So we prioritized other features as we sought to establish our balance between the textual and the material. On a more fundamental level, ISE has created its own XML encoding scheme rather than using a recognized standard, such as the TEI.

The SQA interface provides users with the opportunity to carry out comparative analysis, via either text or image, of different copies of different editions of *Hamlet*. This can be done by comparing images of the different copies side by side, and perhaps most strikingly, by using a page overlay function. This function allows users to lay pages from different copies over each other; variations between copies will in this way be apparent.[19]

---

[19] Due to the lack of standardization in the imaging process, currently not all quartos can be viewed at precisely the same size even using the zoom feature. In order to enable deep zooming (a technique in which an image is copied to several files of incrementally lower resolutions and then divided into small tiles so that a browser need load only the pieces of the image currently in view), the team at MITH initially used the very lightweight solution in the Google code repository, "panojs" (coded by Dan Allen). Although the library was easy to use, problems with cross-browser compatibility (especially in Internet Explorer 6) eventually forced MITH to migrate the code to the open source mapping interface, Open Layers. MITH programmer J. Grant Dickie wrote a script to allow Open Layers to use the tiles generated by panojs so that the images did not need to be retiled (an extremely time-consuming process). Work continues to find a solution to this issue.

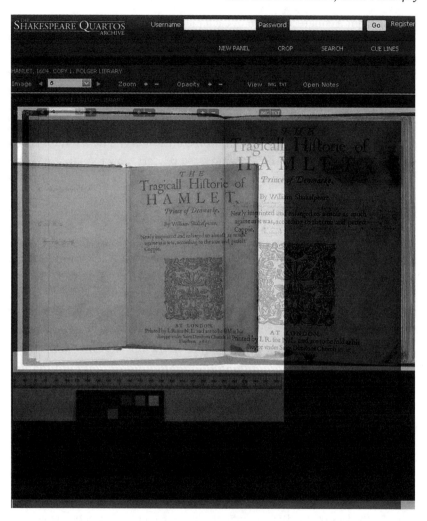

Figure 1. Here, the title pages of two second quartos (Folger STC 22276, copy 1, and British Library, C.34.K.2) are overlaid, with the latter made semi-transparent using the resource's opacity feature.

Encoded *Hamlet* texts also allow comparative analysis to be done in other sophisticated ways. Users can isolate tagged material of particular interest, e.g., stage directions, catchwords, signatures, or a particular character's speeches. From the outset, the aim was to include as much information as possible about each copy within the encoded texts. While the encoded texts exist alongside digital images in the SQA interface, allowing users to approach the texts in whichever format best suits their purpose, the electronic texts can be used without the digital images.

This independent use of electronic texts aids accessibility. We want users to have easy access to our encoding to enable use of the resource however they wish (including outside the user interface). In making these electronic editions freely available for download, we hope users whose approach differs from ours will be able easily to adapt the encoding to suit their purposes. We have not sought to guide users along particular lines of study or interpretation. In the balance between description of the original and interpretation, we favoured the former. There is, naturally, interpretation in any transcription, let alone in an encoded edition: take the italicized "Ham." preceding a speech, say, to mean that the lines following comprise a speech to be spoken by the character Hamlet. A basic level of interpretation was essential to make sense of the text and for the functionality of the underlying document. To this we added markup that is invisible in the default display of the text but present in the XML, including imposing conventional act and scene divisions on the quartos, describing types of stage direction, and expanding abbreviations so that a search for "question" also returns the word "questiō."

We set out, then, to create an accessible resource that would allow detailed comparative analysis of the *Hamlet* quartos, using a combination of image and encoded text. We chose an established, flexible encoding scheme, and where questions arose we aimed to develop our encoding on descriptive rather than interpretative principles. We wanted to include as much information about the material quartos—i.e., their material context— as possible. The play's textual tradition is explored in many excellent editions; our project sought to highlight its early print history and reception through these material artefacts. Our aim, essentially, was to do as much as we could. We had then to establish what precisely that should be.[20]

---

[20] In order to inform our decisions on what to include and what to exclude, we held an Advisory Forum, where a group of experts from a number of fields—editors of Shakespeare, early modern academic specialists, theatre, education and accessibility professionals—met to discuss the work of encoding *Hamlet*. It became clear that while most participants felt that most encoded features suggested to them were desirable, there were some things it was just not possible to do within the project's strict one-year timeline. Further details about the membership, structure, and outcomes of the SQA Advisory Forum can be found at http://quartos.org/info/documentation.html (accessed 15 October 2009). Details can also be found there about the project's message board, set up for the purpose of ongoing encoding policy discussions.

Textual vs. physical: The printed text

It is useful to make a distinction between textual features, that is, features of the play-text itself, and physical or material ones which are manifestations of the printing process. The basic textual features of *Hamlet* are relatively straightforward to encode. Speeches, speakers, stage directions, paragraphs, and verse lines are easily accommodated within the TEI tagging scheme. Some tasks that would have required too much time and/or a level of specialism not held by any of our project partners were excluded. Given our constraints, metrical tagging was not possible; neither was a detailed analysis of whether a line was verse or prose. Looking beyond the textual, a distinguishing feature of SQA is a focus on the physical aspects of the quartos. We preserved the physical layout of the original pages in digital format as far as possible. Line and page breaks of each copy are preserved, the presence and position of forme work such as catchwords, signatures, and running headers are recorded, and the basic position of stage directions (inline or independently lineated) are included as well.

The printing process of the *Hamlet* quartos is also apparent in the electronic texts through the recording of printer errors and other features such as turned-over and turned-under verse lines and dropped or decorated capitals. Printer errors have not been corrected in the SQA texts; where a letter is inverted, <c> (*character*) tags are used, with the @rend attribute value "inverted." Similarly, the presence of turned-over or turned-under verse lines is indicated both in the <lb/> (*line break*) tags and the <c> tags surrounding the brackets that introduce such lines. Examples include the following:

<l>Then Honesty can transfor<c rend="inverted">m</c>e Beauty:</l>[21]

<p>O deere <name type="character" ref="#oph" rend="italic"> Ophelia</name>, I am ill at these numbers, I haue not art to recken
    <lb/>my grones<gap reason="illegible" agent="unclear" extent="1" unit="chars" resp="#fol"/> but that I loue thee best, ô most best belieue it, adew.
    <lb/>Thine euermore most deere Lady, whilst this machine is to him.

---

[21] SQA, ham-1603-22275x-hun-c01.xml. The file naming system for the SQA is intended to be comprehensible by humans as well as unique. Each file follows the pattern: name of play-date-STC number-holding institution-copy number. Abbreviations are taken from the Library of Congress. Copy numbers are taken from the *English Short Title Catalogue*, accessed 12 October 2009, http://estc.bl.uk/.

<lb rend="turnunder"/><c rend="turnunder">(</c><name type=
"character" ref="#ham" rend="italic">Hamlet</name>.</p> </sp>[22]

This is important for users interested in typography, and there are other benefits to an electronic page layout that reflects the original. It enables assistive technologies,[23] which broadens access to a range of users who would be excluded by an image-only resource.[24] We hope that the resource will be used as a teaching aid and that the electronic text in modern font (though with early modern printing conventions) might draw students in, with one less level of difficulty to overcome.

We could not encode some aspects of the printing process within the project's constraints. A detailed analysis of spacing, for example, would have been much too time-consuming; rather than attempt to capture variations in the spaces between words and lines, we have used a single space between words, and the spaces captured between lines are to the modern standard. Such detailed analysis would doubtless be useful for a select few specialists in the field of printing history. To the majority of our users such work would be of little interest or use, and those who are interested are able to look at the matching images.[25] Digital texts of the sort created by the SQA are intended to enable *users* to pursue different kinds of research and study, as opposed to allowing the editors to carry out specific research and study in the course of creating the resource; tagging for detailed metrical analysis or a focus on punctuation and spacing is arguably inappropriate in this context. Certainly, for all practical purposes, it was impossible for the SQA project.

---

[22] SQA, ham-1604-22276x-fol-c01.xml.

[23] Assistive technology (AT) is a term that encompasses "assistive, adaptive, and rehabilitative devices" (http://en.wikipedia.org/wiki/Assistive_technology, accessed 14 October 2009) which enable people with disabilities to gain access to information and study. An example of AT is the screen reader, a device that identifies and interprets text as speech, sound icons, or through a Braille output device (http://en.wikipedia.org/wiki/Screen_reader, accessed 14 October 2009). While screen readers can "read" most modern fonts, they are not normally able to interpret early-modern type.

[24] Although not yet explicitly built into the interface, this form of accessibility is greatly facilitated by our encoding choices.

[25] Such decisions were taken following discussion at the Advisory Forum (see n. 20 above).

Textual vs. physical: Beyond the printed text

Different copies and different editions of the *Hamlet* quartos reveal much about their original printing processes, but, inevitably, their postprinting journeys varied considerably—a fact revealed by, among other things, the amount of damage they sustained in their transmission through the centuries. Sometimes this damage affects the legibility of the printed text, recorded in SQA using the element <gap>, e.g., <gap reason="absent" agent="cropped" extent="1" unit="chars" resp="#odl"/>. Each <gap> contains the attributes @reason indicating why there is a gap, @agent indicating the cause of the damage, @extent (a numerical value) relating to @unit (characters, words, lines, and so on), and @resp (indicating who is responsible for the information contained in the <gap>, in this example, the Oxford Digital Library). Available reasons for a gap are fairly restricted: @reason can have the values "illegible" or "absent." "Absent" is used where something is missing, perhaps cropped, as evidenced by other copies of the edition, and we do not wish to imply its presence by using "illegible." However, causes of damage can vary considerably; @agent can have values such as the following, most of which are self-explanatory:

- ★ abrasion
- ★ bleedThrough
- ★ cropped
- ★ damagedType
- ★ damp
- ★ deletion[26]
- ★ excised[27]

Quartos were transcribed and marked-up from digital images, rather than from the original printed books. One potential drawback of working from digital images is that in some instances it can be difficult to determine the exact nature of particular damage and indeed whether a character or word is truly illegible.[28] All of the damage information was supplied or checked

---

[26] Some methods of deletion have rendered the printed text illegible, hence the need for this value. For discussion of how still-legible deletions were transcribed, see below.

[27] For a full list, consult "Encoding Documentation," *Shakespeare Quartos Archive*, accessed 15 October 2009, http://www.quartos.org/info/encoding.html.

[28] Projects such as the *Digital Image Archive of Medieval Music* (DIAMM), accessed 24 December 2009, http://www.diamm.ac.uk/index.html and the Archimedes Palimpsest Project, accessed 14 February 2011, http://www.archimedespalimpsest.org/, dem-

by experts at the Folger and at the British Library; where they were supplying damage information about quarto copies held by their own institutions, they could of course check against the originals, but where they were working on other institutions' copies they had to rely on the, admittedly very high-resolution, digital images. Our encoding scheme allows us therefore to include the @agent value "unclear" to indicate that the cause of the damage cannot be determined with confidence. Using the <gap> element allows us to record damage affecting legibility of the printed text, but not other kinds of damage. As one would expect, different copies have suffered various kinds of damage over the years; they may be torn, foxed, stained, or faded. Where damage did not affect legibility (for example, on pages or parts of pages with no printing) it was not recorded in the text of the electronic edition. These features are often recorded in the notes on the quartos' condition, supplied by the holding libraries, and reproduced in the TEI headers. Detailed records of this sort of damage would make a valuable contribution to this project, but would require study of each physical quarto (rather than its digital surrogate). The time and travel this would have involved made it impossible.

A TEI header, which must be present in every TEI-conformant text, is prefixed to each of the thirty-two *Hamlet* transcriptions. The TEI header contains information about the file, such as bibliographic details about the source artefact and the creation and revision history of the electronic text. One element of the TEI header, the <msDesc> element, is used for describing the physical make-up of the material book being encoded. This element was designed specifically for description of manuscripts;[29] however, early printed book and manuscript specialists often want to record similar information. The <msDesc> element provides the best place for recording information about the printed book. The SQA contains descriptions of the binding of each quarto; this information is in the <bindingDesc> element, within the <physDesc> element, which itself nests in the overarching <msDesc>, for example:

---

onstrate how much information (including "lost" data from manuscripts damaged beyond what the naked eye can read) can be garnered through digital manipulation of high-quality images. The SQA had neither the resources nor the expertise to carry out similar manipulation and analysis. As the images are available for download, we would welcome users undertaking such work.

[29] TEI Consortium (2010, sec. 10).

```
<msDesc>
   <physDesc>
[...]
<bindingDesc><p>Gilt borders and ornament on <locus facs="#ham-
1603-22275x-hun-c01-image001">front cover</locus>. Title tooled
in gilt reads <quote>HAMLET
   <lb/>SHAKESPEARE
   <lb/>LONDON 1603</quote></p>
 <p>Gilt borders and ornament on <locus facs="#ham-1603-22275x-
   hun-c01-image002">facsimile image 002a</locus>. </p>
[...]
   </bindingDesc>
   <accMat><p>Label on <locus facs="#ham-1603-22275x-hun-c01-
   image002">facsimile image 002a</locus></p></accMat>
[...]
   </ physDesc >
[...]
   </ msDesc >[30]
```

The <accMat> (*accompanying material*) element contains information about other sorts of material associated with the printed book, such as bound-in fragments, bookplates, or library paste-ins.

The <msDesc> element in the TEI header also contains information about the various scribal hands responsible for handwritten annotation throughout each quarto copy; information about each hand is nested within the <msDesc> element using the <handNote> element. The identity of the hands was established by quartos experts at the Folger and the British Library. Naturally, some scribes are not identifiable, but discrimination among scribes (particularly in annotations that do not include written words, for example, underlining) was sometimes possible on the basis of medium or ink color. While the digital images are of excellent quality, the nuances of ink and pencil shade are easier to determine in the original than on the screen. By identifying scribes in this way, we hope to add value to our editions in the ability to trace a scribe's work throughout a text (and ultimately, we hope, throughout all the plays in quarto).[31] The information in <handNote> conforms to this pattern:

---

[30] SQA, ham-1603-22275x-hun-c01.xml.

[31] By assigning unique identifiers to each of the hands present within and across the quartos, it becomes possible for users to easily trace the transmission of a particular

Hand identifier: [e.g. #aa]
Scribe: [Name of annotator, if known]
Script: [secretary, copperplate, Italian etc.]
Medium: [brown [ink], pencil etc.]
Scope: [major or minor] (describes how widely the hand is used in this text)
Description: [further descriptive detail]

For example:

> <msDesc><msIdentifier><repository>Huntington   Library</re-
> pository></msIdentifier>
>   <physDesc>
>   <handDesc>
>
>   <handNote xml:id="#ab" script=" roman" scribe="anonymous"
>   medium="pencil" scope="minor">This post-1700 hand provides
>   numbers and a shelfmark on the pastedown inside the front
>   cover.</handNote>
>   <handNote xml:id="#ac" script=" roman" scribe="anonymous"
>   medium="pencil" scope="minor">This post-1700 hand supplies
>   foliation on the bottom left margin of each leaf, starting on the
>   first page of printed text with the number 27.</handNote>
>   [...]
>   </handDesc>
>   [...]
>   </physDesc>
>   [...]
> </msDesc>[32]

The @xml:id attribute is used to give each hand a unique identifier which is also contained in the body of the text. This provides a link between the annotations in the text and their description in the header.

We shall discuss handwritten annotation in more detail below, but it may already be clear that a distinction is made between manuscript annotation and printed material such as pasted-in catalogue records or library stamps. In

---

quarto as revealed by its owners' annotations. The different personalities of owners such as Edmond Malone are revealed by the kind of annotations they left behind.
[32] SQA, ham-1603-22275x-hun-c01.xml.

some ways this makes for an awkward distinction. Would users find it more useful, more intuitive, for the presence of library stamps to be indicated in the text proper, perhaps using <figure> tags? What is the difference between a later handwritten addition and a later printed one? One could argue that handwritten annotations are integral to the physical quarto, and cannot be removed. But this could also be said of stamped information, which cannot be removed in the same way as pasted-in printed material could be. Handwritten annotation can only, for the most part, be understood in the context in which it appears. Such material would, largely, be meaningless if captured away from the textual feature it is intended to illuminate, but it is not very significant where exactly, in relation to the text, a library stamp appears. To include these features in the body of the text would, perhaps, make the document unduly cluttered. We decided it would be neater to include such non-manuscript-related information in the TEI header, with other similar copy-specific information.

Manuscript annotation

By making available multiple copies of the same quarto editions of *Hamlet*, the SQA provides the opportunity for close comparative analysis. Such analysis could focus on the textual changes made between editions of *Hamlet* or on the printing process across copies and editions, for example. But arguably the most significant aspect of the individual quarto copies, which most differentiates any one from the others, is the physical evidence of what happened to each postprint, the material manifestation of their transmission history: what brought these low-status printed plays to their current richly covered, prized status? Their different bindings and the paste-ins and library stamps reveal much about this, as do the varying sorts of damage and repair they have sustained, but the most compelling evidence of their individual histories is the handwritten annotations that have been added to the pages.

From experience of manuscript encoding projects, we had an idea of some of the complexities we might meet in the quartos' manuscript annotations.

We expected some quartos to be very light on annotation, but for some to require significant work.[33] We were less prepared for the complex negotiation between descriptive and interpretative editing (particularly when set against the need to complete the pilot project on time and on budget). In keeping with our intention to provide a tool for learning and research, we wanted to privilege descriptive encoding; but we soon saw the need to add a further layer of interpretation in order to enable presentation of information as intuitively as possible in the final resource. This tension will be explored more fully as we discuss the detail of our approach to tagging manuscript annotations.

Annotation tagging in detail

Our descriptive encoding includes <add> (*addition*) or <addSpan> (*added span of text*) for all manuscript material added to the printed texts (including material that has later been cancelled) and <del> (*deletion*) and <delSpan> (*deleted span of text*) for all cancelled text. <add> is used for minor additions comprising a few words or characters. <addSpan> is used for larger textual interventions: for longer additions, and for passages which contain more complex features and textual apparatus, such as (though not restricted to) a passage of several lines, entire speeches (of any length), or a sequence of manuscript interventions. Each of these elements includes @resp, @hand, and @place attributes. The @place values were taken from a closed list, for example:

★   for the margins around the text block: *margin-top, margin-bot, margin-left, margin-right*[34]

We thought it worth differentiating types of manuscript addition. If a user is interested in textual emendation by annotators, for example, finding the bibliographic information added by librarians and curators, or scribbles that

---

[33] Some quarto copies have little in the way of annotation. For example, the British Library's first copy of the fifth quarto (ham-1637-22279x-bli-c01) has two cataloguing notes (the author's name and the book's shelf number) and only one other annotation (the letters "g.v." on the title page). By contrast, some of the quartos have a great many annotations, in multiple hands, for example the Huntington's second quarto of 1604 (ham-1604-22276x-hun-c01), which formerly belonged to Charles Kemble and has thirty-four manuscript annotations in nine hands, and the Bodleian's fourth quarto (ham-1625-22278x-bod-c01), formerly Malone's, which has 489 annotations.

[34] For a full list, consult "Encoding Documentation," *Shakespeare Quartos Archive*, accessed 15 October 2009, http://www.quartos.org/info/encoding.html.

appear to be nothing more than nib-tests, would muddy their search results. The possible values of the @type attribute were taken from a closed list, for example:

★ for graphic manuscript representations: *figure*
★ for textual interventions: *intervention*
★ for textual notes: *note*[35]

Although the first iteration of the user interface does not explicitly enable searching across manuscript annotations, the display conventions do make use of the proof-of-concept tagging. It is expected that (funding permitting) subsequent versions of SQA will exploit this rich encoding.

<add> tags cannot float freely in TEI-compliant texts. For this reason they were transcribed within the closest valid tag, including <fw> (*forme work*), <l> (*line*), <p> (*paragraph*) and <speaker>. However this was not always appropriate, for example, where an annotator has clearly indicated the addition belongs elsewhere. Annotators might, for example, like Malone in his copy of the fourth quarto (the most consistently complex of all the project's texts),[36] use a line number or a figure as a note-marker. Malone noted, "This undated copy I have collated with the quarto of 1604, and have placed the variations at the bottom of the page."[37] We wanted to avoid encoding like this:

```
<fw type="catchword" place="foot-right">That
<add><figure/><del>13 there?</del></add> <add>26 our fantasie.</
add>
<add>2. twelfe.</add> <add>4 hart.</add><add>15 leedgemen.</
add><add>7 farwell.</add>
<add>21 Say, what is &c</add><add>30 minuts.</add><add>31. ap-
parision</add>
<add>32. approove</add></fw>[38]
```

This approach would not have been incorrect; however, it struck us as unwieldy and, particularly for people approaching the quartos primarily through the electronic text, indigestible. Instead we opted to transcribe the annotations at their indicated line numbers, embedding the additions in the

---

[35] For a full list, see note 34.

[36] ham-1625-22278x-bod-c01, Bodleian, Arch. G d.41.

[37] ham-1625-22278x-bod-c01-002, Bodleian, Arch. G d.41, manuscript notes on page opposite title.

[38] Bodleian, Arch. G d.41, [A2v].

text at the indicated positions. Each note-marker was transcribed (or, in the case of a figure, described) as the value of an @n (*number*) attribute. Here, for example, Malone supplies four textual emendations on the mount at the foot of a page.[39] The final one reads "35 And either the Devil," indicating that the intervention is intended for the 35th line of the page (which reads, in the print, "And master the Deuill, or throw him out").[40]

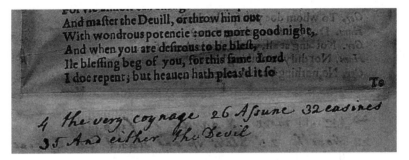

Figure 2. [fig. _ham-1625-22278x-bod-c01-035-4-5-8.TIF]

<l><subst><del type="substitution" hand="#aa" resp="#fol">And master the Deuill</del><add n="35" hand="#aa" place="mount-bot" type="intervention" resp="#fol">And either the Devil</add></subst>, or throw him out</l>[41]

We transcribed the emendation directly in line 35, nesting the <add> and <del> elements in a <subst> (*substitution*), to suggest that Malone offered an alternative, rather than a supplementary, reading (as discussed above). The manuscript addition was verified by Shakespeare experts at the Folger, hence the "#fol" value of the @resp (*responsibility*) attribute. The hash-sign refers back to the header, where the Folger Shakespeare Library is defined, as is the identification of the scribal hands. The hand "aa" refers to Malone. This type of deletion we described as "substitution" (here, the value of @type)

---

[39] Bodleian, Arch. G d.41, [I1v].

[40] This problematic line is from Hamlet's speech beginning "O throw away the worser part of it," where he exhorts his mother to avoid her husband's bed. The first quarto has the speech abbreviated to its first line and interrupted by the entrance of Hamlet's father's ghost. The second and subsequent quartos have the exchange after the ghost has exited, but the second quarto alone has the line (which most editors agree is lacking a word: Thompson and Taylor [2006, 350], for example, suggest "And either *shame* the devil.").

[41] SQA, ham-1625-22278x-bod-c01.xml.

because it is marked only by the presence of the manuscript alternative reading. The type of addition is defined by our transcription guidelines as an "intervention" in the text, marked here by the @type value. The @n value is taken from the annotation's note-marker, giving the line number in the printed text. In this way, every aspect of Malone's note is both transcribed and described by the encoding.

Where figurative illustrations function as note-markers, they are supplied in square brackets (following the editing convention of marking supplied information not present in the original) and taken from a closed list. For example, in his copy of the fourth quarto, Malone inserted two speeches that are present in the first and second quartos and absent in the third, fourth, and fifth. He added these at the foot of the mounted page (with other emendations), marking the place of their insertion in the text with the line number and a double triangle:

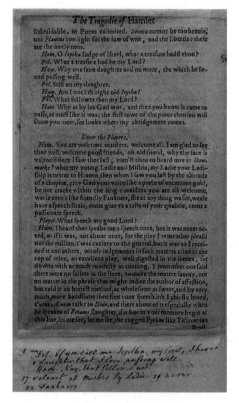

Figure 3. [fig. _ham-1625-22278x-bod-c01-022-3-2-2.TIF][42]

---

[42] Bodleian, Arch. G d.41, [E4v].

The annotation is complex in that its encoding requires <sp> (*speech*) and
<speaker> elements, which necessitates the use of an <addSpan> element and
its accompanying <anchor> (rather than in the simpler <add> element, which
cannot contain the necessary apparatus):

> <addSpan place="margin-bot" n="9 [double triangle]" resp="#fol"
> spanTo="#ham-1625-22278x-bod-c01-005"/>
> <sp who="#pol"><speaker>Pol.</speaker> <p>If you call me Ieptha,
> my lord, I have <lb/>a daughter that I love passing well.</p></sp>
>   <sp who="#ham"><speaker><hi rend="underline">Ham</hi>.</
> speaker> <p>Nay, that followes not.</p></sp> <anchor xml:id="ham-
> 1625-22278x-bod-c01-005"/>[43]

Some @n values include illustrative figures and transcribed words or
numbers, and therefore include both square-bracketed (supplied) text and
transcription.[44] (For the further complication of underlined text, see the
discussion below.) We felt this scheme for recording complex manuscript
additions might be helpful to users who wished to see at a glance where a
textual emendation had been suggested by a scribe, as well as to those who
are unaccustomed to following editing marks in proofed texts.

Throughout our treatment of manuscript annotations, we described how
annotators had intervened in the texts. Our use of <add> and <del> did not
imply that we were giving authority or precedence to one reading over another, only that we were describing what previous editors had indicated.
This was relevant to the next problem: how to provide a legible text. Where
an annotator has supplied a variant, how should we indicate that the manuscript and printed versions are alternative readings? The answer seemed to
be through nesting paired <add> and <del> tags in the <subst> element. Here,
it is important to stress that the use of this construction is not intended to
imply an editorial judgment, but a description of the apparent intention of
the annotator.

---

[43] SQA, ham-1625-22278x-bod-c01.xml.

[44] Where a figurative manuscript marking was not obviously functioning as a note-
marker, it was captured using a <figure> tag, with a <figDesc> inside it, e.g.:

> <add place="margin-right" hand="#ad" type="figure"
> resp="#bli"><figure><figDesc>Manicule.</figDesc></figure></add>
> (British Library, C.34.k.1, [F2r]).

Other examples of the descriptions used in <figDesc>s include arrow, cross, double
triangle, manicule, scribble, and trefoil.

Material marked for cancellation is enclosed in <del> tags, whether in print or manuscript. A <del> tag contains the attributes @hand, @type, and @resp. It may also contain an @n, as with <add> above. The @hand, @resp, and @n attributes function here as in the <add> element. The values of @type, on the other hand, were drawn from another closed list. Examples include *braced* and *crossed*, where cancelled text is indicated with a brace or cross; *obscured*, where text has been partially or completely concealed, e.g., by scribbling; *overwritten*, where text is marked for deletion by a hand which supplies the alternative reading by writing over the original; *substituted*, where another reading is supplied with no other signal to delete the original text.

Where an annotation has been made, and then subsequently crossed out, and so is essentially both an addition and a deletion, we nested the <del> tag within the <add> tag. In this example the book's call number has been revised:

<add place="textblock" type="bibliographic" hand="#ab" resp= "#bli" >C.34 K. 4</add>

<add place="textblock" type="bibliographic" hand="#ac" resp= "#bli"><del type="struckThrough" hand="#ab" resp="#bli">C.34. e.5 </del></add>[45]

Figure 4. [fig. _ham-1611-22277x-bli-c01-004-3-2-2.TIF][46]

Sometimes an annotation has overwritten the printed word, transforming it into something else. In this case the <subst> tag has been used. In this example, "my" has been changed to "thy":

[45] SQA, ham-1611-22277x-bli-c01.xml.

[46] British Library, C.34.k.4, [A2v].

<subst><del type="overwritten" hand="#aa" resp="#odl">m</del><add hand="#aa" place="supralinear" type="intervention" resp="#odl">th</add></subst>y[47]

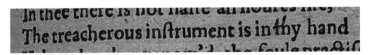

Figure 5. [fig. _ham-1611-22277x-bli-c01-053-4-8-6.TIF][48]

In these cases, the TEI supplied the necessary encoding. In other places, the guidelines supplied solutions that were too complex for our schema. An example of this was how to encode a single manuscript addition functioning as two textual interventions. Edmond Malone, in particular, favoured this approach to annotation. He frequently used two note-markers to refer to the same suggested change in two separate printed lines. Here, he suggests four emendations to the text, noting the line number on the page of each. "Fraunce," Malone's emended spelling of "France," he indicates should be used both at line 20 and 24:

![Handwritten annotations: "9 hartely farwell. 15 hart 20 Fraunce. Antepenult. Hath, my lord, wrong 24)"](image)

Figure 6. [fig. _ham-1625-22278x-bod-c01-007-4-5-9.TIF][49]

In order to highlight our reason for repeating a single (verbal) addition, we chose to record the annotation at both indicated points in the text and include both line numbers in each @n value:

<l>Your leaue and fauour to returne to <subst><del type= "substitution" hand="#aa" resp="#fol"><hi rend="italic">France<hi> </del><add n="[brace] 20 24" hand="#aa" place="mount-bot" type="intervention" resp="#fol">Fraunce</add></subst>,</l>

...

<l>My thoughts and wishes bend againe toward <subst><del type="substitution" hand="#aa"

---

[47] SQA, ham-1625-22278x-bod-c01.xml.

[48] British Library, C.34.k.4, [O1r].

[49] Bodleian Library, Arch. G d.41, [B1v].

resp="#fol"><hi rend="italic">France</hi></del><add n="[brace] 20 24" hand="#aa" place="mount-bot" type="intervention" resp="#fol">Fraunce</add></subst>,</l>[50]

Elsewhere we found the need for a tag which does not exist in the TEI guidelines: a <substSpan> in which we could nest an <addSpan> element paired with a <delSpan> element. This would be invaluable for instances where a seemingly simple annotation calls for a complex change in the encoding apparatus. On the page, an annotation's function might look straightforward: for example, a speech has been printed in its entirety and given to one character, but an annotator indicates that one line of the speech should be given to another character, while the rest of the speech should remain attributed to the first (printed) character.

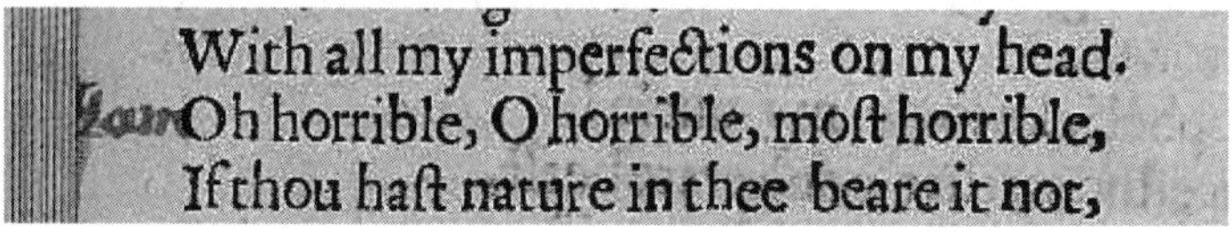

Figure 7. [fig. _ham-1637-22279x-fol-c02-016-3-1-3.TIF][51]

To keep our encoding consistent, we would have liked to nest within such a <substSpan> element the following:

★   a <delSpan> surrounding the original <l>
★   an <anchor> (for the <delSpan>)
★   an <addSpan>
★   a closing </sp> (speech)
★   an opening <sp>
★   an opening <speaker> with its associated attributes
★   the line, in its entirety
★   a second closing </sp>
★   an <anchor> (for the <addSpan>)
★   an opening <sp> (to reopen the printed speech)
★   an opening <speaker> (to repeat the original speaker)

Instead, lacking this element, we left the annotation in its simplest form, merely prefacing a line in one of Horatio's speeches:

---

[50] SQA, ham-1625-22278x-bod-c01.xml.

[51] Folger, STC 22279 Copy 2, [C4v].

<l>With all my imperfections on my head.</l>
<l><add place="margin-left" hand="#af" type="intervention" resp=
"#fol">Ham</add>Oh horrible, O horrible, most horrible,</l>
<l>If thou hast nature in thee beare it not,</l>[52]

This records the annotation where it occurs, but it means that the passage
is not recorded as belonging to either Hamlet or the ghost of his father. It
will only be returned in the results of a search for every speech by the Ghost,
which will suit a user interested in the printed version of the text but not one
who is following the logic of the annotations.

Further complications arose where the printed text is illegible (as opposed
to deleted). Where printed text was partially cropped, or was otherwise inadvertently partially illegible, and completed in manuscript, affected characters have been transcribed once in <add> tags, with the @type "completedCropped," e.g.:

<l><add   hand="#ab"   type="completedCropped"   place="inline"
resp="#fol">W</add>oo't drinke vp Esill, eate a Crocadile?</l>[53]

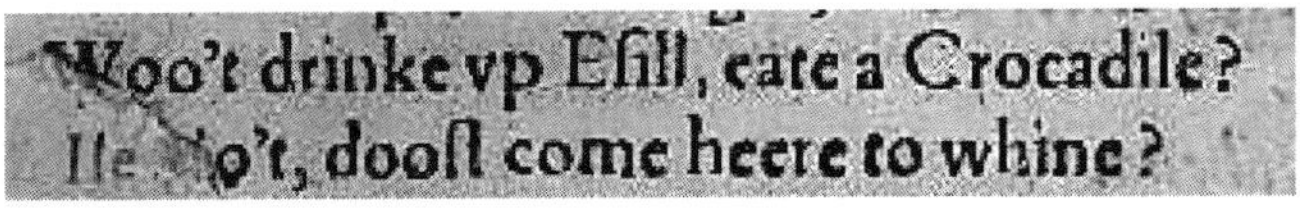

Figure 8. [fig. _ham-1604-22276x-fol-c01-050-3-1-5.TIF][54]

Such <add> tags are not paired with <gap>s because, by definition, "completedCropped" text is partially there, as distinct from completely cropped and
subsequently fully supplied text.

Where printed text has been entirely cropped or torn, as in the second line of
the figure, or is otherwise inadvertently illegible (to the extent that it cannot
be confidently transcribed), and supplied in manuscript, the <add> is paired
with a <gap> of a specified extent, following this pattern:

<l><gap reason="absent" agent="torn" extent="7" unit="chars"
resp="#fol"/><add type="suppliedCropped" place="inline" resp=
"#fol">And wag</add>er o<gap reason="absent" agent="torn" ex-
tent="2" unit="chars" resp="#fol"/><add type="suppliedCropped"

---

[52] SQA, ham-1637-22279x-fol-c02.xml.

[53] SQA, ham-1604-22276x-fol-c01.xml.

[54] Folger, STC 22276, [M4v].

place="inline" resp="#fol">re</add> your heads; he being rem-
isse,</l>[55]

Here the phrase "And wager ore your heads" is partially illegible, because
the page has been torn. An annotator has supplied "And wag" and the "re"
of "ore." We indicated the illegible characters (which total seven, including
the space) in a <gap> and paired it with the <add type="suppliedCropped">.
While the project's stylesheet and documentation account for this, it is a feature we would like to see added formally to the TEI: an element which pairs
<add> with <gap>, in the way the <subst> element pairs <del> and <add>.

Another significant type of handwritten annotation not covered by addition
and deletion tagging is underlining. All underlined text was transcribed as
such, in the most straightforward manner. Where manuscript text was underlined by the same hand as the writing, we transcribed it simply in <hi
rend="underlined"> (*highlighted*) tags. Printed text underlined in manuscript
was transcribed using <addSpan> and <anchor> tags, except when the underlining functions as a deletion mark, which we recorded in the @rend of
the <del> tag.[56] Where manuscript annotation appeared to be underlined in
a hand different from the writing, <addSpan> was also employed, to distinguish between the hands.

In encoding manuscript annotations, then, we strayed far from our original remit of using the encoding to describe as simply as possible what appeared on a page, favouring instead a level of interpretation that we hoped
would augment the usefulness of the online resource and would demonstrate
sound and valid markup. As with encoding printed text, the possibilities of
extending and refining the markup to capture postprint additions seemed
to stretch indefinitely before us, and we were restricted more by time than
by any disinclination to express even more explicitly the textual history and
transmission of the quartos.

---

[55] SQA, ham-1604-22276x-fol-c01.xml.

[56] For example:

> <speaker rend="italic">Bar.</speaker> <l><subst><del hand="#af"
> type="underlined" resp="#odl"><crend="droppedCapital">
> VV</c>Hose</del><add place="margin-right"
> type="intervention" hand="#af" resp="#fol"><hi
> rend="underline">who's</hi></add></subst> there?</l></sp>

(SQA, ham-1611-22277x-fol-c03.xml; Folger, STC 22277 Copy 3 [B1r]).

Conclusion

Overall we tried to capture as much detail regarding the physical book as we could within our project's scope. There remains much that could be done. More detail could be provided on the physical make-up and on the edition and ownership history of the book, particularly if the TEI were to develop guidelines specifically for printed book description. Fuller damage information could be supplied. Furthermore, some aspects of the material quartos cannot be adequately represented in a digital text format; for example, the visual impact of the original font is not there in the digital text. Although the presence of handwritten annotations, library stamps, and paste-ins are recorded in the texts' TEI headers, the "layered" effect of the original printed text cannot be replicated in the digital text. Most obviously, we lose the sensation of holding the original in hand—the weight of the paper, the smell, the sensation of the binding.

Being able to access digital images of the quartos mitigates some of these inadequacies. Digital images allow us to get very close to the visual impact of the original, if not to the feel of the physical object. They allow us a fuller understanding of the condition of the individual quartos and their passage through history and can justify new interpretative and descriptive readings that might conflict with the encoding choices we made. Despite their inherent limitations, digital images are an excellent surrogate for originals, like the Shakespeare quartos, which are precious, widely dispersed, and accessible by very few people.

While the digital images significantly help us to appreciate some of the material qualities of the Shakespeare quartos, we believe their information is most valuable when it is also recorded in accompanying electronic texts. Both elements may be used independently of the other for some kinds of work. The ability to switch easily between the two digitized data forms, electronic text and images, means users can check a transcription, or see what interpretation we have made of a particular feature in the original.

Although time constraints necessarily limited the extent to which full searchability would be enabled in the prototype interface, our encoding of such features as inverted characters, catchwords, and handwritten annotations records their presence in the downloadable XML file. All handwritten material has been encoded, which enables search for, and isolation and analysis of, the work of particular annotators, within and across the copies of *Hamlet*. Should we find funding for a second phase of the project, we would create similar digital editions of all the copies of all Shakespeare's plays in pre-1642 quartos, which would enable even broader searches and comparative analysis, and include this function in the SQA interface. Already study that would previously have been extremely laborious is rendered straightforward and speedy by this encoding. This screenshot is an example of the ease of use the interface currently provides. It includes a small (zoomed-out) image of the title page of Malone's fourth quarto (Bodleian, Arch. G d.41), and two other panels showing the digital image and the electronic text of the opening G2v and G3r.

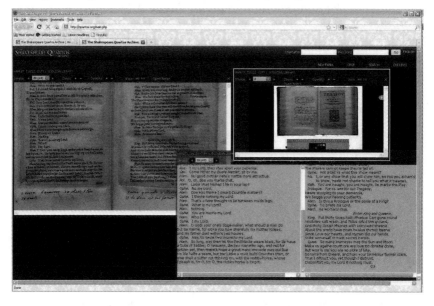

Figure 9. SQA screenshot

The TEI header allows us to record copy-specific information provided by Shakespeare experts; the same is true of the damage information recorded in <gap> tags. Such expert input cannot be accessed via a digital image. The electronic texts open up the quartos in new and exciting ways, allowing different types of study, whether used with the images or independently.

Inevitably, we learned many lessons during the encoding of the quartos in this pilot project. We had not anticipated the complexities of adapting TEI <msDesc> for the description of early printed books. We had, naively, expected that the encoding of handwritten annotations was something that could comfortably be done in our one-year time frame; we quickly discovered that such work required significant time and expertise. On the one hand, our expectations of the amount of work we could do in one year were too high; on the other, our estimation of how complex the work would be was too low. The Shakespeare quartos are so rich, textually and materially, that encoding work could continue almost indefinitely. Nonetheless, on advice from experts in related fields, we have produced a resource that is valuable and innovative, and we hope will provide a platform for further encoding and refinement in the future, both in a second phase of our SQA project and through other people working in the field, but, truly, there is much more in the Shakespeare quartos than was ever dreamt of in our philosophy.

WORKS CITED

Kuhn, Jim. Forthcoming. "A Hawk from a Handsaw: Collating Possibilities with *The Shakespeare Quartos Archive*." In *New Technologies and Renaissance Studies II*, edited by Tassie Gniady, Kris McAbee, and Jessica Murphy. Tempe: Arizona Center for Medieval and Renaissance Studies.

Porter, Dot. 2008. "Extending msDescription to Describe Printed Books (and to Describe Manuscripts Better)." TEI Members' Meeting 2008. Accessed 24 December 2009. http://www.cch.kcl.ac.uk/cocoon/ tei2008/programme/workingpapers/wp_004.html.

Shakespeare, William. 2006. *Hamlet*. Edited by Ann Thompson and Neil Taylor. London: Arden Shakespeare.

TEI Consortium, eds. 2010. "10. Manuscript description." *TEI P5: Guidelines for Electronic Text Encoding and Interchange*. Version 1.6.0. TEI Consortium. http://www.tei-c.org/Guidelines/P5/.

Trettien, Whitney Anne. 2009. "Comment on SQA." *The Digital Reading Room — er, Archive*. HASTAC (Humanities, Arts, Science, and Technology Advanced Collaboratory). Posted 22 November 2009. Accessed 14 February 2011. http://www.hastac.org/blogs/whitneyt/digital-reading-room-er-archive.

_____ 2010. "Disciplining Digital Humanities, 2010: Staging Shakespeare, XMAS, Shakespeare Performance in Asia, Shakespeare Quartos Archive, and BardBox." *Shakespeare Quarterly* 61 (3): 391–400. Accessed 14 February 2011. http://muse.jhu.edu/journals/ shakespeare_quarterly/summary/v061/61.3.trettien.html.

Digitizing Non-Linear Texts in TEI P5: The Case of the Early Modern Reversed Manuscript

Angus Vine
University of Stirling
angus.vine@stir.au.uk

Sebastiaan Verweij
University of Oxford
sebastiaan.verweij@ell.ox.ac.uk

Introduction[1]

In 1731 Richard Turner wrote the following in his commonplace book: "What is wrote at each End of this Book, is by my Uncle, Mr. John Knight / What is wrote forwards is by me—Richard Turner junior commencing 1731" (Glasgow University Library, MS Murray 556, fol. [24v], manuscript unfoliated). What Turner describes here is not unusual: manuscript books often passed through various hands, used and reused by different owners at different times. In this case, the original owner, John Knight, collected a great deal of English poetry, mostly from the late seventeenth century; his nephew then added to the manuscript some thirty years later, copying what he could in the gaps that his uncle had left. What is unusual about Turner's comment, however, is its degree of articulacy: few copyists or scribes have left quite so explicit records of what they actually did. Turner does not just record that he inherited his uncle's book, he also tells what he did to that manuscript once it passed into his hands.

Turner's comment also highlights an important characteristic of a number of manuscript books: non-linearity. Manuscripts do not always document or describe a chronological, historical, or palaeographical progression from the first leaf to the last. Scribal stints[2] play a role here; so too, as in the case of the Glasgow University Library manuscript, do different owners. Where manuscripts do not exhibit a linear progression, terms such as *beginning* and

---

[1] We are extremely grateful for advice on coding to the TEI community on the TEI-L mailing list (particularly Dan O'Donnell and Peter Boot) and also to Leonidas Konstantelos.

[2] A scribal stint describes the portion of work or copying carried out by an individual scribe in a manuscript (*OED*, s.v. "stint," *n.*[1], 7.a).

ISBN 978-0-86698-499-7 (online)   ISBN 978-0-86698-474-4 (print)
New Technologies in Medieval and Renaissance Studies 3 (2012) 113–136

end become arbitrary: they are designations that may reflect the foliation or pagination of a manuscript, but that tell us little about how the manuscript was actually compiled or used. Such manuscripts therefore pose serious questions to editors and perhaps even more serious questions to those working on digital editions. How does one connect single items, whether copied in one sitting or at different times, that are physically separated from one another across a manuscript as a whole? How does one distinguish scribal stints that overlap and intersect with one another? More fundamentally, is it possible to convey the textual sense of a non-linear manuscript while also conveying its physical integrity—and all of this encoded in standardized markup language? Indeed, as Jerome McGann reminds us,

> As we lay the foundations for translating our inherited archive of cultural materials, including vast corpora of paper-based materials, into digital depositories and forms, we are called to a clarity of thought about textuality that most people, even most scholars, rarely undertake. (McGann 2006, 198)

Digitizing miscellanies and commonplace books[3] enforces a consideration of early modern textuality and a profound engagement with non-linearity. That natural language and artefactual textual structures are not always easily captured in digital markup is well known, yet the challenge remains to approximate such structures with the tools that are currently at our disposal.

In this chapter, we shall explore the technological possibilities and challenges of digitizing non-linear manuscripts. We consider both how an editor might present them and how one might encode them in the Text Encoding Initiative (TEI) P5 guidelines, the de facto standard for marking up digital texts and editions in scholarly research projects, as we move from the theoretical and practical problems that this kind of manuscript poses to the range of solutions currently available.[4] To explore these issues we focus on one particular kind of non-linear material: the early modern reversed

---

[3] Strictly speaking, a commonplace book was a collection of witty or memorable quotations or sayings (the *commonplaces*) organized under categories, topics, or heads; for more on this genre, see p. 126 below. A miscellany, by contrast, was a less schematic collection of texts. Also, miscellanies typically contain whole texts rather than extracts from them. For a useful introduction to the phenomenon of the manuscript miscellany, see Love (1993, 5–7 especially).

[4] For more on the use of TEI P5 guidelines for manuscript description, see Cummings's chapter in this volume.

manuscript (a manuscript written in from both ends, such as that of Turner described above). Although this essay arises from our experience in working with reversed manuscripts on *Scriptorium: Medieval and Early Modern Manuscripts Online* (http://scriptorium.english.cam.ac.uk), our hope is that it will offer a best practice guide for digitizing non-linear material more generally.[5] For this reason, therefore, the last part of our essay will consider, more generally, the challenge of conflicting hierarchical structures in TEI-encoded manuscript descriptions.

Scriptorium is a digital archive of twenty English manuscript commonplace books and miscellanies from *c*. 1450 to *c*. 1720, based in the Faculty of English at the University of Cambridge. Our website provides free public access to digital images of these materials as well as extensive critical and descriptive materials, including full technical descriptions, full indices of content of all manuscripts (which wherever possible identify sources), scholarly articles, and partial transcriptions. The manuscripts themselves include, for example, a biblical miscellany kept by King Edward VI (Trinity College, Cambridge, MS R.7.31), a book of husbandry belonging to the regicide Sir William Heveningham (Holkham Hall, MS 685), and the miscellany compiled by Francis Bacon's chaplain and amanuensis, William Rawley (Lambeth Palace, MS 2086). The earliest, a well-known literary manuscript connected with Glastonbury Abbey (Trinity College, Cambridge, MS O.9.38), dates from the mid-fifteenth century (see further Rigg 1968), while the latest, the reading notes of Edward Pordage (King's College, Cambridge, MS 840.5), dates from the early eighteenth century. The manuscripts come from ten different libraries or repositories: Emmanuel, St John's, King's, Queens', and Trinity College, Cambridge; Cambridge University Library; Lambeth Palace; Holkham Hall; Belton House; and Leeds University Library. *Scriptorium* does not therefore represent an actual or historical archive: there is no physical collection that corresponds exactly or even in part with the collection that we have created. But this is the strength of a digital archive such as *Scriptorium*: material produced in different locations and at different times can be brought together and their connections observed. Connections can also be re-established between materials that are now geographically disparate, preserved in different libraries or repositories but which were produced in the same place or at the same time. *Scriptorium*, in short, enables the kind of comparative work that is cru-

---

[5] *Scriptorium: Medieval and Early Modern Manuscripts Online* at Cambridge, further described below, should not be confused with the similarly named *Digital Scriptorium* at Columbia University, accessed 23 October 2009 (http://www.scriptorium.columbia. edu).

cial to the study of manuscript culture but which, without the aid of digital technology, is often difficult for the researcher.

Reversed manuscripts

Reversed manuscripts are not unusual in the early modern period. A manuscript which might be a student's notebook at one end might at the other end be a collection of witticisms, a laundry list, an index, or a record of bills and accounts. A manuscript might be reversed in this way by the same scribe, as in the case of the Glasgow University Library manuscript: before it passed into Turner's hands, his uncle copied items at both ends of the volume. It is easy enough to imagine reasons why a scribe might do this. One obvious reason for entering items at different places in a manuscript is to organize the material, to classify different sorts of material by separating them physically. This is the case, for example, with one of the *Scriptorium* manuscripts: Emmanuel College, Cambridge, MS I.3.2 (James 1904, 47–48). This manuscript is a quarto paper-book of eighty-six leaves, gathered into eleven quires of eights. Most of the items are entered from the same end. Entries into the last quire, however, are reversed: to the reader who has begun with the first leaf, entries appear upside down and back-to-front. The manuscript mainly contains notes and extracts in English, Greek, and Latin, from authors including Petrarch, Platina, Fynes Moryson, and Joseph Scaliger. The reversed material, however, is different: rather than literary commonplaces, it consists chiefly of five synoptic tables and a rudimentary and unfinished theological index (fols. 86v–81v). Reversing the manuscript, in short, might have been a way for the scribe to separate the two different kinds of entry. This conclusion is supported by the fact that the scribe did not prepare the reversed leaves in the way that he did most of the rest of the manuscript: the leaves are not ruled, and the items are not entered within the rubricated margins that appear earlier in the volume.

Another, perhaps more common, explanation for reversed manuscripts is a change of owner. In this scenario, it is clear why a later owner might have chosen to enter items at a different end and in a different direction to a previous one. A good example of this is the commonplace book of Katherine Butler (St Paul's Cathedral, London, MS 52. D. 4). Little is known about Butler apart from what this manuscript tells us. From a note on the flyleaf it is apparent that Butler received the volume in 1693 as a gift from her father, and she continued to add prose and verse to it until 1745. Her entries include classical and contemporary excerpts and also her own translation of Sir Francis Bacon's *In felicem memoriam Elizabethae, Angliae reginae*. But, for our purposes here, what is noteworthy is not so much what she copied (although she was undoubtedly an assiduous and careful copyist), as where she copied it. Before coming into Butler's hands, the manuscript had a previous owner, Knightly Chetwood (1650–1720), the future dean of Gloucester, and his entries, which are sermon notes, including some from John Donne, are copied at the other end of the volume. Butler, in short, reversed the volume, marking her ownership of it by starting to copy from the other end.

Such manuscripts tell us a great deal about scribal culture. They attest to the circulation of manuscripts and books, to reading practices, and to practices of composition. Moreover, this creative use of space may reveal a compiler's attitude towards his or her text. For instance, whether a poem is allotted either a full page, or elsewhere a scrappy margin, reveals much about its perceived value for the copyist. Such manuscripts are therefore just the kind of material that editors might want to reproduce and publish. Moreover, manuscripts, as scholars now recognize, are more than just the sum of their contents (and certainly more than the sum of a handful of canonical poems), and manuscript culture encompasses considerably more than splendid presentation copies and the relatively familiar verse miscellanies. But the kind of manuscript that we describe here also makes serious demands on the reader. The examples discussed so far are comparatively straightforward: in each case, the progress of copy is clear and the reason for reversal apparent. In other manuscripts, however, the order is much less clear. That murkier territory is the concern of the rest of this essay, for not only do such manuscripts present greater demands on the reader, they also present a great challenge to the editor and digitizer.

The reversed miscellanies of Alathea Bethell and Elizabeth Lyttelton

The two reversed manuscripts to be used as a case-study in this essay are Lambeth Palace Library, MS 2240, and Cambridge University Library, MS Add. 8460. The first is a miscellany compiled by Alathea Bethell (1655–1708), containing mostly devotional poems and prose. Bethell started her manuscript at one end and copied fifteen items into it. These items appear on what the modern foliation designates as folios 1r to 36r. The sixteenth and seventeenth items, however, are entered from the other direction: that is to say, they begin on what now appears as the verso of the last leaf in the bound volume (fol. 52v) and continue back towards the middle of the volume (fol. 37v).[6]

---

[6] It is important to remember that "recto" and "verso" here are slightly arbitrary designations: they reflect the modern foliation of the manuscript (the work of a librarian) rather than say anything about its chronology or progress of copy.

It is unclear what motivated Bethell to reverse her manuscript, as the final two items, "Directions for A Pious life" (fols. 52v–50v) and "Directions for for A Pious and usefull life" (fols. 50r–37v), could equally well have followed the "Meditations in Sickness and Afflictions" (fols. 25r–36r) that conclude the front end of the manuscript. A change of copy-text, a desire to set apart the final two items, or simply a different date of entry, may account for Bethell's scribal habits here.

Matters are more complicated in our second miscellany. MS Add. 8460 belonged to the family of the author and physician Sir Thomas Browne. Most of the entries are in the hand of his third daughter Elizabeth Lyttelton (b. c. 1648, d. after 1728; see further Morris 1986; Burke 2003). About a third of the manuscript, however, is in a second, more cursive hand. These items (on what are now pp. 170–104 and 102 reversed) are sermon notes, homilies, and biblical commonplaces and verses, and they are characterized by their idiosyncratic orthography and rapidity. For some time, this second hand went unidentified, and scholars simply referred to the items collectively as "Sermon notes and homilies"; however, Rebecca Bullard has recently proposed, by cross-referring the hand with that of certain Browne family letters held in the Bodleian Library, Oxford, that this scribe was Elizabeth Lyttelton's mother and Thomas Browne's wife, Lady Dorothy Browne (see Bullard 2009). Lyttelton wrote entries from both sides of the manuscript, while her mother entered her sermon notes and homilies from one side only. Beginning from her mother's end, Lyttelton copied poems and prose fragments both preceding and following her mother's notes, but she also reversed the volume to start writing from the other end entirely.

The exact circumstances in which this challenging book was created remain uncertain. In terms of dating, it seems that the manuscript was already in use from both ends before 1676. In this year, Lyttelton's younger sister Mary had died, and her signature is inscribed in the manuscript's flyleaves at both ends. It is not impossible that Lyttelton and her mother used the manuscript simultaneously (and this would provide a rationale for the reversal), but it is more likely that Lady Dorothy passed down the book to her daughter. The first, and the earliest, sermon notes are taken from "Mr Bottman" (170), probably John Boatman, an ejected clergyman from London who in 1656 "addressed multitudes" in Norwich, where Thomas and Dorothy Browne had lived since their marriage in 1641, in support of his preferred candidate for the House of Commons elections (Evans 1979, 217–18). Boatman and George Cock, another preacher well represented in the manuscript, were ministers of St Peter Mancroft in Norwich from 1654 until the early 1670s, and if the sermon notes date to approximately this period, Lyttelton would have been too young to participate in the creation of the book. (The rapidity of the hand, the irregular orthography, and the apparently rough quality suggest that the notes were taken from a live experience, either during the sermons themselves or immediately afterwards.) On the evidence of Lyttelton's source materials and the development of her handwriting, her contributions were compiled during two periods: the majority of items in the 1670s and 80s, and a later set of additions, characterized by a darker ink in a scratchier hand, written after 1687, including a final item as late as 1710. Lyttelton's use of space is particularly challenging in instances where she returned to her manuscript to fill in blank spaces. Her copy of Dr John Dillingham's "hymne to our Redeemer," for instance, was entered over various pages (6, 7, 8, 9, 18, and 19) where previous entries had not filled the page; in other words, some consecutive texts are written over non-consecutive pages, and rub shoulders with non-related material on the same page. Already aware of the challenge that this might pose to a reader, Lyttelton indicated the continuance of her hymn with a series of asterisks across the feet of the pages.

Clearly, the reader of such reversed manuscripts will have to negotiate the physical object carefully, and in a manuscript reading room this causes relatively little difficulty. To the digitizer, however, such non-linear textual structures can create problems. A faithful reproduction of the manuscript would interrupt the logical text flow, and if we were to follow the modern pagination and arbitrarily favour one end as the "beginning," then a large part of the manuscript at the reverse end would be reproduced upside-down. Conversely, if textual integrity and readability (or linearity) of the items is the overriding factor in the production of a manuscript facsimile or digital edition (as would be the case in a traditional text-based diplomatic or critical edition), then a way must be found to extract the texts from the manuscript, which may compromise the representation of its physical make-up, and so, from a codicological perspective, distort the evidence.

Before we discuss this further, and since our editorial and encoding policies are very much dependent upon our chosen mode of dissemination, it will be useful to introduce the *Scriptorium* website interface and its supporting technologies. As a digital archive, *Scriptorium* is oriented towards the representation of a manuscript as a physical object.

Figure 1: "Image View." Manuscript image reproduced with permission of the Lambeth Palace Library.

Our users typically interface with the miscellanies and commonplace books through our "Image View" (see Fig. 1), in which manuscript images (either single page or by openings) occupy the centre of the screen and are accompanied by an item box that describes all the items currently visible on the screen. Items are demarcated units of various kinds, usually, but not necessarily, text-based: for instance a poem, prose note, signature, illustration, or mark of ownership. Complementary to our "Image View" is a "Full Description" that includes a complete item list and bibliographical and technical details (collation, binding, paper, hands, watermarks, etc.), and a tabled and interactive "Contents View" that allows for an alphabetical re-ordering of items by, for instance, author, first line, or title. From "Image View," clicking on a thumbnail opens up a high-resolution image that can be freely enlarged

and rotated to allow extremely detailed investigation of palaeographical features. We also make available selected transcriptions of manuscript items
(organized per item, not per manuscript), and these are dynamically generated from the XML and rendered as PDFs.

A *Scriptorium* manuscript is described in its entirety in an XML document
compliant with the guidelines of TEI P5.[7] Using the "Manuscript Description"
module, each XML document consists of three parts. The first part is the <tei-
Header> element and contains a publication statement, an item list under
the <msDesc> element, a list of physical characteristics under the <physDesc>
element, the manuscript's history under the <origin> and <provenance> elements, and several additional categories: the <listBibl> element for bibliographical references, the <listPerson> element for respondents (authors or
other personages that feature in the manuscript), and finally some encoding
information (see TEI Consortium 2007, sec. 10). Central to our project is a
detailed item-by-item description under the <msContent> element. This is a
list of items ordered according to their occurrence in the manuscript. Each
<msItem> element consists at minimum of a <locus> element tag that cross-
refers to a facsimile (see below), and a descriptive <note> element. More typically, each item also contains a <title> element (where this is different from
a heading given in the manuscript), <author>, <rubric>, <incipit>, <explicit>,
and <finalRubric> elements (the latter four tags encode, respectively, information about an item's heading [or rubric], the first and last lines of the
item [incipit and explicit], and a concluding subscription [final rubric]). It
should be stressed that we do not routinely provide full transcriptions of the
miscellanies and commonplace books, and thus the <msContent> element is
the most complete catalogue of a manuscript's content that we provide. Item
lists may be relatively short (see Trinity College, Cambridge, MS R.7.31, containing only three items over twenty leaves) or very extensive (for instance,
Leeds University Library, Brotherton Collection, MS Lt. 91, consisting of 283
items over 179 leaves).

The second part of the XML document is the <facsimile> element, where each
<surface> element stands for a single page that also gets assigned an identi-
fier tag for cross-referencing. Each <surface> element contains two image
files, one a thumbnail, the other a large JPG. In addition, each single page
<surface> element is also associated with an image file of the opening of
which it forms a part. In order to indicate whether a given <surface> element

---

[7] All *Scriptorium* XML documents have been made available on our website.

represents the recto (right) or verso (left) side of an opening, we use the <zone> element with coordinating attributes.

Example 1:

```
<teiHeader>
<!--->
<msItem n="7">
    <locus facs="#f_10r #f_11r #f_12r">ff. 10r, 11r, 12r</locus>
    <author>A. L.</author>
    <rubric>A Poem for Christmass day by A.L.</rubric>
    <incipit>come wellcome guest &amp; fill The Breast</incipit>
    <explicit>hear. us with speed.</explicit>
    </msItem>
</teiHeader>
<!--->
<facsimile>
<!--->
    <surface n="21" xml:id="f_10r">
    <graphic url="Lamb2240_10r_large.jpg" />
    <graphic url="Lamb2240_10r_small.jpg" />
    <zone ulx="250" uly="0" lrx="500" lry="448">
    <graphic url="Lamb2240_9v_Lamb2240_10r.jpg" />
    </zone>
    </surface>
<!--->
</facsimile>
<text>
    <pb n="21" facs="#f_10r" />
    <div type="item" no="7">
    <!-- text contained for 10r is encoded here -->
    </div>
</text>
```

Example 1 shows a simplified extraction of our code from the miscellany of Alathea Bethell and the three respective parts, an <msItem> element, and corresponding <facsimile>, and <text> elements.

Rationale for reversing and coding the reversed manuscript

Confronted with several reversed manuscripts in our corpus, we have adopted a digitization strategy that has tried to accommodate the manuscript as object, while simultaneously presenting a reading experience that ensures maximum intelligibility. In the case of the Lyttelton manuscript, as we have shown above, Dorothy Browne's sermon notes precede all other materials; however, at some point a librarian has (perhaps arbitrarily) paginated the manuscript from the other end, starting with Lyttelton's later additions. This pagination has then been followed by scholars working on the manuscript (Dobell 1918; Keynes 1919; Burke 2003). The decision about which part of the manuscript to treat as the front has thus been made for us (even if this decision does not reflect the actual order of entries). Our digital edition follows this pagination (1–45) in order to preserve the integrity of the manuscript; however, after the first forty-five pages we have reversed the manuscript and also the images of the individual pages to facilitate consultation and reading. Thus our user will initially open the manuscript from one end, but read it from both ends (pp. 1 to 45, and then pp. 174 to 46). We believe that this decision allows us to replicate both how the original owners used the manuscript and the experience of a modern reader faced with it in the Manuscripts Reading Room of Cambridge University Library. We have, in effect, sought to replicate digitally the process of turning the manuscript physically, which any reader would need to do. Admittedly, this makes for a surprising digital reading experience when, after page 45 the reader clicks on the next page, he/she is taken to the inside back cover (image reversed), and reads the manuscript back towards the middle. Since in a strict sense this approach compromises the cover-to-cover linear flow of the manuscript, we have decided also to include a PDF download of the entire non-reversed object—thus, in this instance the pagination is consecutive and appears at the top right and left where it belongs, yet all text from page 46 onwards appears upside-down. We have followed this approach for the other three reversed manuscripts in our collection as well (Emmanuel College, Cambridge, MS I.3.2, Lambeth Palace Library, MS 2240, and St John's College, Cambridge, MS S.34).[8]

Reversal of our images also necessitates modification of the XML code, particularly in the <facsimile> section. By reversing an opening, what appears as a verso side is in fact (viewed from the original "front end") a recto, and con-

---

[8] See *Scriptorium*, University of Cambridge, accessed 23 October 2009, http://scriptorium.english.cam.ac.uk, where the non-reversed PDFs are available by viewing the abovementioned manuscripts.

sequently, what appears to be a recto is in fact a verso. The XML needs to be adjusted accordingly. As may be seen in Example 1, the <zone> element coordinates for the opening containing MS 2240's folio 10r (a regular non-reversed page) are as follows: <zone ulx="250" uly="0" lrx="500" lry="448">. That is to say, on an image of the opening for folios 9v–10r, measuring 500 pixels wide and 448 pixels high, the upper left corner for folio 10r has as its upper left "x" coordinate 250, upper left "y" coordinate 0, lower right "x" coordinate 500, and lower right "y" coordinate 448. Reversed coordinates allow our XSL stylesheets to process reversed openings as if they were regular openings, and thus properly link to large resolution JPGs from thumbnail openings.

Example 2: Reversed Opening

```
<teiHeader>
<!--->
<msItem n="37">
    <locus facs="#p_173 #p_172 #p_171">pp. 173-171</locus>
    <rubric><name key="#WRAL">S<hi rend="superscript">r</hi>
    Walter  Rawleigs</name> Letter to his wife after his<lb/> Con-
    demnation</rubric>
    <author><name key="#WRAL">Sir  Walter  Raleigh</name></
    author>
    <incipit>you shall receiue my Dear wife my Last words in these
    my</incipit>
    <explicit>Walter Rawleigh</explicit>
</msItem>
</teiHeader>
<!--->
<facsimile>
<!--->
<surface n="50" xml:id="p_173">
    <graphic url="UL_Add8460_87r_large.jpg" />
    <graphic url="UL_Add8460_87r_small.jpg" />
    <zone ulx="0" uly="0" lrx="250" lry="310">
    <graphic url="UL_Add8460_87r_UL_Add8460_86v.jpg" />
    </zone>
    </surface>
<surface n="51" xml:id="p_172">
    <graphic url="UL_Add8460_86v_large.jpg" />
    <graphic url="UL_Add8460_86v_small.jpg" />
```

```
<zone ulx="250" uly="0" lrx="500" lry="310">
    <graphic url="UL_Add8460_87r_UL_Add8460_86v.jpg" />
    </zone>
</surface>
<!-->
</facsimile>
```

Example 2, taken from Lyttelton's manuscript, demonstrates that these zoning values have to be reversed when an image is reversed: the coordinates that normally demarcate a recto would now describe a verso.

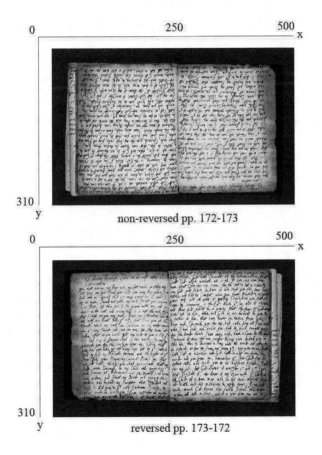

Figure 2: X and Y coordinates of non-reversed and reversed openings. See image plates for a colour version of this figure.

Figure 2 further illustrates how the X and Y coordinates have changed for the reversed openings. Thus for p. 173 (showing as a recto in a non-reversed image, but as a verso after reversal) zoning coordinates are the opposite of those in Example 1: <zone ulx="0" uly="0" lrx="250" lry="310"> (for an image measuring 500 x 310).

Representing non-linear structures in TEI

To the scholar of miscellanies, a linear progression is not always the most important one. If we want to follow a miscellanist's progress, or investigate the accumulative effect of compilation, we need to follow in their footsteps as closely as we can. If a manuscript is written over a considerable period of time, developments in the hand might suggest the order in which items were copied; paper stock, collation, ink, pens, nibs, and ductus (or flow of the pen and formation of the letter) provide further clues. The text layout (one item scribbled around another, for example) can help to establish the order in which a collection is formed. Furthermore, source materials (particularly when printed or otherwise datable) may reveal a *terminus a quo.*

Later additions written around earlier entries occur very frequently in miscellanies that changed ownership during the course of composition, or that were the work of multiple scribes (as is evident from another *Scriptorium* manuscript, Leeds University Library, MS Lt 91). Later additions are, of course, integral to medieval and early modern scribal culture. Many texts were subsequently corrected or glossed; in other cases, scribes wrote continuations of earlier texts, so medieval and early modern scribal practice may usefully be conceived of as dialogic and profoundly non-linear. This is perhaps most usefully observed in the commonplace book. Kept by the greater part of early modern lawyers, writers, natural philosophers, and others, these notebooks provided a space to retain materials for re-use and were often organized by rhetorical or ethical subject headings. Readers were enjoined to note down memorable or pithy quotations (the *commonplaces*) as and when they came across them. As Erasmus put it in his *De ratione studii* of 1512, every student "should have at the ready some commonplace book of systems and topics, so that wherever something noteworthy occurs he may write it down in the appropriate column" (672). Both the way in which a commonplace book was constructed and the manner in which it was used thus defy easy linear reading strategies. A commonplace book does not record reading experiences in a chronological fashion, and nor was it used in this way by its original compiler.

The question that thus arises is how best to represent the conflicting textual structures that define the manuscript commonplace book and miscellany. Besides observing the integrity either of the artefact or of the text in the order in which it appears in the book, a third option presents itself; namely, a genetic approach, one that follows subsequent scribal stints in the order in which they have been written, and that may not simply be observed by turning the page. In other words, the editor must differentiate between the spatial relations of manuscript items on the one hand (i.e., how they physically appear on the page) and their temporal relations (which came first, which came later) on the other. Ideally, the editor would then record both sets of information simultaneously. *Scriptorium* currently takes a rather conservative approach: consecutive item numbers are in exactly the order in which they appear on the page. It is only in the <note> element (within the <msItem> element) that we record whether a given text is a later addition. It would be extremely useful, however, if a manuscript item list would allow for the recording of spatial *and* temporal relations, not by means of a discursive prose <note> element, but by means of a structural organizational principle native to the TEI tag set. Non-hierarchical structures, or structures that conflict with other hierarchies in the markup, are a well known problem in XML. Chapter 20 of the TEI P5 guidelines offers various solutions to specific problems of overlapping hierarchies, yet the guidelines also state up front that

> no current solution combines all the desirable attributes of formal simplicity, capacity to represent all occurring or imaginable kinds of structures, suitability for formal or mechanical validation. The representation of non-hierarchical information is thus necessarily a matter of trade-offs among various sets of advantages and disadvantages (TEI Consortium 2007, sec. 20).

Our particular solution presented below was conceived in relation to the core hierarchy of each *Scriptorium* manuscript XML description (which in turn is based on sec. 10: manuscript description of the guidelines, TEI Consortium 2007), namely the linear sequence of <msItem> elements.

A striking, localized illustration of why, despite these limitations, we might want to record both spatial and temporal relations is to be found in Lyttelton's manuscript (see Fig. 3).

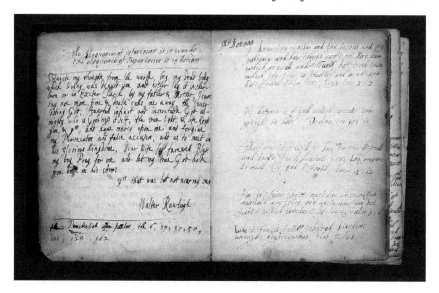

Figure 3: Cambridge University Library, MS Add. 8640, pp. 171–70 reversed.
In Dorothy Browne's hand: maxim on eloquence at top left, and sermon
notes from "Mr Bottman" on right hand page. In Lyttelton's hand: the end
of the Raleigh letter, and a list of the Penitential Psalms at bottom left.
Image reproduced with kind permission from the Syndics of Cambridge
University Library. See image plates for a colour version of this figure.

This occurs towards the "end" of the manuscript (assuming on the basis of its
pagination that p. 1 is the start). On what are now pages 173 to 171, Lyttelton
copied Sir Walter Raleigh's letter to his wife Elizabeth, written in December
1603 as he awaited execution (*The Letters of Sir Walter Raleigh*, letter no. 172).
This item is in Lyttelton's later, scratchier hand, and it seems to have been
added where Lyttelton found space in this manuscript. This time, unlike for
the Dillingham hymn, the space was at her mother's end of the volume. What
are now pages 173 and 172, on which the majority of the letter is copied,
would originally have been among the front flyleaves of the book.[9] Dorothy
Browne's sermon notes do not begin until what is now page 170, with the
first entry from Mr Boatman. But on page 171, where the remainder of the
Raleigh letter is copied, the sequence and progress of copy are more complicated. This page was not blank: Dorothy had already copied an item, a short

---

[9] What is now page 174 would have been the first flyleaf: copied here are signatures,
ownership inscriptions, and the instructions for a card game, just the sort of ephemeral material typically copied on flyleaves.

verse maxim—"The Eloquence of inferiours is in words / the eloquence of Superiours is in Action,"—at the top of it. This maxim was presumably intended to serve as an epigraph to the manuscript as a whole, in imitation of a common print convention. Lyttelton was therefore left with the space below the epigraph, into which she duly squeezed the rest of the Raleigh letter, separating it from her mother's maxim by a horizontal line. She then added another item at the foot of the page—a list of the seven Penitential Psalms—which is in turn separated from Raleigh's letter by a second horizontal line.

In our XML manuscript description the letter to Raleigh, epigraph, list of Penitential Psalms, and sermon notes from Boatman are given the following tags: <msItem n="37">, <msItem n="38">, <msItem n="39">, and <msItem n="40">. These item numbers correspond to where the items appear on the page. The sequence speaks to the physical make-up of the manuscript, not to how it was actually compiled. For the user of the *Scriptorium* website this may not be a problem because there is also a full photographic facsimile alongside. The shift from Lyttelton to Browne and back again is immediately apparent: the two women write very different hands. So long as the user has access to information about their hands—in the case of *Scriptorium*, accessible in the technical description of the manuscript via the "Full Description" tab at the top of the screen—then the scribal stints can be readily inferred.

We might nevertheless still want to organize the material. Within TEI P5 there are various provisions that can help us here, tags that enable us to encode precisely this kind of non-linear structure. The first option is the <handShift> element, designed to "indicate where a change in hand is detected for whatever reason" (TEI Consortium 2007, sec. 11.4). This element, in other words, distinguishes scribal stints and so enables us to differentiate between the material copied by Lyttelton and the material copied by Browne (and also the material copied by the third hand, that of Mary Browne). Moreover, since the <handShift> element also shares a number of attributes with the <handNote> element, which describe aspects of a hand in which a manuscript is written, this option is also desirable from a palaeographical perspective. With the @script attribute, for instance, we could characterize the hands of the two women: both write seventeenth-century round hands, but Browne's is much more cursive. We could also say something about the extent of their hands and also the differences in ink, using the @medium and @scope attributes. We might, in short, have a solution: by organizing our material by scribe rather than by physical location we would come closer to the original chronology of the manuscript.

This approach would enable us to group together all the material in each of the different hands in the manuscript. Unfortunately, though, it would not enable us to differentiate between material in the same hand, but written at different times. This material would still be lumped together, as there would be no discernible change in hand. Stints could be distinguished, but when those stints are non-linear we would not get very far. In the case of the Lyttelton manuscript, this would mean that we would still not be able to indicate the progress of copy, and we would not be able to draw attention to those items inserted by Lyttelton at a later date. Moreover, since the <hand-Shift> element is intended primarily for the transcription of primary sources and the markup of texts, rather than manuscript description, it would be of limited use to a project such as *Scriptorium* anyway (as we do not provide full transcription of our collections). *Scriptorium* is an archive of digital images, which are identified via the item list, not a series of full text online editions, and so we need a solution that is applicable to a TEI description of a manuscript, and that can either be nested within the <msContents> element of a TEI header or allow for a wholesale reorganization of the <msItem> list.

An XSL transformation[10] could effect a reorganization of all items into whichever order we might prefer; however, this still leaves the scribal stints unrepresented within the base XML description, which is where they properly belong. At present there are no specific TEI tags to encode stints within an XML manuscript description. But the problem is more complicated still, for what we are trying to do is also to overlay one hierarchy (scribal chronology of a manuscript) on a hierarchy that is already encoded (physical organization of a manuscript). We therefore need a workaround, a solution that enables overlapping hierarchies of encoding applied to the same information. One option is simply to have two XML documents for the one manuscript, each of which catches a single aspect or view. This is TEI conformant, and the P5 guidelines contain various methods for linking or pointing to multiple documents in this way. This solution, however, is far from ideal: not only does it mean that the information about a manuscript is in multiple places, it also greatly increases the risk of inconsistencies and errors. The same holds true for multiple encoding within the same document (as described in TEI Consortium 2007, sec. 20.1), which effectively repeats all text, thus allowing for alternate encoding structures. This creates much redundant data in a

---

[10] XSL is a language for writing stylesheets that describe how to display and organize the information contained within an XML document that in itself contains no directions for display in a browser or other viewer.

single document, however, and presents the same risks of inconsistency and error (particularly when later changes have to be made).

But all is not lost: there may be a workaround that does allow the simultaneous encoding that we seek. One possibility is to encode the scribal stints as a series of <event> elements, as illustrated in Example 3. The <listEvent> element is nested within the <sourceDesc> element of the <teiHeader> element, similar to our <listPerson> elements of respondents. Each <msItem> element has now been given a unique <xml:id> tag corresponding with its numerical value (that is, a number assigned by the order in which the items are encountered in the manuscript in spatial sequence). Under the <listEvent> element we have also treated each item as a specific event in time (though entries can be copied in one sitting, they will never be transcribed simultaneously). These are now reorganized according to when they were copied into the manuscript. Each <event> element is similarly associated with an <xml:id> assigned in chronological sequence, and the connection between the <event> and <msItem> elements is made through a <ptr/> element (pointer).

Example 3

```
<teiHeader>
<!--->
<msItem n="37" xml:id="#i.37">
    <locus facs="#p_173 #p_172 #p_171">pp. 173-171</locus>
    <rubric>Sr Walter Rawleigs Letter to his wife after his Condem-
    nation</rubric>
    <author>Sir Walter Raleigh</author>
    <incipit>you shall receiue my Dear wife my Last words in these
    my</incipit>
    <explicit>Walter Rawleigh</explicit>
</msItem>
<msItem n="38" xml:id="#i.38">
    <locus facs="#p_171">p. 171</locus>
    <title type="supplied">Maxim</title>
    <incipit>The Eloquence of inferiours is in words</incipit>
    <explicit>the eloquence of Superiours is in Action</explicit>
    </msItem>
<msItem n="39" xml:id="#i.39">
    <locus facs="#p_171">p. 171</locus>
    <title type="supplied">List of Penitential Psalms</title>
```

```
        <incipit>the 7 Penitentiall <del>spa</del> psalms, the 6, 39, 37,
        50,</incipit>
        <explicit>101, 129, 142</explicit>
        </msItem>
    <msItem n="40" xml:id="#i.40">
        <locus facs="#p_170 #p_169 #p_168 #p_167 #p_166 #p_165
        #p_164 #p_163 #p_162 #p_161 #p_160 #p_159">pp. 170-159</
        locus>
        <title type="supplied">Sermon notes and homilies</title>
        <incipit>Mi<hi rend="superscript">s</hi> Bottman</incipit>
        <explicit>all to gether Ignorand of our selues</explicit>
        </msItem>
    <!-->
    <listevent>
        <event n="1" xml:id="#e.1">
                <desc>1st chronological entry by Hand 2</desc>
                <ptr target="#i.38" />
        </event>
        <event n="2" xml:id="#e.2">
                <desc>2nd chronological entry by Hand 2</desc>
                <ptr target="#i.40" />
        </event>
        <!-->
        <event n="79" xml:id="#e.79">
                <desc>79th chronological entry by Hand 1</desc>
                <ptr target="#i.37" />
        </event>
        <event n="80" xml:id="#e.80">
                <desc>80th chronological entry by Hand 1</desc>
                <ptr target="#i.39" />
        </event>
    </listevent>
    <!-->
    </teiHeader>
```

Such a solution makes possible a dual organization of manuscript items, and an XML processor could extract from this information a list ordered either by item number or by event number, and then extract the relevant item information through the <ptr/> element provided. As Example 3 shows, the first two <event> elements refer to manuscript items 38 and 40 respectively:

the maxim and the sermon notes from Boatman, Dorothy Browne's first entries in what was, presumably, a blank book. Lyttelton's entries (Raleigh's
letter and the list of Psalms), though physically preceding her mother's, are
now assigned <event> elements 79 and 80. A more complex example would be
where multiple items were entered in one stint—as is the case elsewhere in
the Lyttelton manuscript—and here the <listEvent> element approach would
work particularly well, since it would enable us to group the items together
as a single event. Unfortunately, though, this solution does not allow for a
reordering of material by scribal stint if the change occurs within a single
item, as is sometimes the case in a long, scribally produced text. Common
sense must prevail here: either the <note> or the <handShift> elements must
suffice in such a situation (or <msItem> elements may be further subdivided).
Before accepting this solution unreservedly, we must first remember John
Lavagnino's warning that "if there isn't already a tag that can be used for
what you need to describe, don't force an existing one into the role" (2006,
336). An <event> element, as the TEI guidelines (sec. 13.3.4.3) attest, "is usually used to record information about a place, or a person; for this reason
the element usually appears as content of a place or person." We would
nevertheless suggest that the <listEvent> element can be usefully employed
to express chronologically ordered events as well as in its more customary
role of describing persons or places within a text. Our workaround, in short,
modifies, but does not force, existing tags, and in doing so it enables the kind
of economical and error-free multiple encoding that a non-linear structure
such as the Lyttelton manuscript demands.

Conclusion

At present, this solution has not been implemented on our live website, and
we offer it as a future direction that the *Scriptorium* project could take. We
also offer it as an illustration of how the digitization of an apparently rar-
efied aspect of early modern manuscript culture—in this case, the reversed
scribal manuscript—might speak to the concerns of digitizers more widely.
Non-linearity, after all, the problem with which this essay has grappled, is
something to be found in other kinds of manuscript. We could think here
of manuscript part-books, or dramatic prompt books. In both cases, either
a musical piece or a play's coherence is dependent on various parts transcribed into different individual books. The digitizer might want both to
retain the integrity of the part-book, and to make the individual part fit into
its larger musical structure, and will thus have to impose several hierarchies
to make this work. By the same token, the <listEvent> element solution that
we are proposing might be applied to other bibliographical matters. Print

historians, for example, have long been interested in identifying the work of individual compositors, and just as we have suggested that scribal stints might be encoded with <event> elements, so the same tag might be used to mark up and distinguish the work of different compositors. The simultaneous encoding that we describe might enable a digital editor to produce a text organized both as it should be read and as it was originally set in the printhouse. (Rather than being set seriatim, most early modern English books were set by formes; a compositor typically set all the pages for one side of a sheet and sent them to be printed before the pages of the other side of the sheet were set.) Having the facility to reorganize an early modern text by formes would certainly be useful. It would not produce a reading edition (hence the need for multiple or simultaneous encoding), but it would tell us a great deal about both print-house practice in general and the practices of individual printers.

The <event> element, in sum, might allow us to encode both textual and bibliographical facts in the same document and at the same time. The attraction of this, as our case-study attests, is obvious. Its broader applicability is also apparent, and we hope that it therefore provides a useful way of addressing the fundamental problem of representing conflicting hierarchical structures in TEI. And at the very least, by attending to scribal stints as well as the physical make-up and pagination or foliation of manuscripts in this way, we can ensure that the *Scriptorium* project lives up to the expectation of the digital facsimile as expressed by Kevin Kiernan:

> The reliability of editors of the future will depend not so much on historical or interpretative introductions bound to a single edition as on the editors' ability to show the relation between the edition and its documentary sources and to bring their readers to an ever-expanding digital library of supporting ancillary material (2006, 265).

The digital edition allows readers to break away from mono-directional reading (as has also been vigorously discussed in relation to hypertext). This breaking-away is precisely what this essay has sought to do, both in its account of a particular problem and in its broader discussion of non-linear structures. There can be no better illustration of this need to break away, we suggest, than the case of the early modern reversed manuscript—and no better defense of the need for digital as well as print editions.

WORKS CITED

Manuscripts:

MS Add. 8460. Cambridge University Library, Cambridge.

MS I.3.2. Emmanuel College, Cambridge.

MS Lt 91. Brotherton Collection, Leeds University Library, Leeds.

MS Murray 556. Glasgow University Library, Glasgow.

MS 685. Holkham Hall Library, Wells-next-the-Sea.

MS 840.5. King's College, Cambridge.

MS 2086. Lambeth Palace Library, London.

MS 2240. Lambeth Palace Library, London.

MS S.34. St John's College, Cambridge.

MS 52. D. 4. St Paul's Cathedral, London.

MS O.9.38. Trinity College, Cambridge.

MS R.7.31. Trinity College, Cambridge.

Printed and secondary sources:

Bullard, Rebecca. 2009. Cambridge University Library, MS Add. 8460. *Scriptorium: Medieval and Early Modern Manuscripts Online.* University of Cambridge. http://scriptorium.english.cam.ac.uk/resources/articles/pdf/Bullard_CUL_MS_Add_8460.pdf.

Burke, Victoria. 2003. "Contexts for Women's Manuscript Miscellanies: The Case of Elizabeth Lyttelton and Sir Thomas Browne." *The Yearbook of English Studies* 33:316–28.

Dobell, Percy John. 1918. *The Literature of the Restoration, Being a Collection of the Poetical and Dramatic Literature Produced Between the Years 1660 and 1700, with Particular Reference to the Writings of John Dryden.* London: P. J. & J. E. Dobell.

Erasmus, Desiderius. 1978. *Literary and Educational Writings 2: De copia / De ratione studii.* Edited by Craig R. Thompson. Vol. 24 of the *Collected Works of Erasmus.* Toronto: University of Toronto Press.

Evans, John T. 1979. *Seventeenth-Century Norwich: Politics, Religion and Government, 1620–1690.* Oxford: Clarendon Press.

James, Montague Rhodes. 1904. *The Western Manuscripts in the Library of Emmanuel College: A Descriptive Catalogue.* Cambridge: Cambridge University Press.

Keynes, Geoffrey. 1919. *The Commonplace Book of Elizabeth Lyttelton.* Cambridge: Cambridge University Press.

Kiernan, Kevin. 2006. "Digital Facsimiles in Editing." In *Electronic Textual Editing,* edited by Lou Burnard, Katherine O'Brien O'Keeffe, and John Unsworth, 262–68. New York: Modern Language Association.

Lavagnino, John. 2006. "When Not to Use TEI." In Burnard, O'Keeffe, and Unsworth, eds., 334–38.

Love, Harold. 1993. *Scribal Publication in Seventeenth-Century England.* Oxford: Clarendon Press.

Latham, Agnes, and Joyce Youings, eds. 1999. *The Letters of Sir Walter Raleigh.* Exeter: University of Exeter Press.

McGann, Jerome. 2006. "Marking Texts of Many Dimensions." In Burnard, O'Keeffe, and Unsworth, eds., 198–217.

Morris, G. C. R. 1986. "Sir Thomas Browne's Daughters, 'Cosen Barker,' and the Cottrells." *Notes & Queries* n.s. 33:472–78.

Rigg, A. G. 1968. *A Glastonbury Miscellany of the Fifteenth Century: A Descriptive Index of Trinity College, Cambridge, MS O.9.38.* Oxford: Oxford University Press.

TEI Consortium, eds. 2007. *TEI P5: Guidelines for Electronic Text Encoding and Interchange.* Version 1.3.0. TEI Consortium. http://www.tei-c.org/ Guidelines/P5/.

Palaeography and the "Virtual Library" of Manuscripts[*]

Peter A. Stokes

King's College London

peter.stokes@kcl.ac.uk

The field of palaeography is one that has been heavily affected by developments in technology, and particularly by photographic reproductions, the cost of which has generally decreased as the number and quality have increased (Boyle 1984, 23–66).[1] Indeed the importance for palaeographers of such facsimiles is reflected in the *Comité international de paléographie latine* which has as one of its two primary objectives the reproduction of scribal hands in all dated and datable manuscripts from the medieval West (Garand 1982, 25–29; Robinson 1988, 1:1). One of many questions that these developments raise is what new opportunities and challenges have come to palaeographers as a result of these "virtual libraries" of manuscripts. This has been discussed before, in the context of print as well as digital reproduction (Petrucci 1984; Tanselle 1989; Kiernan 1994; Ciula 2005, §§6–7; Rumble 2006, 5–9; Stokes 2010), and the implications are many, but rather than address them all, this paper will focus on those of particular relevance to palaeographical method, examining some ways in which palaeography has changed already and some difficulties to be overcome for development in future.

---

[*] The discussion presented here would not have been possible without the generous financial support of the Leverhulme Trust and the Cambridge Isaac Newton Trust.

[1] The term "palaeography" is used in the narrow sense throughout this paper; namely the study of (medieval) handwriting with a view towards its history and development and the identification, localization, and dating of scribes. Much of this discussion also applies to the broader term, however; namely manuscript studies in general, but with the important exception of codicology, or archaeology of the book, which is not considered here. For debate about these terms see especially Spunar (1958), Derolez (1973), Langeli (1978), and Mallon (1982), summarized by Stokes (2010).

ISBN 978-0-86698-499-7 (online)   ISBN 978-0-86698-474-4 (print)

New Technologies in Medieval and Renaissance Studies 3 (2012) 137–169

Some problems in palaeography

It has often been observed that palaeographers tend to express qualitative opinions rather than objective arguments, and they have been accused of issuing vague statements without evidence, or even pronouncements that cannot be debated or engaged with meaningfully (Derolez 2003, 7–8; Davis 2007; Stokes 2009, 311–12). This is not to doubt the accuracy or value of experts who have devoted many years to the study of medieval manuscripts, but, as Albert Derolez has written, "The method applied hitherto in paleographical handbooks has produced an authoritarian discipline, the pertinence of which depends on the authority of the author and the faith of the reader" (2003, 9). Tom Davis expresses similar concern when he contrasts the arguments of palaeographers with the seemingly much more precise and objective ones of forensic document analysts (2007; see also Stokes 2009, 317–19). Although he acknowledges differences between forensic analysis and palaeographical study, Davis still argues that even those palaeographers who do attempt to provide full and detailed arguments usually rely on verbal description, and such descriptions are necessarily imprecise and subjective (2007, 270–73). Both Derolez and Davis therefore identify a methodological problem in how to articulate palaeographical arguments in objective ways that can be evaluated and debated and can thereby gain some level of support: in Derolez's words, "How is it possible to proceed in such a way that the description of a specimen of handwriting is as clear and convincing to its reader as it is to its author?" (2003, 7). Derolez's question is far from trivial. Part of the problem is that subjective impressions are inherently difficult to communicate and cannot be engaged with effectively; but at least some of these difficulties can be reduced, if not overcome, with the prevalence of digital images and the "virtual libraries" of manuscripts.

New opportunities in palaeography

Perhaps the single biggest change that computers, the Internet, and digitization have brought about is the "democratization" of manuscript studies: we can now view a large number of complete, high-quality, full-colour facsimiles of manuscripts anywhere in the world, often for no cost, if we have a modern computer and a good connection to the Internet.[2] In essence these are little different from print facsimiles that preceded them, except that digital im-

---

[2] At the time of writing, the most complete list of online facsimiles is the Center for Medieval and Renaissance Studies, UCLA, *UCLA Catalogue of Digitized Medieval Manuscripts*, accessed 23 October 2009, http://manuscripts.cmrs.ucla.edu/.

ages are (or at least can be) more accurate and are usually cheaper, easier to access, and easier to manipulate. Without reproductions, the study of manuscripts is limited to those who are physically close to libraries or have the financial resources to travel (cf. Page 1992, 79), and to those who can obtain permission to view the most valuable and fragile volumes (Lowe 1972, 2:575–76). Even if a print facsimile does exist, this is often very expensive and held by only the wealthiest libraries.[3] Microfilm is generally cheaper, and indeed some have suggested that microfilms themselves should be digitized and made available (Johnson 2004, 7–11), but the quality is usually poor and the images can be misleading, sometimes with disastrous results (Tanselle 1989, 27–33; Kiernan 1995, 197–98 and 205–11; Page 1992, 79). In contrast, digital images are usually of higher quality than print and especially micro-film and are normally also in full colour.[4] This improved quality can mean that important details become visible that were previously hidden, such as changes in ink, annotations, damaged passages, the range of pigments used, and sometimes even erasures, rulings, or the quality of parchment, all of which can substantially alter arguments about a manuscript and its produc-tion. One implication for this is in scribal identification. Forensic document analysts routinely examine handwriting under microscopes (Kam, Wetstein, and Conn 1994, 12; Davis 2007, 273), but palaeographers have done so very rarely (but see Kiernan 1994, 39–40); now they can view images of manuscript pages under high magnification much more easily, thereby allowing more detailed analysis of scribal practices than was possible, or at least practical, before. It has been observed that no facsimile, however accurate, can ever replace an original (Petrucci 1984; Tanselle 1989), and one must resist the temptation to assert that the latest technology solves all the problems of the previous ones. Nevertheless, these high-quality images do ameliorate at least some of the problems with print facsimiles and particularly with microfilm.

This greater access to high-quality images means first that more people can study the manuscripts, since they can now see details that would previously

---

[3] For example, the paperbound volumes of Early English Manuscripts in Facsimile range from €470–€950 each, and the hardbound €820–€1325 (Rosenkilde & Bagger 2007).

[4] The term "high quality" prompts the question what quality is "high," but the an-swer to this is always changing as demonstrated by Kevin Kiernan's enthusiasm in 1991 for images with "full scale of 256 levels from black to white" (1991, 22). Never-theless, one can normally expect digital images to have better detail and colour ac-curacy than microfilm or even most forms of photography. For current standards in digital imaging see Craig-McFeely and Lock (2006, 12–17) and Craig-McFeely (2007/8, §§13–47), as well as Terras (2008).

have required consulting the original. It also has implications for palaeo-graphical method, bringing us close to an ideal expressed a century ago by Ludwig Traube; namely that palaeographical analysis should consider entire corpora rather than selected highlights or those examples which are easily accessible (Brown 1959–63, 362–63, referring esp. to Traube et al. 1909–20, 1:20–48 and 2:9–13). The proliferation of digital facsimiles is also starting to produce changes in how palaeographical arguments are presented. For example, Davis suggests that palaeographers should use images much more, and specifically grids that present images of different letters together for easy comparison (2007, 258–59 and 267). It is not clear precisely what he has in mind, since his example is no longer accessible, but one possibility is a prototype database of letters from manuscripts shown in Figure 1, below.[5]

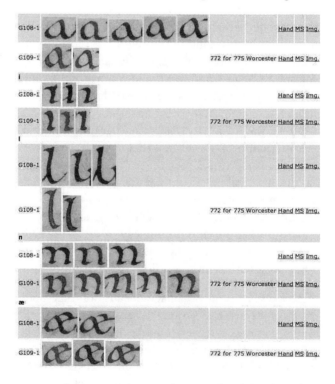

Figure 1. Output from a prototype palaeographical database being developed by the author. The letters are from Cambridge, Corpus Christi College, MS 419 (G108-1) and MS 421 (G109-1), reproduced by permission of the Master and Fellows of Corpus Christi College Cambridge.

---

[5] For the inaccessibility of Davis's example see p. 158 below, and for the example database see pp. 147–48.

Davis does not suggest that visual evidence should or even could replace verbal description entirely. The use of verbal description can probably never be avoided, because any use of a manuscript or facsimile is an act of interpretation (Cameron, Frank, and Leyerle 1970, 79; Page 1992, 79; compare also Tanselle 1989, 33–34). Writing is no more than marks on a page, and to consider those marks as texts or even letters requires an interpretative step. This is not purely a theoretical point but has practical significance: for example, even a diplomatic transcript cannot be completely objective, and to consider it so invests it with a finality and authority that it cannot sustain (Robinson and Solopova 1993, 19–21; Robinson 2009, 43–45). In the case of Davis's grid, although the use of photographs may seem objective, even selecting which letters to reproduce is an act of interpretation; using using this visual evidence to demonstrate an intellectual argument is a further interpretative step, and these steps must be explained if the argument is to be understood and evaluated. We must be told which aspects of the letterforms are considered significant, how these significant differences compare between samples, and so on, and if we are not told this then we are at sea, as is demonstrated by an existing attempt to categorize letterforms by images alone (see below).

This need for interpretation and subjectivity is by no means detrimental to the use of images; on the contrary, the increased use of images should improve the clarity and precision of palaeographical arguments. Illustrations have been used by palaeographers since the field's inception (Stokes 2010; Treharne forthcoming),[6] but this use has been limited in part because of the cost involved in printing them, and so Davis suggests putting images online (2007, 267 and 270). Creating a new web page with images raises the issue of reproduction rights (which will be discussed shortly), but even if one does not reproduce images, one can still provide links to photographs of pages which are already freely available, and these URLs or detailed references can also be provided in a print publication. Indeed, it would be very useful for interfaces to digitized manuscript libraries to include not only facilities to pan and zoom in to images, but also to allow a permanent URL, which enables one to reference not only the image in question but also the region of interest and level of zoom (as is currently possible on sites such as Google Maps). In this way one could provide a link that brings the user not just to the image of a manuscript page, but to a specific part of that page at the appropriate level of zoom, thereby highlighting a particular letter, word, decoration, or anything else so required.

---

[6] I thank Professor Treharne for sending me a copy of her paper in advance of publication.

As well as allowing scholars to illustrate their arguments better, the increased access of a "virtual library" can also lead to greater accountability.[7] A verbal description of handwriting cannot be verified without a lot of effort and access to the appropriate materials, but a manuscript that is digitized and available online can easily be checked by many different scholars. Furthermore, the reproduction of complete manuscripts in full colour allows one to see the larger context of the scribal hand in question. Illustrating particular features necessarily means taking a small and possibly non-representative sample of a scribe's handwriting; however, some palaeographers have argued that one must see the aspect of the whole page rather than the details of particular letterforms to understand a scribal hand (for which see James in Pfaff 1977, 104; Brown 1993, 258). There is also the risk that a given argument is based on too limited a sample of letterforms, and if one can access the whole manuscript then one can check for variation and can judge whether or not this has been taken into account. The layout of a manuscript page, its *mise en page*, is also an important consideration not only in art history but in palaeography and manuscript studies more generally (Bischoff 1990, 27–30; Irvine 1994, 371–93). Despite this, many photographs in print show only a detail of the page, not the page as a whole, meaning that the surrounding context of a decoration or word is lost. One well-known example of this is the *Survey of Manuscripts Illustrated in the British Isles* (Alexander 1975–96), a set of seven large-format volumes that contain many hundreds of illustrations; but most of these illustrations show decorated elements carefully excised from their manuscript context in such a way that almost none of the surrounding page is visible. Even reproducing the whole page is not necessarily enough: as art historians in particular have recently reminded us, books are not designed as disembodied pages but rather as openings, that is, as two facing pages of a book as it lies open before the reader or viewer. This unit of the opening was often exploited by those designing pages and layouts, sometimes by having a single illustration extend across both pages, or by placing elements on one page which reflect or refer to elements on the other (for examples, see Withers 2007; Pierazzo and Stokes 2011, esp. 402). Nevertheless most photographs in print do not show even a full page, let alone a two-page opening, and so this component of the design is lost. Many digitized manuscripts are not presented as openings either, but at least the interested user can access the larger context and even re-create the opening using simple imaging software as required (for which see below). Similarly, although Davis has not suggested this, not only grids of letters but

---

[7] See, however, the caveats presented by Terras (2011).

also images of complete pages or openings could be posted together, thereby overcoming the criticisms given here.[8]

The advantages of "virtual" manuscripts discussed here are not new insofar as the same could be achieved with print facsimiles, albeit at much greater cost. In addition to reduced cost, another benefit of digital images is the ease with which they can be managed and manipulated. It has already been noted that palaeographers need to study large corpora rather than a few exceptional manuscripts, but in practice the quantity of material has proven difficult to manage; that difficulty, although not eliminated, is now significantly reduced. Digital photography is now so widespread that most home computers come supplied with facilities for viewing, magnifying, sorting, arranging, tagging and even annotating images.[9] Even simple magnification should not be underestimated, as already discussed. Tools for annotation and image management are also extremely useful for scholars, allowing one to find images of pages quickly, compare different pages, scale samples of handwriting for comparison, and otherwise manage large volumes of material. Some damaged or illegible manuscripts can also be "restored" relatively easily using standard software such as Adobe Photoshop or the GNU Image Manipulation Program, as long as the resolution and colour-depth is sufficient (Craig-McFeely and Lock 2006; Craig-McFeely 2007/8; Stokes 2011a). Perhaps the most widely publicized example of this restoration is the so-called Archimedes Palimpsest, in which the only known copies of Archimedes' *Method of Mechanical Theorems* and *Stomachion* were recovered using very sophisticated and expensive imaging techniques (Easton, Knox, and Christens-Barry 2003).[10] However, in some cases erasures or faded writing can be recovered with no more than a good photograph and some free or readily available software: texts recovered in this way include some medieval music, part of Cyprian's "Epistolary," the endorsement of an Anglo-Saxon charter, and a

---

[8] For grids of letters see Figure 1, above. The combination of letters and full manuscript pages will be provided in the Digital Resource for Paleography (DigiPal) project, King's College London, accessed 23 October 2009, http://digipal.eu/.

[9] Both Microsoft Vista and Apple Mac OS 10.5 ("Leopard") and above include a "cover flow" visualization for images in folders and also include specialized software for organizing images ("iPhoto" from Apple and "Windows Photo Gallery" from Microsoft). The "Preview" application shipped with Mac OS X includes the facility to annotate images. More sophisticated tools are also freely available, such as those described by Bradley (2008) and Opas-Hänninen et al. (2008, 44–52 and 194–96).

[10] See also The Archimedes Palimpsest Project, accessed 23 October 2009, http://www.archimedespalimpsest.org.

copy of a poem by Donne (Craig-McFeely 2007/8; Schipper 2004; McLeod 2005; Stokes 2008, 66–67; see also Twycross 2008).

Tools are also available that facilitate the online publication of images, as encouraged by Davis (see above). The prevalence of digital photographs and the desire to disseminate them has led to many resources for publishing images online; these range from services such as Flickr[11] and Google's PicasaWeb[12] to such tools as Apple's iWeb and Microsoft's FrontPage, as well as utilities to upload images automatically. Again, however, more sophisticated tools are also freely available. These include the Image Markup Tool which allows users to annotate images and then export the data in TEI-compliant XML or an automatically generated web page.[13] Even more relevant is "Chopper," a tool designed specifically for compiling images of letterforms "chopped out" from digital photographs in much the way that Davis describes.[14] The software has been developed on a proprietary system, but it does allow one to export data in XML which can then be transformed into XHTML or PDF for publication. This is just a sample of the many different methods and tools that are available. It does not claim to be complete and will undoubtedly look dated very soon. The point is that these tools are readily available and that almost all of them are already included on most home computers, or can be downloaded for free and installed easily by the average user. These tools, combined with a growing corpus of publicly available digital images, allow even those with little understanding of technology to work with images in new ways and to produce relatively easily the kind of visual evidence that Davis advocates. Indeed we are already starting to see new resources that utilize these tools, and some of these will be discussed shortly.

Even though no facsimile can replace an original, an online "virtual" manuscript, when manipulated with these tools, can still enable a much better understanding of the original for a much wider audience than was pos-

---

[11] http://www.flickr.com, accessed 23 October 2009.

[12] http://picasaweb.google.co.uk, accessed 23 October 2009.

[13] Martin Holmes, Image Markup Tool, University of Victoria, accessed 23 October 2009, http://tapor.uvic.ca/~mholmes/image_markup. The Image Markup Tool is now being integrated into a new resource, the Text Image Linking Environment (TILE). At the time of writing this project is still in its initial stages but further information is available at TILE, Maryland Institute for Technology in the Humanities and Indiana University, accessed 23 October 2009, http://mith.umd.edu/tile/.

[14] See "Technical Resources," *International Dunhuang Project* (IDP), British Library, London, accessed 23 October 2009, http://idp.bl.uk/pages/technical_resources.a4d.

sible in a print format. However, much of this is simply an easier way of doing "traditional" scholarship, with questions and methods that are not substantially different from those done previously. Even damaged manuscripts were successfully restored well before the "digital age" by using chemical reagents or specialized photography (see, for example, Smith 1938–39), although such methods normally required special equipment and skills, at a cost. Regarding new methods, Willard McCarty, Michael Hart, and others have suggested that increased ease of access (especially in speed and volume) can itself transform scholarship (McCarty et al. 2009), or that simply being able to visualize and manipulate information can allow one to test hypotheses or create new knowledge by exploring material in new ways (Sculley and Pasanek 2008, 421–22; Clement et al. 2008; Jessop 2008). Nevertheless the question remains, what else can be done with these images, and specifically what entirely new approaches are now possible? For example, the tools for analysis discussed so far still rely on the examination of letterforms by the (human) eye. In contrast, some more recent techniques use an entirely different type of comparison: namely, by statistical analysis of quantitative measurements. One of these techniques was pioneered by Léon Gilissen, who took many hundreds of measurements of pen-angle, pen-width, and other quantitative features of scribal hands in order to characterize script (1977). Unfortunately, some details of his method are flawed (Derolez 2003, 8), and taking such small, detailed measurements from an original manuscript or even a photograph proved extremely laborious and often inaccurate. Now, freely available software such as the GNU Image Manipulation Program allows one to measure relative lengths, proportions, and angles accurately and very easily, as long as the image is itself undistorted and of high enough resolution, and as long as the natural expansion and shrinkage of parchment is taken into account (for which see Terras 2011 and Woods 2006, 205–06, respectively). Such tools therefore enable the sort of analysis Gilissen attempted, providing the scale and precision that he needed but could not realistically obtain, and his approach is receiving new interest for this reason.[15] Indeed the

---

[15] For one application see Aussems (2006). Mark Aussems took measurements with a (physical) ruler directly from the computer screen for this study (97–98), but he is now extending this work and is aware of the software and methods described here (Aussems, email message to author, 2008). Compare also Robert Stevick's study of word spacing at Robert Stevick, *Old English Graphotactics*, 1999, revised 2004, http://faculty.washington. edu/stevickr/graphotactics/index.html, and GraphoScop, discussed by Gurrado (2009). It should be noted, however, that none of these projects accounts for page curvature, image distortion, or the natural expansion and contraction of parchment noted above.

principle of quantitative analysis has been extended further in so-called "digital" or "computational" palaeography, where images are analysed by the computer with relatively little human intervention in an attempt to reduce subjectivity and instead use quantitative evidence as much as possible (Stokes 2009, 323–31; see also Ciula 2005; Stokes 2007/8; Bulacu and Schomaker 2007). This area is still very much in development and has yet to produce functional systems that are acceptable to medievalists. It has also been suggested that these and other computational approaches to the humanities tend to provide "answers" that cannot be verified and should rather allow one to explore, suggest, and be surprised (Clement et al. 2009; Davis 2007, 266 n. 27; Stokes 2009, 321–25); whereas this field has come about entirely as a result of the prevalence of digital images and the "virtual libraries" of manuscripts.

New challenges

The increase in "virtual libraries" of manuscripts, along with the tools to make use of these libraries, is in fact providing many new opportunities and starting to change the way scholars work. Nevertheless, there are some substantial difficulties that must be overcome before the potential of these libraries and tools can be fully realized. Rather than trying to survey all possible issues, the remainder of this paper will focus on two in particular: palaeographical searching and image rights.

Image databases: Nomenclature, searching, and encoding letterforms

The first issue that a scholar may well encounter when coming to a virtual manuscript library is how to search it. The obvious answer is through a database or catalogue, ideally a union catalogue of "virtual libraries" through which a single search can return images from different repositories. Unfortunately, such catalogues are difficult to create in practice, and partly because of this the very act of producing them is forcing us to change the way we work as manuscript scholars. One of the biggest difficulties is that vagueness and inconsistency can be tolerated in print catalogues but are unacceptable to a computer, and so digital projects are forcing us to be clearer, more precise, and more consistent, and therefore to revisit old problems with a new urgency.

The simplest example of this need for precision and consistency is terminology. There is no established and widely used palaeographical terminology even for the names of scripts, let alone the finer details such as letterforms. For example, Alexander Rumble's guidelines for describing manuscripts refer to "standard names" for scripts, such as "insular minuscule or pointed, square and round Anglo-Saxon minuscule" (1994, 12). By "round Anglo-Saxon minuscule," Rumble is clearly referring to the script used for writing in the vernacular throughout England for most of the eleventh century; however, a quick survey of scholarship reveals that this same script goes by several other names: "Caroline minuscule" (Ker 1957, xxv–xxvi), "Anglo-Insular minuscule" (Boyle 1984, 75),[16] "Anglo-Saxon Round minuscule" (Brown 1990, 64), "Anglo-Saxon vernacular minuscule" (Dumville 2001, 10–11), "English Caroline minuscule" (Roberts 2005, 85–103, esp. 100–2),[17] "English Vernacular minuscule" (Stokes 2005). This variation is embarrassing, but experts in the field can at least understand what is meant, either by becoming familiar with the different terms or by inferring their meaning from the context. But, as Elaine Treharne has observed in relation to her own online catalogue, this inconsistency is not tolerable in digital systems, and this in turn makes such systems very difficult to produce and use (2007; see also Treharne forthcoming). A sufficiently detailed catalogue should allow a user to find all manuscripts containing what she or he might call "round Anglo-Saxon minuscule," for example, but a search will return nothing if the person who wrote the catalogue called this same script "Anglo-Saxon Round minuscule." The problem is exacerbated with union catalogues, since the various databases and catalogues must communicate with one another, and this presupposes consistent terminology across them all. This is not a new problem, and the *Comité international de paléographie latine* (CIPL) was founded in 1953 partly for the purpose of establishing a standard terminology; but, despite sixteen international meetings to date, it is still nowhere near producing an accepted result (see, however, Muzerelle 2003).

The problem of nomenclature and categorization is even more acute when considering databases not of manuscripts but of handwriting itself, since these require searching not only for scripts but also for letterforms. One such database has been built by the Cuneiform Digital Palaeography Project, which allows users to search for photographs of cuneiform signs by a wide range of criteria such as the language of composition, the museum number of the text vehicle, the date, origin, and provenance of the inscription, the genre of the text, and so on.[18] Users can browse by instance (graph), sign (grapheme), and

---

[16] Note also Boyle's use of "Caroline minuscule" for what seems to be the same thing (1984, 113, no. 747).

[17] Note also "Late Anglo-Saxon minuscule" for what seems to be the same thing (Roberts 2005, 96–98).

[18] Cuneiform Digital Palaeography Project, University of Birmingham and the British Museum, accessed 23 October 2009, http://www.cdp.bham.ac.uk/.

text vehicle.[19] A "Clipboard" feature is provided which allows users to save images of graphs and compare them in a manner similar to that described by Davis (and indeed Davis himself is a member of the project team). Apparently similar to this is the International Dunhuang Project's palaeographical database (see Fig. 2, below): it is not available at the time of writing, but descriptions and published screenshots suggest an approach rather like that of the *Cuneiform Digital Palaeography Project* (IDP Technical Resources). This resource seems likely to be of enormous value to scholars in the field, at least judging by the descriptions published to date, and something like it is very much a desideratum for western palaeography.

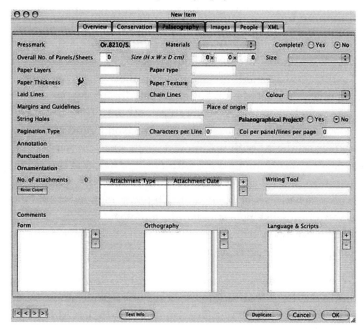

Figure 2. Palaeography Screen for the Dunhuang Database (reproduced from IDP Technical Resources)

---

[19] For the terminology see Davis (2007, 255): "The grapheme /a/ is the letter considered independently of any particular realization of it. An allograph is an accepted version of that grapheme: 'a' and 'ɑ' are allographs of /a/. An idiograph is the way (or one of the ways) in which a given writer habitually writes /a/. A graph is a unique instance of /a/, as it appears on a particular page." "Allograph" is therefore equivalent to the term "letterform" more commonly used by palaeographers, and the two are used interchangeably here.

As useful as these two databases seem, however, neither allows searches for all handwriting that shows a particular allograph or idiograph. Such searches would be extremely useful for palaeographers who want to identify scribal hands or map out developments in script, but how to design an interface that allows this is by no means clear. One possibility is to search using verbal descriptions, and this has been tried in an unpublished database that has been designed, built, and populated by the author (Stokes 2007/8, §§24–25). The database focuses on vernacular English script from the period circa 990 to circa 1035: it therefore includes information about all the manuscripts and charters that contain any script from this period, even if that script is no more than a few words scribbled in a margin; brief records are also included for all the manuscripts without any script from this period but that are in Helmut Gneuss's *Handlist of Anglo-Saxon manuscripts ... written or owned in England up to 1100* (2001). It also contains a list of over 280 distinct palaeographical features such as "flat-topped square **a**," "horned **e**," "long tongue of **f**," and so on, and these features are mapped to 466 scribal hands. The database thereby includes just over 17,000 scribe-feature pairs; that is, 17,000 records of the form "hand G219-1 shows teardrop-shaped **a**." One can then search for scribal hands that show any combination of features, or for all the features that can be attributed to a given time or place (see Fig. 3, below; and Stokes 2007/8, figs. 13–15). The obvious difficulty with this system of categorization is that it depends on a very detailed terminology for handwriting, but, as we have seen, no such standard terminology exists. The nomenclature is therefore idiosyncratic by necessity and is almost impossible for anyone other than the compiler to understand. This difficulty has been partly overcome by providing an illustrated glossary (Stokes 2005, 1:vi–xi), and it is also possible in principle to associate different descriptions with a given feature. For example, the form of "**s**" that we normally use today could be catalogued in the database with at least three different descriptions—round, majuscule, and uncial—so that searches on any of these terms would return a hit.[20] Nevertheless, this ignores the likely possibility that some terms do not equate directly with others but are instead ambiguous or only partially overlap in semantic range. It also ignores the extremely high level of interpretation required to categorize features of handwriting in this way: some forms of "**a**" are clearly Caroline, for example, and others are clearly round, but many are somewhere in between (Fig. 4). The problem on the one hand is again that arguments based on description are very difficult to interpret precisely and unambiguously. On the other hand, manuscripts are written by people, and

---

[20] I owe this idea to Nicholas Pickwood (2009).

people—even when professionally trained—do not always fit neatly into the categories that the computer normally requires.[21]

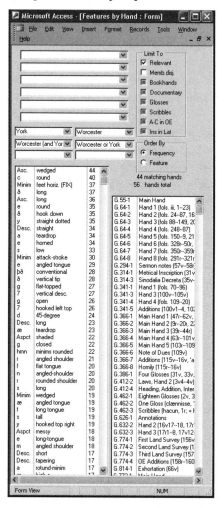

Figure 3. Unpublished database of Anglo-Saxon hands showing those associated with Worcester and York. The column on the left shows that forty-four hands feature wedged ascenders, and the column on the right lists those forty-four hands. For further discussion see Stokes (2007/8).

---

[21] The principle of human variation has been used to argue against any use of digital or quantitative methods in palaeography, an argument that has proved very controversial (Costamagna et al. 1995 and 1996; Pratesi 1998; Gumbert 1998; Derolez 2003, 7–9; Ciula 2005; Stokes 2007/8).

Figure 4. Examples of the letter "a." The one on the left is clearly Caroline, that on the right clearly round, but those in the middle show the range of forms in between, which are harder to classify. Letterforms are from Cambridge, Corpus Christi College MS 383, fol. 57r, reproduced by permission of the Master and Fellows of Corpus Christi College, Cambridge.

The final database to be considered here takes an entirely different approach, eschewing verbal description entirely and relying instead on an index of images. This is the *Palaeography Catalogue* in the Manchester Centre for Anglo-Saxon Studies (MANCASS) C11 database (Scragg et al. 2005).[22] The database as a whole contains some 165 manuscripts or fragments, seventy single-sheet charters, and fourteen continuous glosses (Rumble 2005b, 1). Within that corpus, seventy-five "scriptors" have been identified, where scriptors are defined as "scribes who have written more than one sequence"; a "sequence," in turn, is "a unit of continuous written work by a single scribe." At the time of writing, many sequences in the database contain records of spelling but not of script; although a list of scriptors is provided, there is no list of sequences and so it is difficult to know how many sequences have palaeographical information, but the *Palaeography Catalogue* contains just under seven thousand sequence-letterform pairs. This catalogue consists of about 180 different letterforms (allographs) which are represented both by codes and by "generalized pictorial representations of letterforms used by more than [one] scribe."[23] These "generalized representations" are adapted from images of manuscripts but are not graphs; that is, the images that one sees in the catalogue or associated with a sequence are not direct photographs of any particular scribal hand but are instead generic forms produced by the database compilers and designed to illustrate those features which the compilers consider representative of the particular allograph in question. The compilers have then assigned these representations to the scribal sequences, so that a given sequence has associated with it a set of generalized representations that the compilers consider best represent the actual letters (graphs) on the manuscript page.

---

[22] http://www.arts.manchester.ac.uk/mancass/C11database/.

[23] Alexander R. Rumble, email to author, 29 May 2009.

One can search the palaeography catalogue for a particular manuscript, although there is no way of knowing in advance if a given manuscript contains any palaeographical information. Alternatively one can browse the list of scriptors; this list does include palaeographical information if it is present (Fig. 5). One can also browse the *Palaeography Catalogue* itself. The entry page for this catalogue presents all 180 allographs as generalized pictorial representations and invites the user to select one of them (Fig. 6); when this is done, the user is given a list of all sequences that show this allograph and is enabled to search for combinations of allographs (Rumble 2005b, 224–25; 2006, 14–16). This use of visual indexing therefore follows Davis's recommendations but is difficult to use in practice. The pictorial representations are given without any annotation whatsoever, meaning that one cannot know which features have been considered distinctive of that particular allograph. To take an admittedly extreme example, Figure 7 shows four entries from the *Palaeography Catalogue*, all representing a standard abbreviation for the word *and*; however, these four images look almost identical, and at present there is no way of knowing what distinguishes them. The differences are apparently embedded in the numerical code which is assigned to each allograph; the broad principles involved here have been discussed (Rumble 2005b, [2005]a), but at the time of writing no full description of this code has been published.[24] To illustrate the principles, the catalogue gives the codes of the allographs in Figure 7 as "and_5_2_3_1_1_2," "and_5_2_3_1_1_3," "and_5_2_3_2_1_1," and "and_5_2_3_2_1_2." The "and" component is here used to indicate that the grapheme in question is the abbreviation for "and." The numbers that follow are part of a much larger typology of all Latin scripts: "5_2_3" stands for "Anglo-Saxon minuscule, c. 850–1100," and "d_5_2_3_2_1" represents "d [in Anglo-Saxon minuscule of c. 850–1100] with short and rounded ascender" (Rumble 2005b). Unfortunately we are given no more than a few illustrative examples, and so the perceived difference between the forms of *and* in Figure 7 remains hidden, as does the organizing principle of the catalogue as a whole. In many cases, differences between the allographs seem apparent from the images, and so useful searches can still be made, but this "apparentness" must itself be guessed and there is no way of confirming it. Furthermore, as noted above, the images in the database are not those from any existing manuscript but are instead taken from facsimiles and then modified by hand; this is largely to avoid problems of copyright,[25] but this practice

---

[24] Professor Rumble has informed me that the description is indeed planned for publication (email to author, 29 May 2009). I thank him for his comments on a draft of this paper.

[25] I thank Donald Scragg for clarifying this point in conversation.

also adds yet another layer of interpretation between the user and the manuscript. In this respect it is comparable to an approach taken by the System for Palaeographical Inspections (SPI) described by Arianna Ciula (2005), in which the computer automatically generates "average" letterforms. Both methods seek to highlight those differences between graphs that are perceived to be "essential" and to remove those which are not.[26] The problem with both is not necessarily the use of ideal representations rather than images of "real" graphs, not least because even "real" images would involve interpretation in selection, cropping, scale, and so on. The problem is rather that neither the MANCASS nor SPI makes clear the degree and means of interpretation. This is problematic in both cases, since if one cannot identify the interpretation then one cannot verify it or the results that it gives. However, there is an important difference in purpose. The "average" forms in SPI are intended to be an intermediate stage used by the computer for automatically assessing scribal nearness; this means that one can obtain useful results without needing to understand these images directly, although with the caveats above about verification. In contrast, the representations of letters in the MANCASS system are designed explicitly for the (human) user, and any meaningful use of the *Palaeography Catalogue* requires the user to know the principles captured by each representation. Without this knowledge, one cannot find entries in the catalogue or make sense of those entries once they are found.

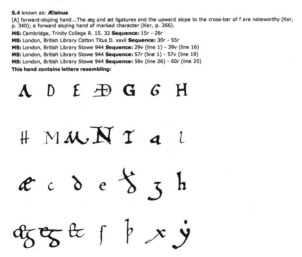

S.4 known as: **Ælsinus**
[A] forward-sloping hand...The æg and æt ligatures and the upward slope to the cross-bar of f are noteworthy (Ker, p. 340); a forward sloping hand of marked character (Ker, p. 266).
MS: Cambridge, Trinity College R. 15. 32 **Sequence:** 15r - 26r
MS: London, British Library Cotton Titus D. xxvii **Sequence:** 30r - 55r
MS: London, British Library Stowe 944 **Sequence:** 29v (line 1) - 39v (line 16)
MS: London, British Library Stowe 944 **Sequence:** 57r (line 1) - 57v (line 19)
MS: London, British Library Stowe 944 **Sequence:** 59v (line 26) - 60r (line 25)
This hand contains letters resembling:

Figure 5. Scriptor 4 (Ælsinus) from the list of scriptors in the MANCASS C11 database.

---

[26] I thank one of the anonymous reviewers of this paper for emphasizing this comparison.

The design of the MANCASS *Palaeography Catalogue* highlights the interpretive element of illustrations as well as words and demonstrates the need for both visual evidence and verbal discussion mentioned above: by presenting only visual information, without a verbal explanation of the compiler's interpretation, the resource is almost unusable. These problems should be alleviated to a large extent when the full description of the numbering scheme is published, at which point the database will provide a hybrid index of both images and words. This, combined with images of the actual graphs written by each scribe rather than a generic type for each allograph, would go a very long way towards addressing these difficulties as they would present both the visual evidence and the verbal explanation of how that evidence has been interpreted.[27]

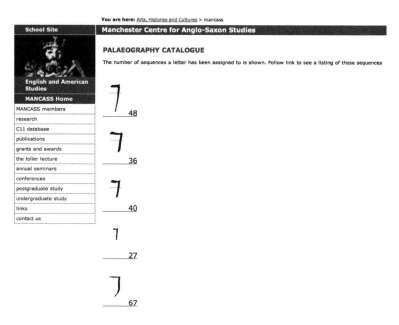

Figure 6. The first five entries in the Palaeography Catalogue from the MANCASS C11 database. Each image here is a link to all occurrences of that letterform in the catalogue.

---

[27] For a new project attempting this integration of descriptive and visual information, along with other forms of visualization, see the reference to DigiPal in n. 8, above.

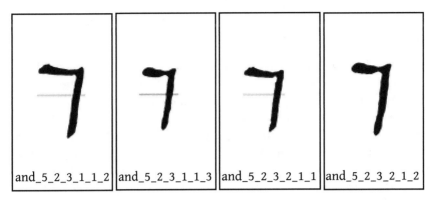

| and_5_2_3_1_1_2 | and_5_2_3_1_1_3 | and_5_2_3_2_1_1 | and_5_2_3_2_1_2 |

Figure 7: Images from the MANCASS C11 *Palaeography Catalogue* used
to represent different allographs

The examples considered so far are not especially sophisticated in terms of
technology, and the more general problem of how to search images is very
familiar to researchers: the opening keynote lecture at the Digital Humanities Conference in Paris in 2006 was on precisely this topic (Seppänen 2006),
and to draw more heavily on computer science and artificial intelligence
seems a fruitful approach. One example of this more sophisticated use of
computer science is a system described by Melissa Terras and Paul Robertson
that incorporates both a schema for the markup of strokes in XML and artificial intelligence to take unknown graphs as input and suggest interpretations (graphemes) as output (2004; Terras 2006, 92–137).[28] Part of this system
involved knowledge elicitation to determine how palaeographers describe
scripts, and using this information to develop a model and encoding scheme
for letterforms, "resulting in an XML representation of each character on a
stroke by stroke basis" (Terras and Robertson 2004, 1; see also Terras 2006,
93–100). Although designed to help read damaged tablets, a system like this
could probably be used to describe letterforms more generally, and perhaps
also to search for instances of them. It would require some considerable extension to be useful for palaeographical analysis of writing with a quill on
parchment, however, as it does not allow for details such as pen-angle or the
contrast between thick and thin strokes, details that palaeographers consid-

---

[28] See now also the continuation of this work as the e-Science and Ancient Documents
project (eSAD), University of Oxford, accessed 23 October 2009, http://esad.classics.
ox.ac.uk/.

er significant to the identification of medieval scribes and which therefore distinguish allographs in medieval script.[29]

Terras and Robertson also make explicit a further use of digital photographs, namely "marking up images of text to generate XML representations of letterforms"; but, as they note, palaeographical markup is not included in current initiatives such as the TEI encoding scheme (2004, 413).[30] One possible model for this is the Character Description Language (CDL) which has been developed by the Wénlín Institute "for precise and compact description, rendering, and indexing of all Han (Chinese, Japanese, Korean, and Vietnamese) characters, encoded and unencoded" (Bishop and Cook 2003, 2004). Chinese and related scripts have associated with them a very detailed vocabulary for the strokes that make up characters and also an established system for breaking down these characters into units; these systems are used both to teach beginners to write and to enable entries to be found in dictionaries. In this sense they already have a proven system for organizing and searching for complex graphs, and the CDL draws heavily on this. Like the encoding system proposed by Terras and Robertson (2004), CDL is also stroke-based, but it characterizes strokes using Han (Mandarin Chinese) terminology, whereas the former system uses coordinates of the sample image. Thus a straight vertical stroke is called *shù* ("vertical") in Chinese and so is represented in CDL by **s**, while a vertical stroke with a hook to the left at its base is represented by **sg** (*shù gōu*, "vertical-hook"), and so on. The specification then gives detailed rules for combining the strokes to form units, and these units are then located relative to one another using a coordinate system to form characters. This system on its own is not sufficient for western palaeography as it distinguishes only between features that bear meaning in

---

[29] For some lists of features considered significant in medieval script see Stokes (2009, 313–15), and compare the list given by Terras and Robertson (2004, 400–2; also in Terras 2006, 98–99). Although quite different in detail and purpose, a similar system is followed by SPI, using artificial intelligence and "average" letterforms as described by Ciula (2005) and discussed briefly on p. 153 above; but this system is designed to find similar scribal hands rather than to search for particular allographs.

[30] The *Script Encoding Initiative*, despite its promising name, aims to encode characters (graphemes), not script in the sense used by medievalists; its purpose is to prepare new proposals for Unicode rather than to represent letterforms. See http://www.linguistics.berkeley.edu/sei, accessed 23 October 2009. The Digital Resource for Palaeography (DigiPal) project has a model of script as one of its research objectives, but at the time of writing it is still some way from producing this: see http://digipal.eu/, accessed 23 October 2009.

the Chinese writing system; that is, it allows the distinction of all graphemes in Chinese but not all allographs in medieval Latin script, with omissions once again including pen-width and pen-angle. Nevertheless, the principle, and particularly the combination of verbal, graphical, and coordinate-based description, seems worth further investigation.

Use of images: Longevity, copyright, and reproduction rights

The second issue to consider is the use of images in publication, particularly with respect to copyright and reproduction rights.[31] As noted several times already, Davis (2007) suggests that digital images should ideally be posted online in order to illustrate palaeographical arguments with a full body of evidence, and methods in "digital paleography" also require images to be made widely available so that results can be repeated and verified (Stokes 2009, 323–24 and 329). There are some difficulties with this, however. One is the risk that argument and evidence become separated. This is not a problem if the evidence is published within the article or book, as has normally been done with print publications and is often found in online ones; digital publications that do this to good effect include some online journals such as *Digital Medievalist*[32] and dual print/digital publications such as the one you are reading now. However, this assumes that publishers can embed the content in their publications, and this may not be possible in practice: perhaps the publication is a print one but the lower cost and higher quality of digital images are desired, or perhaps the evidence in question is a large corpus, or indeed a complete manuscript, and so the volume is too great to be incorporated. In these cases, the discussion must refer to evidence that is stored elsewhere, and this introduces new risks such as a print journal outlasting its digital complement, or simply that the two become disconnected. The difficulty of sustaining extrinsic material like this is well known, not only because resources may move or disappear but also because such links are not well supported by existing standards (Pitti 2004, 484–85). The difficulty is particularly significant when images have been manipulated or removed from their context, in which case the accompanying metadata can be lost, meaning that one cannot necessarily know what manipulations have been made or even which manuscript is being recorded (Besser 2004, 565–69; Lee

---

[31] For general discussion of this topic as applied to the UK see especially Padfield (2007) and, for a more technical treatment, Garnett, Davies, and Harbottle (2005); for the US see Stanford (2008) and Case and Green (2006).

[32] *Digital Medievalist*, accessed 23 October 2009, http://www.digitalmedievalist.org/journal/.

and O'Donnell 2009, 269–70). Indeed, this problem of disappearing evidence has already arisen with Davis's own material, as the URL that he printed in his article now returns an HTTP 404 error ("not found"), and search engines lead to his website but not to the material that he describes.[33] Davis's argument still stands in principle, and there are ways to reduce these problems, such as using institutional rather than personal websites, but the danger remains.

Another difficulty that must be considered is reproduction rights. This is an extremely complex area, and so the discussion that follows should not be considered authoritative in any way—those who require it must seek legal advice—but a brief summary of the current state of affairs can still be presented here. Libraries and museums generally assert copyright on photographs they make of material in their holdings, even though these are faithful reproductions of material that is itself out of copyright. A ruling in the United States maintains that such a reproduction does not convey originality and so is not protected by copyright (Kaplan 1999; see also Case and Green 2006), but the current literature strongly suggests that in the United Kingdom such a photograph probably is so protected (Garnett, Davies, and Harbottle 2005, §§3–142; as well as Garnett 2000; Deazley 2001; and discussion on Wikimedia Commons). Complicating the issue further is the question of "a substantial part" in UK law: if the material in question is "not a substantial part" of the whole then its use may be acceptable even if the item is within copyright, but unfortunately there is no formal definition of what a "substantial part" is (Padfield 2007, 110–13). "Fair use" may allow use for private study, but, at least in the UK, it explicitly excludes any sort of publication (Padfield 2007, 165).[34] Furthermore, whether or not copyright is an issue, contract law almost certainly is (Padfield 2007, 163). Libraries normally require users to agree to their terms and conditions before issuing images, and "virtual libraries" normally have terms of use; in both cases the further reproduction of images without written authorization is expressly prohibited. Furthermore, some libraries charge a yearly subscription for rights to publish images online, a policy that has clear implications for the longevity of the website in question. Databases of letterforms are even more complex: private databases for scholarly research presumably constitute "fair use," but what if the database is then published online? What of small samples

---

[33] The URL Davis provides is http://doiop.com/3mhmia (2007, 252n3); at the time of writing he is apparently migrating to a new website (Davis 2009), but the material for his article does not yet seem to be available there.

[34] A useful starting-point for fair use in the USA is *Copyright & Fair Use*, Stanford University Libraries, 2008, http://fairuse.stanford.edu/.

of script or occasional letterforms extracted for illustrative purposes (for example Lapidge 2000 or Thompson 2006)? It seems unlikely that any library would prosecute for something like this, but one can imagine publishers quite understandably baulking at such usage. The terms and conditions for reproduction and publication are complex and vary widely, so much so that a report from the Max Planck Institute refers to the "confusing patchwork of policies ... [which] is hindering new research and publication in the humanities," as a result of which they have issued a set of recommendations for best practice (2009a, 1; also von Oertzen and Wilder 2008; von Oertzen n.d. [2009]; and the Institute's online discussion platform, 2009b). The point of this is emphatically not to criticize libraries, which are under the pressure of funding cuts and constant demands to become financially self-sustainable. In my personal experience librarians have been very helpful and usually generous in allowing publication, and librarians themselves contributed to the Max Planck Institute's recommendations for open access (von Oertzen and Wilder 2008; cf. Derolez 2003, xv). Nonetheless, these restrictions pose significant challenges to palaeographers, and it remains that to document a thorough palaeographical comparison of scribal hands adequately might well require images from many different pages in different manuscripts held in different repositories, and these could prove very costly and require extensive negotiation and paperwork. Adequate illustration of palaeographical arguments is therefore hampered not by technology but by questions of access and rights to digital images.

Conclusions

That large-scale digitization of manuscripts will bring both opportunities and challenges seems self-evident. Some of these have been addressed here, but it should also be clear that both the challenges and opportunities extend far beyond the few that have been selected for discussion in this paper: these include the separation of images from context, in terms of metadata and the "destruction of the codex as an integral whole" (Lee and O'Donnell 2009, 262 and 269–70); the loss of any sense of materiality and indeed most of the elements relevant to codicology (Stokes 2011b); and accountability and ethics in image enhancement (Craig-McFeely 2007/8, §§62–64). Nevertheless, the issues raised here—of access and "democratization," of copyright and reproduction rights, of searching and nomenclature, and of how to use images to better codify and understand handwriting—all seem particularly pertinent to palaeographical study. Perhaps, then, as we come to understand these digital resources better, and as we resolve the difficulties that are holding us back at present, we may be in a better position to solve the "crisis of paleography" and raise the resulting "low esteem in which paleography is currently held as an academic discipline" (Derolez 2003, 2–3). It seems unlikely that this "crisis" will be solved by any single change in method: simply having more images will not make the field more objective without better use of those images and without more recognition of the need for communicability, reproducibility, and so on (for which see Stokes 2009, 323–25). It should also be noted that palaeography, like all other disciplines, will never be truly objective: we have already seen that any use of a manuscript is an act of interpretation, and Claus Huitfeldt, for example, seems to suggest a further difficulty when he notes that "objectivity of interpretation" occurs when "decisions [are made] on which all (or most) competent readers agree or seem likely to agree" (2006, 196). Furthermore, it is usually difficult or impossible to prove absolutely the veracity of a palaeographer's claim and therefore to test the validity of her or his method (Stokes 2009, 317). Nevertheless, palaeography is too central to medieval studies to be abandoned: instead new methods need to be developed, and the digitization of medieval manuscript culture is likely to go a long way in helping this to happen.

WORKS CITED

Alexander, J. J. G., ed. 1975–96. *Survey of Illuminated Manuscripts in the British Isles.* 7 vols. London: Harvey Miller Publishers.

Aussems, J. F. A. 2006. "Christine de Pizan and the Scribal Fingerprint: A Quantitative Approach to Manuscript Studies." MA diss., University of Utrecht. http://igitur-archive.library.uu.nl/student-theses/2006-0908-200407/UUindex.html.

Besser, H. 2004. "The Past, Present and Future of Digital Libraries." In *A Companion to Digital Humanities*, edited by Susan Schreibman, Ray Siemens, and John Unsworth, 557–75. Oxford: Blackwell.

Bischoff, Berhard. 1990. *Latin Paleography: Antiquity and the Middle Ages.* Translated by Dáibhí Ó Cróinín and David Ganz. Cambridge: Cambridge University Press.

Bishop, Tom. 2004. "Character Description Language (CDL): The Set of Basic CJK Unified Stroke Types." Wenlin Software for Learning Chinese. http://www.wenlin.com/cdl/cdl_strokes_2004_05_23.pdf.

Bishop, Tom, and Richard Cook. 2003. "A Specification for CDL: Character Description Language." Wenlin Software for Learning Chinese. http://www.wenlin.com/cdl/cdl_spec_2003_10_31.pdf.

Boyle, Leonard E. 1984. *Medieval Latin Paleography: A Bibliographical Introduction.* Toronto: University of Toronto Press.

Bradley, John. 2008. "Collaborative Tool-Building with Pliny: A Progress Report." In Opas-Hänninen et al., 65–67.

Brown, Michelle P. 1990. *A Guide to Western Historical Scripts from Antiquity to 1600.* London: British Library.

Brown, T. J. 1959–63. "Latin Paleography Since Traube." *Transactions of the Cambridge Bibliographical Society* 3:361–81.

_____ 1993. *A Palaeographer's View: Selected Writings.* Edited by J. Bately, M. P. Brown, and J. Roberts. London: Harvey Miller Publishers.

Bulacu, Marius, and Lambert Schomaker. 2007. "Automatic Handwriting Identification on Medieval Documents." In *Proceedings of 14th International Conference on Image Analysis and Processing,* 2007, 279–84. Los Alamitos, CA: IEEE Computer Society. http://doi.ieeecomputersociety.org/10.1109/ICIAP.2007.33.

Cameron, Angus, Roberta Frank, and John Leyerle, eds. 1970. *Computers and Old English Concordances.* Toronto: University of Toronto Press.

Case, Mary, and David Green. 2006. "Rights and Permissions in an Electronic Edition." In *Electronic Textual Editing,* edited by Lou Burnard, Katherine O'Brien O'Keeffe, and John Unsworth, 565–88. New York: Modern Language Association.

Ciula, Arianna. 2005. "Digital Palaeography: Using the Digital Representation of Medieval Script to Support Palaeographic Analysis." *Digital Medievalist* 1: http://www.digitalmedievalist.org/journal/1.1/ciula/.

Clement, Tanya, Sara Steger, John Unsworth, and Kirsten Uszkalo. 2008. "How Not to Read a Million Books." University of Illinois. http://www3.isrl.illinois.edu/~unsworth/hownot2read.html.

Craig-McFeely, J. 2007/8. "Digital Image Archive of Medieval Music: The Evolution of a Digital Resource." *Digital Medievalist* 3: http://www.digitalmedievalist.org/journal/3/mcfeely/.

Craig-McFeely, J., and A. Lock. 2006. *Digital Image Archive of Medieval Music: Digital Restoration Workbook*. Oxford: Oxford Select Specialist Catalogue Publications.

Costamagna, G., et al. 1995 and 1996. "Commentare Bischoff." *Scrittura e Civiltà* 19:325–48 and 20:401–7.

Davis, Tom. 2007. "The Practice of Handwriting Identification." *The Library* (7th series) 8:251–76.

_____ 2009. Unask. http://www.unask.com/.

Deazley, Ronan. 2001. "Photographing Paintings in the Public Domain: A Response to Garnett." *European Intellectual Property Review* 23:179–84.

Derolez, Albert. 1973. "Codicologie ou archéologie du livre?" *Scriptorium* 27:47–52.

_____ 2003. *The Palaeography of Gothic Manuscript Books from the Twelfth to the Early Sixteenth Century*. Cambridge: Cambridge University Press.

Dumville, David N. 2001. "Specimina codicum palaeoanglicorum." In *Collection of Essays in Commemoration of the 50th Anniversary of the Institute of Oriental and Occidental Studies*, 1–24. Suita, Osaka: Kansai University Press.

Easton, R. L., Jr., K. T. Knox, and W. A. Christens-Barry. 2003. "Multi-Spectral Imaging of the Archimedes Palimpsest." *Proceedings of the Applied Imagery Pattern Recognition Workshop (IEEE-AIPR'03)* 32:111–16.

Garand, Monique-Cecille. 1982. "Le Catalogue des manuscrits datés: Bilan et perspectives." In *Paläographie 1981: Colloquium des comité international de paléographie*, edited by Gabriel Silagi, 25–29. Munich: Arbeo-Gesellschaft.

Garnett, Kevin M. 2000. "Copyright in Photographs." *European Intellectual Property Review* 22:229–37.

Garnett, Kevin M., Gillian Davies, and Gwilym Harbottle. 2005. *Copinger and Skone James on Copyright*. 2 vols + suppl. London: Sweet & Maxwell.

Gilissen, Léon. 1977. *Prolégomènes à la codicologie: Recherches sur la construction des cahiers et la mise en page des manuscrits médiévaux*. Ghent: Éditions scientifiques E. Story-Scientia.

Gneuss, Helmut. 2001. *Handlist of Anglo-Saxon Manuscripts: A List of Manuscripts and Manuscript Fragments Written or Owned in England up to 1100.* Tempe: Arizona Center for Medieval and Renaissance Studies.

Gumbert, J. P. 1998. "Commentare 'Commentare Bischoff'." *Scrittura e Civiltà* 22:397–404.

Gurrado, M. 2009. "«Graphoskop», uno strumento informatico per l'analisi paleografica quantitative." In *Kodikologie und Paläographie im digitalen Zeitalter — Codicology and Paleography in the Digital Age,* edited by Malte Rehbein, Patrick Sahle, and Torsten Schaßan, 313–42. Norderstedt: Books on Demand.

Huitfeldt, Claus. 2006. "Philosophy Case Study." In *Electronic Textual Editing,* edited by Lou Burnard, Katherine O'Brien O'Keeffe, and John Unsworth, 181–96. New York: Modern Language Association.

IDP. *International Dunhuang Project: Technical Resources.* London: British Library. Accessed 23 October 2009. http://idp.bl.uk/pages/technical_resources.a4d.

Irvine, Martin. 1994. *The Making of Textual Culture: "Grammatica" and Literary Theory, 350-1100.* Cambridge Studies in Medieval Literature 19. Cambridge: Cambridge University Press.

Jessop, Martyn. 2008. "Digital Visualization as a Scholarly Activity." *Literary and Linguistic Computing* 23:281–93.

Johnson, David F. 2004. "Digitizing the Middle Ages." *Literature Compass* 1: http://dx.doi.org/10.1111/j.1741-4113.2004.00041.x.

Kam, Moshe, Joseph Wetstein, and Robert Conn. 1994. "Proficiency of Professional Document Examiners in Writer Identification." *Journal of Forensic Sciences* 39:5–14.

Kaplan, Lewis A. 1999. *Bridgeman Art Library, Ltd., v. Corel Corp., 36 F. Supp. 2d 191 (S.D.N.Y. 1999).* http://www.law.cornell.edu/copyright/cases/36_FSupp2d_191.htm.

Ker, Neil R. 1957. *Catalogue of Manuscripts Containing Anglo-Saxon.* Oxford: Clarendon Press.

Kiernan, Kevin S. 1991. "Digital Image Processing and the Beowulf Manuscript." *Literary and Linguistic Computing* 6:20–27.

_____ 1994. "Old Manuscripts/New Technologies." In *Anglo-Saxon Manuscripts: Basic Readings*, edited by Mary P. Richards, 37–54. New York: Garland.

_____ 1995. "The Legacy of Wiglaf: Saving a Wounded Beowulf." In *Beowulf: Basic Readings*, edited by Peter S. Baker, 195–218. New York: Garland.

Langeli, Attilio B. 1978. "Ancora su paleografia e storia della scrittura." *Scrittura e Civiltà* 3:329–37.

Lapidge, Michael. 2000. "The Archetype of Beowulf." *Anglo-Saxon England* 29:5–41.

Lee, Stuart, and Daniel P. O'Donnell. 2009. "From Manuscript to Computer." In *Working with Anglo-Saxon Manuscripts*, edited by Gale R. Owen-Crocker, 253–84. Exeter: Exeter University Press.

Lowe, E. A. 1972. *Paleographical Papers, 1907-1965*. Edited by Ludwig Bieler. 2 vols. Oxford: Clarendon Press.

Mallon, Jean. 1982. "Qu'est ce que la paléographie?" In *Paläographie 1981: Colloquium des Comité international de paléographie, München, 15 - 18 September 1981*, edited by Gabriel Silagi, 47–52. Munich: Arbeo-Gesellschaft.

Max Planck Institute. 2009a. "Best Practices for Access to Images: Recommendations for Scholarly Use and Publishing." Berlin. http://www.mpiwg-berlin.mpg.de/PDF/MPIWGBestPracticesRecomm.pdf.

_____ 2009b. *Discussion Platform: New Ways of Using Digital Images*. Max Planck Institute. http://fswiki.mpiwg-berlin.mpg.de/doku.php.

McCarty, Willard, et al. 2009. "Looking Back and Speeding Along." *Humanist Discussion Group* 22.645. http://lists.digitalhumanities.org/pipermail/humanist/2009-March/000346.html.

McLeod, Randall. 2005. "Obliterature: Reading a Censored Text of Donne's 'To his Mistress going to Bed'." *English Manuscript Studies 1100-1700* 12:83–138.

Muzerelle, Denis. 2003. *Vocabulaire codicologique*. Institut de recherché et d'histoire des textes. http://vocabulaire.irht.cnrs.fr/vocab.htm.

Oertzen, Christine von. [2009]. "New Ways of Using Digital Images: Recommendations Concerning the Free Use of Visual Media for Scholarly Purposes." Max Planck Institute. Accessed 23 October 2009. http://www.mpiwg-berlin.mpg.de/en/news/features/feature4/.

Oertzen, Christine von, and Kelly Wilder. 2008. "Scholarly Publishing and the Issues of Cultural Heritage, Fair Use, Reproduction Fees and Copyrights." Berlin: Max Planck Institute. PDF. http://www.mpiwg-berlin.mpg.de/PDF/MPIWGWorkshop1-2008Report.pdf.

Opas-Hänninen, Lisa Lena, Mikko Jokelainen, Ilkka Juuso, and Tapio Seppänen, eds. 2008. *Digital Humanities 2008: Book of Abstracts.* Oulu: University of Oulu.

Padfield, Tim. 2007. *Copyright for Archivists and Records Managers.* London: Facet Publishing.

Page, R. I. 1992. "On the Feasibility of a Corpus of Anglo-Saxon Glosses: The View from the Library." In *Anglo-Saxon Glossography: Papers Read at the International Conference Held in the Koninklijke Academie voor Wetenschappen, Letteren en Schone Kunsten van België, Brussels, 8 and 9 September 1986*, edited by R. Derolez, 77–96. Brussels: Paleis der Academiën.

Petrucci, Armando. 1984. "La scrittura riprodotta." *Scrittura e Civiltà* 8:263–67.

Pfaff, R. W. 1977. "M. R. James on the Cataloguing of Manuscripts: A Draft Essay of 1906." *Scriptorium* 31:103–18.

Pierazzo, Elena, and Peter A. Stokes. 2011. "Putting the Text Back into Context: A Codicological Approach to Manuscript Transcription." In *Kodikologie und Paläographie im digitalen Zeitalter — Codicology and Paleography in the Digital Age* II, edited by Franz Fischer, Patrick Sahle et al., 397–430. Norderstedt: Books on Demand.

Pickwoad, Nicholas. 2009. "Bookbindings: The Missing Piece in the Bibliographical Jigsaw." Lecture, University of Cambridge, 16 February.

Pitti, Daniel V. 2004. "Designing Sustainable Projects and Publications." In Schreibman, Siemens, and Unsworth, eds., 471–87.

Pratesi, A. 1998. "Commentare Bischoff: un secondo intervento." *Scrittura e Civiltà* 22:405–8.

Roberts, Jane. 2005. *Guide to Scripts Used in English Writings up to 1500*. London: British Library.

Robinson, P. R., ed. 1988. *Catalogue of Dated and Datable Manuscripts, c. 737–1600, in Cambridge Libraries*. 2 vols. Cambridge: D. S. Brewer.

Robinson, Peter. 2009. "What Text Really Is Not, and Why Editors Have to Learn to Swim." *Literary and Linguistic Computing* 24:41–52.

Robinson, Peter, and Elizabeth Solopova. 1993. "Guidelines for Transcription of the Manuscripts of the Wife of Bath's Prologue." In *The Canterbury Tales Project: Occasional Papers*, edited by N. F. Blake and Peter Robinson, 19–52. Oxford: Oxford University Computing Services, Office for Humanities Communication. PDF. http://www.canterburytalesproject. org/pubs/op1-transguide.pdf.

Rosenkilde & Bagger. 2007. Early English Manuscripts in Facsimile: Price List. http://www.rosenkilde-bagger.dk/Early%20English%20Pricelist.htm.

Rumble, Alexander R. 1994. "Using Anglo-Saxon Manuscripts." In *Anglo-Saxon Manuscripts: Basic Readings*, edited by Mary P. Richards, 3–24. New York: Garland.

_____ [2005]a. "The Paleographical Material in the C11 Database." In Scragg et al. 2005. Accessed 23 October 2009. http://www.arts. manchester.ac.uk/mancass/C11database/data/PalaeogIntro.pdf.

_____ 2005b. "Paleography, Scribal Identification and the Study of Manuscript Characteristics." In *Care and Conservation of Manuscripts: Proceedings of the 8th International Seminar*, edited by Gillian Fellows-Jensen and Peter Springborg, 217–28. Copenhagen: Museum Tusculanum Press.

_____ 2006. "The Study of Anglo-Saxon Manuscripts, Collections and Scribes: In the Footsteps of Wanley and Ker." In *Writing and Texts in Anglo-Saxon England*, edited by Alexander R. Rumble, 1–17. Cambridge: D.S. Brewer.

Schipper, William. 2004. "Digitizing (Nearly) Unreadable Fragments of Cyprian's 'Epistolary'." *In The Book Unbound: Editing and Reading Medieval Manuscripts and Texts*, edited by Siân Echard and Stephen Partridge, 159–68. Toronto: University of Toronto Press.

Scragg, D. G., Alexander R. Rumble, Kathryn Powell, Susan D. Thompson, and Joana Soliva. 2005. MANCASS C11 Database Project. Manchester Centre for Anglo-Saxon Studies. http://www.arts.manchester.ac.uk/ mancass/C11database/.

Sculley, D., and Bradley M. Pasanek. 2008. "Meaning and Mining: The Impact of Implicit Assumptions in Data Mining for the Humanities." *Literary and Linguistic Computing* 23:409–24.

Seppänen, Tapio. 2006. "Multimedia Information Retrieval." In *Digital Humanities 2006: Conference Abstracts*, edited by Chengan Sun, Sabrina Menasri, and Jérémy Ventura, i. Paris: Centre Cultures Anglophones et Technologies d l'Information (CATI).

Smith, A. H. 1938–39. "The Photography of Manuscripts." *London Medieval Studies* 1:179–207.

Spunar, Pavel. 1958. "Définition de la paléographie." *Scriptorium* 12:108–10.

Stanford University. 2008. "Copyright and Fair Use." Stanford University Libraries. http://fairuse.stanford.edu/.

Stokes, Peter A. 2005. "English Vernacular Script, ca. 990 – ca. 1035." 2 vols. PhD diss., University of Cambridge.

_____ 2007/8. "Paleography and Image Processing: Some Solutions and Problems." *Digital Medievalist* 3: http://www.digitalmedievalist.org/ journal/3/stokes/.

_____ 2008. "King Edgar's Charter for Pershore (AD 972)." *Anglo-Saxon England* 37:31–78.

_____ 2009. "Computer-Aided Paleography: Present and Future." In *Kodikologie und Paläographie im digitalen Zeitalter — Codicology and Paleography in the Digital Age*, edited by Malte Rehbein, Patrick Sahle, and Torsten Schaßan, 313–42. Norderstedt: Books on Demand.

_____ 2010. "Scripts." In *Handbook of Medieval Studies: Terms, Methods, Trends*, edited by Albrecht Classen, 2:1217–33. 3 vols. Berlin: De Gruyter.

_____ 2011a. "Recovering Anglo-Saxon Erasures: Some Questions, Tools and Techniques." In *Palimpsests and the Literary Imagination of Medieval England*, edited by R. Chai-Elsholz, T. Silec, and L. Carruthers, 35–60. New York: Palgrave.

_____ 2011b. "Teaching Manuscripts in the Digital Age." In *Kodikologie und Paläographie im digitalen Zeitalter — Codicology and Paleography in the Digital Age* II, edited by Franz Fischer, Patrick Sahle et al., 229–45. Norderstedt: Books on Demand.

Tanselle, G. Thomas. 1989. "Reproductions and Scholarship." *Studies in Bibliography* 42:25–54.

Terras, Melissa. 2006. *Image to Interpretation: An Intelligent System to Aid Historians in Reading the Vindolanda Tablets.* Oxford: Oxford University Press.

_____ 2008. *Digital Images for the Information Professional.* Farnham: Ashgate.

_____ 2011. "Artefacts and Errors: Acknowledging Issues of Representation in the Digital Imaging of Ancient Texts." In Fischer and Sahle et al., eds., 43–62.

Terras, Melissa, and Paul Robertson. 2004. "Downs and Acrosses: Textual Markup on a Stroke Level." *Literary and Linguistic Computing* 19:397–414.

Thompson, Susan D. 2006. *Anglo-Saxon Royal Diplomas: A Palaeography.* Woodbridge: Boydell.

Traube, Ludwig, Franz Johannes Boll, Paul Joachim Georg Lehmann, and Samuel Brandt. 1909–20. *Vorlesungen und Abhandlungen von Ludwig Traube.* 3 vols. München: Beck.

Treharne, Elaine M. 2007. "Writing the Book." Presented at English Manuscripts 1060–1220 Conference, 2 August 2007, London.

_____ Forthcoming. "The Good, the Bad, the Ugly: Old English Manuscripts and their Describers." In *The Genesis of Books: Studies in the Scribal Culture of Medieval England in Honour of A. N. Doane,* edited by Matthew Hussey and John D. Niles, chap. 11. Turnhout: Brepols.

Twycross, Meg. 2008. "Virtual Restoration and Manuscript Archaeology." In *The Virtual Representation of the Past,* edited by Mark Greengrass and Lorna Hughes, 23–48. Aldershot: Ashgate.

Wikimedia Commons. "Why Do We Allow the PD-Art Tag to be Used for Photographs From Any Country?" When to Use the PD-Art Tag.

Accessed 23 October 2009. http://commons.wikimedia.org/wiki/
Commons:When_to_use_the_PD-Art_tag#Why_do_we_allow_
the_.7B.7BPD-Art.7D.7D_tag_to_be_used_for_photographs_from_any_
country.3F.

Withers, Benjamin C. 2007. *The Illustrated Old English Hexateuch, Cotton Claudius
B.iv: The Frontier of Seeing and Reading in Anglo-Saxon England.* London:
The British Library.

Woods, Christopher S. 2006. "The Conservation of Parchment." In *Conservation
of Leather and Related Materials*, edited by Marion Kite and Roy Thomson,
200–24. London: Butterworth-Heinemann.

A Probabilistic Analysis of a Middle English Text[*]

Jacob Thaisen

Adam Mickiewicz University, Poznań / University of Stavanger

jacob.thaisen@uis.no

With the Norman Conquest of 1066, written English ceased to be employed for administrative and other official purposes, and the normative spelling conventions established for the West Saxon variety of Old English fell into disuse. When the language eventually began to regain these crucial domains around three centuries later, a supralocal norm for spelling in English no longer existed. The only models available to writers were the practices of other languages known to them or, increasingly as English strengthened its position, the conventions adopted in English texts to which they were exposed. As a result of the interaction of all these factors, Middle English—the vernacular of the period from the Conquest to William Caxton's 1476 introduction of printing from movable type—is characterized by considerable variation in spelling, even within the output of a single individual. There is nothing at all unusual about a single writer of this period representing one and the same word in more than one way, including frequent words such as the definite article and conjunctions. Writers could even use the availability of variants to their own advantage in carrying out the task of committing words to parchment, for example, to adjust the length of lines or speed up the writing process.

The variability of Middle English spelling practices means it would be misguided to assume that two texts penned by a single individual necessarily follow, or should follow, identical spelling conventions, especially in terms

[*] The research reported in this paper is financially supported by the Polish Ministry of Education, grant N104 045 32/4256. I am grateful to my former colleagues in the Department of the History of English at Adam Mickiewicz University, Poznań, Merja Stenroos and other Stavanger-based members of the Middle English Grammar Project, as well as Karina van Dalen-Oskam, Nila Vázquez, Robert Lew, the four anonymous readers, and especially the editors of the present volume for their helpful feedback. I thank the editors of *Boletín Millares Carlo* for permission to reproduce Figure 2.

ISBN 978-0-86698-499-7 (online)   ISBN 978-0-86698-474-4 (print)

New Technologies in Medieval and Renaissance Studies 3 (2012) 171–200

of the proportional usage of variants for the same word. It is more prudent to view the spelling habits of any specific writer as characterized by variation within bounds. One should therefore be cautious in using spelling as a basis for stylometric analysis of Middle English, for example for attribution of a particular text to a particular individual.

A fundamental in stylometry is the concept of the *writer-invariant*: the assumption that specific properties of a given writer's texts are near-constant and so can be used to discriminate one writer from another. Examples of properties that scholars have proposed as invariant include frequency of various function words and preference for specific lexical items. For Middle English literary materials, the variation inherent in a writer's spelling is, however, only one of the two reasons why this assumption does not hold true. The other reason is that the bulk of these materials are scribal copies containing a mixture of forms carried over from the exemplar and forms introduced by the scribe. The work of Angus McIntosh, which culminated in *A Linguistic Atlas of Late Mediaeval English* (McIntosh et al. 1986), has shown that the late medieval scribe who set out faithfully to reproduce his exemplars at the level of spelling was a rare creature. Typically, scribal copies are near-duplicates of their exemplars only at the levels of the lexicon and syntax, especially word order.

Scribes felt free to impose their own spelling habits on the text they were copying, but they inserted their own forms with varying degrees of thoroughness and under certain constraints of their exemplars. Rhyming position, for example, was so strong a constraint that it often produced distinct usage; indeed, Michael Benskin and Margaret Laing (1981) draw a parallel to the sociolinguistic situation of diglossia (the use of distinct dialects or languages for non-overlapping purposes within a language community) in describing the effects of constraints on a scribe's selection of spelling form in a given position in a verse line. A particularly well-known instance comes from folio 41r of British Library, MS Cotton Nero A.x with the unique copy of the anonymous poem *Pearl*. This page contains the line "More and more and ʒet wel mare" with *more* spelt with "o" initially and medially but with "a" finally. A reasonable hypothesis is that the "a" form was found in the exemplar in all three positions, but that in line-final position a desire to preserve the rhyme with "fare" *go* (preterite) two lines further on overrode the scribe's tendency to introduce forms from his own repertoire. These conditions require that stylometric comparison of texts for the purpose of identifying and isolating distinct usage(s) be based on probability rather than certainty. The probabilistic methods that are a keystone in statistically based machine translation, spell-checking, optical character recognition, and other natural language processing applications have the desired ability to predict the possible variations on a single datum.

This chapter describes how a probabilistic modeling method can be applied in stylometric analysis to trace a change in spelling in a manuscript copy of a longer Middle English literary work in a single scribal hand and ultimately determine the number of exemplars drawn upon in the production of that copy. In what follows, I contrast conventional, more qualitative methodology with the quantitative one I here propose, before turning to that scribal copy as a case study to evaluate the evidence it provides. My principal argument is that while quantitative and qualitative methods may produce equivalent results, greater promptness and ease characterize the application of the former.

Linguistic mixedness in medieval English texts

A scholar may wish to study the spelling practices preserved in a scribal copy of a text. Knowing the spelling habits of the author of the text or of the scribe of the copy, or scribes of previous copies in the text's transmission history, would aid the scholar in this study, as this knowledge would provide a standard of reference. But the many influences on how a scribe spells, which include the exemplar(s), mean that the copy furnishes the scholar with no direct evidence of the unconstrained spelling habits of either the author or scribes past or present. What the scholar can readily identify, isolate, and use as the starting point for analysis are stretches of text that are distinct from other stretches of text with respect to spelling. It may be presumed that the various influences on the scribe's selection of spelling form were constant during the production of such a stretch, which I refer to as an "orthography."

A shift from one orthography to another, be it gradual or abrupt, accordingly indicates that some influence made itself felt on the scribe. The exemplar being such an influence, one orthography may result from a given scribe copying under the influence of exemplar A and another orthography from the same individual copying under the influence of exemplar B. A categorical switch between orthographies might, therefore, signal a change of exemplar. A gradual transition, on the other hand, might show the scribe increasingly either picking up forms from a single exemplar as he copies ("progressive transcription") or introducing his own forms in place of those he encountered in that exemplar ("progressive translation") (Benskin and Laing 1981).

Orthodox methods applied by historical linguists to separate orthographies from each other may be described as predominantly qualitative. Spelling forms are typically collected from samples of manuscript texts in response to a predesigned questionnaire and then arranged into tables for visual analysis. The various forms of the questionnaire items are sometimes recorded merely as being present or absent, but at other times their occurrence is quantified in absolute or relative terms; such quantitative data customarily are subjected only to simple statistical tests. It is apparent that the eventual outcome hinges on the amount of text analysed and the number of items considered.

A key method within this research tradition, centred on *A Linguistic Atlas of Late Mediaeval English*, is that of linking a text's spelling forms to their geographic distribution to assess that text's dialectal purity. This method was developed for the purpose of dialect mapping, but it can also be applied in studies of textual transmission to separate forms originating in the exemplar from forms introduced by the scribe, provided the two sets are dialectally distinct from one another. With the line from *Pearl*, for instance, consultation of a dialect map would reveal the spelling of the word *more* with the letter "a" used to represent the strongly stressed vowel to be typical of locations so much more northerly than those characterized by the "o" form that the historical linguist would hesitate to accept both forms as falling comfortably within the spelling habits of a single individual.

To separate a text into dialectal subsets, the researcher identifies the spelling forms with a specific set of lexical, phonological, and morphological variables with known geographically significant distributions, notably the few hundred mapped out in *A Linguistic Atlas of Late Mediaeval English*. This set contains powerful discriminators of dialect; yet variables from other classes could discriminate dialects equally powerfully. The example of the modern English quantifier *any*, which in Old English was the adjective *ǣnig*, illustrates this possibility. It is conventional in dialectal analysis to concentrate on the quality of the initial vowel in this word because of geographic variation in the operation, a century or two after the Norman Conquest, of a phonological process known as "trisyllabic shortening," which affected certain of its declensional forms, such as dative ones in "-um"; this is the sound change ultimately responsible for the stem vowel alternation in present-day standard British English *south* : *southern* and *Christ* : *Christmas*. It is, however, also conventional to pay little attention to the phonologically invariant medial consonant (spelled "n, nn") or final vowel (spelled "i, y, ie, ye"),[1] which might equally be subject to individual scribal preference or have dialectal distribution, as is recognized by Angus McIntosh (1963, 1974, and 1975) and Margaret Laing and Roger Lass (2006 and 2007).[2]

The practical feasibility of supplementing the established, predominantly qualitative methods for identifying and isolating orthographies with further variables and more data increases with the digital availability of diplomatic transcripts of medieval manuscripts. The same is true of the practicability of applying quantitative methods to the same problem or to related ones, such as how to reconstruct a text's transmission history from linguistic data. Recent years have witnessed a steady increase in the volume of such digital materials. The digital humanities community has responded by subjecting the lexical variation present in the texts to sophisticated computer-assisted analysis, although medieval spelling practices have attracted less attention. Computer-assisted quantitative studies of large bodies of medieval linguistic data are thus still few, but their potential for manuscript studies is significant.

A potential practical obstacle to the application of a quantitative method on a large data set is that the method may require prior qualitative classification of the data, such as lemmatization or part-of-speech tagging.[3] Meeting this requirement may come at an expense of time which should be weighed against the gain in accuracy as compared with more qualitative methods based on sparser data. Probabilistic modeling is different in that it requires

---

[1] Angus McIntosh et al. (1986, 4:28–29) record thirty-three different spelling forms for *any*, including forms with unhistorical initial "h," a variable not mentioned in my discussion.

[2] The use of a single symbol for both "y" and "þ" has been shown to have dialectal distribution (Benskin 1982).

[3] Examples of quantitative studies requiring substantial qualitative pre-processing of medieval linguistic data include Kari Anne Rand Schmidt (1993), Peter Robinson (1997), Antonio Miranda-García and Javier Calle-Martín (2005), and Karina van Dalen-Oskam and Joris van Zundert (2007). The texts tagged by the editors of *A Linguistic Atlas of Early Middle English, 1150–1325* (http://www.lel.ed.ac.uk/ihd/laeme1/laeme1.html, 2007) and *A Linguistic Atlas of Older Scots, Phase 1: 1380–1500* (http://www.lel.ed.ac.uk/ihd/laos1/laos1.html, accessed 23 October 2009) may likewise be mentioned, as may those comprising the MEG-C corpus available from the Middle English Grammar Project, March 16, 2011, http://www.uis.no/research/culture/the_middle_english_grammar_project/meg-c/.

very little pre-processing of data, and no pre-selection of variables. The discussion now turns to this family of methods.

Probabilistic modeling

Attributing a text to a writer, be it an author or a scribe, on linguistic grounds involves comparing it with other texts associated with that writer. For materials dating from before the introduction of printing from movable type, those other texts may be found within the same manuscript as the text for attribution, or they may be found in other manuscripts. It is, however, difficult to define a set of variables to compare because texts differ lexically. A frequently adopted solution is to make texts comparable by restricting the inquiry to specific variables within a specific lexical subset which texts may reasonably be expected to share, such as common lexical items like the words *more* and *any*. The probabilistic methods advocated in this chapter, by contrast, attain greater comprehensiveness because they exclude no available data. Since a particular text always is a sample of a particular orthography, one can use that text to estimate that orthography and then use this estimate—the probabilistic "model"—as the basis for comparison with other texts. This section explains how these methods assign probability to data.[4]

First one needs a text on which to base or "train" a model:

{min myne þin fyn nine pine wine}

With these training data and with the letter as the basic unit, the unconditional probability of the letter "p" is a quantification of the possibility of it occurring; that is, it is the letter's relative frequency in the training text. However, relative frequency alone has little potential as a distinctive attribute of this text. How "p" is used in context in the text has greater potential as a distinctive attribute. Context can be taken into consideration by working with conditional probability, but there is a question of how much context to consider. With these training data, the conditional probability of the letter "p" is a quantification of the possibility of it occurring after the specific, ordered sequence of letters "min myne þin fyn nine" and no other. But when the training data are a longer text with multiple occurrences, it becomes impracticable always to take account of the full sequence of preceding letters in computing conditional probability, so approximations are introduced as substitutes. A common way of approximating is to shorten the

---

[4] For a fuller introduction to probabilistic modeling, see chapter 6 of Gernot A. Fink (2008).

preceding sequences used in calculating conditional probability. A 2-gram probability is thus a widely used substitute in which the sequence of preceding letters is one letter long, and a 2-gram model is correspondingly simply an exhaustive listing of the 2-gram probabilities for all the training data. With 3-grams the sequence is two letters long, while with 4-grams it is three letters long, etc. With a 2-gram model built from the present training data, an accepted estimate of the probability of meeting the form "pine" is thus the product of each constituent letter's 2-gram probability:

$$P_{ML}(\text{"pine"}) = \frac{c(\text{"p"}|\text{BOW})}{c(\text{BOW})} \times \frac{c(\text{"i"}|\text{"p"})}{c(\text{"p"})} \times \frac{c(\text{"n"}|\text{"i"})}{c(\text{"i"})} \times \frac{c(\text{"e"}|\text{"n"})}{c(\text{"n"})} \times \frac{c(\text{EOW}|\text{"e"})}{c(\text{"e"})}$$

$$= \frac{1}{7} \times \frac{1}{1} \times \frac{5}{5} \times \frac{4}{8} \times \frac{4}{4}$$

$$= 1:14$$

Here "c" (for "count") denotes absolute occurrence in the training data, and "BOW" and "EOW" respectively mark the beginning and end of a word. The notation "$b|a$" indicates a 1-gram b given an immediately preceding 1-gram a (that is, a 2-gram ab).

A probability estimate is standardly expressed not as a probability, as might be expected from the foregoing, but instead as "perplexity." The two measures are equivalent, as the perplexity of the model is the reciprocal of the average probability per form—"14" in "1:14" in the above calculation. It is convenient to work with perplexity, as the measure is always a positive integer larger than 1, rather than a decimal. In the present paper, I prefer to talk in terms of probability when discussing forms and of perplexity when discussing models.

The resolution of training data into their constituents enables a model to assign probability to forms having those same constituents but missing from the training data. The higher the probability an unattested form receives, the more likely it is that the form belongs to the same orthography as the training data. The form "pyne" is thus unattested in the present training data but seems possible given that those data include a precedent for both the constituent "BOW-p" and the constituent "yne-EOW." The form seems, furthermore, more probable than the likewise possible but unattested form "ympen," since it constitutes a lesser violation of the graphotactics (the rules for how letters combine) inferable from the training data. However, a 2-gram model based on the present training data cannot resolve "pyne" satisfactorily:

$$P_{ML}\ (\text{"pyne"}) = \frac{c(\text{"p"}|\text{BOW})}{c(\text{BOW})} \times \frac{c(\text{"y"}|\ \text{"p"})}{c(\text{"p"})} \times \frac{c(\text{"n"}|\ \text{"y"})}{c(\text{"y"})} \times \frac{c(\text{"e"}|\ \text{"n"})}{c(\text{"n"})} \times \frac{c(\text{EOW}|\ \text{"e"})}{c(\text{"e"})}$$

$$= \frac{1}{7} \times \frac{0}{1} \times \frac{2}{2} \times \frac{4}{8} \times \frac{4}{4}$$

$$= 0$$

The subscript "ML" stands for "maximum likelihood" because the training data themselves have highest probability according to the estimates of this model, as indeed they should have intuitively, since they constitute the entire attested data. But it is unrealistic that "pine" should appear once in every fourteen words and "pyne" never occur at all in other natural-language texts attesting the same orthography as the training data. The maximum likelihood estimates themselves, therefore, inadequately model the orthography the training data represent.

A more realistic model can be constructed from the same training data by weighting them. The term used to describe this process is "smoothing." As this term suggests, weighting the data increases their uniformity: the overestimates for the attested forms ("pine") are lowered and the underestimates for forms which happen to be unattested ("pyne") are raised.[5] No form receives a zero probability, including forms comprising unattested constituents. Importantly, key properties of the training data stay intact so that, for example, a relationship like P("pine") > P("pyne") > P("ympen") continues to hold. No doctoring of data happens, only the employment of statistical means to simulate what the researcher does intuitively when working with spelling, such as accepting "pyne" but rejecting "ympen." What are those statistical means?

A simple example of a means of smoothing is to modify the equation for computing probability by adding the constant 1 to the total absolute occurrence for every item recorded in the training data:

---

[5] The maximum likelihood probability of the form "pyne" was zero because the constituent "py" was unattested in the training data. Since both "p" and "y" were attested, their respective probabilities could perhaps have been inserted as a substitute, a solution known as "back-off" which is used in certain methods.

$$P_{ADD}(b|a) = \frac{1+c(b|a)}{|V| + c(a)}$$

Here "$|V|$" (vocabulary size) is the number of distinct letters the training data include. Since $|V| = 9$ in the present case, applying this technique gives:

$$P_{ADD}(\text{"pine"}) = \frac{1+c(\text{"p"}|BOW)}{|V| + c(BOW)} \times \frac{1+c(\text{"i"}|\text{"p"})}{|V| + c(\text{"p"})} \times \frac{1+c(\text{"n"}|\text{"i"})}{|V| + c(\text{"i"})} \times \frac{1+c(\text{"e"}|\text{"n"})}{|V| + c(\text{"n"})} \times \frac{1+c(EOW|\text{"e"})}{|V| + c(\text{"e"})}$$

$$= \frac{1+1}{9+7} \times \frac{1+1}{9+1} \times \frac{1+5}{9+5} \times \frac{1+4}{9+8} \times \frac{1+4}{9+4}$$

$$\approx 1:825$$

$$P_{ADD}(\text{"pyne"}) = \frac{1+c(\text{"p"}|BOW)}{|V| + c(BOW)} \times \frac{1+c(\text{"y"}|\text{"p"})}{|V| + c(\text{"p"})} \times \frac{1+c(\text{"n"}|\text{"y"})}{|V| + c(\text{"y"})} \times \frac{1+c(\text{"e"}|\text{"n"})}{|V| + c(\text{"n"})} \times \frac{1+c(EOW|\text{"e"})}{|V| + c(\text{"e"})}$$

$$= \frac{1+1}{9+7} \times \frac{1+0}{9+1} \times \frac{1+2}{9+2} \times \frac{1+4}{9+8} \times \frac{1+4}{9+4}$$

$$\approx 1:2{,}593$$

It is a more reasonable simulation of real-life spelling preferences to estimate that the form "pine" should be produced once in every 825 words than it is to maintain it should turn up once in every fourteen words. It is also reasonable that the unattested form "pyne" now has a probability and that this probability is lower than that for the attested form "pine," which intuitively is correct given that the sequence "yn" is rarer than the sequence "in" in the training data.

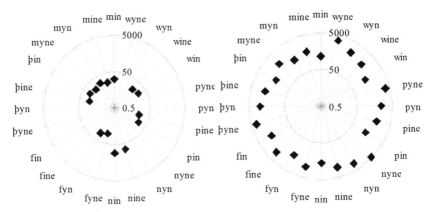

Figure 1: Unsmoothed (maximum likelihood, left) and smoothed (additively, +1, right) probabilities for a range of forms.

Figure 1 above shows the unsmoothed (maximum likelihood, "ML") and smoothed (additively, +1, "ADD") 2-gram probabilities for the forms hosted by the present training data as well as for other, similar forms. It can be seen that a number of forms, such as "wyne," "pyn," and "nyn," are absent from the unsmoothed series but present in the smoothed series. This is due to their maximum likelihood 2-gram probabilities being zero, just like that for the form "pyne," and for the same reason: lack of attestation of a constituent 2-gram in the training data. It can also be seen that the smoothed probabilities are lower and more evenly distributed than are the unsmoothed ones. And it is noticeable that a relationship P("Cin(e)") > P("Cyn(e)") holds for any consonant C, except in the case of the words *fine* and *mine*. The reason is that their forms "fyn" and "myne" are the only attested forms spelled with "y" in the training data: all other forms have "i." Figure 1 thus confirms that smoothing produces greater uniformity without loss of key properties of the training data.

Imagine a test text written in the same orthography as the training text but differing from it lexically. It is clear that an additively smoothed model is able to resolve this test text more satisfactorily than is an altogether unsmoothed model; that is, the smoothed model has a lower perplexity, as it is capable of assigning the test text a probability that is more realistic in view of the variable spelling habits characteristic of real-life Middle English. More refined smoothing techniques (several exist) lower a model's perplexity further, thus improving its ability to resolve test data.[6]

One of these techniques is that developed by Frederick Jelinek and Robert Mercer (1980), who weight training data according to the following equation:[7]

$$P_{JM}(b|a) = \lambda P_{ML}(b|a) + (1 - \lambda) P_{ML}(b)$$

(where $0 < \lambda \leq 1$)

Here, the smoothed probability of the 2-gram *ab* is based partly on the unsmoothed probability of the 2-gram *ab* and partly on the unsmoothed probability of the 1-gram *b*, the value of the constant λ determining the relative contributions of the addition's two parts. The innovation is that the 1-gram

---

[6] For a description of various smoothing techniques and a comparison of their performance, see Stanley F. Chen and Joshua T. Goodman (1998). See also the work referred to in n. 4.

[7] The equation is simplified.

level is brought into play, or "interpolated" to use the term found in the literature.

To illustrate why bringing in the 1-gram level improves the realism of a model of spelling, consider the analogous case of a model of lexis seeking to emulate naturally occurring present-day English. The lexical model is constructed from training data hosting identical occurrence of the word sequences "good time" and "good thyme," leading to their having equal maximum likelihood probability. Since, however, "time" is more frequent than "thyme" in actual usage, their identical occurrence in the position after "good" is evidently due to chance. The skew caused by the chance factor can be compensated for in modeling to achieve a more realistic distribution by factoring the occurrence of the individual words into the calculation of the probability for their occurring in sequence. Interpolation by means of the Jelinek-Mercer equation effects this factoring in and thus rectifies such accidentally unrepresentative distributions in training data. This rectifying ability of interpolation makes it a key instrument in modeling spelling data collected from a Middle English manuscript, since letters collocate just like words do: for instance, as in today's standard spelling, the letter sequence "sl" was more frequent in medieval times than "sr," and a word-separating space was more likely to be preceded by the letter "e" than "o." The other reason it is advantageous to interpolate is that distributions of letters that accidentally misrepresent the spelling habits they exemplify are likely to be prominent in training data because of the restricted length of a manuscript text. The more diverse the training texts and the greater their volume, the more representative they are of the orthography they represent.

Another technique, introduced by Ian Witten and Timothy Bell (1991), is the one applied in the present study. This technique smoothes according to an equation resembling that developed by Jelinek and Mercer but including a mechanism for treating a 2-gram like a 1-gram. It is useful to do so when a 2-gram contains a 1-gram that hardly ever occurs outside the context of that particular 2-gram. Such a behaviour characterizes the right-hand element in "accent aigu," "bar mitzvah," and "cast aspersions" from present-day English lexis, while instances from medieval English spelling practices include the right-hand element in the forms "þᵉ" (for the word *the*), "þᵘ" (for the word *thou*), "þˢ" (for the word *thus*), and "wᵗ" (for the word *with*) (the superscript symbols are regarded as distinct from the alphabetic letters they resemble). Middle English also comprises now-obsolete symbols representing fixed sequences of two or more letters. Among these symbols, "ₚ" (for the letter sequence *pro*) and "9" (for the sequences *con* or *com*) are further instances of bound distributions since they will nearly always be preceded by a space (a space is regarded as a letter with no probability of its own). In smoothing the probability of a given 2-gram *ab*, Witten and Bell handle such collocations by letting the value of λ, which determines the relative contributions of the two addends in the smoothing equation, be dictated by how many alternatives to the constituent *a* can occupy the slot immediately to the left of constituent *b* according to the training data. Taking the number of alternatives into account redefines λ as a variable rather than a constant, since its value will vary from one 2-gram to another. The redefinition increases the realism of a model because, without it, these fixed 2-grams are underestimated as the result of their receiving the product of the probability of their constituents as their probability. Witten and Bell, however, worked in text compression and did not have Middle English spelling in mind when they developed their smoothing technique. Their fundamental idea in deriving their equation was that unattested 1-grams could be best estimated from the occurrence of rare 1-grams in training data.

3-grams are used for the stylometric analysis of the present data, rather than the 2-grams used in these introductory remarks for ease of illustration. The probability computed for a given 1-gram *c* is thus not made conditional upon the immediately preceding 1-gram *b* but the immediately preceding 2-gram *ab*. The reason for building 3-gram models rather than 2-gram ones is that piloting has established that the longer grams yield a clearer result, although the difference is slight.

Stylometric analysis of Middle English spelling practices would benefit from improved smoothing of models. As compared with unsmoothed models, models smoothed according to the Jelinek-Mercer or Witten-Bell methods attractively offer probability estimates that are more independent of the training text's lexis. Yet, the improved independence is unequally distributed in a model. The Witten-Bell method of smoothing, for example, addresses fixed 2-letter sequences in which the sequence's first letter is predictable from its second letter. Fixed 2-letter sequences of this type are certainly common in Middle English, but so are ones in which the sequence's second letter is predictable from its first letter; thus "ꝉ" (for *l* or *le*), "ħ" (for *h* or *he*), "ꝛ̃" for (*r* or *re*), "n̄ꝺ" (interpretation unclear), "p̄" (for *p* or *ppe*), "ꝭ" (for *is*), "ꝰ" (for *us*), and "⁊" (for *et*) will all almost invariably be followed by a space in just the same way as, at the lexical level, "abominable," "bated," and "litmus" will precede "snowman," "breath," and "test," respectively, in most contexts in present-day English. In addition, both smoothing techniques lack a means to normalize the length of spelling forms. Since the techniques essentially assign to a form the product of the individual probabilities of its constituent letters as its probability, the longer forms "sche" (for the word *she*) and "shaƚƚ" (for the word *shall*) receive a lower probability than their shorter counterparts "she" and "shal." Both smoothing techniques thus underestimate longer forms and correspondingly overestimate shorter ones. The realism of a model and its accuracy in resolving test data would improve if the technique used for smoothing it treated both types of fixed 2-letter sequence as if the sequence was a single letter, and if it held the probability of functionally equivalent forms to be constant irrespective of how many letters they contain.

A known corpus: A copy of The Canterbury Tales *containing two orthographies*

To show the applicability of probabilistic methods in stylometric analysis of Middle English for identification and isolation of orthographies, I set up a controlled study with a copy of Geoffrey Chaucer's unfinished composition *The Canterbury Tales* as the corpus. The particular copy of interest (*Gg*, henceforth) is found in Cambridge University Library, MS Gg.4.27, part 1, alongside other texts, and the control is the knowledge that *Gg* is written in a single scribal hand but contains two orthographies, almost certainly as the result of a change of exemplar (Thaisen 2005–06).[8] Moreover, the diverse poetic forms and miscellaneous narrative contents make the work linguistically diverse and thus good material for testing the ability of probabilistic models to reduce the effects of this diversity through smoothing of the models.[9] The composition is a collection of tales individually narrated by a motley company of personages and linked one to the next through the framework of a pilgrimage (invoked in the prologues). This content is organized in a prologue-tale-prologue-tale pattern and is commonly described as a poem, although parts are in prose. The verse parts mostly take the shape of open heroic couplets (enjambed rhyming couplets with a line-medial caesura), and they are usually written in pentameter, although some lines lack the initial stressed syllable. Two tales are in rhyme royal (seven-line stanzas rhyming "ababbcc"). If Witten-Bell smoothing can successfully produce comparability between sections of *Gg* in spite of its linguistic eclecticism and lexical diversity, and if perplexity of models is an adequate measure at all in comparative analysis of Middle English spelling data, the present analysis should confirm the existence of the two orthographies in *Gg*.

---

[8] The present section echoes Thaisen (2005–06), but rectifies several infelicities of presentation in that article.

[9] I recognize that optimum test data would of course have only one variable.

The various manuscript copies of *The Canterbury Tales* are non-identical: Some copies include text commonly attributed to Chaucer that others exclude, while still other copies add non-Chaucerian text ranging in length from single words to whole tales; the authorship of certain passages is disputed. Copies with otherwise identical poetic content order the content differently, and authorial variants exist; no manuscript copy contains all text accepted as Chaucerian. *Gg* comprises only text which editors would consider as belonging to the poem and include in a regular edition, whether or not Chaucer in fact wrote every word. *Gg* is, however, incomplete, for many folios containing both text and decoration (miniatures) have been excised. What survives of the poem does so mostly written on folios without decoration. The poem follows *Troilus and Criseyde* and is followed by the *Legend of Good Women*. It begins abruptly at line A37 on the final folio of quire 11 and may originally have been preceded by a frontispiece.[10] It ends with the *explicit* (words closing a textual unit) to "The Parson's Tale" on the first verso of quire 37 and may originally have been followed by the *Retraction*.

The manuscript (481 vellum folios) collects most of Chaucer's longer poetical works and several of his shorter poems into a single volume.[11] The customary dating of its production, which primarily rests on palaeographic and decorative features, is the second half of the first quarter of the fifteenth century (Parkes and Beadle 1979–80, 3:6–7), which is within a generation after the death of the poet. Scholars normally associate its production with East Anglia on various grounds. This date and place of origin make the manuscript an important witness to the early transmission of Chaucerian poetry outside the London-Westminster area from which the earliest copies stem.

It was *Gg*'s combination of two orthographies that occasioned the selection of this text as the corpus for the present study. In my previous study (Thaisen

---

[10] The line numbering system here used is that of the Riverside editions (F. Robinson 1933 and 1957; Benson 1987), which is standard in Chaucer scholarship, although competitors exist. The system divides the poem into a number of fragments "A" to "I" and through-lineates the lines within each fragment. Hence, A37 refers to line 37 of Fragment A. See also the concluding section to the present chapter.

[11] A facsimile of the manuscript containing *Gg* was edited by Malcolm Parkes and Richard Beadle (1979–80) and includes a comprehensive account of the manuscript's palaeography, codicology, illumination, and other features. Other bibliographical descriptions of it are available in John M. Manly and Edith Rickert (1940), Daniel W. Mosser (1996), and Michael C. Seymour (1997). The manuscript has received a fair amount of scholarly attention; see Takako Kato (2008) for a recent overview.

2005–06), I identified and isolated the two orthographies by visual analysis of a comprehensive map showing how several hundreds of spelling forms are distributed in the text. Semi-automatic compilation of this map was made practicable by the availability of an electronic transcript of *Gg* and the index of spelling forms per word included on Peter Robinson's (2004) all-witness CD-ROM edition of "The Miller's Tale." This index includes every spelling form of every word found in the fifty-eight extant pre-1500 witnesses to both the tale and its prologue. To generate the map, I arranged some 23,000 possible spelling forms of the 280 headwords in the questionnaire developed for *A Linguistic Atlas of Late Mediaeval English* into a MySQL table, and next executed a script to record, in another MySQL table, which of those forms occurred in which locations in *Gg*. The map provided examples of random fluctuation in distribution between variants for the same headword, as may be expected from the amount of spelling variation generally found in Middle English. However, this map also revealed that a shift from one form to another took place in the same location in the text for numerous headwords, and visual comparison of the forms concerned permitted me to isolate the variable features in them and subsequently chart their occurrence irrespective of headword. Such coincident shifts are unlikely to be random in origin. Since codicological and textual evidence also indicated a discontinuity in the same location in *Gg* and palaeographic evidence favoured a single scribal hand, I attributed the shift to a change of exemplar.

The changeover falls near the junction of the narratives of the Summoner ("SU") and the Clerk ("CL"). It is especially visible in a reversal of the preference for "þ" and "eCe/oCe" as against "th" and "eeC/ooC" (where "C" represents any consonantal letter), as can be gleaned from Figure 2 below, which shows the distribution of "þ," "ee," and "oo" in *Gg*. It is also observable in a similar reversal of the forms used for certain less-frequent headwords: for example, "be-" in *before* and *between*, "sen(e)/sens" for *since*, and "nat" for *not* relative to "bi-/by," "sith-/syth," and "not," respectively. Note that the two sets include spelling differences that are phonologically invariant ("þ" vs. "th") as well as ones that are phonologically variant ("a" vs. "o" in *not*).

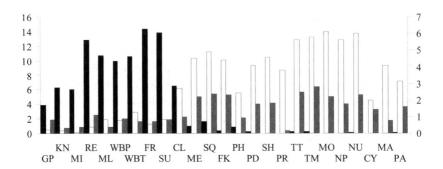

Figure 2. Occurrence, by tale, of "ee" (White: 2,677 Occurrences), "oo" (Grey: 1,327 occurrences), and "þ" (Black: 3,263 occurrences) in *Gg* (per thousand characters.) "ee" and "oo" plot on the right vertical axis. *Note*: In figures 2, 3, and 4 all prologues except for the *Wife of Bath's Prologue* are omitted from consideration. "The Cook's Tale" is lost through the mutilation to *Gg*. *Source*: Reprinted, by permission, from Thaisen (2005–06, 384).

My identification and isolation of the two orthographies was thus achieved by extending conventional, predominantly qualitative methodology in a quantitative direction. To begin with, the forms were exclusively analysed for their distribution within *Gg*, never for their dialect, as is traditionally the case. Their distribution was typically not considered independently but rather in relation to that of other forms with which they could be substituted, like "oCe" can be with "ooC" in *book, took*, and similar lexical items. Moreover, it was discovered that spelling differences between forms not readily elicited by the questionnaire used for *A Linguistic Atlas of Late Mediaeval English* in fact had significant distributions. The phonologically invariant spelling differences are a specific example. Visual comparison of forms led me to isolate the variable features in them and then chart the distribution of those features. This process effectively generated a revised questionnaire through collapsing forms originally collected under items separate in the questionnaire used for *A Linguistic Atlas of Late Mediaeval English*. The features were always shorter than the word hosting them, such as "ee" in any lexical item, resulting in higher numbers of attestations and therefore more robust distributions. Since the availability of an electronic transcript made it practicable to collect all forms of all questionnaire items, the volume of data far exceeded what is typically collected from manuscripts. Data collection was, however, still a prolonged process, and it required some investment of time to effect the iterative process of first visually identifying and isolating variable features and then collapsing questionnaire items. By contrast, probabilistic models can be constructed and perplexities obtained both effortlessly and expeditiously.

It is useful to review the non-linguistic evidence supporting the change of exemplar, so as to contextualize it. This evidence comprises (a) codicological features, which I analysed visually from digitized images in conjunction with descriptions in manuscript catalogues,[12] and (b) textual features examined by other scholars. To begin with the former, there is evidence to suggest a hiated copying process in how the text of *Gg* is arranged on the quires it occupies. A manuscript's quires always provide important clues to the order of their copying and any physical divisions present in the source materials. One such clue is a blank at the end of a quire in combination with the start of a new textual unit at the top of the first recto folio of the subsequent quire. Such a coincident quire/textual boundary may come about accidentally, but it more typically results from hiated, possibly non-consecutive, copying of text onto quires which were only subsequently arranged in the intended order due, for example, to piecemeal reception of source materials. The scribe of a manuscript thus copied may have attempted to remove the blank at the time the order of quires was decided so as to achieve an aesthetically pleasing presentation of the text he was copying, but he would have been unable to do so successfully unless a suitable number of lines were available to fill the blank.

In *Gg*, the junction of the Summoner's and Clerk's tales arguably coincides with a quire boundary, for before the mutilation, the prologue to "The Clerk's Tale" almost certainly commenced on the final folio of quire 20 after the last lines of "The Summoner's Tale," while the tale proper evidently started on the first recto of quire 21. The content of these two folios, both missing today, can be reconstructed with considerable confidence from that of the surviving folios that precede and follow them (fols. 241 and 244), and from the presence on the stub of folio 243 of a horse's tail, which is most probably what remains of a miniature once placed at the top of the page before line E57, where the Clerk's narrative begins after the prologue.

Signatures provide further codicological support for the *Gg* change of exemplar. These are annotations to indicate the intended order of the folios and quires. In the present manuscript, like in most other manuscripts, they are placed in the footer area on the individual folio. Up to and including quire 20, every recto folio found in the first half of the quires containing text from *The*

---

[12] See n. 11 above.

Canterbury Tales is signed in the standard format "alphabetic letter + Arabic numeral," as if these quires somehow constituted an independent production unit (the quires being made up of sheets each folded once to make two folios, it was unnecessary to sign the folios in the latter half of the quires). From quire 21 to quire 37 (containing the end of the poem), the format of signatures is "arbitrary symbol + Roman numeral," if the quires and folios are signed at all.[13] Quire 21 also marks the beginning of a separate unit in terms of the preparation of the writing surface, as quires 17–19 and 21–23 were each batch-ruled, the latter twice because the original ink flaked off (Parkes and Beadle 1979–80, 3:39–40).

Lastly, in addition to this codicological support, the boundary between the two tales is coincident with a change in the textual affiliations. *Gg* is independently descended from the presumed archetype up to and including "The Summoner's Tale," but is related to the *Hengwrt* and *Ellesmere* manuscripts in all the remaining tales, according to textual scholars John M. Manly and Edith Rickert (1940, 1:175–76).[14] Textual agreement between manuscript copies could arise accidentally in individual locations, but repeat agreement over many folios is more likely to be genetic in origin.

Modeling the corpus: Gg's spelling

To enable me to compute and compare perplexity for sections of *Gg* against one another, the Canterbury Tales Project made available a digital transcript of this text conformant with the transcription principles detailed by Peter Robinson and Elizabeth Solopova (1993).[15] These principles are very suitable because they are designed to reproduce manuscript text faithfully at the level of the letter. They thus uphold a one-to-one relation between text and transcript at this level, except that they preserve the distinction emphatic (uppercase) versus non-emphatic (lowercase), which strictly is a feature

---

[13] I assume here that the signatures are contemporary with the scribe's work, although Malcolm Parkes and Richard Beadle (1979–80, 3:62–63) cautiously suggest that they were possibly added by a binder at work later in the fifteenth century, along with the catchwords. If these annotations post-date the scribal contribution to the manuscript, they served as an aid to the binder in assembling the manuscript, but it is difficult to see any reason for the first series to terminate with quire 20.

[14] *Hengwrt* and *Ellesmere* are, respectively, Aberystwyth, National Library of Wales, Peniarth MS 392 D, and San Marino, Huntington Library, MS El.26.C.9.

[15] The Canterbury Tales Project, Institute for Textual Scholarship and Electronic Editing, University of Birmingham, accessed 23 October 2009, http://canterburytalesproject.org.

of presentation. This faithfulness also extends to symbols unknown to the present-day English alphabet, such as the already mentioned "ᵱ" (for the letter sequence *pro*), "ꝯ" (for *con* or *com*), "ſ" (for *is*), and "ꝰ" (for *us*). Most other transcription systems reproduce the runic letters "þ" (thorn) and "ȝ" (yogh) and the emphatic form "ff" of the letter "f" but translate the remaining symbols into modern alphabetic form. Many systems accordingly replace the runic letter "ꝥ" (wynn) with "w," and where relevant they insert letters to expand abbreviated spelling forms ("ᵱ" = "pro," "wᵗ" = "with" with underlining used to represent editorially inserted letters) and suppress strokes deemed decorative in function in the particular context (the bar in "ƚɬ" and "ħ"). The values editors assign in interpreting these symbols, which pervade the Middle English corpus, can influence the validity of a probabilistic model, especially if the expansions are effected silently ("wᵗ" = "with" or "wyth"?).

My modeling tool is the SRI Language Modeling Toolkit (SRILM, henceforth; Stolcke 2002). SRILM is a Unix-based collection of scripts for estimating and evaluating language model types based on *n*-gram statistics and is freely available for non-commercial purposes from SRI International.[16] The toolkit takes a plain text file with the training data as its exclusive required input. Lists of context markers, permitted *n*-grams, and the like can also be optionally supplied as additional input in separate files.

In preparing the *Gg* transcript for modeling, I modified it slightly. One alteration was to insert a marker for word and verse-line boundaries. Another was to prune the transcript of all features irrelevant to the spelling of the Middle English comprised in the text of *The Canterbury Tales*: all words and phrases in Latin, punctuation marks, transcriber's annotations, and numerals. I also made emphatic letters non-emphatic and took out all words containing a special symbol indicating an illegible letter.

Next, I segmented the transcript of *Gg* into two separate series: one with the text divided into nineteen sections of equal length (40,000 bytes in terms of file size) to obtain data volumes deemed sufficient to produce reliable models and another with the division into tales maintained (the tales vary in length, from less than three hundred lines to more than 2,200) to represent the literary structure of the text. To demonstrate the applicability of probabilistic methods in stylometric analysis of Middle English texts, it was of interest to show that two segmentations of the same material would produce congruent results. Before dividing up the text, I removed all prologues

---

[16] SRI Language Modeling Toolkit, SRI International, accessed 23 October 2009, http://www.speech.sri.com/.

from both series, except for the tale-length "The Wife of Bath's Prologue" (all other prologues are much shorter). Issues in the textual history of the poem motivated this decision, including the disputed authorship of certain prologues, the fact that transposition of prologues is a feature of the poem's manuscript tradition, and the sometimes weak narrative integration of the prologues with the tales they introduce. Lastly, I instructed SRILM to build and smooth (using the Witten-Bell method) a 3-gram model for every section and tale, in each case by using the modified transcription of the given section or tale as the training data.

The toolkit could now use the transcriptions of the same sections and tales as test data and assign probability to all the forms occurring in them based on the models; it did so for every combination of model and section/tale in the two series. SRILM returned the average probability per form in the given section or tale, expressed as a perplexity. For the series with the nineteen equal-length sections, this computation produced a separate model for each section, and for every such model, a separate perplexity for every section. I established the mean perplexity and standard deviation for the nineteen perplexities obtained for each model, and repeated the procedure for the series with the tales. The box and whisker graphs in Figures 3 and 4 below present the results, with the diamond representing mean perplexity and the T-bar representing half a standard deviation, so that one upright T-bar and its reverse together indicate an interval of one standard deviation from the mean.

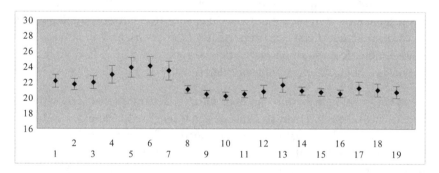

Figure 3. Mean perplexity and standard deviation,
by equal-length section, in *Gg*

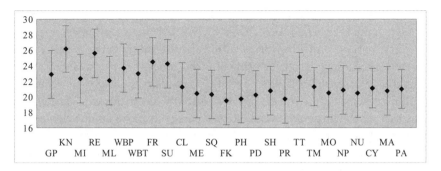

Figure 4. Mean perplexity and standard deviation, by tale, in *Gg*

In every case as one moves from left to right in Figure 3, the standard deviation interval for a section always imbricates the standard deviation interval for the following section. This distribution suggests the sections are samples of the same population. The sole exception is found between sections 7 and 8, where the pattern of continuous overlapping is interrupted. The interruption is coincident with a sudden drop in the length of the intervals, and the sections coming before it all have above-average mean perplexities, while only that of section 13 among the later ones rises slightly above this value. The "U test" devised by Henry B. Mann and Donald R. Whitney (1947) statistically assesses whether two population means come from the same population and is appropriate for the present data, since it does not presume test data are normally distributed. Its application returned a probability of less than 1:1,000 for the hypothesis that sections 1–7 and 8–19 of *Gg* are drawn from a single population (U = 84, n^1 = 7, n^2 = 12, P < 0.001, two-tailed). It will be recalled that the change of exemplar coincided with the junction of the Summoner's and Clerk's tales. Section 7 runs from line D1807 early in the *Summoner's Tale* ("SU") to line E708 late in the *Clerk's Tale* ("CL").

Figure 4, representing the series divided by tale, presents a similar picture with a drop in mean perplexity between the *Summoner's Tale* ("SU") and the *Clerk's Tale* ("CL"), again with the tales coming before this textual boundary invariably expressing a higher mean perplexity than those coming after it, except for the *Tale of Sir Thopas* ("TT"). The Mann-Whitney "U test" again gave less than 1:1,000 as the probability that one and the same population is present on either side of the boundary (U = 142, n^1 = 9, n^2 = 16, P < 0.001, two-tailed). The two series, therefore, provide congruent evidence for *Gg*'s containing two orthographies. However, in this second series, the tales of the Knight ("KN") and the Reeve ("RE") are aberrant, with unusually high mean perplexities. The extreme sparseness of the present training data renders models based on them especially vulnerable to local unevenness in the distribution of spelling forms within these training data. One may reasonably expect such local clustering of forms to characterize a tale or other narratively coherent unit, since specific vocabulary is likely to be repeated within each such unit. The *Reeve's Tale* certainly meets this expectation, for this narrative incorporates as an integral part of its plot a unique element in a pseudo-Northern dialect beside the regular element in the southerly dialect characterizing all other parts of the poem. Since this dialectal mixedness is conveyed through spelling, the tale includes a relatively high number of spelling variants by design, which raises the perplexity of a model founded on it. The deviation of the *Knight's Tale* is less readily explicable but may be to do with the amount of training data it supplied, the tale being much the longest verse tale.[17]

The alternative segmentation into equal-length units produces models that are more robust. This is because this division cuts across the poem's narrative boundaries and therefore supplies more evenly distributed training data; witness the absence of fluctuation in the pattern of imbrications around sections 1 to 5 in Figure 3 with the tales of the Knight and Reeve. So, while the evidence is unambiguous for *Gg*'s containing two orthographies, it is at the same time clear that the sparseness of the available data cannot be ignored in stylometric comparison of Middle English texts based on probabilistic models of their spelling patterns.

Evaluating the perplexities: Gg's two orthographies and the textual tradition *of Chaucer's* Canterbury Tales

Much previous scholarship maintains that the text of Chaucer's *Canterbury Tales* circulated as independent narrative units—commonly referred to as "fragments"—among scribes, even at several removes from the presumed archetype.[18] This is because comparison of how the various manuscripts order the poetic contents reveals fixed sequences of prologues and tales to be the basic units of transposition and inclusion/exclusion throughout the

---

[17] Both prose tales ("TM" and "PA") are longer than the *Knight's Tale*, yet have average mean perplexities and short standard deviation intervals. The likely reason is that the prose tales contain more repetition of phrasing than the verse tales.

[18] No book-length account of the textual tradition of Chaucer's *Canterbury Tales* has appeared in the past twenty years. For an argument favouring a single archetype, see Norman F. Blake (1985). For an argument favouring independent textual traditions for different parts of the poem, see Charles A. Owen (1991).

poem's manuscript tradition. The literary structure permits transposition because in the prologue-tale-prologue-tale pattern not every tale is linked to another through its prologue; indeed some tales have no prologue. The frequent reordering of the contents in the chain of scribal copying suggests that the narrative units of the poem reached scribes in a physical form readily permitting reordering. Loose sheets and quires have such a form, while bound codices do not.

One series of fragments identified through comparison of tale orders in the early manuscripts runs from "A" to "I" and is embodied in the line numbering system devised by Frederick Furnivall (1868) and adopted in the Riverside editions (F. Robinson 1933 and 1957; Benson 1987) with the "received" text. The correspondence between the fragments in this series and the inferable physical units of transmission is inexact, especially with respect to a few of the prologues; for example, despite their belonging to different fragments, lines E2419–2440 and F1–8 often occur in conjunction with one another in the manuscripts and could have occupied a separate exemplar sheet. As another example of the lack of exactitude in the proposed boundaries for the units of the poem's scribal transmission, John M. Manly and Edith Rickert (1940) use the line numbering system of the Riverside editions, but their exhaustive collation of the variations in text and tale order in all the surviving manuscripts leads them regularly to posit changes of exemplar within fragments.

That the poem circulated in such fragments is further suggested by their boundaries being sometimes discernible from breaks in the physical makeup of the individual manuscripts copied from them. An example is the breaks in the patterns of the signatures, quiring, and ruling which coincide with the boundary between the *Summoner's Tale* and the *Clerk's Tale* in *Gg*, as this location also forms the boundary between what are fragments "D" and "E" in the nomenclature of the Riverside editions. Similar breaks are found already in the earliest known manuscripts, such as Hengwrt, Ellesmere, and British Library, MS Harley 7334, all of which may have been started under Chaucer's supervision, although he may have died before their assembly was completed (Stubbs 2000 and 2007; Mooney 2006; Blake and Thaisen 2004). Regardless of precisely how many fragments there were, where their exact boundaries fell, and even what specific poetic material they included,[19] their occurrence so early in the textual tradition strongly suggests that a series of

---

[19] The issue of how to define the canonical text is open to interpretation, for slight differences exist in poetic contents (irrespective of their ordering) between the earliest known manuscripts.

them constituted the presumed archetype itself, which makes sense in the light of the unfinished nature of *The Canterbury Tales.*

However, a peculiarity about the possible derivation of most late medieval copies of the poem from fragments is that practically every scribe manifestly was able to obtain the complete canonical text (give or take a prologue or two) irrespective of his date and location, judging by the record of the surviving copies themselves. The eighty-four extant scribal copies are almost exclusively either complete codices or individual folios, rather than units corresponding more closely to any proposed fragment. This fact suggests that early in the textual transmission of the poem the fragments stopped circulating independently, even though they possibly remained physically distinct. *Gg*'s two orthographies are telling: they constitute evidence of multiple fragments having come together to form just two exemplars within a provincial area, already within a generation after Chaucer's death.

Conclusion

This chapter has exemplified the applicability of an established quantitative method from the domain of natural language processing—probabilistic modeling—in stylometric analysis of Middle English for identification and isolation of what I have termed orthographies—stretches of text that are distinct from other stretches of text with respect to spelling. There are no living consultants to draw on for Middle English, only written texts. That the sources for the language and its literature are all written makes their accurate decoding a primary task, but the variability of medieval spelling practices compels the researcher to practise the historical linguist's "art of making the best use of bad data" in pursuing this task (William Labov 1994, 1:11). An orthography is a key aid in this pursuit: because an orthography is relatively homogeneous, the presumption is that the various influences on its writer's spelling preferences were constant during its production. A shift from one orthography to another, be it gradual or abrupt, accordingly indicates that a parameter changed.

Such parameters are many and varied. As has been discussed above, a mere handful of the surviving Middle English texts record the naturally occurring or unconstrained spelling practices of an individual. Only a few texts are authorial holograph compositions. The bulk are scribal copies at one or more removes from the author. Scribes in the medieval period partly perpetuated spelling forms from their exemplars and partly inserted their own forms in their stead. The spelling conventions of any specific scribe or author were at the same time themselves variable without being random. Moreover, the influences on a scribe's or author's spelling also included the genre conventions of the text he was working on, its intended audience and function, his script, his writing implement, and his writing surface, as well as the more general circumstances of his text's production, such as whether a supervisor was present, a house style existed, payment was promised, or a deadline was approaching. Studying orthographies can thus provide insight into medieval text production and material culture.

Accurate decoding of Middle English materials is therefore not just about making sense of the actual symbols on the page. It is about establishing the evidential value of the materials as sources for the Middle English language and its literature. Applying a probabilistic modeling technique in stylometry can aid the scholar in determining the number of exemplars drawn upon in the production of a given scribal copy. The techniques can thus be useful for textual editors seeking to reconstruct the transmission history behind their scribal copy and its relationship with the presumed archetype. The historical linguist may likewise benefit from knowing how many orthographies a given scribal copy contains, so as to be able to assess its value as evidence for the written usage of an individual at a specific point in time and space.

However, orthodox, more qualitative means of analysis also serve this same purpose. In fact, applying a probabilistic modeling technique in stylometric analysis of Middle English does not in itself lead to identification and isolation of orthographies undetectable by those orthodox, more qualitative means. It is fair to claim, however, that its application considerably facilitates their objective detection. My original analysis included collection and subsequent visual analysis of a larger body of data than has tended to be standard. This first step led to formation of a hypothesis that two orthographies were present in *Gg* and to identification and isolation of the spelling features that show their likely presence. This step was followed by a second round of data collection from the electronic transcript of *Gg*, recording only attestations of those features. This second step amounted to tailoring the general questionnaire used for *A Linguistic Atlas of Late Mediaeval English* to the specific materials at hand and involved extending the questionnaire to include new features. A specific class of these new features comprises pairs of forms that show an orthographic contrast but no phonological one; this class of forms appears to contain strong indicators of the presence of distinct orthographies, but has yet to be shown to be of value in dialect mapping. The second step strengthened the hypothesis that *Gg* contained two orthographies, and consideration of textual and codicological data confirmed it. The insight was not easily gained.

By contrast, data collection for the probabilistic analysis was both speedy and exhaustive. It was effected entirely automatically and required little pre-processing of the *Gg* transcript. Every gram was collected, rather than spelling forms of pre-selected items only. Perplexity was automatically computed on the basis of all the collected grams to obtain a quantified measure of similarity between the sections of *Gg*. This similarity would in a more conventional analysis be argued from visually identified correspondences between the sections with respect to the occurrence of spelling forms. Visual identification of correspondences characterized this probabilistic analysis too, but only at a later stage in the data analysis: the formation of the hypothesis about the existence of the two orthographies in *Gg* was based on visual analysis of the plots contrasting the mean perplexities and standard deviations for the sections and models (Figs. 3 and 4). Statistical testing subsequently confirmed this hypothesis. A probabilistic analysis might therefore be considered more objective.

With the potential to gain fresh, or at least more accurate, insight and with the practical advantage that transcripts of many important texts are already digitally available, a desideratum in future probabilistic modeling of Middle English spelling is the development and software implementation of improved smoothing techniques. The absolute frequency of occurrence of letters and letter sequences in a training text determines their unsmoothed probability in a model based on that training text; but absolute frequency characterizes an orthography poorly, since it is a function of the training text's lexis. Smoothing seeks to solve this issue by statistically manipulating a model of spelling forms to make it independent of the training text's lexis. The Witten-Bell equation produces this independence by factoring in what is effectively a qualitative element: the number of different combinations in which the given letter or letter sequence is found in the training data. However, while sufficient for successfully identifying and isolating the two orthographies present in *Gg*, the equation inadequately models certain characteristics of medieval English spelling practices: it assigns too low a probability to longer spelling forms and fails to recognize the bound distribution of certain letters.

It would be feasible, with comparatively little investment of time, to construct probabilistic models of every digitally available text dating from before the standardization of English spelling with a view to computing and comparing their perplexity. However, a cautionary note is in order, as even reliable editions of Middle English manuscript materials differ in transcription principles. For example, when a manuscript has "nacoñ" for *nation*, the representations accepted by editors include "nacoun" and "nacion" with editorially inserted letters underlined, not to mention "nacion" with silent expansion of "ñ." Differences of this kind matter little when one bases a probabilistic analysis on a single source, as the editor will have imposed a consistent representation. But they complicate comparative analysis of texts from different sources, as they mean that the requirement of full compatibility between the transcripts of those sources is not met. One should therefore exercise caution in identifying what manuscript transcripts constitute a suitable basis for stylometric analysis of Middle English.

WORKS CITED

Benskin, Michael. 1982. "The Letters 'þ' and 'y' in Later Middle English, and Some Related Matters." *Journal of the Society of Archivists* 7:13–30.

Benskin, Michael, and Margaret Laing. 1981. "Translations and 'mischsprachen' in Middle English Manuscripts." In *So Meny People Longages and Tonges: Philological Essays in Scots and Mediaeval English Presented to Angus McIntosh*, edited by Michael Benskin and Michael L. Samuels, 55–106. Edinburgh: Middle English Dialect Project.

Benson, Larry D., ed. 1987. *The Riverside Chaucer*. Boston: Houghton Mifflin.

Blake, Norman F. 1985. *The Textual Tradition of the "Canterbury Tales."* London: E. Arnold.

Blake, Norman F., and Jacob Thaisen. 2004. "Spelling's Significance for Textual Studies." *Nordic Journal of English Studies* 3:93–107.

Chen, Stanley F., and Joshua T. Goodman. 1998. *An Empirical Study of Smoothing Techniques for Language Modeling*. Technical Report TR-10-98, Harvard University. http://research.microsoft.com/en-us/um/people/joshuago/publications.htm.

Dalen-Oskam, Karina van, and Joris van Zundert. 2007. "Delta for Middle Dutch: Author and Copyist Distinction in 'Walewein'." *Literary and Linguistic Computing* 22:345–62.

Fink, Gernot A. 2008. *Markov Models for Pattern Recognition: From Theory to Applications*. Berlin: Springer.

Furnivall, Frederick J. 1868. *A Temporary Preface to the Six-Text Edition of Chaucer's "Canterbury Tales": Part I, Attempting to Show the True Order of the Tales, and the Days and Stages of the Pilgrimage, etc., etc.* London: Trübner.

Jelinek, Frederick, and Robert Mercer. 1980. "Interpolated Estimation of Markov Source Parameters from Sparse Data." In *Proceedings of the Workshop on Pattern Recognition in Practice*, edited by Edzard S. Gelsema and Laveen N. Kanal, 381–97. Amsterdam: Elsevier.

Kato, Takako. 2008. "Corrected Mistakes in *MS Gg.4.27*." In *Design and Distribution of Late Medieval Manuscripts in England*, edited by Margaret Connolly and Linne Mooney, 61–87. York: York Medieval Press.

Labov, William. 1994. *Principles of Linguistic Change: Volume 1: Internal Factors*. Oxford: Blackwell.

Laing, Margaret, and Roger Lass. 2006. "Early Middle English Dialectology: Problems and Prospects." In *Handbook of the History of English*, edited by Ans van Kemenade and Bettelou Los, 417–51. Oxford: Blackwell.

_____, comps. 2007. *A Linguistic Atlas of Early Middle English, 1150–1325*. University of Edinburgh. http://www.lel.ed.ac.uk/ihd/laeme1/laeme1.html.

Manly, John M., and Edith Rickert, eds. 1940. *The Text of the "Canterbury Tales": Studied on the Basis of All Known Manuscripts*. 8 vols. Chicago: Chicago University Press.

Mann, Henry B., and Donald R. Whitney. 1947. "On a Test of Whether One of Two Random Variables Is Stochastically Larger Than the Other." *Annals of Mathematical Statistics* 18:50–60.

McIntosh, Angus. 1963. "A New Approach to Middle English Dialectology." *English Studies* 44:1–11.

_____ 1974. "Towards an Inventory of Middle English Scribes." *Neuphilologische Mitteilungen* 75:602–24.

_____ 1975. "Scribal Profiles from Middle English Texts." *Neuphilologische Mitteilungen* 76:218–35.

McIntosh, Angus, Michael L. Samuels, and Michael Benskin, with the assistance of Margaret Laing and Keith Williamson. 1986. *A Linguistic Atlas of Late Mediaeval English.* Aberdeen: Aberdeen University Press.

Miranda-García, Antonio, and Javier Calle-Martín. 2005. "The Validity of Lemma-Based Lexical Richness in Authorship Attribution: A Proposal for the *Old English Gospels.*" *ICAME Journal* 29:41–55.

Mooney, Linne R. 2006. "Chaucer's Scribe." *Speculum: A Journal of Medieval Studies* 81:97–138.

Mosser, Daniel W. 1996. "Witness Descriptions." In *The "Wife of Bath's Prologue" on CD-ROM*, edited by Peter Robinson. Cambridge: Cambridge University Press.

Owen, Charles A. 1991. *The Manuscripts of the "Canterbury Tales."* Cambridge: D. S. Brewer.

Parkes, Malcolm B., and Richard Beadle, eds. 1979–80. *The Poetical Works of Geoffrey Chaucer: A Facsimile of Cambridge University Library MS Gg.4.27.* 3 vols. Norman: Pilgrim Books, in association with D. S. Brewer, Cambridge.

Rand Schmidt, Kari Anne. 1993. *The Authorship of the "Equatorie of the Planetis."* Cambridge: D. S. Brewer.

Robinson, Fred N., ed. 1933. *The Complete Works of Geoffrey Chaucer.* Boston: Houghton Mifflin.

_____, ed. 1957. *The Works of Geoffrey Chaucer.* Boston: Houghton Mifflin.

Robinson, Peter. 1997. "A Stemmatic Analysis of the Fifteenth-Century Witnesses to the *Wife of Bath's Prologue.*" In *The "Canterbury Tales Project" Occasional Papers*, Vol. 2, edited by Norman F. Blake and Peter Robinson, 2:69–132. London: Office for Humanities Communication.

_____, ed. 2004. *The "Miller's Tale" on CD-ROM.* Leicester: Scholarly Digital Editions.

Robinson, Peter, and Elizabeth Solopova. 1993. "Guidelines for Transcription of the Manuscripts of the *Wife of Bath's Prologue.*" In *The "Canterbury Tales Project" Occasional Papers*, Vol. 1, ed. Norman F. Blake and Peter Robinson, 1:19–52. Oxford: Office for Humanities Communication.

Seymour, Michael C. 1997. *A Catalogue of Chaucer Manuscripts: Volume 2: The "Canterbury Tales."* Aldershot: Scolar Press.

Stenroos, Merja, Martti Mäkinen, Simon Horobin, and Jeremy Smith, comps. 2009. *The Middle English Grammar Corpus. MEG-C base.* Version 2009.1. University of Stavanger. http://www.uis.no/research/culture/the_ middle_english_grammar_project/meg-c.

Stolcke, Andreas. 2002. "SRILM: An Extensible Language Modeling Toolkit." In *Proceedings of the 7th International Conference on Spoken Language Processing*, edited by John Hansen and Bryan Pellom, 901–4. Denver: Casual Productions.

Stubbs, Estelle, ed. 2000. *The Hengwrt Chaucer Digital Facsimile.* Leicester: Scholarly Digital Editions.

_____ 2007. "'Here's One I Prepared Earlier': The Work of Scribe D on Oxford, Corpus Christi College, MS 198." *Review of English Studies* 58:133–53.

Thaisen, Jacob. 2005–06. "Orthography, Codicology, and Textual Studies: The Cambridge University Library Gg.4.27 *Canterbury Tales.*" *Boletín Millares Carlo* 24–25:379–94.

Williamson, Keith, comp. 2008. *A Linguistic Atlas of Older Scots, Phase 1: 1380–1500.* University of Edinburgh. http://www.lel.ed.ac.uk/ihd/laos1/laos1.html.

Witten, Ian H., and Timothy C. Bell. 1991. "The Zero-Frequency Problem: Estimating the Probabilities of Novel Events in Adaptive Text Compression." *IEEE Transactions on Information Theory* 37:1085–94.

The Digitization of Bookbindings

Athanasios Velios
University of the Arts London
a.velios@camberwell.arts.ac.uk

Nicholas Pickwoad
University of the Arts London
npickwoad@paston.co.uk

Introduction

When we talk of digitization, it is often in reference to books, whether manuscript or printed, medieval or modern. Many digitization projects deal with the textual content of volumes held in libraries, and although the benefits of such projects can be justified by the importance of the digitized text, inevitably most of them are incomplete as digitization projects because they focus on only one aspect of the book: its content. However, the book as an object, of which the binding is a major component, holds a wealth of information beyond the content of the book. The leaves of a manuscript or a printed book were often bound in response to the owner's choice and at his or her expense. The binding can therefore reflect the financial status of the owner or the intended use of the book. It will often give information about where and when the book was first used, and in fact, this information is sometimes more important than the information offered by the content itself. This chapter summarizes recent work done on the digitization of medieval and early modern bookbindings, focusing on a case study from the library of St. Catherine's Monastery in Sinai, Egypt.

An important aspect of the digitization of bookbindings is that it is done not by a machine but by a human expert: a binding surveyor. Bookbinding digitization is the process of producing an extensive set of metadata for a book based on specific guidelines. Photography is often used to supplement the metadata—the reverse of most other approaches to digitization, where metadata supplements photographic evidence. Digital imaging of books is a well-researched field, covered elsewhere in this volume. In this chapter we survey the study of bookbindings and present guidelines for their description, which primarily includes physical dimensions, bookbinding techniques, and materials. Although this work was initiated and developed for the study of a medieval library, it applies also to later periods, because although binding traditions have changed over time, the overall format of the codex has

ISBN 978-0-86698-499-7 (online)   ISBN 978-0-86698-474-4 (print)
New Technologies in Medieval and Renaissance Studies 3 (2012) 201–228

remained the same. We begin by explaining the importance of bookbinding to historical study.

The value of historic bookbindings

For centuries the study of books has been almost entirely devoted to their textual or graphical content and, by extension, to the support materials on which the texts have been written or printed (e.g., papyrus, parchment, paper, etc.). Occasionally, bindings of particular beauty or lavish decoration have been included in such studies, but their descriptions were mostly concerned with the decoration of the binding (a typical example is Nixon 1956).[1] In recent years, however, the more detailed examination of bindings of all sorts has revealed a wide variety of structures and materials. This has opened the possibility of dating and giving provenances to bindings by means other than their decoration, thus adding important information to what was already known about the texts that they contain and how these texts were received and used. Each process in the production of a handmade binding is subject to wide variations; and, like other manually produced artefacts, a binding is likely to contain marks of its manufacturing process which are unique to individual binders. Such marks can be used like signatures to identify the work of usually unnamed individuals. In addition, the quality of a binding, as deduced from its structure and materials as well as its decoration, can greatly enhance our understanding of the status and function of individual books within the literate world that produced them, whether it be a treasure on the altar of a major cathedral church or a humble schoolbook carried around in a child's satchel. Bindings also often record evidence of ownership, handling, and storage practices which can throw additional light on the history of individual texts, their damage and repairs, and their changing value over the centuries.

The well-established practices of bibliography, palaeography, and codicology have been established over decades of descriptive and analytical development. In order for the description of bindings to take its place alongside these disciplines, we have to establish its scope and develop its methodologies in a much shorter period, as this discipline has only evolved recently. To this end, the library of the monastery of Saint Catherine on Mount Sinai in Egypt has proved a fertile testing ground.

---

[1] An example of such a collection is that of the library formed by the kings of France at Fontainebleau (Lafitte and Le Bars 1999). Often these bindings are important for their associative value, such as provenance that includes a significant historical figure.

The library of St. Catherine's Monastery

The Monastery of St. Catherine in the Sinai peninsula is one of the earliest Christian monasteries in the world. It can claim continuous monastic life from the fourth century. Previously published work (Brock 1996; Manafis 1990) has showcased the importance of the monastery and its treasures—the collection of manuscripts and early printed books being among them.[2] The library contains over 3,300 bound manuscripts and about twelve thousand printed books. Although there are manuscripts from as late as the nineteenth century, the majority date from before the sixteenth century, and most of these are in their first or early bindings, making it one of the largest collections of early bindings in the world and hence ideal for the study of medieval and early modern bookbinding. The manuscripts found in the library carry mostly *Greek* bindings (we will explain later why this term is better avoided), but they also cover a large range of different binding techniques and features from Western Europe, the Mediterranean, and the Middle East. They cover a range of subjects, including mathematics, astronomy, and music, but the vast majority of them are biblical, theological, and liturgical books. Many of these have been produced at the Monastery; but during periods when the Monastery's bindery was inactive, books travelled from important monastic centres in Greece, including Crete and Mount Athos. Links with European centres of book manufacturing have been established, although palaeographical research is still under progress.

In 2001 the library, in collaboration with Camberwell College of Arts, initiated a preservation program which demanded the need to understand the collection and its condition. A means of recording the bindings was therefore necessary, and this led to the work described in this chapter. The first stage here is to describe the principles for digitizing bookbindings.

Describing bookbindings

The scale of the task

It is the nature of observation that the longer one spends looking at an object the more details one notices and the longer the description one produces. A book can be described as a stack of sheets often bound together. The description of this seemingly straightforward object can evolve to a multipage document with extensive reports of binding materials and features. The detail in

---

[2] For catalogues of the manuscript collection see Gardthausen (1886); Kamil (1970); Weitzmann and Galavaris (1990).

which a researcher is prepared to describe a book depends on the anticipated uses of the data (often based on agreed observation criteria) and logistics (such as time and cost). If a record does not contain enough information, its potential as a resource will be limited. In our work, the binding descriptions we propose are detailed enough to cover most requirements for the historical study of a binding: in general, the descriptions continue until an indivisible piece of binding material has been described. Therefore our descriptive methodology has evolved because of the need for surveying bindings in detail to extract useful historical and conservation related conclusions about collections. At a time when work at such level of detail is not adopted anywhere else, interoperability was not our initial concern. As we explain next, we have developed a multilingual glossary of bookbinding terms to record these descriptions. We have arranged these terms in a hierarchical tree structure where the terms for general bookbinding features (such as *endleaves*) correspond to large branches of the tree, and terms for detailed bookbinding features (such as *method of endleaf edge treatment*) correspond to small branches under a large branch. For short binding descriptions, early generations of the hierarchy are sufficient (i.e., only general terms). For extensive descriptions, the generations of the hierarchy can be exhausted. This hierarchy is implemented using the eXtensible Markup Language (XML).

Our intention was to produce a working system for recording bookbinding information, and the glossary structure helped with the arrangement of the numerous terms. We did not intend to produce an ontology of bookbinding structures, which would require universal approval and more time-consuming analysis. Although in the following sections we discuss the glossary as a collection of concepts, we do that only to emphasize that we are not limited to one language and not to indicate ontological structure. An ontology would, however, be the next step to the formalization of our glossary as a universal standard.[3]

The level of detail to which a binding should be recorded can be debated, but the validity of its description should not. Both short and long binding descriptions should be valid and consistent. This was a major consideration during our survey and the reason for developing our glossary, which acts as a blueprint for producing records and as a way for checking their validity. The following paragraphs explain the challenges we met in our effort to develop this glossary.

---

[3] Work on this has already begun with the formation of an international group of experts and an EU consortium under the name "Language of Bindings."

Bookbinding terminology and free-text descriptions

Perhaps the most systematic work in developing a bookbinding glossary was done by Roberts and Etherington (2009) in *Bookbinding and the Conservation of Books: A Dictionary of Descriptive Terminology*. This work is an invaluable reference for bookbinding historians and conservators. Entries are arranged alphabetically, making the dictionary ideal for looking up definitions of terms as they occur in the literature. Bookbinders or bookbinding historians can refer to the dictionary to resolve disputes regarding the use of terms. Essentially, Roberts and Etherington produced a reference resource for describing bindings using the English language (and no other language) in the form of simple text—similar to what we see in catalogue descriptions or conservation records. Our glossary builds on Robert and Etherington, but with a different objective.

Roberts and Etherington's glossary is developed for English speakers who use prose to describe their bindings. It inherently has two disadvantages: 1) it cannot be used by non-English speakers; and 2) it cannot be used by computer software to categorize and search bookbinding descriptions automatically. The latter disadvantage is not a limitation of this glossary specifically, but of free-text in general: it is extremely difficult for a piece of software to extract useful information for a bookbinding description written in free-text. By "extracting useful information" we mean transferring information from the text to a structured document or a database. A structured document places certain types of information in predictable locations, making it easy to extract. A typical structured document is a web page written in HTML. The title of the page and the author are located in a specific part in the beginning of the document which makes classifying HTML pages based on title or author possible. Structured documents do not normally follow the syntax of a spoken language. Soderland (1999) identified the problem of extracting information from unstructured free-text by developing an information extraction system and testing it on semi-structured text (such as news stories).[4] Because promising results were achieved only after lengthy and tedious training of the information extraction system, he concluded that the software is still immature for extracting systematic and organized information from free-text. Since then, considerable work has been done in the field of information extraction, especially in bioscience, but recent reports[5]

---

[4] A semi-structured document is loosely defined as a document of which the information is stored based on some kind of document structure, but also includes information "hidden" in free-text.

[5] See for example Mooney and Bunescu (2005).

indicate that extracting information from free-text is still a difficult challenge. Chang et al. (2006) in their review of methods for extracting information from the Web conclude that unsupervised extraction, i.e., collection of information without prior training of the software by a user, has very limited applications. If these conclusions are true for the biosciences, which rely on strict terminological rules (such as rules for naming amino acids), then they are certainly true for bookbinding where terminology is not formed in the same way and varies significantly. Therefore, based on the available bibliography, extracting bookbinding information from free-text is impractical.

This limitation in processing free-text is the reason for the evolution of structured text in a variety of standards (including that for HTML). Structured text allows the retrieval of data based on complex queries which at the moment require user input. For example, retrieving instances of books bound in limp bindings is possible by a user only through a keyword search and continuous reviewing of results. Software is unable to do this automatically unless structured documents of binding descriptions exist. Following the idea of structured documents, our approach offers a detailed data-structure for describing bookbindings which allows both humans and computer software to search through binding structures automatically. We have borrowed terms from Roberts and Etherington (2009) (as well as other publications) and we have created new ones, but instead of keeping them in an unstructured, flat, alphabetical order (suitable for free-text), we have arranged them in a hierarchical structure which is based on the structure of the bound book (suitable for structured documents). Therefore the terms used in other glossaries are placeholders of bookbinding concepts in our structured documents. Our structured approach guides the surveyor through the description process, so that the only requirements are access to the binding and reference to our proposed vocabulary. To our knowledge this is the first time this approach has been adopted in the field.[6]

A common misconception about the use of controlled vocabularies is that because they are made for computer use, the potential for a good variety of words (thesaurus) is limited and therefore only partially covers human requirements for data presentation. However, because the vocabulary used for our structured bookbinding description matches the concepts involved in a

---

[6] An important Dutch publication (Gnirrep, Gumbert, and Szirmai 1992) has broken its glossary of bookbinding terms down into sections related to the major components of bindings, but, as a printed book, it is limited in its ability to utilize a fully hierarchical structure.

bookbinding, a variety of spoken-language terminologies can be deployed at the user's request. For example, the term *endband* in the structured vocabulary represents the idea of the endband and not the English-language word.[7] Therefore the fact that Roberts and Etherington prefer the word *headband* to describe the same idea is irrelevant to our structured description. The concept of endband can be represented on a screen in a multitude of ways according to the preference of the user (it can be labelled *endband, headband, head*, etc.); however, its representation to the computer is consistent because of the underlying conceptual structure, and therefore we can easily instruct the computer to search for it regardless of which spoken-language term is used. This approach frees the description process from linguistic arguments over the suitability of particular terms. Another important benefit of this approach is the possibility for supporting multilingual descriptions. Although the underlying conceptual structure of the document is created using terms from a chosen spoken language (we are using mostly English), if labels for a different spoken language (e.g., Greek) are produced and matched to the conceptual structure, then the document can be published in that language automatically. The huge advantage of this approach is that the structured bookbinding documents are language independent. For example, an endband will be presented as κεφαλάρι to a Greek user, and descriptions made in English can be searched by users in other languages. The actual production of the labels in different languages still needs to be done manually.

Another misconception is that structured vocabularies have limited capacity for producing free-text (prose). In the case of library catalogues, for example, binding descriptions are included in free-text for better readability. This can cause problems for a limited vocabulary because of their lack of grammatical syntax (Fig. 1). However, previous and recent work in Natural Language Generation[8] shows that a set of data can be automatically transformed either through templates (Wilcock 2001) and/or with more complex techniques (Van Deemter, Krahmer, and Theune 2005) to produce a report which follows a syntactically and grammatically correct structure.[9] This means that binding descriptions made using structured documents could be automatically

---

[7] The fact that we have chosen the English language term *endband* to describe our concept is only because of convenience. In theory we could have chosen any other convenient term to describe the same concept.

[8] Natural Language Generation (NLG) is the process of generating natural language from a machine representation system such as a database or a structured document.

[9] A good summary of such techniques and systems was given by Reiter and Dale (1997) and by Theune (2003).

converted into suitable entries for a catalogue. In our approach, the structured documents for binding descriptions offer the important advantage of automatic information retrieval by a computer without compromising the presentation of data to audiences from different scholarship fields and different languages in a structured way.

Non-descriptive terms

Before we proceed to the development of structured documents for bookbinding descriptions, we need to emphasize an important characteristic of traditional bookbinding descriptions using free-text: the use of a single term to describe numerous bookbinding features. A typical example is the term *Greek-style binding*, which often indicates the existence of protruding endbands, an unsupported sewing structure, interlaced straps, boards with grooved edges, and a textblock which is cut flush with the boards (Fig. 2). The term has been used loosely: for example, even if a binding carries only two out of these four characteristics, a researcher may still call it *Greek-style.* Detailed observation may prove that these characteristics are partially present. Therefore, although the initial description as a *Greek-style* binding is somewhat correct, the binding is really a variation of this style, i.e., *Greek-style binding with sewing supports* and our description suffers as the binding "almost conforms to a style, but not quite." To avoid such confusions, we propose describing a binding based on the examination of a set of features, and we do not permit assumptions about style or structure before the complete set of features has been recorded. Therefore, terms such as *Greek-style* are ambiguous, and we have decided not to use them in our structured documents. However, because these ambiguous terms have been used extensively in the past, it is appropriate to preserve them as part of the traditional use of the language. We will explain later how this is done.

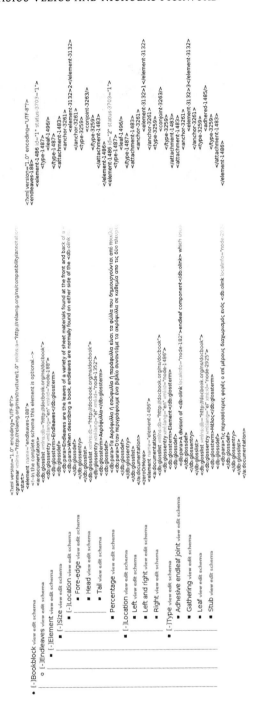

Figure 1. The use of the glossary for producing bookbinding descriptions. Terms as they appear in the Glossary Content Management System (left), Glossary terms as they appear in the automatically produced RelaxNG schema (middle) and an example bookbinding description based on this schema (right). All examples have been truncated due to the verbosity of XML.

Figure 2. Greek 1563, an example of a Greek-style binding from the library
of the St. Catherine Monastery in Sinai, Egypt.

Deconstruction of bookbindings

In the previous section we explained how the ambiguity of some terms used
traditionally can lead to inaccuracies or confusion during descriptions, and
this is the reason why we have decided to use terms that describe specific
features of a binding rather than its overall style. In an effort to formalize
this principle we have attempted to break down the binding structure and
describe its individual components. We have abandoned terms that refer to
the whole binding; instead, we build the "image" of the binding by adding
together many detailed descriptions of individual features. These descriptions can be considered as the "building blocks" of the overall structured
document. We go further and describe the characteristics of each building
block (such as material, technique, colour, etc.) and we arrange these building blocks relative to each other so that the more detailed descriptions follow the more general ones. This produces a hierarchical structure with the
so-called parent-child relationships. To avoid using the term *Greek-style*, we
produce a hierarchical description of the building blocks (endbands, unsupported sewing, straps, boards, textblock edges, etc.) which eventually indicate whether, or to what degree, the book is *Greek-style*.

The idea of hierarchical levels of detail is important in our methodology and
has been the subject of many lengthy discussions during the production of
our document structure. Initially, we were influenced by our experience
of working with popular binding structures. When producing the glossary
structure we inadvertently made assumptions about how bindings are actu-

ally structured. For example, in the case of endleaves, we began by assuming that endleaves are attached as a group (or groups) to the binding in some way (usually sewn). It seemed reasonable that a useful division of the endleaf structure would be the endleaves *unit* which we defined in our glossary as a group of sheet material attached together in one action to the book. This was then broken down into endleaf *components*, which were single sheets of material folded to form one or more leaves, and finally the endleaf *element* which was a part of a component, typically a stub or a leaf. For example, Figure 3 is a way of showing the arrangement of endleaves in a book. The endleaves are shown in cross section with the black bar corresponding to the first gathering and the lines to individual endleaves. The short line through the fold of the endleaves indicates that the endleaves are sewn through the fold on the spine, whereas a dotted line would indicate that the endleaves are adhered to the spine.

Figure 3. Simple example of endleaves arrangement.

Hierarchically, the same endleaves arrangement is shown in Figure 4. This hierarchical structure worked remarkably well for the majority of endleaves; however, when testing the same structure for unusual endleaves arrangements, we discovered that it was unworkable because of our initial assumptions. One such unusual arrangement is when endleaves are not attached to the binding directly but through other endleaves. This is important information for a bookbinding historian which was lost in our initial structure. Figure 5 shows an example of an arrangement where a unit is attached to another unit instead of being attached to the spine directly. In examining unusual cases, such as this one, we had to revise our initial assumptions about how endleaves are attached. We created a more flexible structure where the building block is the <endleaf> element, thus removing the layers of *units* and *components*. The <endleaf> element in the new structure is defined as a layer of sheet material attached to the endleaves or book in some way. In our revised structure, we number and describe the endleaves sequentially (inwards) as shown in Figure 6a. An extract of the RelaxNG schema for endleaves is shown in Figure 6b. This structured description is successful because it allows any combination of endleaves. The description is also sufficient for software to reconstruct the endleaf arrangement and make reasonable comparisons with other endleaf arrangements.

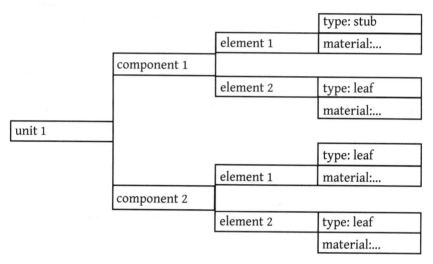

Figure 4. Hierarchical arrangement of endleaves.

Figure 5. Complex example of endleaves arrangement.

Figure 6 (a and b) gives examples of a hierarchy and definition of endleaves, below.

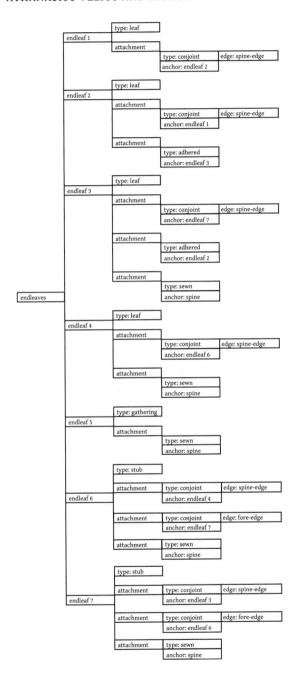

Figure 6(a): New hierarchical arrangement of endleaves.

```
<element name="endleaves">
    <oneOrMore>
      <element name="endleaf">
        <attribute name="id"><text/></attribute>
        <element name="type">
          <choice>
            <element name="stub"><empty/></element>
            <element name="leaf"><empty/></element>
            <element name="gathering"><empty/></element>
          </choice>
        </element>
        <oneOrMore>
          <element name="attachment">
            <element name="type">
              <choice>
                <element name="adhered"><empty/></element>
                <element name="sewn"><empty/></element>
                <element name="conjoined">
                  <choice>
                    <element name="foredge"><empty/></element>
                    <element name="spine"><empty/></element>
                    <element name="head"><empty/></element>
                    <element name="tail"><empty/></element>
                  </choice>
                </element>
              </choice>
            </element>
            <element name="anchor">
              <attribute name="id"><text/></attribute>
            </element>
          </element>
        </oneOrMore>
      </element>
    </oneOrMore>
  </element>
```

Figure 6(b): RelaxNG definition of endleaves.

Although not shown in our figures, there is potentially a larger range of information that can be recorded for each endleaf. This includes:

a) material (paper, parchment, textile, etc.);
b) formation (patched, pieced, etc.);
c) edge treatment (cut, folded, torn, etc.);
d) location (left, right, or both); and
e) size (as a percentage of the overall textblock size in one dimension).

In fact, each of these items can be recorded in more detail. For example, for *edge treatment*, if the endleaf was *cut*, it may be possible to identify the *tool* and the way it was cut, the *shape* of the cut, and so on. If resources allow, one can record all the characteristics of each element in full, and if resources are limited, simply indicating the number of elements present could be enough. In both cases, the same basic document structure will be used ensuring compatibility of records.

It is also important to note that information such as *location* and *material* is often required for many binding features. Although the descriptions of *material* for *endleaves* and *material* for *textleaves* are made based on the same document structure, these materials still apply to different binding features. Context is important and the hierarchical structure of the glossary ensures that it is preserved, since identical child materials will have different parents.

The level of detail to which the glossary is compiled is a matter for debate, but in principle, if a binding feature will never be searched for, then analyzing it and generating a description is probably a pointless task. A good example is the case of *patched* endleaves. These are endleaves which have been created by putting together smaller pieces of paper in a random fashion. This has never been normal practice, but sometimes necessary due to lack of materials. The arrangement of patches could be recorded in a structured way by measuring the coordinates and dimensions of the pieces and reconstructing their geometry. This would allow for searching patched pieces based on coordinates and dimensions. We believe this search would probably never yield meaningful results for historical conclusions. Therefore it is better to summarize this information in a drawing. This way one would be able to see a good representation of the patched endleaf, and we would not consume valuable resources in working out the exact geometry of each patch. We will later propose a way of embedding drawings in our structured documents through the Scalable Vector Graphics (SVG) standard.[10]

---

[10] SVG specifies an XML file format that stores two-dimensional vector graphics. Vector graphics use a set of geometrical entities (e.g., point, line, shape, etc.) to represent an image. The advantage of vector graphics is that they are scale independent

In this next section we describe an example of how our document structure evolved. Discussions on the adequacy of this structure for mapping all possible binding structures still continue, but they all follow the same route: we often build the document structure for a binding component based on a popular variant of that component; we test it, and make adjustments to allow more flexibility. This document structure is implemented using XML tools as explained below.

XML Schema development

Having explained how our structured descriptions follow a hierarchical arrangement of terms based on the way books are bound, we will now investigate how best we can implement these structured descriptions based on current technologies. A suitable solution for our implementation is XML. XML documents are designed for system interoperability and for Internet publishing and searching. They offer the necessary tools for semantic retrieval of information (namespaces) and document standardization (XML schemas). XML documents must be structured hierarchically and therefore are suitable for mapping our terminology's parent-child relationships.[11] Each parent and child constitutes a separate XML document element. In the field of humanities XML has been used extensively, especially for encoding text.[12] The Text Encoding Initiative (TEI Consortium 2010) has been setting the standard in the field. TEI offers a set of XML elements that can be used to identify the structure (e.g., the grammar or pagination) of text, by wrapping segments of text with these elements. In a similar fashion we propose the use of XML for describing bookbindings, but as we have chosen not to use free-text, the XML elements in our descriptions do not have any text as contents. Instead the XML elements themselves describe the bookbinding structure.

Because XML documents can be used to describe anything, it is important that each document conforms to a standard for describing the given entity. These standards are often implemented in an XML schema which acts as

---

and therefore preserve their quality when magnified (this is not the case with raster pictures which are stored as arrays of pixels and therefore lose their quality when magnified).

[11] There is extensive literature on XML, both online and in print. Among others, a good introductory book is by Morrison (2005), and reference documentation is offered by the World Wide Web Consortium (W3C, http://www.w3.org/standards/xml, accessed 23 October 2009).

[12] Text encoding is the process of annotating text, using XML or other technologies, for digital representation and semantic enrichment.

the definition for XML documents. The first step in our implementation was to build the definitions of our glossary using a schema language. We chose RelaxNG for its simplicity and flexibility. RelaxNG is an ISO standard (International Standardards Organization 2008) for document schema definitions which is easy to learn and use (Van der Vlist 2004). Using RelaxNG to define our schema, we faced a number of challenges:

a) Naming convention. Our XML elements were given indicative names for the binding features or concepts they represented. As mentioned earlier, the glossary terms that correspond to the XML elements are not terms of a specific language (such as English), and arguably it would be sufficient to use any form of identification for the name of an element, for example a random id number. In the case of the interchangeable terms *headband* and *endband*, the element corresponding to this concept could be given any number (e.g., no1). Both these spoken language terms would then correspond to concept/ element no1. In other words, although discussions of the suitability of *headband* or *endband* might lead to different conclusions, discussions about the suitability of a random number are not applicable, thus eliminating the time-consuming problem of choosing a term. The risk of this method is that when hundreds of elements acquire random numbers, the resulting document would be impossible for a human to follow. Computer software would have no problem reading a document based on this schema, but given that one of the advantages of XML is human readability, we felt we should not remove it. For this reason we adopted mostly English terms for element naming combined with an identity number like this: *<endband-1502>*. This solution allows both the computer software and the human eye to follow the XML document. The choice of the word *endband* instead of *headband* for the element name is purely down to our preference, but the element name *<endband-1502>* can still be mapped to any term (*endband, headband, head*, etc.). If future discussions about the use of our onomatology[13] for XML elements conclude that *<endband-1502>* must change, then this would be possible provided that the identity number remains the same. If *headband* becomes the preferred element name, the old element name can be updated from *<endband-1502>* to *<headband-1502>*. However, changing the element name should not be encouraged, since the change would have no effect on users. We anticipate that description of bookbindings will never be done without a graphical user interface.

---

[13] Onomatology: the study of the origin and forms of proper names.

Although encoding text can be done effectively in a text editor, a binding surveyor should not need to edit an XML file directly because there is no text to input. Therefore it is unlikely that one would need to type the element names directly: thus the complication of looking up the corresponding number is removed.[14] One would instead use a graphical user interface to fill in a survey form that would present the available elements together with documentation, which is described next.

b)   Documentation. Explanations were produced for each term to define its concept within a given context. We also allowed for these descriptions to be multilingual. The explanations could include all possible options for terms as preferred by different audiences. So far, the included recommendations for the terms used have not been the subject of extensive discussion, but should such discussions take place the concluded terms may be altered within the documentation text. Therefore the definition of a concept is fixed, but the term one chooses to give this definition might change, if absolutely necessary. Our concept definitions are intended for humans and therefore they are done in text. In order to improve the usability of this text (links to other terms, emphasis, paragraphs, etc.) we chose to use an encoding standard for text: the docbook standard (Walsh and Muellner 2008). Docbook is a standard way for encoding text in XML. For elements that are translated in many languages, there is a separate entry for each language, thus allowing an element to be presented in a user's preferred language. The docbook standard was chosen for its simplicity; however, other equally efficient systems do exist, such as TEI which was mentioned earlier. Since our documentation is not complex, shifting from one documentation standard to another would be a relatively straightforward task, and given the popularity of TEI with the academic community, this is something that we are currently considering.

The extent of the documentation and the large number of people working on it simultaneously from different locations created a logistical problem for managing the XML schema and its documentation. Although sophisticated tools from the software development community are widely available, we discovered that our requirements were adequately covered by the content

---

[14] Moreover, a plethora of modern XML editors allow guided typing and features such as auto-completion which solve that problem when directly editing XML documents.

management system Drupal (http://www.drupal.org) which organizes content and revisions of content, and handles users. Because it manages both the production of the schema and its documentation, Drupal also functions as an online reference publication and as the repository of our XML schema. It offers sophisticated tools for keeping translations synchronized, and it requires very basic training for non-experts. The details of our customization of *Drupal* are beyond the scope of this chapter, and we intend to publish them shortly in a separate paper (Velios forthcoming).

Generic terms: XML Queries

In previous sections we explained why generic terms such as *Greek-style binding* are not useful for our binding descriptions. We also said that these terms have been extensively used in the literature and therefore it would be unreasonable to ignore them. We can include these terms in our descriptions indirectly by transforming them into XML queries. We define a set of criteria that should be fulfilled in order for a generic term to suffice in describing a binding. In the case of *Greek-style binding*, we agree that if a binding has *raised* endbands and *straps* and *grooved boards*, and the textblock is cut *flush* to the boards, then it is considered as *Greek-style*. This definition may be arbitrary, and some people will not agree with it; however, because these traditional terms are not strictly defined we prefer to use them as wrappers of clearly defined XML queries, which can change if required.

Drawings and photography

An important part of a bookbinding record is a set of drawings to hold information that cannot be recorded in the hierarchically structured description. We referred earlier to the problem of *patched* endleaves which are put together in a random fashion such that the patches are not worth recording systematically; however, a representation of a *patched* endleaf might be useful for conservation records, and therefore we opt for drawings. We propose to use, as part of a bookbinding description, the well-established standard for drawings using vector graphics based on XML: SVG (XML Graphics for the Web, http://www.w3.org/Graphics/SVG/). Because SVG is essentially XML, it can be merged with a bookbinding description in XML. We intend to publish the logistics of the integration of SVG with our records at a later date. Photography is also essential for a bookbinding record, and we have a system for taking standard shots of a book which capture essential information about a binding. This system has been described elsewhere (Velios and Pickwoad 2006). The methodology described here evolved during a major bookbinding recording project at St. Catherine's Monastery which acted as a test bed (St. Catherine's Library Conservation Project at Ligatus, http://www.ligatus.org. uk/stcatherines). This is described in the next section.

Application of methodology

Working in an active monastery

The active religious life of St. Catherine's Monastery is the main reason why their books have been kept in good condition until today. The book as an object is appreciated and treated with great respect in the Greek Orthodox tradition, added to which is the dry and stable environment of the desert. The monastery has always prioritized religious life instead of the role of a research institution as far as the library is concerned. Scholars have been welcomed to the monastery, and various research projects have been successfully completed there, but this has always been peripheral to the main function of the community. Our work was no exception, and many logistical issues had to be resolved for us to be able to examine the bindings. These mostly involved arranging our work schedule to fit around the daily monastic program and negotiating the fathers' personal time to accompany us in the library. This often disrupted our work, and we had to allow ample time during our trips to cover for possible delays. Although from a research point of view this is difficult to justify and often frustrating, it does mean that it allows time for thinking and puts the work in the correct perspective within the monastery's life.

Surveying historical collections of bindings

As mentioned in the introduction, bookbinding digitization is similar to text-markup in that it is performed by humans, which inevitably introduces some challenges:

a) Quality monitoring. In digitization projects, it is often the case that quality can be monitored through calibration of equipment and checking the results with appropriate devices. In digital photography, for example, it is possible to measure the resolution, noise,[15] and colour

---

[15] Noise in digital photography is the evidence of variance in colour values where there should not be any. It is often observed when photographing a "flat" colour of a constant colour value, where the resulting digital image appears to have a range of such values instead of only one. Typically noise is introduced when the signal received by the camera sensor is amplified.

accuracy achieved in a shot by including a suitable reference target[16] in the frame (Williams and Burns 2006). It is impossible to employ such techniques to assess human observation and description. One way of monitoring quality is by making an observation multiple times and confirming that it is the same every time. In practice this is feasible by having more than one person make the same observation; and for this reason, when surveying bookbindings, it is best to work in teams. In our case at the St. Catherine's Monastery, observations were made by at least two surveyors.

b)   Positive negative. In an inspection of a bookbinding record, it is often the case that an expected binding feature is not present. An example is a binding which appears to have boards but not a cover. There are a number of possibilities: i) the binding is unfinished for some historical reason; ii) the binding originally had a cover but it was lost; iii) the surveyor accidentally forgot to include the cover in the record; or iv) the surveyor could not decide whether the binding has a cover or not. In order to clarify this uncertainty, we need to confirm the *positive negative* where items that were never present in a binding are marked as such. To do this, each element of our binding record includes an attribute that clarifies the status of a component that is not present. Depending on that status, a software process representing the binding might chose to ignore the element or indicate that it was never present. This is because the historic description of a binding record should reflect so far as is possible the state of the binding when it was produced and not be affected by the state of preservation of the item or the ability of the surveyor.

c)   Cost, time, and planning. In any digitization project, handling the items to be digitized can be the most time-consuming task, the duration of which can be difficult to calculate. This is the case with the digitization of bookbindings where handling is a key aspect of the whole process for fear of damaging the books, especially rare material. Another uncertainty in calculating the time needed for digitizing a collection of bindings is the complexity of the structures. In other digitization projects, the time required for photographing, for example, a painting with a rough paint surface versus a painting with a smooth

---

[16] A reference target in digital photography is a flat patch of typical colours and geometrical shapes that is included in the shot. The appearance of the target in the resulting image allows the evaluation of its quality.

paint surface under the same photography specifications will differ, but not dramatically. In the case of bookbinding digitization, this difference may be dramatic as the time required to digitize an item depends on the complexity of the structure, which is unknown until it has been examined. Therefore, a sequence of extremely complex binding structures will slow the digitization procedure, and it is usually impossible to assess in advance the required time for a whole collection. In the case of the St. Catherine's Library, the average time it took to collect a reasonable amount of information for a book was one hour.

d) Training. In any digitization project, operators may require training in order to complete digitization tasks. In some cases these tasks are simple but repetitive and the training lasts from a few hours to a few days. Bookbinding digitization relies on specialist experience in recognizing binding features. This means that professionals are required for the work. In our project, only trained book conservators and bookbinding historians participated in the digitization of the books.

Potential of XML bookbinding records

Apart from the obvious use as a resource for the study of historic bookbinding, the digitization of a collection of bindings can be a valuable resource for a range of practical applications. Like any XML document, the binding descriptions can be published online. There is a variety of tools which allow data retrieval from XML documents, mainly XML databases for isolated resources. Because the Web predominantly offers semantically poor documents, tools for semantically indexing distributed XML documents have hardly appeared. However, as we move towards a wider adoption of structured documents (especially with the Semantic Web),[17] the isolated efforts to search XML documents semantically will grow and may deliver widely useful tools. Producing the binding records in XML and publishing them online will eventually allow the retrieval of binding information from collections held in different libraries provided that a common schema is used. This will be an invaluable tool for historical bookbinding research, as it will allow scholars to match the binding description they have in front of them with binding descriptions from around the world.

---

[17] The Semantic Web is an initiative to allow computer software to perform tasks online without the direction of a user and by using structured documents.

On a local scale, interesting results can be extracted from data collected from single libraries, as we have discovered in the St. Catherine's Library. In historical research, a PhD study by Nikolas Sarris (2010) on the tooled decoration of the manuscript bindings in the library at St. Catherine's has benefited from the digitized records of the bindings. Sarris has identified possible groups of manuscripts based on earlier bibliographical and palaeographical study. He has also consulted the binding records to compare binding features of these groups of books. In many cases the comparisons enabled him to confirm the bibliographical and palaeographical study and in others to identify new historical evidence and extract significant conclusions about the history of the monastery.

A recent study on board production in the library has relied solely on the digitized bindings. Honey and Velios (2009) examined the records of book-boards from the library's manuscript collection and extracted useful statistical information about composite boards.[18] This data confirms the lack of available binding materials in the monastery over the centuries, but also proves the monastery's continuous care for the manuscripts by employing early "conservation" techniques. The examination of the records showed that old boards are not discarded but repaired and kept (e.g., often broken boards are adhered and/or sewn).

Digitized bindings are also useful for practical tasks. For example, the value of the books in the library at St. Catherine's and the requirement for their preservation has initiated a project to produce protective boxes. These need to be produced according to the size of each book. A simple query of our digitized binding records on book size offers this information. It can also be combined with queries of other details of the binding which indicate the requirement of extra space in a box. These binding features include metal furniture or raised endbands. The added benefit of the survey is that a lot of useful information has been collected, and the books do not need to be handled again, thus reducing the risk of damage.

Similar benefits have been observed during a project to rebuild the library and rehouse the collection. The amount of shelving needed in the new building, the position of the books on the shelves for optimum use of the limited space, and the material and people needed for packing and storing are a few of the questions that have been answered using data from our digital records.

---

[18] Composite boards are boards that consist of more than one piece of board material joined to one another by a variety of techniques which mostly involve threads.

Another example of the use of the digitized material for practical work has been the selection of planks of cedar wood for new book boards. A query on the size of boards from our database of digitized bindings indicated an average aspect ratio and size for boards and the variance of this data. This information allowed a more informed judgment about which would be the most useful pieces of cedar wood and thus avoid unnecessary waste.

Further work

The value of the digitized bindings for both the practical management of collections and scholarly questions is clear. We believe that we have explored only a fraction of the possibilities digitization offers. Some new ideas we have begun to research are described here.

Our glossary of bookbinding terms addresses a practical problem of bookbinding description, but it has not been developed as an ontology. This makes it unlikely that our glossary will be widely adopted, despite the limited focus of the field. Our next step will be to investigate the best path for the transformation of the glossary to a recognized standard and map it using ontology tools, with the CIDOC Conceptual Reference Model[19] being an obvious candidate.

A binding record can be overwhelmingly detailed and therefore difficult to visualize. Photography alone, on the other hand, captures only the exterior of a binding and perhaps some details which are not always possible for a researcher to interpret. These two types of binding records work best when combined. We are working on a tool that will allow this combination of photography and binding records by relating elements of an XML binding record to what is seen on a photograph. This will allow the detailed annotation of a photograph using the binding record (similar tools have been produced by a number of popular websites, e.g., http://www.fotonotes.net).

Another promising application is the automatic visual reconstruction of bindings, based on their digitized XML record. This will allow an XML description of a binding to be transformed into a series of linear drawings and possibly 3D models which will resemble an ideal representation of the original binding, but will not necessarily be realistic. A useful application of this technology would allow the surveyor to double-check the record as it is being built by comparing the reconstructed model to the real binding. Another

---

[19] *The CIDOC Conceptual Reference Model* (CIDOC-CRM), International Council of Museums, updated 7 October 2011, http://www.cidoc-crm.org.

application would be the production of visual material for education when photographs are not available or are unclear.

The limited resources at the St. Catherine's Monastery precluded the use of the Internet in our workflow. As Internet connections become faster and more reliable in Sinai, we intend to produce an online interface in the form of a dynamic web page that will offer a convenient tool for digitizing bindings. This tool will retrieve the glossary/schema from our online content management system, display the terms and documentation in the user's preferred language or vocabulary, and guide the user through the hierarchical structure for completing the binding record. We have decided on an online tool, running on web server software, because of the logistical advantages for technical support and deployment as well as platform independence and standards compliance. This server software can run in a local network for libraries without Internet access, although synchronization of data might be an issue.

In this chapter we have explained the importance of bookbinding descriptions for historical study and have described a methodology for recording bookbindings using XML. We have shown how descriptive concepts of bookbinding components can be used as XML elements of the descriptions and how our XML schema combines both the mapping of a binding structure and a multilingual glossary. Finally, we have described some new ideas of how this work can be extended with better visual representation of our records. We believe that such applications will further promote the digitization of bindings as a critical element for historical study of libraries and archives, and we hope that the work we have done so far is a useful starting point.

WORKS CITED

Brock, Sebastian. 1996. "A Venerable Manuscript Collection." In *The Monastery of Saint Catherine*, edited by O. Baddeley and E. Brunner, 85–97. London: The Saint Catherine Foundation.

Chang, Chia-Hui, Mohammed Kayed, Moheb Ramzy Girgis, and Khaled Shaalan. 2006. "A Survey of Web Information Extraction Systems." *IEEE Transactions on Knowledge and Data Engineering, TKDE-0475-1104.R3*: 1–18. http://www.csie.ncu.edu.tw/~chia/pub/iesurvey2006.pdf.

Drupal. Accessed 23 October 2009. http://www.drupal.org/.

Gardthausen, V. 1886. *Catalogus Codicum Graecorum Sinaiticorum.* Oxford: Clarendon Press.

Gnirrep, W. K., J. P. Gumbert, and J. A. Szirmai. 1992. *Kneep en Binding: een terminologie voor de beschrijving van de construkties van oude boekbanden.* The Hague: Koninklijke Bibliothek.

FotoNotes. Accessed 23 October 2009. http://www.fotonotes.net/.

Honey, Andrew, and Athanasios Velios. 2009. "The Repair and Re-Use of Byzantine Wooden Bookboards in the Manuscript Collection of the Monastery of St Catherine, Sinai." In *Holding it All Together: Ancient and Modern Approaches to Joining, Repair and Consolidation,* edited by Catherine Higgit and Janet Ambers, 68–77. London: Archetype.

International Standards Organization. 2008. ISO/IEC 19757-2: 2008. *Information Technology--Document Schema Definition Language (DSDL) Part 2: Regular-Grammar-Based Validation-RELAX NG.* ISO. http://standards. iso.org/ittf/PubliclyAvailableStandards/index.html.

Kamil, M. 1970. *Catalogue of All Manuscripts in the Monastery of St Catherine on Mount Sinai.* Wiesbaden: Harrassowitz.

Lafitte, M., and F. Le Bars. 1999. *Reliures Royales de la Renaissance: La Librairie de Fontainebleau 1544-1570.* Paris: Bibliothèque nationale de France.

Manaphes, Konstantinos. 1990. *Sinai: Treasures of the Monastery of Saint Catherine.* Athens: Ekdotike Athenon.

Mooney, Raymond J., and Razvan Bunescu. 2005. "Mining Knowledge from Text Using Information Extraction." *SIGKDD Explorations. A Special Issue on Text Mining and Natural Language Processing* 7 (1): 3–10.

Morrison, Michael. 2005. *Sams Teach Yourself XML in 24 hours: Complete Starter Kit.* Indianapolis: Sams Publishing.

Nixon, Howard M. 1956. *Broxbourne Library: Styles and Designs of Bindings from the Twelfth to the Twentieth Century.* London: Maggs Brothers.

Reiter, Ehud, and Robert Dale. 1997. "Building Applied Natural Language Generation Systems." *Natural Language Engineering* 3 (1): 57–87.

Roberts, Matt, and Don Etherington. 2009. *Bookbinding and the Conservation of Books: A Dictionary of Descriptive Terminology*. Conservation Online. http://cool.conservation-us.org/don/don.html.

Sarris, N. 2010. "Classification of Finishing Tools in Byzantine/Greek Bookbinding: Establishing Inks for Manuscripts from the Library of the St. Catherine's Monastery in Sinai, Egypt." PhD diss., University of the Arts, London.

Soderland, Stephen. 1999. "Learning Information Extraction Rules for Semi-Structured and Free Text." *Machine Learning* 34:233–72.

TEI Consortium, eds. 2010. *TEI P5: Guidelines for Electronic Text Encoding and Interchange*. Version 1.6.0. TEI Consortium. http://www.tei-c.org/Guidelines/P5/.

Theune, Mariët. 2003. *Natural Language Generation for Dialogue: System Survey*. Enschede: University of Twente.

Van Deemter, Kees, Emiel Krahmer, and Mariët Theune. 2005. "Real Versus Template-Based Natural Language Generation: A False Opposition?" *Computational Linguistics* 31 (1): 15–23.

Van der Vlist, Eric. 2004. *RelaxNG*. Sebastopol: O'Reilly & Associates.

Velios, A. Forthcoming. "Customising Drupal for Developing Structured Glossaries."

Velios, A., and Pickwoad, N. 2006. "The Digitization of the Slide Collection from the Saint Catherine Library Conservation Project." Presented at IS&T Archiving 2006, 22–27 May, Ottawa, Canada.

Walsh, Norman, and Leonard Muellner. 2008. *DocBook 5.0: The Definitive Guide*. Sebastopol: O'Reilly Media, Inc.

Weitzmann, Kurt, and George Galavaris. 1990. *The Monastery of Saint Catherine at Mount Sinai: The Illuminated Greek Manuscripts, From the Ninth to the Twelfth Century*. Vol. 1. Princeton: Princeton University Press.

Wilcock, Graham. 2001. "Pipelines, Templates and Transformations: XML for Natural Language Generation." In *Proceedings of the First NLP and XML Workshop*, 1–8. Tokyo.

Williams, Don, and Peter Burns. 2006. "Evaluating Digital Scanner and Camera Imaging Performance." In *IS&T Archiving 2006.* Springfield: Society for Imaging Science and Technology.

World Wide Web Consortium. Accessed 23 October 2009. http://www.w3.org.

W3C SVG Working Group. Scalable Vector Graphics, XML Graphics for the Web. Accessed 23 October 2009. http://www.w3.org/Graphics/SVG/.

Digitizing Collection, Composition, and Product: Tracking the Work of Little Gidding

Paul Dyck

Canadian Mennonite University

pdyck@cmu.ca

Ryan Rempel

Canadian Mennonite University

rgrempel@gmail.com

with
Stuart Williams
Independent Scholar

stuart@swilliams.ca

Introduction

Given the universal ascension of the Internet search as a primary method for initiating almost any inquiry, including academic research queries, and the development of image and text bases such as *Early English Books Online* (EEBO) that bring together vast historical resources and make them available on the scholar's desk, it is hardly necessary to claim that digitization has something important to offer the study of early modern material culture. We will argue in this paper, though, that digital tools offer much more than most scholars are currently taking. In particular, we have found that XML and digital images offer an effective way not only of delivering information about material culture but, more importantly, of doing primary research on cultural objects. Our ideal method is digital from the ground up, aimed at a process rather than a product, or put another way, a product that is always produced by a scholarly process. An important correlative of this process is that, from beginning to end, our goal is to keep central the material object of study. On the back-end, then, we have a set of XML-encoded texts being dynamically combined in imitation of the material object, and on the front-end, we have the image of the object itself. In designing this interface, we are blurring the distinction between editing

ISBN 978-0-86698-499-7 (online)   ISBN 978-0-86698-474-4 (print)

New Technologies in Medieval and Renaissance Studies 3 (2012) 229–256

and presentation: we imagine the presentation interface as a version of the editing interface rather than as a new project.[1]

Our project involves a group of books made by hand by the extended Ferrar family at Little Gidding in the 1630s.[2] These books were made by cutting and pasting text and images from other books and from prints. Thus, we study not simply the books, but also the extensive range of material sources for those books. Our project is in a formative stage: we have closely studied one of the Little Gidding books, a gospel harmony made for King Charles I, identifying many of the materials used in it, and we have developed XML encoding schemes for it as well as an interface.[3] We plan to digitize this first book and to produce a digital edition of it in the coming years. We also look ahead to the much larger project of editing all the extant Little Gidding concordances and their many sources within a single research tool, allowing as full an exploration as possible of the activities of the Little Gidding workshop as a remarkable node of early modern compilation and production.[4]

The Ferrars' method shares with today's electronic compositional culture some important and mutually enlightening similarities. Most notable is the transportability of the text or image fragment and its redeployment in new compositions. While subsequent centuries witnessed the addition of images to printed texts and the assembly of various cut-outs in scrapbook form, the Little Gidding concordances stand out as serious books made entirely of fragments from other books. They are the apotheosis of the commonplace book; the proof that a most important text—and simultaneously a rare object—can be compiled out of commonly available materials. Since the textual transportability that they employ relies upon a vigorous system of textual encoding, they supply the model for their own digitization, allowing us in turn to model their material process of composing the page.

---

[1] This is in contrast to the tendency noted by Matthew G. Kirschenbaum for interface to be the final phase of a project, thus distancing the end-users' experience of the material from that of the editors (2004, 525).

[2] For the standard (though hagiographically misty) introduction to Little Gidding, see A. L. Maycock (1980). Recent work by Joyce Ransome, especially her new monograph on the topic (2003, 2005, 2011), as well as work by D. R. Ransome (2000) and A. M. Williams (1970) does much to fill out the historical picture.

[3] British Library C23e4.

[4] The best account of all extant concordances is J. Ransome (2005).

The Little Gidding books and their materials

In the 1630s, in the countryside northwest of Cambridge, the extended Ferrar family, in an intentional retreat from the world, found a "new way of printing" admirably suited to the family's needs. This wealthy merchant family, faced with severe financial difficulties (brought on in large part by the Crown's seizure of the Virginia Company in which they were heavily invested), devoted themselves to a monastically shaped life (see Maycock 1980, 195–226). Nicholas Ferrar, one of the family's leaders, devised an activity that would keep his nieces occupied both physically and mentally: the construction of "harmonized" gospel books, made by hand from printed resources. The family called these books "concordances," though they did not list words as concordances commonly do, but rather brought the four gospel accounts into concord. The books are thus gospel harmonies, a textual practice of reconciling the four Gospels going back to Tatian's second-century *Diatessaron* (Peterson 1990). These books were the site of physical and spiritual labour. In addition to keeping their makers from the sin of idleness, the books kept them thinking about the words of the Gospel. Also, their organization of the four Gospels into a continuous 150-chapter account of Christ's life provided a single narrative that could be memorized and recited at five daily hours of prayer, and thus repeated monthly, in its entirety. Finally, in their advanced form (the books grew in complexity as the community made more) the books provided a way to study the four Gospels at once. The concordances were suitable, then, as a communal work project, as matter for public worship, and as a resource for personal biblical study. To these uses another was added from outside: the use of these books as gifts, most notably to King Charles I, at his request.

The Little Gidding concordances and their history have been described at length elsewhere, but we will give a short account of their physical and textual construction here in order to establish the challenges and opportunities involved in producing an electronic edition of one of these books.[5] The most striking fact of the concordances is that they are made almost entirely out of pieces of other publications, either books or collections of engravings: the concordance made for Charles I contains two copies of a 1633 duodecimo New Testament, two copies of a 1631 quarto New Testament, two copies of

[5] See J. Ransome (2005) and Henderson (1982) as well as Dyck (2003, 2008). There are fifteen extant concordances, including nine dealing with the Gospels (including a polyglot), three with the Pentateuch, two with Kings and Chronicles, and one with Acts and Revelation.

Henry Garthwait's 1634 gospel harmony, titled *Monotessaron*, two copies of a third New Testament, leaves from a folio Bible, and over five hundred biblical illustrations, primarily engravings produced in Antwerp. The present-day book they most resemble, if only in their method of construction, is the scrapbook. But they go far beyond anything in the scrapbook mode in their attempt to create a serious or "true" book by such a method. They are meant to be books, produced locally and individually, but with the effect of print. Keeping this effect in mind, it is remarkable that these pages contain not only large pieces taken from other books, but often hundreds of small fragments, creating a cornucopia of image and text.

The concordances were, in their time, highly regarded books: King Charles personally requested one and reportedly called it "a rich present for even the greatest king upon earth" (Muir and White 1996, 77). George Herbert described another of the books as "a rich jewel worthy to be worn in the heart of all Christians" (Muir and White 1996, 76). By the high-print era of the early twentieth century, however, the books could be disregarded: one of them, currently in the collections of Harvard University, was to be sold as blotting paper before it was recognized, and the concordances in general were described by one scholar as "dreadful monuments of misdirected labour" (Hobson 1929, 122). These books, which could be described in the early twentieth century as dreadful monuments, are now the locus of increasing scholarly investigation. The research of the past few decades has brought to light the particularities of early modern book culture, and in particular, its profound mixture of what we tend to describe as manuscript and print practices. For all their oddity, the Little Gidding concordances can now be seen as strangely typical of their time: they bring together traditional practices of composition with the new experience of relatively cheap print. Rather than copying by hand, the makers used scissors and glue to form a new text out of the material of the source. In this way, the broadly circulated text of the Gospels was made into a private book and circulated as a manuscript might.

A *representative page*

Figure 1. Chapter 13 of the king's book © The British Library Board. C23e4
See image plates for a colour version of this figure.

Figure 1 shows a single page from the king's concordance. Chapter 13, significantly, is the first of the 150 chapters to combine multiple gospel accounts, and the layout acknowledges this fact by using the traditional evangelist symbols: a lion with Mark, an ox for Luke, and an angel with Matthew.[6] It thus provides a powerful visual identity for each account as well as figuring the quality of the combination: this is one text from four; it is both one and four. The page contains the story of Jesus's baptism by John. Yet its pictures show the coming of the Holy Spirit at Pentecost and a woman giving food to other women and children, cut from engravings by Michael Coxie and Maarten de Vos.[7] These images move beyond illustration of Christ's baptism, to the working out of the significance of the event, and are linked to the text by manuscript additions. On the top right image, the Ferrars have written "He shall baptize y^u wth the Holy Ghost and with Fire," repeating the text of Matthew 3:11 below. On the lower centre image, the Ferrars have copied Luke 3:11, to the right: "And He y^t hath meat let him doe likewise." The first figure looks biblically forward and historically back to the coming of the Spirit, while the second figure demonstrates the practical action connected to the event.

The central textual engine of the king's concordance as well as the other three extant gospel harmonies made by the Ferrars at about the same time (the mid-1630s) uses a technique the Ferrars called "Collection."[8] This method presents in a single column both a readable composition from the four Gospels and everything left over as a basis for comparison. It does this through two textual categories marked by typeface:

---

[6] The images of Mark and Matthew were cut from the title page of *Vita, Passio, et Resvr-rectio Iesv Christi*, a series of fifty-one illustrations of Christ's life designed by Maarten de Vos. The Ferrars employed other prints from this series elsewhere in the king's book. So far, we have not identified the print from which the ox has been cut.

[7] Maarten de Vos's subject is the feeding of the hungry, from a series on the seven acts of mercy. See Schuckman (1996, 622). The Ferrars used another print from the same plate later in their book, chapter CXXVII "The IVDGEMENT," cropping the Latin text at the bottom: "ESVRIVI ENIM ET DEDISTIS MIHI MANDVCARE." For the Coxie design, engraved by Aegidius Sadeler, see Strauss and Shimura (1986, 108).

[8] In addition to the collection, the king's concordance also provides two other arrangements of the Gospels. The first, called the "comparison," gives the separate gospel accounts in parallel columns; the second, called the "composition," gives a single account made of multiple gospels. These were probably added to ensure the satisfaction of Charles that he was getting the whole gospel text. For a picture showing all three arrangements, please see an earlier version of this paper, Dyck and Williams (2008).

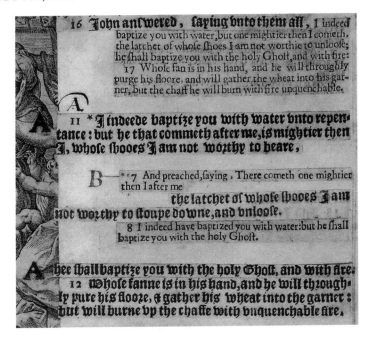

Figure 2. Detail of "Collection"
© The British Library Board. C23e4

The first, in black letter, is named "context," and the second, in roman letter, is named "supplement." The context consists of a composition of the various Gospels into a single story, while the supplement consists of all the leftover matter, primarily repeated material. In the figure above, the Ferrars have combined the accounts of Luke, Matthew, and Mark, choosing Matthew's version of John the Baptist's words over Luke and Mark's versions, except for a detail from Mark. Among other relevant details, all three record John's description of his relative importance to Christ in terms of his relation to Christ's shoes. In Matthew's version, John says that he is not worthy to bear Christ's shoes, while the other two have him refer to "unloosing" the "latchet" of the shoes. In this case, Mark's otherwise minimal account has been brought into the context because it adds the detail of "stooping down," missing from the other two accounts. Again, the Ferrars were guided in this intricate selection of textual fragments by the goal of constructing the fullest possible account, even to the tiniest of details, while leaving the other accounts in play on the page, inviting further study. As a way of displaying the similarities and differences between gospel accounts, the Ferrars' method is strikingly effective.[9] In particular, it foregrounds a textual quality of current interest to multimedia theory and practice—intertextuality—which points out that any text can only be read in relation to other texts. The Ferrars, in building their own multimedia mixes, would have likely understood their practice within the theory of commonplaces, the gathering of materials under common heads, allowing their employment to particular rhetorical ends. The concordances in fact use the word "head" to describe the 150 chapters: these heads each contain a collection of materials. Unlike other early modern commonplace books, though, these have narrative profluence. They thus serve simultaneously as narrative and as a storehouse of materials, fit for reemployment toward emergent occasions.[10]

The "collection" stands out as an elegantly encoded text, unobtrusively demonstrating its complicated structure through the aforementioned alternation of typefaces and by marginal alphanumeric markers indicating gospel source and chapter (e.g., B1, C3, and A3 in Fig. 1 refer to Mark chapter 1, Luke 3, and Matthew 3). Notably, this Little Gidding reference system—what we might generatively think of as Little Gidding markup—has been layered on top of the canonical markup of the biblical text, that is, the marking of the text into books, chapters, and verses. This is all to point out that the Little Gidding community began with one of the most structurally encoded texts available and then restructured it, using the biblical text's canonical markup as an ordering system, but also using typeface as markup. This latter use is striking, in that black letter and roman faces were culturally significant as codes of authority, but had also previously been used as structural marks: for

---

[9] This effectiveness depends, though, on the order of the book. Some seemingly parallel passages are not "collected" here, such as the stories of Christ's chasing the animal sellers and money-lenders out of the temple. Since this occurs late in the first three Gospels, but early in John, the harmonizer has a problem. The Ferrars, following Jansen, solve it by treating John's as a separate incident in chapter 19 and the other Matthew and Mark together in chapter 111, as a "Second Casting Out."

[10] Jonathan Culler's discussion of intertextuality in *The Pursuit of Signs* (2001) helpfully tracks the many uses of the word. It seems most useful here as a way of naming the way that this material object draws attention to the fact that each of its words and pictures has already been read in some other textual *and* material place. The tracking of these material sources in this project does not in any way solve the question of intertextuality (what have these words and images already said?), but rather makes the question more available. In doing so, it takes up the Ferrars' reading of the four Gospels as an overtly intertextual activity. For early modern commonplace theory, see Cave (1979), Crane (1993), and Lechner (1962).

example, in the use of roman faces in early black letter King James Bibles to indicate additional material, such as chapter summaries. In these books, the Little Gidding community gave neither typeface precedence of authority (in some other concordances that the community made, the context is in roman, and the supplement in black letter), but otherwise used it innovatively, to encode a structure within the biblical text itself.

Digitizing the concordances: a brief overview

This project takes up the tasks of scholarly annotation and linking of discreet materials. Large-scale projects, including the Text Image Linking Environment (TILE) (Porter, Reside, and Walsh) and the Open Annotation Collaboration (Cole et al.), as well as many editions set the context for this sort of work. Our materials, though, offer a particular challenge in that they are not only themselves an annotation project, but one that is materially constituted in a peculiar way. The goal of our project is to reveal the creative work of Little Gidding as primarily annotation: the material linking of a multitude of fragments that comment upon each other to form the text's multilinear readings. With a digital approach we can encode these annotations as a compositional structure and encode the fragments. This encoding does not produce a static facsimile, but rather scripts a process, allowing the user to virtually unmix the remix and, in seeing how the books were constructed and from what, to discover much about the Little Gidding methods, answering questions including what gospel sources were favoured over others, which images from a series were included or left out, and what choices were made in shaping the overall effect of the books.

Ad hoc XML as a medium for primary research

Even at the note-taking stage we observed that the encoded electronic environment is well suited to describing the complex content of the king's book. When we began studying the book, both on microfilm and in person, we used a word-processing document with a table to record chapter titles and numbers, scriptural contents, images, manuscript additions, and so on. At the point, however, when we started using XML to describe the book, the description became much more precise, in that XML's extensibility makes possible a customized set of elements and attributes far more sensitive and complex and, finally, usable than any table could be. Our first move was to create a document that, as simply as possible, would describe the book's textual compilation: harmony chapters and their constitutive gospel chapters and verses, in order, noting typeface:

```
<?xml version="1.0" encoding="UTF-8"?>
<hchapter n="XIII" title="JOHNS BAPTIZING &amp; PREACHING/His RAYMENT &amp; FOODE" col="37">
    <excerpt source="b 1:1-3" type="context"/>
    <excerpt source="b 1:4-6" type="supplement"/>
    <excerpt source="c 3:1-6" type="context"/>
    <excerpt source="a 3:1" type="supplement"/>
    <excerpt source="a 3:2-7a" type="context"/>
    <excerpt source="a 3:7b-10" type="supplement"/>
    <excerpt source="c 3:7-16a" type="context"/>
    <excerpt source="c 3:16b-17" type="supplement"/>
    <excerpt source="a 3:11a" type="context"/>
    <excerpt source="b 1:7a" type="supplement"/>
    <excerpt source="b 1:7b" type="context"/>
    <excerpt source="b 1:8" type="supplement"/>
    <excerpt source="a 3:11b-12" type="context"/>
    <excerpt source="c 3:18" type="context"/>
</hchapter>
```

Figure 3: Our first XML for the king's book

We thus created an ad hoc XML structure, one directed to this particular material object, that would most accurately and efficiently describe this book without reference, at this stage, to other markup structures.[11] We designed this DTD as we worked with the book, using the oXygen XML editor's "learn structure" feature, which produces a DTD to fit the document.[12] Throughout this initial encoding, we changed our XML document structure (via the DTD) as the source material dictated. At times while working with the book in the archive, Paul made several DTD changes a day. The XML editor served not to arrange previously gathered information within a previously established structure, but as an arena in which to record information as that information was gathered and simultaneously to experiment with encoding structures. Earlier versions of oXygen had a "learn structure" command that had to be applied manually, while newer versions automate this function. It is important for our purposes to be able to control this function manually. In this way, the scholar can make structural changes as the material demands, but then be bound by these structural rules as he or she proceeds, able to

---

[11] See Bart (2006) for a discussion of the use of experimental markup as a way of handling a particularly problematic manuscript in the *Piers Plowman* Electronic Archive. Because the text in question conflates the three established versions of the poem, it vexes normal editorial process and, consequently, TEI markup. Bart's method uses experimental markup to describe the text's eccentricity, making rigorous study of the text possible, and raises the question of how experimental methods can be brought into the practices of TEI.

[12] See oXygen XML Editor, SyncRO Soft, accessed 23 October 2009, http://www.oxygenxml.com.

change these rules if a change is justified by the material. If "learn structure" is automatic, then any change will automatically become part of the rule, disabling XML's usefulness as a disciplinary tool. The judicious use of sophisticated XML editors such as oXygen is itself an act of research, helping the scholar gather, structure, and articulate new intellectual content. As a tool for gathering information on the Little Gidding book, our XML editor was vastly superior to the word processor that we had used earlier, especially in that it could contain the entire original textual structure (and later the whole gospel text itself) without overwhelming the writing space. Our Word file used a table that captured the bare-bones structure of the king's book; whenever we wanted to note anything about the book, we needed first to describe what part of the book we were noting. Using an XML editor, we were able instead to notate and build a facsimile of the king's book, a facsimile that began as a skeleton, giving the structure of the document without the actual gospel text, which we later fleshed out with the text itself. Starting with a structural skeleton allowed us to work backwards through the Little Gidding process, establishing first what *they* had established first: namely, a plan of how the four Gospels would fit together. As mentioned above, this skeleton also facilitated our documentation of the book's images. Before we added text to the structure, we added notes on the images, a workflow that allowed us to specify the images' textual locations without us having to navigate the text at the same time.

Two examples of the kinds of information we were able to record accurately within our XML structure through ad hoc elements follow. The first is the manuscript writing on images referred to above.

Figure 4. Manuscript on images
© The British Library Board. C23e4

In this example from chapter 13, the <figure> element provides a reliable container for all information about that figure, and Paul added a manuscript element within it:

```
<figure col="40">
  <figDesc>Tongues of Fire (Pentecost), woman in center of group of men and women, in frame with
   incense spelling ABBA PATER</figDesc>
  <head>PARS TOTIVS ET DE TOTO FIDES . et dedit dominus hominibus,</head>
  <text>Hod hakadosh (Hebrew: "divine favour")</text>
  <ms>He shall baptize yu' wth' the Holy Ghost and with Fire</ms>
</figure>
```

Figure 5. An added element

Likewise, whenever one of the four gospel accounts breaks off and does not continue on the next page, but rather several pages later, the Ferrars add a note to this effect:

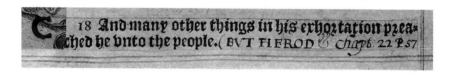

Figure 6. A manuscript "link"
© The British Library Board. C23e4

This figure shows the end of Chapter XIII, in column 40, which ends with Luke 3:18. The manuscript "link" indicates that the Luke narrative continues with the words "But Herod ..." in Chapter XXII, column 57. We encoded this as follows:

```
<excerpt source="c.3:18" type="context"/>
<link col="40">
  <hi rend="letter(roman)">(BVT HEROD &amp; chapt: 22 P 57</hi>
</link>
```

Figure 7. Encoding the "link"

The transition to a full text

In starting with a skeletal structure and then populating it, we have an opportunity to reconstruct in part the Little Gidding compositional process itself, in a highly computing-assisted way. The canonical structure of the Gospels and their free availability on the Web made it possible to automate the first step in the transition from structure to full text. Once we had encoded the basic structure of the king's book, Stuart Williams developed his own cut-and-paste technique—something we playfully called "gospelgrab"—as a midway step in the development of our transcription of the gospel text.

He wrote a program (in Python) to pull a modern-spelling, public domain version of the King James text into the Little Gidding structure.[13] Our XML reference thus becomes populated with the full text:

<verse book="b" cnumber="2" id="b.1.1-c" type="context" vnumber="1">¶ The beginning of the Gospel of Jesus Christ the Sonne of God, </verse>

<verse book="b" cnumber="2" id="b.1.2-c" type="context" vnumber="2"> As it is written in the

Figure 8. Populating the structure

This automated, high-speed re-enactment of the Little Gidding concordance-making process provided a base text (modern in spelling, punctuation, and other textual features) that we could then conform to the early modern text as found in the king's book, using an XML editor.

TEI/VRA conversion

It has never been our goal to finally publish this edition using our original ad hoc markup. Rather, even as the canonical book-chapter-verse reference system of the Bible works precisely because it is a shared standard, so we are committed to encoding our material in as standard a format as possible. The Text Encoding Initiative (TEI) provides a remarkably wide-ranging set of elements with which to mark a text, and it is the standard to which we aim.[14] This said, there is much about the Little Gidding books that pushes the limits of a markup structure, and so we anticipate doing some customization, following TEI guidelines. While TEI provides a highly nuanced structure for text, it does not attempt to do so for images, and so we are using the Visual Resources Association (VRA) scheme to describe the images in the book, which effectively form not a single work, but a collection of works.[15] By using these standards, we hope to give our work a measure of accessibility and,

---

[13] Python is an open-source, general purpose, high-level programming language. See Python Software Foundation, Python, accessed 23 October 2009, http://www.python. org. The King James Version text was encoded by Wolfgang Shultz and was down-loaded in 2006 from Zefania XML Bible Markup Language Files, Sourceforge, Geeknet, accessed 23 October 2009, http://sourceforge.net/projects/zefania-sharp/. Specific-ally, we excerpted the Gospels from kjv.xml, which was in sf_kjv.zip.

[14] TEI Consortium, "TEI Guidelines," accessed 23 October 2009, at http://www.tei-c. org/Guidelines/.

[15] Visual Resources Association (VRA), accessed 23 October 2009, http://www.vraweb. org/.

consequently, permanence. While we are designing an interface around the particularities of the Little Gidding book, our goal is to make our data itself as open as possible to other tools, both present and future, so that that data can be put to many uses, including display in future interfaces.[16] We see the standard structures of the TEI and VRA as the best way of addressing this goal.

Besides the openness of the data, standards provide a more immediate benefit. TEI and VRA provide not only an agreed upon method, but ones positively grounded in good scholarly practice. In other words, these standards have a positive disciplinary effect, at times suggesting and at other times demanding that we ask certain questions of our material. The TEI header in itself provides an implicit tutorial in the accountability required to produce a scholarly edition. Likewise, the attributes available within elements can pose helpful questions. For instance, our ad hoc XML had used an <ms> tag, which is not a TEI element, to note handwritten material on images. In converting the structure to TEI, we settled on the "hand" attribute in TEI to indicate the handwriting, and this then immediately posed the question whether different hands could be detected in the document (something which the original research had not systematically tracked). Another suggestive possibility within TEI has proved central to the direction we have taken with our textbase: this is the process of "inclusion," which we discuss at length below.

Deconstructing our textbase into multiple documents

A central concern of our project is to handle the Little Gidding concordance as well as all its sources as objects in their own right. Our ad hoc XML does a good job of describing the Little Gidding concordance, but it does not describe sources themselves, only the materials derived from those sources, as they appear in the concordance. Once we had run our gospelgrab procedure and matched our text to the original, we faced a choice. Would we treat the resulting text as a single unit, the product of a cut-and-paste process, which we would then edit in a standard way, or would we construct a system that cuts-and-pastes the concordance every time it is used? Paul initially assumed the former: as a textual scholar he wanted a stable text upon which he could work. Stuart and Ryan, working on this project at different times, have both consistently favoured the latter. Significantly, they as programmers without specialist knowledge of early modern materials have been able to go much further than the literary specialist in imagining ways to computationally

---

[16] All of our programming is open source. We will explore the usefulness of a Creative Commons licensing structure for our transcription and encoding, while all images we use will be by agreement with the institutions owning the original documents.

serve the primary materials, developing tools that address the particularity of the materials.

We can helpfully address the possible ways of handling the concordances in terms of depth. The concordances themselves have been constructed from a vast and potentially chaotic collection of pieces. These have been ordered, glued, and pressed to form a book that has lasted some 375 years. In order to form a functioning book, these many pieces have been deliberately, laboriously, and effectively formed into a single material object. But what does one now do with the book as a scholar? The scholarly task attempts to follow the process, working backwards to identify positively all the constituent parts and bring the material under a kind of scholarly control. The critical fact, however, is that the completed concordances, though a unity, are not functionally or even physically a single piece. While they are admirably well fitted and smooth, this smoothness is that of the well-made mosaic: it does not disguise the pieces but rather demonstrates a kind of marvellous multiplicity. The pages of the concordance present both a singular object and a collection of materials standing dynamically, on the page—dynamically, that is, in that they have each been placed there to a particular end. In this way, the edges (of each pasted segment) matter; they in fact make all the difference between this and a conventionally produced book. The edges, we argue, act rhetorically to suggest the multiple ways of reading described in the book's preface, indicating not a text that has been finally arranged, but an endlessly rearranging text.

When does modern scholarship go too far in flattening the text and how might it track the dynamics of the page? The only currently available representation of the king's concordance is a British Library microfilm, and it makes a good example of the two-dimensional nature of imaged texts. The microfilm successfully captures the biblical text and most marginal letters and headings. It predictably loses shading details in the prints, but gives a workable representation of them. However, due to its relatively low resolution and poor capturing of grayscale values, it makes the handwriting barely legible and barely shows the gold lettering used for some initial letters in the headings as well as for the marginal Ds that indicate John's Gospel, presumably because of the reflectance of the gold. More critically, the microfilm washes out almost all of the edges, effectively presenting not a cut-and-paste page, but rather a poorly printed conventional one. The handwork has been erased, and the effect is ugly, communicating little of this book's appeal to Charles I.[17] The flatness of this representation becomes most obvious at chapter 120, where a large flap on the original page reveals a second image beneath, a function about which the user of the microfilm can only guess. This missing information captures the overall effect of the microfilm: given the lack of a better representation, the microfilm is invaluable, but it is at best a dim memory of the artefact.

The next order of depth comes with the high-resolution photographic facsimile. Notably, obtaining funding for such images is a significant material challenge facing the production of this digital edition. In the few images we have ordered from the British Library so far, though, we have been pleased to see that they display the cut-and-pasted quality of the page, clearly showing the edges of the pieces. A full printed photographic facsimile of the book would have some appeal: it would immediately communicate the size of the original and something of what would have been involved in using it. No matter how clear, though, the photographs would remain two dimensional, not only missing the tactile sense of the original, but also giving the overall sense of the original as a *modern* book, a singular object rather than a collection of texts. On a practical level, a full printed photographic facsimile would also be prohibitively expensive.

Significantly deeper would be a digital photographic facsimile accompanied by a single XML file, in the form of many current electronic editions. This would allow a user to see photographs of the original while also viewing, for example, a transcription of the text, a table of contents, and information about the prints. These last three components would be encoded in the XML file, with regularized spelling and cross-referencing of sources, allowing a user to follow active hyperlinks for the links added by the Ferrars (Fig. 6), to search the text and images for recurring words or motifs, or to find prints by a particular artist, such as Maarten de Vos, among other functions. This would go a long way to representing the dynamic qualities of the original, but it would still treat the original as a single object, and in so doing, would resist the cut-and-paste structure of the materials.

The Little Gidding concordances provide us with an ideal opportunity to push digital tools and methodology deeper than we otherwise might, for they demand an edition made of many editions, in which one is always view-

---

[17] We are not suggesting that this appeal was uniquely aesthetic, for this book could hardly have competed with most objects in Charles's extensive art collection on aesthetic grounds alone. At the same time, its status as a handmade, artistically rich, devotional book cannot be separated from its aesthetic appeal.

ing at least two books at once. The achievement of the concordances is in their presentation of a single text-object via the collection of materials from many text-objects, a complexity that is always present to the reader through the physical make-up of the page. Rather than model this as a single XML file (albeit one with links to source materials), we are working back to something like our initial gospelgrab document, producing a document that contains very little content, but that instead records what pieces of what sources the Ferrars put where; that is to say, an order:

```
- <joinGrp targFunc="start end">
    <join type="context" targets="bible1631.xml#c.3.16.a bible1631.xml#c.3.16.a" />
    <join type="supplement" targets="bible1633.xml#c.3.16.b bible1633.xml#c.3.17" />
    <join type="context" targets="bible1631.xml#a.3.11.a bible1631.xml#a.3.11.a" />
    <join type="supplement" targets="bible1633.xml#a.3.11.b bible1633.xml#b.1.7.a" />
    <join type="context" targets="bible1631.xml#b.1.7.b bible1631.xml#b.1.7.b" />
    <join type="supplement" targets="bible1633.xml#b.1.8 bible1633.xml#b.1.8" />
    <join type="context" targets="bible1631.xml#a.3.11.b bible1631.xml#a.3.12" />
    <join type="context" targets="bible1631.xml#c.3.18 bible1631.xml#c.3.18" />
  </joinGrp>
```

Figure 9. TEI structural document

As the excerpt above shows, this ordering document uses empty markup to indicate, in the case of each biblical fragment, the edition, book, chapter, and verses that make up that fragment. In the case of the images, we will assign an identification code as well as a brief description to each print or print fragment. These elements refer to other documents, in this case, XML transcriptions and photographs of the Gospels from both 1631 and 1633 New Testaments, as well as various series of prints, also encoded in XML and, if possible, photographed.[18] The only content in this structural document is what the Ferrars wrote themselves: the table of contents, the preface and title, the chapter titles, the commentary, the marginal references, and the links.

Our separation of the many sources that make up any Little Gidding concordance, effectively deconstructing it, allows the scholar to consider more thoroughly its construction, making immediately available the sources as much as possible in their own right, and making apparent the compositional choices of the Ferrars, as those choices were enacted on the sources. The sources will be available to be browsed and searched as individual documents; but, just as importantly, they will also be used alongside the concordance, allowing the re-enactment of the Ferrars' snipping and arrangement

---

[18] We hope to work with various archives, including the Museum Plantin-Moretus in Antwerp and the Archives and Special Collections of the University of Manitoba in Winnipeg, to acquire these images.

of them on the page. This will demonstrate what has been selected in both its former and new contexts, as well as what has been left out. In some cases, parts of single prints have been used in diverse places in the concordance. Our process, in imitating that of the Ferrars, will open their process—one of lively rhetorical employment of a wide range of rich materials—to further scholarly investigation.[19]

One question that arises out of the separation of the ordering document from the source documents concerns the particular and minute choices of the Ferrars. If the Ferrars had only ever used whole verses or whole prints—in other words, units already recognized in bibliographic convention—then the ordering document could simply refer to these units with no further scholarly intervention. In fact, though, the Ferrars very often used partial verses and partial prints. What is the best location, then, for the information concerning this particular and idiosyncratic subdivision of bibliographical parts? Take for instance, the case of Mark 1:7, which in the king's book is split into two sections, one in roman typeface (indicating supplement) and the other in black letter (indicating context).

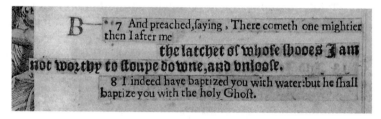

Figure 10. Splitting verses
© The British Library Board. C23e4

To the left of this verse, coincidentally, the Ferrars have pasted a section from a larger print, showing a woman giving food to the poor (see Fig. 1). Should these divisions, namely the division of Mark 1:7 and the division of the print, be recorded in the ordering document? This would have the advantage of keeping all of the Ferrars' compositional choices in this document and would not interfere with the natural structure of the source document, both of

---

[19] We came to this approach in part through a conversation with Daniel O'Donnell, who put a similar concept to work in his edition of Caedmon's Hymn (2005), which generated several display texts from several manuscript witnesses through XSLT processing that enacted editorial decisions, eliminating duplication of texts while separating editorial choices from materials.

which fit our editorial goals. One could use Xpointer and count words, indicating that only the first ten words of verse 7 are included in the supplement and that every word after that is in the context. Likewise, one could indicate the coordinates of the excerpt from the source print. However, this would also require inventing a reference system that would exist in the absence of the source document itself, an absence that is troubled both in principle and in practice. Numbering words, for instance, requires that words follow modern typographical conventions. In the example above, though, they do not. How does one count "preached,saying?" We read this as two words and one comma, which are present, but we also read a word space, which is not there. While we have not yet decided how to handle irregular word spacing in our XML, the issue points to a larger problem with such a reference system: that it is fragile. In theory it is possible to get it right, but very small errors would be difficult to detect and would ruin our representation of the original text.

The problem in principle with noting all the cuts in the order document is that this separates the action of cutting from the thing being cut. The issue is how to respect and represent the two kinds of information, that is, the design of the Little Gidding book including all of its cuts and the uncut primary materials. We want an edition that conserves both. We think that we can do this by marking the Ferrars' cuts in the images of the primary materials, but in non-obtrusive ways. To address the issue of verse subdivisions, we are currently marking the divisions as segments called "subverses." The black letter 1631 New Testament file contains these lines:

```
- <ab type="verse" n="7" xml:id="b.1.7">
    <seg type="subverse" n="a" xml:id="b.1.7.a">And preached, faying, There commeth one
    mightier than I after me,</seg>
    <seg type="subverse" n="b" xml:id="b.1.7.b">the latchet of whofe fhooes I am not worthy
    to ftoupe downe, and vnloofe.</seg>
```

Figure 11. 1631 New Testament. Note placement of third comma.

The roman 1633 New Testament file contains these lines:

```
- <ab type="verse" n="7" xml:id="b.1.7">
    <seg type="subverse" n="a" xml:id="b.1.7.a">And preached, faying, There cometh one
    mightier than I after me</seg>
    <seg type="subverse" n="b" xml:id="b.1.7.b">, the latchet of whofe fhoes I am not
    worthie to ftoupe down, and vnloofe.</seg>
```

Figure 12. 1633 New Testament. Note placement of third comma.

The two are joined in the Little Gidding structure document in this way:

```
<join type="supplement" targets="bible1633.xml#b.1.7.a bible1633.xml#b.1.7.a" />
<join type="context" targets="bible1631.xml#b.1.7.b bible1631.xml#b.1.7.b" />
```

Figure 13. How the two "subverses" are joined.

While this markup does add information to the source material, it follows the Ferrars' practice of not cutting across verse boundaries, but only within them, so that there are no overlapping elements (that is, while they frequently use partial verses, they never produce a new "verse" by joining the final section of one verse with the initial section of another). Both the Ferrars' cuts and our subverses follow the grain of the biblical verse divisions, naturally extending them. The subverse segments allow us both to point reliably to the exact textual fragment used by the Ferrars and to present the source text with the subverse markup suppressed. It also will allow a user to take an alternate approach to the materials, starting with a source and seeing how it was cut, rather than starting from the finished book. Likewise, we will mark image fragments, encoding them with their spatial coordinates, both so that we can reliably point to specific fragments and also so that users can browse prints, see which ones were cut (rather than pasted whole), and then see exactly how they were cut.

The project requires any number of decisions (large and small) when it comes to XML encoding practices. These end up involving a curious mixture of computational, representational, editorial, and practical considerations. For instance, we considered using XInclude to mark our inclusions, which would have had some computational advantages (since the actual inclusions could have been handled by various software frameworks with no additional programming on our part). However, this computational advantage has a representational disadvantage. We do not need an inclusion mechanism merely to be a convenient method to handle a large text; we are interested in the inclusions themselves, not in simply performing inclusions. Yet the XInclude technique would force us to choose, at the computational stage, between having the inclusions performed invisibly, so that our own programming would not even see the boundaries, or not at all.[20] We need a computational approach that is more visible, such as the TEI <join> tag, whose

---

[20] XInclude is a mechanism for general purpose inclusion. See "XInclude Current Status," World Wide Web Consortium (W3C), accessed 23 October 2009, http://www.w3.org/standards/techs/xinclude#w3c_all.

representation can be flexibly chosen with appropriate programming (at the cost of having to actually do that programming).

We also considered using the <anchor> tag as an empty element to mark subverses without imposing an additional hierarchical level on the source document. This would have worked reasonably well, but the editorial references it implied seemed awkward. If we were to follow the usual practice of referring to the first part of a subverse as "a" and the second as "b," would the empty element dividing the verse be labelled "a" or "b"? If it is to mark the end of an excerpt, it would be natural to label it "a," since that would allow us to specify that an excerpt ran until the end of the "a" division. Yet if it is to mark the beginning of an excerpt, it would be natural to label it "b," since that would allow us to specify that an excerpt ran from the start of the "b" division. The label is, of course, in one sense arbitrary, and either scheme could be made to work; however, one advantage of XML encoding is that it combines, in varying degrees, human-readability with the precision necessary to support useful computation. By using subverses with content, we are able to preserve this advantage, using labels such as "a" and "b" in ways that are consistent with editorial instincts and sufficiently precise for computation.

User interface

Even before transitioning to the TEI and reconstructed source documents, we prototyped an interface to the materials using HTML in conjunction with a JavaScript framework at the front-end and a backend based on the "Ruby on Rails" framework.[21] Our initial effort focuses on two goals: the effective navigation of the material and support for scholarly collaboration in the identification of the prints used by the Ferrars. The navigation interface presents four separate views of the materials: a table of contents (top left), the transcription (bottom left), a facsimile of the current page (centre), and a column of thumbnails (right) (see Fig. 14). The key feature is that each view is synchronized with the others. So for instance, when users click on a chapter heading in the table of contents, the chapter view scrolls to display the current chapter, the facsimile view displays the current page, and the thumbnail view shows the current page and those near it. Even at this early stage, this interface is already the most accessible manner in which to browse the document. It also begins to represent the document's cut-and-paste means of production by reunifying the list of figures.

---

[21] Ruby on Rails is an open source web framework. See David Heinemeier Hansson, Ruby on Rails, accessed 23 October 2009, http://rubyonrails.org/.

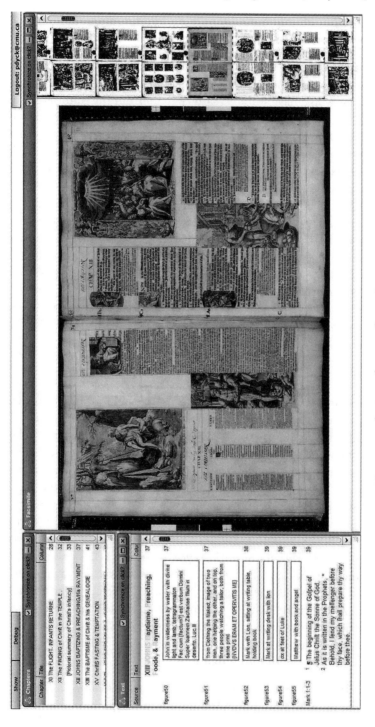

Figure 14. The Interface as of March 2010, at
http://littlegidding.pauldyck.com

The further we get in developing the interface, the more we will be able to accommodate the contributions of a wider group of scholars. Identifying the hundreds of engravings used in the concordance is one of our greatest immediate scholarly tasks, and so we are currently testing a mechanism to allow users to add comments on figures. Originally our plan was to have someone edit the XML sources separate from the interface; however, it quickly became apparent that it would be more productive to modify the XML file via the user interface (given adequate attention to issues of authorization and version control). This desire for specialized editing tools was intensified when we split the document into multiple sources, since it was much easier to track the relationship between the sources computationally than by using a generic XML editor manually.

In continuing to develop a user interface that faithfully represents the complex structure of the source material, we imagine a set of interface elements that represent each document (the Bibles, the prints, and the concordance itself) as a navigable whole in its own right, but also as synchronized with each of the others. Clicking on a figure as represented in the concordance ought, for instance, to display information about the print from which it comes, and, if possible, display that print in its various contexts: its original series; others by the same designer, engraver, or printer; or others of the same biblical scene. In this way, we can represent the dynamism inherent in the construction of the concordance itself. Perhaps techniques of animation can be applied to represent the integration of elements into the concordance even more dramatically.[22]

So, how might this project come to fruition? Thus far, it has been possible because of the personal interest of two programmers not in academic positions (and thus in no professional way rewarded for their work) and because of the generous support of Canadian Mennonite University, which has funded research travel and a research assistant. At this point, though, we face an apparent hump: while we have done considerable groundwork, we need greater resources in order to take the project further. Primarily, we lack high-resolution images of BL C23e4, as well as the funding required to purchase such images. We have applied for research funding for the project, including digital images, from the Canadian government, receiving positive reviews

---

[22] Given that the multiple materials of the concordances seem to us to call for an enriched spatial approach, it is interesting to note that John B. Krygier describes cartography itself as intertextual, and finds that computers make "applied intertextuality easy" (1999, 248).

but no funds as yet. At the same time, it is possible that institutions owning other Little Gidding scriptural harmonies may be better positioned than the British Library to partner with us by providing images. We are beginning to explore these options. Since this project would ideally and ultimately include all the extant Little Gidding books, which together would provide the best basis for their study, it does not especially matter where we begin. That said, since BL C23e4 is the most complex and richly illustrated of the books, its inclusion is particularly important.

In addition to starting with images of a Little Gidding book, we also need to have images of the source materials—especially the biblical editions and the biblical illustrations—used in making that book. This is important to the extent that the materials have been modified by cutting: the less intact, the more important that we provide an image of the original object. Some of these images are available in online databases, particularly ARTstor, and we plan to investigate the possibilities of linking to these images from within our interface.[23] Ideally, though, if and when we can scan original materials and include them in our project, we will.

We have not yet thought a great deal about eventual delivery. We would prefer that this project be freely available so that its materials will gain a larger audience, but we are also aware that for-fee publication may provide more reliable funding for the maintenance of the project.

Conclusion

In conclusion, while this project presents many unique scholarly and computational challenges, it does seem to us to bring to the fore some common truths. The overarching observation here is that scholars in general do not take all they can from XML. The Little Gidding books highlight just how appropriate a tool XML can be not only at a project's delivery stage, but from the beginning of its conceptualization. As an ad hoc tool, XML has proved suitable to our materials. In fact, even if we lacked computation altogether, XML would still be a better way philosophically of representing the Little Gidding books than any other method known to us. This suitability has mostly to do with the thousands of data points in this material: so long as the ad hoc XML categorizes these data points in a structured and precise way, it can provide an effective base for a smooth transition to further project stages—given a consistent naming system, names can be changed, and each name

---

[23] ARTstor, Andrew W. Mellon Foundation, accessed 23 October 2009, http://www.artstor.org.

change provides an opportunity for examination. The ad hoc XML anchors this structure in the most accurate description of the materials themselves. We also think that this suitability brings out the non-modern quality of any early text: early books are perhaps as much like present-day text and image bases as they are like present-day books. Since any edition, whether print or digital, is a representation, the digital edition has the advantage of making the material strange rather than making it familiar. Significantly, one of the indications to us that this project is worthwhile is the great extent to which it pushes us to rethink both the book and the text- and image-base, perhaps most clearly in the way that the material has pushed us not only to represent the product of this work in a user interface, but also to develop a photograph/XML interface as a working tool, one that allows us both to construct this edition and to model the original material process of the Ferrars.

WORKS CITED

The New Testament ... Newly Translated Out of the Original Greek, etc. 1633. Edinburgh: By the Printer to the Kings Majestie [Robert Young].

The New Testament ... Newly Translated out of the Originall Greeke, etc. 1631. Robert Barker & the Assignes of Iohn Bill: London.

Bart, Patricia R. 2006. "Experimental Markup in a TEI-Conformant Setting." *Digital Medievalist* 2 (1): http://www.digitalmedievalist.org/journal/2.1/bart/.

Cave, Terence. 1979. *The Cornucopian Text: Problems of Writing in the French Renaissance*. Oxford: Clarendon Press.

Cole, Tim, Neil Fraistat, Jane Hunter, and Herbert Van de Sompel. The Open Annotation Collaboration. University of Illinois. Accessed 23 October 2009. http://www.openannotation.org.

Crane, Mary Thomas. 1993. *Framing Authority: Sayings, Self, and Society in Sixteenth-Century England*. Princeton: Princeton University Press.

Culler, Jonathan. 2001. *The Pursuit of Signs*. London: Routledge.

Dyck, Paul. 2003. "'So Rare a Use': Scissors, Reading, and Devotion at Little Gidding." *The George Herbert Journal* 27 (1–2): 67–81.

_____ 2008. "'A New Kind of Printing': Cutting and Pasting a Book for a King at Little Gidding." *Library: The Transactions of the Bibliographical Society* 9 (3): 306–33.

Dyck, Paul, and Stuart Williams. 2008. "Toward an Electronic Edition of an Early Modern Assembled Book." *Computing Humanities Working Papers* A (44): n.p.

Early English Books Online. 2003–10. ProQuest LLC. http://eebo.chadwyck.com/home.

Ferrar Family. 1635. *The Actions & Doctrine & Other Passages Touching Our Lord & Sauior Iesus Christ, as They Are Related by the Foure Euangelists, Reduced into One Complete Body of Historie, Wherein That, Wch Is Seuerally Related by Them, Is Digested into Order, and That, Wch Is Jointly Related by All or Any Twoe or More of Them Is, First Expressed in Their Own Words by Way of Comparison, and Secondly Brought into One Narration by Way of Composition, and Thirdly Extracted into One Clear Context by Way of Collection ... to Wch Are Added Sundry Pictures, Expressing Either the Facts Themselues or Their Types & Figures ... 1635*. [Compiled by Nicholas Ferrar and His Family.]. British Library C23e4.

Henderson, George. 1982. "Biblical Illustration in the Age of Laud." *Transactions of the Cambridge Bibliographical Society* 8 (2): 173–216.

Hobson, G. D. 1929. *Bindings in Cambridge Libraries*. Cambridge: Cambridge University Press.

Kirschenbaum, Matthew G. 2004. "'So the Colors Cover the Wires': Interface, Aesthetics, and Usability." In *A Companion to Digital Humanities*, edited by Susan Schreibman, Ray Siemens, and John Unsworth, 523–42. Oxford: Blackwell.

Krygier, J. B. 1999. "Cartographic Multimedia and Praxis in Human Geography and the Social Sciences." In *Multimedia Cartography*, edited by William Cartwright, Michael P. Peterson, and Georg F. Gartner, 245-56. New York: Springer.

Lechner, Sister Joan Marie O. S. U. 1962. *Renaissance Concepts of the Commonplaces*. New York: Pageant.

Little Gidding Test Site. 2010. http://littlegidding.pauldyck.com.

Maycock, A. L. 1980. *Nicholas Ferrar of Little Gidding*. Grand Rapids: Eerdmans.

Muir, Lynette R., and John A. White, eds. 1996. *Materials for the Life of Nicholas Ferrar: A Reconstruction of John Ferrar's Account of his Brother's Life Based on All the Surviving Copies*. Leeds: Leeds Philosophical and Literary Society.

O'Donnell, Daniel Paul. 2005. "The Ghost in the Machine: Revisiting an Old Model for the Dynamic Generation of Digital Editions." *HumanIT* 8 (1): 51–71.

Peterson, William L. 1990. "Tatian's Diatessaron." In *Ancient Christian Gospels: Their History and Development*, by Helmut Koester, 403–30. London: SCM Press.

Porter, Dot, Doug Reside, and John A. Walsh. Text Image Linking Environment (TILE). Digital Humanities Observatory and Maryland Institute for Technology in the Humanities. Accessed 23 October 2009. http://mith.umd.edu/tile/.

Ransome, D. R. 2000. "John Ferrar of Little Gidding." *Records of Huntingdonshire* 3 (8): 16–24.

Ransome, Joyce. 2003. "Prelude to Piety: Nicholas Ferrar's Grand Tour." *The Seventeenth Century* 18:1–24.

_____ 2005. "Monotessaron: The Harmonies of Little Gidding." *The Seventeenth Century* 20:22–52.

_____ 2011. *The Web of Friendship: Nicholas Ferrar and Little Gidding*. Cambridge: James Clarke.

Schuckman, Christiaan. 1996. *Hollstein's Dutch & Flemish Etchings, Engravings, and Woodcuts 1450-1700: Maarten de Vos*. Edited by D. De Hoop Scheffer. Vol. 44. Rotterdam: Sound & Vision Interactive.

Strauss, Walter L., and Tomoko Shimura, eds. 1986. *The Illustrated Bartsch: Netherlandish Artists: Cornelius Cort*. New York: Abaris Books.

TEI Consortium, eds. *TEI P5: Guidelines for Electronic Text Encoding and Interchange*. TEI Consortium. Accessed 23 October 2009. http://www.tei-c.org/release/doc/tei-p5-doc/en/html/index.html.

_____, eds. "16. Linking, Segmentation, and Alignment." In *TEI P5: Guidelines for Electronic Text Encoding and Interchange.* TEI Consortium. Accessed 23 October 2009. http://www.tei-c.org/release/doc/tei-p5-doc/en/html/SA.html.

Williams, A. M. 1970. *Conversations at Little Gidding: "On the Retirement of Charles V," "On the Austere Life."* Cambridge: Cambridge University Press.

Vexed Impressions: Towards a Digital Archive of Broadside Ballad Illustrations

Patricia Fumerton
University of California,
Santa Barbara
pfumer@english.ucsb.edu

Carl Stahmer
University of California,
Santa Barbara
cstahmer@gmail.com

Kris McAbee
University of Arkansas,
Little Rock
kxmcabee@ualr.edu

Megan Palmer Browne
University of California,
Santa Barbara
meganpalmerbrowne@gmail.com

The time is ripe to bring cheap art, beloved in its day by the masses, back into the early modern picture, even if that picture needs to be a digital image. Today's increasing scholarly interest in ephemera puts us on the road to such a recovery. A notion of the ephemeral was first embraced by New Historicist and Cultural Materialist critics in the 1980s under the guise of the "marginal" or "out-of-the-ordinary" and placed in the service of "high" or court culture.[1] But more recent consideration of ephemeral artefacts recognizes their value as a reflection of the "low" or popular, if also of the crude and impermanent. Still, resistance among art historians has been strong. As art historian Kevin Murphy observes,

> Scholars of early modern culture have been increasingly energetic in mining ephemeral artifacts for insights into political, cultural,

---

[1] It is ironic that the New Historicism of the 1980s often turned to the curious, the obscure, and the momentary in the service of the cultivated, the high, and the enduring (court politics, canonical literature—including Shakespeare's plays—or esteemed art, such as Holbein's *The Ambassadors* portrait, made even more famous by Stephen Greenblatt's extensive discussion of the painting). See Patricia Fumerton's evaluation of the first phase of New Historicism and her early call for a move away from a single focus on high culture (1999). For Greenblatt's discussion of *The Ambassadors* portrait, see Greenblatt (1980, 17–26).

ISBN 978-0-86698-499-7 (online)   ISBN 978-0-86698-474-4 (print)
New Technologies in Medieval and Renaissance Studies 3 (2012) 257–285

social and religious life during the period. At the same time, however, art historians—and particularly historians of the print—have continued to focus on the work of a few renowned masters and to eschew cheaper and less artistically ambitious works, despite all they have to teach us.[2]

Leading the way for serious study of ephemeral printed art, Murphy, together with Sally O'Driscoll, organized a 2009 conference at the Graduate Center CUNY, "Ephemera: Impermanent Works in the Literary and Visual Culture of the Long Eighteenth Century," 12–14 March (http://web.gc.cuny.edu/dept/ArtHi/eph.pdf). This three-day event brought together renowned curators and scholars of the seventeenth through the nineteenth centuries to engage seriously with such transient artefacts as manuscript drafts, almanacs, advertisements, trade cards, watch papers, bookplates, currency, sheet music, playing cards, comic books, oral songs, and of course, printed broadside ballads. A panel of curators jump-started the event, consisting of Georgia Barnhill, Curator of Graphic Arts at the American Antiquarian Society; Henry Raine, Head of Library Technical Services at the New-York Historical Society; and—what might appear the odd woman out—Patricia Fumerton, Professor of English and Director of the *English Broadside Ballad Archive*, or EBBA, at UCSB (http://ebba.english.ucsb.edu/). While no curator by any traditional stretch of the definition, Fumerton's presence on the panel acknowledged what is perhaps the major facilitator of access to ephemeral artefacts—the Internet.

Online archives, such as the immense *Early English Books Online* (EEBO) (http://eebo.chadwyck.com/home) and *Eighteenth-Century Collections Online* (ECCO) (http://gdc.gale.com/products/eighteenth-century-collections-online/), have spawned new awareness of thousands of non-canonical texts and images that might never have otherwise been seen by scholars or the general public (the originals not only in most cases unknown but obscured by being tucked away in boxes or back rooms of often hard-to-access rare book rooms). Even more important in promoting access to ephemera are the more specialized archives determined to bring attention to cultural artefacts either lost among the millions of bits of data of EEBO and ECCO or not yet, and perhaps never to be, digitally archived in those large databases precisely because they are perceived to have only passing value next to works with more name recognition. *The Proceedings of the Old Bailey* (http://www.oldbai-

---

[2] We are grateful to Dr. Murphy for allowing us to quote his insights, made in email conversation with Patricia Fumerton.

leyonline.org/), for instance, is dedicated to making the marginal, in this case court records, matter. Such also is the objective of the EBBA.

EBBA's grappling with the challenge of digitally archiving ephemeral art is the subject of this essay, which is written collaboratively by several key members of the EBBA team, including its director, Patricia Fumerton.[3] Funded in large part by the National Endowment for the Humanities, EBBA is dedicated to mounting online all surviving early ballads printed in English, with priority given to black-letter broadsides of the seventeenth century—the heyday of the printed broadside ballad. The single most printed medium in the literary marketplace of seventeenth-century London, broadside ballads (called "broad-sides" because they were printed on one side of a large or "broad" sheet of paper) were a form of mass communication. Tessa Watt (1991) estimates that as early as the late sixteenth century they were possibly printed in the millions,[4] and then sent onto the city's streets or out into the provinces in the packs of peddlers along with other cheap fare. Indeed, one could not travel from point A to point B in London without hearing ballads sung on street corners or seeing them pasted up on posts and walls. Broadside ballads thus touched all levels of society; yet they were decidedly aimed at and embraced by the "low." They were printed on the cheapest paper using recycled, worn woodcuts (in addition to recycled tunes for ready familiarity) so as to be affordable to all but the very poorest of society. They cost on average a mere penny. To increase their allure, ballads towards the end of the sixteenth and beginning of the seventeenth century became increasingly ornamental, with decorative lines and many pictures. People of the lower to middling sort would buy ballads to paste them up on their walls as ornaments. Finally, ballads of this period were sung to simple, well-known tunes (so well-known that just the tune title needed to be printed on the ballad), which also made them more accessible to the less educated. And to make sure they lured people of all tastes, they addressed every possible topic from every possible angle, including the always popular tabloid-like news story. As a medium of mass communication, the importance of broadside ballads can scarcely be overestimated.

---

[3] Patricia Fumerton is Director of EBBA, Carl Stahmer is Associate Director, and Megan Palmer Browne is EBBA Impressions Specialist. Kris McAbee was Assistant Director of EBBA when she mostly wrote her contribution to this piece; on assuming the position of Assistant Professor at the University of Arkansas, Little Rock, in 2010, McAbee became EBBA's UALR Project Manager.

[4] Watt (1991, 11).

EBBA's goal is to make these ephemera come alive for modern readers/listeners/viewers in approximations of the ways they resonated for contemporaries in their own time. Our goal is to make broadside ballads fully accessible as texts, songs, cultural records, and art of the period. EBBA thus provides online images of each ballad in high-quality facsimiles as well as "facsimile transcriptions" that preserve the original ballad illustrations while transcribing the unfamiliar font into easily readable modern type. In addition, visitors to the site can find recordings of ballads, background essays that place the ballads in their cultural context, TEI/XML encodings of the ballads, and search functions that allow users easily to find ballads as well as their constituent parts or makers.

The process of building EBBA has been a vigorous scholarly act precisely because it must at all times wrestle with the impermanent and changing nature of the ephemeral artefact that makes it a moving target. This is especially the case in the area of cataloguing and creating search mechanisms for the many illustrations to the ballads. As noted above, these visuals were much beloved by contemporaries but have been much neglected by modern art historians. Indeed, in its treatment of broadside ballad illustrations, about which so little has been written, EBBA has entered unchartered territory. The challenges we face are made more difficult, not easier, by the digital nature of the archive. As with all projects before the digital era that worked with objects in a mediated form (e.g., through photographs or reproductions in books), we are at a necessary remove from the originals. We are thus unable in our digitization of broadsides to distinguish between fine woodcut strokes or to identify with any certainty specific woodblock sources, the originals of which are now mostly lost. The solutions we have found to these problems have often led to more questions than answers, but the fruits of our labours are great in that they allow scholars to appreciate anew early modern cheap print and the manifold cultural issues it reflects, as some sample readings will show. However, even as we fine-tune our cataloguing and search mechanisms of broadside ballad illustrations—or what, more accurately, should be called "impressions," as further explained below—we constantly look forward to new possibilities for expanding access to cheap digitized art as well as to its highbrow cousins.

Most scholars not directly engaged with digital humanities work will be surprised to learn that the technical challenges associated with creating a scholarly digital archive are minor in comparison to the host of theoretical ones presented by the very nature of the artefacts being archived. Creating a digital version of an analogue artefact is, at its root, an act of translation.

A binary image file that uses a coded sequence of ones and zeros to store and deliver directions about how to render, on-screen, a representation of a seventeenth-century broadside ballad is something quite different from the ballad itself.[5] This very difference presents one of the prime benefits of digital scholarship.[6] The migration of the information (textual, visual, material) contained both in and on the paper ballad to its digital form forces the scholar to confront a series of fundamental questions about the nature of the artefact of study—questions that are frequently otherwise elided.[7]

The most significant of these questions is, "What, exactly, are we archiving?" This would seem an obvious question with an obvious answer, but it isn't. When one is forced to look closely at any aesthetic object, it becomes obvious that the bounds of the object itself are not nearly as stable as one would wish. Is the edge of an image the edge of the ink or paint, the edge of the paper or canvas on which it is printed or painted, the edge of the book in which it is bound, or of the framing ornament on the book's page? A long line of scholars, including the likes of Derrida (1994), Barthes (1977), and Foucault (1984), have dealt extensively with this problem at an abstract level, noting the necessity with which any symbolic action, in Foucault's words, "invariably goes beyond its own rules and transgresses its limits" (1984, 102). The printed artefact, as such, stands not as a stable object of study but as what Derrida dubs "a differential network, a fabric of traces referring endlessly to something other than itself" (1994, 84). When one sets out to create a digital representation of a printed text, image, or combination thereof, this problem moves quickly from the realm of the abstract to the material. As Derrida tells us, "[I]f we are to approach a text ... it must have a board, an edge"

---

[5] The fact that reading electronically presents a different reading experience from that of reading from print is much commented on both by scholars and the public at large. One of the best scholarly treatments of this difference remains Raymond Kurzweil's short essay, "The Future of Libraries," in which he details a host of biologic and cognitive bases for the experiential difference between reading a print text in its original print form versus a digital rendition. See Kurzweil (1992).

[6] Lavagnino (1995) still presents one of the most clearly stated treatments of the scholarly advantage of examining a text from outside of its original material form of production—a critical act which frees itself from the interpretive assumptions inherent in the materiality of text, thereby revealing new knowledge. See also Deegan and Tanner (2002), particularly 1–57.

[7] See McGann (2001), particularly chapter 2, for a discussion of the limitations of scholarship that attempts to understand the structure of a work of literature from within the confines of its own "bookish" form.

(81), and the digital archivist must, in fact, decide, exactly where the edge of the artefact being digitized lies before it can be scanned, photographed, catalogued, transcribed, etc.

This problem is particularly vexing for EBBA, as broadside ballads are, adopting Derrida's terminology, uniquely edgeless aesthetic artefacts in their original, printed form, consisting of fluid aggregations of sub-objects. Whereas each individual illustration, ornamentation, and textual unit that appears on a broadside ballad can and should be considered an independent aesthetic object in its own right, each must additionally be considered as part of the unified aesthetic composition that is the broadside. Taken as a whole, the form of broadside ballads is relatively standardized.[8] Metal typeset was used to print the text of a ballad (for most of the seventeenth century, in black letter or "gothic" type) onto a coarse folio or half-folio sheet. The ballad title was typically printed, often in a different font from the text proper, above the ballad text, accompanied by a designation of the tune to which the ballad was to be sung. In addition to the ballad's textual elements, woodcut illustrations were often presented below the title and tune designation. When present, imprint information appeared at the conclusion of the text of the ballad. Finally, a variety of ornamental borders and margins were frequently used to segregate portions of the ballad and to provide an overall, visually appealing aesthetic.

Each of the various constituent elements of the broadside identified above— title, tune, ballad text, illustrations, ornamental dividers, and imprint—is both part of the whole and an independent object of study in its own right. This multiplicity is highlighted by the fact that individual printing blocks and moveable typeset were often used and reused on multiple broadsides in combination with different ballad texts, tune designations, and ornamentation; individual vocal melodies, identified by either recognizable tune titles, printed musical score, or both, were likewise reused such that multiple ballads were written and printed to be sung to the same tune. As broadside ballad printing was first and foremost a commercial venture, printers were inclined to get absolutely as much use out of their mechanical means of production as possible in order to minimize cost and maximize profitability. There was a financial and physical trade in woodcuts such that the same cut, or a reproduced version of the cut, was frequently used by multiple printers. Similarly, the reuse of known tunes as the melodic base for multiple ballads facilitated not only the singing of the ballads by consumers, but also, more importantly,

---

[8] See Rollins (1919, 262).

the singing of the ballads by the balladeers who peddled the printed broadside ballads in the city streets. Object reuse and exchange at multiple levels thus improved the economics of the broadside ballad industry.

The broadside ballad is more collage than single aesthetic whole, as noted by Alexandra Franklin (2002, 329) and Fumerton (2002, 501); however, despite the fact that much of the content of an individual broadside (including major portions of the ballad text that appears on it) was likely to be sampled from previous broadsides, the individual broadside was also meant to be aesthetically pleasing when taken as a whole. The rich ornamentation, the frequent depiction of upper-class figures in woodcut illustrations (even in the face of the overall poor quality of the woodcuts themselves), the adoption of ornate, black-letter print on an object whose primary audience (the middling and poor) consisted of many who would have been unable to read it, ornate borders and flourishes—all these features were present primarily as a way of creating an overall visual effect that would entice even the illiterate to purchase the broadside.[9] The broadside ballad, in fact, served as the primary form of ornamental art and aesthetic engagement for the illiterate and semi-literate of the day.

Adding to the aesthetic "edgelessness" of the basic form of the broadside ballad is its provenance. With few exceptions, extant broadside ballads were preserved to the present day by collectors from their period of production, or shortly thereafter, most of whom not only physically collected the broadsides but attempted to organize, catalogue, and preserve them by pasting or otherwise fixing them into album books.[10] EBBA's current holdings include the five volumes of broadsides started by John Selden and completed by Samuel Pepys, and the four volumes (in five album books) started by Robert Harley and augmented by successive owners, including the Earl of Roxburghe. Together, these two collections represent several thousand broadsides; however, in both cases, there is not a one-to-one correlation between single album pages and single broadsides. In both collections, the collectors adopted the curatorial practice of trimming and often cutting the original broadside sheets into their constituent parts and then pasting these parts onto album-book pages. This process frequently involved the removal and/or addition of graphical elements and, sometimes, spatial reorganization of

---

[9] For a fuller discussion of the aesthetic aspects of the broadside ballad, see Fumerton (2002, 498–99).

[10] See Rollins (1919, 262) for a full discussion of the collectors and collections of broadside ballads.

the constituent parts of the broadside. As they became part of these collections the broadsides were recollaged, as it were.

It is tempting to consider this material reorganization of the broadside as an intrusion into its aesthetic authenticity; however, the collected form, in and of itself, represents an aesthetic object worthy of scholarly study for two primary reasons: first, because it provides a window into how readers more contemporary than ourselves understood, organized, and catalogued the broadside ballad, and second, because in most cases the collected form represents the sole access that readers have had to broadside ballads for several hundred years. Each broadside ballad has, seemingly, two forms of incarnation—the broadside itself and the album page—each of which, while deeply connected to the other, has its own material and interpretive history that must be preserved and catalogued.

In confronting these difficulties, it was necessary for EBBA to formulate a theory of Derridian "edgeness" for the broadside ballad that would determine exactly which elements and/or sub-elements relating to an individual broadside ballad would be collected and catalogued. Would we, for example, consider the entire album page as the artefact of study, or would we attempt to digitally reconstitute the original broadside, or independently catalogue sub-elements of the broadside, such as illustrations and ornamentation, etc.? After travelling for some time down various avenues of trial and error along these lines, we settled ultimately on a consciously abstracted theory of the "impression" as the defining aesthetic edge of the archive. In printmaking scholarship, an impression designates any print made from a wood block (Hind 1935).[11] The distinction here is between the block itself (which contains an image on it) and the printed images (impressions) that are created by the block. While not all print elements that appeared on the original broadside were printed by block, the basic concept of the impression as designating a distinct visual element produced by a discrete, interchangeable block, cut, stamp, or typeset arrangement can be applied to all visual elements of a broadside ballad, and has proven a workable scholarly means for identifying the most basic material units that compose each broadside ballad.

This conception of "impression" abstracts the image created by a block (the impression) from the physical block itself. EBBA's method of cataloguing further abstracts this abstraction by completely decoupling the block or typeset used in the printing process from the impressions created. EBBA makes no claims regarding the actual block/cut or typeset used to create an impres-

---

[11] See also Griffiths (1996, 9–12) and Parshall and Schoch (2005, 2).

sion, focusing instead only on the visual image or textual unit as it appears on the page. Each abstracted impression is granted object status in EBBA's cataloguing database, and the reappearance of an impression is tracked across broadside and album book manifestations with no regard paid to the question of whether the exact same block or typeset was actually used to create the impression.[12] This may seem like an unnecessarily subtle, theoretical distinction, but it provides a practical means of defining the edges of the base collection of objects that comprise a particular broadside (a printed poem, a musical score, an image, etc.) and of cataloguing them both independently and as they relate to other visual content on the page without being bound by the materiality of the physical block or typeset used in the printing process. It allows us to note, at the level of database and markup, that "this functions like that" and that "this is like that" without claiming that "this is that."

EBBA's process for cataloguing the pictorial impressions produced by woodcut printing on the broadside sheet provides a good example of the practical advantages for both cataloguers and, more importantly, end-users in adopting an abstracted theory of the impression as a general cataloguing principle. The usefulness of any cataloguing function is necessarily dependent upon the quality and consistency of tagging and description across the entire catalogue. For the print history aspect of the ballads (from publishing data to page condition) EBBA has developed rigorous scholarly cataloguing standards based on bibliographical principles and grounded in precedents set by ballad scholars such as Helen Weinstein (1992). Yet precedent systems for the cataloguing of illustrations seem inadequate for the cataloguing of woodcut impressions on ballads. Existing ontologies and systems are insufficient for organizing information about the frequently unsophisticated and degraded black-and-white ballad impressions and making that information searchable through a sophisticated digital web interface.

EBBA has attempted several means of cataloguing ballad woodcut impressions and ultimately discovered that the most consistent and productive form of digital cataloguing of early modern illustrations is not, ironically, entirely based on computational cataloguing systems. EBBA has endeav-

---

[12] Tracking the history and use of specific blocks or cuts would, of course, stand as a useful addition to our catalogue, but such determinations cannot be adequately made given the current state of the forensic technologies that can be applied to extant collections given their, by and large, extremely fragile state. The inclusion of such information in the database would not, however, if it were available, invalidate a more abstract-based cataloguing structure for reasons explained further in the essay.

oured to use free-association, cataloguer-generated keywording, longer nested-descriptions to accommodate general and more specific terms, as well as a taxonomic classification system (all of which we discuss in more detail below), and found each of these methods to be inadequate for the cataloguing of woodcut impressions. Yet experimenting with each of these techniques in dealing with thousands of ballads contributed to EBBA's development of a fixed set of fifty standard keyword concepts, a controlled vocabulary specific to the ballads, which are exposed to the user for the purposes of searching on EBBA's advanced search (http://ebba.english. ucsb.edu/search_combined/).

Keyword tagging is frequently the first step towards creating and organizing data about content, and EBBA's initial attempts to capture information about woodcut impressions relied heavily on cataloguer-generated keywords without the use of a structured vocabulary.[13] Keywords can be very reliable for organizing one's own images, since in these cases the user is also the cataloguer, but such is not the case for EBBA. Most users of EBBA are not cataloguers, and because in 2003, at the inception of the archive, social computing as a scholarly practice was on a distant horizon, folksonomic tagging of the woodcut impressions, such as that investigated by *Steve: The Museum Social Tagging Project* (http://steve.museum), was not supportable and would have likely engendered similar difficulties.[14] Hence, at the early stages of cataloguing the Pepys ballads, with which EBBA began, those compiling the information—even though they were early modern scholars—had no way of knowing exactly what sets of terms and concepts would be most relevant for other ballad scholars and users of the site.[15] As pop-cultural, aesthetic,

---

[13] Such ad hoc keywording takes the form of cataloguers listing simple noun forms, of their own choice, to describe the most salient aspects of the image depicted in the woodcut impression. Because EBBA's earliest cataloguers were working from Weinstein's existing catalogue (1992), which was developed specifically for the Pepys ballads but which only lists dimensions for the woodcut impressions, cataloguers generated the initial keywords in conjunction with longer narrative descriptions modelled on the *Blake Archive* (discussed below). The full narrative descriptions quickly became too time-consuming and unwieldy for the first pass of cataloguing, so not all of the woodcut impressions were keyworded in the first pass.

[14] EBBA's in-house keyword cataloguing and folksonomic or collaborative 2.0 tagging in ontology development frequently ran into similar problems: namely spelling, synonymy/homonymy, and mismatching. See Braun et al. (2007).

[15] Studies of search log data of other online archives indicate a lack of correspondence between archives' metadata and the terms that users employ to search. See

and print-historical artefacts covering a long period (primarily 1550–1750), EBBA's ballads potentiate scholarly interests in a variety of fields. How then can cataloguers generate keywords that are as varied as the ballads—and the ballad scholars—themselves? They can't. Once keyword information is generated, it epitomizes the dilemma Baudrillard expresses of the information revolution: "Information can tell us everything. It has all the answers. But they are answers to questions we have not asked, and which doubtless don't even arise" (1990, 219).

The issue of providing useful information in EBBA's cataloguing of the woodcut impressions becomes two fold: on the one hand, anticipating the user's needs and, on the other, accurately addressing those needs. However, the solution to this problem is singular: providing for both the cataloguer and the user a defined set of keywords. Curtailing the keywords to a standardized list ameliorates the difficulty of, on the one hand, correctly identifying items in crudely rendered impressions and, on the other, assigning the most useful vocabulary to those items. Useful keyword tagging should anticipate precisely those user questions that might arise. Alternatively, limiting the tagging and the search to a standard set of keyword concepts acknowledges that most questions of users cannot be anticipated, and so, instead, invites specific lines of inquiry.

Without a standard vocabulary from which to catalogue, keyword tagging inevitably becomes inconsistent and, therefore, inadequate for searching purposes. Take, for example, the keyword lists produced, without a standard vocabulary, by two different cataloguers for variant impressions of one of the most common pictures to appear on early modern ballads: a woman with a fan (Figs. 1 and 2).[16]

Trant (2009) for a fuller review of the intervention of social tagging and folksonomy in this problem.

[16] Variant impressions of this woman holding a large feathered fan appear fifty-four times in the Pepys collection alone.

Figure 1. Woman-with-fan impression from "A goodfellowes complaint against strong beere," Pepys 1.438–439

Figure 2. Woman-with-fan impression from "The faythfull Louers resolution," Pepys 1.256–257

These two impressions are very similar, suggesting that they may both be from the same woodcut block. However, because we have no access to the original woodcut blocks themselves, EBBA cannot know whether the minor variations in the woman's face, the outline of the fan, the shoe on the left, and the top of the farthingale are the result of vagaries in inking or pressing of the same block, or whether they appear because different, nearly identical, woodcut blocks were used, in which case it would be impossible to tell which is the original and which the "copy." To avoid claiming that both impressions were made from the same woodcut block, yet still acknowledge the similarity and relative "sameness" of these two illustrations, EBBA calls such impressions "variants" of each other.[17] Two different cataloguers generated keywords for these nearly identical variants, and both lists include "lady" and "woman" as well as "dress," "feather," "flower," "fan," and "necklace." These keywords seem to cover the central items depicted in the impressions, with some variety to accommodate for synonyms (e.g., "lady" and "woman"). Both cataloguers also include "branch" and "tree," apparently after consultation with each other and some confusion over whether the fan is feathered or a tree branch. Although it is unlikely that the fan is made of tree branches, since feathered fans were the norm for the period, cataloguers cannot be certain of what is either rendered or evoked in this image so their inclusion of "branch" is understandable. Yet this level of granularity in keywords inevitably leads to inaccurate search results: someone looking for images of trees would also get this image. Moreover, only one cataloguer, using her specialized knowledge of fashion of the period, included "wide ruff" and "farthingale" in her list of keywords for one of the impressions. A search run on these keywords would then return only one woodcut impression, errone-

---

[17] The term "variant" describes impressions that depict essentially the same illustration with only minor variations. For example, not all images of a woman holding a fan are variant impressions, since some women holding fans may be illustrated with different fans, hairstyles, dresses, poses, backgrounds, etc. Yet, in instances where impressions seem similar enough to be considered essentially the same or very closely imitated, EBBA groups them as variants by assigning them the same numerical identifier in the mySQL database (this grouping is discussed in more detail below). Such grouping necessitates scholarly calls about what qualifies as similar enough to be a variant. In her catalogue of the Pepys ballads, Weinstein (1992) also makes such scholarly judgments in her appraisal of variant editions of ballads in the collection, marking only those ballads as variant editions that are at least 80 percent similar. As a rule of thumb, EBBA's impression cataloguers followed the same method, grouping variant impressions based on estimations of at least 80 percent similarity.

ously implying that variants of this woodcut impression do not include the more specific fashion elements.

One possible solution to the varied amount of specificity in such catalogue-generated lists of keywords is to increase granularity by grouping general terms with more specific terms. However, such long, nested descriptions—an approach to which EBBA repeatedly returned—only redoubled many of the same problems of shorter keyword lists. Inspired by the success of the *William Blake Archive* (http://www.blakearchive.org/blake/), we imitated the narrative style of their descriptions of Blake's designs, with the hope that capturing a wealth of detail (e.g., "dress or farthingale") would increase the reliability of our searches. However, we quickly discovered that these descriptions tended not only to lead to false-positives (like the example above), they would also balloon to an unwieldy size. Moreover, they suggested a degree of certainty that could not, in fact, always be guaranteed by the frequently crude images. Like the *Blake Archive*, EBBA acknowledges that users can always go to our reproductions of the images themselves to inform their own analysis of the impressions. The *Blake Archive* has also recognized the potential for error in their design descriptions, noting that "many interpretations have been based on weak, partial, or mistaken impressions of what appears in the designs."[18]

EBBA's intention for these narrative descriptions was that they could be useful to non-specialists and beginning scholars, particularly undergraduates, by providing context and pointing out distinctive features that might be lost to an eye unpractised in reading such images. But as with the more free-form keywording efforts, the sheer number of images made it impossible for a single individual to do the job, again resulting in discrepancies in the descriptions of associated impressions. Further, the idiosyncrasies of the images themselves—some carefully employing conventions of realism and classicism, some flat in perspective and awkward in draftsmanship, some static, some narrative, some solemn, some whimsical—made it difficult for an interdisciplinary team of scholars to agree on a method of logical, systematic description. This meant that the long descriptions, when completed, were uneven in detail and inconsistent in terminology, length, and accuracy. As an attempt to remedy this, a single member of the team (Palmer Browne) went back through all of the descriptions, attempting to bring consistency and accuracy to the archive as a whole. By this time, the richest descrip-

---

[18] See "Editorial Principles," *The William Blake Archive*, revised 14 August 2008, http://www.blakearchive.org/blake/public/about/principles/.

tions included detail on costume, architecture, and the like. In an attempt to keep this richness and remain consistent, her retooling of the long descriptions resulted in an excessive glut of detail, because standardizing across the impression descriptions required that details addressed in one description be included in all subsequent descriptions to avoid false-positives. Finally, it became apparent to all that such narrative descriptions were neither particularly useful to the non-specialist nor an efficient use of archivists' time, and they were removed from the active version of the database.

The *Blake Archive* seems to have found their narrative descriptions similarly unwieldy and not in strict accordance with users' needs. They have now implemented an image search based solely on a list of 1,039 terms grouped by eight categories.[19] This latest attempt is similar to the taxonomic structure provided by other image classification systems, such as Iconclass, which hierarchically orders 28,000 image subject terms.[20] Although Iconclass has the valuable asset of being widely available (including online, via the Iconclass 2100 Browser, http://www.iconclass.org/) and is widely used, EBBA has not found its granularity to be manageable or applicable when cataloguing ballad woodcut impressions. The "stock" character of many of these impressions resists attempts to pin down individual subjects, such that cataloguers are at a loss where to begin with such a huge list of terms. Likewise, users have too many points of entry for searching illustrations tagged by so many terms. EBBA's list of fifty keyword concepts, tailored to ballad impressions specifically, streamlines the process for the users. Furthermore, large sets of subject terms, like those used by Iconclass and the *Blake Archive*, do not solve problems of inconsistency, neither among cataloguers (since any cataloguer may choose a different set of foci than another), nor across impressions (since what might be deemed the "subject" of one impression may be faded, warped, or lost in a variant impression).

For example, what happens when the "woman with fan," discussed above, loses her signature item, as she does in Pepys 1.296–297 (Fig. 3)? This impression differs more distinctly from the impressions of women with fans seen in

---

[19] The categories consist of Figure Type (62 terms), Figure Characters (115 terms), Figure Postures and Gestures (253 terms), Figure Clothing and Other Attributes (98 terms), Animal (92 terms), Vegetation (73 terms), Object (294 terms), and Structure (52 terms). See http://www.blakearchive.org/blake/imagesearch.html, accessed 23 October 2009.

[20] See the official Iconclass website for a fuller description of its components: http://www.iconclass.nl, accessed 23 October 2009.

Figures 1 and 2, and is more likely to be from a different woodcut block, but in the absence of certainty and in the face of such striking similarity despite the variations, EBBA considers them all variant impressions. Cataloguers for the impression in Figure 3 would not have reason to include the Iconclass notation 41D262, which is the classification code for "fan."[21] Resultantly, a keyword search for impressions with "fan" as subject would not return this impression. Hence, were EBBA to rely solely on Iconclass for cataloguing the woodcut impressions, we would leave out this notation and would thus fail to associate this woman with her fellow fan-holding variants. Likewise, any cataloguing system based solely on keywording individual impressions overlooks features that fade or break off over time. However, the fan is a salient factor in the other variants of this impression. Though the fan itself may not appear in this particular impression, it is implied by association with the numerous variants in which the fan does appear. Indeed, the fact that the fan is missing is perhaps the most interesting aspect of this impression, but keywording alone, especially through hierarchical systems like Iconclass, does not capture information about subjects that do not appear on the impression. EBBA thus needed a cataloguing system that not only treats these impressions as individual objects but that also matches variant impressions in order to bring such noteworthy differences to the fore.

---

[21] The hierarchical nature of Iconclass notations is evinced by the number of characters in the classification code. Each of the six characters represents a level in the hierarchy: 4 Society, Civilization, Culture; 41 material aspects of daily life; 41D fashion, clothing; 41D2 clothes, costume; 41D26 accessories (~ clothing); 41D262 fan.

Figure 3. Woman-with-fan impression from "The Discourse betweene A
Souldier and his Loue," Pepys 1.296–297

To match these variants, EBBA's database includes woodcut impressions
groups. Developed out of our revisitation of the woodcut impression metadata, all variant impressions of similar illustrations—that is, impressions that
may be from either the same, copied, or closely imitated woodcut block—are
assigned to the same group. Thus, in EBBA's improved interface, users do
not need to happen upon the best search term to find any given impression: they can either choose from a drop-down list of search terms on EBBA's
advanced search or, when viewing any given ballad, they will be able to opt
to see ballads with variants of that ballad's woodcut impressions. For ease of
cataloguing, groups are given descriptive names and, after the initial pass of
grouping, the cataloguing interface, shown in Figure 4, employs a drop-down
menu listing all possible groups, to avoid the creation of duplicate groups.
EBBA is currently in the process of standardizing its drop-down impressions
group list and plans to make it available to users from the advanced search
page. EBBA's improved user interface will also use these groupings in the
database to give users the option (through a button on the citation page)
to see variant woodcut impressions where available. Only through EBBA's
repeated revisiting of the impressions have we been able to gain the intimate
familiarity with them necessary to group the impressions by variants in the
database.

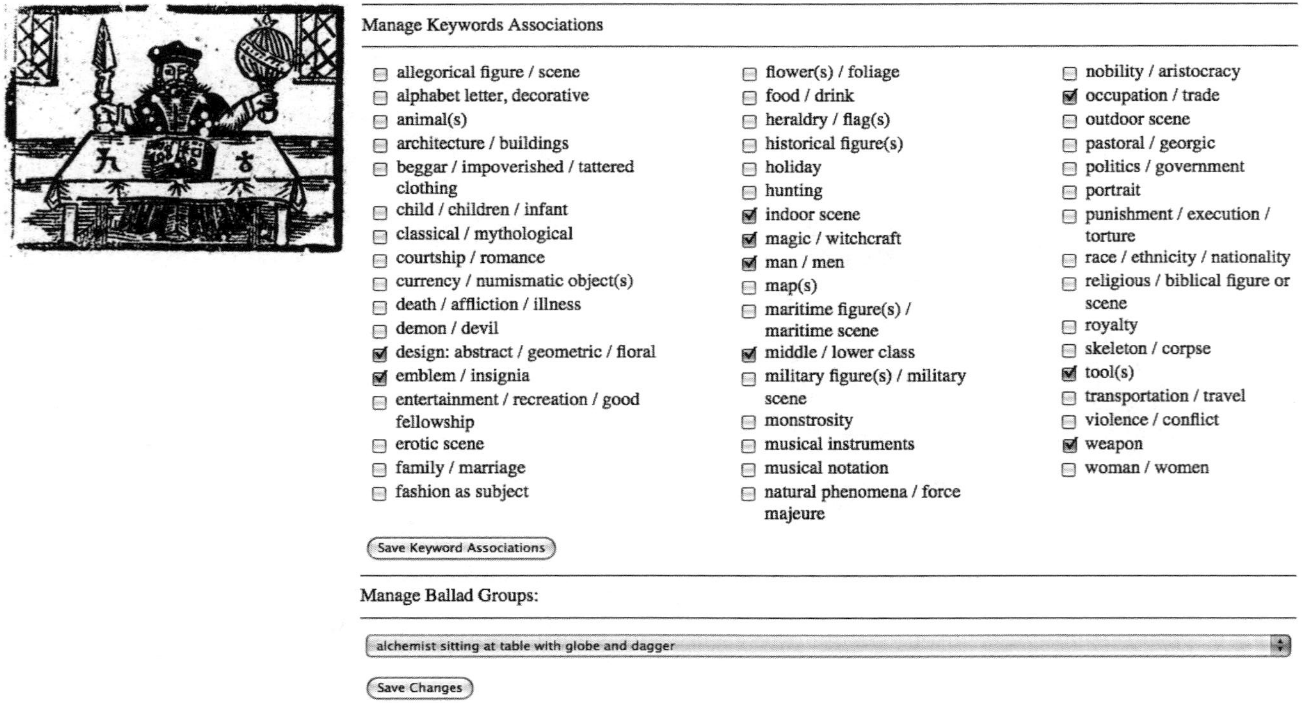

Manage Keywords Associations

- ☐ allegorical figure / scene
- ☐ alphabet letter, decorative
- ☐ animal(s)
- ☐ architecture / buildings
- ☐ beggar / impoverished / tattered clothing
- ☐ child / children / infant
- ☐ classical / mythological
- ☐ courtship / romance
- ☐ currency / numismatic object(s)
- ☐ death / affliction / illness
- ☐ demon / devil
- ☑ design: abstract / geometric / floral
- ☑ emblem / insignia
- ☐ entertainment / recreation / good fellowship
- ☐ erotic scene
- ☐ family / marriage
- ☐ fashion as subject

- ☐ flower(s) / foliage
- ☐ food / drink
- ☐ heraldry / flag(s)
- ☐ historical figure(s)
- ☐ holiday
- ☐ hunting
- ☑ indoor scene
- ☑ magic / witchcraft
- ☑ man / men
- ☐ map(s)
- ☐ maritime figure(s) / maritime scene
- ☑ middle / lower class
- ☐ military figure(s) / military scene
- ☐ monstrosity
- ☐ musical instruments
- ☐ musical notation
- ☐ natural phenomena / force majeure

- ☐ nobility / aristocracy
- ☑ occupation / trade
- ☐ outdoor scene
- ☐ pastoral / georgic
- ☐ politics / government
- ☐ portrait
- ☐ punishment / execution / torture
- ☐ race / ethnicity / nationality
- ☐ religious / biblical figure or scene
- ☐ royalty
- ☐ skeleton / corpse
- ☑ tool(s)
- ☐ transportation / travel
- ☐ violence / conflict
- ☑ weapon
- ☐ woman / women

(Save Keyword Associations)

Manage Ballad Groups:

alchemist sitting at table with globe and dagger

(Save Changes)

Figure 4. Impressions management system with standardized keywords and drop-down menu for groups of variants (for Pepys 4.357, Impression 2)

The granting of object status to each impression in EBBA's cataloging database, discussed above, allows us to associate variants of that impression with no regard paid to the question of whether the same block was actually used to create the impression. This type of cataloguing, in which EBBA does not claim that any impression is an "original" or "copy" of any other woodcut, allows a shift of focus to the semiotic relationship between impressions that bear significant similarity. Take, for example, the impressions on Pepys 4.20, "The Swimming Lady": an impression of a man with two bathers perched on the bank of a body of water and a separate impression of a bathing woman (Fig. 5). The break between the two images makes clear that these are two separate impressions. Yet their close placement aligned next to each other suggests that they might be ancestors of a once single woodcut block, now broken in two.[22] This constructed composite invites speculation about printing practices that would be very hard to verify in the absence of access to the whole woodcut block, but EBBA's focus on the object status of impressions allows for cataloguing as the pictures appear in the particular instance, as two separate impressions rather than one singular illustration of a man looking at a woman. In this way, EBBA's catalogue of the impressions allows for the semiotic association between the two impressions without concretizing assumptions about the origins of the illustration.

Figure 5. Impressions from "The Swimming Lady," Pepys 4.20

---

[22] In fact, in her catalogue of the Pepys ballads, Weinstein identifies each of these two sets of impressions as "two blocks arranged as composite cut," pointing to them as a counter-example of a broken block (1992, xlii).

Two very similar impressions appear on Pepys 4.4, "The Happy Lovers Pastime," again placed together to form a composite image, a compound illustration consisting of two separate but aligned impressions (Fig. 6). The constructed nature of this composite image is evident in comparison of the illustrations from "The Swimming Lady" (Fig. 5) with those on the "Happy Lovers Pastime" (Fig. 6). Subtle differences between the two impressions of the bathing woman on the right (including facial expression, etching marks on the forearm, and leaf-shape of the foliage) suggest that these two impressions do not come from the same woodcut block. They, like the numerous women-with-fan impressions discussed above, are variants of each other. That the bathing woman impression does not appear in the Pepys collection in a singular impression that contains as well the man who seems to be gazing at her exemplifies why EBBA identifies these as individual "impressions" as opposed to "woodcuts" (the vernacular shorthand for such illustrations, which is more evocative of the item used to make the illustration than the single instance on the page itself). The variant impressions of the bathing woman are clearly related to each other, but due to their obvious differences they probably would not be linked in the database if EBBA were to attempt to catalogue woodcut blocks.

Figure 6. Impressions from "The Happy Lovers Pastime," Pepys 4.4

The ability to find variants of these impressions becomes especially valuable when the individual parts of the implied composite appear on their own. The impression of the man on the left appears alone, for instance, on Pepys 3.352,

"Loves Lamentable Tragedy." Without the bathing woman seated next to him, the implication of his pose shifts: rather than furtively spying on a woman in a state of undress, the man seems to be turning away from the nude figures behind him as he looks toward the edge of the water (and, indeed, of the very ballad). Yet, even when the bathing woman does not appear as the object of the man's gaze, her connection to him in so many other ballads places her in a semiotic chain with this illustration. For example, she also appears without the gazing man in Roxburghe 4.22, "Love's Unspeakable Passion: Or, The Youngman's Answer to Tender hearts of London City." The fact that this ballad is a response ballad to "Love's Lamentable Tragedy," where he appears alone, further supports her implicit connection to him—a connection sustained by a search of variant impressions. The bathing woman also emerges on Pepys 3.187, "The Charming Eccho," and on Pepys 3.342, "The Musical Shepherdess," both times without her voyeuristic male counterpart. EBBA's matching of variants provides modern scholars with an experience that early modern ballad consumers were likely to have, since they probably would have seen the bathing woman and the gazing man placed together on other ballads or perhaps even as a single, whole woodcut impression on another text. Such knowledge of the illustration of the bathing woman placed compositely elsewhere as a titillating object of a voyeuristic gaze highlights the erotically charged effect of this half-naked woman in these ballads, drawing a connection between her appeal to the man watching her in the composite image and her appeal to the audience of the ballad itself.

The iconographic significance of some woodcut impressions is so powerful that the message of the ballad text is lost without them. This can be seen not only within and between EBBA's ballads but also when EBBA impressions are matched with impressions from other sources, a process which at the moment can only be done on a case-by-case basis. It is to be hoped that, in the future, full integration with other databases will be possible. A poignant example of the benefits of such matching, drawing on EEBO (the *Early English Books Online*) as well as the EBBA database, is the 1612 ballad, "The good Shepheards sorrow for the death of his beloued / Sonne," Pepys 1.352–353.[23] Before discussing how the impressions on this broadside are indispensable to the meaning of the ballad, it is useful to examine the ballad text. The first part of the ballad is spoken by a bereaved father, who laments in the second stanza,

---

[23] Date from *English Short Title Catalogue*; Weinstein lists an R. Johnson as the possible author (1992).

> In Sable roabes of night,
> My dayes of joy aparreld bee,
> My sorrow sees no light,
>   my light through sorrowes nothing see,
> And now my sonne his date hath runne,
> And from his Sphere doth goe,
> To endless bed of foulded lead,
>   and who can blame my woe?

This is highly crafted, literary language. The Donne-like punning on son/sun results in a sophisticated planetary metaphor which enhances the already evocative picture of sorrow and night as a rich sable garment. The son/sun has unnaturally and wrenchingly left his sphere; brightness and joy are gone, and only a dull and inescapable "bed of lead" remains. This internal rhyme has the effect of reinforcing the bleakness of the situation. Not only are we reminded of the former brightness and promise of the young man, but a third, unspoken, rhyming word haunts the end of the stanza: "dead." The speaker's simple refrain—"and who can blame my woe?"—both pulls the narrator from his grief for a moment and brings the ballad's audience into the song. This sophisticated bereaved father asks us a direct question; our compassion or condemnation become part of the ballad's narrative structure.

The ballad's second part is spoken by a different, unnamed narrator, who consoles the father both by trying to quiet the griever's lament and by acknowledging the heaviness of the loss. This speaker acknowledges that no man "Can well forbeare, / To shed a teare" for the loss of the bright youth. But at the end of the ballad, he offers words of compassion and hope:

> Thy woes I cannot blame,
>   but in thy sorrowes beare a part,
> Yet now to patience frame,
>   and see the salve cures all our smart:
> This bud is dead,
> Is gone, is fled,
>   but in his place doth grow
> A Flower as faire:
> As fresh as rare,
>   and he cures all our woe.

This speaker thus answers the question the father had posed in the first half of the ballad: no one will "blame his woe," not only because the father's own personal loss is great, but because the speaker himself bears a part in the father's bereavement. In the last line, the sorrow is not, as in the first part of the ballad, "my woe"; nor is it, as in the earlier stanzas of the second part, "your woe." It is "our woe." Here, the second speaker aligns himself with the father and also responds on behalf of the ballad's entire audience: all of us have been affected by this death. The undeniable emotional appeal and the final assertion of hopeful renewal make this ballad compelling, but the insistence that the shepherd's grief should be shared by all is perhaps puzzling to a modern audience until we listen to the story being told by the impressions.

This broadside has three woodcut impressions: the first, a fairly simple cut of a generic king; the second, a highly ornamental picture of a young man in a plumed hat and lace collar; and the third, a portrait of a young man in profile holding a lance (see Fig. 7). The king and the man in the lace collar appear at the top of the first part of the ballad, and the youth with the lance appears at the top of the second part. The impression of the king has not yet been possible to trace or match with other impressions, but his symbolic function (kingship) is clear. The second impression is identifiable as a specific individual: Frederick, future king of Bohemia, who was married to Princess Elizabeth in 1613. A very similar alternate of this impression appears on a broadside announcing the couple's marriage.[24] But it is the third impression that is the key to the story: an intense-looking young man in elaborate armour, hair windblown from the top of his head, holding a lance that cuts horizontally across the top half of the pictorial space, its ends vanishing beyond the edges of the frame (Fig. 8). This, too, is a portrait: the young Prince Henry. The impression is a copy of the top three-quarters of a full-length engraving by Simon Van de Passe; another woodcut impression of the same engraving appears in a 1612 edition of Michael Drayton's *Poly-Olbion*, which is dedicated to the young prince and can be found in the EEBO database.[25] The reason this image is so powerful in connection with the ballad is, of course, that Prince Henry died in November of 1612, at the age of eighteen, from an illness that is now believed to have been typhoid fever. The fact that the impression indicates definite signs of wear on the woodblock (large breaks in the top and bottom left-hand borders and a wormhole visible in the hilt of the sword Henry wears at his side), along with the existence of the original engraving and at least one other woodblock copy, suggests that this image of Henry was frequently printed and probably widely circulated. It would have borne

---

[24] Maxwell (1613); date from STC.

[25] At present, the only way to locate such correspondences between EEBO and EBBA database impressions is by individual scholarship.

almost iconic status. To Londoners in 1612, then, the juxtaposition of the ballad images with its text would have had a clear and moving topical meaning. The shepherd is James; the lost son is Henry; the new bud is Charles. The contemporary audience is invited to mourn this national loss not only by the unnamed second speaker but by the king himself, ventriloquized through the title's "Shepheard." The shepherd/king/father's tragic loss is emphatically their loss too, and it is clear that the king is woefully grieving indeed. Of course, a ballad whose text claims to speak for the current king might have seemed seditious and in need of censure, but because the speaker is shown to be the king only by way of the impressions, the ballad is free to circulate with impunity, and its audience is invited to mourn alongside James. The unstated purpose of this song, which would have been clear to an audience in 1612, might have been lost without the significant supratext provided by the impressions and the possibility of matching such impressions across early modern media. The provenance of these impressions indicates how the work as a whole functioned as part of the complex iconography of this period.

Figure 7: "The Good Shepheardes sorrow for the death of
his beloued Sonne"

Figure 8. Third impression from "The good Shepheards sorrow for the death of his beloued Sonne," Pepys 1.352–353

The process of associating such variant impressions not only within but beyond EBBA's holdings, even as it depends upon new technologies to organize, analyse, and display information, ultimately relies heavily on scholarly expertise. Only an intimate familiarity with the impressions across the thousands of ballads in the archive can produce what is perhaps EBBA's most valuable archival feature: the matching of variant impressions. Consequently, the chief function of EBBA's current technological infrastructure is accessibility: to expose and make useful to a wider audience our scholarship on the seventeenth-century broadside ballad, in all of its rich complexity. For now, the process of building this resource, and especially of making these connections between variant images, must still be done manually. As EBBA looks towards the not too distant horizon, however, new technologies loom which offer the potential to liberate the process of variant recognition from the necessity for pre-existing scholarly knowledge. Whereas to date most image catalogue/search interfaces have relied on image tagging (whether by scholars or the public at large) as a means of organizing and navigating image collections, we have already entered an era where the computer itself can, independently, examine a collection of images and determine which ones are similar to others and in which ways. Research in computer vision and visual pattern recognition dates back many decades; however, as a result of the United States Department of Homeland Security's desire to develop automated systems for identifying particular individuals on film, an historically unprecedented level of funding has been devoted over the past decade to Artificial Intelligence (AI) research in the area of computer vision. Specifically, advances in the areas of image segmentation and recognition—processes whereby computers are able to examine an image at a binary level, identify the edges of discrete objects that appear in the image, and then compare these objects either with a known database or with objects found in other images—offer important (and unimagined, no doubt, by the Department of Homeland Security) potential for digital archivists.[26] Taking the previously discussed case of a woman holding a fan, for example, we have existing computer models that would be capable of accurately "looking" at every image in the ballad collection and returning a list of all images in the catalogue that contain not only versions of the woman holding a fan, but also images that contain the fan without the woman or the same woman without the fan.

Such potentially automated systems are not the stuff of science fiction. Both the algorithms and the computational code needed to perform this kind of analysis have already been developed and are beginning to seep into the commercial software arena.[27] They have yet, however, to be leveraged by digital archivists. At EBBA, we see great potential in doing just that. Such AI processes would not replace the kind of deep, scholarly engagement that is reflected in EBBA's current tagging system, but would enhance it. We imagine a system whereby EBBA scholars, EBBA end-users, and the computer itself would work as collaborators in an ongoing process of building

---

[26] For more information on Image Segmentation and recognition see the UC Berkeley Computer Vision Group, accessed 23 October 2009 (http://www.eecs.berkeley.edu/Research/Projects/CS/vision/) and MIT's Computer Science and Artificial Intelligence laboratory (CSAIL), accessed 23 October 2009 (http://www.csail.mit.edu/).

[27] The newly announced "Google Goggles" service, accessed 23 October 2009 (http://www.google.com/mobile/goggles/#landmark) is the most widely known example of the commercial application of this newer technology. Other examples include Attrasoft image recognition search-engine, accessed 23 October 2009 (http://www.attrasoft.com/); TagCow image tagging service, accessed 23 October 2009 (http://www.tagcow.com/); and Mobvis vision technologies and intelligent maps for mobile attentive interfaces in urban scenarios, accessed 23 October 2009 (http://www.mobvis.org/), all of which are early stage commercial ventures in the area of computer-assisted image recognition and comparison.

not only literal but also semiotic webs of association between impressions in the archive. Such a system would, interestingly, simultaneously concretize the user experience by making it easier and faster to find what one is looking for, while at the same time playing more freely with the ephemerality of the archive itself, serving to further destabilize the integrity of the broadside proper by facilitating navigation across impressions according to constantly shifting points of focus rather than scholar-defined hierarchies. Such a digital archive would allow us to have our scholarly cake and eat it too, preserving the ephemeral through an architecture that drives towards destabilization.

One might dub what we foresee through the interaction of machine and human intelligence a "systemized destabilization" which seeks to capture the very essence of the early modern broadside ballad. The printed ballad, as we have seen, was made up of mobile collage-like pieces—changing titles, tunes, texts, ornaments, and woodcut impressions. Each of those component pieces might migrate and mutate as it moved from broadsheet to broadsheet. Though there may well have been an element of arbitrariness to the selection by which such movable parts were assembled by printers on any particular broadside, as we have seen, they together form a potentially self-reflexive whole that could communicate special meaning to audiences in their own time and still speak to scholars who study them today. The illustrations to broadsides are perhaps their most vexing features because we rarely have original woodcuts to prove that one impression is in fact the same as another. This is also why we rely heavily on EBBA scholarly judgments made by the interpretative eye. Even once we enter the age of computer-generated match-ups of impressions or parts of impressions on broadside ballads, the human eye of the experienced scholar must interpret the potential connections identified by the computer. Only the trained scholarly eye can meaningfully read the association of images, as we have offered in this paper in the readings of associated impressions held within the EBBA database as well as between those impressions and other holdings, electronic or not. EBBA's goal is to make a database that can best capture impressions and their variations in a systematic way precisely by incorporating the EBBA scholar in evaluating image variations, and ultimately (indeed, continually) prompting a retooling of the database so as to better associate impressions, in a supportive feedback between human and machine.

WORKS CITED

Barthes, Roland. 1977. "The Death of the Author." In *Image, Music, Text*, translated by Stephen Heath, 142–48. New York: Hill and Wang.

Baudrillard, Jean. 1990. *Cool Memories.* Translated by Chris Turner. London: Verso.

Braun, Simone, et al. 2007. "Ontology Maturing: A Collaborative Web 2.0 Approach to Ontology Engineering." In *Proceedings of the Workshop on the Collaborative Construction of Structured Knowledge (CKC) at the Sixteenth International World Wide Web Conference (WWW 07)*, Banff, Canada.

Deegan, Marilyn, and Simon Tanner. 2002. *Digital Futures: Strategies for the Information Age.* New York: Neal-Schuman Publishers.

Derrida, Jacques. 1994. "Living On." In *De-Construction and Criticism*, edited by Harold Bloom et al., 75–176. New York: Continuum.

Early English Books Online (EEBO). 2010. http://eebo.chadwyck.com/home/.

Eighteenth-Century Collections Online (ECCO). 2010. http://gdc.gale.com/products/eighteenth-century-collections-online/.

English Broadside Ballad Archive (EBBA). 2010. http://ebba.english.ucsb.edu/.

Foucault, Michel. 1984. "What is an Author?" In *The Foucault Reader*, edited by Paul Rabinow, 101–20. New York: Pantheon.

Franklin, Alexandra. 2002. "The Art of Illustration in Bodleian Broadside Ballads before 1820." *Bodleian Library Record* 17 (5): 327–52.

Fumerton, Patricia. 1999. "Introduction: A New New Historicism." In *Renaissance Culture and the Everyday*, edited by Patricia Fumerton and Simon Hunt, 1–17. Philadelphia: University of Pennsylvania Press.

_____ 2002. "Not Home: Alehouses, Ballads, and the Vagrant Husband in Early Modern England." *Journal of Medieval and Early Modern Studies* 32 (3): 493–518.

Greenblatt, Stephen. 1980. *Renaissance Self-Fashioning: From More to Shakespeare.* Chicago: University of Chicago Press.

Griffiths, Antony. 1996. *Prints and Printmaking: An Introduction to the History and Techniques*. Berkeley and Los Angeles: University of California Press.

Hind, Arthur M. (1935) 1963. *An Introduction to a History of Woodcut with a Detailed Survey of Work Done in the Fifteenth Century*. Vol. 1. Reprint, New York: Dover Publications.

Iconclass 2100 Browser. 2010. http://www.iconclass.org/.

Kurzweil, Raymond. 1996. "The Future of Libraries." *Library Journal* 171 (1): 80–82.

Lavagnino, John. 1995. "Reading, Scholarship, and Hypertext." http://www.stg.brown.edu/resources/stg/monographs/rshe.html/.

Maxwell, James. 1613. *The Imperiall and Princely Pedegree of the Two Most Noble and Vertuous Princes Lately Married*. London: E. Allde for Henry Gosson.

McGann, Jerome. 2001. *Radiant Textuality: Literature after the World Wide Web*. New York: Palgrave Macmillan.

Parshall, Peter, and Ranier Schoch. 2005. *Origins of European Printmaking: Fifteenth-Century Woodcuts and Their Public*. New Haven, CT: Yale University Press.

The Proceedings of the Old Bailey. 2010. http://www.oldbaileyonline.org/.

Rollins, Hyder E. 1919. "The Black-Letter Broadside Ballad." *PMLA* 34 (2): 258–339.

Steve: The Museum Social Tagging Project. 2008. http://steve.museum/.

Trant, Jennifer. 2009. "Studying Social Tagging and Folksonomy: A Review and Framework." *The Journal of Digital Information* 10 (1): http://journals.tdl.org/jodi/article/view/269/.

Watt, Tessa. 1991. *Cheap Print and Popular Piety, 1550-1640*. Cambridge: Cambridge University Press.

Weinstein, Helen. 1992. *The Pepys Ballads: Catalogue of the Pepys Library at Magdalene College, Cambridge*. Woodbridge: D.S. Brewer.

A Virtual Museum or E-Research?
British Printed Images to 1700 and the Digitization of Early Modern Prints[*]

Stephen Pigney
Goldsmiths, University of London
s.pigney@gold.ac.uk

Katherine Hunt
The London Consortium
katherinehunt@hotmail.co.uk

British Printed Images to 1700 (bpi1700) is a project that makes available an online digital library of sixteenth- and seventeenth-century British prints.[1] There is a compelling need for such a resource: although prints are important examples of early modern visual and material culture, the study of British prints has suffered from insufficient foundational research. As a research-directed project, bpi1700 set out to do more than simply digitize a large corpus of objects. It aimed to present these objects in ways useful both to specialists, such as print scholars, and to general students and researchers of early modern Britain, and in doing so, to contribute significantly to the wider understanding of the period and its visual and material culture. The bpi1700 website provides various resources that contextualize prints, such as surveys of print history and historiography, an introduction to print genres, and directories of printmakers and publishers; and it presents original research, through essays on individual prints and a listing of all book illustrations between 1604 and 1640. The heart of the project is, however, the database itself, containing records for several thousand prints with the

---

[*] We wish particularly to acknowledge the contribution of Hafed Walda from the Centre for Computing in the Humanities at King's College London to this essay. We have also benefited from valuable discussions with Professor Michael Hunter—the director of *British Printed Images to 1700*—and John Bradley, William Schupbach, and Mary Wills.

[1] British Printed Images to 1700, accessed 23 October 2009 http://www.bpi1700.org.uk. Directed by Professor Hunter from Birkbeck, University of London, bpi1700 is a collaboration between Birkbeck and the Centre for Computing in the Humanities at King's College London, accessed 23 October 2009 (http://www.kcl.ac.uk/artshums/depts/ddh/about/index.aspx). It was funded by a three-year award from the Arts and Humanities Research Council of the United Kingdom.

ISBN 978-0-86698-499-7 (online)   ISBN 978-0-86698-474-4 (print)
New Technologies in Medieval and Renaissance Studies 3 (2012) 287–312

potential for ongoing expansion; here, above all, the project team wished to create a resource informed by research.

In what follows we discuss two features of the database that required careful consideration: the creation of a structure allowing for a more rational presentation of multiple objects and a fuller understanding of prints and their production; and a subject thesaurus facilitating sophisticated iconographic and historical research. Planning and designing these features posed various challenges—both practical and conceptual—and we consider some of these below. In particular we discuss the organization, classification, indexing, and presentation of prints; how to fulfil these tasks in ways that create a resource useful to non-specialists while simultaneously furthering specialist research; and—an issue crucial to the project's long-term research potential—how best to structure a database and develop indexing of metadata suitable to the particular research aims of the project yet also compatible with other resources. Our discussion of these issues is framed by a distinction between the "virtual museum" and "e-research," a distinction we believe is helpful in considering the approach to digitization of projects such as bpi1700 whose institutional "home" is the world of academic scholarship rather than the museum or collection. We suggest that the experience of bpi1700 sheds light on various questions and challenges posed by the creation of digital repositories of objects by academic researchers.

Virtual museums and e-research

Given the ambitious goals of bpi1700, the choice of an electronic rather than printed resource is natural: modern databases, as highly sophisticated organizational tools enabling data retrieval in a multiplicity of ways, have potential benefits unavailable to traditional, printed resources such as catalogues and surveys, both for researchers preparing the data and users of the resource. The well-designed digital resource, particularly when available online, can widen accessibility[2] and promote complex interaction with data. Indeed, the potential of the digitization of material and visual culture is such that it is tempting to regard the research possibilities it opens up as almost limitless, particularly for enabling multi- and interdisciplinary work; however, there can sometimes be a mismatch between the expectations of this research potential and some of the realities and challenges, and conse-

---

[2] Not least through digital imaging, which provides a useful alternative for scholars unable to access collections. bpi1700, for example, uses a Zoomify flash interface to enable detailed viewing of images, usually with magnification in excess of the actual size of the object.

quently the decisions and choices, faced by a digitization project. We think a useful way of considering these research possibilities and their challenges is by making a distinction between the "virtual museum" and "e-research."

There are many types of virtual museum,[3] and it would be unwise here to attempt too comprehensive a definition. Essentially they are online collections of objects. They typically stem from physical museums, and they involve the application of information technology to the concerns of the curator: the organization, management, and presentation of objects, and the development of learning resources. The virtualization of objects and their digital classification and publication are the principal goals of the virtual museum, realized through such essential tasks as photography, scanning, and cataloguing. Many virtual museums are little more than the websites of physical museums, usually with a digitized sample (at least) of the collection. At the other end of the spectrum are "collections of collections," for example resources such as the Virtual Museum of Canada[4] and ibiblio.[5] A collection of collections may act primarily as a portal, or it may build thematic links stretching across collections along with tools enabling extensive user interactivity. The latter approach brings virtual museums close to our notion of e-research. By e-research we understand the application of information technology to the concerns of academic scholarship, for example through the fostering of shared resources and research. In relation to the field of visual and material culture, an e-research approach emphasizes the development of collaborative, interdisciplinary research, organizing and contextualizing objects materially, visually, and historically, facilitating and undertaking complex analysis driven by the demands of scholarship.[6]

The differences between a virtual museum and e-research can be understood, for example, in the various ways a digitization project may prepare

---

[3] For a directory of virtual museums, see the *Virtual Library Museums Pages*, updated 1 September 2006, http://icom.museum/vlmp/.

[4] Virtual Museum of Canada, 2009, updated 2011, http://www.virtualmuseum.ca/.

[5] ibiblio, University of North Carolina at Chapel Hill, 2000, updated 2011, http://www.ibiblio.org/.

[6] For a general discussion of some of these issues, see Jankowski (2009). It is beyond the scope of this essay to discuss more fully the nature of e-research, particularly its relationship to e-science, but a good example illustrating this relationship and the wider aims of e-research is the Oxford e-Research Centre, accessed 23 October 2009, (http://www.oerc.ox.ac.uk/). The Centre for Computing in the Humanities (see n. 1 above) is another example of an institution dedicated to e-research.

and present an early modern printed text. The virtual museum approach may consist principally in the presentation of a digital facsimile of a single copy of the text. The e-research approach, on the other hand, may attempt to prepare an online critical edition through the collation of various editions and copies. Furthermore, although the virtual museum may well provide ancillary contextual material to aid understanding of the text and advanced functionality for searching the text, we believe these features to be essential aims of e-research: ideally, the text prepared by the e-research project would enable the user to compare various editions and copies, it would be fully searchable, and it would be indexed and annotated in sophisticated ways.

The virtual museum and e-research are not, of course, mutually exclusive—indeed, considerable overlap between the two approaches is to be expected—and it would be wrong to suggest that museums, whether physical or virtual, do not embody and develop important research. Nevertheless, we feel it is possible to distinguish broadly between the different emphases, demands, and goals of the virtual museum and e-research. A digitization project can aspire to both, and indeed this has been the aim of bpi1700: to classify, index, and present prints so that a virtual museum is created, and to add depth and contextualization to these tasks such that the resource constitutes e-research.

The scholarly context to bpi1700

To understand the rationale behind some of the decisions taken by bpi1700, it is worth commenting briefly on the scholarly context to the study of early modern British prints. Until comparatively recently the visual culture of sixteenth- and seventeenth-century Britain was a somewhat underdeveloped field. More recent scholarship, however, has increasingly emphasized the richness and cultural importance of images in early modern Britain and the complex historical and social contexts in which those images were situated. Central to much of this work has been an appreciation of the printed image.[7] Prints survive in a wide variety of genres and treat a diverse range of subject matter: from single-issue prints to book illustrations and title-pages; from maps to playing cards, trade cards, and ballads; from elaborate reproductions after Old Master paintings aimed at the "high end" of the print market to mass-produced woodcuts affordable to even humble consumers; from por-

---

[7] A good example of recent scholarship that uses British printed images within a broader historical thesis is Watt (1991), a consideration of popular religion through the extensive trade in ballads and chapbooks in Elizabethan and early Stuart England. Some other recent examples of interdisciplinary research using prints are Knights (2005), Monteyne (2007), Pierce (2008), Jones (2010), and Hunter (2010).

traits to landscapes; from devotional subjects to bawdy entertainment; from political propaganda to scandalous satire. Their significance extends beyond the visual to their role as material objects: they existed in a complex relationship between printmakers, artists, publishers, printsellers and booksellers, consumers and collectors, and much can be learned from them about early modern publishing, commerce, and trade. Interesting in their own right, prints also provide a fascinating insight into the broader history and culture of the period, and they are particularly fertile ground for interdisciplinary research. Arguably deserving of centre stage in any study of the visual history of the period, they certainly warrant serious attention in more general historical accounts.

As promising as much recent work is, scholarship remains at an early stage; it is also striking that some extremely valuable work on prints is still largely neglected by the wider scholarly community, possibly (and unjustifiably) regarded as too specialist.[8] A major problem frustrating attempts to incorporate printed images within more general British cultural history is the patchiness and often seriously underdeveloped scholarly foundations of British print studies, a state of affairs that contrasts strikingly with continental European print studies. For Dutch, Flemish, German, and Italian print studies the scholarly groundwork has long been established: the twenty-one volumes of Bartsch's *Le Peintre-Graveur* (1803-21) represent a magisterial scholarly achievement, large parts of which have still to be superseded;[9] Bartsch has been supplemented and often improved upon by *Hollstein's Dutch and Flemish Etchings, Engravings and Woodcuts, ca. 1450-1700* (1949–) and the equivalent volumes for German prints (1954–);[10] and for French prints there are the eleven volumes of Robert-Dumesnil's *Le Peintre-Graveur Français* (1835-71).[11] There is no equivalent to this foundational work for early modern British print history, as Antony Griffiths has commented: "The need for a survey of seventeenth-century British printmaking is self-evident... But not only has no general history ever been written; for large areas the ground-work has never been laid, and a disheartening amount of the existing coverage,

---

[8] For example, Griffiths (1998) and O'Connell (1999) both deserve a more prominent place in the wider study of the early modern period.

[9] A new series, complete with illustrations and commentaries, was begun in 1978 under the title *The Illustrated Bartsch*.

[10] Both are currently being revised as *The New Hollstein* (1993–, 1996–).

[11] For a survey of catalogues and other books on printmaking, giving some indication of the gap between work on early modern British and contemporary continental European prints, see Griffiths (1996, 128–33).

repeated again and again without a check of original sources, is extremely inaccurate" (1998, 6). There *are* a number of important catalogues dealing with sixteenth- and seventeenth-century British prints, but each is limited in focus, and, in certain cases, in need of significant revision: John Chaloner Smith's *British Mezzotinto Portraits* (1878–83),[12] a general catalogue on British mezzotint engraving from its origins in the 1680s, but confined to portraits; A. M. Hind's *Engraving in England in the Sixteenth and Seventeenth Centuries* (1952–64),[13] an important descriptive catalogue of engravings in Tudor and early Stuart England, but by no means complete; the first two volumes of Stephens's *Catalogue of Political and Personal Satires* (1870–83), covering satirical prints in the collections of the British Museum and British Library up to 1733; Pennington's catalogue of the etchings of Wenceslaus Hollar (1982); Fagan's catalogue of the engravings of William Faithorne the elder (1888); and Globe's extraordinary catalogue of the mid-seventeenth-century printseller Peter Stent (1985). This brief list indicates some of the lacunae in the general scholarship: most etchings other than by Hollar, engravings from the second half of the seventeenth century, and mezzotint genre prints,[14] to name only three important areas in need of major foundational work.

One of the long-term aims of bpi1700 is to rectify this lack of adequate groundwork for print studies: the project presents the first catalogue of any kind aspiring to a complete survey of sixteenth- and seventeenth-century British printed images. Although significant and valuable material can be found in several other online resources—the most important of which are the *Bodleian Library Broadside Ballads*,[15] the *Wenceslaus Hollar Digital Collection* at the University of Toronto library,[16] *Collage*, the database of the City of London Libraries and Guildhall Art Gallery,[17] and the online collections of the National Portrait Gallery[18] and the British Museum[19]—with the exception of

---

[12] Supplemented by Russell (1926).

[13] The third volume, covering engraving during the reign of Charles I, was compiled from Hind's notes by Margery Corbett and Michael Norton.

[14] Ganz (1994) has gone some way to improving scholarship on mezzotint genre prints.

[15] *Bodleian Library Broadside Ballads*, 2011, http://www.bodley.ox.ac.uk/ballads/ballads.htm.

[16] *Wenceslaus Hollar Digital Collection*, University of Toronto, accessed 23 October 2009, http://link.library.utoronto.ca/hollar/.

[17] *Collage*, City of London Libraries and Guildhall Art Gallery, accessed 23 October 2009, http://collage.cityoflondon.gov.uk/collage/app.

[18] National Portrait Gallery, 2011, http://www.npg.org.uk/collections.php.

[19] British Museum, accessed 23 October 2009, http://www.britishmuseum.org/research.aspx.

the Toronto Hollar catalogue, these resources are not devoted to the printed image alone.[20] A notable feature of these catalogues is that they are based on single collections, and as such exemplify various features of the "virtual museum" as discussed above: they itemize, classify, and present, with essential information, numerous objects within particular collections. As a project that is not based on a single collection,[21] bpi1700 has a different set of criteria, purposes, and possibilities. Above all, bpi1700 has greater scope to present, organize, and classify its corpus in ways driven by academic research.

Inventory catalogues and catalogues raisonnés

Major considerations for bpi1700 and its aim of adopting a research-driven approach to its corpus concerned the organization of data, database structure, and the interface following from these. Database design relates to cataloguing principles: the intention behind cataloguing influences design requirements for a database. We identified two types of catalogue which correspond broadly to the distinction we have made between virtual museums and e-research. The first type is the inventory catalogue of the particular collection, such as those electronic resources mentioned above, a primary purpose of which is to itemize and manage holdings within that collection. Such catalogues have invariably grown out of internal catalogues within libraries and museums operating according to standards of collection and curatorial management.[22] *Cataloging Cultural Objects* (Baca et al. 2006), probably the most important data standard dealing with cultural objects, is primarily intended for professionals working within collections, and is especially suited to the inventory catalogue.[23] The increasing public availability of such catalogues has been of huge benefit to scholarship. Nevertheless, as research resources they are by

---

[20] The image is prominent in the *Bodleian Library Broadside Ballads*, which, through its use of the Iconclass iconographic system (see n. 30 below), treats images in a sophisticated way. But since many ballads were text only, images are not its central focus.

[21] The overwhelming majority of the bpi1700 database stems from the collection held at the British Museum's Department of Prints and Drawings, with supplementary material from other sources, notably the National Art Library at the Victoria and Albert Museum; however, bpi1700 is not in principle restricted to particular collections.

[22] An important British standard is McKenna and Patzatzi (2007). Also relevant, although primarily designed for library cataloguers, is Betz (1982).

[23] *Cataloging Cultural Objects* (Baca et al. 2006). See the CCO Commons website, which makes *Cataloging Cultural Objects: A Guide to Describing Cultural Works and Their Images*, 2006, available for free download, at the CCO website hosted by the Visual Resources Association, http://cco.vrafoundation.org/.

their very nature subject to certain limitations: they are generally restricted to the holdings of a single collection, and they are guided first and foremost by the need to identify, locate, and manage objects within a collection.

Figure 1. John Smith, Portrait of Lucy Manners, Duchess of Rutland. Mezzotint. c. 1699. c. 350 mm x 249 mm. The three impressions show changes of state between printings: (i) The first state. British Museum 1902,1011.4817 (ii) The second state. British Museum 1902,1011.4818 (iii) The third state. British Museum 1902,1011.4819

The second type of catalogue is the catalogue raisonné, most typically the comprehensive and authoritative catalogue of the output of an artist, print-maker, or publisher. In print scholarship, examples are the various founda-tional works such as Bartsch and Hollstein, and the important catalogues of early modern British prints mentioned above, such as those by Hind, Pennington, and Globe. A key concern of catalogues raisonnés of prints has been to identify the various states and impressions of each print. Much of our thinking about database design has been informed by the reproducibility of prints: from a single block or plate multiple impressions can be printed. These impressions might be used in different ways: the same print might be issued, without alteration, as a single print or as part of a series, or it might be used as an illustration to a book (and sometimes to more than one book). Furthermore, the printing matrix—the plate or woodblock—can be altered between printings, thereby generating different states. Often these altera-tions are minor, for example the retouching of the design, or the addition of lettering. But in many instances major alterations are made: significant details may be added or removed, and there are numerous examples of por-traits in which the sitter is changed between states. A fairly straightforward example illustrating these differences is a 1699 mezzotint portrait of Lucy Manners, Duchess of Rutland, engraved by John Smith after a portrait by Godfrey Kneller (see Fig. 1). The print survives in four known states and at least sixteen known impressions. The following description of the different states is typically found in a catalogue raisonné:

I.   Unlettered and unfinished proof. Before the landscape background and rock on left side. Single flower in left hand.
II.   Lettered with title and production details. Landscape and rock added.
III.   Reworked, and additional flower added to left hand.
IV.   Posthumously published.

This is a fairly typical, relatively unproblematic example of changing print states: an unpublished proof state by which the printmaker can check the progress of the design; a lettered and published state; a reworked state after the plate had worn down, in which the opportunity was taken to add a further detail; and a later published state, possibly after some further retouching of the plate. Even here there is some guesswork as to the nature of the fourth state—impressions from it seem hard to find—for example, whether it genuinely constitutes a new state or whether it is simply a later impression of the third state. And it is interesting that there is an unfin-ished proof but not a finished proof. Proofs survive most commonly in a finished state lacking only lettering: this raises the possibility that there may have been an intermediary state between the first and second.

Questions about what constitutes a change of state can often be controversial, not least because the identification of different states is an important part of print scholarship and central to the catalogue raisonné. The production history of a print can be illuminating not only about the printmaking process but also about the print trade itself: it can shed light on the relations between engravers and publishers, and between different publishers (for example, it can establish instances where a stock of plates have been sold by one publisher to another and the different ways plates may have been used and reused). Although these are among the most challenging areas of print scholarship, they are also among the most rewarding. An understanding of the full history of the production of a print—not only who made the print, but who designed it, who published it, and the various ways in which a print was sold and used—is a contribution not merely to the specialism of print scholarship but more generally to the role of the print as a material object in its wider social and cultural context. The ideal resource for studying early modern British prints would be a catalogue not only as comprehensive as possible in the scope of its corpus and the data presented about individual prints, but also able to identify the various impressions and states, provide as full a history of their production as the evidence allows, and link these impressions and states together in an intelligent and useful way. Such an ideal is a daunting task, and would require the work of numerous scholars over many years even to get close to realization.[24] Yet this ideal is worth pursuing, not only because of its intrinsic value, but also because digitization lends itself precisely to this type of large-scale, ongoing research, and to the challenge of the complex visual and material relations to be found in print history.

We decided, therefore, that bpi1700 could most appropriately aspire to be an electronic catalogue raisonné. Its value lay less in the itemization and presentation of as many individual prints as possible and more in its ability to group prints together in intelligent ways that offer greater contextualization of them as material objects. To illustrate a fairly simple advantage of such a database over the inventory catalogue for the end user, we can consider the way results are generated from searches. Of the various impressions of the John Smith portrait of Lucy Manners, five are in the British Museum print collection: one first state, two second state, and two third state

---

[24] An indication of the vastness of such a task is provided by the scale and duration of the ongoing Hollstein printed catalogues: more than one hundred volumes for the two series of Dutch and Flemish, and German, published over more than half a century.

impressions. In an inventory catalogue of the museum's collection, a search for this portrait will generate all five results, one for each impression: useful for knowing what the collection holds, but an unwieldy outcome less useful for research. By contrast, the type of database structure favoured by bpi1700 would generate a single result, with full information on the different states recorded in one record, and a means to access images and further information on individual impressions via that single record (see Fig. 2).

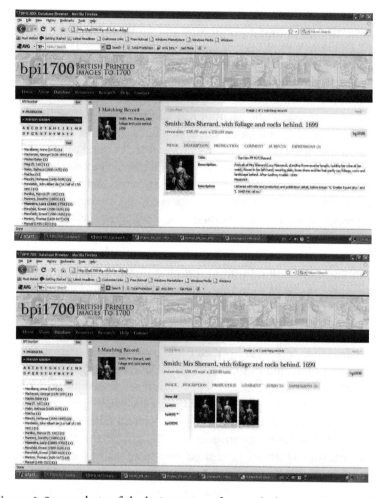

Figure 2: Screenshots of the bpi1700 interface with the record for Smith's mezzotint portrait of Lucy Manners, illustrating how the print-impression structure of the database appears to the user. (i) The description of the print. (ii) Thumbnails of the three impressions of the print in the database.

Clicking on the bpi number for an impression will open up impression-specific information. The preferred impression, which is used as a basis for the single print record, is marked with an asterisk.

FRBR and database design

Designing a database informed by a catalogue raisonné approach presented a number of challenges. Although a well-established part of scholarship, few models of the catalogue raisonné can be found either in electronic resources or in guides to cataloguing standards. As mentioned above, most standards have been developed with the cataloguing needs of the museum, archive, or library in mind, and, since they are designed to accommodate all forms of cultural object, specific issues relating to particular objects (such as the reproducibility of prints) tend not to be addressed.[25] Among resources dealing with printed images, none of them groups different states and impressions together in a single record, although most acknowledge and either link or refer to other impressions and variant states.[26] In the absence of models among the literature and resources dealing with cultural objects, bpi1700 investigated instead bibliographic approaches to cataloguing and databases. Bibliography has long developed international cataloguing standards to distinguish among the generic "work" (e.g., Shakespeare's *Hamlet*), different editions and translations of that work (e.g., the first folio edition of *Hamlet*), and the individual examples of that work held in library collections (e.g., a copy of the First Folio in the British Library). There are good reasons why print cataloguers should seriously consider the principles, methods, and standards of bibliography: not only do prints share with printed books the ability to be reproduced, often with variations between printings, but since prints were so frequently used as title-pages and book illustrations, and since

---

[25] A resource that does address print cataloguing is the *Prints and Printmaking Australia Asia Pacific* database, accessed 23 October 2009; for their conventions see http://www.printsandprintmaking.gov.au/Conventions.aspx. Its emphasis is on cataloguing individual items, not on creating a structured database linking items together. For an example from *Cataloging Cultural Objects* (Baca et al. 2006) of a recommended record for a print (an etching by Hollar), see http://www.vraweb.org/ccoweb/cco/example42.html, indicating the emphasis on recording at the level of the individual object within a collection.

[26] Among other material objects, an example of the model desired by bpi1700 is *Roman Provincial Coinage Online*, a numismatic resource that distinguishes between coin types and specimens of that type: *RPC Online*, University of Oxford, 2005, http://rpc.ashmus.ox.ac.uk/.

print publishers and sellers often had close connections to book publishers and sellers, the principles of bibliographic cataloguing would seem a promising approach for print cataloguing.

The set of standards most influential on bpi1700 is that presented in *Functional Requirements for Bibliographic Records* (FRBR),[27] which, despite its title, offers a model relevant beyond book cataloguing, as indicated by its many examples from a wide range of cultural forms. FRBR's methodology "is based on an entity analysis technique that is used in the development of conceptual models for relational database systems." The most relevant of the FRBR entities for the present discussion are those which deal with "the products of intellectual or artistic content": there are four such entities, "works," "expressions," "manifestations," and "items," of which the first two "reflect intellectual or artistic content," while the latter two "reflect physical form." By a *work* FRBR understands an "abstract entity." There is no single material object which can be pointed to as the work: "We recognize the *work* through individual realizations or *expressions* of the *work*, but the *work* itself exists only in the commonality of content between and among the various *expressions* of the *work*." A work is always realized through one or more than one expression, an expression being "the specific intellectual or artistic form that a *work* takes each time it is 'realized.'" An expression can be the realization of one and only one work. *Manifestation* and *item* concern "physical form." A manifestation is "the physical embodiment of an *expression* of a *work*." There may be only one instance of a manifestation (an author's manuscript copy, for example) or several instances (a printed edition, for example). Finally, an *item* is "a single exemplar of a *manifestation*." It is usually a single, unique physical object (though it can be more than one, such as a monograph issued as two separately bound volumes, or a recording issued on several separate compact discs) (FRBR 1998, 12–23).

These entities can be illustrated in the example of the Smith portrait of Lucy Manners (w=work; e=expression; m=manifestation; i=item):

w: John Smith's portrait of Lucy Manners after Godfrey Kneller.
    e: The mezzotint print by John Smith.
        m1: The first state, unlettered and unfinished.
            i1: Impression in British Museum (1902,1011.4817).
            i2: …

---

[27] IFLA Study Group on the *Functional Requirements for Bibliographic Records* (1998). Referred to as FRBR in the text. All italics in original.

m2: The second state.

    i1: Impression in British Museum (1902,1011.4818).

    i2: Impression in British Museum. (Smith, vol. 2, p. 40), cropped.

    i3: Impression in National Portrait Gallery, London (D11621).

    i4: ...

m3: The third state, reworked and with alterations.

    i1: Impression in British Museum (1902,1011.4819).

    i2: Impression in British Museum (1855,0512.66).

    i3: Impression in Bibliothèque Nationale, Paris (Ec. 84, fol. 37), cut.

    i4: ...

m4: The fourth state, posthumously published.

    i1: ...

As this example shows, in the FRBR structure actual objects are only described within the entities of manifestation and item, corresponding here with actually existing states and impressions. So in this example the structure establishes a relationship between the abstract "portrait of Lucy Manners by Smith" (the work) with no reference to the form this portrait takes, to the realization of this work in the form of a mezzotint print (the expression), the manifestations of this expression in the different states in which the print is found (manifestations), and the individual impressions of each state as held in various collections (items).

The type of structure outlined by FRBR is ideal for print cataloguing, since it accommodates the different states in which prints can be found and the impressions of those states. Although bpi1700 considered a threefold structure of *prints*, *states*, and *impressions*, corresponding to FRBR's *expressions*, *manifestations*, and *items*, it was eventually decided for practical and presentational reasons to implement a twofold structure based on the entities of *prints* and *impressions*, with full state information recorded within the print entity in a field dedicated to production history, and state number (or description) of individual impressions recorded in a field within the impression entity. In the case of the Smith mezzotint of Lucy Manners, the bpi1700 database contains a single print record with a preferred image and full information about the different states in the production history of the print. This print record also itemizes each impression within the database relating to it (in this example, three impressions of the portrait in the bpi1700 database), with corresponding images and brief impression-specific information.

Even in this simplified form, such a structure allows multiple states and impressions of individual prints to be grouped together within a single record, enabling prints to be more fully understood as complex material objects. The print entities, which are the records intended to be displayed first and foremost on the interface, are in effect not records of individual objects, but rather of the abstract cultural form realized in the individual impressions among the impression entities. We believe this is an innovative method of electronic cataloguing of cultural objects, one designed explicitly to facilitate a more research-driven approach. Certainly it raises many challenges, not least of which are the resources required not only to catalogue prints but also to identify and explain the relationships between them. In addition, this approach raises questions concerning compatibility. The ways in which the bpi1700 database structure might link to similarly structured bibliographic databases (desirable for research into the seriously understudied area of book illustrations) remain to be explored, as does the compatibility between bpi1700 and other databases of cultural objects, a vital consideration both for the export, import, and sharing of data, and for the overall research potential of the resource. Much work is still required in answering such questions of database compatibility, but one area of the project which required immediate engagement with issues surrounding compatibility concerned indexing and the subject thesaurus.

Subject indexing and compatibility

One of the aims of bpi1700 is the sophisticated indexing of objects. Not only does such indexing make the resource more useful, enabling rich and complex user-searches of the data, but it also enhances research by contextualizing the images. We needed to develop an index suitable to our particular materials and catering to the needs of our anticipated users, without losing sight of the value of compatibility with other indexing systems.

In its guidelines for describing objects, *Cataloging Cultural Objects* (Baca et al. 2006) defines two types of subject. One is termed the "of-ness" of an object: "what would be seen in the work by an objective, nonexpert viewer," that is, what is depicted on or by an item. The other type of subject relates to the broader concepts relevant to, if not immediately visible from, the object: its "about-ness," which is described as "its iconographical, narrative, thematic, or symbolic meaning."[28] Both types of descriptive subject are relevant to the material with which bpi1700 is concerned, and both enable rich contextualization of the objects. Examples of the types of context that need to be captured are the often complex social and political messages that prints were intended to convey (satirical prints being notable in this respect), and the texts that many prints were designed to accompany or illustrate (title-pages and book illustrations being obvious examples).

An example of a print in which both types of subject are highly relevant is "The Embleme of England's Distractions," or "Cromwell between Two Pillars," a 1658 engraving by William Faithorne after a drawing by Francis Barlow (see Fig. 3).

Figure 3. William Faithorne, "The Embleme of England's Distractions." Engraving. 1658. 562 mm x 422 mm. British Museum 1935,0413.184

---

[28] http://www.vraweb.org/ccoweb/cco/parttwo_chapter6.html.

Here Oliver Cromwell is shown trampling the Whore of Babylon and a serpent personifying "faction." He is flanked by pillars representing the rule of
law and the allegiance of England, Ireland, and Scotland, and a dove of peace
hovers above. At the top are biblical scenes, including Noah's ark coming to
rest at Mount Ararat. Below left are scenes of country tranquillity (including a helmet being used as a beehive, a long-standing emblematic device for
peace), and below right scenes of subversion—plotters egged on by Jesuits
hacking at the pillar and laying gunpowder to it. Some examples of the "of-
ness" of this print include "sun," "dove," "armour," and "beehive," while
subjects that convey the "about-ness" might include "legitimacy," "the rule
of law," "peace," and "subversion." A complex print like this is an important
and fascinating cultural and material object that is revealing not only to the
print historian, but also to, for example, the political historian. To achieve
this usefulness, however, its subject indexing has to be both inclusive and
correct, which demands a sophisticated, research-driven thesaurus.

In developing such a thesaurus, we considered several existing subject indexes. We can again make a useful comparison between the research aims
of bpi1700 and the type of thesaurus often attached to museum inventory
catalogues. In many cases these collections are simply too large and too
broad to make a set of subject categories that will be substantially useful for
research. In large museum collections, which might, for example, include
archaeological and anthropological material alongside fine and decorative
arts, from prehistory to the present day, it is difficult to identify categories
that will be meaningful or appropriate across the entire corpus, or that will
be sufficiently sensitive to the specialist needs of specific parts of it. Effective subject-indexing also requires uniformity of use which is likely to be
difficult across such a large institution. A notable exception to this, and an
example of a collection that has successfully created its own set of subject
terms, is *Insight*, the online database of the Tate collection.[29] *Insight* classifies
the collection by both objects and broader themes. Its hierarchy of information has a manageable three-level structure, and the objects have been
tagged with terms in ways that generate useful search results. So, to take
some similar terms to those suggested above for the Faithorne print of Oliver
Cromwell, *Insight* presents hierarchical arrangements of terms such as "History–Government and Politics–Political tension," and "Nature–Animals and
Birds–Dove." Although *Insight* tends to be more helpful in describing what is
depicted in an image (the "of-ness") than the broader themes of the image

---

[29] Tate Insight, accessed 23 October 2009, http://www.tate.org.uk/collections/in-
sight.htm.

(the "about-ness"), it is nevertheless an excellent example of a classification system that successfully combines usability with huge research potential.

What is less clear about a bespoke thesaurus such as *Insight* is the extent to which it is compatible with other classification systems. Balancing compatibility with specificity is one of the principal challenges faced by projects like bpi1700. An entirely tailor-made set of subjects might make the database difficult to sustain in the long term and is likely to render the database impossible to integrate with other resources; there are huge benefits in one database being able to "talk" easily to another, and in the sharing of data and research. However, projects such as bpi1700 need to develop a set of subjects sensitive to the material and the intended scholarly aims, and which promote advanced research. Although bpi1700 considered a similar bespoke solution to the problems of classification as that exemplified by *Insight*, we ultimately decided that the advantages of compatibility with other resources weighed against the benefits of an entirely custom-made thesaurus. To ensure a high level of compatibility with other projects, the bpi1700 subject indexing system makes use of two authorities: Iconclass and Library of Congress Subject Headings. Both are important standards used in many comparable resources, but neither is a perfect fit for the corpus of material covered by bpi1700. A careful balance had to be made between compatibility and specificity, between the need to adhere to these authorities and the appropriate freedom to depart from them.

Iconclass was devised as "a systematic overview of subjects, themes and motifs in Western art," and has a strongly iconographic approach.[30] It consists of more than 28,000 definitions, ordered hierarchically and keyed with alphanumeric codes, which identify and classify objects depicted in works of art; the alphanumeric codes are ideal as a basis for compatibility and are an excellent solution to linguistic differences. Iconclass's structure and classifications have been adopted by many collections to subject-index their objects, from the *Bodleian Library Broadside Ballads* project to the Musée d'Orsay. Iconclass has many hierarchical levels, and the level of detail can be extremely useful, both for specialist researchers and general users: for example it includes a code for "bows on clothing" (41D2654) and also one for "hushing," i.e., putting a finger to one's lips (31B623591).[31] On the other

---

[30] Iconclass 2011, http://www.iconclass.nl/.

[31] At times, perhaps, there are too many levels in the hierarchy; the term "foot," for example, is reached only after seven layers of the hierarchy: 3 Human Being, Man in General—31 man in a general biological sense—31A the (nude) human figure; "Cor-

hand, Iconclass sometimes lacks detail on some of the broader themes we felt important to include in bpi1700. For example, the researcher interested in the concepts of "legitimacy" and "the rule of law" (themes illustrated by the Faithorne print above) will find many specific terms relating to concrete, visual features of law and jurisprudence, but no code relating to the sought-after abstract concepts.

While the Iconclass system has many virtues, particularly in relation to compatibility, the codes are not the most intuitive means of searching for many users, and we felt that developing an authoritative and precise scholarly terminology based on natural language remains important. For terminology we relied, where possible, on terms preferred by Library of Congress Subject Headings (LCSH), a decision based on its status as the predominant international bibliographic indexing standard, familiar to and used by libraries and cataloguers worldwide. It has also been applied to inventory databases of cultural objects: at the Wellcome Collection in London, for example, whose library and iconographic collection both use LCSH. A particularly useful feature of the Library of Congress system—and one that enhances its compatibility—is its comprehensive terminology, particularly as it accompanies its "preferred" terms with non-preferred "used for" terms. In general, the bpi1700 subject thesaurus uses the LCSH-preferred term: so, for example, "author" is a preferred term to which a search for "writer" will be directed, because "author" is preferred in LCSH.

LCSH terms are generally useful to describe the "about-ness" of a print; for example, both "rule of law" and "legitimacy of governments" are included in LCSH. They are less strong in the often rich and detailed "of-ness" of visual images. For example, there is no authorized term for "doves" (a cataloguer having to use the more general term "pigeons" instead), nor is there an authorized term for "sunsets," only the rather the less specific "sun—rising and setting." Since subjects in LCSH derive from bibliographic material—that is, the LCSH list is made up of subjects of books in the Library of Congress collection—such gaps in specificity are not surprising, but they can be problematic to the cataloguer of visual material. For example, there are many books on "gestures," an authorized LCSH term, but probably none on the specific gesture of "hushing," which therefore lacks a term within LCSH. A further limitation of LCSH is that it is not as sensitive to historical context as would

---

po humano" (Ripa)—31A2 anatomy (non-medical)—31A22 parts of the human body (skeleton excepted)—31A225 legs—31A2255 foot. See http://www.iconclass.org/rkd/31A2255, accessed 23 October 2009.

be ideal for a project such as bpi1700, and frequently tends towards anachronism: for example, it prefers the terms "working class" and "middle class," notoriously controversial terminology in early modern studies and generally avoided by scholars who consider alternatives such as "middling sort" and "labouring class" more appropriate. Furthermore, the LCSH "used for" terms are occasionally inappropriate for the purposes of iconographic classification, often failing to capture nuanced but significant differences between similar subjects. A striking example is "hills," which is not a preferred term, but is "used for" "mountains": not only might many cartographers raise their eyebrows at this blurring, but iconographically a hill is certainly different enough from a mountain to warrant its own term in a subject thesaurus.

Nevertheless, the ability to include "used for" terms within the bpi1700 subject thesaurus is very useful. The subject thesaurus has been encoded in XML to allow substantial cross-referencing, with non-preferred terms automatically directed to the chosen term within the index; this enables anachronisms and other non-preferred terms to be included and searchable even though they are not visible to users at the thesaurus front-end. Entering the term "working class," for example, will automatically direct a user to the more appropriate "labouring class" instead—this enables the resource to be useful to specialist and non-specialist alike. At the same time, to enable compatibility with Iconclass the bpi1700 thesaurus also uses Iconclass codes, with a view to allowing those too to be searchable. For example, we hope to develop functionality for the user so that by entering "46A17," the Iconclass code for "working class, labourers," the user will be directed to "labouring class" in the bpi1700 thesaurus.

For such a subject-rich project as bpi1700 there are clear and valuable benefits to developing a thesaurus compatible with both Iconclass and LCSH, but as we have indicated above, both authorities have certain limitations: there are numerous terms that we felt were important for bpi1700 material but which neither authority covers. Among such terms are some key concepts of interest to the scholar of early modern Britain, such as "sociability," and terms that capture important abstract ideas and the wider context in which the print can be located, but that are not immediately obvious iconographically, such as "subversion" (for example, an image illustrating text specifically concerned with subversion). Since we aimed to create a subject index that can satisfy both the specialist and the general user, we wished to develop a thesaurus that is scholarly, precise, and inclusive. The depiction of dress is an example of a particularly complicated area. Many terms that users might want to search by (for example, "jacket") are likely to be anachronistic, but some correct terms used by the dress historian (for example, "doublet" or "jerkin") are likely to be unfamiliar to or not fully understood by the general user. Including specialist terms like this not only captures historical and scholarly precision, but is intended to be of educational and research value to the general user. There are also items of dress which, though easily recognizable, lack a precise name of their own. An example of this is the swathe of material draped over a sitter who wears a simple shift underneath, as in Isaac Beckett's mezzotint portrait of Catherine "Orinda" Phillips (see Fig. 4).

Figure 4: Isaac Beckett, Portrait of Catherine "Orinda" Phillips. Mezzotint. 1683–88. 238 mm x 177 mm. British Museum 1902,1011.155

This type of fashionable undress was a convention of portraiture often found in late seventeenth-century mezzotints: no woman would ever have actually received guests in this way. In the absence of a proper name for this garment, we chose to call it simply a "draped garment," following the advice of *Catalog-*

ing Cultural Objects (Baca et al. 2006) that "it is better to be broad and accurate rather than specific and incorrect."

Developing such a rich taxonomy, while also attempting to build in compatibility, is one of the most difficult challenges for a research-driven digitization project. Nor do the challenges stop at the stage of developing the thesaurus: among the questions that we believe e-research has to confront—but which fall outside the scope of this essay to address properly—are how, given resource limitations, the requisite expertise can be harnessed; and the extent to which more collaborative approaches, such as those found in folksonomies and social tagging, may offer interesting solutions to the demands of e-research. In turn, such questions raise further problems relating to compatibility, especially compatibility between the needs of specialists and those of the general user.

Conclusion

As we have suggested here, digitization is the obvious choice for the type of scholarship intended by bpi1700. As a means of making a large body of material available to a broad user group, while at the same time organizing and presenting this material in ways driven by research, the digitization project has immense potential. But there are a number of challenges to realizing this potential. bpi1700 has had to confront some of these, as we have outlined above: how to develop database and cataloguing standards in the absence of clearly agreed international standards; and how to build compatibility into the resource while also remaining faithful to the subject matter and research requirements of the project. As we have argued, digitization offers an array of choices, but with those choices comes the necessity to think carefully about balancing innovation with compatibility, and about how best to meet a wide range of research and learning needs. We do not believe there are straightforward answers to many of these questions, but we do think it useful to consider the features of different types of digitization project, and particularly, as we have suggested above, the differences between the virtual museum approach and that of e-research. Certain tensions follow from these differences: most cataloguing of prints has been done within museums and galleries, and the curatorially driven nature of this cataloguing is not always a good fit for the needs of the e-research approach. The problems are compounded in the field of print studies by the lack of consistent adherence to recognizable international standards of cataloguing. For an academic project such as bpi1700, this creates a number of challenges, for example the importing and sharing of data. The digitization of prints involves a constantly evolving process of engagement with the conventions established by com-munities of scholars, curators, and librarians; it demands the development of working tools that deliver information and create useable resources; and it promises innovative approaches to the organization and sharing of data and the construction of thesauri in ways that reveal relationships between the different interested communities and promote inter- and multidisciplinary research. The realization of these aims—without loss of data and scholarly integrity—requires both conceptual and technical solutions, and a commit-ment to openness, sharing, and compatibility.

WORKS CITED

Baca, Martha, et al. 2006. *Cataloging Cultural Objects: A Guide to Describing Cultural Works and Their Images.* CCO Commons. Chicago: American Library Association. http://www.vrafoundation.org/ccoweb/index. htm.

Bartsch, Adam von. 1803–21. *Le peintre-graveur.* 21 vols. Vienna: J. V. Degen.

_____ 1978–. *The Illustrated Bartsch.* Edited by Walter L. Strauss. New York: Abaris Books.

Betz, Elisabeth W. 1982. *Graphic Materials: Rules for Describing Original Items and Historical Collections.* Washington, DC: Library of Congress. http:// www.loc.gov/rr/print/gm/graphmat.html.

Fagan, Louis. 1888. *A Descriptive Catalogue of the Engraved Works of William Faithorne.* London: B. Quaritch.

Ganz, James A. 1994. *Fancy Pieces: Genre Mezzotints by Robert Robinson and his Contemporaries.* New Haven, CT: Yale Center for British Art.

Globe, Alexander. 1985. *Peter Stent, London Printseller, circa 1642-1665: Being a Catalogue Raisonné of his Engraved Prints and Books.* Vancouver: University of British Columbia Press.

Griffiths, Antony. 1996. *Prints and Printmaking: An Introduction to the History and Techniques.* 2nd ed. London: British Museum Press.

_____ 1998. *The Print in Stuart Britain 1603-1689.* London: British Museum Press.

Hind, Arthur Mayger, et al. 1952–64. *Engraving in England in the Sixteenth and Seventeenth Centuries.* 3 vols. Cambridge: Cambridge University Press.

Hollstein, F. W. H., et al. 1949–. *Hollstein's Dutch and Flemish Etchings, Engravings and Woodcuts, ca. 1450–1700.* Amsterdam: M. Hertzberger.

_____ 1954–. *Hollstein's German Engravings, Etchings and Woodcuts, ca. 1400–1700.* Amsterdam: M. Hertzberger.

_____ 1993–. *The New Hollstein: Dutch and Flemish Etchings, Engravings and Woodcuts, 1450–1700.* Roosendaal: Koninklijke van Poll.

_____ 1996–. *The New Hollstein: German Engravings, Etchings and Woodcuts, 1400–1700.* Rotterdam: Sound and Vision Interactive.

Hunter, Michael, ed. 2010. *Printed Images in Early Modern Britain.* Aldershot: Ashgate.

IFLA Study Group on the Functional Requirements for Bibliographic Records. 1998. *Functional Requirements for Bibliographic Records: Final Report.* Munich: K. G. Saur. http://www.ifla.org/publications/functional-requirements-for-bibliographic-records.

Jankowski, Nicholas W., ed. 2009. *E-Research: Transformation in Scholarly Practice.* London: Routledge.

Jones, Malcolm. 2010. *The Print in Early Modern England: An Historical Oversight.* New Haven, CT, and London: Yale University Press.

Knights, Mark. 2005. *Representation and Misrepresentation in Later Stuart Britain: Partisanship and Political Culture.* Oxford: Oxford University Press.

Library of Congress Subject Headings. Accessed 23 October 2009. http://authorities.loc.gov/.

McKenna, Gordon, and Efthymia Patzatzi, eds. 2007. *SPECTRUM: The UK Museum Documentation Standard: Version 3.1.* Cambridge: Museum Documentation Association.

Monteyne, Joseph. 2007. *The Printed Image in Early Modern London: Urban Space, Visual Representation and Social Exchange.* Aldershot: Ashgate.

O'Connell, Sheila. 1999. *The Popular Print in England 1550–1850.* London: British Museum Press.

Pennington, Richard. 1982. *A Descriptive Catalogue of the Etched Work of Wenceslaus Hollar 1607-1677.* Cambridge: Cambridge University Press.

Pierce, Helen. 2008. *Unseemly Pictures: Graphic Satire and Politics in Early Modern England.* New Haven, CT, and London: Yale University Press.

Robert-Dumesnil, A. P. F. 1835-71. *Le peintre-graveur Français.* Paris: G. Duplessis.

Russell, C. E. 1926. *English Mezzotint Portraits and Their States.* 2 vols. London: Halton & T. Smith.

Smith, John Chaloner. 1878–83. *British Mezzotint Portraits, from the Introduction of the Art to the Early Part of the Present Century.* 4 vols. London: H. Sotheran.

Stephens, Frederic George. 1870–83. *Catalogue of Political and Personal Satires in the British Museum.* 4 vols. London: Chiswick Press.

Trant, Jennifer. 2009. "Tagging, Folksonomy and Art Museums: Early Experiments and Ongoing Research." *Journal of Digital Information* 10 (1): http://journals.tdl.org/jodi/article/view/270/277.

Watt, Tessa. 1991. *Cheap Print and Popular Piety, 1550-1640.* Cambridge: Cambridge University Press.

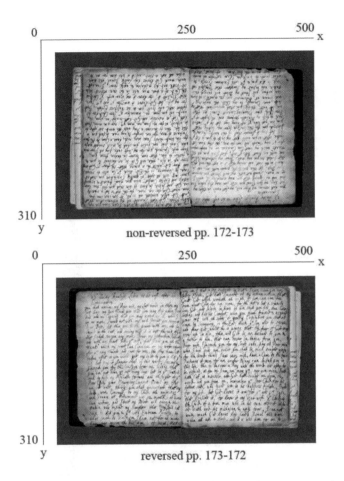

0   250   500 x

310

y

non-reversed pp. 172-173

0   250   500 x

310

y

reversed pp. 173-172

Vine and Verweij Figure 2: X and Y coordinates of non-reversed and reversed openings

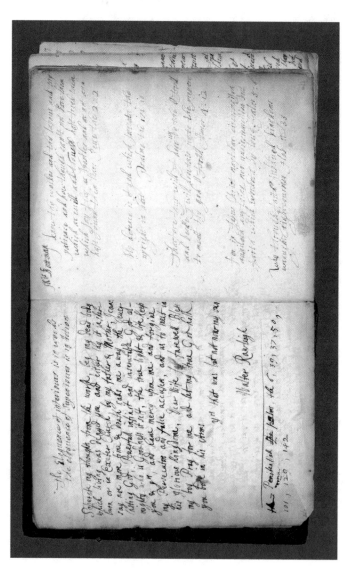

Vine and Verweij Figure 3: Cambridge University Library, MS Add. 8640, pp. 171–70 reversed. In Dorothy Browne's hand: maxim on eloquence at top left, and sermon notes from "Mr Bottman" on right hand page. In Lyttelton's hand: the end of the Raleigh letter, and a list of the Penitential Psalms at bottom left. Image reproduced with kind permission from the Syndics of Cambridge University Library.

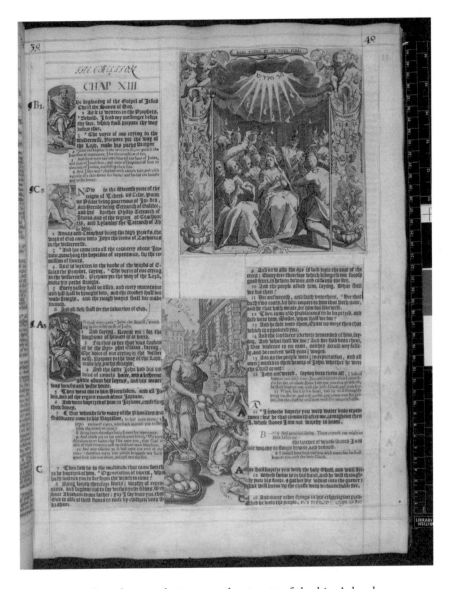

THE GOSPEL

CHAP XIII

The beginning of the Gospel of Iesus Christ the Sonne of God.

2 As it is written in the Prophets, Behold, I send my messenger before thy face, which shall prepare thy way before thee.

3 The voyce of one crying in the wildernesse, Prepare yee the way of the Lord, make his paths straight.

...

Dyck and Rempel Figure 1. Chapter 13 of the king's book
© The British Library Board. C23e4

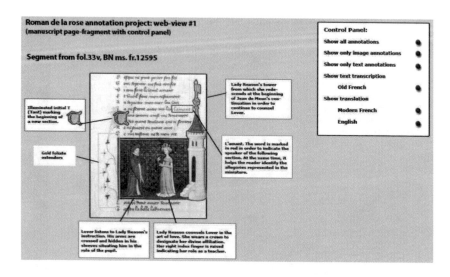

Jakacki and McWebb Figure 3. Screenshot 1: Annotation Capability

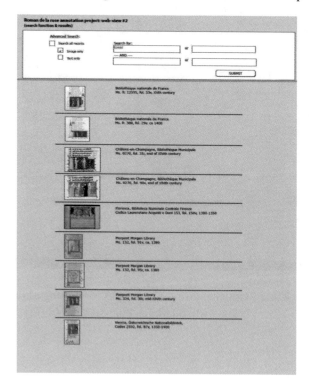

Jakacki and McWebb Figure 4. Screenshot 2: Search Function and Results

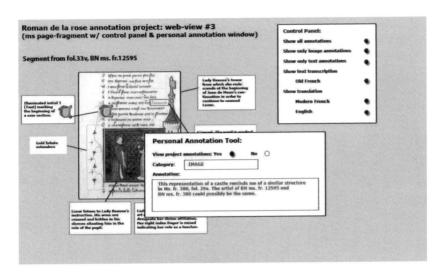

Jakacki and McWebb Figure 5. Screenshot 3: Personal Annotation Capability

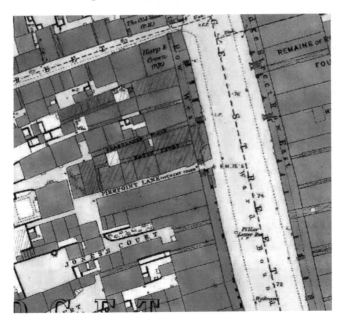

Vetch Figure 2. Extract from OS 1:500 scale plan of Chester (1871–73), showing part of Bridge Street and its associated plot-patterns, largely unchanged
from the medieval period, stretching along both street frontages, with
buildings individually and separately identified (coloured pink in the original) (Source: Chester Record Office / "The Digital Mapper")

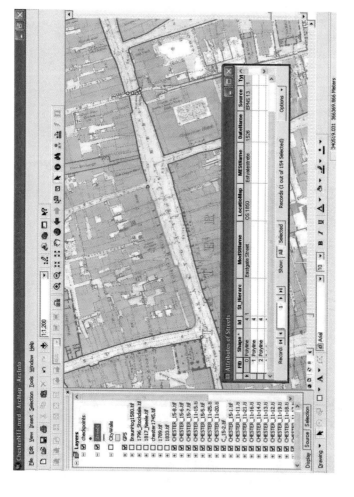

Vetch ofFigure 3. Screenshot from the medieval Chester GIS in its developmental stage showing layers of historic map images ("rasters," in the list, left) and (in the map window on the right) the vectorizing of features underway, as denoted by the turquoise/green coloured lines. In this example Eastgate Street is being digitized from the OS 1:500 plan, together with an example of the associated attribute data (for Eastgate Street, with information about it held in the database).

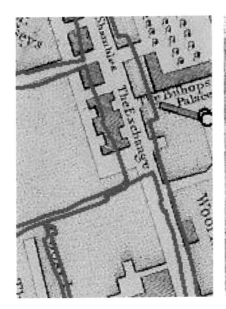

Vetch Figure 5. Examples of overlaying different geo rectified historic map layers to establish earlier urban topographies: left, streets digitized from the OS 1:500 plans (shown in green), overlaid on Lavaux's 1745 plan; right, OS 1:500 plan of 1872–73 overlaid onto earlier (1780s) map in the area of Castle Street and Bridge Street, and clearly showing the diagonal line of the new Grosvenor Street inserted in the early 1830s cutting through earlier street and plot-patterns. The yellow spots on both images indicate points at which GPS data was gathered in the field-survey described above.

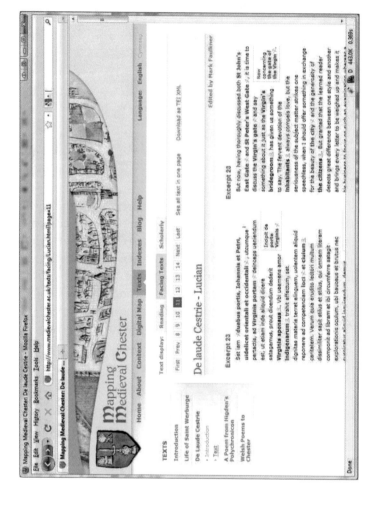

Vetch Figure 7. "Facing Texts" view of the Lucian, showing an example of marginal apparatus ("Incipit de porta Virginis"). Text highlighted in green (with "northings" icon) denotes a cross-reference to the map or to the index of places; text high-lighted in red (with person icon) denotes a cross-reference to the person index.

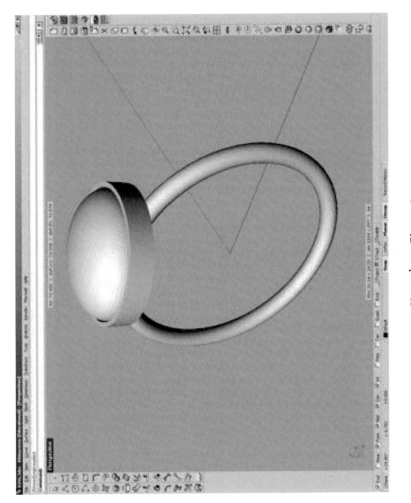

Humphrey Figure 1

Humphrey Figure 2

Humphrey Figure 3

Humphrey Figure 4

Humphrey Figure 5

Humphrey Figure 6

Humphrey Figure 7

Humphrey Figure 8

Humphrey Figure 9

Rose Tools: A Medieval Manuscript Text-Image Annotation Project

Christine McWebb
University of Waterloo
cmcwebb@uwaterloo.ca

Diane Jakacki
Georgia Institute of Technology
diane.jakacki@lcc.gatech.edu

Introduction

With the now widespread availability of digitized data, researchers in the humanities are learning to go about their work in new ways and requiring new research tools to do so. Responding directly to this changing research environment, Rose Tools proposes to develop a sophisticated modular integrated text-image annotation suite of tools. In 2002, Jerome McGann cautioned digital humanists that "[t]he general field of humanities education and scholarship will not take up the use of digital technology in any significant way until one can clearly demonstrate that these tools have important contributions to make to the exploration and explanation of aesthetic works." Since then, an ever-increasing number of works in the humanities and the fine arts (literary texts, artefacts, paintings, etc.) have been made available in digitized form by libraries, universities, and research groups from all over the world. Google Books, for example, aims to scan over 30 million books and by 2008 had already accomplished well over fifty per cent of its task (Clement et al. 2008). Increasingly, researchers, including humanists, turn to the Web as a starting point for their research in order to access these materials.

Yet, despite the existence of numerous digital humanities (DH) tools that have been developed to assist with such data searches, most of us nevertheless tend to revert to traditional practices in the scholarly interpretation of the digitally available data, such as taking notes in a word processor, printing or saving web pages, perhaps going so far as to use bibliographic software programmes like EndNote to organize our materials. To underscore this disconnect between what is digitally available and what, in reality, is used by humanities researchers, the 2005 Summit on Digital Tools for the Humanities reported that "only about six percent of humanist scholars go beyond general purpose information technology and use digital resources and more complex digital tools in their scholarship" (2006). Though this figure has

ISBN 978-0-86698-499-7 (online)   ISBN 978-0-86698-474-4 (print)
New Technologies in Medieval and Renaissance Studies 3 (2012) 313–334

most likely increased in the last three to four years, it follows nonetheless that in order to significantly enable humanist scholars to effectively apply DH tools for research on large-scale datasets, we need data analysis tools:

★ that are simple to use, and user-friendly in order to allow the humanist scholar with little or no knowledge in DH to understand and apply them quickly;

★ that offer the possibility of self-directed knowledge and personalized use in the form of note taking and data storage;

★ tools that are not corpus-specific but rather exportable and adaptable to datasets that share similar characteristics and therefore allow for a wide range of application.

With these needs in mind, Rose Tools plans to contribute to this "next step" in cyberscholarship by developing a sophisticated modular integrated suite of text-image annotation tools, a resource that will enable a broad array of humanists to concentrate on the benefits of incorporating digital data into their research without having to teach themselves complex and ever-evolving computer languages. Since the proposed suite of tools will be developed using medieval manuscript datasets, it will not only enable textual studies, but will also contribute to the study of materiality. Beyond transmitting basic textual information about a given work, the medieval manuscript has long been regarded as a physical object and artefact. As Stephen G. Nichols and Siegfried Wenzel state, a medieval manuscript "speak[s] to us about its social, commercial, and intellectual organization at the moment of its inscription" (1996, 1). Sylvia Huot has convincingly demonstrated that form and content and, by extension, the arranging and rearranging of text and image are inherent components of the medieval *opus* (1987). In what follows, we will describe this modular suite of tools for which we have now completed the conceptualization and which we will begin to develop.

Objectives and anticipated outcomes

Rose Tools will explore and develop manual and semi-automated ways of enriching images and text in an integrated fashion in order to provide an infrastructure for novel forms of humanities research. Our team comprises literary scholars, programmers, and computer scientists from the United States and Canada. We will draw on the following three existing and established text-image annotation tools which will be described in more detail below:

★ Image Markup Tool (IMT) (http://www.tapor.uvic.ca/~mholmes/image_markup/) developed by Martin Holmes (Humanities Computing and Media Centre, University of Victoria, Canada).

★ Image-Based XML (IBX), an Eclipse-based image annotation tool developed by Kevin Kiernan, Emeritus, University of Kentucky, and Emil Iacob, Georgia Southern University (http://eppt.org).

★ Pliny, John Bradley's (King's College, University of London) prototype for personalized annotation (http://pliny.cch.kcl.ac.uk/).

For the creation of a tool prototype, it is essential to focus as a first step on a coherent set of data in order to be able to take into account not only textual variants but also the theoretical implications of text-image interaction, and in the case of our datasets, the physicality of the object. Initially, we will use a small dataset of images available on the site of the MARGOT project (http://margot.uwaterloo.ca) of the most widely reproduced and read work in French medieval literature, the *Roman de la rose*, which was written jointly by Guillaume de Lorris and Jean de Meun (1236, 1269–78), containing 27,000 lines of verse (see below for a description of the digital corpus). We have worked out the concept of the annotation tool and its components, which will be explained in detail in the section titled "Background and Conceptualization." The tool development began in January 2011 and is to be completed by March 2012.

In the second step, we plan to apply our suite of tools to large repositories of multirepresentational data; potential beneficiaries of this application include ARTstor (http://www.artstor.org/), which presently is only searchable by keyword in the captions, and *Early English Books Online* (EEBO, http://eebo.chadwyck.com/home), which despite being an image-based resource does not recognize visual elements in its search function. Rose Tools will provide the means for sophisticated and robust image-text annotation allowing image-fragment searching and extensive comparative analysis. Consequently, in the short term, we will further *Roman de la rose* scholarship and enable scholars to pursue research questions that require the analysis of large numbers of *Rose* manuscripts. In the longer term, we will enable researchers of any image-based dataset to apply our suite of tools for robust data enrichment.

The corpus

As a test bed for development of the tool prototype, we will initially use the small dataset of one hundred medieval manuscript miniatures of the well-known French *Roman de la rose*.[1] These images have been made available in high-resolution scans on MARGOT and are an integral part of Christine Mc-Webb's "Reading the *Roman de la rose* in Text and Image" project (http://margot.uwaterloo.ca/ROMAN/index.html), complementing her critical anthology *Debating the Roman de la rose* (2007). The *Roman de la rose* is commonly seen as a precursor to Dante's *Divine Comedy*, though in its day it was more popular than Dante's work. It is a long poem of 21,000 lines in the form of a dream allegory that serves as a vehicle for new, and often unorthodox, thinking about current issues in religion, philosophy, and politics. In particular its second author, Jean de Meun, not only created a new form of literary romance, but also challenged prevailing attitudes about how poets could talk about love in literature.

Guillaume de Lorris and Jean de Meun's conjoined *Roman de la rose* is one of the foundational pieces of French medieval literature. The *Rose* has provoked much controversy, debate, and scholarship in the past as well as today.[2] It comprises two fundamentally different parts. In the first 4,000 lines, written by Guillaume de Lorris in 1236, the narrator embarks on a dream voyage during which he falls in love with a rose, enclosed and protected by a walled garden. The protagonist's narration plunges the reader into an ocean of courtly conventions as the frame of the allegorical dream vision sets up a fierce battle between seductive sexual forces. All the courtly topoi designed to enchant the medieval reader with the magic of a springtime world are present. But Lorris's text ends rather abruptly upon a scene in which Jealousy has locked the Rose in a tower in order to secure her from the Lover's advances. The poem remained at this point for about forty years, until, around 1275, the scholastically trained Jean de Meun, deploying a markedly different literary rhetoric, added another 17,000 lines.

With Jean de Meun the tone moves from the courtly to the philosophical, thus reflecting the interests of late thirteenth-century scholasticism. The topical breadth of his continuation includes treatises on planetary forma-

---

[1] Copyright for images on the MARGOT site, of which Christine McWebb is co-director, remain reserved to the library of origin.

[2] For example, McWebb (2007); Bel and Braet (2006); Huot (1993); Brownlee and Huot (1992); Badel (1980).

tions and musings on the positions of the sun, the moon, and stars and their metaphysical effects on humans, to name but a few areas of scientific debate that the reader would encounter and would read alongside the wide range of topics discussed in this work. Guillaume de Lorris's so-called guiding allegory of courtly love is often pushed to the sidelines, and we are reminded of the Rose's fate only from time to time, until she is finally defeated by the Lover's wooing and succumbs to her fate which is the plucking of her rosebud, the loss of her virginity.

A great number of the 360 extant manuscripts are richly illuminated and, consequently, provide a useful dataset for scalability. As a starting point, however, this small dataset lends itself well to the development of the functions that make up the tool we will create because the images are relatively homogeneous, as they all stem not only from the same literary work but also from a defined number of excerpts from Jean de Meun's continuation and from manuscripts spanning a period of about seventy years. This step in the development will show the value of the tool for large data repositories and will turn our collection of *Rose* miniatures into an interoperable repository of images targeted for annotation. Further, a small dataset will make back-tracking easier when programming and coding errors need to be located, and it will simplify the task of indexing the terms used in the annotations. However, our software will be designed to be scalable to allow for application with large datasets.

Background and conceptualization

The question that arises is why use a medieval text and its manuscripts as a test bed for a suite of tools that will have a much wider range of application? Our intellectual interest in the medieval *Roman de la rose* aside, we have come to realize that it is crucial to turn to previous forms of communication in order to conceptualize successfully the suite of tools we have in mind. In fact, Raymond Siemens formulated this historic approach recently when explaining the mandate of a new major collaborative initiative called INKE (Implementing New Knowledge Environments): "From ancient cave paintings to hand-printed books to Facebook, people have been reading in various forms for thousands of years. But what will the act of reading look like in the future and what can we learn from the past to ensure digital applications enhance and expand the reading experience?"[3]

---

[3] Raymond Siemens, "$2.5 Million Grant with an Additional $10.4 Million Funding in Institutional and Research Partner Support to Study Reading in the Digital Age," blog, Digital Literacy Centre, 17 March 2009, http://blogs.ubc.ca/ubcdlc/2009/03/17/25-

The beginning of the electronic age and the invention of the Internet, without a doubt a revolutionizing force in the way we communicate, are frequently compared to the last major communication revolution, the perfection of the printing press around 1450 by Johannes Gutenberg. The shift from the handwritten page of the medieval manuscript to the printed page arguably transformed the way we read and process information.[4] Print technology had many long-term consequences, one of which was that it enabled linearity in reading through the gradual reduction and elimination of miniature images and illustrations. The medieval book was often interspersed with paratextual information in the form of marginalia, illuminations, miniatures, annotations, rubrication, and so forth. Instead of reading the text in linear fashion, which is what the modern reader would naturally assume, the medieval reader habitually connected the various textual and paratextual components with one another in order to create meaning. Many studies on iconography and the relation between text and image have convincingly shown that medieval illuminated manuscripts of works such as the *Roman de la rose* discouraged linear reading of text.[5] Quite to the contrary, the often polysemous interaction between the miniature content and the written text was crucial for the understanding of the work. Yet, most of the pictorial elements found in the medieval manuscript were largely replaced with unadorned text once the printing press took hold across Europe at the end of the fifteenth and the beginning of the sixteenth century. Gradually, most modern editions of medieval and early modern texts, originally produced with integral visual elements, have been stripped of all but perhaps a few representative images. We would follow the argument of Roger Chartier (1982), Henri-Jean Martin (Martin and Chartier et al. 1982), Marshall McLuhan (1968), and others who show that the predominance of linearity in reading and processing of information was largely a consequence of print technology's emphasis on mass production, literacy, and economic practicality.

Conversely, the digital age has reinstated to a certain extent the functionality of the illustration, the icon, and the pictorial symbol. Few are the websites that offer a purely linear textual interface; rather, they are inter-

---

million-grant-with-an-additional-104-million-funding-in-institutional-and-research-partner-support-to-study-reading-in-the-digital-age/.

[4] See Crick (2004); Rouse and Rouse (2000); Martin (1995); Hindman (1991); Chartier (1987); Martin and Chartier et al. (1982).

[5] With particular focus on the *Roman de la rose* we refer to Sylvia Huot (1993). In the broader context of the literature of the high and the late Middle Ages, see also Camille (1992); Hindman (1991); as well as Desmond and Sheingorn (2003).

spersed with images of all kinds reminiscent of the medieval illuminated manuscript where textuality and paratextuality interact with one another on several semiotic levels. The invention of the Graphical User Interface (GUI), out of which the most current consumer-oriented operating systems were born, has implicitly espoused this interaction of the written and the pictorial on the one hand and the artificiality of linearity in reading on the other by creating an architecture where one application is superimposed on the next. It goes without saying that the analogy between text-image interaction on websites and medieval manuscripts quickly reaches its limits. The usefulness of such a connection, however, lies in the enduring presence of imagery alongside text in the medieval manuscript and its resurfacing in web culture. If we accept then that linearity is "unnatural" to human thought processing, it follows that linear representation of information will have its drawbacks as well. Recent developments in print culture, where we frequently find references to websites, and new reading technology such as the Sony Reader or Amazon Kindle, although modelled after the traditional book, allow more freedom in delinear, fragmented reading experiences as we can hop around within the "book," conduct keyword searches, call up information as we read, simultaneously and conveniently peruse a variety of texts, and so forth.

The graphic conceptualization of the medieval manuscript and by extension of the suite of tools we will develop can best be described conceptually by referring to cinema theory as it was formulated by Erwin Panofsky and Sergei Eisenstein: the crux of the usability and the successful implementation of this product is the principle of co-expressibility, or as we would more accurately call it "poly-expressibility"; in other words we provide narrative, symbolic, and pictorial expressibility where the image is integrated into the text.[6] The images, the text, and the marginalia as well as the annotations that we provide will be "read" as fragments creating among themselves and in relation to the text what Eisenstein termed a "harmonic montage" (Aumont 1987, 32). Harmonic montage takes into consideration all of the stimuli of a fragment. In every constellation of images and texts there is a vertical dimension consisting of a fragment as well as a horizontal or diachronic dimension, where the relation between the fragments is considered. To continue, there is the syntax whereby a narrative is created from one fragment to the next. It is at this point where Panofsky and Eisenstein's theory fails in its adaptation to the online representation of the artefact because, and this is crucial, contrary to cinematic structure the narrative that we create with this sort of

---

[6] See most notably *Montage Eisenstein* (Aumont 1987).

expandable product is much more characterized by fluidity and malleability than a set of cinematic images that still must adhere to a certain linearity.

To take the link between cinema and Web further, we will turn our attention to the concept of hypermediacy. The Web relies upon the intrinsic incorporation of all available media types—text, graphics, audio, video—to create a "hypermedial" experience that is distinct for each user. As articulated by Jay David Bolter and Richard Grusin (1999), all media since the Renaissance have incorporated within them multiple media, and as they developed they have fluctuated between immediacy and hypermediacy, between transparency and opacity. It is the very nature of this oscillation that enables each medium to reform those that have come before it and to provide us with the key to recognizing it as a medium. However, this reliance of each new medium on previous and concurrent media to establish itself (film on photography, television on radio, by example) implies that rather than creating a unique experience, new media invariably recall for us elements of their predecessors. Ultimately, and especially with a medium so heavily reliant on hypermedia as the Web is, we experience a reformation or remediation of one medium by another. Examined thus, the powerfully hypermedial Web allies itself more closely with the delineal manuscript than the straightened book (Bolter and Grusin 1999, 59).

Specifically in the context of the medieval manuscript, then, *Rose Tools* will mimic the medieval commentary tradition, where text, gloss, miniature, and marginalia form a composite book-space in a palimpsest of information that will engender meaning:

Figure 1. "The Open Missal," Ludger Tom Ring the Younger, 16th century. ©
By permission from The Frances Lehman Loeb Art Center, Vassar College.

When looking at this painting of an open missal by Ludger Tom Ring the
Younger, we get a glimpse of several pages all containing highly diverse information, from rubricated text, to musical score, to a full-size frontispiece-
style miniature. The book, as depicted in this painting, is held in this static
semi-open state by an invisible hand allowing us to view multiple "windows"
at the same time. In other words, one could argue, as does Johanna Drucker,
that although it is pysically made out of paper or parchment, it can be abstracted as a virtual book, where "[t]he literal 'spaces' are shown in such a
way as to create a figurative and phenomenal *e-space* of exchanges and relations" (2007, 232).[7]

---

[7] Note from the authors: the identification of this painting is erroneous in Drucker's
article (2007) where the artist is identified as anonymous.

Differing reading strategies are required for the medieval codex, with all of its inherent and multifaceted textual and iconographic components, and the interactive e-space of the web page, where information, and by extension interpretation, is created and manipulated through the superimposing structure of windows, scroll-over pop-ups, and so forth. In the electronic environment linearity is broken completely. Rose Tools, consequently, will allow the reader/viewer to participate more actively in the interpretative act; he/she will function as the creator of the interpretation by making decisions as to what annotations to read and where to add his/her own commentary. The interpretive act, then, is inductively steered by the user's decisions.

Arriving at interpretations is the quintessential activity of humanistic research. Though considerable work has been done in this area, more in-depth research needs to be conducted with the goal of defining what qualitative research methodology humanists use when doing research.[8] To put it in very reductive terms, the consensus from the sources below is that "a central component of scholarly research is centered on extensive reading" (Bradley 2008). To take this further, reading for scholarly purposes most often generates ideas which, in turn, are cognitively linked with previously acquired knowledge (a process sometimes characterized as "reading and musing"). In other words, when reading, the humanist establishes intra- and intertextual connections with other information that is available to him/her. These connections will eventually build up to a layered artifice of meaning which will be sorted out in logical fashion in the final research outcomes, be it an article, a conference paper, a monograph, and so forth.

In a way, and to go back to the question of the medium in use, this description of the process of scholarly reading is not so different from what the book (the humanist's most used object of study) does in itself: the book can usefully be described as a "knowledge machine."[9] That is to say, the finished book contains many layers of information which are either referenced through notes, bibliographies, indexes, etc., or referred to implicitly as we continue to read around the topic of the book at hand. In other

---

[8] The most recent effort is the creation of the Digital Literacy Centre at the University of Victoria and the University of British Columbia, Canada. See also John Bradley (2008); Willard McCarty (2002); W. S. Brockman et al. (2001); and John Unsworth (2000).

[9] In his keynote address at the 2009 SHARCNET Research Day (University of Waterloo, May 2009), Raymond Siemens used this term to describe what a book does, and how it is perceived and used by the humanities researcher.

words, the book is intrinsically connected to much more than its reader: it is integrated conceptually within the research library in its broadest sense, the physical place but also the web of knowledge connected to the subject it explores. Consequently, the humanist's creation of an intelligent interpretation that is informed by multiple strands of interrelated and intersecting information mimics the concept of the book in that it, too, implicitly points to layered information outside of itself. Book and researcher, therefore, interact and form a kind of conceptual *mise en abîme* or a mirror image of one another. The so-called bookwheel invented by Agostino Ramelli in the sixteenth century is an early example of knowledge integration on a material, pragmatic level:

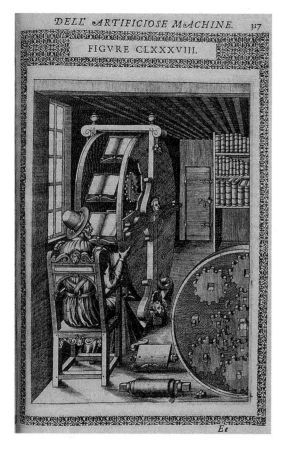

Figure 2. "Bookwheel." Source: Smithsonian Institution Libraries, Washington, DC. Ramelli, Agostino, *Le Diverse et Artificiose Machine*, 1588. © By permission from the Smithsonian Institution Libraries.

The wheel enabled a scholar to consult an array of volumes by placing them on rotating shelves and then turning the wheel from one volume to another, thereby allowing for a proto-hypertextual reading of pertinent texts. In theory, this was a revolutionary approach to intertextual research. In reality, the wheel was a complex and rather clunky contruction of gears and counterbalances that sought to make easier a process that scholars already practiced by picking up and putting down (most commonly on a table or desk) a set of books related to a common subject of research. It had disappeared from use by the early eighteenth century. However, it represents for us a useful metaphor for the limitations on research that *Rose Tools* aims to address: the isolation of the humanities scholar from the desired resources and the disconnect between primary sources (or reasonable facsimiles thereof) and the research process. We envision the personal annotation component of *Rose Tools* (see below) to enable scholars to examine elements of the manuscripts that are uniquely pertinent to their research and to enable them to track their discoveries in an overlaid notetaking system that can be saved individually or shared with other humanists, thereby encouraging more correspondence of ideas. Our point of departure for the creation of our tool suite then must be a computational model of the book as an integrated and multilayered "knowledge machine." Our final product, on the other hand, will be to develop an innovative and dynamic reading environment that will respond to the intuitive process already used by humanist scholars, one that relates to the books' character as a potential "e-space."

Description of Rose Tools

Rose Tools will involve three levels of usage to address a variety of scholarly research requirements. First, it will allow researchers to use large-scale datasets with a particular focus on European medieval literature, culture, history, linguistics, and art history in order to investigate research questions where comparative analyses across many manuscripts/images are required. Multiple layers of annotation, information, and interpretation will break down a linear mode of reading and, ultimately, will further mimic the methodology we use to do research in many humanities disciplines. We will offer the researcher not only the possibility of calling up superimposed layers of annotation on a given data fragment, but also of comparing all instances of the same phenomenon, as seen in Screenshot 1 and 2 below. These images are mock-ups of what *Rose Tools* will look like. Screenshot 1 shows the level of annotation and the possible search functions, and in Screenshot 2 we demonstrate how the user will be able to retrieve (for example) all occurrences of the same allegory, in text and image, or even of a component (a piece of clothing, a colour, etc.) of that same allegory.

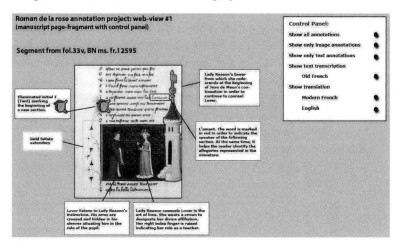

Figure 3. Screenshot 1: Annotation Capability. See image plates for a colour version of this figure.

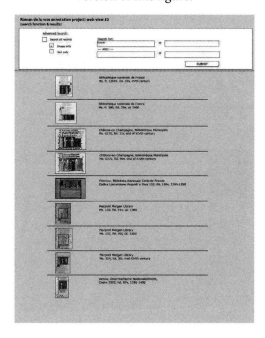

Figure 4. Screenshot 2: Search Function and Results. See image plates for a colour version of this figure.

We will be able to offer a tool not only to allow and facilitate novel forms of research but also to pave the way for developing new research paradigms, such as demonstrated in Screenshot 2, for example, where art historians will be able to identify artistic currents and trends in illumination techniques and styles across time (the identified manuscripts date from the end of the thirteenth century to 1520) by calling up certain images across a range of manuscripts. Another potential use for art historians would be to allow them to examine workshop practices better and identify particular artists at work in different manuscripts, and so more broadly study the manuscript-making community in and around Paris in the fourteenth and fifteenth centuries. They will also presumably be able to explore important changes in iconography and determine which scenes and parts of manuscripts are most frequently illustrated.

Second, Rose Tools will allow researchers to extend the dataset in order to add their own comments, reactions, interpretations, and insights to our data for their own personal annotation. Screenshot 3 demonstrates this feature of *Rose Tools* where self-organizing knowledge can be shared. This feature will be made available in an online environment in order to facilitate and encourage collaboration in the scholarly community.

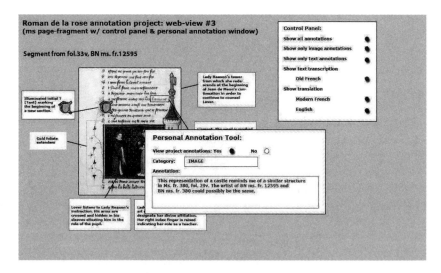

Figure 5. Screenshot 3: Personal Annotation Capability. See image plates for a colour version of this figure.

Third, Rose Tools will be adaptable to other datasets by plugging information into the tool infrastructure in an online environment. No downloading will be required. Rose Tools, therefore, will provide an easy-to-use application that will further enhance the infrastructure for cyberscholarship. *Rose Tools* will be based on a back-end and a front-end web interface environment complete with tutorials and help files.

The three existing tools mentioned above (IMT, IBX, Pliny) will serve as conceptual models for *Rose Tools* as we will identify their limitations and draw on their strengths. The developers of all three tools participated in early discussions of *Rose Tools*.

Image Markup Tool (IMT)

According to its website (http://tapor.uvic.ca/~mholmes/image_markup/goals.php), the goal of IMT is "to be able to describe and annotate images, and store the resulting data in TEI XML files" and "to produce a tool which creates conformant TEI P5 XML files, but which has a simple enough interface that it can be used by people with little or no experience in editing XML code." Although IMT provides a model for an open-source, simple-to-install, and simple-to-use tool, it suffers from certain limitations that Rose Tools plans to address. As it is, IMT allows only one image to be annotated at a time. Further, as can be seen in Screenshot 4, IMT has no capability for polygonal zones; in other words, it is only possible to segment the image into rectangular surfaces. Our aim is to facilitate comparative research with extensive multiple image functionality including polygonal zones.

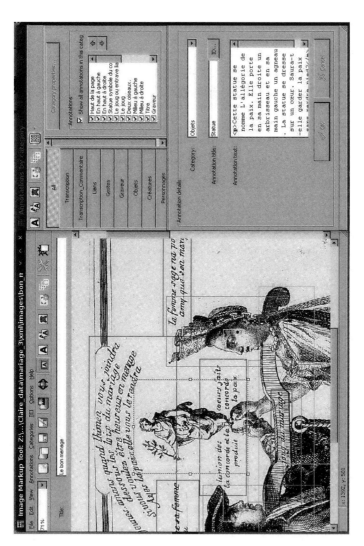

Figure 6. Screenshot 4: Rectangular Zones in IMT[10]

[10] We thank Martin Holmes for giving us permission to use this screenshot.

Image-based XML (IBX)

IBX, as it is now called (formerly EPPT: Edition Production and Presenta-tion Technology, http://www.eppt.org), "is . . . designed to integrate images and text through XML, to make them available for use by any image-based electronic project."[11] While IBX's remote-server access and versatility (it produces XML encodings using any DTD or schema, for example) lend them-selves to Rose Tools's stated goal of adaptability, it is an Eclipse-based ap-plication that requires advanced program configuration knowledge and does not work with XML schemas (the current standard for TEI).[12] Screenshot 5 offers a view of the multilevel functionality of IBX where one can call up an image, its corresponding textual transcription, and XML-markup. Here, we have a demonstration of IBX as it is applied to manuscript Bodleian Library, Douce 195 of the *Roman de la rose.*

Figure 7. Screenshot 5: EPPT- Trial

Pliny

Pliny (http://pliny.cch.kcl.ac.uk) is free downloadable software that facili-tates note-taking and annotation. It allows readers to integrate their initial

---

[11] *Electronic Facsimilies and Texts,* Ionut Emil Iacob and Kevin Kiernan, 2005, updated 18 November 2011, http://www.eppt.org.

[12] We thank Emil Iacob for giving us permission to use this screenshot.

notes into a representation of an evolving personal interpretation, and it can be used with both digital and non-digital materials. Further, Pliny enables the particular kind of interconnection between tools that annotation requires. For example, the annotation can be in the form of a PDF, a URL, or text in a pop-up window, as we demonstrate in the screenshot below, where the green text boxes refer to websites.[13] The image is a miniature of manuscript Bibliothèque nationale, fr. 12595 of the *Roman de la rose.* Pliny is also a stand-alone "Eclipse" application, though it is easier to use than IBX. Thus far, it only serves as a prototype model.

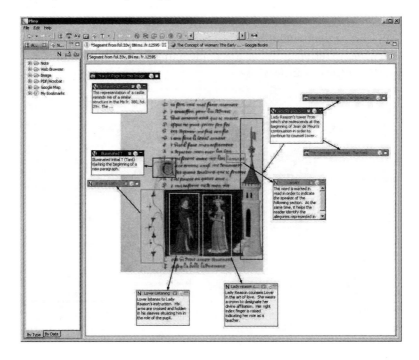

Figure 8. Screenshot 6: Annotation in Pliny[14]

It is not our aim to integrate these three tools, but to build a new suite of tools that will use IMT, IBX, and Pliny as conceptual models. Using IMT's overriding advantage, namely its user-friendliness, and IBX's principle of encoding versatility, we will build the web interface for Rose Tools using TEI

---

[13] For a description of Pliny as a platform for personal annotation and its role in scholarly interpretation, see Bradley (2008).

[14] We thank John Bradley for creating and giving permission to use this screenshot.

P5 Guidelines because TEI is a widely-used, stable standard.[15] It contains a set of tags that are designed expressly for the identification of surfaces (pages, etc.) and zones on those surfaces. It has an established set of methods (primarily using @corresp and @facs attributes) for linking transcriptions, annotations, and commentary to zones and surfaces. We will create polygonal zones (see Screenshots 1, 3 above). The data will be stored in an eXist XML database that gives us many options for writing a front-end web application. Using the note-taking capability of Pliny as a prototype model will help us to develop the third level of Rose Tools, which will be to facilitate personal annotation either of the *Rose* manuscripts or of other datasets, which can be plugged into our sophisticated reading environment.

We plan to begin user testing in collaboration with the Open Annotation Collaboration project (OAC, PI: Timothy Cole, http://www.openannotation.org/index.html), with whom we have entered into a partnership for this purpose. OAC plans to release a prototype of its web and Resource-centric interoperable annotation environment by summer 2011. Rose Tools will serve as a use case for interoperability testing. Based on the results, we will then further develop and refine the three levels of annotation described above. This will be completed in prototype form by December 2011, at which time we will begin user testing by contacting members of the DH community and asking them to try our tool suite and fill out a survey. We aim at March 2012 for the completion of the tool development and the annotation of a limited number of manuscript images.

Conclusion

Rose Tools constitutes the "next step" in cyberscholarship commensurate with advances in hardware and software, and a new conceptualization of the role of digital tools in relation to long established, and successful, practices in humanities and related disciplines. It will provide the scholarly community with an infrastructure for comparative analysis of hitherto disparate texts and image datasets. It is an annotation tool complete with sophisticated content on a specific corpus that will undoubtedly lead to the revision of many commonplace notions in *Rose* scholarship. Based on its fundamental principle of interoperability, Rose Tools will enable a wide range of potential applications for content non-specific data sets and provide scholars, students, and researchers with unique tools to analyse images and text in an integrated fashion using methodologies with which they are already familiar.

---

[15] TEI Consortium, "TEI P5: Guidelines for Electronic Text Encoding and Interchange," accessed 23 October 2009, http://www.tei-c.org/Guidelines/P5/.

WORKS CITED

Aumont, Jacques. 1987. *Montage Eisenstein*. Edited and translated by Lee Hildreth et al. Bloomington: Indiana University Press.

Badel, Pierre-Yves. 1980. *Le Roman de la rose au XIVe siècle: Etude de la réception de l'oeuvre*. Geneva: Droz.

Bel, Catherine, and H. Braet. 2006. *De la rose: Texte, image, fortune*. Leuven: Peeters.

Bolter, David J., and Richard Grusin. 1999. *Remediation: Understanding New Media*. Cambridge, MA: MIT Press.

Bradley, John. 2008. "Thinking about Interpretation: *Pliny* and Scholarship in the Humanities." *Literary and Linguistic Computing* 23:263–79.

Brockman, W. S., et al. 2001. *Scholarly Work in the Humanities and the Evolving Information Environment*. A Report from the Council on Library and Information Resources. Washington, DC: Digital Library Federation. http://www.diglib.org/pubs/dlf095/.

Brownlee, Kevin, and Sylvia Huot. 1992. *Rethinking the Romance of the Rose*. Philadelphia: University of Pennsylvania Press.

Camille, Michael. 1992. *Image on the Edge: The Margins of Medieval Art*. Cambridge, MA: Harvard University Press.

Chartier, Roger. 1982. *Pratiques de la lecture*. Marseille: Rivages.

_____, ed. 1987. *Les usages de l'imprimé: XVe–XIXe siècle*. Paris: Fayard.

Clement, Tanya, Sara Steger, John Unsworth, and Kirsten Uszkalo. 2008. "How Not to Read a Million Books." University of Illinois. http://www3.isrl.illinois.edu/~unsworth/hownot2read.html.

Crick, Julia, ed. 2004. *The Uses of Script and Print, 1300–1700*. Cambridge: Cambridge University Press.

Desmond, Marilynn, and Pamela Sheingorn. 2003. *Myth, Montage, and Visuality in Late Medieval Manuscript Culture: Christine de Pizan's Epistre Othea*. Ann Arbor: University of Michigan Press.

Drucker, Johanna. 2007. "The Virtual Codex from Page Space to e-space." In *A Companion to Digital Literary Studies*, edited by Raymond Siemens and Susan Schreibman, 216–32. Malden, MA: Blackwell.

Hindman, Sandra. 1991. *Printing the Written Word: The Social History of Books, circa 1450–1520.* Ithaca, NY: Cornell University Press.

Holmes, Martin. Image Markup Tool. University of Victoria. Accessed 23 October 2009. http://tapor.uvic.ca/~mholmes/image_markup/goals. php.

Huot, Sylvia. 1987. *From Song to Book: The Poetics of Writing in Old French Lyric and Lyrical Narrative Poetry.* Ithaca, NY: Cornell University Press.

_____ 1993. *The Romance of the Rose and its Medieval Readers: Interpretation, Reception, Manuscript Transmission.* Cambridge: Cambridge University Press.

MARGOT. Accessed 23 October 2009. http://margot.uwaterloo.ca.

Martin, Henri-Jean. 1995. *Histoire et pouvoir de l'écrit.* Paris: Albin Michel.

Martin, Henri-Jean, Roger Chartier, et al. 1982. *Histoire de l'édition française.* Paris: Promodis.

McCarty, Willard. 2002. "A Network with a Thousand Entrances: Commentary in an Electronic Age?" In *The Classical Commentary: Histories, Practices, Theory*, edited by Roy K. Gibson and Christina Shuttleworth Kraus, 359–402. Leiden: Brill.

McGann, Jerome. 2002. Ivanhoe Game Summary. http://www. speculativecomputing.org/ivanhoe/framework/summary.html.

McLuhan, Marshall. 1968. *The Gutenberg Galaxy: The Making of Typographic Men.* 2nd ed. Toronto: University of Toronto Press.

McWebb, Christine. 2007. *Debating the Roman de la Rose: A Critical Anthology.* New York: Routledge.

Nichols, Stephen G., and Siegried Wenzel. 1996. *The Whole Book: Cultural Perspectives on the Medieval Miscellany.* Ann Arbor: University of Michigan Press.

OAC: Open Annotation Collaboration. Accessed 23 October 2009. http://www. openannotation.org/index.html.

Pliny: A Note Manager. Accessed October 23 2009. http://pliny.cch.kcl.ac.uk.

Rouse, Mary A., and Richard H. Rouse. 2000. *Manuscripts and their Makers: Commercial Book Producers in Paris, 1200-1500.* Turnhout: Brepols.

Summit on Digital Tools for the Humanities. 2006. *Report on Summit Accomplishments.* University of Virginia, 28–30 September 2005. http:// www.iath.virginia.edu/dtsummit/SummitText.pdf.

TAPOR: Text Analysis Portal for Research. Accessed 23 October 2009. http:// tapor.ca.

Unsworth, John. 2000. "Scholarly Primitives: What Methods Do Humanities Researchers Have in Common, and How Might Our Tools Reflect This?" Presented at a Symposium on Humanities Computing: Formal Methods, Experimental Practice, King's College, London, 13 May. http://www3.isrl.illinois.edu/~unsworth/Kings.5-00/primitives.html.

Digitization of Maps and Atlases and the Use of Analytical Bibliography[1]

Wouter Bracke
Royal Library of Belgium
Université libre de Bruxelles
wouter.bracke@kbr.be

Gérard Bouvin
Royal Library of Belgium
gerard.bouvin@kbr.be

Benoît Pigeon
Royal Library of Belgium
benoit.pigeon@kbr.be

From 2006 to 2008 the Royal Library of Belgium (http://www.kbr.be/) participated in a European Commission-funded project for the development of research services in the field of old maps. This chapter presents this new Internet-accessible scientific tool (http://www.digmap.eu/), evaluates its possibilities and flaws, and makes suggestions for the future, specifically in reaction to (or better, in line with) Anthony Grafton's critical observations on digital libraries. The introductory section will concentrate on the nature of maps and the history of cartography in relation to digital databanks of map images. For practical reasons, in describing Digmap we take examples mainly from the collection of the Royal Library of Belgium.

Introduction

The creation of digital online databanks may have many particular goals, from the conservation or preservation of a collection to its substitution, but its most prominent aim certainly is to improve the collection's accessibility. This implies facilitating access to information about that collection, in other words, improving communication on the collection's content. This commu-

---

[1] This contribution benefited by a short correspondence between W. Bracke and Tony Campbell in December 2007 when preparing the first Digmap workshop, accessed 23 October 2009 (http://www.digmap.eu/workshop). This topic is also addressed in Bouvin and Bracke (2008). This essay and its research were completed in October 2009.

ISBN 978-0-86698-499-7 (online)   ISBN 978-0-86698-474-4 (print)
New Technologies in Medieval and Renaissance Studies 3 (2012) 335–362

nication requires structured information, and structuring information is essentially what digital (as well as other) databanks are about.

Digitization of the written word is, if we may believe Anthony Grafton in his *The New Yorker* article on the future of reading, but "one of a number of critical moments in the long saga of our drive to accumulate, store and retrieve information efficiently" which can be traced back to the third millennium before Christ when Mesopotamian scribes began to catalogue the clay tablets in their collections (2007). In this process, books, and henceforth libraries too, became the information-storage devices that have proved the most practical and therefore the most successful. Until the arrival of the Internet, their prime position has never been questioned. With the Internet, things have clearly changed: the Web not only offers much larger storing capacity than any existing library, it also offers a relatively rapid and easy retrieval of all kinds of data, including images: anyone, from the highly specialized professional to the simple layperson, can use its services without training. It allows browsing through its steadily growing collections by simple search keys or advanced searches in no time. And although books and libraries are far from being dead and forgotten, e-books and virtual libraries more and more compete with their physical counterparts.[2]

Improving the collection's accessibility also means reaching a larger public than is served by more traditional communication tools in this field, such as card indexes, surveys of holdings, printed and manuscript inventories and catalogues, bibliographies, or other such finding aids. Access to information is indeed essential not only to the users but also to the providers of that information. Without that access, no communication is possible, and without communication no conveyance of whatever kind can be established between the information provider and its receiver. Digital databanks not only can improve access to information and reach more people, but they can also improve the communication process itself. Indeed, in matters of communication, visualization is an important and effective tool. Data vi-

---

[2] Virtual libraries can be digital or digitized. Digital libraries propose a single virtual copy of a book; digitized libraries are the result of the digitization of complete libraries without leaving out one single copy in the library. John Brown and Paul Duguid (2000) stress the impossibility of digitized libraries and note the logical shift in research towards digital libraries. They furthermore distinguish digital libraries from electronic libraries in that the former (predominant in the United States) severs many connections to the conventional library which they actually want to substitute, while the latter seeks to complement paper resources (180ff.).

sualization by means of photographs, drawings, maps, diagrams, or tables enhances the users' understanding of the message transmitted by them. It is no surprise then that digital databanks of figurative documents and objects tend to attract more users than those of simple texts.[3] Indeed, one grasps more easily the sense of a message when put in a figurative form than when it is presented as simple reading texts. In 1801, William Playfair, pioneer in the graphical representation of statistics, had already stated in his preface to *The Statistical Breviary*, when discussing the principles on which his study was based, that "making an appeal to the eye when proportion and magnitude are concerned, is the best and readiest method of conveying a distinct idea" (1801, 4). Perhaps more than any other means of data visualization or representation, maps easily combine different sorts of information (not only geographical) and complex meaning in a way that is easier to understand than statistical charts or tables as they are overall more accessible to the general public. The "appeal to the eye" also accounts for the rapid spread of thematic cartography in nineteenth-century Europe (Palsky 2008, 414ff.).[4]

In historiography too, as in other disciplines, maps have been used to aggregate information in a graphic way to sustain an argument, or to illustrate one's point. Most of these maps are modern maps representing geographical information of previous times. Such maps have a long history. If not the founder then at least a very celebrated representative of the genre is none other than the Antwerp editor Abraham Ortelius (1527–98) who in 1579 published his first historical maps in the *Parergon*, a small corpus of historical maps of Belgium, Italy, Greece, Egypt, Palestine, the Roman Empire, and Saint Paul's peregrinations, which Ortelius added to the main body of his

---

[3] Of course, in comparison to speech, texts can be considered images themselves (cf. Goody 1977).

[4] Recently Bertrand Daugeron (2009) has discussed the relationship between classification in natural history and cartography. For further reading see Harley's contribution on the development of the history of cartography (1987, 1ff.). The idea that maps can be used for structuring information is foundational in the development of Geographic Information Systems (GIS). On GIS see chapter 13 in this volume. The Electronic Cultural Atlas Initiative, accessed 23 October 2009 (http://ecai.org/) is a fine example of how cultural data can be ordered geographically and accessed in a single interface. Ray Larson of the University of California at Berkeley presented the initiative at the first workshop organized by the Digmap partners in Lisbon in 2007. See note 1, above. The templates of his conference can be visualized at http://www.digmap.eu/workshop, accessed 23 October 2009. For GIS in historical research, see also Knowles and Hillier (2008).

atlas in 1584.[5] Early and old maps on the contrary have long been neglected in historiography.[6]

Even if the use of early maps as a means of illustrating or even emphasizing a point of view has never been questioned, their reliability as historical documents has been subject to much discussion. Historian John H. Parry went as far as calling old maps slippery witnesses (1976, 33–34).[7] Historians have indeed long neglected systematic recourse to early maps. This can partly be explained by a very limited, and essentially antiquarian and bio-bibliographical, interest in the history of early maps before the nineteenth century. Consequently, the history of cartography is a relatively young discipline which developed in the first place outside academic circles, in national learned societies and libraries or with private collectors and map dealers. Here the focus was on bio-bibliography and the publication of facsimile atlases. In academe its development was long dependent on the growing interest in and institutionalization of geography. Only from the 1930s onwards did the history of cartography gain its scholarly independence, with the foundation in 1935 of *Imago Mundi*, the first international scholarly journal in the field, by Leo Bagrow.[8] For a long time, the multiplicity of their uses and purposes and the complexity of their language made maps very untrustworthy as historical documents, and thus they did not receive the same attention by scholars as other sources. As pointed out before, maps are indeed an effective and pow-

---

[5] On Ortelius, the maker of the "first atlas," entitled *Theatrum Orbis Terrarum* (1570), see van der Krogt (2003, 33ff.). For an overview of his map production see also van den Broecke (1996). For the history of the genre see Kretschmer (1986, s.v. Geschichtskarte); Skelton (1972, 62 ff.).

[6] Although the epithets "old" and "early" (and even "historical") are often used indistinctly to indicate premodern maps, we prefer to follow the definitions proposed in the *Multilingual Dictionary of Technical Terms in Cartography* (International Cartographic Association 1973), where a distinction is made between an old map, "which no longer serves the purpose for which it was produced and is now only of historical or artistic interest" (815.1); an early map, defined as "a map produced before the first systematic survey of the area it represents" (815.2); and a historical map, being "a map which represents features or phenomena which existed, or which are believed to have existed, in some past period of time" (823.24).

[7] Cf. Harley (2001). In 1967 the second Conference on the History of Cartography held in London had as its main theme "Early Maps as Historical Evidence." Some of the papers were published in *Imago Mundi*: cf. Harley (1968) and Cornelis Koeman (1968).

[8] First edited by Leo Bagrow and Hans Wertheim in Berlin, the journal is now published by Imago Mundi Ltd, London.

erful communication tool. They not only represent space but can simultane-ously be used (and misused) for political, economical, or societal reasons. They are works of art, but can also be bearers of ideas. To be fully understood, maps have to be studied thoroughly, not just for their geographical content, but as a product of their time, and the whole production process (intellec-tual, manual, and technical) should be analysed. Only then can the study of old and early maps help the historian to understand the reasons (other than geographic representation) for their production. This approach, where the map itself becomes a scholar's focus of interest and study, is effective only when the history of cartography is accepted as a discipline of its own.

For many years, partly due to its inherent relationship with geography, car-tography was evaluated according its degree of correctness in representing geographical reality. Little or no investigation went into these other aspects of early cartography. With Leo Bagrow, who among his various interests par-ticularly cultivated the study of printed maps of the fifteenth and sixteenth centuries, historians of cartography became more involved with the study of the formal qualities of maps and their evolution (Skelton 1972, 99ff.). The early map was finally studied for what it really was, a visual cultural artefact. Since then, the social aspects of mapmaking have been a matter of interest to an ever-growing group of scholars, and maps have become an historical document as valuable as the written word. In this respect, one cannot stress enough the importance of the initiative taken by Brian Harley and David Woodward in the mid-1970s, when they started to plan the publication of a multivolume encyclopedia on the history of cartography.[9] Their work is based on the idea that the history of the map is like the history of the book and that "[m]aps—like books—can be regarded as agents of change in his-tory" (Harley and Woodward 1987, 5). In recent decades, scholars of litera-ture have taken this idea a step further and have approached maps as texts, applying to them the same critical treatment as is used in literature. They then consider maps to belong to traditions of graphic rhetoric, representing social processes.[10] In short, the study of early maps has evolved from the

---

[9] Harley and Woodward (1987). The long-awaited third volume, dedicated to cartog-raphy in the European Renaissance, came out in 2007 (Woodward 2007a). See also Knowles and Hillier (2008).

[10] Particularly interesting in this respect are the chapters on literature and maps in the third volume of The History of Cartography (Woodward 2007a, 401–76). Recently, Denis Wood and John Fels (2008) have demonstrated the inseparability of cartograph-ic and non-cartographic elements in maps featuring nature.

analysis of their geographical content to the historical contextualization of cartographical production.

Where does the digitization of maps fit into this discursive analysis, and how does it contribute to a better understanding of maps as agents of change? Even more, how does the digitization of maps support the growing interest in their non-geographical aspects?

Old and early maps are all over the Web. Most sites that have a historical dimension display them, where they typically serve illustrative purposes only. Other sites are exclusively dedicated to maps: there are sites with maps of a particular city, region, or country and sites of map collections, map sellers, and other merchants. The problem with maps on the Internet is thus not so much a question of availability as a matter of dealing with the enormous amount of images of maps (i.e. of structuring mass information). Some portals have attempted to organize the information on early maps, the most important of which is without doubt the portal created and updated by Tony Campbell, honorary map librarian of the British Library. It bears the title *Map History/History of Cartography* and, as is stated by its subtitle, it is "THE Gateway to the Subject."[11] This portal proposes, among many other sorts of information related to the history of cartography, a selection of 2,500 annotated links to websites containing images of old and early maps. In the introduction to this list of sites containing images of maps, Campbell argues that "there is no index to the images of individual early maps on the web. It is likely that there are now (December 2007) several hundred thousand early map images."[12] Based on his experience of examining thousands of sites and being confronted with their variety and great range of quality and usefulness, Campbell offers to those who host maps some fundamental suggestions as to image selection and quality, accessibility, indexing, and metadata.[13] Campbell's suggestions have been very stimulating to the developers of the Digmap services. According to Campell's analysis, the best online catalogues of map images are usually structured in a traditional bibliographic manner, offering lists of maps ordered by geographic location or other subject, and searchable by means of indexes. Only a small number of them allow users to browse their cartographic images through geographic localization tools, which make use of the maps' geographic coordinates, scale, names of places

---

[11] Tony Campbell, *Map History/History of Cartography*, 1996, updated December 2011, http://www.maphistory.info/.

[12] http://www.maphistory.info/aboutim.html, accessed 23 October 2009.

[13] http://www.maphistory.info/aboutim.html#hosts, accessed 23 October 2009.

or areas, and historical events related to the toponymy.[14] David Rumsey's website of twenty thousand old maps is perhaps the most advanced of all cartographic webites.[15] It proposes several interactive services, such as a GIS browser which shows detailed overlays of maps and geospatial data. It also uses a high-performance viewer where the map image covers the whole screen, allowing access to more visual data on the screen. Rumsey's website is now also accessible through the *European Cultural Atlas Initiative* website (http://ecai.org/). As this collection mainly concerns eighteenth- and nineteenth-century maps, the site is not of immediate use to Renaissance scholars. However, as with Campbell's website, Rumsey's work has greatly influenced the Digmap project.

Most digitization projects still privilege the map's image, that is, the geographical or cartographical information it contains. Metadata is mostly limited to author/editor, title, and date, and even these are often simply deduced from the map itself. Little attention is given to the map's formal aspects. Yet the importance of extensive and correct metadata is nicely illustrated by an example posted by Peter van der Krogt on the Maphist list, an email discussion group whose primary focus is old and early maps, atlases, globes, and other cartographic documents.[16] Van der Krogt addresses the problematic description of a seventeenth-century map of Africa available on the website of a university library. The library offers an image of the map and of its verso, which is covered with French text. The presence of an image of the map's verso is already quite exceptional: most images of maps on the Internet are limited to their cartographical representation. The metadata accompanying the map's image also are fairly rich, with a description of the map's title, author, place and date of publication, and information on the document's size and origin. In consequence, the user's first impression is very positive: this is a useful site with high-quality images, which provides a functional viewer, and is respectful of the document's history. Yet van der Krogt detected several errors in the document's basic description (wrong title, wrong author, and wrong date). It is obvious that without good metadata a database, and certainly a digital database, cannot work effectively. The problem of errors in metadata will be addressed further on, where the discussion of Digmap's

---

[14] For a survey see Fernández-Wyttenbach et al. (2007).

[15] *David Rumsey Map Collection*, Cartography Associates, 2009, http://www.davidrumsey.com.

[16] Peter van der Krogt, email discussion group, 13 January 2007, http://mailman.geo.uu.nl/pipermail/maphist/2007-January/009067.html.

future will lead us to stress the effectiveness of the attention paid to the document's physical features.

The treatment of the enormous mass of already available images of maps on the Internet, the differences in quality of the images and their descriptions, and the variety of individual and uncoordinated initiatives in the field made it apparent that an integrated tool for the viewing and analysis of early maps and related information should be created. This led to the founding of the Digmap project.

The Digmap project (http://www.digmap.eu)

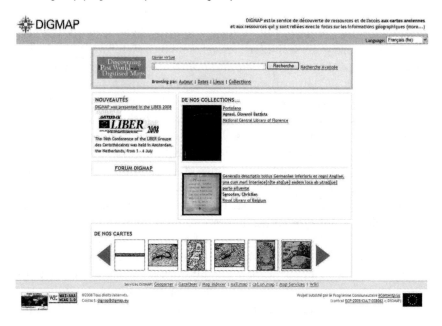

Figure 1. Web page of the Digmap portal

Digmap stands for *Discovering our Past World with Digitized Maps* (Fig. 1). The project was run by an interdisciplinary consortium of seven European partners that can be divided into two groups. The first group comprised partners with technical skills in information systems design and development, with a particular interest in geographic information processes: the Instituto Superior Técnico of Lisbon, the project's coordinator; the Universidad Politécnica de Madrid; and the Institute of Mathematics and Informatics at the Bulgarian Academy of Sciences. The second group was composed of national libraries holding relatively small but qualitatively important map collections: The Biblioteca Nazionale Centrale di Firenze, the National Library of Portugal, the National Library of Estonia, and the Royal Library of Belgium.[17] These were the data providers. The partners of the Digmap project wanted to offer the general public a tool that would combine digital information retrieval through geographic coordinates with the traditional search engines using indexing systems of library catalogues. Geo-localization of the maps is essential in the project. It is also very useful in research as it allows overlapping, linking, and manipulation of geographic information and of maps in particular.[18]

The project, co-funded by the European Commission program eContent*Plus*, a multiannual community program to make digital content in Europe more accessible, usable, and exploitable, lasted roughly for two years, from October 2006 to the end of 2008.[19] At the present time almost fifty thousand cartographic resources are available through the website. In addition to the metadata offered by the data providers in the project, these resources come from associated partners who graciously offered their own collections for harvesting (the national libraries of Spain, Scotland, and Iceland, and the Spanish National Geographic Institute) and through direct harvesting of cartographic resources on the Internet by OAI-PMH.[20] Not all resources are images of maps. In fact, the database also includes bibliographic records for which no image is yet available and records of reference works and other specific studies related to cartographical material. Every image is related to one copy of a map, but that does not mean that all images concern different maps. Indeed, different collections may have a copy of the same map. Still, every copy with its own image and bibliographical record has been recorded in the database. Cartographic resources in the Digmap database cover all

---

[17] A presentation of these partners can be found in the fourth newsletter of the Digmap project, which presents at the same time the final project's report, 2008, at http://www.digmap.eu/doku.php?id=wiki:digmap_newsletter, accessed 23 October 2009.

[18] On the advantages of geo-referencing see Christopher Fleet's paper delivered at the map curator's workshop of the British Cartographic Society (2008).

[19] The eContent*Plus* program expired on 31 December 2008, but its goals continue to be pursued through the Information and Communications Technologies Policy Support Programme (ICT PSP).

[20] OAI-PMH stands for Open Archives Initiative Protocol for Metadata Harvesting, a protocol providing an application-independent interoperability framework for metadata harvesting. More information at http://www.openarchives.org/OAI/openarchivesprotocol.html#Introduction, accessed 23 October 2009.

kinds of maps and contents, ranging in time from the fifteenth to the twentieth century: manuscript and printed maps, large-scale and small-scale maps, world maps, celestial maps, maps of the continents, national, regional, and local maps, thematic maps, and more. This database can easily be extended thanks to the services offered by the Digmap website which will be discussed later on. In fact, there is no limit to its extension. It must be stressed though that for the time being the development of the Digmap website and its implementation has stopped. In the near future local repositories will be installed in the national libraries that participated in the project. Every partner will then be able to decide to close its repository to the world outside and use it as a kind of personal database, or open it to all and continue the role the coordinator has played during the project, harvesting on a regular basis the metadata and images of maps available through the Internet, graciously offered by future partners or even proposed by individuals. The latter will need an authorization to do so from the local administrator. The choice between an open or a closed system will most probably depend on the partners' investment policy and especially their willingness to invest on a long-term basis in further developing and maintaining the services offered by Digmap. In the long run, though, Digmap as a web service should be integrated into the European Digital Library, along the lines of the European Digital Libraries Initiative.[21]

What does Digmap offer its users already and what will become possible in the near future? Some Digmap services are accessible to all users; other users need a personalized username and password which, for the time being, are given only to the participants in the project. The most important service freely accessible to all is without doubt the Digmap portal (http://portal.digmap.eu). The portal offers simultaneous and remote access to the different cartographical collections present in the database. The user interface offers simple and complex queries. An example: looking for cartographical information on Europe, users just have to type the name in the white box on the portal's welcome page and click on "search." They will then get all resources related to Europe, maps, books, etc., with a short description of the docu-

---

[21] See Digital Libraries Initiative, European Commission, 2005, updated 2011, http://ec.europa.eu/information_society/activities/digital_libraries/index_en.htm. The European Library is a free multilingual service that offers access to both digital artefacts (books, posters, maps, sound recordings, videos, etc.) and bibliographical resources of the forty-eight national libraries of Europe. The vision behind this project is to provide equal access in order to promote worldwide understanding of the richness and diversity of European learning and culture.

ment and indication of the library or institute that provided the metadata
(Fig. 2). In cases where the resource has been digitized, a thumbnail appears
on the left of the screen. On the right, statistical information can be found
related to the number of documents present in the different collections of
the database responding to the request. For more detailed information on
one of the resources, Digmap connects the users to the description of the
provider's catalogue. If the users click on the thumbnail or the image's URL
(uniform resource locator), they will get a larger image and, if available, a
quality image which can be magnified thanks to the provider's local viewer.
If they look for a specific author or have a specific date, place, or collection in
mind, they can also browse through the corresponding indexes.

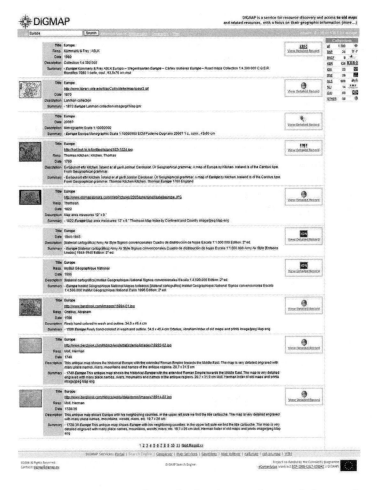

Figure 2. First page with results for the simple search (Europe)

The advanced search offers the opportunity of refining a search, be it biblio-graphical, geographical, or temporal.[22] This can help in comparing similar maps or different copies of the same map and their descriptions. Combining "author's name=Ortelius" and "map's subject=Belgium," for instance, gives a list of eight documents, all belonging to the Royal Library of Belgium. All eight maps have the same subject (the Netherlands in ancient times) and the same geographical outline (Fig. 3).[23] They all bear the same title which makes clear that their production is somehow related to Ortelius. Indeed, Ortelius made two plates of it, the first in 1584 which was replaced in 1595. Both maps appeared in various editions in different languages (Latin, Ger-man, French), which can be identified by the text on the verso (Van den Broecke 1996, 197ff.). However, some maps in the list cannot be identified with one of these published by Ortelius. They were produced later on by dif-ferent cartographers who copied and edited Ortelius's map or used his plate, as in the case of Claes Janszoon Visscher (1587–1652) who bought the plates from Pieter van den Keere (1571–after 1646) (van der Krogt 1997, 1:620–21 and 2003, 3B:770–71). Through the Digmap list, its images, and descriptions, a whole story comes thus to life, that of Ortelius's map of the Netherlands in Roman times and its editorial success. Its history is emblematic for the map trade in the Renaissance period (and later), when copperplates moved from one editor to another and maps were often copied. Variants of different editions or printing states are sometimes hardly detectable, making correct attributions very difficult. A list of images with their full description can thus be of help in determining the maps' identity.

---

[22] Search keys for bibliographical searches are: title, author, contributor, date, pub-lisher, subject, description, identifier, and contents. All are combinable. Geographic searches can be done by latitude and longitude, or north-south and east-west limit. Searches in time can be done by indicating a period, from or to a specific year. Search-es can be done in the whole database or limited to certain collections.

[23] It should be mentioned that although the name Belgium is mentioned in the docu-ment's title, the map depicts the former Netherlands of which Belgium was a part until the end of the sixteenth century. If one were to look for the Netherlands, he or she would obtain the same list.

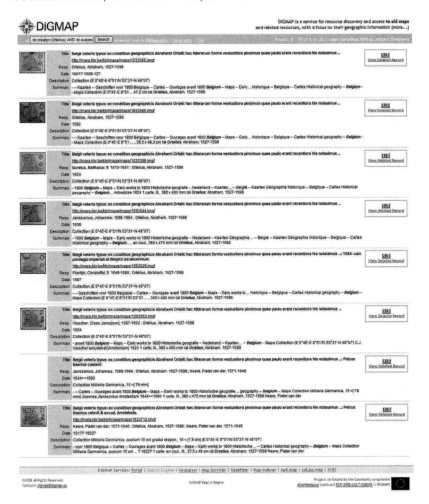

Figure 3. List of resources for the combined search by author (Ortelius) and subject (Belgium)

One does not have to be a map specialist to profit from the Digmap services, as illustrated by the following sample. Looking for information on the sixteenth-century cartography of America, for instance, users may fill in the word "America" and the dates 1550 and 1600 in the advanced search in time. They will then get a list of seventeen items, including images of maps of America by Ortelius, Sebastian Münster (1488–1552), Gerard Mercator (1512–94), Theodore de Bry (1528–98), and others, a reference to a portulan atlas by Giovanni Battista Agnesi of around 1550, and two identical maps of

Florida present in two different libraries and harvested thanks to the OAI protocol. The list also mentions a map by Ortelius kept at the Royal Library of Belgium for which there is no image, but the map can be most probably identified with the one offered by the National Library of Australia, of which a picture is indeed available. The latter happens to possess the 1964 facsimile edition of an earlier version of the map. In a few clicks the users will get a very nice idea of the different representations of America between 1550 and 1600 and enough information for further research. Providing access to a rich and diversified but well-structured cartographic heritage, Digmap is potentially a virtual library of maps and related documents.

Besides the Digmap portal, other services are provided on the Digmap website. Those related to the database input, however, are restricted to authorized users. Still, corrections to metadata can be suggested to the website's administrator by any user by way of comments to specific documents. The administrator will then intervene in the databank, accordingly. The Record Editor (RED) gives the possibility of editing bibliographical records from any online collection that has adopted the OAI protocol, and the service called "cat.on.map" allows the registration of relevant online resources (i.e., pages with digitized maps, websites related to cartography, geography, etc.). These resources are referenced in the database as "external resources." In this system, authorized users can register and edit resources themselves by providing the respective metadata, associate geographic coordinates, and other geographic details. Geo-indexing can be done with the help of GeoIndexer, a geographic indexing service using the Google Maps API to embed Google Maps.[24] The final insertion of their data, however, is still decided by the administrator. The Digmap gazetteer integrates information from multiple data sources and enables queries by place names, place types, footprints (the area covered by a geographic place), relations to other places, time frames and other associated metadata. It offers the possibility of converting current and historic place names into locations on the earth's surface, or vice versa. The GeoParser automatically identifies the names of places and historical periods and assigns the resources to the corresponding geo-temporal scopes. It uses the gazetteer for reference recognition. Both the gazetteer and GeoParser are automated tools for enriching the existing metadata. Additional geographical and temporal search tools are offered: GeoTimes is a service that combines spatial browsing and timeline browsing by using GeoBrowser and Timeline, respectively. GeoBrowser shows the subset of records that have geographic coordinates on the map, while Timeline provides a visual under-

---

[24] Google Maps, accessed 23 October 2009, http://maps.google.com.

standing of the record dates for the subset of resources that have valid dates. The "nail.map" service supports the generation of thumbnail images. The thumbnails can either be reference maps with place markers added to them, or screenshot renderings of online resources (i.e., web page thumbnails). Finally, the Image Feature Extractor (FTX) is a service that enables extraction of features from images that have geographic meaning, such as cartouches, map orientations, marine monsters, mermaids, etc.[25]

The Digmap service is based on a metadata repository called Repox, an XML metadata repository for storing, preserving, and managing metadata sets. Repox supports a translation functionality to transform the original metadata format (MARC21, UNIMARC or any other common format) into another format. The transfer of records between Repox and the data providers is assured by OAI-PMH. Once the Digmap software and database are installed in the partner institution, Digmap could become in the long term a real virtual library of cartographic metadata offered by associated partners and registered users, whose number can be extended without limit, as well as harvested independently from the Internet.

Digitization and analytical bibliography

Grafton in his article on "Future Reading" (2007) expresses the idea that digital libraries will never be able to replace real ones, because every copy of a printed book is different and has a different story to tell. To study a book, it is not enough to read the text it contains: one must also study its different editions, even its translations. A book's history is reflected in its dissemination, in the traces of its readers left in the book's preserved copies. Therefore, the book historian also needs information about ownership and will want to see the marginal notes in the book's copies. This kind of information is hard to find in digital libraries, which digitize only one copy of a book. What the book historian really needs are digitized libraries, i.e., libraries of which every single copy is digitized.[26] David Rothman (2007), recognizing the elusiveness of digitizing complete libraries and other collections, still dreams of seeing "every book, every other document of importance, digitized someday—not just the texts but the full images." As long as this remains wishful thinking (and will it ever be different?), the book historian will want to consult directly all existing copies of a book. On the other hand, digital libraries can contribute to a better understanding of a book's history. Indeed, Grafton's plea (2007)

---

[25] The different services are highlighted in the fourth and last newsletter of the project (see n. 17).

[26] See n. 2.

in defense of the direct study of books and other material writings does not mean he neglects or denigrates the importance of technical improvements in the field of classification. Instead, he stresses the compatibility and even more so the complementarity of both digital information retrieval and the direct study of a book's copy (or copies). In a way, a parallel may be drawn here with what happened in the field of mapping in the Renaissance when graphics became as important in geographical descriptions as the written word, and portulans became portulan charts, itineraries became route maps, and cadastres became cadastral maps. Indeed, all of these were written descriptions—of sea coasts, distances between road stations, and land measurements respectively—before being represented on maps. The image did not replace the text, but a new idiom was added to the old and both became complementary (Woodward 2007b, 11ff.).

Still, the virtual universe becomes bigger every day and increases our possibilities of exploiting documents. In a paradoxical way, the creation of digital surrogates at the same time dematerializes the physical object and gives us new ways of interrogating the material object. At the same time, the computer interface is adopting more and more the tactile and visual characteristics of the physical information source.[27] So, virtual documents increasingly resemble their physical model and offer practical advantages over the material exemplar: faster access to information; simultaneous access by different users to the same document; remote access; access to the document's content; preservation and conservation of the original document and its content; enriched media and interactivity. Yet, as things stand today, there are still important qualitative and quantitative differences between the virtual document and its exemplar, especially in the case of graphic documents. An image is not enough to supplement the original; it has to be accompanied by a detailed description of the physical object in an extensive set of metadata.

As noted above, historians of cartography have changed their focus from the geographical content of maps to the historical significance of the map as cultural artefact. Research into the material culture of maps offers new insights into their production and their role in society. This change of interest is paralleled by a revolution in analytical bibliography, where bib-

---

[27] In 2008 LG Philips LCD developed a flexible A4 size e-paper display (http://www.lg-display.com accessed 23 October 2009), and in 2009 Sony Corp. launched its first wireless electronic reader with tactile screen, called the Reader Daily Edition (Nilay Patel, "Sony announces Reader Daily Edition, free library ebook checkouts," 25 August 2009, http://www.engadget.com/2009/08/25/sony-announces-daily-edition-reader/).

liographic records now include descriptions of the material characteristics of the document, characteristics which often vary significantly from copy to copy.[28] The analysis of the production process, the transmission and the reception of texts in all their forms necessitate the systematic inventory of the objects' material characteristics. These can be divided into three main categories: characteristics related to the map's fabrication (e.g., different states of the plate), characteristics related to the map's dissemination (e.g., casing, slipcase, binding, mounting on canvas), characteristics related to the map's use (e.g., assembly, annotations, marks of propriety). These characteristics provide information on the document's history and can explain the presence or absence of certain other features of the material object, and even the document's content. In other words, these descriptive annotations provide information about the document as such and also help to put its content in the right perspective. For instance, in the list of maps of Europe of the seventeenth century (cf. supra), the Digmap database references a folio map of Europe by William Jansz. Blaeu (1571–1638), the founder of a famous dynasty of cartographers and editors in Amsterdam (Fig. 4). The map is well known for its rich borders illustrating plans of the most important European cities of the time and its depiction of local clothing fashions in various European countries. Blaeu edited his first folio map of Europe in 1617. Different states are known of this map, and no date is given for this particular edition. Several indicators, not all of which are geographic, enable us to date this copy after 1648 and even after 1660: the name of the Republic of the Seven United Netherlands, a political entity confirmed by the Peace of Westphalia in 1648, is added on the map and the political boundaries depicted on the map are those which resulted from the treaties of 1648; on copies published after 1660 the hypothetical island Frisland east of Iceland has been removed, as is the case on this map (Bracke et al. 2007, 59ff.). To paraphrase Brown and Duguid, the periphery of the geographical information guides us to what's central, in this case, a positive identification of the map. Context shapes content (2000, 202).

---

[28] On analytical bibliography see Chartier's preface to the French translation of McKenzie (1991); Delaveau, Sordet, and Westeel (2005). For the analytical bibliography of maps in particular see Pacha (1996).

Figure 4. *Europa recens descripta à Guilielmo Blaeuw* (XII – Europe gén. – XVII
s. – III 10920 CP). Copyright Royal Library of Belgium

Even if essential bibliographical information is to be found on the map itself,
it is not necessarily correct, as is shown by the following example.

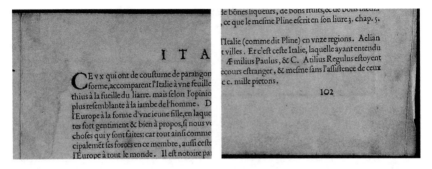

Figure 5. The southern part of Italy (XIV Italie Gén. – 1587 – Ortelius – III
11396 CP). Copyright Royal Library of Belgium

This sixteenth-century map of Italy, entitled *Italiae veteris specimen*, by Ortelius, depicts Italy in ancient times (Fig. 5). It was part of the *Parergon* (cf.
supra). This map is explicitly dated 1584 in its cartouche. Thus, a description
based on the cartographic image alone would date this map 1584. A cataloguer interested in analytical bibliography, however, would also look at the
back of the map and come to a different conclusion. Indeed, on the basis
of the typeset text printed on the back of the map, particularly the page's
incipit, "*Italie…*," and the page number in the lower right corner, "102," we
can attribute the map to the fourth French edition of Ortelius's atlas, called
the *Théâtre de l'Univers*, of 1587.[29] But we can make this attribution only if we
have access to both sides of the artefact.

As maps and atlases were read and used for practical purposes, annotations
and corrections were often added by the author himself or by some other
user, often anonymous. These annotations give us precious information
about a book's history and dissemination. For instance, this small atlas of
the Netherlands in Dutch by Abraham Goos, *Nieuw Nederlandtsch Caertboeck*
(Amsterdam, 1616), was still read at the end of the eighteenth century, as is
illustrated by its annotations (Fig. 6).

---

[29] [7000H:31A] in van der Krogt (2003). Description of the atlas in van der Krogt (2003,
196ff.).

Figure 6. Abraham Goos, *Nieuw Nederlandtsch Caertboeck* (VH 30691 A). Copyright Royal Library of Belgium

These are signed by a certain Nicolas Petit of Luxemburg, a priest and lawyer, and dated 1787. In the online catalogue of the Royal Library of Belgium, the information concerning the annotations is given in the annotation field, a field that is generally neglected in the indexing process.[30]

Digitization projects today tend to neglect the potential richness of bibliographic records, preferring short descriptions of documents. These are usually limited to title, creator (author, editor, or publisher), and place and year of publication. This is not the case with the Digmap website, which transfers the user who is looking for more detailed information on a document to the local catalogue of a determined library. Technical limitations and questions of feasibility and budget are often invoked to explain certain omissions of information in library catalogues. Indeed, export of complete records, including zones of notes and information on the level of analytical bibliography, from one library system to another—and in Digmap from the local provid-

---

[30] More examples in Harley (1968) and Koeman (1968).

ers' system to Repox—is a time- and money-consuming business.[31] It seems that choices have to be made as to the amount of information one wants to convert, choices which depend on manpower and budget. Yet, if digitization programs want to reach the scholarly community, they will have to evolve with the changes in cataloguing and making of bibliographies which libraries have been operating over the last twenty years or so.

Digmap and the future

Although the Digmap portal is accessible to all users of the Internet, Digmap's full functionality is available only to partner institutions that install its services locally. A last example will show what the utility of Digmap promises to become as more institutions get involved as contributing participants. Although not as well known as his contemporary cartographers Mercator or Ortelius, Jacob van Deventer (1500–1575) is without doubt one of the major cartographers of the Renaissance.

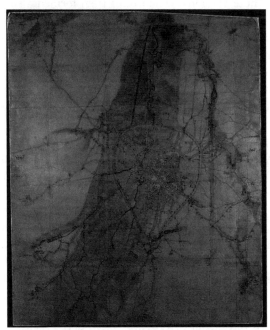

Figure 7. Map of Brussels by Jacob van Deventer (Ms 22090). Copyright Royal Library of Belgium

---

[31] See for instance Michael Seadle's (2008) viewpoint in the first issue of *World Digital Libraries* and the interim report on digital preservation in the Netherlands, published in July 2009 under the title *A Future for our Digital Memory.*

Deventer was probably the first to use triangulation in drawing his maps. His production is composed of regional maps and city plans that cover the territory of what is now roughly the Netherlands, Belgium, Luxemburg, and Northern France (Fig. 7). His maps, the majority of which are preserved only in manuscript, excel in preciseness and detail.[32] The maps, together with his city plans, were made for Charles V and his son and successor Philip II, king of Spain (and of the Low Countries), and other official bodies for military purposes, which is why most of them were never published or printed. Consequently, copies of Deventer's work are rare and hard to come by. Over two hundred cities from the Low Countries were measured and depicted by Deventer officially from 1559 onwards. At his death in 1575, Deventer still had not finished the volumes destined to the king. Most of his city plans survive in two versions, a "minute" or draft version (or what is considered as such by today's scholars) and a final version. The final version of the maps that have come to us is now in the National Library of Madrid. In the nineteenth century the minute versions, which until then formed a single collection, were sold publicly and dispersed: today the city plans of the Netherlands are preserved in the different local or regional archives of the cities concerned, and the minute versions of the Belgian and other cities are all preserved in one volume at the Royal Library of Belgium. Partial facsimiles have been made through the years, but to this point there is still no edition covering all city plans in their minute and final versions (if both have been preserved). Through the services offered by Digmap the whole collection could easily become accessible with little effort. This could be accomplished in one of the following ways: all of the institutions concerned could furnish the Digmap database with an image and basic description or other metadata of the plan in their possession; or, because most of these institutions already have an image of their Deventer plan on their own website, anyone interested in the subject could easily harvest the image and metadata using the Cat.on.map service described above. All images (with their metadata) grouped together in one virtual library would offer great possibilities for research on Deventer. Indeed, besides the traditional advantages of digitization listed here, the permanent accessibility of these maps' images could contribute significantly to finding answers to some fundamental questions which still haunt Deventer specialists and historians of cartography, such as the relation between both versions, the process of mapmaking itself and the copying of maps.[33]

---

[32] A short introduction to Deventer, with bibliography, can be found in Bracke (2008).

[33] For further references, see the bibliography in Bracke (2008) where these questions are touched upon.

As mentioned before, the Digmap website is not a final product. Even after the local installation of its services, further developments will be necessary. Local administrators will have to polish the existing indexes and refine search keys. Furthermore, the insertion of new metadata by authorized users (institutions and individuals alike) will ask for a thorough follow-up, as the database's quality will depend on the quality of the metadata and the descriptions of the cartographic resources. International standards are at hand to improve the metadata's interoperability, but their application requires some bibliographical education.[34] National and academic libraries are in principle best placed to provide reliable metadata. The van der Krogt example, however, shows that even here no guarantee can be given. The Digmap database unfortunately suffers from a lack of coherence in the harvested databanks. Indexing thus remains a major problem. If, for example, you browse the indexes by author in search of Abraham Ortelius, you will have to look under A. Ortelius, Abraham Ortelius, Ortel (Abraham), Ortelius, and Ortelius (Abraham). All these forms are found in the metadata and indexed as such. It is apparent that some harmonization is necessary here. More attention also needs to be given to representing the maps' material features. Transferring the reader to the online description supplied by one of the libraries is not enough. More images should be added: the 1587 map of Italy by Ortelius, for example, should be represented in both recto and verso. Only then would physical consultation of the material document become superfluous. Although Digmap gives access to high-quality images through the partner institutions' individual viewers, it does not allow the user to download these images and appropriate them. In this the program respects the copyright policy of every participating institution. The rather conservative attitude of most (but not all) libraries and other institutions is understandable, but perhaps a more generous policy would benefit both the user and the contributing institution.[35] Indeed, in the context of shrinking budgets, interactivity could constitute a solution. Work that nowadays cannot be done by the institutions' personnel because of lack of time or budget, from correcting images over geo-referencing to making databases of extracted features on images, could be done by the interested user.

---

[34] For international standards related to bibliographic descriptions of cartographic material see the International Standard Bibliographic Description (ISBD), a set of rules produced by the International Federation of Library Associations and Institutions (IFLA), accessed 23 October 2009 (http://www.ifla.org/).

[35] This is certainly not the place to discuss the complex matter of copyright. On this subject see Georgia Harper's plea for more free content on the Web (Harper 2008).

Conclusions

The results of the Digmap project are practical, proposing solutions for geo-localized digital libraries of early and old maps and related documents. The website offers flexible services for registering, searching, and browsing in collections of digitized early maps. Maps can be registered by their geographic boundaries and easily classified, indexed, and searched, thanks to multilingual geographic and other thesauri. All services are available on the Internet through simple "click and go" actions. All software solutions are reusable and available in open-source.

Digmap provides an answer to two main demands by users of cartographic material, both casual browsers and dedicated researchers: it constitutes a central repository of map resources offering a global index to identified early maps on the Web; and it offers access to freely available high-resolution scans facilitating the visual juxtaposition of maps. In addition to high-resolution scans, Digmap also offers access to a full description of the visualized document, if it exists in one of the library catalogues connected to the Digmap database. The automatic indexing tools are without doubt one of the main assets of Digmap, and through its Image Feature Extractor, Digmap offers something parallel to type-proof searches in scanned texts. Interactivity, although not yet fully developed, will enhance the website's utility. Indeed, every registered user can participate actively in the creation of a real virtual library of early and old maps by adding images of maps, filling in, completing, or correcting records with metadata of newly added or already existing images, and enriching the library of reference works on the subject. Thanks to a control system of administrators, and cataloguers at the partner institutions, new data are fully checked before being definitely integrated in the repository. Finally, a forum permits users to put questions or pass expertise or other information to the scientific community or even to the larger public interested in or involved with old maps.

Digmap is already an important tool for research and information retrieval and as such complementary to the direct study of the material document. It could become even more important if it can respond to the changing demands of book professionals, librarians, and cataloguers, stressing the importance of a document's material description. For Digmap to become an efficient virtual library of cartographic documents it will have to respect much more the maps themselves, their formal features, and their history, and not only concentrate on their geographic content.

WORKS CITED

Bouvin, Gérard, and Wouter Bracke. 2008. "Digitization and Analytical Bibliography." *E-Perimetron* 3 (2): 77–85.

Bracke, Wouter. 2008. "Jacob van Deventer e l'atlante di città dei Paesi Bassi." In *Le città dei cartografi: Studi e ricerche di storia urbana*, edited by Cesare de Seta and Brigitte Marin in collaboration with Marco Iuliano, 38–48. Naples: Electa Napoli.

Bracke, Wouter, et al. 2007. *Formatting Europe, Mapping a Continent: Dix siècles de cartes d'Europe dans les collections de la Bibliothèque royale de Belgique.* Edited by W. B., Lisette Danckaert, Caroline De Candt, and Marguerite Silvestre. Brussels: Royal Library of Belgium.

Broecke, Marcel P. R. van den. 1996. *Ortelius Atlas Maps: An Illustrated Guide.* Netherlands: HES Publishers.

Brown, John Seely, and Paul Duguid. 2000. *The Social Life of Information.* Boston: Harvard Business School Press.

Campbell, Tony. 1996–2010. Map History/History of Cartography. http://www.maphistory.info/.

Chartier, Roger. 1991. "Textes, formes, interprétations." Preface to *La bibliographie et la sociologie des textes* by D. F. McKenzie. Luçon: Éd. du Cercle de la librairie.

Daugeron, Bertrand. 2009. "L'usage méthodique de la carte en botanique: Classer en histoire naturelle au XVIIIe siècle." *Le Monde des Cartes* 199:97–104.

Delaveau, Martine, Yves Sordet, and Isabelle Westeel. 2005. "Penser le catalogage du livre ancien à l'âge du numérique." *Bulletin des bibliothèques de France* 50:52–61.

Digmap Project. 2007. European Community. http://www.digmap.eu/.

Fernández-Wyttenbach, Alberto, M. Álvarez, M. Bernabé-Poveda, and J. Borbinha. 2007. "Digital Map Library Services in the Spatial Data Infrastructure (SDI) Framework: The DIGMAP Project." In *Proceedings of the 23th International Conference in Cartography, International Cartographic*

Association (ICA-ACI). Moscow, (Russia) August 4-10: http://www.digmap. eu/doku.php?id=wiki:papers.

Fleet, Christopher. 2008. "Putting Old Maps in Their Place? Practicalities of Geo-referencing and Delivering Historical Maps Online." Presented at the Conference of the Map Curators' Workgroup 2008, organized by the British Cartographic Society. http://www.cartography.org.uk/ default.asp?contentID=834.

Goody, Jack. 1977. *The Domestication of the Savage Mind.* Cambridge: Cambridge University Press.

Google. Google Maps. 2010. http://maps.google.com/.

Grafton, Anthony. 2007. "Future Reading: Digitization and its Discontents." *The New Yorker,* 5 November. http://www.newyorker.com/ reporting/2007/11/05/071105fa_fact_grafton.

_____ 2008. *Codex in Crisis.* New York: Crumpled Press.

Harley, John Brian. 1968. "The Evaluation of Early Maps: Towards a Methodology." *Imago Mundi* 22:62–74.

_____ 1987. "The Map and the Development of the History of Cartography." In Harley and Woodward, eds. 1987, 1–42.

_____ 2001. "Text and Contexts in the Interpretation of Early Maps." In *The New Nature of Maps: Essays in the History of Cartography*, edited by P. Laxton, 33–49. Baltimore: Johns Hopkins University Press.

Harley, John Brian, and David Woodward, eds. 1987. *Cartography in Prehistoric, Ancient, and Medieval Europe and the Mediterranean.* Vol. 1 of *The History of Cartography*, edited by John Brian Harley and David Woodward, 1987-. Chicago: University of Chicago Press.

Harper, Georgia K. 2008. "Mass Digitization and Copyright Law, Policy and Practice." http://www.umuc.edu/cip/learningopportunities/ archivedsymposia/upload/Keynote2_Harper_Mass_Digitization_PPT. pdf.

International Cartographic Association. 1973. *Multilingual Dictionary of Technical Terms in Cartography.* Wiesbaden: Franz Steiner Verlag GMBH.

International Standard Bibliographic Description. 2007. *International Standard Bibliographic Description (ISBD)*. Preliminary consolidated edition. IFLA Series on Bibliographic Control, vol. 31. Munich: K.G. Saur. http://www.ifla.org/files/cataloguing/isbd/isbd-cons_2007-en.pdf.

Knowles, Anne Kelly, and Amy Hillier, eds. 2008. *Placing History: How Maps, Spatial Data, and GIS Are Changing Historical Scholarship*. Redlands, CA: ESRI Press.

Koeman, Cornelis. 1968. "Levels of Historical Evidence in Early Maps (With Examples)." *Imago Mundi* 22:75–80.

Kretschmer, Ingrid, et al., eds. 1986. *Lexikon zur Geschichte der Kartographie von den Anfängen bis zum ersten Weltkrieg*. Wawrik, Vienna: Franz Deuticke.

Krogt, Peter van der. 1997. *Koeman's Atlantes Neerlandici*. Vol. 1. 't Goy-Houten: HES & De Graaf Publishers.

_____ 2003. *Koeman's Atlantes Neerlandici*. Vol. 3, parts A–B. 't Goy-Houten: HES & De Graaf Publishers.

McKenzie, Donald Francis. 1986. *Bibliography and the Sociology of Texts*. London: British Library.

[Netherlands Coalition for Digital Preservation]. 2009. *A Future for Our Digital Memory: Permanent Access to Information in the Netherlands*. Interim Report—Summary in English. Netherlands Coalition for Digital Preservation. http://www.ncdd.nl/en/documents/Englishsummary.pdf.

Pacha, Béatrice. 1996. "La carte, instrument et objet: Essai de bibliographie matérielle." In *Cartes et plans imprimés de 1564 à 1815: Collections des bibliothèques municipales de la région Centre*, edited by B. Pacha and L. Miran, 35–41. Paris: Bibliothèque nationale de France.

Palsky, Gilles. 2008. "Connections and Exchanges in European Thematic Cartography: The Case of Nineteenth-Century Choropleth Maps." *Belgeo* 3–4:413–26.

Parry, John H. 1976. "Old Maps Are Slippery Witnesses." *Harvard Magazine*. April:33–34.

Playfair, William. 1801. *The Statistical Breviary; Shewing, on a Principle Entirely New, the Resources of Every State and Kingdom in Europe; Illustrated with*

Stained Copper Plate Charts, Representing the Physical Powers of Each Distinct Nation with Ease and Perspicuity. To Which is Added, a Similar Exhibition of the Ruling Powers of Hindoostan. London: J. Wallis.

Rothman, David. 2007. "The *New Yorker* Is as Wrong about e-Libraries as Martin Luther Apparently Was About Paper Books." *TeleRead: Bring the e-books home.* 30 October: http://www.teleread.org/2007/10/30/ the-new-yorker-is-as-wrong-about-e-libraries-as-martin-luther-apparently-was-about-paper-books/.

Royal Library of Belgium. Accessed 23 October 2009. http://www.kbr.be/.

Seadle, Michael. 2008. "Digital Libraries: Economics and Archiving." *World Digital Libraries* 1:vii.

Skelton, Raleigh A. 1972. *Maps: A Historical Survey of Their Study and Collecting.* The Kenneth Nebenzahl, Jr. Lectures in the History of Cartography at The Newberry Library. Chicago: University of Chicago Press.

Wood, Denis, and John Fels. 2008. *The Natures of Maps: Cartographic Constructions of the Natural World.* Chicago: Chicago University Press.

Woodward, David, ed. 2007a. *Cartography in the European Renaissance.* Vol. 3 of Harley and Woodward, eds. 1987–.

_____ 2007b. "Cartography and the Renaissance: Continuity and Change." In Woodward 2007a, 3–24.

Between Text and Image: Digital Renderings of a Late Medieval City

Paul Vetch
Department of Digital Humanities,
King's College London
paul.vetch@kcl.ac.uk

Catherine Clarke
Swansea University
c.a.clarke@swansea.ac.uk

Keith Lilley
Queen's University Belfast
k.lilley@qub.ac.uk

Introduction

The Mapping Medieval Chester project brings together scholars from the fields of literary studies, historical geography, and humanities computing[1] in order to explore the ways in which material and imagined urban landscapes construct and convey a sense of place-identity.[2] The project's focus is the city of Chester, situated in northwest England on the border with Wales, and the identities that its inhabitants formed between c. 1200 and 1500; its primary aim is the juxtaposition and interconnection of geographical and lit-

---

[1] The project team includes Catherine Clarke, Helen Fulton, and Mark Faulkner, Swansea University; Keith Lilley and Lorraine Barry, Queen's University Belfast; and Paul Vetch and Eleonora Litta at the Department of Digital Humanities (DDH), King's College, London. See further http://www.medievalchester.ac.uk/about/team.html, accessed 23 October 2009. See also "Mapping Medieval Chester," Digital Humanities, King's College London, accessed 23 October 2009, http://www.kcl.ac.uk/artshums/depts/ddh/research/projects/mmc.aspx.

[2] The full title of the project is Mapping Medieval Chester: Place and Identity in an English Borderland City c. 1200–1500; it was funded by the UK Arts and Humanities Research Council (AHRC) from September 2008 to September 2009. Full details of the project grant can be consulted at the Arts & Humanities Research Council website, accessed 23 October 2009, http://www.ahrc.ac.uk/FundedResearch/Pages/ResearchDetail.aspx?id=135992.

ISBN 978-0-86698-499-7 (online)   ISBN 978-0-86698-474-4 (print)
New Technologies in Medieval and Renaissance Studies 3 (2012) 363–393

erary "mappings" of the medieval city, using both cartographic and textual sources to extend our understanding of how place-identities were forged in the medieval city through local association and relationships with imagined and material urban landscapes.

The digital activities of the project have focused on three key areas: firstly, the development of a Geographical Information System (GIS) to create and publish a new map of Chester as it was c. 1500; secondly, the creation of new scholarly digital editions of a number of significant but little-known and inaccessible contemporary texts; and finally, the setting of these two very different primary sources in apposition within the context of an integrated online digital publication. The project has consistently sought to use information technologies as a means not only of expressing but also of interrogating and indeed generating "mappings" of medieval Chester. This approach is important because it is still relatively unusual in medieval studies to make use of digital media in the processes of interpretation and understanding, rather than of simply storing or democratizing access to, the visual and textual cultures of the Middle Ages. While computational methods and techniques that support the capture and facsimilar reproduction of fragile manuscripts or the diplomatic editing and publication of complex medieval texts are ubiquitous and well understood, for the moment at least their role remains largely an enabling or supporting one, facilitating the more mechanical aspects of scholarly activity.[3] In this context, the Mapping Medieval Chester project's use of historical GIS techniques alongside more established tools of digital humanities (such as the TEI) will, we believe, prove significant both in providing a clear demonstration of medieval studies' potential for enabling users to consult literary and cartographic sources in digital media, and more generally in fostering transferable methodologies and working models for integrating geographical and textual data. This paper explores the methodological and technical underpinnings of our approach and considers also the theoretical questions and practical challenges that the remediation of medieval notions of space and cartography evokes.

Disciplining urban spaces: Placing Chester in the medieval cultural imagination

Medieval literary and cultural studies have recently seen a significant growth of interest in place, space, and their representations. Informing

---

[3] For two recent and particularly thought-provoking pieces in this context see Flanders (2009) and Sutherland (2008).

much of the current work on medieval place, space, and identity are the seminal writings of Henri Lefebvre and Michel de Certeau. These cultural theorists call attention to the ways in which space, rather than existing as a neutral basis of, or backdrop to, culture and society, is actively *produced* through usage, social practice, and interpretation (Lefebvre 1991; de Certeau 2002, especially part 3). Recent studies of literature and the medieval city have drawn on these theoretical frameworks, with influential volumes including Hanawalt and Reyerson (1994) and Butterfield (2006). David Wallace and Paul Strohm have also been particularly prominent voices in critical conversations about how the medieval city was experienced, imagined, and represented by contemporary writers and audiences. David Wallace's study *Premodern Places: Calais to Surinam, Chaucer to Aphra Behn* emphasizes the fundamental interrelationship between the geographical and material realities of medieval landscapes and their resonances at imaginative levels, stressing that "the locales in [Wallace's] book ... are both geographic sites and ideas, dreams, and feelings about places" (2004, 16). Paul Strohm's study, *Theory and the Premodern Text*, opens with the chapter "Three London Itineraries," which seeks to imagine and recover the experiences of medieval walkers as they moved through the medieval city, responding to and interpreting the features of urban layout, architecture, and topography around them (2000). Drawing clearly on de Certeau's theoretical exploration of "Walking in the City" (2002, part 3, 91–110), Strohm notes that while the postmodern walker may be free to renegotiate and remake the meanings of city space according to his/her own experiences and perceptions, "with the *premodern* walker, the balance shifts from improvisation toward regulation and a lessened freedom with respect to established social signifiers" (2000, 4). Strohm suggests instead that "the peculiarity of medieval space involves the extent to which it is already symbolically organised by the meaning-making activities of the many generations that have traversed it" (2000, 3). The Mapping Medieval Chester project is a conscious attempt to renew attention to the connections between the material fabric of the medieval city and the ways in which it is invested with meanings—and how those meanings are regulated and represented—by medieval texts. As Robert Allen Rouse has observed, drawing on the metaphor of the city-as-text, "We read a city almost as a manuscript, with the buildings, statues, memorials, and place-names acting as a tangible script in which the public history of a city is written" (2005, 135; see also Duncan 1990).

Medieval Chester presents a particularly rich opportunity for the investigation of medieval practices of space and the role of the material fabric of the city in the production of urban identity. Many early (though no medieval) maps of the city survive, along with much detailed archaeological and documentary evidence; and in addition to sources for the material fabric of the city, the medieval literature includes a rich and diverse range of textual "mappings" of the city produced by authors from different backgrounds and perspectives. Located on the (often troubled) border between England and Wales, medieval Chester is a site of cultural diversity, exchange, and tension, reflected in the diverse, multilingual texts relating to the city produced by authors both Welsh and English, secular and monastic, citizen and outsider. These diverse texts offer disparate symbolic organizations of the medieval city, presenting different configurations and interpretations of the urban space and its materiality. The Mapping Medieval Chester project has focused on three main texts or bodies of texts for editing and examination, selecting sources that reflect the different perspectives of different cultural and ethnic communities within this medieval frontier town. First, the *De Laude Cestrie* ("In Praise of Chester"), written by Lucian, a monk at the Benedictine Abbey of St Werburgh (now Chester Cathedral), offers a monastic perspective on the city. Written around 1195 and the earliest of our chosen texts, Lucian's urban work seeks to demonstrate how the material fabric of the city may yield deep spiritual meanings and truths through exegetical reading (see Clarke 2006, 105), yet Lucian's text often misrepresents the reality of the urban landscape in order to heighten its allegorical potential (see Barrett 2009, 30). The much later *Life of Saint Werburge* by Henry Bradshaw is the work of another monk of St Werburgh's. Written around 1513, it survives in the 1521 London edition printed by Richard Pynson. Like Lucian's encomium, Bradshaw's hagiography also gives detailed attention to the urban space and layout of the medieval city, emphasizing the central role of the Benedictine Abbey and of St Werburgh herself as the city's patron.[4] Bradshaw reads the fabric of the city chronologically, giving an account of its building, development, and many phases of renovation, and he also focuses on the city's role as a fortress against attacks from the Welsh "and other barbarike nacions."[5] The project's third textual group is a collection of Welsh poems, many never before edited from the manuscript sources, which reflect the importance of

---

[4] For Bradshaw, writing shortly before the Reformation and in the context of the increasing power and authority of the city's secular authorities, this insistence on the central importance of the Abbey probably reflects anxieties about its waning status. See Barrett (2009, 47–51).

[5] All quotations from Bradshaw's *Life of St Werburgh*, Lucian's *De Laude Cestrie*, and the Welsh poems are from *Mapping Medieval Chester*, 2008, http://www.medievalchester.ac.uk/texts/index.html.

Chester across medieval Wales.[6] Many of these texts centre on the relics of the true cross at Chester (a focus for Welsh pilgrimage) as well as on the themes of travel into the city, roads, and journeying. The poems also feature satire on Chester's citizens and their trades, including a short verse that mocks the weakness of Chester beer. Thus these poems reflect Chester as a significant location for Welsh writers, offering a different perspective on the city from those who were not afforded the status and rights of citizens and who came from a different cultural and ethnic background as well as a different literary tradition.

The importance of these texts has remained largely unrecognized because they have not, in the past, been readily available or accessible. Bradshaw's *Life of Saint Werburgh* was last edited in 1887; *De Laude Cestrie* was only partially edited in 1912, and no English translation has ever existed; and the Welsh poems relating to Chester were little known to scholars outside medieval Welsh studies. Accordingly, a significant output of the Mapping Medieval Chester project has been the preparation of new scholarly editions of each of these texts to a consistent standard, a process which (in the case of the Lucian and Welsh poems) has included making new transcriptions from (single) extant witnesses, and the creation of new English translations. Taken together, these eclectic medieval texts, from Lucian to the Welsh poems, demonstrate the very different ways in which the material fabric of the city could be read in the medieval period. As subjective representations of the urban, they reveal much about the varied spirituality, politics, cultural and literary traditions of medieval writers and audiences, yet their meaning-laden textual mappings often stand in stark contrast to the material realities of the medieval city.

Urban mappings: Cartography and rematerializing Chester's late-medieval landscape

The earliest cartography to show Chester's local topography and landscape dates from the end of the sixteenth century (Fig. 1).[7] Despite this early mapping of the city, there is no map contemporary with medieval Chester. This means that modern commentators have relied upon adapting modern street maps, marking on medieval street names, the city's walls, and other key

---

[6] Chester was of course the administrative centre for North Wales in the medieval period, and was involved in campaigns of conquest, as well as longer-term processes of control and regulation. See for example Thacker (2003, 34–38).

[7] For a list of printed maps and plans for Chester, see Cheshire and Chester Archives and Local Studies (2001).

landmarks, such as the bridge across the Dee, and Chester's distinctive con
tribution to medieval architecture, the "Rows."[8] Maps like these often feature in historical or archaeological studies of the city as illustrative devices
to show, albeit approximately, the relative positions of the city's medieval
institutions and the framework of streets that interconnected them.[9]

Figure 1. Extract of William Smith's (1588) plan of Chester from his *The
Particuler Description of England. With the portratures of certaine of the cheiffest
citties & townes* (Source: British Library, MS Harley 1046, fol. 173).

In Mapping Medieval Chester, the use of maps and mapping consciously de-
parted from providing maps simply as illustrations. Working back from the
extant post-medieval maps and the archaeological and historical evidence,
our goal was to piece together the physical and topographical features that
comprised Chester at a particular moment in its past, and thus synthesize

---

[8] The Chester "Rows" are a unique architectural feature of the city, an elevated and
covered walkway running parallel on both sides of the city's two main axial streets.
See Brown (1999).

[9] A case in point is Laughton (2008), where such a map appears opposite the title page.

a new map of Chester's medieval urban landscape.[10] Fundamental to this is the process of "town-plan analysis," which uses post-medieval cartography as a source from which to reconstruct medieval urban topographies.[11] A succession of maps and plans of Chester, from Smith's late-sixteenth-century manuscript plan through to detailed Ordnance Survey (OS) maps of the mid- to late nineteenth century, provides a set of temporal snapshots charting the evolving geography during the transformation of the city's early urban antecedents into an expanded and industrialized city of the 1800s. Of these map sources, the large-scale OS 1:500 scale plans of 1871–73 are without doubt the most accurately drawn and surveyed, showing in great detail the urban landscape of Victorian Chester, including individual buildings and their respective property boundaries (Fig. 2).

Although far removed in time from the medieval city, the urban landscape documented in the OS maps clearly reveals relict urban features dating from the Middle Ages: many of Chester's streets, particularly those within the city's walls, owe their layout to this period; similarly, the plot-boundaries, city walls and gates, ecclesiastical buildings, and other topographical features recorded by the Ordnance Surveyors also remain largely unchanged (Alldridge 1981–83). These detailed nineteenth-century plans are thus an invaluable and viable cartographic source from which to begin the process of reconstructing Chester's late medieval urban landscape.

Conversely, a comparison of the OS plans and Smith's plan of the city of 1588 reveals the extent to which certain areas and features of late-medieval Chester have disappeared over time. The extant intermediate historic maps and plans, such as that drawn by Alexander de Lavaux in 1745, chart these gradual erasures from the landscape and their subsequent redevelopment, but here too the city's enduring medieval skeleton remains (at least partially) visible. Where Chester's medieval features were more successfully obliterated, notably after the Reformation in the case of monastic houses, the work of local archaeologists over the past half a century has done much to fill the lacunae: mapping the boundaries of former monastic precincts, for example, and establishing the ground plans for their conventual buildings (see Ward 1990).

---

[10] For a comparable worked-through example, see Lilley, Lloyd, and Trick (2005), accessible via the Archaeology Data Service, University of York, 2005, http://ads.ahds. ac.uk/catalogue/specColl/atlas_ahrb_2005.

[11] On the principles of this approach see Lilley (2000).

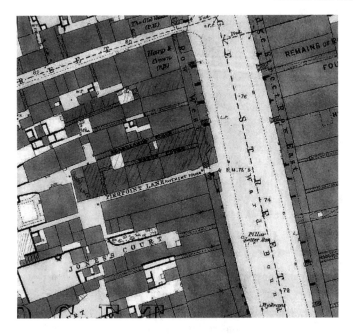

Figure 2. Extract from OS 1:500 scale plan of Chester (1871–73), showing part
of Bridge Street and its associated plot-patterns, largely unchanged from
the medieval period, stretching along both street frontages, with buildings individually and separately identified (coloured pink in the original)
(Source: Chester Record Office / "The Digital Mapper"). See image plates for
a colour version of this figure.

While the combination of archaeological evidence and the sequence of historic maps outlined here provides a firm basis for a projection of the urban
topography of Chester c. 1500, equally it represents a hugely varied, and
indeed variable, set of cartographic, historical, and archaeological data. The
use of a Geographical Information System (GIS) allows this data to be compiled faithfully, and with editorial integrity, into a map that is, we believe,
as accurate and detailed, both geographically and historically, as possible.

*Reassembling the city: Mapping out Chester's medieval urban topography
using GIS*

The spatial technologies used to create digital maps are well known to cartographers and surveyors working in geology, planning, archaeology, and
geography, but are comparatively new to medievalists and urban historians.
For the creation of historical maps, GIS offers distinct advantages over the

traditional method of drafting (using tracings and paper) owing to its inherent ability to store and dynamically represent data from multiple sources.[12]

The cartographic, archaeological, and documentary sources from which a new map of Chester must be pieced together are diverse, as we have noted, and in most cases not contemporary with the Middle Ages. Moreover, the archaeological and documentary sources typically provide evidence which is good for some areas of a city, but poorer or non-existent in others (Chester is typical in this regard). This presents a problem when trying to map the whole city, since it is undesirable to leave blank areas, which, although accurately reflecting a lack of current knowledge, could equally (and incorrectly) imply to an observer a lack of medieval occupation or activity. Such *terrae incognitae* need therefore to be clearly represented on a map, and a GIS makes it possible not only to include them (using later map evidence and a degree of informed conjecture) but also to alert users of the map to the origins of the data from which interpolation has been derived. This degree of cartographic transparency is difficult to achieve using printed maps.

The process begins in the GIS as a series of map layers built up by importing digital scans ("rasters") of paper maps. The plans used in the Chester GIS include the OS 1:500 plans, Lavaux's 1745 plan, and others from the late 1500s to mid-1800s. These raster images are used as the basis for the creation of spatial data from selected elements of the image—a process analogous to tracing (known in GIS as digitization or "vectorizing"). In the GIS each component of the data is visualized as a separate "layer," which can be then georectified—that is, placed in a modern geographical coordinate system. This process works much better for more modern maps than it does for early historic maps since the latter were usually surveyed and drawn using projection systems that do not translate easily into modern geographical (i.e., latitude and longitude) coordinate systems that are used by GIS software.[13] This presents a methodological problem, but in theory at least these historic maps should all sit one above the other, each representing urban topographic "strata" of particular periods or dates (Fig. 3).

---

[12] On the uses of GIS in archaeological and historical research see Gregory and Ell (2007) and Wheatley and Gillings (2002); in the context of studying medieval urban landscapes see Lilley, Lloyd, and Trick (2007).

[13] Mapping Medieval Chester's GIS was developed using ESRI ArcGIS: http://www. esri.com/software/arcgis/, accessed 23 October 2009.

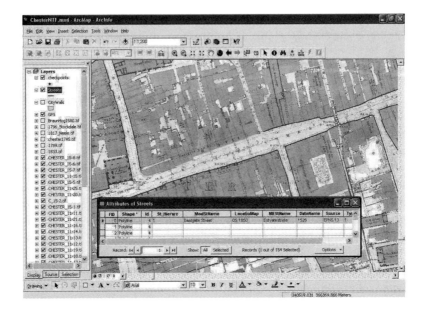

Figure 3. Screenshot from the medieval Chester GIS in its developmental
stage showing layers of historic map images ("rasters," in the list, left) and
(in the map window on the right) the vectorizing of features underway, as
denoted by the turquoise/green coloured lines. In this example Eastgate
Street is being digitized from the OS 1:500 plan, together with an example
of the associated attribute data (for Eastgate Street, with information about
it held in the database). See image plates for a colour version of this figure.

Of the historic maps used in this exercise, the OS 1:500 1870s plans georectified to modern geographical coordinates with least difficulty. The process
of georectification of historic map layers was undertaken by incorporating
field-survey data, gathered by the project team in September 2008 using
a differential Global Positioning System (dGPS), into the GIS,[14] thus establishing the precise geographical positions of Chester's key topographical
features and locations (such as towers on the city's walls). From positional
survey data of this sort, it is possible to establish the relative degrees of "distortion" in the various historic cartographic layers imported into the GIS.
This is useful as it indicates which historic maps are more (or less) accurately
surveyed, and thus which of them are more reliable in the digitization process as sources of topographical information. In the case of Chester, the GPS
survey data confirmed that the 1870s 1:500 OS sheets are the city's earliest

---

[14] For description of the use of dGPS in urban surveys see Lilley et al. (2005).

accurate cartography, and thus they, in preference to earlier maps, were used as the basis for our map-digitization work.

With the historic map layers imported into the GIS, selective digitization ("vectorizing") of those urban features known to be of medieval antecedence could begin. Digitization on screen focused on particular known medieval urban features, including street patterns for the city as a whole, and proceeded through other constituent urban topographical features, such as the circuit of city walls; other standing medieval structures, such as churches, gates and towers on the walls; plot-patterns along the medieval streets; the Rows; the bridge over the Dee; and the course of the Dee itself. Each of these features was stored as a separate layer in the GIS, partly to afford eventual users of the map the ability to toggle the display of individual layers, and partly because separation of each of the topographic features into layers allows them to be visualized differently in the GIS in terms of line-weight, colour, shade, and so forth, which helps to communicate more effectively the different cartographic information contained in the GIS (Fig. 4). The available historical evidence was used as a guide to help identify historically and geographically appropriate urban features: for example, to identify which of the streets shown on the OS plans were known (from documentary sources and archaeology) to have existed in 1500, and to establish where post-medieval changes affected their alignment and orientation. The same checking process extended to other urban features too: for example, in ensuring that the alignments of the city's walls, the locations and ground-plans of parish churches and the abbey, the plot-patterns, Rows, and narrow lanes (all shown by the 1:500 plans) were the same as those present in 1500. Such a detailed interrogation of the evidence was vital to ensure the credibility of the finished map.

From the digitizing process, numerous holes in our emerging map of late-medieval Chester became apparent, particularly in those areas along the western side of the city, just within the walls, where the majority of the city's religious houses had stood (as well as the castle, which survives today). To map these "lost" details we relied primarily upon scanning archaeological plans of excavated and surveyed features.[15] Once imported into the GIS, these enabled the restoration of the outlines of former medieval structures, such as the city's lost religious houses and their precincts. The dual advantage of using these archaeological plans is that they are drawn to modern cartographic standards, and so easily georectified, yet also accurately reveal how these urban features appeared at the end of the Middle Ages.

---

[15] These were kindly made available by the city archaeologist, Simon Ward.

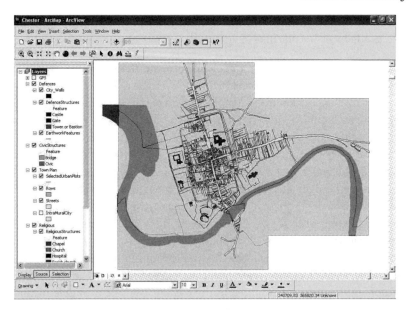

Figure 4. Screenshot from the Chester project GIS showing topographic layers (left) and digitized features in the map window (right). This is the GIS in its final stages with the map showing the city's topography and layout c. 1500.

Nevertheless, even with this archaeological data, significant topographical gaps remained in the digital map, especially in cases where post-medieval redevelopment had changed the alignment of a street, or obliterated known medieval buildings, including the city's gates. In some cases, the locations and shapes of such missing medieval features are shown by certain of the city's historic town plans. However, vectorizing from these early maps is not straightforward since they georectify poorly (compared to the OS 1:500 plans), and generally they lack the level of topographical detail required for accurate digitization. The need to include these lost features necessitated a pragmatic approach, using earlier map-sources selectively. In some cases this required "locally" georectifying part of an historic map-layer to locate a particular lost feature, and then digitizing from it, rather than from the OS 1:500 plans. This method was used, for example, to help re-create the earlier alignments of once narrow streets that were widened and "improved" in the eighteenth and nineteenth centuries, as well as to add streets that had disappeared altogether, as in the case of Capel Lane near Bridge Gate, and part of Castle Street (Fig. 5). If even earlier maps had to be relied upon to substitute a lost feature, a different process was used. This involved redrawing a lost feature (in the GIS) and locating it not exactly where the georectified historic map suggested it ought to be, but where it seemed more correctly (historically and topographically) to belong. This was the case for the demolished market hall, for example. Similarly, locating the sites of the city's former medieval gates (demolished in the eighteenth century) was accomplished by extrapolating from the extant alignments of the city walls shown on the OS 1:500 plans, rather than using the position of gates as shown by the poorly georectified earlier maps.

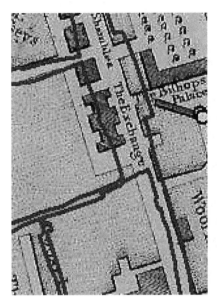

Figure 5. Examples of overlaying different geo rectified historic map layers to establish earlier urban topographies: left, streets digitized from the OS 1:500 plans (shown in green), overlaid on Lavaux's 1745 plan; right, OS 1:500 plan of 1872–73 overlaid onto earlier (1780s) map in the area of Castle Street and Bridge Street, and clearly showing the diagonal line of the new Grosvenor Street inserted in the early 1830s cutting through earlier street and plot-patterns. The yellow spots on both images indicate points at which GPS data was gathered in the field-survey described above. See image plates for a colour version of this figure.

Despite the care with which this process of selective restoration was conducted, features introduced back onto the map in this way must be seen as being to some extent speculative and provisional in status. It is in this respect that the inherent cartographical transparency of GIS can be brought to bear to ensure the integrity of the map, since each vector shape in the GIS—line, polygon or point—is annotated in detail with attribute data (visible in Fig. 3), typically including the map source, from which the feature was digitized, and the documentary or archaeological evidence that establishes its medieval provenance. Additionally, the visualization tools available in the GIS software allow for the visible demarcation of layers and features interpolated from secondary evidence, from those for which more unequivocal evidence has been found, providing an effective means of communicating to a viewer the cartographical status of the different regions or features asserted on the map.

Alternative topographies: Locating "the cross" in mappings of medieval Chester

A primary goal of Mapping Medieval Chester was to bring together visual and textual mappings of the medieval city in order to reveal to a user the complexity of the relationship between the physical reality of the city and its identity as projected through the contemporary literature. At the same time, we sought to make this relationship a tangible one by joining the texts to the map at each point of spatial correlation, such that users would be able to move from text to map and vice versa in order to trace ligatures from one resource to another. For the most part this process was straightforward: textual references to buildings or streets were easily and unambiguously located on the map. In a few cases, however, the task of establishing direct correlations between texts written specifically to be evocative and allusive rather than topographically precise, and a map offering at times only a partial outline of the city, proved challenging.

One particularly interesting instance of this problem arose in trying to locate the "cross" which is referred to by various contemporaries in their written accounts of the city. The "cross" appears, for example, in late-medieval Welsh poems describing Chester as a focus of pilgrimage and devotion, including "Y Grog i bob dyn o gred" ("The Cross, for every man of Christendom") by Guto'r Glyn in the fourteenth century and "Y Grog odidog y doded dy lun" ("Outstanding Cross, may your image be set") by Llawdden in the fifteenth century (see Williams and Williams 1939, 283; Daniel 2006, 78). A fourteenth-century poem by Gruffudd ap Maredudd celebrates the miraculous arrival in the city of the "true cross" housed in St John's Church:

> Llyna'r ddelw fyw a elwir,
> Llanw a'i dug dduw Llun i dir.

Llawenydd i'r dydd a'r don
A'i llywiodd i Gaerlleon,
Lle daeth nerth a gallu dwys
O law Agla i'w eglwys.

There it is, called a living image,
a tide brought it on a Monday to the land.
Joy to the day and the wave
that steered it to Chester,
where strength and solemn power came
from the hand of the Lord to its church.

The cross's functions as toponym and symbol in fact recur across diverse texts edited and examined by the project and raise a number of challenging and significant questions.

For example, on the western approaches to the city a cross was sited in the Roodee outside the city walls, prominently for all to see, particularly for those approaching Chester from Wales.[16] This particular (western) cross, which is shown on some historic maps, such as the OS 1:500 plans, signified an intersection between two medieval parishes, perhaps predating them in origin, with the cross being used as a parochial marker (Dodgson 1981, 63). But it is not the only locatable cross in Chester. A more obvious cross lay at the city's centre, in the street outside St Peter's church. This cross, known as the "high cross" of Chester, is clearly shown on Smith's plan of 1588, as well as others of around that time. It was typical of the period to have a "high cross" in the centre of a city, and this was not necessarily always a market cross (indeed the main market place in Chester was to the north, outside the abbey's gates) (Dodgson 1981, 12). It is the "high cross" which gave rise, in Chester's case, to the local street-name "The Cross" which appears on the OS 1:500 plans. Significantly, "The Cross" was also the intersection of the city's four main axial streets which cut Chester into four quarters. The image of a "high cross" situated at the centre of a distinctive cruciform shape of intersecting streets possessed a powerful allegorical potential which was not lost on (English) contemporary writers. In his description of the city, Lucian uses it as a metaphor for Christ and for the crucifixion:

Habet eciam plateas duas equilineas et excellentes in modum benedicte crucis, per transuersum sibi obuias et se transeuntes, que deinceps fiant quattuor ex duabus, capita sua consummantes

---

[16] As recently noted by Lewis (2005, 1).

in quattuor portis, mistice ostendens atque magnifice, magni Regis
inhabitantem graciam se habere, qui legem geminam noui ac ueteris
testamenti per misterium sancte crucis impletam ostendit, in quattuor euangelistis.

Chester also has two perfectly straight streets intersecting like the
blessed cross, which form four roads, culminating at the four gates,
mystically revealing the marvellously innate grace of the Great
King, who, through the four evangelists, showed the twin law of the
old and new testaments to be completed through the mystery of the
holy cross.

Lucian metaphorically maps Christ's body onto Chester's urban topography
in a clear allusion to the crossroads at the town centre. Lucian's "cross" is not
just an intersection of streets, but a manifestation of Christ's enduring temporal and spatial presence in the urban world Lucian observes. The city thus
"crosses itself" as a sign of Christ's body. But at the same time, in adducing
Chester's metaphorically and literally cruciform streets, Lucian also extends
the semiotic potency of the cross *beyond* one topographical location so that it
encompasses the whole city and its people, employing an evident and quotid-
ian feature of the city's topography to connect Chester with Christ, and so
to the wider Christian world (Lilley 2009). While it is *possible* to see Lucian's
"cross" as spatially locatable as a place on the map centred on a street called
"The Cross," in topographically locating it we move from the allegorical to
the literal, and this significantly diminishes the effect of Lucian's more richly
suggestive "mapping" of Chester's topoi.

The attempt to locate Chester's polysemous medieval crosses exposes some
difficult methodological challenges. Firstly, can we be sure when the same
cross is being referred to in each of these texts, given that several other crosses featured prominently in the local urban landscape? The textual sources
give evidence of several possible crosses, some of which can be geographically located with certainty, while others cannot. Secondly, even where it is
possible to locate and map a cross, the process of doing so may well prove
reductive or inadequate. There are, then, alternative topographies arising
from these two very different kinds of urban mapping: the deterministic process of modern cartography and map-making, and the figurative potential of
textual signs and the spaces they map out.[17]

---

[17] On this point see Edney (2005, 9).

An integrated digital publication: Bringing everything together

The intangible nature of the relationship between Lucian's figurative, allegorical cross and a specific point in the city—nuanced and powerful, but also resistant to direct, literal expression—illustrates a challenge faced by the project in attempting to bring together a disparate set of source materials within a single coherent online publication. In translating the multivalent, alternative topographies described above from analogue to digital, it seems inevitable that a process of attrition must occur, given that the mechanism afforded by the Web for expressing relationships—the hyperlink—allows only for the expression of simple, direct, and unqualified reference. In setting out to design the Mapping Medieval Chester web resource, our goal was to mitigate this loss as far as possible by employing strategies to help propagate and catalyse in the mind of the reader or user the activity of drawing out the richer connections between the sign and the signified, between map and texts.

A significant obstacle to building a unified web publication from the diverse materials represented by Mapping Medieval Chester has been that the two major components of the resource (i.e., texts and map) demand very different types of presentation and are derived in turn from two different technical methodologies: on the one hand, TEI XML and the substantial tradition of electronic scholarly textual editing; and on the other, GIS. Both are well established within their usual domains of application, but, to date, not often brought together.[18] A typical approach was taken for the digitization of the texts, which, having been transcribed, were encoded in XML using the TEI P5 guidelines.[19] A customized RELAX NG schema was developed both to accommodate the fairly wide variety of textual features and characteristics exhibited by the different texts,[20] and to allow "project-specific" features (specifically, references to persons and places) to be recorded. The editorial work

---

[18] Indeed the only specific example of GIS and TEI being used in close context we know of is the defunct BerGIS project in Norway, accessed 23 October 2009 (http://bergis.uib.no/). For details of this specific aspect of the work, see Bruvik (2006).

[19] P5 guidelines available online at TEI Consortium, "TEI: P5 Guidelines," accessed 23 October 2009, http://www.tei-c.org/Guidelines/P5/.

[20] RELAX NG is a language for expressing XML schemas (a schema defines a set of grammatical rules that apply to an XML document). The most recent version of the TEI guidelines introduced the possibility of using RELAX NG (as opposed to the older DTD model), which confers a number of technical benefits. For more information on RELAX NG, see http://www.relaxng.org, accessed 23 October 2009; on its use in TEI P5, see n. 19, above.

was carried out entirely in XML and was the responsibility of the literary scholars who were given a tailored training program prior to the start of the project. We employed a characteristic multipass workflow for XML editing, whereby the editors applied basic structural markup to each text in a first pass, and subsequently performed more detailed markup (encoding person/ place information together with cross references, editorial commentary, references, and translated texts where appropriate) over the course of two or more subsequent iterations. The work concluded with the finalizing of the authority lists of persons (which recorded each unique person referred to within the texts) and of places (likewise recording each unique place mentioned in the texts, and thereby forming the basis of data for interconnection of text and map).

The texts are rendered via a dynamic, Apache Cocoon-based web application, which handles the textual visualizations in addition to managing the overall web publication framework, including common navigation, indexing, and searching, as well as the display of help and contextual and scene-setting material for the website.[21] Even within the relatively small corpus of texts drawn upon by Mapping Medieval Chester, the task of providing a consistent user experience in presenting the texts is complicated by the vastly different types and styles they represent. The texts are in (sometimes more than one of) Middle English, Middle Welsh, and Latin, between them representing the very different textual traditions of scholarly treatise, narrative prose, and poetry; while the corpus itself is composed of a mixture of complete texts and extracts from much larger works. Accordingly, each text brings with it the heritage of a different editorial convention, ranging from the relatively light touch required for Bradshaw's *Life of Saint Werburge*, for example, where only glosses and critical apparatus are necessary, to the considerably more formalized approach demanded by the Lucian text, which not only requires full translation but is an inherently complex text in terms both of its *mise en page* and its structure.[22] The first challenge then was to present each of these disparate texts in a way that allows some degree of consistent reading experience while satisfying different types of users: those who want to simply read and understand the texts, those who may have very specific scholarly

---

[21] The web application was built on version 2.0 of DDH's xMod XML publication tool (subsequently renamed Kiln). Kiln Documentation, accessed 23 October 2009, at https://github.com/kcl-ddh/kiln/wiki/.

[22] *De Laude Cestrie* includes marginal *apparatus fontium* and *apparatus criticus* which can appear in all four of the margins of the page; as is customary, each annotation is positioned in close proximity to the passage of text to which it refers.

interests in the texts themselves, or those who may wish to use them as a basis for pedagogical activity and for whom the presence of a thorough and contextually appropriate critical apparatus is highly desirable.

The overriding goal with the texts then was to create both credible and usable editions. Our solution is to offer the texts to the user in either two or three "views" or fixed perspectives, each suited to a specific mode of use. The *Life of Saint Werburge*, for example, is offered in both a "Reading" (Fig. 6) and a "Scholarly" view; the former shows a full line-by-line gloss of the Middle English and includes textual apparatus discretely (by means of references that pop up), while the latter view suppresses the glossing and outputs the scholarly textual apparatus in full beneath each "page" of text.

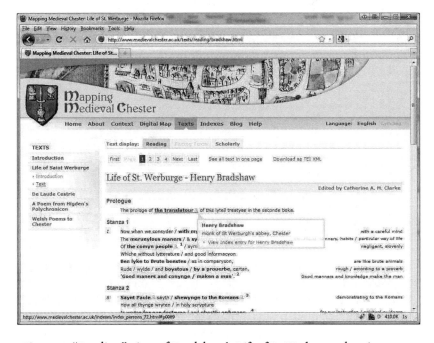

Figure 6. "Reading" view of Bradshaw's *Life of St. Werburge*, showing marginal glossing and (in the pop-up) an annotated cross-reference to an index of persons.

In fact, substantially the same information is available in both of these textual views: the difference lies primarily in the different visual emphasis given by making some information explicit (and therefore permanently visible) and other information visible on demand (as when moving the mouse over certain words or footnote markers).[23]

Lucian's *De Laude Cestrie* necessitated a more complex approach. It too was offered in "Reading" and "Scholarly" versions, but also in an aligned "Facing Texts" rendition setting the Latin original and its English translation side-by-side (Fig. 7).

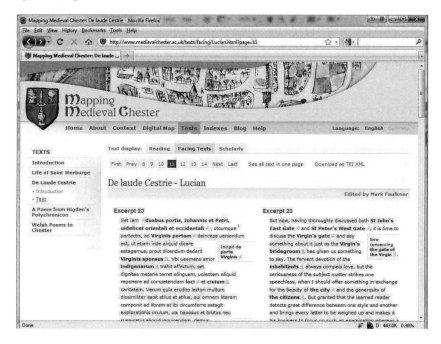

Figure 7. "Facing Texts" view of the Lucian, showing an example of marginal apparatus ("Incipit de porta Virginis"). Text highlighted in green (with "northings" icon) denotes a cross-reference to the map or to the index of places; text highlighted in red (with person icon) denotes a cross-reference to the person index. See image plates for a colour version of this figure.

---

[23] The decision to present a fixed number of preset views, as opposed to giving the user the ability to customize the display more freely, was based on the findings of two user engagement exercises and additional research conducted by DDH in the context of two other projects: *Out of the Wings*, accessed 23 October 2009 (http://www.outofthewings. org/) and *Nineteenth Century Serials Edition* (NCSE), accessed 23 October 2009 (http://www. ncse.ac.uk). This research revealed, somewhat surprisingly, a high level of indifference among users towards tools and functionality allowing information to be shown, hidden or rearranged. Vetch (2010) reports on these findings.

Each view presents a semi-diplomatic edition of the text which visualizes the position of the marginal apparatuses. In addition, both the "Facing Texts" and "Scholarly" views preserve the line breaks and page layout from the original manuscript—an unusual approach for a text of this type, but one which allows a more faithful positioning of the apparatus with respect to the original source (and which additionally allows line references to the text to be meaningfully resolved). Longer texts are paginated by default, but the user can elect to view the entire text in a single page if desired. In addition, the underlying TEI XML file for each text is available for download from the website, allowing users to explore the markup and apply their own analysis or visualization.

In preparing the underlying map data for online publication, our goal was to propagate the same degree of flexibility and transparency inherent to GIS through to the presentation of the maps online. In particular we were concerned to preserve the ability to separate out the map data into individual topographic layers (parish boundaries, plots, structural features) and to ensure that the evidence that had allowed lost or missing features to be restored or interpolated onto the map could be consulted.

The viewing of maps on the Web is now ubiquitous, but GIS-derived maps look quite different from the sorts of web-based maps that are commonly encountered online. Typically they employ more complex interfaces, designed to be familiar to users who are already comfortable with desktop GIS applications and terminology, which allow for navigation and some manipulation of the map data (minimally by showing or hiding the topographical layers and other information).[24] We needed to visualize the map data in a way that would suit both a "lay" user and a GIS specialist, and this meant that the use of the most obvious and ubiquitous tools for web-based display of maps (most notably Google Maps and its accompanying API) were not suitable.[25] The leading commercial tool for web-based rendering of GIS data at the time of writing remains ESRI's ArcIMS tool;[26] it is, however expensive, and would have required considerable customization in order to

---

[24] For numerous examples of maps delivered via ESRI's ArcIMS / ArcGIS tools which typify what is described here see http://www.esri.com/apps/showcase, accessed 23 October 2009.

[25] One reason for this is the sheer number of layers of data that are present on the Chester map. Some further explanation is offered at http://blog.medievalchester. ac.uk/2009/07/06/a-new-map-of-medieval-chester/.

[26] See http://esri.com/software/arcims/index.html, accessed 23 October 2009.

sit comfortably within the *Mapping Medieval Chester* resource.[27] We chose
instead to explore the potential of the Open Source MapServer software,[28]
coupled with the OpenLayers client-side delivery framework,[29] both of
which were already in use at DDH to map prosopographical data from the
Domesday Book as part of the PASE (Prosopography of Anglo-Saxon England) project.[30] Unlike Google Maps, MapServer is a platform for building
custom mapping applications, rather than a ready-to-use, off-the-shelf
visualization tool, but the development effort required to deploy it is expi-
ated by the ability to custom-build an application. Moreover, MapServer's
compatibility with GIS data sources makes it possible to build an interface
in which different layers of data can be toggled on and off by the user, and
its native capabilities further allow presentation of maps in two ways: as
navigable, but essentially static images generated on request by the server,
and (via OpenLayers) as a full-screen, fluid map view with an interaction
model and user experience broadly familiar to anyone who has used Google
Maps. The *Mapping Medieval Chester* website offers end users a choice between these two modes of presentation: the static delivery mechanism has
been used to provide what has been called a "low bandwidth" version of
the map (Fig. 8), which is undemanding in terms of browser requirements,
computer performance, and speed of Internet connection; while a "high
bandwidth" version of the map allows much greater interactivity and offers a more intuitive interface (Fig. 9).

---

[27] Additionally, ESRI indicated in 2009 that ArcIMS development is now ceasing in
favour of the more feature-rich ArcGIS server package.

[28] MapServer (currently at version 5.4.2) is available, with documentation, at http://
mapserver.org, accessed 23 October 2009.

[29] OpenLayers is available from http://openlayers.org, accessed 23 October 2009.

[30] Original (2004) version available online at http://www.pase.ac.uk/; a heavily revised new version with mapping was published in winter 2009.

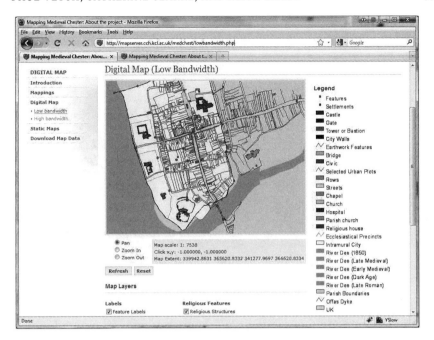

Figure 8. The "Low Bandwidth" version of the digital map, with layer legend to the right and basic zoom and pan controls. Each layer can be toggled on and off using controls at the bottom of the screen.

Both versions of the map offer the user the ability to customize which map layers are visible, allowing, for example, a user to see the shape of the River Dee across five different time periods, or to simplify the map by showing individual layers as required.

In addition to the interactive maps, a set of seven very high-quality "themed" maps have been created and are available for use under a Creative Commons licence.[31] They each present particular views on the new map data. For example "Ritual Chester" shows the route taken by the Whitsun Plays, "Civic Chester" shows the locations of the principal civic structures, and so forth. As with the texts, the underlying raw data is also available for download in the form of GIS shape files, which include all of the attribute data revealing the sources used to compile the map.[32]

---

[31] The maps are freely available (under a Creative Commons licence) from http://www.medievalchester.ac.uk/mappings/static.html, accessed 23 October 2009.

[32] The GIS data is available for download from http://www.medievalchester.ac.uk/

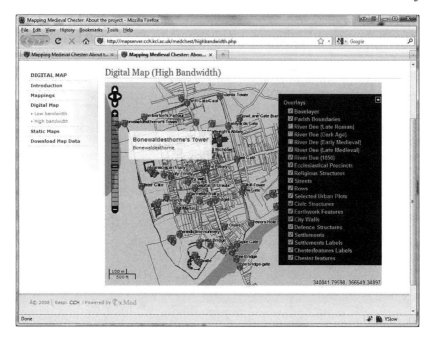

Figure 9. The "High Bandwidth" map, which can be manipulated in real time
and includes pop-up cross-references to the place index.

In visualizing both the texts and the maps, we have consciously endeavoured
to strike a balance among editorial intervention, flexibility, utility, and to
some extent familiarity, in borrowing both from established print analogues
for textual presentation, and conventions for the presentation of map data
familiar from desktop GIS applications. Notwithstanding this overarching
conceptual approach, there of course remain fundamental differences in both
the interfaces to, and the underlying technical basis of, the textual and cartographic material, which pose a number of technical and conceptual challenges
in bringing these data together in a coherent and effective way. Whereas a
typical electronic textual edition might usefully juxtapose a hypertext with an
accompanying digital facsimile image, viewing textual editions together with
GIS data necessitates switching between two completely different web applications (in this case Apache Cocoon and MapServer) in a way that inevitably and
conspicuously exposes the differences between these two very different domains of scholarly enquiry and methodology, and thus fracturing the user experience for someone passing from text to map. We have attempted to counter

mappings/download.html, accessed 23 October 2009, where there is also information
about free viewing tools.

this, in effect, by changing the nature of the problem and removing the need to "jump" between resources so often. Thus, interconnections between text and map are mediated by an interstitial view, a pop-up tooltip which shows, superimposed over the text, a partial representation of the GIS map image centred on the location referred to in the text (Fig. 10).[33]

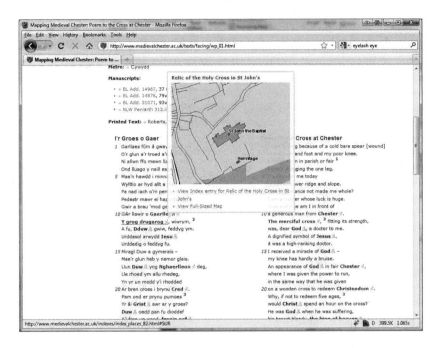

Figure 10. Moving the mouse over the highlighted text "Y grog drugarog," "the holy cross," in the Welsh poem shown here reveals a preview of the map, centred on the location as mapped. At this point the user can then choose to see an index entry for the location term (to find other textual references to it); to move through to consult the full size map; or to move the mouse to un-focus the pop-up window, and return to consulting the text.

This allows the referent term to be seen in juxtaposition with the physical location to which it has been assigned, and thereby (it is hoped) provides sufficient information to obviate the need for frequent switching between

---

[33] There are, of course, a small number of situations where the location might either be unclear in a way impossible to resolve (as is the case, for example, with some references to "the church"), or beyond the scope of the map (i.e., "Jerusalem"); in these instances a note is displayed accordingly.

the full-text display and the full-size map, a process that would, for example, be disruptive for a user attempting to work systematically through one of the texts.[34] Moving in reverse, from map to text, presents a slightly different problem in that most locations on the map are adduced many times within the different texts. To work around this difficulty we provide a clickable list (in the same large tooltip) of the passages within the text that refer to the point on the map the user has clicked (Fig. 11). Should the list of references be too long to be readily or comfortably displayed in this format, the list is truncated and the user has the option to view the full list within the place index.

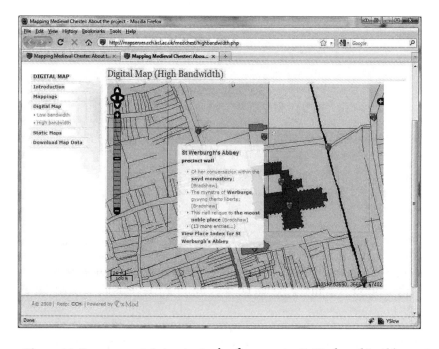

Figure 11. Pop-up containing textual references to St Werburgh's Abbey, allowing the user to move through to view the individual textual references shown in context, or to go to the relevant place index entry to consult the full list.

The approach outlined here could by no means be thought of as an "integration" of map and text; but it allows the sketching out of a smoother func-

---

[34] This technique for using pop-ups is very similar to a viral marketing technique sometimes seen on the Web, where brand names include "IntelliTXT" and "Context-Link." For more on this technique and its potential see Vetch (2006).

tional and cognitive ligature between what are two very different resources while solving a difficult usability issue in affording only a *preview* of the map or text (often all that is required) that allows a user to move through to a more detailed full map and text display if desired.

Conclusion

To date, the Mapping Medieval Chester project has resulted in a range of tangible outcomes which will enable future work on the medieval city and the city literature. The project website now offers the first editions of many Welsh poems, the first scholarly (partial) edition of Henry Bradshaw's *Life of Saint Werburge* since 1887, as well as the first edition of much of Lucian's *De Laude Cestrie* and its first modern English translation. The linkage of these texts to indices, as well as to the interactive map, allows users to explore the different representations and interpretations of urban space by different medieval writers and the ways in which the material fabric of the medieval city was "symbolically organized" in divergent and sometimes competing ways. The digital publication is already proving to be of use in undergraduate and postgraduate classroom teaching, as well as in scholarly research, and will bring a new dimension to study of the medieval Chester Cycle Plays now that the route of the Corpus Christi procession can be more accurately visualized, and more clearly seen in the context of contemporary accounts of the city.[35] Other outputs include a major international, interdisciplinary colloquium held in July 2009,[36] as well as a volume of essays by the project team and other contributors, *Mapping the Medieval City: Space, Place and Identity in Chester, c. 1200–1500* (forthcoming, University of Wales Press). Plans for future work also include a proposed full edition of the Lucian *De Laude Cestrie* (both in print and digital, building upon the XML encoding model created for the present project) by the project's post-doctoral researcher, Mark Faulkner. Additionally, some members of the project team will be involved in a further project, The Gough Map,[37] which will effectively continue the work doc-

---

[35] A PDF version of a map tracing the procession route is available at http://www.medievalchester.ac.uk/redist/pdf/ritualchester.pdf, accessed 23 October 2009.

[36] For information on the colloquium and launch event, see http://blog.medieval-chester.ac.uk/category/colloquium/.

[37] The Gough Map is one of the earliest maps to show Britain in a geographically recognisable form. This AHRC-funded project began in April 2010 with Keith Lilley as the Principal Investigator, and Paul Vetch and Nick Millea (University of Oxford) as Co-Investigators. Linguistic Geographies: The Gough Map of Great Britain and its Making, accessed 23 October 2009, http://www.goughmap.org/.

mented here in exploring map and text integration while taking advantage of some alternative technologies.[38]

It is always to be hoped that the conversations, methodologies, and processes that a project such as this entails will become more important and enduring than any of the specific outputs. The *Mapping Medieval Chester* project has successfully initiated dialogues with users both within and outside academia, deliberately including features that enable interaction, evaluation, and continuing development. The project blog, for example, continues to communicate our work in progress with multiple audiences, including medieval scholars, students, and the wider public.[39] The website also continues to expand through the addition of images supplied by members of the public who attended our Mapping Medieval Chester Festival, uploaded via Flickr and embedded in the interactive map.[40] These pictures provide further new perspectives on the juxtapositions between text and image, place and identity, medieval and modern which the project's digital resources seek to explore. Mapping Medieval Chester represents only a snapshot in time of a nascent dialogue between subject disciplines which looks set to evolve very rapidly over the course of the next few years not only with the evolution of technology, but as we grow better attuned to the ways in which it can enable new modes of scholarly enquiry.

---

[38] The project will evaluate use of GeoServer, accessed 23 October 2009 (http://geoserver.org) and offer map data for export in KML format (a widely used XML schema for expressing geographical data).

[39] Blog visible at http://blog.medievalchester.ac.uk.

[40] For more details and photographs of the Festival, see http://blog.medievalchester.ac.uk/tag/festival/. Those who took part in the tours were encouraged to publish their photographs via the photo-sharing website Flickr, and they have been embedded onto the online map to establish a visual correlation between the modern and medieval town. Flickr group visible at http://www.flickr.com/groups/1204980@N21, accessed 23 October 2009. The photographic layer is available via the "High Bandwidth" map on the Mapping Medieval Chester website.

WORKS CITED

Alldridge, N. J. 1981-83. "Aspects of the Topography of Early Medieval Chester." *Journal of the Chester Archaeological Society* 64:5-31.

Barrett, Robert W. 2009. *Against All England: Regional Identity and Cheshire Writing, 1195-1656.* Notre Dame: University of Notre Dame Press.

Brown, A., ed. 1999. *The Rows of Chester: The Chester Rows Research Project.* English Heritage Archaeological Report 16. London.

Bruvik, Tone Merete. 2006. "TEI in an Historical GIS." Accessed 2 October 2008. http://gandalf.aksis.uib.no/bergis/Forelesninger/TEI%20in%20 an%20histoical%20GIS.pdf.

Butterfield, Ardis, ed. 2006. *Chaucer and the City.* Cambridge: D. S. Brewer.

Certeau, Michel de. 2002. *The Practice of Everyday Life.* Translated by Steven Rendall. Berkeley: University of California Press.

Mapping Medieval Chester. Blog. Accessed 23 October 2009. http://blog. medievalchester.ac.uk.

Cheshire and Chester Archives and Local Studies. 2001. *Printed Maps in the Cheshire Record Office.* Chester: Cheshire County Council.

Clarke, Catherine A. M. 2006. *Literary Landscapes and the Idea of England, 700-1400.* Cambridge: D. S. Brewer.

Daniel, R. Iestyn, ed. 2006. *Gwaith Llwadden.* Aberystwyth: Canolfan Uwchefrydiau Cymreig a Cheltaidd Prifysgol Cymru.

Dodgson, J. McN. 1981. *The Place-Names of the City of Chester.* Part 5, sec. 1:i of *The Place-Names of Cheshire.* 5 vols. English Place-Name Society, Vol. 48. Cambridge: Cambridge University Press.

Duncan, James S. 1990. *City as Text: The Politics of Landscape Interpretation in the Kandyan Kingdom.* Cambridge: Cambridge University Press.

Edney, Matthew H. 2005. "The Origins and Development of J. B. Harley's Cartographic Theories. Cartographica Monograph 54." Special issue, *Cartographica* 40 (1-2).

Flanders, Julia. 2009. "The Productive Unease of 21st-Century Digital Scholarship." *Digital Humanities Quarterly* 3 (3). Accessed 24 October 2009. http://digitalhumanities.org/dhq/vol/3/3/000055.html.

Gregory, Ian N., and Paul S. Ell. 2007. *Historical GIS: Technologies, Methodologies and Scholarship.* Cambridge: Cambridge University Press.

Hanawalt, Barbara A., and Kathryn L. Reyerson, eds. 1994. *City and Spectacle in Medieval Europe.* Minneapolis: University of Minnesota Press.

Laughton, Jane. 2008. *Life in a Late Medieval City: Chester 1275-1520.* Oxford: Windgather Press.

Lefebvre, Henri. 1991. *The Production of Space.* Translated by Donald Nicholson-Smith. Oxford: Blackwell.

Lewis, Barry James. 2005. *Welsh Poetry and English Pilgrimage: Gruffudd ap Maredudd and the Rood of Chester.* Aberystwyth: University of Wales Centre for Advanced Welsh and Celtic Studies.

Lilley, Keith D. 2000. "Mapping the Medieval City: Plan Analysis and Urban History." *Urban History* 27:5–30.

_____ 2009. *City and Cosmos: The Medieval World in Urban Form.* London: Reaktion Books.

Lilley, Keith D., Christopher D. Lloyd, and Steven Trick. 2005. "Mapping Medieval Townscapes: A Digital Atlas of the New Towns of Edward I." University of York. http://ads.ahds.ac.uk/catalogue/specColl/atlas_ahrb_2005.

_____ 2007. "Mapping Medieval Townscapes: GIS Applications in Landscape History and Settlement Study." In *Medieval Landscapes,* edited by Mark Gardiner and Stephen Rippon, 27–42. Bollington, UK: Windgather Press.

Lilley, Keith D., Christopher D. Lloyd, Steven Trick, and Conor Graham. 2005. "Analysing and Mapping Medieval Urban Forms Using GPS and GIS." *Urban Morphology* 9:1–9.

Rouse, Robert Allen. 2005. *The Idea of Anglo-Saxon England in Middle English Romance.* Cambridge: D. S. Brewer.

Strohm, Paul. 2000. *Theory and the Premodern Text*. Minneapolis: University of Minnesota Press.

Sutherland, Kathyrn. 2008. "Being Critical: Paper-Based Editing and the Digital Environment." In *Text Editing, Print and the Digital World*, 12–26. Farnham: Ashgate.

Thacker, A. T. 2003. "Later Medieval Chester 1230–1550." In *A History of the County of Cheshire*. Vol. 5, part 1 of *The City of Chester*, edited by C. P. Lewis and A.T. Thacker, 34–89. London: Boydell & Brewer.

Vetch, Paul. 2006. "Connecting Web Resources With Deep Hyperlinking." Presented at Digital Humanities 2006, Paris-Sorbonne. http://staff. cch.kcl.ac.uk/~pvetch/permalink/dh2006.pdf.

_____ 2010. "From Edition to Experience: Feeling the Way Towards User Focussed Interfaces." In *Electronic Publishing: Politics and Pragmatics*, edited by Gabriel Egan, 163–76. Toronto and Tempe, AZ: Iter/Arizona Center for Medieval and Renaissance Studies.

Wallace, David. 2004. *Premodern Places: Calais to Surinam, Chaucer to Aphra Behn*. Oxford: Blackwell.

Ward, Simon M. 1990. *Excavations at Chester: The Lesser Medieval Religious Houses, Sites Investigated 1964-1983*. Chester: Chester City Council.

Wheatley, David, and Mark Gillings. 2002. *Spatial Technology and Archaeology: The Archaeological Applications of GIS*. London: Taylor & Francis.

Williams, Ifor, and John Llywelyn Williams, eds. 1939. *Gwaith Guto'r Glyn*. Cardiff: University of Wales Press.

Virtual Reality for Humanities Scholarship

Lisa M. Snyder
The Urban Simulation Team, the Institute for Digital Research
and Education, and the Experiential Technologies Center,
University of California, Los Angeles
lms@ucla.edu

Virtual reality (VR) stands poised to challenge the dominance of two-dimensional drawings and static images in the research, study, and teaching methods related to architectural and urban form. The availability and growing ubiquity of spatially based and three-dimensional (3D) technologies is creating new forms of scholarship and publication. Within virtual environments created to academically rigorous standards, it is now possible to explore reconstructed buildings and urban spaces, re-create the experience of citizens from other eras, challenge long-held reconstruction theories, and gain insights into the material culture of past civilizations in ways never before possible. The purpose of this essay is to provide a framework for developing research projects that exploit virtual reality and consider the unique challenges of using this new technology for the study of material culture.

Broadly defined, the term "virtual reality" can be applied to a wide range of technologies, the common thread being that they involve three-dimensional computer-generated environments that respond to user actions. The use of VR technologies for the study of material culture is theoretically applicable to the replication of any element of the physical world, either in its current state or as it existed at some defined moments in its past. The object of study could, therefore, range from small-scale artefacts to large-scale natural landscapes, or any point in between. User engagement within this range could be anything from the ability to manipulate digital representations of artefacts to pedestrian navigation through virtual space. For the following discussion, primary consideration will be given to the historically accurate, academically vetted reconstructions of the built environment—individual structures, urban complexes, and cityscapes—that are the hallmark of VR research at UCLA. In this context, Willard McCarty's definitions of a "model" as "a representation of something for the purposes of study" and "modelling" as "the heuristic process of constructing and manipulating models" are honed

ISBN 978-0-86698-499-7 (online)   ISBN 978-0-86698-474-4 (print)
New Technologies in Medieval and Renaissance Studies 3 (2012) 395–428

to very specifically refer to three-dimensional computer representations of geometric form and their creation (2004, 255).

The first section of this chapter explores the basics of developing an academic VR project, beginning with identifying the research questions to be addressed and ending with a discussion of the workflow typical for the creation of a virtual environment or computer reconstruction. Two large-scale VR projects are then used to illustrate the real-world applicability and possible variations of this development cycle. The first, the real-time Temple Mount installation at the Davidson Center in Jerusalem, was initiated and built for public consumption; the second, a reconstruction model of Santiago de Compostela, began as a classroom experiment but shifted focus to give primacy to the academic process behind the effort. The chapter concludes with an exploration of the pedagogical and academic potential of this technology and a discussion of the challenges that may limit future development of large-scale, academically vetted VR projects.

Developing a virtual reality project

The research question

Virtual reality technologies can contribute in significant ways to the study of material culture, but, like any other toolset, they should be employed only after careful consideration has established that their use will further the project's research objectives. The mere availability of new and interesting technology is not enough. Once clearly defined, the research questions to be investigated become a valuable scoping mechanism for the project by establishing both the expected outcomes and the desired deliverables.

Taking a cue from educational theory, the research questions most commonly addressed through VR projects typically fall into one of two categories. *Process-based* questions are addressed through the analytical act of creating the virtual artefact or environment with little or no expectations for the longevity of the data beyond the life of the project. *Product-based* questions may include process-based elements during the construction of the VR environment, but are more focused on interaction with the finished product and long-term public dissemination of the research.[1] In truth, most projects

---

[1] In studies on teaching and learning, these terms have a variety of meanings. *Process-product research* "attempts to define relationships between what teachers do in the classroom (the processes of teaching) and what happens to their students (the products of learning)" (Anderson, Evertson, and Brophy 1979, 193). *Process* is also used

involve both process- and product-based components, but with varying degrees of emphasis. A project to document the visible remains of a Byzantine settlement as a means towards predicting the location of the long-vanished city wall, for example, may be largely focused on the data gathering process, but will also generate a simple VR environment to explain the project results. Conversely, a product-based project to examine how online users interact with a virtual Byzantine settlement may include a significant portion of time dedicated to construction of the virtual environment, but will do so in a fashion and with technology that is markedly different from that chosen by a project team focusing primarily on process with little concern for a publicly available deliverable. The challenge is to articulate clearly the research objectives at the onset of the project in order to make intelligent decisions about the scope of the work required, the technology to be used, methodology, the expertise required on the project team, hardware and software purchases, dissemination of the research results, and funding.

Early VR projects tended to be process-based with research agendas that looked to build knowledge about the physical world from the process of constructing and manipulating the 3D computer surrogate. Archaeologists were early adopters of the technology, with the lessons learned from creating the computer environment directly informing ongoing archaeological activities and augmenting academic publications.[2] VR projects lend themselves to

---

to identify the steps through which a learner builds knowledge, as opposed to the actions of a teacher. Maria Roussou in her article "Learning by Doing and Learning Through Play: An Exploration of Interactivity in Virtual Environments for Children" builds a case for interactivity in VR by citing the learning theories of Jean Piaget and Seymour Papert wherein learners "construct their own knowledge by testing ideas and concepts based on prior knowledge and experience, applying them to a new situation, and integrating the new knowledge with pre-existing intellectual constructs" (2004, 4). *Product*, defined above as the end result of teaching, is also used in the business sense to describe a tangible and marketable object such as a piece of instructional technology or a textbook.

[2] The use of VR applications for archaeology has been well documented, beginning with Reilly (1991), as have standards for archaeological use of VR and three-dimensional computer modeling to explore research questions specific to a single artefact, structure, or site. See Barceló, Forte, and Sanders (2000), Gill (2009), Goodrick and Gillings (2000), and the proceedings associated with cultural heritage computing including the Computer Applications in Archaeology (CAA) conferences and the Virtual Reality, Archaeology, and Cultural Heritage (VAST) conferences (Niccolucci 2000); and the various publications dealing with computing and quanti-

process-based inquiry because creating the 3D model requires a deep understanding of the physical artefacts and extant remains, their history, and all related textual and material evidence. Scholars are challenged to think about materiality, structure, the interrelation of building elements, possible physical manifestations of cultural practices, and vernacular building traditions as part of a complex web of data that informs the creation process and grounds the material evidence. Questions in process-based VR research might focus on a single archaeological site as a way to analyse physical remains, generate lighting or structural studies, compare different scholars' reconstruction ideas, challenge long-standing interpretations, or use the technology to reconstruct specific building elements from excavated features and artefacts. Process-based projects often include an end product beyond the knowledge gained from the exercise. The primary research objective of The Digital Michelangelo Project (Levoy et al. 2000), for example, was to test applications for laser rangefinder technology, but the resulting static illustrations from the 3D laser scan have subsequently been used to illustrate the project's website and a number of papers on the technical aspects of the project (Godin et al. 2001; Davis et al. 2001; Ikemoto, Gelfand, and Levoy 2003). Datasets from this project are also available, but have limited value for the general humanities researcher because they are geared more towards computer science research.[3] The product in this example is secondary to the underlying computing problems such as manipulating or visualizing large-scale datasets, designing lighting and rendering algorithms, and creating cohesive meshes from 3D laser scans.

The recent explosion of 3D modeling software, online virtual worlds, and other spatially based technologies has opened up this fertile area of research to the broader academic community and created a wealth of product-based VR projects. These product-based projects may address process-based research questions during the creation of the virtual environment, but their primary focus is to provide ongoing public access to the research results and facilitate new lines of research within the finished environment.[4] Examples of

---

tative methods in the British Archaeological Reports (BAR) published by Archaeopress.

[3] In July 2009 the team released a full-resolution model of Michelangelo's *David* that contains about one billion polygons, and they suggest that "it may be the largest geometric model in existence of a scanned object" (Levoy 1997–2003).

[4] Certainly in the United States, this wealth of VR projects has been fueled by the combination of available online toolsets and a push for the dissemination of research results by our major federal and private funders.

"in-world" research questions include how interaction with a digital facsimile of the physical world facilitates new discoveries; how experiencing the space, albeit virtually, builds new knowledge about the historical environment being represented; how this new visualization tool can be used to teach and learn about architecture and urban space; and how the 3D environment can be used as a publishing platform.[5] Impacts of the technology on users would also be considered product-based research and might include questions such as how the user's ability to navigate through the virtual space impacts his or her understanding of the modelled environment. A common thread through these product-based projects is the expectation of a publicly available suite of deliverables that extend beyond the life of the project—a web presence that provides learning and teaching resources, for example, or long-term access to the modelled environment through a for-profit virtual world vendor.

Technology

Virtual reality technologies can be grouped according to the degree the user is immersed in the environment: early VR research focused on single-person experiences that approximated total perceptual immersion in a computer-generated environment through the use of head-mounted displays and user interaction made possible with data gloves. Cave Automatic Virtual Environment (CAVE) technology advanced VR research by placing the user inside the projection space by displaying the computer-generated environments on each surface of a small chamber. Depending on the application, users may interact with the virtual space via motion sensors or devices that track head or hand movements (e.g., goggles or data gloves). The development of desktop VR marked the shift away from single-user systems and towards more functional tools for humanities and social science scholarship. Recent advancements in computer and graphics processing power and ever-widening bandwidth enabled a surge in online virtual worlds for social-networking and game play[6]

---

[5] Johanson (2009, 414) includes an example of the staging of gladiatorial games in the Roman Forum during the Roman Republic; other examples would include a viewshed analysis that uses a VR environment to study what is visible from any fixed vantage point.

[6] Virtual worlds has become a well-defined subset of VR research. In the inaugural issue of the *Journal of Virtual Worlds Research*, Mark Bell proposed the following definition: "a synchronous, persistent network of people, represented by avatars, facilitated by networked computers" (2008, 2). Examples include Kaneva (2006–10), Second Life, Whyville (1999–2010), There (2010), Sirikata (2010), Open Simulator (2010), and SDForum's Virtual World SIG (1999–2007).

with sites like Second Life,[7] Whyville, and Stanford's Sirikata; while sophisticated online mapping programs such as Google Earth and Microsoft Research
Maps (2010) provide interaction with rich geographical content on a global
scale.

Selecting the most appropriate technological solution for any given project
is one of the most critical decisions that the academic team will be required
to make, and one that should be made with a firm understanding of the
project's primary research objectives and desired end product. At the heart
of all virtual reality technologies are three-dimensional computer models:
digital geometry that exists in three-dimensional virtual space and represents its physical counterpart. There are many options for creating digital
representations of physical objects, extant structures, or hypothetical reconstructions, each with its own strengths and limitations. Laser scanners,
such as those used by the Center for Advanced Spatial Technologies (CAST)
at the University of Arkansas, allow researchers to create large-scale data
meshes that replicate entire archaeological sites.[8] At the opposite end of the
spectrum, small-scale artefacts can be scanned on a rotation table and the resultant meshes combined to create a 3D digital facsimile.[9] Three-dimensional
modeling packages that facilitate the creation of virtual environments are
available for all budgets and skill levels: Google freely distributes SketchUp[10]
to facilitate the development of simple 3D content for Google Earth; more sophisticated modeling software packages such as Rhino (2007) and AutoDesk's

---

[7] Second Life website, accessed 23 October 2009, http://www.secondlife.com. For subsequent web publications mentioned in the text, see the bibliography for location and
site information.

[8] At the time of this writing, CAST was using an Optech ILRIS and a Minolta Vivid 9i.
Their website includes links to technical information and project examples including
a description of high-density survey of the Incan ruins of Machu Picchu (CAST 2010).

[9] Whether these tools fit our definition of virtual reality will depend on their eventual
use: the digital representation of a small-scale artefact embedded onto a museum
website that can be rotated by the viewer could be considered VR (the object is
computer-generated and is responding to user interaction); a large-scale terrain mesh
used as the basis for scoping an archaeological dig would not (the terrain is computer-
generated but is not presented to the user in a fashion that allows interaction); the
same terrain, incorporated into simulation of the site would be considered VR, if that
simulation was freely navigable by the user.

[10] SketchUp website, accessed 23 October 2009, http://sketchup.google.com. For subsequent software products mentioned in the text, see the bibliography for vendor and
site information.

3D Studio Max (2010a) are geared towards professional architects and include toolsets for creating photorealistic single-frame renderings and fixed animations; Autodesk's Maya (2010b) is best suited for character animation and rendering; and Presagis's Creator (2007–10) is designed for flight simulation and real-time interaction. Online virtual worlds typically include their own rudimentary modeling packages while giving primacy to avatar interaction and communication. Interactive panoramas are another popular option for providing virtual tours of extant urban environments.[11]

Choosing technology appropriate to the project's research objectives and desired end products allows the team to focus its efforts in an intelligent and efficient manner. Knowing at the onset that the desired end product is an online virtual world that includes avatar interaction will narrow the list of available technologies. Similarly, the work required to create a computer model that will be used to generate a five-minute animation is very different from the work required to create a model to be used in a real-time simulation. In the former, the project team would choose a modeling program with toolsets for generating animated sequences; the computer model would need to include only elements visible in the finished animation, constructed at a level of detail appropriate to the size of the object or structure in the final rendered scene.[12] A real-time simulation, in contrast, presumes that the user has the ability to interrogate the environment at will; the computer model needs to be constructed accordingly, with careful attention to data efficiency, spatial organization, and controlled levels of details. Shifts in project goals and desired end products become increasingly difficult to accommodate and potentially expensive to implement as the work progresses.

---

[11] See examples in Mapping Gothic France (2010) and the Ashes2Art project (2005).

[12] Detail, in the parlance of computer models, can be expressed in terms of the number of polygons (the individual faces that make up the object in 3D space) and textures (the digital imagery that is "mapped" onto the polygons to give them form). The number of polygons (and the amount of texture) used in a model can vary widely. An initial massing model may be simply a box consisting of six polygons. A highly detailed model of a complicated classical building could easily involve 150,000 polygons. In their directions for modellers creating content with SketchUp, Google (2010) suggests that "less than 500 [polygons] is ideal for most buildings" being loaded into GoogleEarth.

Multidisciplinary team

The team required for a VR project will be dictated by the goals of the research, the scope and complexity of the project, available funding, and the desired end product. With nominal training and free software, a small team of students could easily build a simple model of their campus (or a reconstructed ancient city) in SketchUp as part of a class assignment and upload it into Google Earth. At the opposite end of the spectrum, the development of a large-scale VR project requires a multidisciplinary team of scholars, administrators, and technologists. The scholars bring to play the necessary knowledge of the subject matter, the literature of the discipline, and the location of textual and material evidence critical to the reconstruction. Administrators and project managers facilitate the ongoing development and ensure the day-to-day advancement of the project. The job title "technologists" here refers to a broad category of scholars or research staff focused on the technical elements of the project, be they 3D computer modeling, website or database development, or systems support. Architecturally trained computer modellers, for example, will be able to ground reconstruction questions with real-world knowledge of building systems and structure. Subject experts may also be required to help steer the project team towards the most rigorous solution for specific questions of fact or conjecture. In the end, the skill sets necessary to complete a project successfully will be driven by the research, and it is imperative that project directors understand the requirements of the project and are realistic about the availability of that talent (and/or the time required for training personnel).

The training of project team members (and the next generation of VR scholars) is serious business. It is unrealistic to think that handing a graduate student the manual for a complicated piece of software is going to result in a beautifully crafted virtual environment. An appropriate training program for the next generation of VR scholars should be analogous to more traditional scholarly research. Academics producing monographs and peer-reviewed articles employ graduate students as research assistants and graduate them from simple tasks (gathering library books, online journal entries, and illustrations for works-in-progress) to those requiring deeper discipline-specific knowledge and that result in significant contributions to the field. These students learn about scholarly production under the tutelage of their academic mentor, and through involvement with the process commensurate with their skill level. The same paradigm is applicable to computer modeling and the creation of VR projects.

Workflow

The process required to construct a VR project will vary depending on the scope of the project, the technology being used, the amount and availability of textual and material evidence, and the size of the project team. A hypothetical small-scale project may involve a lone researcher creating rudimentary geometry, or "massing," of Alberti's Santa Maria Novella[13] to illustrate the mathematical relationships between building elements, with the intent to produce a model overlaid with textual commentary that can be accessed by students in Google Earth. Working with architectural line drawings available in any introductory architectural history textbook and using Google's SketchUp, this task could easily be accomplished in a few weeks. A hypothetical large-scale project might look to re-create the entire city of Florence as it existed at key moments in the Renaissance so that users could freely navigate through the virtual space and investigate the changes to the city over time. Instead of simple massing models, the project team wants to focus on very detailed, high-fidelity models of key architectural monuments and urban interventions.[14] An undertaking of this scale would likely take years to complete and involve a variety of subject experts to provide guidance on the different aspects of the project; architectural historians, Renaissance scholars, urban historians, technologists, and archaeologists would all be of equal importance. The amount of evidentiary resources required to build these models to any degree of veracity would be daunting. Sophisticated software would be required for both the modeling and user interaction with the VR environment. The point to be taken is that our two hypothetical projects have some base similarities—both involve buildings in Florence—yet their objectives and scope are vastly different and would require vastly different resources to be realized. It is, therefore, very important that researchers have a clear understanding of their objectives, the technology to be used, how it works, and how it will be applied to the project at hand. This will determine the work that will be required to complete the project, the time that it will take, and the project team that will be required to achieve a positive result.

---

[13] Completed between 1448 and 1470, Alberti's design for Santa Maria Novella in Florence was commissioned by the Rucellai family and incorporated elements of a prior Gothic structure with new Renaissance ideals of proportion and beauty.

[14] An exemplar of this type of high-fidelity model is the beautifully detailed Biblioteca Medicea Laurenziana in 3D (2005) created by the Italian company Panebarco & C. for the Italian Ministry of Cultural Assets. The project is freely available online through the Internet Culturale website, but requires installation of the Exhibits3D player; a gallery of images from the computer model is also posted.

Technical issues of user interaction and project dissemination aside, the creation of any virtual environment or computer reconstruction effort will move forward in predictable and iterative stages:

Research and information gathering. The first and most important task for the project team is to assemble all available materials about the site that might inform the reconstruction model or environment to be constructed. This dataset could include, but is not limited to, photographs of the site/building as it currently exists; historic photographs of the site/building; all books, articles, or unpublished work on the site/building; all primary and secondary textual references to the site with a specific focus on the time period to be represented in the computer model; excavation reports; any and all measured drawings of the site/building; any and all maps, drawings, or satellite images that reference the building or area to be reconstructed; documentation of prior reconstruction designs; documentation of contemporary structures that could be used as a stylistic or material reference; and any general references to the culture that might inform the ongoing project. This archive will be the primary resource for the scholars and modellers working on the reconstruction, and it will continue to grow through the life of the project. When the goal of the computer simulation is to provide users with a high-resolution re-creation of an architectural space that can sustain prolonged exploration and discovery, the veracity of the virtual environment must be beyond reproach. The importance of the initial research and the depth of the data archive, therefore, cannot be overemphasized.

Computer modeling. The 3D modeling portion of the VR project is analogous to crafting a work of non-fiction. Construction of a simple massing model establishes the framework for the work to follow, in the same fashion as the first draft outline of a book establishes the direction of the textual argument. For our hypothetical virtual Florence, a first step might be to choose the most appropriate historical map of the city to use as the base image, scale it in the virtual space to match the true dimensions and geographical coordinate system of the city itself, and add basic geometric shapes to represent buildings in the urban fabric. This phase of work will uncover gaps that are not fully addressed in existing research materials, reveal areas of uncertainty, and establish the direction of future work. From the initial massing models, highly detailed versions of the key architectural monuments could then be developed individually as one might work through the chapters of a book. Each monument would present its own challenges depending on its circumstances: a structure unchanged since the thirteenth century could be re-created based on images and as-built dimensions; one that exists but has been modified over time would require significantly more research to uncover and represent its various phases accurately; and a building that no longer exists but was critical to the architectural development of the Renaissance city will require deeper research, consultation with subject experts, and consideration of a different set of interpretive issues. Adhering to an acceptable level of academic rigour during the creation of a reconstruction model is often difficult because the modeling process demands concrete decisions from vague textual evidence and limited visual material. The London Charter project (2009), led by the Centre for Computing in the Humanities at King's College London and developed by a consortium of cultural heritage institutions involved with computer-based visualization, has established guidelines for best practices organized around implementation, aims and methods, research sources, documentation, sustainability, and access. Any VR project that involves reconstructed elements should be familiar with the objectives and recommendations of the charter, specifically those portions that deal with the documentation and dissemination of the project's methods and outcomes.

Formative discussion and development. In the editing stage of a print publication project, the author may write and rewrite passages to accommodate new information and new ideas. Similarly, during the development of a virtual environment, the work will alternate between traditional academic scholarship and computer modeling as the project matures and new questions are revealed, researched, analysed, and resolved. Throughout this cycle, research focused on specific areas of uncertainty will inform the modeling and augment the data archive. The scope of the questions posed in formative discussions with other members of the project team, subject experts, and members of the scientific committee will eventually narrow as knowledge about the modelled environment coalesces, the pieces of the digital puzzle fall into place, and the geometry is finalized and locked.

Dissemination. The project and its planned end product will dictate the development requirements for work beyond the creation of the 3D virtual environment. This final optimization and dissemination phase should be a part of the project plan from the onset, with time and money allocated appropriately. The end product for a process-driven project may simply be an academic publication that positions the new work within a discipline-specific knowledge base: development would be locked, the lessons learned documented, and graphics created from the computer model to illustrate the written text. At the opposite end of the spectrum, creation of the virtual environment may be only one piece of a larger-scale project to develop a first-person computer game that teaches players about history. An example is Europa 1400–The Guild (2002), a game that immerses players in a fanciful medieval European environment and allows them to generate their own characters, train in one of twelve different occupations (smith, tincture mixer, cleric, thief, banker, merchant, etc.), and interact with computer-generated characters and situations.[15] Beyond creation of the computer model, this project team had to design and animate characters, craft the storylines that the action follows, design and build the software interface, and package the game for distribution.[16]

Limited dissemination or controlled educational use may be possible at any stage of the construction, insofar as the state of the model accommodates the needs of the users and/or the lesson's stated learning objectives, but broader dissemination requires that the project be tested, user-hardened, and documented, and that the team has in place a release management plan and infrastructure for long-term user support. Developing projects that use established software from commercial companies is one strategy to simplify dissemination requirements. Building in-world in Second Life may have limitations, but once completed, Linden Lab has the software in place for users to create avatars, navigate through the virtual space online, and interact with other users. The First World War Poetry Digital Archive, for example, is an exemplary academic project that has been developed in Second Life.[17] Exhibition visitors are encouraged to explore archival materials within the three-dimensional context of a simulation of areas of the Western Front. Critical to the experience are Second Life's established tools for streaming audio and video. Similarly, GoogleEarth has the infrastructure in place to load simple SketchUp models, embed imagery on top of the three-dimensional models, and create pedagogical narratives with geo-referenced annotations and sequenced view points.

---

[15] Developed by German software company Cranberry Production GmbH (a subsidiary of dtp entertainment AG and the continuation firm of 4HEAD Studios) and released by Austrian game developer JoWooD Entertainment AG.

[16] Another gaming example that was inspired by history is Assassin's Creed 2 (2009) developed and released by Ubisoft (2001–08). Set in Venice in 1486, the game features "the look and feel of Italian Renaissance" and plays with some of the "what ifs of the time period" by allowing players to purchase devices designed by Leonardo da Vinci.

[17] *The First World War Poetry Digital Archive* (2010) is housed at the University of Oxford and focuses on materials related to the major British poets of the First World War. The website home page includes a link to information about the Second Life exhibition.

Case studies

The following cases studies illustrate the complexities of the development of large-scale VR projects. Of particular importance for this discussion is how the objectives of the research changed (or not) over the life of the project, how those objectives defined the choice of technology, the scope of the work, the project teams assembled, the workflow, and the end product.

The real-time Temple Mount installation at the Davidson Center, Jerusalem

At its onset, the real-time visual simulation model of the Temple Mount developed jointly by the Israel Antiquities Authority (IAA) and the Urban Simulation Team at UCLA and installed in 2001 at the Ethan and Marla David-son Exhibition and Virtual Reconstruction Center in Jerusalem (1996–2010) was defined by its eventual end product—a virtual environment that provides visitors to the Center an understanding of how the Temple Mount site might have appeared in the first century. In 2007, an expanded version of the simulation model was unveiled that includes a reconstruction of the eighth-century early Islamic structures on and around the Temple Mount. What is important to note is how the process of building the computer model became a significant knowledge-building exercise for the two IAA archaeologists involved—the renowned biblical scholar and archaeologist Ronny Reich on the first-century Herodian version of the project,[18] and Yuval Baruch, Jerusalem district archaeologist, on the Umayyad (660–750 CE) version (Figs. 1 and 2). Working with the author, each archaeologist was forced to internalize and analyse all available research on their respective eras in order to make informed reconstruction decisions.

The creation of the Umayyad version of the Temple Mount project involved almost two years of work for team members in both Los Angeles and Jerusalem. Jerusalem district archaeologist Yuval Baruch was the subject expert from the IAA responsible for gathering the evidentiary material, consulting with other subject experts in Israel as reconstruction questions were uncovered, and making the final reconstruction decisions. He was assisted by Liat Weinblum, website developer for the IAA, and a team of scholars across Israel that reviewed the material evidence and provided feedback on the computer model as it developed. In Los Angeles, the author was the primary modeller, supported by the administrative and technical personnel of the Urban Simulation Team. Development of the project followed the stages previously de-

---

[18] For additional discussion of the Herodian version of this project, see the papers by Fisch, Reich, and Snyder in Mattusch, Donohue, and Brauer (2006).

scribed. The terrain from the existing model of the first-century Herodian Temple Mount was used as a reference for the initial Umayyad massing. AutoCAD files of the excavation plans and elevation points gathered in the field were then imported into the 3D modeling software and used to position the main Umayyad buildings and the main north/south road of eighth-century Jerusalem relative to the southwestern corner of the Temple Mount platform.[19] As the model progressed, an archive of digital reference images was assembled by the team that included both site photographs and images of well-preserved contemporary Umayyad structures in the Trans-Jordanian desert and Syria. Construction on the individual areas of the model alternated with periods of intense research as new material was required. Work-in-progress files were made available to the project team in Israel, and these were shown interactively to the subject experts for comments and formative evaluation. Once the geometry was locked, the focus shifted to the visual elements of the model and optimizing the geometry for run-time efficiency.[20] In the final stage of the project, an overlay of site images was embedded into the model for use in presentations in the interactive classrooms at the Davidson Center in Jerusalem,[21] and historic notes and resources about the Umayyad period were posted on the Jerusalem Archaeological Park's website (2001–10). Additional IAA technologists and education department personnel joined the team in the months prior to the project launch to install new computer systems and train the archaeologist guides at the Davidson Center.[22]

---

[19] The modeling package used was a polygonal-surface modeller called Multi-Gen Pro (now Presagis Creator), chosen because it allows the type of data control required for real-time interaction.

[20] This involved revisiting the data structure and implementing nested levels of detail triggered by the user's position within the modelled environment (i.e., the distance of the user to a modelled building element determines the amount of detail that is displayed in the simulation).

[21] This technique allows visitors to immediately compare images of the extant ruins to the reconstruction simulation and provides a reference for their later explorations in the excavations.

[22] At the Davidson Center, both the Herodian and Umayyad reconstructions are shown in classrooms outfitted with benches to accommodate moderate-sized groups of people. Archaeologist guides talk with each group and lead virtual tours through the real-time reconstruction models to prepare the visitors for their exploration of the nearby excavation area. In the 2001 installation, the model was run on an SGI Oynx II IR-4 (the only computer capable at the time of running the simulation); at the time of the 2007 unveiling of the early-Islamic version of the reconstruction model, the SGI hardware was replaced with commodity personal computers running a Linux

Figure 1. The second phase of the real-time model developed by the Urban Simulation Team at UCLA for the Israel Antiquities Authority focused on the Umayyad (660–750 CE) buildings once adjacent to the Temple Mount platform in Jerusalem. Archaeologist guides at the Davidson Center give virtual tours through the model to prepare visitors for their explorations of the nearby excavation area.

Figure 2. Construction of the Umayyad model was informed by excavation data, artefacts uncovered on the site, and examination of well-preserved contemporary Umayyad structures in the Trans-Jordanian desert and Syria. Shown is the courtyard of Building 2 in the completed Umayyad model.

operating system. This combination of VR technology and infrastructure allows the guides the flexibility to tailor their virtual tours to the interests and knowledge base of unique groups of visitors.

The reconstruction model of Santiago de Compostela

Similarly, the UCLA reconstruction model (2005) of the Romanesque cathedral of Santiago de Compostela was initiated with a product-based agenda,
but principal investigator John Dagenais has come to give primary value to
the construction process. For the medieval visitor, the Cathedral of Santiago de Compostela was the culminating experience of their often arduous
pilgrimage, housing relics reputed to be the body of St James the Apostle
that were "rediscovered" in the ninth century in the northwesternmost
part of the Iberian Peninsula. The cathedral quickly became a destination
for pilgrims from Europe and beyond because of its importance as one of
two sites in Western Europe housing the remains of an apostle. After several
pre-Romanesque structures were built around the tomb, the Romanesque
basilica was constructed from about 1075 through the date of its consecra-
tion in 1211. At the onset of the digitization project, the goal was to provide
undergraduate students reading medieval Iberian literature for the first
time the experience of entering the church of St James in Compostela at the
conclusion of their ten-week course on the medieval pilgrimage (Figs. 3 and
4). After a less-enthusiastic-than-expected response from his students at the
unveiling of the computer model, Dagenais said that he "came to the conclusion that the use and value of such a thing as a VR Romanesque cathedral
would have to come from something other than my dreamed-of recreation of
a 'medieval' experience. In the end, what was important about it was not the
model one created, but what the process of this creation allowed one to do."[23]
Dagenais's work on the cathedral continues, with a new emphasis on including students in the reconstruction process and on the dialogue between subject experts as they collectively consider alternative reconstructions for the
earlier phases of the complex.

The team involved in the reconstruction model of Santiago de Compostela has
been a mix of technologists, scholars, and students. The first phase of the project was initiated in 2000 and completed in 2004.[24] Dagenais was the primary
scholar, coordinating the research that informed the reconstruction of the
Romanesque cathedral and interfacing with a team of subject experts in the

---

[23] John Dagenais, quoted from an unpublished essay shared with the author, August
2009.

[24] This initial phase was constructed under the auspices of the UCLA Cultural Virtual
Reality Lab (CVRlab) and co-directors Bernard Frischer (Classics) and Diane Favro
(Architecture and Urban Design). At UCLA, the Experiential Technologies Center
(2005) has succeeded the CVRlab.

Figure 3. The first phase of the Santiago de Compostela project focused on the Romanesque incarnation of this important cultural heritage site.

Figure 4. Users are able to freely navigate through the highly detailed virtual cathedral, exploring the space at will. Shown is the nave of the cathedral, looking east toward the choir and apse.

United States and Spain. Dean Abernathy, then a graduate student in the UCLA Department of Architecture and Urban Design, was the primary modeller on the project, supervising a small team of student workers and coordinating research trips for students enrolled in Dagenais's summer field sessions in Galicia. Work began with a significant amount of data collection. Drawings, photos, and texts were located, digitized, and archived. These textual and image references were combined with two-dimensional plan and section drawings to create the 3D geometry of the building. The process of constructing the virtual cathedral from excavation or theoretical reconstruction drawings brought to light a number of questions and issues regarding the accuracy of the archeological drawings. As a result, the team spent considerable time reconfiguring the geometry of the computer model as they explored a number of possible iterations and reconstruction theories. Once the modeling was completed, texture maps were built from photography of the modern-day cathedral and from similar sites taken by the modeling team and undergraduate students assisting on the project. This first phase of the project was used exclusively in classes at UCLA and for presentations at academic conferences. The current

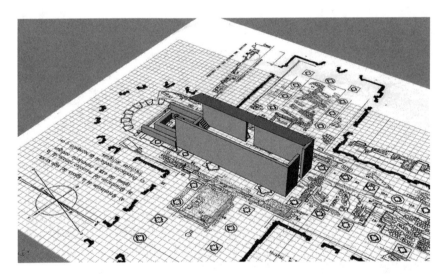

Figure 5. The second phase of the Santiago de Compostela project includes work on the pre-Romanesque versions of the building. Shown is an early test of the schematic massing of the Church of Alphonso II superimposed on a summary drawing of the archaeological excavations under the Romanesque cathedral from *Exploraciones arqueológicas en torno al Sepulcro del Apóstol Santiago* (Guerra Campos 1982, fig. 87).

work on the project involves an equally large professional team that includes Itay Zaharovits, a computer modeller with the ETC, a UCLA graduate student research assistant, technologists from the UCLA Center for Digital Humanities, and subject experts on two continents. This second phase of the project includes more work on the Romanesque, as well as reconstructions of the pre-Romanesque phases of the cathedral, and thus far has followed the same development cycle (Figs. 5–8). Negotiations are underway to include the revised model in an installation at the cathedral that will make the project available to a wider audience.

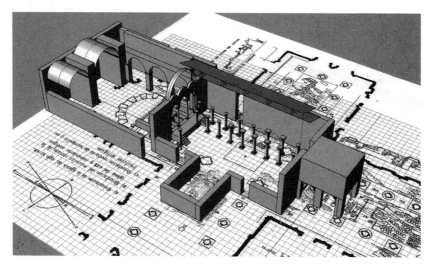

Figure 6. Simple schematic massing is the first step towards developing a viable reconstruction plan that successfully marries all known textual data with the extant remains. Shown is a possible reconstruction of the church of Anteltares (left) and the Church of Alphonso II (center mass) superimposed on a summary drawing of the archaeological excavations under the Romanesque cathedral from *Exploraciones arqueológicas en torno al Sepulcro del Apóstol Santiago* (Guerra Campos 1982, fig. 87). Within the Church of Alphonso II, rows of columns illustrate two different spacing options.

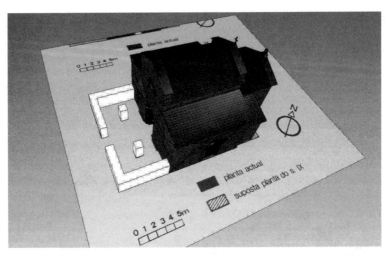

Figure 7. Digital images are placed on the base geometry to suggest the stone and tile building materials used in the region. Shown is the extant Chapel of Corticela superimposed on a plan of the original ninth-century structure from "La arquitectura prerrománica en Galicia" (Núñez Rodríguez 1975). (The white arms extending from the building suggest the foundations of the chapel prior to its modification to make room for the Romanesque cathedral.)

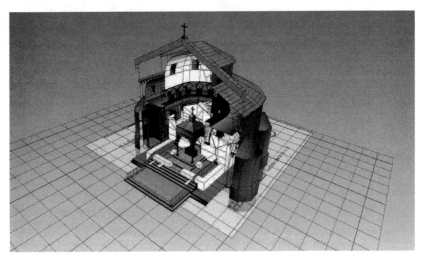

Figure 8. The 3D modeling process allows formal comparisons of buildings from different time periods. Here, two structures from the Santiago de Compostela complex are superimposed to allow comparison of scale and plan. Shown in white is the destroyed Antealtares church within the original Chapel of Corticela. The base plan is from Núñez Rodríguez (1975).

Opportunities for future VR work

VR and the 21st-century learner

The educational potential for academically-created virtual reality environ-ments far exceeds the process-based benefits enjoyed by the project teams. User exploration of VR environments has the potential to revolutionize the study of the built environment because it allows opportunities for teaching and learning that are not possible with other forms of instructional tech-nology. While there is little empirical evidence that specifically addresses student learning gains, one could easily make the argument that interac-tion with the VR environment would result in a probable increase in spa-tial, scale-related, temporal, and holistic understanding of the represented architectural space over use of static images and two-dimensional draw-ings. In educational situations where the use of the VR model is intended to build knowledge about the historic urban environment, it is also prob-able that highly detailed environments are more likely than their rudimen-tary online counterparts to engender student interest because they more closely replicate the actual experience of the physical world. Inferences can be drawn from the growing body of peer-reviewed publications on gam-ing and literature on online virtual worlds that report positive learning outcomes from student encounters with VR technologies: student engage-ment, motivation, and the accommodation of different learning styles are offered as selling points for EduGames such as Harvard's River City project (Virvou, Katsionis, and Manos 2005), and boosters for online virtual worlds point to opportunities for collaboration, exploratory learning, and engag-ing learning experiences (De Freitas 2008; Oblinger 2006; Wilson 2009).

Significant work is needed, however, to conceptualize and realize a frame-work wherein academically generated VR content can be repurposed for broader pedagogical use. Theatre historian Richard Beacham successfully used Second Life as a platform to test the use of virtual worlds for research, learning, and teaching with his Theatron 3 project (2009), developed through the King's Visualisation Lab (Theatron 2004). But, at the time of this writing, academic product in online worlds is far outweighed by substandard content. In his review of VR tools and their impact on the teaching of history, John Allison focuses on online worlds and acknowledges the pedagogical potential of the technology, stressing the need for history educators to engage with the technology in order to understand and help shape the circumstances under which it may best be used. He is, however, critical of the "vaguely his-torical and vaguely real worlds" currently available (2008, 343). That there is a limited selection of academically created and vetted digital work accessible to educators, students, and the general public can be explained in part by the dearth of options for easily sharing 3D content. It is far easier, and therefore more likely, for researchers to distribute static images and video clips generated from highly detailed models than to provide access to the models themselves.[25] A secondary problem is that the computer models, by themselves, are essentially raw data. Unless they were specifically created for pedagogical or public consumption, they are not going to include the contextual material, subject-expert commentary, and academic analysis that would make them engaging and effective tools for teaching and learning. Ideally, scholars would be able to share their content with educators through a vetted repository that also would host the run-time software necessary to integrate the 3D environments into the classroom, and to allow user-generated annotations and commentary. At minimum, this software would need to provide scholars and educators the mechanism to explore, annotate, craft narratives, and build arguments within the 3D space—in essence, facilitating the creation of virtual learning environments that could be broadly disseminated to educators and learners across grade levels and humanities disciplines. This software should also allow the raw computer models to be used as the basis for classroom learning activities, so that students can actively engage with the content to build knowledge by creating a personalized virtual learning environment.

Secondary research

There is also great potential for secondary research within academically generated VR environments, but at the time of this writing, the obstacles for sharing 3D work far outweigh the rewards. Koller and Humphreys outline a vision for "centralized, open repositories of scientifically authenticated virtual environments of cultural heritage sites" (2009, 7.4) in order to provide "efficient access to, interoperability between, and scientific authentication of the 3D models" (2009, 7.1). The authors recognize the many unresolved challenges inherent in this effort (digital rights management, metadata standards, visualization standards, version control, the development of analytic tools, mechanisms for indexing and searching within the 3D archive, interoperability of software/file formats, long-term preservation, and the

---

[25] For examples, see the Digital Roman Forum (2005) and Digital Karnak (2008) projects developed at the Experiential Technologies Center (2005) at UCLA. Other exemplars include the image-based projects developed by the Visual Media Center (2010) at Columbia University.

organizational complexity of coordinating peer-review), but do not address how scholars will actually use the 3D content once it is made available to them. To date, very little secondary research is being conducted with existing 3D work, outside of limited partnerships formally established with the original content producers.[26] To the extent that products—images, animations, and simple web versions of the 3D content—are being made publicly available, scholars can build knowledge from the visualizations and use them pedagogically, but VR environments have yet to facilitate the creation of actual substantive original work.

If providing access to 3D models and virtual environments is intended to enable scholars to build (literally and figuratively) upon the original content, then perhaps the more important unresolved challenge is to clarify the types of secondary research that might be conducted within a VR environment. How might scholars use VR environments for original research and what kind of interaction with the 3D model might they need to successfully undertake that research? There is, unfortunately, no single answer to those questions, and that is part of the challenge to enabling secondary research in VR environments. Functionality developed for one researcher could annoy another; the software necessary for one spatially based study may be at complete odds with the file format of the available VR world. Art historians might be interested in how a certain work of art was originally displayed in a historic structure: they would need access to the 3D model of that structure, a digitized version of the artwork, the software to manipulate the computer model, and the skill set to "hang" the artwork and interact with the results. A second set of scholars might be interested in re-creating an historical event: presuming a model of that environment exists, they would need access, the tools, and skill sets to populate the VR world, and run-time software to visualize the event over time. Other scholars may want the ability to measure distance in the VR environment (already possible in Google Earth), impose a grid on a representation of a building to enable a formal analysis, engage in discussions with other scholars in the context of the virtual world, or compare the characteristics of 3D objects from archaeological excavations across the globe.

It will never be possible to create a perfect interface or toolkit that will address the research questions of every humanities scholar. As evident from

---

[26] Here the term secondary research is broadly used to describe research conducted by a scholar not involved with the initial construction of the 3D model or VR environment.

the examples provided above, there are simply too many variants and too wide a range of possible interactions. Instead, standard tools that will work with specific types of 3D or VR content are in the process of being defined for cohorts of academics with common research goals. Ozmen and Balcisoy (2008), for example, have created virtual calipers for use on a laser scan of an archaeological artefact. We look to the next generation of VR developers to analyse the academic needs more fully, identify the toolsets necessary for scholarly interrogation of the various types of virtual environments, and create the necessary functionalities to open up access to secondary researchers in ways that will allow them to conduct their own experiments and interrogate the VR content in meaningful ways.

The challenges faced by large-scale VR projects

Difficulties scoping projects

Failure to fully grasp the technical requirements of a VR project could lead to its eventual downfall, a likely problem when the lead scholar has limited technical expertise or is pushing a project into uncharted territory. A case in point is the saga of *Arden: The World of William Shakespeare*, an ambitious project led by Edward Castronova from Indiana University to create a MMOG (Massive Multiplayer Online Game) in a virtual Elizabethan world that would allow players to interact with Shakespearean characters and participate in an online crafting economy, while at the same time provide researchers with a virtual laboratory for economic experiments.[27] Expectations in the virtual-worlds community were high, but after the first year of significant funding, the team began to pull back on the scope of the project. Writing on *Terra Nova* (2007), a blog about virtual worlds, Castronova cautioned his supporters to

> think "small Dungeons-and-Dragons world with a Shakespeare layer," not "World of Warcraft but with Hamlet." When we have built a small world that people like to play in, we will do some experiments. Small, limited objectives. The bigger objectives of the Arden project are on indefinite hold.

Castronova has been forthright about the lessons learned from the experience, citing technology and staffing problems and a project out of scope with the available budget (Talamasca 2009). To this, technology blogger Hiro Pendragon (2008) responded, "They should have known."

---

[27] For more background on the Arden project, see Castronova (2009) and Noah (2008).

Expense

There are a number of challenges that will limit future development of large-scale academic VR projects, the greatest of which is the enormous cost and time commitment required. The level of necessary infrastructure is considerable: hardware with high-end graphics-processing power, potentially expensive specialty modeling software, scanning equipment, a robust network, and data storage and network capabilities. The soft costs are even more onerous, considering the sheer number of people involved: project PIs, multidisciplinary subject experts and consultants, student researchers, administrators, modellers, designers, and other technologists as needed by the specific project. The most significant soft costs are those associated with research and modeling, i.e., the person-time required to extract the necessary data from the known archival materials and craft the 3D model into a cohesive virtual environment.

One strategy to minimize modeling work that is being promoted by Procedural, a commercial company that supports the film, television, gaming, and simulation communities, is to use typological rules to create computer-generated urban infill. The website for their CityEngine software describes the process:

> From various GIS (Geographical Information Systems) data given as input, such as population density, land usage, street network and building footprints, the CityEngine assigns type and style of the buildings to its footprints and calls the corresponding shape grammar rules to efficiently create detailed large-scale models. The shape grammar rules which are responsible for the creation of the actual building geometries are manually derived from photos and plans of remaining buildings, archaeological excavation data, and (historical) paintings (2009).

The viability of this approach for an academic VR environment would depend on the project's stated research goals and how (or if) the automatically generated content was explained to the user. With the case study of the Cathedral of Santiago de Compostela it is easy to imagine a time when it becomes desirable to build out the low-scale medieval town simply to illustrate the prominence of the church in the community. In the absence of a historical map or excavation data that details the town layout c. 1211, auto-generated geometry may be acceptable, but only if—as recommended by the London Charter—it is in some fashion made clear to the user that the "town" is a hypothetical reconstruction and details are provided that outline "the extent and nature of any factual uncertainty" (2009, 8).

Skill set required for content creation

The time required to train and nurture team members is another challenge. In personal correspondence, Dagenais has remarked upon the skill-set required to build VR projects:

> At the moment, the creation of these models is largely in the hands of a relatively small group of scholars. And it requires a level of technical skill that takes time to develop. It remains in the hands of the few. The tools for creating such models need to become much easier to use. Students should be able to build their own virtual medieval spaces, not just visit them. Scholars should be able to model their ideas of a structure and work interactively with other scholars in refinements or alternative solutions.[28]

Rather than expecting a wholesale democratization of VR modeling, perhaps the solution is merely to acknowledge the tiered levels of projects previously defined. There are certain tools and certain tasks that are appropriate for novices; a project to create a simple SketchUp model and load it in Google Earth is well within the comfort level of an average high school student.[29] More advanced students can take on more advanced projects with more complicated software and VR tools. But, as a project grows in scope and complexity, a skilled multidisciplinary team is required. To suggest otherwise is to diminish the intellectual demands of the task. The process of creating a virtual environment is in-and-of-itself valid, important scholarship. The amount of research required on large-scale projects is extensive, with an easy 5:1 ratio for time spent on research versus computer modeling.[30] Beyond this significant amount of traditional book-and-archive research, the modeling process requires technical skill, spatial awareness, knowledge of architectural form and history, and a certain level of computer competence.

---

[28] John Dagenais, to author quoted from an unpublished essay shared with the author, August 2009.

[29] In fact, Google has posted extensive content to facilitate the classroom use of Google technology in an educator's forum. Their website includes "getting started" tutorials and lesson plans with pre-made .kmz files.

[30] Time estimate based on the author's current project—a reconstruction of Chicago's World's Columbian Exposition of 1893 being developed through the Urban Simulation Team at UCLA (1996–2010).

There is merit to the suggestion that students and all interested scholars be involved in the making process. At some point in the future, perhaps there will be a technology shift that will enable opportunities for all, but until then, getting students involved at a high level may have to be limited to a fabricated experience. Pollini et al. (2005) proposed a "Virtual Reconstruction Console" created in Macromedia Flash that would allow users the opportunity to select from a list of reconstruction options. In Pollini's example, users analysing a visualization of the Mausoleum of Augustus can select different options for the statuary crowning the summit of the mausoleum (either a monumental statue of Augustus or a Roman horse-drawn chariot), the tree specimens planted on the mid-level structure (cypress, oak, or a combination of oak and laurel), and four different options for decorations around the ground-level entry. Another possible fabricated experience might include providing students with an archive of data from which they could conceivably develop a simple computer model. The point in either case is to engineer a low-risk situation that involves the users in the reconstruction process and has a high probability for a successful outcome.

Students' expectations for visual material

Promoting academic VR projects for broad pedagogical use is valid only in so far as students will willingly (and happily) embrace the environments as a form of instructional technology. Of concern is the constant exposure of today's students to Hollywood films laden with special effects and high-budget video games, genres that enjoy multimillion-dollar budgets. Dagenais relates his disappointment at the student reaction to the Compostela model:

> One of the first things I learned when I excitedly revealed the 3D model to my students in UCLA's Visualization Portal for the first time was that such a model, so thrilling to me, was no big deal for them. Many of them had spent much of their young lives moving through just such virtual spaces. What my VR cathedral lacked was the intensity of experience that made the virtual spaces and physical rules of 3D computer games so captivating and memorable.[31]

True, students are exposed to media, but that doesn't mean they can't distinguish between a fabricated environment and a scholarly reconstruction. In personal discussions with students and lifelong learners after experiences with a range of UCLA VR projects, the importance that they placed on the

---

[31] John Dagenais, quoted from an unpublished essay shared with the author, August 2009.

academic rigour employed in the creation of the virtual space was apparent. It was most important to them that the environments were based on factual evidence: they wanted to know that what they were seeing was as "real" as possible. Interest in details and visual fidelity were distant second and third to academic rigour. The objectives of Hollywood movies and the gaming world are different than those of the academic world, and users of VR environments appear to respect that difference.

Sustainability

A final challenge for VR projects is their long-term sustainability and preservation. In championing the need for an archive for 3D cultural heritage models, Koller and Humphreys suggest that "even digital models that are only two or three years old are losing their original functionality and information richness" (2009, 7:14). This issue is multifaceted and includes long-term preservation of project data, its resultant 3D model, and any products generated from the environment; project standards to enable such preservation; user access that preserves intended functionality; and the forward migration of software and hardware as technologies evolve. While a detailed discussion of the complexities of this issue is beyond the scope of this chapter, it is important to note that this is a serious challenge for VR projects. Efforts are underway to build specialized data archives. The Internet Archive (2001) includes a virtual world component "dedicated to the academic investigation and historical preservation of documentation of virtual worlds," and Koller and Humphreys (2009, 7:6) list a number of archives for very specific content (e.g., 3D scans of cuneiform tablets). Old-school computer games—admittedly not the focus of this essay—are enjoying resurgence in popularity through emulation software that recaptures their original look and feel, a strategy that may be applicable to VR environments (Gooding and Terras 2008). But for the vast majority of VR projects, long-term preservation and access is the responsibility of its original developers, and it is impossible to speculate whether this content is being preserved and to what extent it will be accessible in ten years.

Summary

Academically generated VR projects are uniquely suited to the study of the built environment and material culture. For educators, virtual environments such as the reconstruction model of Santiago de Compostela developed at UCLA offer students an experience impossible to replicate with static images and 2D drawings. Digital technology is also forging new ideas of scholarship:

multi-disciplinary work is more commonly accepted, new modes of publication are emerging, and new questions are being revealed by opportunities made possible only by digital work. The impact of these new paradigms on medieval and Renaissance scholars will undoubtedly increase as the technology becomes more accessible, new VR tools are developed, and new academically generated projects are made available for pedagogy and secondary research. But the realities of developing a VR project are daunting, and scholars considering this type of investigation should first familiarize themselves with the technological options, the range of extant projects, and the project development cycle so that they make informed decisions about project objectives, scope, and long-term dissemination strategies. The challenges for VR content creators are also significant, but surmountable; students and scholars are already engaging with VR technologies to explore reconstructed historical environments and gain insights into past civilizations. The task for future VR developers is to identify and build the toolsets necessary to more fully exploit the pedagogical and academic opportunities inherent in virtual reality.

WORKS CITED

Allison, John. 2008. "History Educators and the Challenge of Immersive Pasts: A Critical Review of Virtual Reality 'Tools' and History Pedagogy." *Learning, Media and Technology* 33 (4): 343–52.

Anderson, Linda M., Carolyn M. Evertson, and Jere E. Brophy. 1979. "An Experimental Study in Effective Teaching in First-Grade Reading Groups." *The Elementary School Journal* 79 (4): 193–223.

Ashes2Art. 2005. Coastal Carolina University. http://coastal.edu/ashes2art/florence/index.html.

Assassin's Creed 2. 2009. http://assassinscreed.uk.ubi.com/assassins-creed-2/#/menu.

Autodesk, Inc. 2010a. Autodesk 3ds Max. http://usa.autodesk.com/3ds-max/.

_____ 2010b. Autodesk Maya. http://usa.autodesk.com/maya/.

Barceló, Juan A., Maurizio Forte, and Donald H. Sanders, eds. 2000. *Virtual Reality in Archaeology*. Oxford: Archeopress.

Beacham, Richard. 2009. *THEATRON Final Report.* http://www.english. heacademy.ac.uk/archive/projects/theatron/theatron_final_report. pdf.

Bell, Mark W. 2008. "Toward a Definition of 'Virtual Worlds.'" *Journal of Virtual Worlds Research* 1 (1): 2–5.

Biblioteca Medicea Laurenziana in 3D. 2005. Internet Culturale, Ministry for Cultural Heritage and Activities, General Direction for Libraries, Cultural Institutes (ICCU). http://www.internetculturale.it/opencms/ opencms/it/pagine/percorsi/pagina_813.html.

Castronova, Edward. 2007. "Arden Slows Down, Takes Breather." *Terra Nova.* Blog. http://terranova.blogs.com/terra_nova/2007/10/arden-slows-dow.html.

_____ 2009. Home Page. Indiana University. http://mypage. iu.edu/~castro/.

Center for Advanced Spatial Technologies (CAST). 2010. University of Arkansas. http://www.cast.uark.edu/home.html.

Creator. 2007–10. Presagis Canada Inc./Presagis USA Inc. http://www. presagis.com/products_services/products/ms/content_creation/ creator/.

Davis, James, et al. 2002. "Filling Holes in Complex Surfaces Using Volumetric Diffusion." In *Proceedings of the First International Symposium on 3D Data Processing, Visualization, and Transmission.* http://graphics.stanford. edu/papers/holefill-3dpvt02/.

De Freitas, Sara. 2008. *Serious Virtual Worlds Report.* Joint Information Systems Committee (JISC): http://www.jisc.ac.uk/publications/documents/ seriousvirtualworldsreport.aspx.

Digital Karnak. 2008. University of California, Los Angeles. http://dlib.etc. ucla.edu/projects/Karnak.

Digital Roman Forum. 2005. University of California, Los Angeles. http://dlib. etc.ucla.edu/projects/Forum.

Experiential Technologies Center. 2005. University of California, Los Angeles. http://etc.ucla.edu.

Fang, Shiaofen, B. George, and M. Palakal. 2008. "Automatic Surface Scanning of 3D Artifacts." In *Proceedings of the 2008 International Conference on Cyberworlds*, 335–41. Washington, DC.

The First World War Poetry Digital Archive. 2010. University of Oxford. http://www.oucs.ox.ac.uk/ww1lit.

Gill, Alyson A. 2009. "Digitizing the Past: Charting New Courses in the Modeling of Virtual Landscapes." *Visual Resources* 25 (4): 313–32.

Godin, Guy, et al. 2001. "An Assessment of Laser Range Measurement on Marble Surfaces." In *Proceedings of the Fifth Conference on Optical 3-D Measurement Techniques*, 49–56. Vienna, Austria. 1–4 October 2001.

Gooding, P., and M. Terras. 2008. "'Grand Theft Archive': A Quantitative Analysis of the Current State of Computer Game Preservation." *The International Journal of Digital Curation* 2 (3): 19–41.

Goodrick, Glyn, and Mark Gillings. 2000. "Constructs, Simulations and Hyperreal Worlds: The Role of Virtual Reality (VR) in Archaeological Research." In *On the Theory and Practice of Archaeological Computing*, edited by G. Lock and K. Brown, 41–58. Oxford: Oxford University Committee for Archaeology.

Google. 2010. Google Earth. http://earth.google.com.

Guerra Campos, José. 1982. *Exploraciones arqueológicas en torno al Sepulcro del Apóstol Santiago.* Santiago de Compostela: Cabildo de la S.A.M. Iglesia Catedral de Santiago.

The Guild. 2002. JoWood Productions. http://www.the-guild.com/main.php.

Ikemoto, Leslie, Natasha Gelfand, and Mark Levoy. 2003. "A Hierarchical Method for Aligning Warped Meshes." In *Proceedings of the Fourth International Conference on 3D Imaging and Modeling.* http://graphics.stanford.edu/papers/mesh-dicing/.

The Internet Archive. 2001. http://www.archive.org/details/virtual_worlds.

The Jerusalem Archaeological Park. 2001–10. Israel Antiquities Authority. http://www.archpark.org.il/index.asp.

Johanson, Christopher. 2009. "Visualizing History: Modeling in the Eternal City." *Visual Resources* 25 (4): 403–18.

Kaneva. 2006–10. http://www.kaneva.com.

Koller, D., B. Frischer, and G. Humphreys. 2009. "Research Challenges for Digital Archives of 3D Cultural Heritage Models." *ACM Journal on Computing and Cultural Heritage* 2 (3): Article 7.

Levoy, Mark. 1997–2003. The Digital Michelangelo Project. Stanford University. http://graphics.stanford.edu/projects/mich.

Levoy, Mark, et al. 2000. "The Digital Michelangelo Project: 3D Scanning of Large Statues." In *Proceedings of SIGGRAPH 2000*, 131–44.

London Charter for the Computer-Based Visualisation of Cultural Heritage. 2009. King's Visualisation Lab and King's College London. http://www.londoncharter.org.

Mapping Gothic France. 2010. Media Center for Art History, Columbia University. http://www.mappinggothicfrance.com and http://www.learn.columbia.edu/mgf/test.html.

Mattusch, Carol C., A. A. Donohue, and Amy Brauer, ed. 2006. *Common Ground: Archaeology, Art, Science and Humanities. Proceedings of the 16th International Congress of Classical Archaeology.* Oxford: Oxbow.

McCarty, Willard. 2004. "Modeling: A Study in Words and Meanings." In *A Companion to Digital Humanities*, edited by Susan Schreibman, Ray Seimens, and John Unsworth, 254–70. Oxford: Blackwell.

Microsoft Research Maps. 2010. Microsoft Corporation. http://msrmaps.com/Default.aspx.

Niccolucci, Franco, ed. 2000. *Virtual Archaeology: Proceedings of the VAST Euroconference.* Oxford: Archeopress.

Ward, M. Noah. 2008. "Arden: World of Shakespeare Interview." Channel Massive. 5 March. http://www.channelmassive.com/blog/?p=105.

Núñez Rodríguez, Manuel. 1975. "La arquitectura prerrománica en Galicia." PhD diss., Santiago de Compostela Universidad, Facultad de Geografía e Historia, Departamento de Historia del Arte.

Oblinger, Diana G. 2006. "Simulations, Games, and Learning." ELI White Paper, EDUCAUSE Learning Initiative. http://www.educause.edu/ELI/SimulationsGamesandLearning/156764.

Open Simulator. 2010. Open Simulator. http://opensimulator.org/wiki/Main_Page.

Ozmen, C., and S. Balcisoy. 2008. "A Software System to Work with 3D Models in Cultural Heritage Research." In *Beyond Illustration: Digital 2D and 3D Technologies as Tools of Discovery in Archaeology*, edited by B. Frischer and A. Dakouri-Hild, 87-97. Oxford: Archaeopress.

Pendragon, Hiro. 2008. "Arden: A Tragedy of Errors." Second Tense. Blog. 27 March. http://www.secondtense.com/2008/03/arden-tragedy-of-errors.html.

Pollini, John, Lynn Swartz Dodd, Karen Kensek, and Nicholas Cipolla. 2005. "Problematics of Making Ambiguity Explicit in Virtual Reconstructions: A Case Study of the Mausoleum of Augustus." In *Theory and Practice: Proceedings of the 21st Annual Conference of CHArt: Computers and the History of Art*, edited by Anna Bentkowska, Trish Cashen, and Hazel Gardiner. London: British Academy. http://www.chart.ac.uk/chart2005/papers/pollini.html.

Procedural City Engine. 2009. Procedural, Inc. http://www.procedural.com/cityengine/.

Reilly, Paul. 1991. "Towards a Virtual Archaeology." In *CAA90: Proceedings of the 18th Conference*, edited by K. Lockyear and S. Rahtz, 133–39. Oxford: Tempvs Reparatvm.

Rhinocerous. 2007. McNeel. http://www.rhino3d.com/.

Roussou, Maria. 2004. "Learning by Doing and Learning Through Play: An Exploration of Interactivity in Virtual Environments for Children." *ACM Computers in Entertainment* 2 (1): 1–23.

Santiago de Compostela project website. 2005. University of California, Los Angeles. http://www.etc.ucla.edu/research/projects/compostela.htm.

Sirikata. 2010. http://www.sirikata.com.

Surendran, NK, et al. 2009. "Contemporary Technologies for 3D Digitization of Maori and Pacific Island Artifacts." *International Journal of Imaging Systems and Technology* 19 (3): 244–59.

Talamasca, Akela. 2008. "Edward Castronova Reveals Lessons Learned from Arden." *Massively.* Blog. 23 March. http://www.massively. com/2008/03/23/edward-castronova-reveals-lessons-learned-from-arden/.

Theatron – Theatre History in Europe. 2007. King's Visualisation Lab, Centre for Computing in the Humanities, King's College London. http://www. kvl.cch.kcl.ac.uk/THEATRON/.

There. 2010. Makena Technologies, Inc. http://www.there.com.

Ubisoft. 2001–08. Ubisoft Entertainment. http://www.ubi.com/US/default. aspx.

The Urban Simulation Team at UCLA. 1996–2010. University of California, Los Angeles. http://www.ust.ucla.edu/ustweb/ust.html.

_____ 1996–2010. Temple Mount Project. University of California, Los Angeles. http://www.ust.ucla.edu/ustweb/Projects/israel.htm.

_____ 1996–2010. "The World's Columbian Exposition of 1893." University of California, Los Angeles. http://www.ust.ucla.edu/ustweb/Projects/columbian_expo.htm.

Van Eck, Richard. 2006. "Digital Game-Based Learning: It's Not Just the Digital Natives Who Are Restless." *EDUCAUSE Review* 41 (2): 17–30.

Virtual World SIG. 1999–2007. *Digital Media SIG.* SD SV Forum. http://virtualworldsig.com/.

Virvou, Maria, George Katsionis, and Konstantinos Manos. 2005. "Combining Software Games With Education: Evaluation of its Educational Effectiveness." *Educational Technology & Society* 8 (2): 54–65.

Visual Media Center. 2010. Department of Art History and Archaeology, Columbia University. http://www.learn.columbia.edu.

Whyville. 1999–2010. Numedeon Inc. http://www.whyville.net/smmk/nice.

Wilson, Lee. 2009. *Best Practices for Using Games and Simulations in the Classroom: Guidelines for K-12 Educators.* SIIA (Software & Information Industry Association). Education Division. http://www.spa.org/index. php?option=com_docman&task=doc_download&gid=610&Itemid=318.

Simulating Splendour: Visual Modelling of Historical Jewellery Research

David Humphrey

Royal College of Art, London

david.humphrey@rca.ac.uk

In the absence of a substantial body of extant objects[1] dating to late medieval and early Renaissance Northern Europe, developing knowledge of the period's jewellery as a cohesive body, and details of its individual jewels, has traditionally relied on text-based works such as inventories and wills. These resources are often given additional support by depictions of jewels in painted or sculpted works, augmenting what may be revealed by analysis of the relatively few objects that have survived. This approach relies heavily on provenance[2] in substantiating claims relating to a range of issues, from ownership to physical form. Harnessing text- and image-based resources has resulted in outstanding findings from scholars including John Cherry (1992), Ronald Lightbown (1978, 1992), and Éva Kovács (2004): these, and others, have brought considerable new light to bear on aspects of ownership, stylistic change, and to some extent design development during the late medieval and early Renaissance periods. Cherry's work, across a wide range of issues from jewellery to poetry in the late medieval period, has brought much-needed cohesion to what previously had been disparate areas of study. Both Lightbown and Kovács have examined and analysed archival records of ownership of medieval jewellery with a degree of precision and depth almost unrivalled in the field. Their works may be seen as outstanding examples of a methodological approach to research traceable to eighteenth- and nineteenth-century antiquarianism, if not

---

[1] For examples of extant jewellery objects from the period, see for example Fliegel et al. (2004), and Scarisbrick et al. (2007). See also object collections in the British Museum, London, Musée National du Moyen Âge, Paris, and the Victoria and Albert Museum, London.

[2] In the context of this work *provenance* is taken to mean evidence, including inventory entries or items in wills, that validates or corroborates claims of ownership, historical association, or physical form.

ISBN 978-0-86698-499-7 (online)   ISBN 978-0-86698-474-4 (print)

New Technologies in Medieval and Renaissance Studies 3 (2012) 429–453

earlier, but still relevant today.[3] In their approach, text-based sources are examined, interpreted, and applied in support of an argument or to explain aspects of the history of a specific object or collection. No criticism of such a methodological approach is suggested here; that approach may be seen as providing the academic rigour underpinning more technologically-driven methods that engage digital modeling and visualization as a means of exploration and analysis. Image-based material is often approached in a similar way, but too often researchers of lesser caliber than those mentioned above incorporate the presence of images in academic output in an illustrative or supportive role, rather than in pursuit of analysis.

Both text- and image-based approaches have been augmented in the past one hundred years by the application of scientifically-driven analysis to historical objects in what may be thought of as object-based pathology. The work of Sheridan Bowman and Colleen Stapleton (1998) is a high-quality example of the advancement of knowledge and context through the application of such an approach. Their work on the All Souls' Jewel, including the use of metallurgical and scanning electron microscope analysis, revealed much about the nature of the materials and techniques of construction employed in fabricating the piece. More significantly, their findings point to the wider use of such techniques in considering other artefacts dating to the late medieval period in Northern Europe. Reinhold Baumstark's detailed analysis of the Goldenes Rössl—a 62cm high example of sculptural goldsmithing made in 1405 that includes a horse and figures modelled in three dimensions—has demonstrated what may be achieved through the combination of traditional and scientifically-driven methodologies employing X-ray and UV-light analysis (1995). Baumstark's work has revealed much about how the object was constructed together with considerable insight into the techniques associated with that construction, particularly so in relation to the use of enamel on three-dimensional forms, and the often crude workmanship employed in areas that would not be seen on the finished object.

Text-based, image-based, and scientifically-driven methods make use of logical, often sequential, patterns of analysis. Text sources, such as inventories and wills, are trawled for data pointing to provenance and details of ownership history: such data are usually bound together into a narrative format

---

[3] Many publications, including the leading academic journal in the field, *Jewellery Studies*, published by the Society of Jewellery Historians in London, feature research that is carried out using this type of approach to the gathering, distillation, and projection of new knowledge.

for publication. Image sources are subjected to scrutiny for indications of the physical form and structure of objects, for connections to descriptions in text-based inventories, and for their possible value as historical visualizations of individual jewels still extant today. Scientifically-driven approaches are often structured via sequential processes: samples are taken from objects that are then subjected to either destructive or non-destructive examination, such as reduction by fire or, in the latter case, examination by X-ray. Individually, and collectively, these methods yield much useful data, but they do not serve to show, for example, how objects interacted with their physical surroundings, the actual lighting conditions in which they were experienced, or the pull a jewel may have exerted on a garment when worn. Digital modeling and visualization systems that harness the power of software to simulate real-world physical properties offer the opportunity to build on the knowledge provided by traditional approaches through the creation of simulated objects which can be interrogated in ways not possible using those traditional approaches. For example, what might the back of a brooch depicted in a painting look like, and how might that brooch have moved in relation to the garment it was attached to? A three-dimensional digital simulation can model the back of the brooch based on expert knowledge of how such objects were generally constructed. A digital simulation allows the attachment of that modelled brooch to a simulated garment. Both the brooch and the garment can then be given digital equivalents of their true material characteristics so that when they collide, they will interact as they would do if made of real materials. Digital research methods of this nature offer the opportunity to pose questions and explore answers about objects and their use that cannot be examined by traditional methods.

Further augmentation of established approaches to research

Unless they are fortunate enough to be able to handle museum objects, most researchers experience the physical presence of historical jewels via museum display: captive inside showcases, often mounted in a way that reveals the front of an object but not its back, and rarely displayed in the context of their actual deployment on the surface of an appropriate garment. Such approaches to display fail to provide the supporting and contextualizing environment in which jewels were originally worn and experienced by wearers and those who viewed them. Considered from the perspective of those who design environments for the display of historical jewellery, practical constraints make it impractical to re-create the true circumstances of how such objects interacted with their original owners and their day-to-day environments. Most museum displays use lamp types and illumination levels of electric-based spotlighting to emphasize the brilliance of gemstones and metalwork; however, historical evidence suggests that even the most magnificent of jewels were not experienced in the equivalent of spotlighting, but in diffused, often poor-quality daylight, moonlight, and dim artificial light in various forms, including candlelight. Different lamp types, and their associated temperature characteristics, have an enormous impact on how colour, reflection, refraction, and polish are experienced. The visual experience created by most museum lighting situations hinders an accurate understanding of how jewels were experienced in the context of their original use.

How historical jewels are displayed in museums raises the issue of authenticity of *siting*.[4] Many, if not most, museums, in addition to confining jewels inside glass cases, mount items by their back face onto the front face of some form of board. This is done for many reasons, including security, viewability for the public, and to display a selection of pieces in close proximity to one another. Such an approach fails to locate the objects in even a vague representation of their original environments of fine fabrics and human bodies. To attempt to re-create such environments physically would be prohibitively costly even to achieve a modicum of simulative authenticity and would produce a potential minefield of controversy concerning what may, or may not, constitute an authentic environment. For such reasons, the way that historical jewels are displayed in public collections and special exhibitions is the result of practical considerations driven by cost, time, and the expertise available to mount them. Museums will not display jewels on actors, in correct period clothing, or via an animatronic dummy (a figure in a display made to simulate human movement through a combination of electronics and robotics) in the foreseeable future, except perhaps in circumstances in which the jewels are part of some form of performance art.

In the field of historical jewellery research there is growing interest in finding alternative or additional ways to expand our experience and understanding into a broader contextualized view that gets closer to the experiences of people living in the distant past. How to facilitate this contextualization is problematic given the well-established methodologies that pervade research in the field and the to-be-expected resistance to change. The key objection

---

[4] *Siting* is concerned with the precise location of jewels on garments and those locations in relation to the underlying human body. Many jewels of the period were positioned for practical reasons (e.g., the joining of two open edges of a garment) or had locations that had long histories as sites for jewels (e.g., a jewel worn over the heart, possibly as a focus of psychological protection).

to the use of research strategies that take a more speculative approach is centred on a powerful argument: any approach that seeks to "re-create" the mindset of, for example, an individual in late medieval society risks creating an invention or illusion incapable of support to any degree of rigour acceptable to even the most receptive of thinkers in the field.[5] Such concerns are right and proper, but should not be seen to preclude attempts to examine aspects of the contemporary circumstances that played on the formation of attitudes: in essence, aspects of what today we consider as "lifestyle."

The digital domain can be applied to historical jewellery scholarship to examine text- and image-based sources in new ways. Traditional approaches to those very same sources have met with logistical, financial, and/or physical constraints; whereas digitally based research methodologies can pursue new insights by exploiting the adaptable nature of digital data. Moreover, the academic rigour of these new research methods can be established. Organizations such as The London Charter have begun to set common standards for digital approaches to historically related research against which the emerging methods can be tested.[6]

Digital resources and historical jewellery research

Digital resources offer historical jewellery research opportunities to create illusions of reality directly through modeling and visualization and to sort, match, and contrast data via the analysis of text, images, database, or spreadsheet entries and volumetric data. The successful positioning of such resources into the various methodological approaches in use within the field is an issue of integration in the first instance and not one of substitution: digital resources need to work in conjunction with other approaches. "Integration," considered more expansively, cloaks the even more central issue of collaboration, which in its various forms is increasingly becoming both a necessary, as well as a desired, strategy in developing more contextualized views of historical objects. Digital resources, acting as mediating agents, not only facilitate collaborative human activity, but also function as conduits through which data can be configured and reconfigured according to the demands of research. Within the bounds of what current technology can de-

---

[5] Trying to understanding medieval attitudes is a constant problem for those working in all strands of medieval history. For research that examines aspects of those attitudes, see for example Le Goff (1988) and Schmitt (1990).

[6] See The London Charter website, accessed 22 November 2010, http://www.londoncharter.org/bibliography.html for a useful range of relevant literature and other resources.

liver, the same data can be displayed as numbers in a spreadsheet or as a visualized object via a rendering application.[7] It is this flexibility, coupled with the mediating opportunities that digital technologies in general can provide, that makes them of significant value in augmenting existing, and more established, historical jewellery research methodologies. Databases, spreadsheets, and similar tools offering search-and-retrieve, formulae-based calculation, and statistical analysis, although of potential value, remain at present largely unexplored for reasons that are not altogether clear. The lack of data to populate them with is certainly one reason, as is the more basic question of what might be done with results. For example, the occurrence of rubies (and their cuts, where noted) in a particular inventory is in itself interesting, but from a statistical point of view, given the usually small number of items listed in inventories, what is revealed is no more than that the owner had so many rubies. Ultimately, perhaps such an analytical approach may be at odds with our natural inclination to enjoy such objects visually rather than as pieces of data. Digital modeling and visualization systems, however, have a direct relevance to, and clear potential for, expansion of our knowledge not only of the physical nature of historical jewellery but also of *how* items were worn and the conditions in which an item was experienced. The digital domain offers researchers a location in which objects, environments, and situations can be modelled, animated, visualized, and questioned in the context of the imitation of gravity, different types of fabric, mounting constraints such as pins, clips, clasps, and hooks, the relevance of lighting conditions, and the effects of human locomotion on the physical choreography of an object worn on a garment. Taken together, such capabilities provide researchers with the means to exploit the potential of digital simulation.[8]

---

[7] Although it may be considered an early work in presenting the use of digital technologies in relation to both real and virtual reconstructions of historical objects, Higgins, Main, and Lang (1996) is still a key publication for those working in the field. Of the more recent publications in the field, see for example Denard (2005). The issue is also addressed in Humphrey (2009).

[8] *Digital simulation* is a term used throughout this work. It is considered here as the creation of digitally based entities that seek to be structural and/or visual equivalents of either their real-world counterparts, or entities with no real-world counterpart that are built and displayed using techniques and technologies that strive to equivalence of real-world entities. For a generic view on digital simulation in historical research, see for example Fernie and Richards (2004).

Simulating splendour: Visual modelling of historical jewellery research

The use of digital modeling and visualization systems in historical object research can be traced back to the late 1960s.[9] The author has been involved in the field, as well as in a parallel career as a goldsmith and jeweller, for twenty-five years and probably qualifies as something of a pioneer. Work by other pioneers impacted on the development of the author's work described here at its germination stage: principally that carried out by Mark Bloomfield and Louise Schofield in the mid-1990s on the Treasury of Atreus at Mycenae (1996) and specifically Bloomfield's model and visualization of a Mycenaean inlaid dagger. By today's standards both the model and its visualization are primitive, but by the standards of the time they demonstrated what could be achieved through a combination of technology and incisive thinking deployed in pursuit of greater historical understanding. That combination is still a worthy touchstone for high-quality research today and was a cornerstone in the development of the Simulating Splendour project.

Simulating Splendour: Visual Modelling of Historical Jewellery Research,[10] is the most recent aspect of long-term research begun by the author in 1996 with his doctoral work at the Royal College of Art in London, titled "iReEn: Integrated Research Environment. An innovative computer-based, collaborative, research-to-prototype environment for use in the decorative and applied arts, with specific focus on its application in historical jewellery research." Aspects of that research were refined with the aid of a grant award from the British Academy in 2003 for a project titled "The development and application of digital animation techniques to the study of jewellery and clothing worn at the Valois Burgundian court, c.1364–c.1477." Both projects focused on developing and exploring the use of digital modeling, simulation, and visualization to reveal more about jewels and their use at the courts of the Valois dukes of Burgundy between c. 1364 and c. 1477. The Simulating Splendour project was devised to bring together, and develop further, aspects of the previous projects: rationales for modeling strategies, the role of light and lighting in the process of viewing jewels, and, more significantly, the latter's possible role in determining both the design and surface char-

---

[9] For a comprehensive bibliography of major works of more recent date, see the London Charter website, accessed 23 October 2009, at http://www.londoncharter.org/bibliography.html.

[10] The Simulating Splendour project was funded by the Leverhulme Trust, beginning in October 2005. Additional funding, specifically for hardware, was provided by the London Development Agency.

acteristics of the various elements composing individual jewels in works of the late medieval to early Renaissance period. Recent advances in modeling, such as the introduction of subdivision modeling[11] in various software applications, and the development of so-called unbiased rendering engines,[12] were seen as being of major value to the level of visual fidelity that could be achieved.

Locations, sources, and issues of data acquisition

Burgundian ducal courts were famed throughout Europe for their magnificence, opulence, and sumptuous excess.[13] What remains today from that world is only a minute percentage of what was produced for it—which means, for researchers, a greater dependence on historical representations of jewellery in other art forms with their attendant problems of artistic licence in representation. The most productive of those sources are the works of early Netherlandish painters, including Jan van Eyck (before c. 1395–before July 9, 1441), Rogier van der Weyden (1399/1400–1464), and Petrus Christus (c. 1410/20–1475/76). Works by these and other artists of the period contain information about jewels that varies in its veracity from relatively accurate representations of geometrical structure to more gestural depictions of the effects of light on, or through, surfaces and objects. In any case, paintings, of however high a degree of visual fidelity, are ultimately interpretations resulting from an artist's translation of what is seen and captured through the use of brushes and paints onto a panel or canvas. This is a crucial point in assessing their reference-value to any attempt at integrating that value into the development of simulations of the jewels to which they allude. A three-dimensional digital simulation of a jewel, constructed solely on the basis of data extracted from a pictorial representation, will be no more than a simulation of what is depicted in the representation: a two-dimensional planar image of a dinosaur's head printed on a cereal packet, when cut out and folded, will be no more than the two-dimensional image folded into a

---

[11] Subdivision modeling is a technique for creating smooth models without necessarily increasing the number of polygons required to define a model to an unacceptably high count. A good introduction to subdivision modeling may be found at *Subdivision-modeling.com: a sub-division modelers primer*, http://www.subdivision.org. Accessed 17 February 2012.

[12] For an overview of this form of rendering technology, see for example Maxwell Render, accessed 22 November 2010, http://www.maxwellrender.com/.

[13] There is extensive literature on the Burgundian court between c. 1364 and c. 1477. On the sumptuousness of the court itself, see for example Fliegel et al. (2004).

three-dimensional form; it will not magically become a fully formed three-dimensional head convincing in its accuracy for any viewer located in any orientation to it.

Antonio Criminisi's (2001, 2002) work on metrology (the science and study of measurement), and its application to the study of historical painting, has established techniques for the extraction of data from two-dimensional images that offers considerable potential for the three-dimensional digital simulation of objects. His more recent research with Martin Kemp (2006) extends those possibilities. Criminisi's approach is a technically sophisticated one that generates convincing results, but it is precise only in relation to the particular image it is based on and does not compensate for the interpretation of the artist. The value of metrology to Simulating Splendour was appreciated from the planning stage, but as one tool in a large array of tools and techniques, rather than as a key or core element. Metrological techniques cannot supply detailed data on gemstone cuts and the precise details of how such stones were mounted; neither can any other technique of data extraction. Even the works of Jan van Eyck are not accurate enough in their detail to be capable of revealing with total accuracy what was being recorded.

In the light of such shortcomings, it was evident from the earliest stages of the project that paintings and sculpted works were of considerable value as general works of reference, but that they required supporting or clarifying data to make them of primary value to the research. These data are contained in pieces of jewellery that have survived from the period, which, although limited in number, contain materials and technical details that can be taken as being close to ubiquitous during the period. Gold, for example, was generally of a consistent hue from object to object because most objects were constructed using metal conforming to the so-called "touch of Paris" (19.2 carat quality). Specific gemstones display colouration appropriate to their type (within understood patterns of modulation);[14] and as naturally occurring materials are time-period independent, their colour does not change over time except in extremely rare cases. Finally, gemstone cuts have an established historical timeline of technical development: as a consequence, the physical forms of gemstones found in jewels at the Valois Burgundian courts can be extrapolated directly or inferred with an acceptable level of accuracy by reference to extant objects from the period which have not suffered remodeling between then and now.

---

[14] For technical details on gemstones, see for example Webster (1998).

What eventually emerged from a detailed and rigorous consideration of what data were needed, and how to gather that data, was a methodological structure combining technical methods and, in the greater part, a methodology employing a combination of heuristic and imitative approaches to data gathering and usage. When coupled with the technical resources of the software applications to be used to simulate the real-world physical characteristics of specific materials—including reflection characteristics of metal, indices of refraction associated with certain gemstones, and the ability to apply digital simulations of physical constraints to mechanisms such as hinges so that they operate in the digital domain as a real-world equivalent would operate—a powerful suite of tools, techniques, and methods was established.

Methods, theoretical issues, technical detail, and outcomes

The approach followed throughout the project consisted of the following stages:

★ identification of specific aims and objectives for each modeling and visualization scenario;

★ extraction of data from sources including paintings and illuminated works and the development of strategies for handling that data. Data extracted included information on the physical structures of objects and the cuts of gemstones;

★ modeling of the object, or objects, in a scene using a combination of Robert McNeel and Associates's Rhinoceros[15] software (commonly known as "Rhino"), Skymatters's Mudbox (now an Autodesk product)[16] and Pixologic ZBrush.[17] These applications were used in combination: Rhinoceros for the basic modeling of objects exploiting both its NURBS-modeling capabilities and its dimensional accuracy, and Mudbox and ZBrush for their support of subdivision modeling[18] and its application to selected areas of objects for local detailing of geometry. Models originated in Rhino were freely passed to Mudbox and ZBrush and back to Rhino for export to the next stage in the process;

---

[15] Rhinoceros, NURBS modeling for Windows, accessed 22 November 2010, http://www.rhino3d.com.

[16] Autodesk USA, accessed 22 November 2010, http://usa.autodesk.com/#.

[17] Pixologic, accessed 22 November 2010, http://www.pixologic.com.

[18] In NURBS-modeling, objects are defined by curve and resulting surface data rather than by polygon data.

★ export of modelled objects to Avid Softimage XSI (now an Autodesk product)[19] in circumstances that required the use of its Ageia NovodeX physics simulation engine to examine object-to-object collisions and the deformations that might result from, for example, a brooch coming into contact with the material of a garment, and then to Next Limit Technologies' Maxwell Render[20] for rendering. If simulation was not required, then the objects were passed directly to Maxwell Render for rendering;

★ the simulation and rendering of objects and scenes using the 16-node renderfarm[21] in the Royal College of Arts Centre for Jewellery Research, managed via Microsoft Windows Server 2003[22] and Virtual Vertex Muster[23] distributed processing software; and

★ the final output in a still or moving image format appropriate for the required purpose.

All of the software applications used in the course of the research were "out of the box": they were not modified, customized, or adapted in any way for the purposes of the research. In all cases the resources (tools, file output types, etc.) within specific applications were perfectly adequate to carry out the work.

The following sequence (Figs. 1–4) shows examples of output following the sequence described above. In Figure 1 the model of a ring, found in much the same basic form in various paintings from the period, has been modelled as a perfect object using Rhino: its hoop is perfectly symmetrical, its gemstone equally so. Global and local signs of usage and wear are not considered in this example: such detail can be added either via "colliding" it with a modelled

---

[19] See n. 16, above.

[20] Maxwell Render, accessed 22 November 2010, http://maxwellrender.com.

[21] A renderfarm is a group of computers used to render computer animation or, for example, compute the effects of collisions between objects in a scene. Individual frames of an animation may be processed on the basis of one frame to one computer, or one frame may be distributed across the group. Renderfarms are controlled and managed using software that distributes the frames to the computers that make up the farm.

[22] Microsoft Windows Server 2003 R2, http://technet.microsoft.com/en-us/windows-server/bb512919. Accessed 17 February 2012/.

[23] Virtual Vertex, http://www.vvertex.com/muster-details.php. Accessed 17 February 2012.

representation of a finger or other object using Softimage XSI to simulate natural distortion and to create a new geometry resultant from that collision. Alternatively, or additionally, the model may be altered directly in Mudbox or ZBrush using a graphic tablet and pen to push and pull the digital geometry. This approach is particularly suited to simulating construction techniques such as hammering and the use of others tools including pliers, saws, and files.

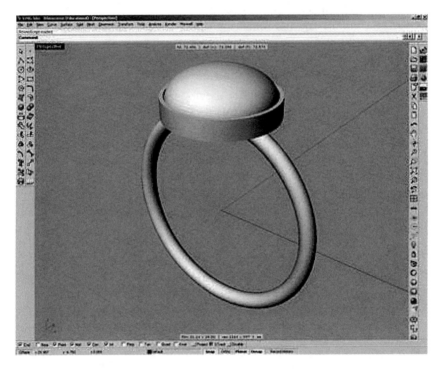

Figure 1. See image plates for a colour version of this figure.

The model, when developed to a final stage, or in an in-progress state, was saved as a DXF file and exported, in this case directly to Next Limit Technologies Maxwell Render. Maxwell Render is arguably the most sophisticated of a new generation of rendering applications that produce images (and animations) by simulating the physical properties of light. Although not foolproof, given sufficient time this approach will generate images of extraordinary accuracy with the bonus of a massive reduction in the inclusion of visual aberrations (known as artefacts in computer visualization terminology) in the completed render.[24]

Figure 2 shows the model imported into Maxwell Render. The various sections of the interface allow fine control of the camera through which the final render will be viewed. The lower half of the interface provides controls for selecting and applying the materials of which the ring is composed—in this case, gold and either ruby or emerald. The rendering itself is managed by other parts of the interface, as are the characteristics of the light sources employed to illuminate the scene.

Figure 2. See image plates for a colour version of this figure.

Figure 3 is a close-up of the ring without any material characteristics applied to it, but lit with light data captured from a photograph and mapped, or decaled, onto its surface. The HDRI (High Dynamic Range Imaging) im-

---

[24] Visual aberrations (or artefacts) appear as faults in a finished render. They may result from a number of different causes including incorrect processing by the software or inter-surface interaction within the rendered scene.

age behind the ring is the source from which the lighting data in the scene was extracted. HDRI seeks to bring to digital visualization accurate representations of light and lighting situations as experienced in the real world.[25] Longer established techniques for the use of light in digital scenes, such as radiosity and ray tracing, use algorithm-based techniques to simulate light and its distribution in a scene and are prone to inaccuracy. Such techniques lack the technical accuracy and resultant sense of realism associated with the use of HDRI.

Figure 3. See image plates for a colour version of this figure.

Figure 4 shows the fully rendered image with the structural elements of the ring presented as yellow gold and the small, round, cabochon stone as a pale emerald. The introduction of simulated materials with their appropriate qualities of colour, reflectance, and indices of refraction increased the overall brilliance of the ring through the interaction of those materials with the light data in the scene, transforming the ring's rather dull appearance in Figure 3, where it was assigned an overall, low reflecting, generic surface.

---

[25] For a detailed discussion of HDRI imaging see Bloch (2007).

Although Figure 3 lacks the detailed material qualities seen in Figure 4, the value of the object's response to lighting data in Figure 3 is of considerable interest. Viewed without complex reflections and their interaction within the scene, the ring has a sense of presence[26] that is lacking in Figure 4: its underlying form is more easily appreciated which in turn provides pointers to aspects of historical design and decision making. This issue will be returned to later in the context of surface finish and inter-object reflection.

Figure 4. See image plates for a colour version of this figure.

Simulating Splendour was never seen as research targeted primarily at the production of breathtakingly impressive images of long-lost jewels or jewels that might have been. From concept it sought to establish a practical and flexible method for the application of digital technologies and software applications in pursuit of increased understanding of the nature and usage of jewels in the late medieval to early Renaissance period in Northern Europe. In the light of this approach, the two most important outcomes to date concern levels of polish applied to metal surfaces and gemstones and the way in

---

[26] Presence is considered to be the quality of "being there" that some digitally-based objects appear to exude. See Sheridan (1996).

which objects and groups of objects were experienced under different lighting conditions.

Figure 5, which is a version of the same basic ring form shown in Figures 1–4 but with a simulation of a ruby rather than an emerald, illustrates what happens if metal surfaces have high levels of reflectance through fine polishing: mirrorlike qualities bring a sense of self-camouflaging to the object. It becomes decreasingly distinct in terms of its form and presence as the level of reflectance increases. It has always been a puzzle as to why many, if not most, jewellery objects from the period under consideration had relatively dull surfaces given that the technologies and techniques were available to goldsmiths to produce highly reflective surfaces.[27] This aspect of Simulating Splendour's outcomes suggests that one rationale for such an approach is that it mirrors the goldsmiths' own thinking about design: in their pursuit of making jewels highly visible indicators of rank or affluence, they used a low level of polish to project the physicality of the jewels in an extremely proactive way. Highly polished objects, especially when worn against highly figured fabrics, were likely to be visually absorbed into those fabrics through the phenomenon of self-camouflaging owing to the inter-surface reflection.

Figure 5. See image plates for a colour version of this figure.

---

[27] Given the high gold purity content found in many works of the period (19.2 carat, whereas 24 carat is the standard for pure, or fine gold as it is known), the dullness of many of the surviving works from the period cannot be accounted for by tarnishing due to atmospheric action or by a pollutant.

Figure 6 uses modelled simulations of an emerald, a ruby, and a diamond, with cuts of contemporary validity sourced from various painted works, framed in a gold band, to show how, with even a relatively low level of polish on both stones and metal, when placed in close proximity to each other—and in relation to a figured fabric in diffused light—the forms of the objects are visually affected. The orientation of the gold band's geometry in particular is difficult to "read" in places. The lighting used in the scene is taken from data collected by the author. It is positioned as if coming through the equivalent of a clerestory window.

Figure 6. See image plates for a colour version of this figure.

Figures 7–9 shows a sequence of images that were generated using the same approaches to modeling and lighting data as in Figure 6. The working hypothesis for this aspect of the research was that, far from being experienced as collections of stones and metal that sparkled, shimmered, and bedazzled, jewels were more often seen by both wearers, and viewers, in lighting conditions that made them anything but spectacular. It was often the sense of presence that came with their physical form that impressed, rather than any other qualities.

As with the levels of surface polish on metals, the technologies and techniques available to gem workers of the period are important in the context of the visual qualities that could be imparted to gemstones by working them. In the early part of the period, techniques practised by European gem workers were confined to the polishing of naturally occurring forms, such as the cabochon or pyramid. Many of the stones with more complex cuts recorded in contemporary paintings (with varying degrees of veracity) were imported

ready-cut and/or polished at their point of origin. As time progressed, European workers absorbed and developed techniques imported from the Orient
and Asia to enable stones to exploit more fully those qualities of reflection,
refraction and so on, that we are used to experiencing today. Figure 7 shows
a group comprising emeralds, rubies, and a diamond lit through the equivalent of a clerestory window with natural daylight, very intense and bright in
its characteristics.

Figure 7. See image plates for a colour version of this figure.

Figure 8 shows the same scene with a reduced level of brightness—in effect
the simulation of a much duller day.

Figure 8. See image plates for a colour version of this figure.

Figure 9 shows the scene again but with a light level commensurate with dusk.

Figure 9. See image plates for a colour version of this figure.

This sequence of simulations demonstrates how levels of natural light affect how translucent, or semi-transparent, objects are visually experienced. The same may be shown using simulations of artificial light types.

The tentative conclusion drawn from this aspect of the research is that the most common conditions for lighting under which jewels were viewed, as demonstrated in Figures 8 and 9, did not allow gemstones to be experienced at their most dazzling. The implication of this may be seen as another potential impact on design thinking: how to make the most of the constituent parts of a jewel given the restricting conditions under which it would be worn and thus displayed to the wearer's audience. Both polish and light levels point to an intriguing association with the developments in fashion in the late medieval period: specifically the rise of the garment known as a *houppelande*[28] to a level approaching ubiquity at the courts of Northern Europe after c. 1390 and before c. 1450. Many images showing the *houppelande* depict it as a garment made from a single-coloured fabric, with the highest-fashion examples in

---

[28] The *houppelande* was a form of full overcoat with baggy sleeves. As worn by men it could either be full-length or reach only down to the knee, and was usually open at the front. The version for women was always full-length with the front closed. In some cases it had a train at the back. It was made in a range of materials including wool and velvet.

black.[29] Such a garment, especially in a dark colour, was an ideal landscape on which to site jewels: it provided basic contrast that resulted in visual attention being directed at the jewels on its surface. In that respect, a *houppelande* could provide, through the qualities of contrast, a way of compensating for poor lighting conditions. This is currently being explored by the author, with the aid of a grant from The Pasold Research Fund.

Future development

No digitally generated object—whether extrapolated from data contained in a painting, illuminated work, or sculpture, or one digitized from a real object—can get to a fine enough grain of detail to claim to be a true simulation, nor can any visualization environment offer a perfect simulation of how a piece of jewellery might have moved on the surface of a garment. No amount of processing power or skillful choreography of software (at least in the foreseeable future) will help to position a simulation as anything more than an attempt to *approach* real-world equivalence. The topography of an object's surface revealed by an electron microscope, for example, is of an order of complexity beyond the capabilities of today's modeling and visualization systems to simulate. But should the pursuit of perfect simulation be the key goal for using digital technologies to further knowledge and contextual understanding of historical artefacts? From its point of conception, the research detailed here took the approach of using digital tools as agents of interpretation, not of replication. That decision impacted not only on how the research was to be conducted, but also the types of sources that were used to provide data and how these data were extracted and extrapolated into visualizations. To a large extent the types of sources available to researchers are fait accompli in nature, consisting of extant objects, paintings, sculptures and illuminated manuscripts as core source material.

Building on the work considered here, the author is employing the same underpinning approach to examine the use of mathematics and geometry in the design of late medieval jewellery. On the basis of extant objects from the period, as well as those implied through pictorial representation, we can see that through the fourteenth and fifteenth centuries jewels grew progressively more complex in their design and in the technologies used to produce them. Goldsmiths developed new techniques to meet changing demands in

---

[29] Many excellent images of this, and other types and styles of contemporary garments, may found in the online illuminated manuscript collections of the Bibliothèque nationale de France, accessed 22 November 2010, http://www.bnf.fr/.

design, many of which by the end of the period required levels of technical skill undreamt of at its beginning.

Virtual reconstruction, or simulation as described here, offers a range of possibilities to areas of historical object research outside of the world of jewellery: ceramics[30] and stained glass[31] are excellent examples from within the applied arts. Beyond the applied arts lies a range of fields of study in which digital simulation or visualization are being, or might be, harnessed: from portable objects to buildings and cities.[32] The techniques of software-based modeling and visualization developed in the course of the *Simulating Splendour* project are capable of realizing portable objects of considerable complexity. It is difficult to envisage any object with supporting historical source material that could not be simulated. The tools available today for modeling and visualization, within applications such as ZBrush, Mudbox, and Maxwell Render, contain sufficient options and operational flexibility to answer most questions posed to them by researchers: the only constraint is perhaps the limit of hardware processing power and the skills required to employ such an approach. Working with the type of digital methodology described here requires not only considerable skills in the specialized software, but more significantly, a well-developed understanding of the interpretative processes involved in turning ideas or concepts about real or historically illustrated objects into digital entities. Both needs can be addressed with sufficient training.

Predicting future developments in digital technologies and associated ap-plications is itself an industry driven by large-scale players including the gaming, film, and automotive industries. The modeling and visualization of historical jewellery is, in relative terms, a very minor application. It is most unlikely that future developments in digital modeling, simulation, and vi-sualization systems will be aimed specifically at, or tailored to, the needs of research into historical objects. This field will remain a niche. Those working in it will continue to have to make generic software applications fit their methodologies and, if necessary, develop plug-ins for generic applications or develop their own stand-alone applications to supply the tools that are needed. Such developments are beginning to take place. At present these

---

[30] See for example Kampel and Sablatnig (2003).

[31] See for example Salemi, Achilli, and Boatto (2008).

[32] A good starting point in considering other possibilities in the application of histor-ical virtual reconstruction is the King's Visualisation Lab website, at King's College, London, accessed 22 November 2010, http://www.kvl.cch.kcl.ac.uk/index.html.

developments are in hardware rather than software, and the focus is on the digital simulation of goldsmithing techniques rather than the objects themselves. The Scottish silversmith Kathryn Hinton, for example, is developing a hand-held interface in the form of a hammer which, when used in the real world in conjunction with a flexible tablet acting as a receiving surface, has its actions replicated within a digital environment in real time. The swinging and striking motion of the hand-held interface mimics that of a traditional hammer, but rather than a real blank of metal being deformed, a simulated blank is deformed in a software application such as ZBrush.[33] The resulting objects can be exported to the real world through the process of rapid prototyping.[34] Such development of innovative hardware devices for interfacing with sophisticated modeling applications must be seen as the way forward for research in the field. Simulation of the actual tools of the craft will bring a closer alignment with the processes and techniques of goldsmithing and the objects they produced. As a consequence, the precision of the simulation of objects will become more historically and physically accurate. At the same time, the technology employed in pursuit of knowledge and understanding is only as valuable as the quality of the material that is presented to it. This material results from scholarship and the intellectual labour of those involved in research. As noted at the beginning of this essay, traditional methods of research have generated outcomes of high academic quality and will continue to do so, but future development is dependent on the increasing integration of traditional and digital methods. If the advantages and best practices found in both approaches can be fully combined into a third way, what may be revealed in the future of jewellery's past appears a fascinating prospect.

Further details of Simulating Splendour: Visual Modelling of Historical Jewellery Research may be found on the Royal College of Art's website, accessed 23 October 2009, at http://www.rca.ac.uk.

---

[33] Details of this research are currently not available in the public domain.

[34] Rapid Prototyping is a process that converts the data contained in digitally generated objects into three-dimensional real-world prototypes. Depending on the particular technology employed, models can be made in a variety of materials ranging from wax to titanium.

WORKS CITED

Baumstark, Reinhold. 1995. *Das Goldene Rössl: Ein Meisterwerk der Pariser Hofkunst um 1400.* Munich: Hirmer Verlag.

Bloch, Christian. 2007. *The HDRI Handbook: High Dynamic Range Imaging for Photographers and CG Artists.* Santa Barbara: Rocky Nook.

Bloomfield, Mark, and Louise Schofield. 1996. "Reconstructing the Treasury of Atreus at Mycenae." In Higgins, Main, and Lang 1996, 227–34.

Bowman, S. G. E., and C. P. Stapleton. 1998. "The All Souls' Jewel: The Enameller's Art, Deliberate or Accidental Tinting." *Jewellery Studies* 8:5–10.

Cherry, John. 1992. *Medieval Craftsmen: Goldsmiths.* London: British Museum Press.

_____ 2001. "Healing Through Faith: The Continuation of Medieval Attitudes to Jewellery into the Renaissance." *Renaissance Studies* 15 (2): 154–71.

Criminisi, Antonio. 2001. *Accurate Visual Metrology from Single and Multiple Uncalibrated Images.* London: Springer-Verlag.

_____ 2002. "Single-View Metrology: Algorithms and Applications." 2002 Deutsche Arbeitsgemeinschaft für Mustererkennung Symposium. September. http://research.microsoft.com/apps/pubs/default. aspx?id=67279.

_____, and Martin Kemp. 2006. "Computer Vision and Painter's Vision in Italian and Netherlandish Art of the Fifteenth Century." In *Perspective, Projections and Design Technologies of Architectural Representation*, edited by Mario Carpo and Frédérique Lemerle, 31–46. London: Routledge.

Denard, Hugh. 2005. "'At the Foot of Pompey's Statue': Reconstructing Rome's *Theatrum Lapideum*." In *Images and Artefacts of the Ancient World*, edited by Alan K. Bowman and Michael Brady, 69–76. Oxford: Oxford University Press.

Fernie, Kate, and Julian D. Richards, eds. 2004. *Creating and Using Virtual Reality: A Guide for the Arts and Humanities.* Oxford: Oxbow Books.

Fliegel, Stephen N., et al. 2004. *Art from the Court of Burgundy: The Patronage of Philip the Bold and John the Fearless 1364-1419.* Exhibition catalogue. Paris: Éditions de la Réunion des musées nationaux.

Higgins, Tony, Peter Main, and Janet Lang, eds. 1996. *Imaging the Past: Electronic Imaging and Computer Graphics in Museums and Archaeology.* British Museum Occasional Paper, no. 114. London: The British Museum.

Humphrey, David. 2009. "Digital Simulation, Mediating Agents and the Implied Historical Object." *Archaeological Review from Cambridge. Invention and Reinvention: Perceptions and Archaeological Practice* 24 (1): 95–107.

Kampel, Martin, and Robert Sablatnig. 2003. "Virtual Reconstruction of Broken and Unbroken Pottery." Presented at Fourth International Conference on 3-D Digital Imaging and Modeling (3DIM '03), Banff, Alberta.

Kovács, Éva. 2004. *L'âge d'or de l'orfèvrerie parisienne au temps des princes de Valois.* Dijon: Éditions Faton.

Le Goff, Jacques. 1988. *The Medieval Imagination.* Chicago: University of Chicago Press.

Lightbown, Ronald. 1978. *Secular Goldsmiths' Work in Medieval France: A History.* London: The Society of Antiquaries.

_____ 1992. *Mediaeval European Jewellery: With a Catalogue of the Collection in the Victoria & Albert Museum.* London: Victoria & Albert Museum.

Musée du Louvre. 2004. *Paris 1400: Les Arts sous Charles VI.* Exhibition catalogue. Paris: Éditions de la Réunion des musées nationaux.

Salemi, G., V. Achilli, and G. Boatto. 2008. "3D Virtual Modelling of a Gothic Stained-Glass panel." In *The International Archives of the Photogrammetry, Remote Sensing and Spatial Information Sciences* Beijing 37 part B5:297–302. http://www.isprs.org/proceedings/XXXVII/congress/tc5.aspx.

Scarisbrick, Diana, Christophe Vachaudez, and Jan Walgrave, eds. 2007. *Brilliant Europe: Jewels from European Courts.* Exhibition catalogue. Brussels: Mercatorfonds.

Schmitt, Jean-Claude. 1990. *La raison des gestes dans l'Occident médiéval.* Paris: Bibliothèque des Histoires, Gallimard.

Sheridan, Thomas B. 1996. "Further Musings on the Psychophysics of Presence." *Presence: Teleoperators and Virtual Environments* 5 (2): 241–46.

Webster, Robert. 1998. *Gemmologists' Compendium.* 7th ed. London: NAG Press.

Coinage, Digitization, and the World Wide Web: Numismatics and the COINS Project*

Jonathan Jarrett
The Queen's College, Oxford
jonathan.jarrett@queens.ox.ac.uk

Sebastian Zambanini
Vienna Institute of Technology
zamba@caa.tuwien.ac.at

Reinhold Huber-Mörk
Austrian Institute of Technology
reinhold.huber-moerk@ait.ac.at

Achille Felicetti
PIN ScRL., Università di Firenze
achille.felicetti@pin.unifi.it

As this paper was first being finalized, a search for "ancient coins" on eBay.com retrieved 7,829 results, the first of which was a lot of uncleaned coins,

* This paper derives from work done in the COINS Project, which was funded by the European Commission under the Community's Sixth Framework Programme, contract no. 044450. However, this publication reflects only the authors' views, and the European Commission is not liable for any information contained herein. The authors must thank Martin Kampel of Pattern Recognition and Image Processing Group, Technische Universität Wien, for his readiness to share material and expertise, on which this paper relies heavily. Other members of the COINS Project were: Franco Niccolucci, Andrea d'Andrea, Sandro Saccenti, Marco Sifniotis, and Hubert Mara (PIN); Robert Sablatnig, Maia Zaharieva, Florian Kleber, and Herrmann Czedik-Eysenberg (PRIP); Dorothea Heiss (AIT), Fiorenzo Catalli (Soprintendenza Archeologica di Roma), Armando Sisinni (Comando Carabinieri Tutela Patrimonio Culturale), Mike Vandamme (Vartec nv BE), Ernest Oberlander-Tarnoveanu (Muzeul National de Istorie a României), and Mark Blackburn; Martin Allen and Elina Screen (Fitzwilliam Museum, Cambridge), all of whom contributed more than mere citation makes clear. Sadly, Mark Blackburn died very shortly before this paper went to press; the authors would like to dedicate it to his memory. Thanks are also due to Professor Ralph Mathisen of the University of Illinois for allowing us to reproduce parts of his 2008 paper and to Julie Hofmann of the University of Shenandoah for putting us in touch with him. During the life of the COINS Project, Jonathan Jarrett was employed at the Fitzwilliam Museum, Cambridge, and Sebastian Zambanini at PRIP, and the Austrian Institute of Technology was known as Austrian Research Centres.

ISBN 978-0-86698-499-7 (online)   ISBN 978-0-86698-474-4 (print)
New Technologies in Medieval and Renaissance Studies 3 (2012) 455–485

probably straight from an archaeological site. No clue to their origin was given by the seller.[1] Other, cleaned coins—silver, gold, and bronze, struck all over Europe and beyond but many with equally little provenance—constituted the thousands of other items for sale. This trade is not confined to eBay: many other sites could be mentioned. Of the coins on sale through these portals, at least some will have been illegally obtained from protected sites and exported illegally from the countries in which they were found; some may even have been stolen from heritage collections or archaeological agencies. The problem is well known, and the development of the WWW as a marketplace has magnified it considerably, but new web technologies can address the problem, in the process adding considerably to the resources available for numismatic and historical study. This chapter describes the work of an EU-funded project, Combat Online Illegal Numismatic Sales, or COINS, in which police, archaeological, heritage and computing agencies, and research teams were all involved, both to address the problem and to maximize consequent benefits for the humanities. The result is a connected set of software tools that can harvest images from the Web, identify coins from those images, and compare those coins against a reference database. Software to assemble and manage this reference database, by data-sharing over a range of institutions and individuals, promises to make it easy for curators and numismatists to assemble and also contribute such datasets with benefits both for law enforcement and for historical scholarship, some of which are outlined in what follows.

Coins as objects, numismatics as source

Although not all scholars realize it, coins have a great importance as historical evidence (Jarrett 2009a, §§2–17; more widely, Grierson 1975). This importance derives from the twofold nature of a coin: it is both a material object, representing a stored amount of value, and a document, bearing the marks and message of the issuer by whose guarantee it is recognized as holding that value. This combination of material and text allows coinage integrally to hold answers to questions that with other medieval and early modern sources are

---

[1] eBay, accessed 12 October 2009, http://coins.shop.ebay.com/?_from=R40&_trksid=p3907.m38.l1311&_nkw=ancient+coins&_sacat=11116; the uncleaned lot OldCoinMan, "Uncleaned ancient Roman coins, very fast shipping," eBay, accessed same date, http://cgi.ebay.com/UNCLEANED-ANCIENT-ROMAN-COINS-VERY-FAST-SHIPPING_W0QQitemZ310172329148QQcmdZViewItemQQptZLH_DefaultDomain_0?hash=item4837b624bc. On the scale and import of the problem see Elkins (2008).

often a matter of inference, such as point of origin, date of manufacture, maker identity, and, of course, value.

In terms of practical application, of course, archaeologists are happy to find coins in their sites because they can provide a close date for the layer of finding. This can be problematic, as date of manufacture and date of deposition can be far apart: some late Roman coins may have circulated for a century or more, for example, and some reused as Anglo-Saxon grave-goods may have had a longer life even than that (King 1988). The use of Roman and Byzantine prototypes in the final coinage of King Edward the Confessor (1042–66), indeed, alerts us to the fact that coin collecting may predate the Norman Conquest of England, if not more (Metcalf 1982, 205). The use of coin, rather than bullion, however, testifies to an authority whose ability to maintain a coinage was recognized. When such coins have travelled far from their mint of origin, we can see that the reputation of that authority was far-reaching, and we can see some suggestions of the trade routes (or other exchange vectors: see Grierson 1959) involved and their change over time. The spread of minting also testifies to the breadth of that authority: the uniformity of the silver denier struck by the Carolingian kings, for example, over hundreds of mints in what is now tens of countries, has led it to be called "the first single European currency," a claim that is not as exaggerated as it may sound (Coupland 2002, 1990).

Because it is usually possible to attribute a mint to a coin, these objects make easy the work of tracing geographical links that have to be inferred from other forms of artwork such as painting styles, and such links have genuine historical importance. Thus, for example, the few suggestions of Roman trade with India in our written sources are much augmented by the number of finds of silver *denarii* in the province of Kerala. Likewise, there exist from the period of the Napoleonic wars Spanish silver dollars ("pieces of four") struck in the name of King Charles IV, but counterstamped with the head of George III of England. These coins testify both to British success at sea and to a shortage of money at home that led this foreign loot to be pressed into currency, where it was, however, ill-received. Contemporary doggerels described this reaction: "Two Kings' heads and not worth a crown" or "The head of a fool stamped on the neck of an ass" (Davies 1996, 294).

At its most basic, a coin tells us that at the time and place of its manufacture there was surplus wealth that could be parcelled up thus for exchange, but when this is multiplied by the thousands of pieces surviving from most currency issues, information is imparted on a much larger scale. Using documentary analysis of mint accounts or, failing these, extrapolations from the number of dies—hand-engraved and therefore unique—involved in the striking of premechanical coinages, estimates of relative currency sizes can be formed that may allow economic historians to plot rises and falls of prosperity and drains or inflows of commercial wealth (Smith 1995; Allen 2006; cf. Buttrey 1993).

Lastly, coins carry messages. They give us the titles and portrait of the issuer, be he an emperor issuing coins for most of Europe or a rural merchant issuing his own trade tokens around two or three English towns during a change shortage (Grierson 1975, 165–70; Mathias 1962). Sometimes political statements like this are made explicitly, and sometimes they are implicit in the design. Coins often speak through the iconography of their design. A process of nearly three millennia of cultural reappropriation is illustrated in the repetition of the archetype of a helmeted and seated warrior goddess, in the persons of Athena in Athens, Roma in Rome, and Britannia in the modern United Kingdom (Bell 1963, 108–9). The portraiture on coins may tell us something about political self-presentation, and occasionally even actual historical appearances (Jarrett 2009a, §13). These meanings and significances can be teased out of coins as with other artworks, but the context of coinage, in which a value must be guaranteed, means that a reading in terms of political or economic power can always be made, which is easy to understand and significant when seen in action.

It is for reasons like this, as well as artefactual interest, that museums and collectors seek out and assemble collections of coins. It is also, alas, why coins are valuable to thieves and smugglers, who evade international export regulations or national restrictions on metal-detecting or similar means of discovery in order to bring ancient money to an ever-eager and sometimes incautious market. This was the problem that the COINS Project was created to meet, but the resulting solutions may allow the exploitation of numismatic evidence in other, previously unprecedented ways.

The COINS Project: Genesis and partners

The project was born out of a specific demand: to help with the policing of sales of ancient coins that were being illegally exported from, in the first instance, Italy.[2] This explains some of the choice of partners, not least the

---

[2] The COINS Project maintains a website at http://www.coins-project.eu, last accessed 12 October 2009, on which its activities are documented and its binaries are progressively being made available.

Italian Carabinieri, but also the University of Florence, in particular their PIN laboratory, and the Soprintendenza Archeologica di Roma (SAR). The solutions that were being considered, however, guided the choice of the other participants: two groups from Austria, the Pattern Recognition and Image Processing (PRIP) Group at the Technical University of Vienna, and a similar section at the Austrian Institute of Technology (AIT), GmbH; a commercial company from Belgium, Vartec nv BE; and two other heritage collections with strong numismatic interests, the National History Museum of Romania in Bucharest (MNIR) and the Fitzwilliam Museum in Cambridge, United Kingdom. This choice of partners made sense because what the project contemplated was a combination of tools that would allow law enforcement officials to scan the Web for images of coins for sale and test them against reference images of known coins, thus eliminating a great many images of no relevance and saving hours of labour, while also gathering the relevant ones together and perhaps even identifying stolen pieces. For such a scheme, expertise was gathered in web-searching and dynamic database construction (PIN and Vartec); in image recognition (PRIP and AIT); and in the coins themselves (SAR, MNIR, and Fitzwilliam). An initial meeting in Cambridge in late 2007 coordinated objectives, and subsequent meetings and demonstrations occurred in Kaprun and Vienna in Austria, Sorrento in Italy, and Uzilina in Romania during the course of 2008, with each team working to its separate agreed schedule between times. The project was formally concluded in January 2009, though the project website has continued to be updated.

Regrettably, the Carabinieri had to withdraw their contribution to the project at an early stage. Their organization did not allow them to meet the demands of the EU for accounting of moneys allocated, and although they initially planned to fund their contribution to the project internally, and to give the project access to the Tutela Patrimonio Culturale's database of stolen artefacts, ultimately the relevant resources had to be redeployed. The Project continued as intended despite this setback, however, and none of its deliverables was affected by the Carabinieri's withdrawal. In any case, at the earliest stages of planning it was intended that the project outputs would have relevance in a much wider sphere than simply theft prevention. We were contemplating tools that could recognize, perhaps even classify, coins from images alone, partly automating the process of numismatic study. Our tools would automatically assemble reference collections, interpreting a wide range of data schemas and making them accessible online. Also, as a fruit of the collaboration among three heritage collections with historically different practices, there was planned a booklet giving suggestions for collections management to holders of coin collections both public and private. Since that is now available (Jarrett 2009b), this paper endeavours instead to explain the workings behind, and the results of, the software components of the project, and to suggest how these might be developed in future and how they will advance the historical study of coinage.

Image recognition

Classification versus identification

The problems to be overcome for the coin-recognition component of the project involved the complication that two very different goals are often understood as part of the same process (Huber-Mörk et al. 2008a for what follows; see also Kampel 2008). These goals are classification and identification, that is, firstly, putting the coin successfully into a group of similar coins and, secondly, distinguishing it among those similar coins. Work has been done on the classification of modern coins, and considerable success achieved with programs like Coin-o-matic (van der Maaten and Poon 2006), but these approaches rely on a factor that is lacking with ancient and medieval coins: the regularity of shape and design ensured by machine manufacture (Kampel 2008, 137). Preindustrial coins, made not with machines but with hammered dies on metal blanks or "flans" cut individually from a sheet or rod, have much less regularity, and coins of the same denomination, type, and issue, even from the same dies, can vary considerably in their shape and the positioning of their design on the flan (Grierson 1975, 94–123), which renders shape-based techniques much less useful. This presents obvious difficulties for a classification approach, as the gross physical similarities on which such approaches are predicated often do not exist. On the other hand, for identification purposes these features and differences make it much easier to tell one coin from a number of like coins, which with modern coinage produced to a uniform design is very much harder. Our subject matter therefore gave the Austrian teams an incentive to concentrate on identification methods in a way that few other research teams investigating such problems had.

Figure 1. Variety within a single coin type, demonstrated with early Athenian silver tetradrachms. Photograph by the authors, copyright © 2007 COINS Project.

Working with test data provided by the Fitzwilliam Museum and the Kunst-historiches Museum in Vienna (KHM), PRIP began their part of the project by testing existing methods. There were two datasets assembled: an initial one harvested from the Fitzwilliam's, KHM's and MNIR's websites, comprising 92 images of variable quality and set-up; and a subsequent and larger one of c. 2,400 images from around 250 coins supplied by the Fitzwilliam and described in the next section. There was also a range of XML datasets with matching images from the Fitzwilliam, MNIR, and SAR that were used for the database sections of the project and are discussed separately below (see Blackburn, Catalli, and Felicetti 2008).[3] Method testing in the image recognition project component was usually performed on the small dataset, but final results as quoted here were all obtained with the larger set and can be considered experimentally significant.

Segmentation

It was found that much existing work had been done with professional-standard images, with uniformly good lighting and exposure conditions and uniform processing (Kampel, Zaharieva, and Zambanini 2008, referencing van der Maaten and Poon 2006, Reisert, Ronneberger, and Burkhardt 2006, and

---

[3] The datasets now form the basis of the material contained in the online version of the COINS Management Tool, discussed below: http://www.coins-project.eu/COINS-MT/bin-debug/main.html# as of 12 October 2009.

Nölle et al. 2003). The goals of the COINS Project made this unrealistic: the desired software would need to recognize coins photographed in many different ways, in a variety of conditions, on a range of equipment. For testing under these conditions, the Fitzwilliam was called upon to contribute a new set of images, which they supplied from their coins in the name of Alexander the Great, nearly 250 specimens almost all of which bear the head of Heracles in a lion-skin right on their obverse side and Zeus enthroned left with a sceptre on the reverse (see Fig. 2). The reverse fields are clustered with a range of extra designs and symbols and one of two inscriptions disposed in a number of ways. These constitute the marks by which a numismatist can classify the coin.[4] To the untrained eye, however, and also to underdeveloped software, these coins basically all look the same in terms of design, if not of execution, and were thus ideal for the project's purposes.

Figure 2. Eight of the Fitzwilliam's test dataset in the name of Alexander the Great, here all silver tetradrachms, imaged in various rotations and lighting conditions. Images by Jonathan Jarrett (left) and Carl Impey (right). Copyright © 2007 Fitzwilliam Museum.

---

[4] For these coinages, see Price (1991), though even this dataset contained pieces not there catalogued.

The test images were largely made with a flatbed scanner, using a lightbox to obliterate background, at three arbitrary rotations so as to give images of the same coin lit from different angles and thus with different patterns of light and shade. A subset of coins was also photographed with a fixed digital camera under a variety of lighting conditions, and an even smaller set with the camera from a mobile phone, a likely origin for many of the images that COINS will have to process (Jarrett 2009a, §30; Jarrett 2009b, 33–39).

This deliberate variety made considerably more complex the first and most basic problem of image recognition, segmentation, or distinguishing the item in question from its background. As a working numismatist, the lead author often had to deal with images of coins taken against textured cloth backgrounds, or on the finder's hand fresh from the earth—both the coin and the hand—which involved trying to pick around the edge in Photoshop. Even in photographs against a clear or uniform background, however, the shadow caused at the edge of a coin by oblique lighting presents difficulties. We have the advantage of already recognizing a coin when we see one, but the kind of organic learning required to do intelligent internal comparisons against stored stereoscopic experience, used by a human being in identifying a seen object, is not yet replicable in software, which must recognize coins on the basis of purely logical or mathematical criteria. The process of segmentation is, however, vital for the next steps of recognition and classification, as it chooses the area of interest in an image on which those tools will work. Challenges in segmentation are principally caused by shadows that make the edge of that area hard to determine, although digital artefacts such as pixelation and compression and problems of scale relative to the image background are also factors.

AIT pursued a modified shape-based approach to this problem (based on Huber et al. 2005), but the PRIP team's approach was different (Zambanini and Kampel 2008; cf. Huber-Mörk et al. 2008a, 6–8 and 13–15). Their solution rested on the assumption that in most cases, the section of the image that interests us, to wit, the coin, will contain more local information than the rest of the image. That is, the design of the coin means more variety in a concentrated area than does the background. By measuring the levels of variation per unit area ("entropy levels") and gray values of the image and overlaying the zones of the image that these identified as significant, a good basis was established for "thresholding," that is, converting to black-and-white on the basis of measurements of light and shade. The final thresholding was tested by measuring its "formfactor," a measurement based on the coherence of the final shape, derived from statistical confidence in the genuine existence of the shape in the data. A shape with outlying wisps or fuzz was deemed less coherent and less likely to be a successful segmentation; those with higher formfactors were preferred. To test this process the small set of ninety-two images were segmented from their backgrounds by eye and used to provide human-validated "ground-truth" values of known accuracy for comparison to the automated segmentation done with PRIP's process. When tested, the automated process achieved an average overlap with the ground-truth segmentations of 98.3 per cent. This was reckoned adequate to be incorporated into the final tool in the next stages of the recognition process (Huber-Mörk et al. 2008a, 14).

Figure 3. Screen capture of a completed segmentation by the COINS segmentation Photoshop plugin. Image by Sebastian Zambanini. Copyright © 2010 COINS Project.

Identification

Because the best area to break ground in appeared to be that of coin identification, this was pursued as a primary goal and classification as a secondary
one. The results of the two groups' work on classification therefore stemmed
from those on identification, and it makes sense to report on identification
first.

Figure 4. A silver tetradrachm of Alexander the Great coin and its shape.
Image by Reinhold Huber-Mörk. Copyright © 2007 COINS Project.

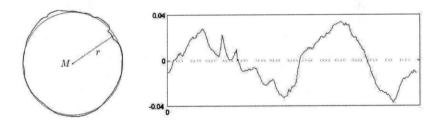

Figure 5. Contour mapping of the same coin's shape profile. Image by
Reinhold Huber-Mörk. Copyright © 2007 COINS Project.

The methods for identification were developed in separate parallel projects
by AIT and PRIP and the results then combined. AIT's method was entitled
"deviation from circular shape matching" (DCSM), and took advantage of the
same factor that defeats easy classification of ancient and medieval coins,

their lack of regular circularity. By establishing a centre point and measuring the distance from centre to edge in a number of directions, a highly individualized contour of each test coin's shape was created that was unaffected by rotation. This contour could be expressed as a vector and stored in a reference database (Huber-Mörk et al. 2008a, 8–11 and 15–18).

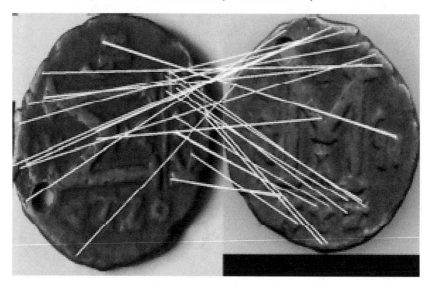

Figure 6. Reverse of a silver tetradrachm in the name of Alexander the Great with local shape descriptors matched. Image by Reinhold Huber-Mörk. Copyright © 2007 COINS Project.

With this vector established for each coin in the test dataset, the method then used this database to test any given image by repeating the measuring process for the new image and comparing it to known specimens. The method was refined by also examining the image on the basis of local shape descriptors, values recording the occurrence of specific patterns in the image data. These were obtained by calculations involving the process known as fast Fourier transform (a range of mathematical techniques that allow the transformation of one complex value into another value more useful for a given process). The DCSM and descriptor methods were then applied one after the other to each image to give a final measure of individual dissimilarity for each one. Once tested against the full dataset, however, it became clear that although this method was competitive compared to others available, it was not by itself capable of a sufficient grade of successful recognition to be useful for the COINS Project's purposes.

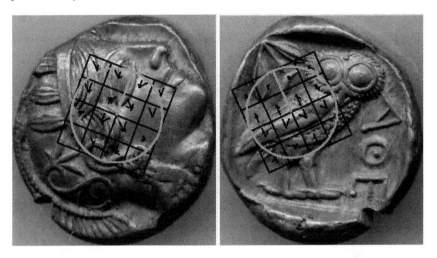

Figure 7. Depiction of mapping of SIFT descriptors on an Athenian stater.
Image by Reinhold Huber-Mörk. Copyright © 2007 COINS Project.

In the meantime the PRIP team had proceeded with a different approach based on "local image descriptors" (LID) (Huber-Mörk et al. 2008a, 11–13 and 15–18). This involved dividing the coin image into a grid and characterizing the sum of the data in each grid section, rather than searching for specific patterns. Two different published descriptors with different bases were used. These are called SIFT, Scale Invariant Feature Transform, and SURF, Speeded-Up Robust Features (Lowe 2004; Bay, Tuytelaars, and Van Gool 2006). SIFT is considerably slower than SURF, which as its name suggests was designed to minimize processing time for such operations. In SURF, also, various parameters can be set to determine what level of response is deemed significant and what ambiguity can be permitted in the results. The concomitant of SURF's faster run-time, however, is a considerable difference in precision: the PRIP team's tests showed that although SURF ran through their test data between three to five times faster than SIFT, it also detected 80 per cent fewer interest points on average. It was therefore perhaps not surprising that when run with the full test dataset, SIFT outperformed SURF by some margin, identifying 71.77 per cent of coins correctly as against SURF's 56.24 per cent (Huber-Mörk et al. 2008a, 15–17; Kampel and Zaharieva 2008; Huber-Mörk, Zaharieva, and Czedik-Eysenberg 2008b; cf. earlier tests in Kampel 2008, 142–43, using SIFT alone). Again, however, these margins were insufficient for COINS purposes.

The obvious consequent step, and one that had always been anticipated by the project, was the combination of the two teams' approaches. Construction of routines using both DCSM and LID matching on the same interrogations of the database showed a considerable step up in accuracy: DCSM + SIFT returned an accuracy of 94.11 per cent and DCSM + SURF 95.16 per cent (Huber-Mörk et al. 2008a, 15–17). The faster performance of SURF, and its marginally greater accuracy in combination with DCSM, determined the adoption of these tools by the COINS Project. While, of course, results in the wider world will depend very greatly on the size and quality of the reference database, according to the hoary computing maxim "garbage in, garbage out," a 95 per cent reduction in a sample of, say, eight thousand images downloaded from the Web is a reduction with immense impact in terms of labour and associated fatigue and performance in the parts of the task that remain to be done by human means.[5]

Figure 8. Screen capture of a completed identification using the COINS Shape-Matching Tool. Image by Reinhold Huber-Mörk. Copyright © 2007 COINS Project.

Classification

In the field of classification, analysing the target coin by means of its shape is unhelpful, but proceeding by local image descriptors is still effective, as

---

[5] Some limited user feedback is now available in the form of Snible (2009).

the type of a coin consists largely in the combination of the sort of design features on which this method operates. For this coarser grade of recognition, in fact, tests by the PRIP team revealed that the existing SIFT and SURF methods performed surprisingly well on ancient coins without modification (beyond adjustments to parameters and so forth). In tests on the large dataset correct classifications were achieved by SIFT in 90.57 per cent of cases and by SURF in 90.86 per cent. That is, the differences between the two methods were negligible and not significantly distinguishable, and both were of an adequately high order.

Output and deliverables

At project completion these processes had been developed into two software tools designed to run on Microsoft Windows and a third written for Unix systems. The first of these is a segmentation program, also packaged within the second tool, which is a shape-matching suite. The third tool incorporates the LID method into a stand-alone command-line or GUI tool for Unix systems. At the time of writing the publically available versions of these tools consisted of Windows versions of AIT's Shape-Matching Package and the PRIP Image Recognition Tool, and a set of plug-ins for Adobe Photoshop for measuring and segmenting coin images.[6] These tools constitute the agreed deliverables for the COINS Project's initial aims, but clearly further development to incorporate the combination of shape-matching and LID methods is desirable. The PRIP team expects to be able to refine their methods on the basis of spatial constraints to a level that might allow the automation of not just coin identification, but mint or die identification (Huber-Mörk et al. 2008a, 27). Meanwhile the two teams are continuing research in this area and further developments can be expected.

---

[6] For further details on these software tools see Huber-Mörk et al. (2008a, 18–26); download packages with documentation are available on the COINS Project website at http://www.coins-project.eu/index.php?Itemid=53&option=com_content, as of 12 October 2009. The Shape-Matching Package requires Windows XP SP2 and Microsoft .NET framework 2.0, the Image Recognition Tool Windows 98, 98 SE, 2000, ME, XP or Vista and the .NET framework 2.0, the last of which is downloadable for free from Microsoft via the link on the page just mentioned. The Photoshop plugins run in Adobe Photoshop CS3.

Harvesting images from the WWW

One of the problems involved in using these tools for a wide range of identifications is that it is difficult to assemble a reference database from museum collections, which usually have many coins of different types rather than a large number of similar coins. Many forms of numismatic study, however, rely on analysis of coinages in bulk. For both these purposes a much larger collection of images is advantageous, and the obvious way to assemble such a collection is by harvesting the WWW. Searching for images on the Web is, however, in its infancy (Saccenti and Sifniotis 2008, 4 and *passim* for what follows). Any habitué of Google Image Search will be aware of its limitations: because it relies on associated text to identify images, rather than analysing the image files themselves, irrelevant results are common. Although some image formats can carry text tags embedded within the file that give useful metadata for such searches, the vast majority are not so tagged. Analysis therefore needs to proceed along the same logical and systematic lines as with the image recognition processes described above: first, an image must be gathered, having been located according to context in the normal way or by knowledge-directed human searching, and then the image content must be separated from its background to make the image suitable for processing. The technology for the latter stages, as described above, now exists, but in applying it to images gathered from the Web a new problem arises. In the tests of the image-matching software above, we were able to assume that any given image actually contained a coin, but current web search technologies do not permit us to be sure of this, as discussed above. Many results gathered by conventional text-based search techniques contain quite irrelevant images.

There are two ways to limit this number of false positives. The first, as with all web searching, is to look in the right place. The PIN team who worked on this part of the COINS Project therefore began by assembling a list of target websites, beginning with seeds contributed from the knowledge of the Fitzwilliam, SAR, and MNIR—such as WildWinds and eBay's ancient coins sales—and designing their routines to follow links from those sites to others and so on out to other parts of the Web.[7] Indexing stops once the return of likely images has diminished to a level set by the user (Saccenti and Sifniotis 2008, 5–6). The second way to eliminate irrelevant results is to employ recognition software. The methods deployed in the COINS software tools, despite their high grade of performance, are not yet suitable for such high-density

---

[7] WildWinds, last modified October 6, 2009, accessed 12 October 2009, http://www.wildwinds.com/; for eBay see n. 1.

operations but, as might be expected, tools are being developed outside the project for content-based image retrieval from the Web, the most successful again using techniques based on local features descriptors (Jing and Baluja 2008). These tools were not advanced enough to be employed in the Project's timescale, however, and so the COINS team resolved to take advantage only of logical profiling by website.

The COINS Web Spider

The COINS Project's approach here relied on a spider program based on the open-source Webcrawler Nutch, which was chosen from several possibilities after careful evaluation (Saccenti and Sifniotis 2008, 6–7, citing Benedict 2004).[8] To Nutch's own indexing and tagging facilities the team at PIN added a plug-in adapted for image searching (Saccenti and Sifniotis 2008, 9). In the simplest terms, this plug-in causes Nutch to examine the code of all web pages that it reaches for the "<img>" tag that indicates an image in the page. It then checks the URL of the web page to ensure that it has not already been indexed, discards any images of less than 90 by 90 pixels (firstly because these are likely to be background or banner images, secondly because they will be too small for parsing by recognition software anyway), then saves the image with a series of tags derived from the code relating to the image itself (e.g., alternate text, title, or caption tags) and also the immediate context of the page. In the case of the seed sites, the context was supplied manually to build profile sets relating to the categories of item displayed thereon, one profile set for example identifying eBay US's ancient coins page. These profiles then served as comparators, along with other sources of information, to assign a probability score to each subsequent website visited, indicating how likely the system thinks each image from that site is of a coin. No image recognition was applied at this stage.

In testing, the spider was deployed on eBay US, doing a variety of slow crawls over the space of a week (so as to keep stress on eBay's servers to a polite level) until the whole site was crawled and indexed. This gave 13,450 URLs, of which 10,906 were actual eBay items; 2,544 were marked as potential coins, and with duplicate URLs pruned this number dropped to almost half. The result of this was that 1,279 images were fetched for inspection, of which only fourteen per cent were not coins (some being coin books, busts of Cæsar, or other things for which keywords were insufficiently distinctive). This means that without image recognition, and with processing that was complete

[8] Nutch, last modified 19 August 2009, accessed 12 October 2009, http://lucene.apache.org/nutch/.

within two hours, eBay US was harvested for coin images and more than eighty per cent was winnowed in processing, leaving a set of images of which eighty-six per cent were relevant (Saccenti and Sifniotis 2008, 10). (It is of course not clear how many correct images were not fetched, as the team did not manually index the whole of eBay in parallel!)

With these results the COINS Spider was deemed adequate for the project's purposes, and it is now available for download from the project's website.[9] This tool provides, therefore, to any numismatist with a certain amount of computing support (or willingness to run one's own Linux machine) the ability to assemble a substantial reference database of images from a far wider basis than any single museum or private collection.

Data inwards: Databases and standards of record

Coin cataloguing database issues

Throughout these aims a key role is played by databases. Databases are an obvious necessity for the heritage sector. At the most basic, every museum needs to have some kind of catalogue, and the advantages of electronic cataloguing are obvious whether one uses a simple spreadsheet or an expensive custom-built collections management system. Each specialist area, however, has its own requirements, and numismatics is no different. Indeed, the data required by a student of modern European coinage would be very different from that wished for by a student of early Islamic coinage, and the differences between machine-made, and therefore uniform, modern coins and hand-hammered coins of earlier periods, every one of which can be a unique piece, complicate matters considerably. However, there are certain things that numismatists the world over would probably like to have recorded of any given item. These particularly include a coin's size, weight, metal content, denomination, issuing authority, and date (Jarrett 2009b, 26–31).

Cataloguing such data for a whole coin collection is not simple. Old weight measurements in grains rather than grams may still mislead those used to

---

[9] The COINS Web Spider is so far only available to run under Linux, from http://www. coins-project.eu/index.php?Itemid=53&option=com_content, as of 12 October 2009. It requires the Sun Java Development Kit 1.4 or higher, Apache Webserver 2.0 or higher and the graphic library set ImageMagick; download links for these, which may be in the user's Linux install already, are supplied on the COINS Spider Installation page at http://www.coins-project.eu/index.php?Itemid=53&option=com_content, as of 12 October 2009.

International Standard units, and square or irregular coins may challenge someone who has been told to record diameter. Complications, however, go beyond simple measurement. Die-axis—the difference in rotation between the two faces of the coin—is a good example. For a great many coins this is uniform inside an issue or has little historical value, but at the level of research where individual mints and moneyers are a concern, die-axis, and the practices thereof, can help untangle mysteries. For example, for much of both the Anglo-Saxon and Anglo-Norman periods in England, English coinage bore a cross on one or both sides. This naturally inclined those striking the coins to align the coin dies they used, at intervals of ninety degrees following the arms of the crosses. This practice was so general, in fact, that any coin not conforming to it must be regarded with great suspicion: die-axis thus becomes one way to spot a likely cast forgery (Larson 2004, 146–51). Such differences can also be authentic, and if a certain practice is spotted from one production centre and not from another, it can lead to important deductions about the number of coins in an issue and the spread of coins from a workshop, and therefore the economy in which the coins operated (e.g., Hollstein 2000, cited in Rosenstein and Morstein-Marx 2006, 68). Die-axis is laborious to measure, frequently but not always approximated, and almost irrelevant to modern coinage; but for certain sorts of work it is vital information.

Further semantic problems can arise with issuing authority. This is sometimes concealed, and even where not so, it is sometimes ambiguous. For example, on a modern British coin, the head and title of Queen Elizabeth II (1952–) invariably appear, and the coins are struck by the Royal Mint, but that is a government company; its coinage is honoured by the Bank of England, and issued by the Exchequer, of which the queen is only notionally head (Challis 1986; Royal Mint 2008). So under what name should it be catalogued? And how may someone else have catalogued it? And so on.

Ontologies, thesauri, and the COINS Management Tool

For museums and collections that are still facing these dilemmas, the COINS Project's most important offering is open-source database software designed to accommodate data of various standards and present it for use in a uniform way. This software, COINS Management Tool (COINS-MT), was designed on the basis of test data submitted to PIN from SAR and the Fitzwilliam in XML format, extracted from the institutions' own catalogues (Felicetti 2008, 4–5). The Fitzwilliam sent a selection of high-standard Greek and Roman coins comprising 1,200 records with a pair of images in each. SAR offered an archive of 600 Roman, Etruscan, and early Italian coins. As may be expected, the standards and terminology used by the two museums differed considerably, not least because each was done in a different language.

A way to link all of these systems is provided by a standard known as CIDOC-CRM, the Comité International pour la Documentation des Musées Conceptual Reference Model, which according to its creators, "provides definitions and a formal structure for describing the implicit and explicit concepts and relationships used in cultural heritage documentation."[10] By focusing on the events that have affected an object—its creation, use, and deposition, as well as its discovery, accession, and consequent storage and inventorying—and relating to each object those entities and qualities that characterize and describe those events, CIDOC-CRM provides "a common and extensible semantic framework that any cultural heritage information can be mapped to" (Felicetti and d'Andrea 2008a, 4). Since CIDOC-CRM has been the International Standard for recording heritage object information since 2006, its adoption for COINS seemed an obvious choice. Further work still had to be done, however, to adapt and extend CIDOC-CRM for COINS's purposes. First, a selection was made of standard CIDOC fields that were already useful for numismatic information, and then other fields in the COINS datasets that were not covered by this first selection were mapped to the most relevant CIDOC fields remaining.[11]

Using this pattern for dealing with heritage objects, it was possible for PIN to create a shared domain ontology that linked all the institution's various catalogue fields to a central thesaurus. This thesaurus was then used as the foundation of the Management Tool (Felicetti and d'Andrea 2008b).[12] It is built on a hierarchical structure in which individual terms can be related to others by equivalence, association, or as super- or subsets of each other,

---

[10] Quoted from *The CIDOC Conceptual Reference Model*, last modified 15 December 2006, accessed 12 October 2009, http://cidoc.ics.forth.gr/; the current version of CIDOC-CRM can be downloaded as a RAR archive at http://cidoc.ics.forth.gr/docs/ver_cidoc_4.3_nov_08_db.rar, last modified 18 February 2009, accessed 12 October 2009.

[11] An example of this process can be found in the mapping done by Achille Felicetti of the Soprintendenza Archeologica di Roma's XML template to CIDOC-CRM, downloadable in Microsoft Excel format at http://www.coins-project.eu/downloads/documentation/SAR_MAPPING.xls, last modified September 9, 2008, accessed 12 October 2009.

[12] The ontology itself, by Achille Felicetti and Andrea d'Andrea, can be downloaded in Microsoft Excel format at http://www.coins-project.eu/downloads/documentation/COINS-ONTOLOGY.xls, last modified 9 September 2008, accessed 12 October 2009.

and follows ISO standards for such exercises.[13] In fact it was discovered that, outside already-international terms such as measurement units, a relatively narrow set of top-level terms could be employed, these being "coin," "denomination," "mint," and "authority." All other terms in the submitted datasets could be subsumed under one of these top-level terms, and it is expected that, although the thesaurus is open to revision for each new collection that the project is allowed to adapt, this range of terms will continue to suffice for most if not all numismatic collections, including those with no existing digital catalogues. The agreed set of terms for record is as follows:

- ★ Denomination
- ★ Provenance (city, province, region)
- ★ Mint
- ★ Date
- ★ Makers
- ★ Category (coin or medal)
- ★ Material
- ★ Dimensions (height, width) or average dimensions
- ★ Weight
- ★ Inscriptions
- ★ Obverse and reverse descriptions
- ★ Bibliographic references
- ★ Catalogue references
- ★ Type references
- ★ Museum's specific identification numbers
- ★ Accession information
- ★ Related images

Encoding of this data is done in the Resource Description Framework (RDF) format, a derivative of XML designed to provide a flexible and extensible framework of modeling and describing information through a variety of syntax formats.[14] Conversion to RDF from existing legacy databases can be done

---

[13] The thesaurus, by Andrea d'Andrea, is visible at: http://www.coins-project.eu/coins_thesaurus.owl, last modified 19 December 2008, accessed 12 October 2009, and can be downloaded in OWL format from http://www.coins-project.eu/index.php?option=com_content&view=article&id=36&Itemid=48, accessed 12 October 2009.

[14] RDF: http://www.w3.org/RDF/, last modified 29 August 2009, accessed 12 October 2009.

either by conversion into a duplicate database, or in real time per query. The disadvantage of the former method is of course that subsequent changes in the data need to be reflected in both versions, and it is easy for the two formats to fall out of step; the advantage would be performance, but in fact, an open-source tool called D2R exists that, on the basis of a predefined mapping, can rapidly convert RDF and HTML queries into SQL that most databases can resolve (Bizer and Cyganiak 2009). Since an adequate mapping for COINS-MT already existed in the form of the ontology and thesaurus described above, this technology was found highly suitable for the project's purposes (Felicetti 2008, 6–8).

With the structure thus established, the actual data, which was often considerably more complex, had to be dealt with. Since much of the data was subjective or descriptive, it had to be stored so as to be accessed semantically rather than structurally, and for this purpose a framework known as Managing Archaeological Data (MAD) was adopted (Felicetti 2006), which in its most recent form comes with a semantic engine able to store and manage data organized in an ontology and allow it to be queried in RDF. This suited COINS's purposes perfectly (Felicetti 2008, 8).

The final internal component of the management tool deals with the associated images, which are stored in high-resolution and low-resolution formats and linked to the records using one of the CIDOC-CRM properties. Only low-resolution images are made available in the user presentation of the Management Tool, but those with higher-level rights can access the high-resolution images or make new low-resolution ones from ingressed high-quality images without the need to import both sets for each item (Felicetti 2008, 9–15).

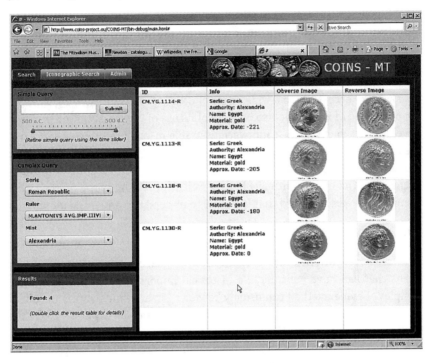

Figure 9. Screen capture of the COINS-MT database in action. Image by
Jonathan Jarrett. Copyright © 2008 COINS Project.

User interaction with the COINS Management Tool is fast and simple.[15] This
is in part due to the simplicity of the basic data structure described above,
but otherwise largely owing to the methods employed to deliver data to the
user's computer. Using a technology known as Asynchronous JavaScript +
XML (AJAX), much of the computing that is usually dealt with by servers in
a classic HTTP session, such as page layout and presentation, is handled by
a client-side JavaScript download that is installed per-session in the user's
browser at log-on. Subsequently the server has only to provide data in raw-
text format, which is parsed client-side by the JavaScript. This technology
converts the user's browser into a session manager that maintains page layout and text presentation itself, greatly speeding interaction and allowing

[15] See n. 3 above for a link to the online demo version. The full software is downloadable in
a ZIP package from http://www.coins-project.eu/index.php?Itemid=53&option=com_
content, last modified 3 February 2009 as of 15 October 2009. It can be run under Windows XP and higher or Mac OS X or higher. The Tool's documentation is to be found
in Felicetti (2008).

immediate response to scrolling, sliders, and other such dynamic controls (Felicetti 2008, 9–15).

The COINS Management Tool is therefore an innovation in terms of containing an adaptable structure based on the latest work in ontologies and thesauri so as to be accessible to a wide range of other formats, presenting a usable format in and of itself, but also because of its use of the latest in web browser development to make these innovations usable in existing Internet software. We can hope that the availability of such an outwardly simple and dynamic tool will result in the recording of more data, and greater usability for others of that data than we might have had, as well as providing non-experts with a numismatic data standard that is simple to understand and implement.

Data out: sharing and study through COINS tools

As has been mentioned above, there are many facets of numismatic study, facets that can have considerable historical import but that require larger samples of evidence than can usually be viewed in any single museum collection. Indeed some private collections have been assembled expressly to enable such a study to be made. Even if one is content to assemble such a dataset in the form of notes, photographs, and catalogue records, it can take years and a great deal of expense in terms of travel and purchasing. Nowadays, however, such samples and datasets can often be accessed not just in coin rooms, but across the Internet, in exactly the sort of coverage required for reference and for examination by the technologies developed in the COINS Project. With our Web Spider and the COINS Management Tool, for example, an institution or an individual scholar can assemble on their desktop a study corpus of thousands of pieces that can be organized for them to a great extent, with both catalogue data and images searchable, in a uniform way despite variation in the standards of record of the websites of origin. This technology, therefore, will enable many different collections already catalogued to be combined into a library of information that will not only greatly increase the *comparanda* available for the COINS Project's initial purpose, but enable academic sharing of data on an unprecedented scale.

The value of such a resource is well known at the Fitzwilliam Museum, whose *Early Medieval Corpus of Coin Finds* database tries to record all single-finds of coins from between 400 and 1180 in Great Britain.[16] With this kind of sample,

---

[16] The *Early Medieval Corpus* was programmed by Sean Miller, whose web page is at http://www.seanmiller.ca, last modified 4 August 2008, accessed 18 August 2008; the *Corpus* itself can be found at http://www.fitzmuseum.cam.ac.uk/dept/coins/emc/,

distribution maps and plots of finds over time take on new significance. The Museum's collection of coins of King Alfred the Great of Wessex (871–99) has one or two examples of most varieties, twenty-two in total, but the EMC/SCBI database increases this haul to 358, with images and findspots where they are known. The findspots can be mapped, and histograms of distribution over time generated. This kind of information lets numismatists come to conclusions about the spread of coinage, its worth, its origins, and its use that would be impossible without such an aggregated dataset. This can also give relative ideas of the size of whole coinages, which tells us a great deal about the state of a region's economy and its political control (Grierson 1975, 155–57; cf. Buttrey 1993). Indeed, although it has not been part of the COINS Project's aims, one side benefit of the image recognition technology it has developed may be the automation of the process of die-linking, that is, identifying coins struck from the same die. And so on: more data makes more possible, and sharing across the Web makes more data possible—the benefits are incremental, but the COINS Project's web harvesting components already make it possible for a scholar to build a hitherto impossible study corpus almost automatically.

For the possible value of that resource, and a closing example, let us quote Professor Ralph Mathisen of the University of Illinois. Professor Mathisen, who has kindly allowed us to borrow this story from a paper of his, is a numismatist by training but also a respected scholar of late Antiquity.[17] He is thus alive to the possibilities of coins as historical evidence, and alive too to what the Web means for such work. We quote:

> The increasing availability of numismatic sale records on the Web, coupled with the easy availability of very high resolution photographs, is leading to an explosion of new scholarly research—in my class on ancient coins, it has become much easier, for example, even for undergraduate students to do cutting edge research.

In 2008 at the International Congress on Medieval Studies in Kalamazoo, Michigan, Professor Mathisen presented a paper that demonstrates both what can be done and what could be much easier, and that ties up strangely well with the COINS Project's initial aims (Mathisen 2008; Bezlov and Tzenkov 2007, 178–91). Again, we give his explanation verbatim:

---

last modified 8 January 2009, accessed 3 March 2009, and is discussed in print in Blackburn (2005).

[17] Professor Mathisen's web page is at http://www.history.uiuc.edu/people/ ralphwm/, last modified 1 August 2008, accessed 18 August 2008.

I've always kept an eye on electronic sales in general and on eBay in particular to see what was passing through the market, and the genesis of the Kalamazoo talk ... was when I noticed back in 2004 that a large number of Theodosius II/Valentinian III consular *solidi* [Roman gold coins of about 4.5 g] had come onto the market. The rest, as they say, is history. After collecting the eBay records, we constructed a corpus of over 300 examples of these and related *solidi* that had passed through other dealers (primarily via the very useful sales records preserved on CoinArchives) that, after accounting for normal background sales, indicated that a hoard of several hundred *solidi* had appeared on the market in the early 2000s. Based on correspondence with dealers (most of whom played things very close to the vest, but a few of whom were candid), I concluded that the hoard originally had been deposited near Philippopolis (Plovdiv). An analysis of contents placed its date of deposit quite firmly ca. 440, putting it squarely in the context of the historically attested raids by the Huns at just that time.[18]

It is immediately easy to see how the COINS Project tools could have helped with this research. Professor Mathisen's example demonstrates how the sort of laborious collection of data that previously had to be done in a range of libraries and auction houses in several different countries can now be done through the Web, though the automation provided by the COINS Project's tools will speed this even further. It also demonstrates how the assembly of such data can have genuine historiographical outcomes. A hoard of coins that was never reported, that was presumably removed from its country illegally and dispersed through sales, can now be reconstituted, approximately dated, and located via the Web and some careful enquiries. We see here the uses of harvesting the Web for images and records, of zeroing in on particular types in a morass of information, and the historical significance that can be got from putting all these pieces together. With the technologies that this project is developing, therefore, it is not just museum cataloguing and collections management that will be advanced; it is what we know about the world and the past, on a level that perhaps only such technologies can make accessible.

---

[18] The CoinArchives site to which Professor Mathisen refers is located at http://www.coinarchives.com/, last modified 15 July 2009, accessed 15 October 2009.

WORKS CITED

Allen, Martin. 2006. "The Volume of the English Currency, c. 973–1158." In *Coinage and History in the North Sea World, c. AD 500–1200: Essays in Honour of Marion Archibald*, edited by Barrie Cook and Gareth Williams, 487–523. Leiden: Brill.

Bay, Herbert, Tubbe Tuytelaars, and Luc Van Gool. 2006. "SURF: Speeded Up Robust Features." In *Proceedings of the 9th European Conference on Computer Vision, 7–13 May 2006, Graz, Austria*, edited by Aleš Leonardis et al., 404–17.

Bell, Robert Charles. 1963. *Commercial Coins 1787–1804*. Newcastle-upon-Tyne: Corbitt and Hunter.

Benedict, Lyle. 2004. "Comparison of Nutch and Google Search Engine Implementations on the Oregon State University Website." Modified 23 June 2004. http://www.misterbot.fr/OSU_Queries.pdf. Current location: modified 18 October 2007. http://web.archive.org/web/20071018222744/.

Bezlov, Tihomir, and Emil Tzenkov. 2007. *Organized Crime in Bulgaria: Markets and Trends*. Sofia: Centre for the Study of Democracy.

Bizer, Chris, and Richard Cyganiak. 2009. D2R Server: Publishing Relational Databases on the Semantic Web. Modified 10 August 2009. http://www4.wiwiss.fu-berlin.de/bizer/d2r-server/

Blackburn, Mark. 2005. "Disseminating Find Evidence: the British Corpus of Early Medieval Coin Finds." In *Actas del XIII Congreso Internacional de Numismática (Madrid 2003)*, edited by Carmen Alfaro et al., 1:169–71. Madrid: Ministerio de cultura.

Blackburn, Mark, Fiorenzo Catalli, and Achille Felicetti. 2008. *Report on Reference Collections*. Modified 9 September 2008. http://www.coins-project.eu/downloads/reports/Coins-044450-D8.pdf.

Buttrey, Theodore. 1993. "Calculating Ancient Coin Production: Facts and Fantasies." *Numismatic Chronicle* 153:335–51.

Challis, Christopher. 1986. "A New Beginning: Llantrisant." In *A New History of the Royal Mint*, edited by Christopher Challis, 661–72. Cambridge: Cambridge University Press.

Coupland, Simon. 1990. "Money and Coinage under Louis the Pious." *Francia* 17:23–54. Reprinted in Coupland 2007, III.

_____ 2002. "The Medieval Euro." *History Today* 52:18–19.

_____ 2007. *Carolingian Coinage and the Vikings: Studies on Power and Trade in the 9th Century.* Aldershot: Ashgate.

Davies, Glyn. 1996. *A History of Money from Ancient Times to the Present Day.* Revised edition. Cardiff: University of Wales Press.

Elkins, Nathan T. 2008. "A Survey of the Material and Intellectual Consequences of Trading in Undocumented Ancient Coins: A Case Study on the North American Trade." *Frankfurter elektronische Rundschau zur Altertumskunde* 7:1–13. Modified 2 October 2008. http://s145739614.online.de/fera/ausgabe7/Elkins.pdf.

Felicetti, Achille. 2006. "MAD: Managing Archaeological Data." In *The E-volution of Information: Communication Technology in Cultural Heritage. Where Hi-Tech Touches the Past: Risks and Challenges for the 21st Century,* Project papers from the joint event CIPA / VAST / EG / EuroMed 2006, 30 October–4 November 2006, Nicosia, Cyprus, edited by M. Ioannides et al., 124–31. Budapest: Archaeolingua.

_____ 2008. Tool for Coin Data Management. Modified 10 September 2008. http://www.coins-project.eu/downloads/reports/Coins-044450-D7.pdf.

Felicetti, Achille, and Andrea d'Andrea. 2008a. *Deliverable D4: Domain Ontology.* Combat On-Line Illegal Numismatic Sales (COINS) Project. Modified 12 September 2008. http://www.coins-project.eu/downloads/reports/Coins-044450-D4.pdf.

_____ 2008b. *Deliverable D5: Multilingual Thesaurus.* Combat On-Line Illegal Numismatic Sales (COINS) Project. Modified 15 September 2008. http://www.coins-project.eu/downloads/reports/Coins-044450-D5.pdf.

Grierson, Philip. 1959. "Commerce in the Dark Ages: A Critique of the Evidence." *Transactions of the Royal Historical Society,* 5th Series, 9:123–40. Reprinted in Grierson, *Dark Age Numismatics: Selected Studies,* II. Collected Studies 96. London: Variorum, 1979.

_____ 1975. *Numismatics*. Oxford: Oxford University Press.

Hollstein, W. 2000. "Die Stempelstellung — ein ungenutztes Interpretationskriterium für die Münzprägung der Römischen Republik." In *XII. Internationaler Numismatischer Kongress: Berlin 1997*, edited by B. Kluge and B. Weisser, 487–91. Berlin: Staatlichen Museen zu Berlin—Preussischer Kulturbesitz.

Huber, Reinhold, Herbert Ramoser, Konrad J. Mayer, Harald Penz, and Michael Rubik. 2005. "Classification of Coins Using an Eigenspace Approach." *Pattern Recognition Letters* 26:61–75.

Huber-Mörk, Reinhold, et al. 2008a. *Deliverable D10: Image Recognition Tool.* Modified 25 July, 2008. Combat On-Line Illegal Numismatic Sales (COINS) Project. http://www.coins-project.eu/downloads/reports/Coins-044450-D10.pdf.

Huber-Mörk, Reinhold, Maria Zaharieva, and Holger Czedik-Eysenberg. 2008b. "Numismatic Object Identification Using Fusion of Shape and Local Descriptors." In *Advances in Visual Computing: 4th International Symposium, ISVC 2008, Las Vegas, NV, USA, December 1-3, 2008, Proceedings, Part II*, edited by George Bebis et al., 368–79.

Jarrett, Jonathan. 2009a. "Digitizing Numismatics: Getting the Fitzwilliam Museum's Coins to the World-Wide Web." *The Heroic Age* 12. Modified 3 June 2009. http://www.heroicage.org/issues/12/foruma.php.

_____ 2009b. *Coins in Collections: Care and Use.* Cambridge: Fitzwilliam Museum.

Jing, Yushi, and Shumeet Baluja. 2008. "PageRank for Product Image Search." In *Proceedings of the 17th International World Wide Web Conference (WWW 2008) April 21-25, 2008 Beijing, China.* Geneva: International World Wide Web Conference Committee. Modified 7 April 2008. http://www2008.org/papers/pdf/p307-jingA.pdf.

Kampel, Martin. 2008. "Computer Aided Analysis of Ancient Coins." In *Digital Cultural Heritage — Essential for Tourism: Proceedings of the 2nd EVA 2008 Vienna Conference, Vienna, August 25-28, 2008*, edited by Robert Sablatnig et al., 137–44. Vienna: Österreichische Computer Gesellschaft.

Kampel, Martin, and Maria Zaharieva. 2008. "Recognising Ancient Coins Based on Local Features." In *Advances in Visual Computing, 4th International Symposium of Visual Computing, December 1-3, Las Vegas, Nevada, USA: Proceedings, part 1*, edited by George Bebis et al., 11–22.

Kampel, Martin, Maria Zaharieva, and Sebastian Zambanini. 2008. "Segmentation and Classification." Presented at COINS Internal Review Meeting, 28 January, Kaprun, Austria.

King, M. D. 1988. "Roman Coins from Early Anglo-Saxon Contexts." In *Coins and the Archaeologist*, edited by P. J. Casey and Richard Reece, 224–29. 2nd ed. London: Seaby.

Larson, Charles M. 2004. *Numismatic Forgery*. Irvine: Zyrus.

Lowe, David G. 2004. "Distinctive Image Features from Scale-Invariant Keypoints." *International Journal of Computer Vision* 60:91–110.

Maaten, Laurens van der, and P. J. Poon. 2006. "Coin-o-matic: A Fast System for Reliable Coin Classification." In *Proceedings of the MUSCLE CIS Coin Competition Workshop, September 11 2006, Berlin, Germany*, edited by Michael Nölle et al., 7–18. Vienna: TU Wien. Modified 30 January 2008. http://muscle.prip.tuwien.ac.at/coin_workshop2006_proceedings/maaten.pdf.

Mathias, Peter. 1962. *English Trade Tokens: The Industrial Revolution Illustrated*. London: Abelard-Schulman.

Mathisen, Ralph. 2008. "Reconstructing a Hoard of Late Roman Gold *Solidi*." Presented in session "Late Antiquity I: Art, Architecture, and Material Culture in Late Antiquity," International Congress of Medieval Studies, 9 May 2008, Western Michigan University, Kalamazoo, MI, USA.

Metcalf, Michael. 1982. "Anglo-Saxon Coins 3: Edgar's Reform to the Conquest." In *The Anglo-Saxons*, edited by James Campbell et al., 204–5. Harmondsworth: Penguin.

Nölle, Michael, Reinhard Granec, Igor Hollander, Konrad J. Mayer, Harald Penz, and Michael Rubik. 2003. "Dagobert – A New Coin Recognition and Sorting System." In *Proceedings of the 7th International Conference on Digital Image Computing - Techniques and Applications (DICTA '03). Macquarrie University, Sydney, Australia*, edited by C. Sun et al., 329–38.

Sydney: CSIRO. Modified 2 December 2003. http://www.aprs.org.au/dicta2003/pdf/0329.pdf.

Price, Michael. 1991. *The Coinage in the Name of Alexander the Great and Philip Arrhidaeus: A British Museum Catalogue*. London: British Museum.

Reisert, Marco, Olaf Ronneberger, and Hans Burkhardt. 2006. "An Efficient Gradient Based Recognition Technique for Coin Recognition." In *Proceedings of the MUSCLE CIS Coin Competition Workshop, September 11 2006, Berlin, Germany*, edited by Michael Nölle et al., 19–31. Berlin. Accessed 19 March 2009. ftp://ftp.informatik.uni-freiburg.de/papers/lmb/re_ro_bu_CISCoin06.pdf.

Rosenstein, Nathan, and Robert Morstein-Marx. 2006. *A Companion to the Roman Republic*. Oxford: Oxford University Press.

Royal Mint. 2008. "An Introduction to Our History, People, Services and Processes." Modified 1 August 2008. http://www.royalmint.gov.uk/Corporate/AboutUs/AboutUsHome.aspx.

Saccenti, Sandro, and Marco Sifniotis. 2008. *Deliverable D9: Numismatic Web Search Tool*. Combat On-Line Illegal Numismatic Sales (COINS) Project. Modified 9 September 2008. http://www.coins-project.eu/downloads/reports/Coins-044450-D9.pdf.

Smith, Douglas. 1995. "Die-Links: A Tool for the Numismatist." *Celator* 9:12–17.

Snible, Ed. 2009. "Software from COINS." *A Gift from Polydektes*, 7 June 2009, accessed 12 October 2009. Blog. http://digitalhn.blogspot.com/2009/06/software-from-coins.html.

Zambanini, Sebastian, and Martin Kampel. 2008. "Segmentation of Ancient Coins Based on Local Entropy and Gray Value Range." In *Proceedings of the 13th Computer Vision Winter Workshop, Moravske Toplice, Slovenia*, edited by J. Perš, 9–16. Ljubljana: Slovenian Pattern Recognition Society.

Contributors

Wouter Bracke is professor of Latin literature and Latin palaeography at the Université libre de Bruxelles (Free University of Brussels). He is also head of the Map room and the Prints cabinet of the Royal Library of Belgium. His research focuses on the history of cartography and the world of the Latin manuscript book in the Renaissance.

Megan Palmer Browne, PhD candidate in English and Medieval Studies at the University of California, Santa Barbara, is woodcut impressions specialist for the Early English Broadside Ballad Archive. Her research focuses on poetic explorations of animal consciousness in the medieval and early modern periods, and on the ways in which these explorations intersect with the changing technologies of these periods. Palmer Browne has an essay forthcoming in the collection *Chaucerian Beasts*, edited by Carolynn Van Dyke (part of the New Middle Ages series from Palgrave Macmillan).

Gérard Bouvin is a certificated librarian at the Royal Library of Belgium since 2004. He obtained a BA in history from the Université libre de Bruxelles (Free University of Brussels). He is a specialist of early maps and actually responsible for cataloguing old and early maps in the Map room of the library.

Catherine A.M. Clarke is Senior Lecturer in English and Associate Director of the Centre for Medieval and Early Modern Research at Swansea University. Her research centres on earlier medieval literature and culture, with particular attention to questions of place, power, and identity and an emphasis on interdisciplinary approaches. Her publications include the monograph *Literary Landscapes and the Idea of England, 700-1400* (Cambridge, 2006), and the edited collection *Mapping the Medieval City: Space, Place and Identity in Chester, c.1200-1600* (Cardiff, 2011). She was Principal Investigator on the AHRC-funded 'Mapping Medieval Chester project' (http://www.medievalchester.ac.uk).

James Cummings co-manages the InfoDev Team at the University of Oxford which provides data solutions, web projects, research support and advice. He is usually an elected member to the Text Encoding Initiative (TEI) Technical Council. James undertook a BA and MA in Medieval Studies from the University of Toronto and a PhD on the archival records of medieval drama from the University of Leeds. He is the elected director of the Digital Medievalist project which runs an open access journal, wiki, mailing-list, and conference sessions. James bridges both Medieval Studies and Digital Humanities in his publications, conference papers, and posters.

Richard Cunningham is a professor of early modern English literature, rhetoric, and Digital Humanities in the Department of English and Theatre at Acadia University in Wolfville, NS. He has published on Shakespeare, John Foxe, and on a variety of DH topics. Since 2008, he has been the Director of the Acadia Digital Culture Observatory. He is the administrative lead of, and a researcher on, the Textual Studies team, and a member of the executive board, of the Implementing New Knowledge Environments research initiative.

Paul Dyck is Associate Professor of English Literature at Canadian Mennonite University in Winnipeg, Canada. He did his doctoral dissertation on early seventeenth-century habits of reading and George Herbert's *Temple* (1633) with particular attention to early editions and what they suggest about the ways in which the poems were originally read. His work has focused on the theological functions of early modern material textuality as found in Herbert and the Little Gidding community led by Nicholas Ferrar, which has been published in several journal articles and book chapters. He is beginning work on the topic of revenge in drama and cinema.

Achille Felicetti is an archaeologist with a degree in Topography of Ancient Roman Italy and is involved, since 2004, in the activities of the VAST-LAB (Standards and Tools for Cultural Heritage) at the University of Florence (Italy). His work mainly concerns the development of technologies and standards for the management of archaeological excavation information and the design and implementation of digital archives of archaeological data. In past years he was involved in the creation of cultural heritage ontologies and standards for the EPOCH project and participated in the COINS project as a developer of semantic digital archives of ancient coins. He is currently involved as coordinator of the metadata activities within the 3D-COFORM project, and is part of the metadata mapping team at the Italian Ministry of Cultural Heritage.

Patricia Fumerton is Professor of English at the University of California, Santa Barbara and Director of UCSB's online English Broadside Ballad Archive, or EBBA <http://ebba.english.ucsb.edu>, which has to date won three large NEH Collections and Resources grants as well as the British Society for Eighteenth Century Studies' first annual *BSECS Digital Eighteenth Century Prize* (2009). Fumerton is also author of the print monographs *Unsettled: The Culture of Mobility and the Working Poor in Early Modern England* (Chicago, 2006) and *Cultural Aesthetics: Renaissance Literature and the Practice of Social Ornament* (Chicago, 1991) as well as co-editor of *Broadsides and Ballads in Britain, 1500-1800* (Ashgate 2010) and *Renaissance Culture and the Everyday* (Pennsylvania, 1999). In addition, she is bringing out a print companion to EBBA, *Broadside Ballads from the Pepys Collection: A Selection of Texts, Approaches, and Recordings* (forthcoming, MRTS), which includes two CDS of song recordings. She continues to expand EBBA while also working on a monograph that investigates the formal, social, and geographical mobility—over 200 hundred years and across the Atlantic—of one particularly popular, if also gruesome, broadside ballad, "The Lady and the Blackamoor."

Alan Galey is Assistant Professor in the Faculty of Information at the University of Toronto, where he also teaches in the collaborative program in Book History and Print Culture. His research focuses on intersections between textual scholarship and digital technologies, especially in the context of theories of the archive. He has published on these topics articles in journals such as *Shakespeare Quarterly, Literary and Linguistic Computing*, and *College Literature*, and in the book collections *Electronic Editing: Politics and Pragmatics* (Iter/Arizona Centre for Medieval and Renaissance Studies), *Text and Genre in Reconstruction* (Open Book), and *The History of Reading* (Palgrave MacMillan; forthcoming). He is co-editor of a special issue of *Shakespeare* (with Ray Siemens, on "Reinventing Digital Shakespeare"), and of the book collection *Shakespeare, the Bible, and the Form of the Book: Contested Scriptures* (with Travis DeCook; forthcoming from Routledge).

David Humphrey is Visiting Tutor in the Department of Goldsmithing, Silversmithing, Metalwork and Jewellery at the Royal College of Art, London. Between 2005 and 2008 he was Deputy Director of the College's Centre for Jewellery Research. His work into aspects of late medieval European goldsmithing has received funding from the Leverhulme Trust, the British Academy, and the Pasold Research Fund. He has presented invited lectures at institutions including the Victoria and Albert Museum, London; Institute d'Histoire Université de Paris IV, La Sorbonne; the University of Cambridge; University College, London and the Courtauld Institute of Art, London. Recent publications include contributions to *AVISTA Journal, Archaeological Review from Cambridge*, and volumes from Cambridge Scholars Publishing and Universal Publishers. He is currently working on aspects of the deployment of geometry in late medieval European goldsmiths' work.

Reinhold Huber-Mörk is a scientist at the Austrian Institute of Technology (AIT) in the field of high-performance image processing. He obtained a PhD in Computer Science from the University of Salzburg, Austria. Before joining AIT, he worked on remote-sensing data analysis at the German Aerospace Research Center in Oberpfaffenhofen and on industrial computer vision at the Advanced Computer Vision GmbH in Vienna, Austria. He is author of approximately 50 scientific papers in the fields of pattern recognition, image processing, computer vision, and remote sensing. He is mainly working on applied research projects including applications in cultural heritage, e.g. automatic identification of ancient coins and digital preservation for libraries. His current research interests are in the field of color image processing, digital preservation, and machine vision.

Katherine Hunt has held curatorial positions at the Victoria and Albert Museum and Tate Britain, and was a research assistant on the AHRC-funded British Printed Images to 1700 Project. She is writing a PhD at the London Consortium, University of London, about English church bells in the seventeenth century, and is a founding editor of Teller Magazine (http://www. tellermagazine.com).

Diane Jakacki is a Marion L. Brittain Postdoctoral Fellow and Instructor at the Georgia Institute of Technology, where she teaches early modern drama, popular culture and media studies. Her research focuses on the examination of illustrated title pages as marketing instruments in the sale of early English play-texts, as well as the application of humanities computing methods for pedagogy and research projects. She has published an article on clues about theatrical practice in the Spanish Tragedy title page illustration in Early Theatre and an edition of John Redford's "The Play of Wit and Science" in the Broadview Anthology of Medieval Drama. She is also the online consultant and designer of the graphical user interface and website for the imageMAT (MARGOT Annotation Tool) project, PI: Christine McWebb.

Jonathan Jarrett is a Departmental Lecturer in the Faculty of History at Oxford University and a Career Development Fellow at the Queen's College. He is author of Rulers and Ruled in Frontier Catalonia, 880-1010: Pathways of Power (2010) and a number of articles on power relations and the use of the past in early medieval Catalonia. He also writes the academic blog A Corner of Tenth-Century Europe and publishes on the propagation of academic research through informal channels. His contribution to this volume is an outcome of work done as a Research Assistant at the Department of Coins and

Medals of the Fitzwilliam Museum in Cambridge, where he was employed before his move to Oxford.

Keith Lilley is Reader in Historical Geography at Queen's University Belfast. He has written extensively on both medieval and modern urbanism. His recent publications include *City and Cosmos: The Medieval World in Urban Form* (Reaktion Books, 2009), as well as a number of online historical resources using distributed GIS, such as Mapping Medieval Chester (http://www.medievalchester.ac.uk), Mapping Medieval Townscapes (http://ads.ahds.ac.uk/catalogue/specColl/atlas_ahrb_2005/) and Linguistic Geographies (http://www.goughmap.org). He is coordinator of a new pan-European research network on "Spatial Technologies and the Medieval City", and is collating a series of papers on this topic for PostClassical Archaeologies in collaboration with Alexandra Chavarria (University of Padua).

Kris McAbee is Assistant Professor of English at the University of Arkansas, Little Rock. She is the former Assistant Director of and the current Technical Consultant for the English Broadside Ballad Archive. McAbee's essays on the printed circulation of ballads, on Love ballads, and on Frolics are forthcoming in *Broadside Ballads from the Pepys Collection: A Selection of Texts, Approaches, and Recordings* (forthcoming, MRTS). Her research focuses on popular verse trends of the early modern period, from sonnets to ballads, and the literary representations of the petty poets who write such verse. She also maintains a critical and pedagogical interest in digitally inflected modes of inquiry, especially in digital archives, teaching with social media, and digital visualization tools. Her recent article on Michael Drayton's repeatedly revised sonnet sequence, *Idea*, appears in *Early Modern Culture* and uses digital motion charts to depict the sonnet vogue.

Christine McWebb is Director, Global Business and Digital Arts at the University of Waterloo Stratford Campus and Associate Professor of French at the University of Waterloo. Her main research interests are in late French medieval literature, culture and iconography as well as the Digital Humanities. She is also the director of the internationally recognized MARGOT project and currently leads two major projects in manuscript digitization and image annotation software development. She has published extensively on the French medieval author Christine de Pizan, the *Roman de la rose* and the relationship between text and iconography in medieval manuscripts. Her most recent monograph, *Debating the Roman de la rose: A Critical Anthology* was published by Routledge in 2007.

Brent Nelson teaches seventeenth-century literature in the Department of English at the University of Saskatchewan. He is the director of the John Donne Society's Digital Text Project and a collaborator on INKE: Implementing New Knowledge Environments. He has published on John Donne and rhetoric and Thomas Browne and the culture of curiosity (among other things) and is currently building an on-line archive of seventeenth-century collections of curiosities.

Nicholas Pickwoad is the founder and director of the Ligatus Research Centre, University of the Arts, London. He was awarded the Royal Warrant Holder Association's 2009 Plowden Medal, in recognition of his work in the study and conservation of historic libraries and rare books. He gave the 2008 Panizzi Lectures under the general title "Reading Bindings" in the British Library in November and December 2008 ("The Art of Bookbinding: bookbindings in art and art on a bookbinding", "The binder who was not Vincent Williamson: working habits and their use in identifying who actually bound the book," and "On the deckle edge: indications of status and economy"). He is an elected fellow of the Society of Antiquaries in the UK and a Council Member of the Bibliographical Society of Great Britain. He has led the library survey at the St. Catherine's Monastery in Sinai, Egypt and has written extensively on the history of bookbinding. He has also given many lectures on the same subject around the world and is currently leading the development of the Ligatus glossary of bookbinding terms.

Benoît Pigeon is a certificated librarian and metadata specialist at the Royal Library of Belgium since 2009. He is in charge of digitization projects in the Map room and the Prints cabinet of the library.

Stephen Pigney is a Lecturer in History at Goldsmiths, University of London and a Sessional Lecturer at Birkbeck, University of London. Previously he was a Research Assistant on the British Printed Images to 1700 project. He has also worked as an academic librarian, a print cataloguer, and a researcher on an editorial project. His research interests focus primarily on early modern intellectual (particularly philosophical and theological) and cultural (particularly literary and visual) history; he is also interested more broadly in issues relating to historiography and digital technologies.

Ryan Rempel is a lawyer with the Canadian Department of Justice, a computer programmer for Isomorphic Software (the makers of the SmartClient Javascript framework), and, on occasion, a sessional lecturer for Canadian Mennonite University, in political studies and the digital humanities. He has collaborated with Paul Dyck on several projects in the digital humanities, exploring techniques for the construction of rich user interfaces for the visualization and modification of XML-encoded documents.

Judith Siefring is a digital editor at the Digital Library of the Bodleian Library at Oxford University, working on encoding projects including the Early English Books Online Text Creation Partnership (EEBO-TCP) and the Shakespeare Quartos Archive (SQA).

Ray Siemens (http://web.uvic.ca/~siemens/) is Canada Research Chair in Humanities Computing and Professor of English at the University of Victoria with cross appointment in Computer Science. Editor of several Renaissance texts and founding editor of the electronic scholarly journal *Early Modern Literary Studies*, Siemens has written numerous articles on the connections between computational methods and literary studies and is the co-editor of several humanities computing books such as *Blackwell's Companion to Digital Humanities* and *Companion to Digital Literary Studies*. He serves as Director of the Implementing New Knowledge Environments project and the Digital Humanities Summer Institute, is Chair of the Alliance of Digital Humanities Organisations' Steering Committee, and is Vice President, Research Dissemination, of the Canadian Federation for the Humanities and Social Sciences; he has served as President (English) of the Society for Digital Humanities/ Société pour l'étude des médias interactifs (SDH/SEMI), Chair of the Modern Language Association's Committee on Information Technology and of the MLA Discussion Group on Computers in Language and Literature.

Lisa M. Snyder is a senior member of the Urban Simulation Team (UST) at the University of California, Los Angeles, and also works with UCLA's Office of Information Technology, Academic Technology Services, Institute for Digital Research and Education, and the Experiential Technologies Center. Her research is focused on the design and use of interactive computer models for the teaching of architectural history. Through the UST, she developed the real-time reconstruction models of the first-century Herodian and eighth-century Umayyad Temple Mount commissioned by the Israel Antiquities Authority and installed at the Davidson Center adjacent to the Temple Mount platform in the Jerusalem Archaeological Park. Snyder is currently working on a computer reconstruction of the World's Columbian Exposition held in Chicago in 1893.

Carl Stahmer, PhD, holds a Research Scientist Appointment at the University of California, Santa Barbara where he serves as the Associate Director of

English Broadside Ballad Archive (http://ebba.english.ucsb.edu). Stahmer has been working in the field of humanities computing since the mid-1990s, when he began constructing the Romantic Circles website (http://www.rc.umd.edu), named by the National Endowment for the Humanities as one of the top twenty educational websites in the world. In addition to creating and maintaining a host of academic websites, Stahmer has also worked as a computer programmer and system architect for a variety of governmental, academic, and commercial technology initiatives over the past twenty years. He has served as the Associate Director of the Maryland Institute for Technology and the Humanities at the University of Maryland, as a member of the Advisory Board of the Networked Infrastructure for Nineteenth-Century Studies (NINES), and as Director of Technology for Lynchinteractive Inc., where he was lead developer and system architect for a variety of internet-based, advanced data-integration solutions, including medical, distance learning, and government information systems. Stahmer's work has been funded by various organizations and institutions, including the National endowment for the Humanities, the Institute of Museum and Library Services, the University of California Humanities Research Institute, the Andrew W. Mellon Foundation, and the British Society for Eighteenth-Century Studies.

Peter Stokes is Senior Lecturer at the Department of Digital Humanities at King's College London, where he leads the Digital Resource and Database of Palaeography, Manuscripts and Diplomatic. After degrees in Classics and English Literature and in Computer Engineering, he completed a PhD at Cambridge on English Vernacular minuscule c. 990-c. 1035. He then worked on the LangScape project at King's College London before receiving a Leverhulme fellowship in Palaeography at Cambridge and then returning to King's. He teaches at the Department of Digital Humanities, the Institute of English Studies, London, and the University of Cambridge; he is Associate Editor of the Digital Medievalist journal; and he is principal coordinator of the Medieval Manuscript Studies in the Digital Age training programme.

Melissa Terras is the Reader in Electronic Communication in the Department of Information Studies, University College London, and the Co-Director of UCL Centre for Digital Humanities. With a background in Classical Art History and English Literature, and Computing Science, her doctorate (University of Oxford) examined how to use advanced information engineering technologies to interpret and read the Vindolanda texts. Publications include *Image to Interpretation: Intelligent Systems to Aid Historians in the Reading of the Vindolanda Texts* (2006, Oxford Studies in Ancient Documents. Oxford University Press) and *Digital Images for the Information Professional* (2008, Ashgate). She is a general editor of DHQ and Secretary of the Association of Literary and Linguistic Computing. Her research focuses on the use of computational techniques to enable research in the arts and humanities that would otherwise be impossible.

Jacob Thaisen is Associate Professor of Literacy Studies at the University of Stavanger, where he is involved in the Middle English Grammar Project, a long-term research effort aimed at producing a reference grammar of Middle English. For the autumn of 2011, he is a visitor in the Medieval Institute Library at the University of Notre Dame (financially supported by the Medieval Institute). He was formerly attached to the History of English section in the School of English at Adam Mickiewicz University, Poznań, and was a researcher with the Canterbury Tales Project in Leicester. With Hanna Rutkowska, Jacob is the editor of *Scribes, Printers, and the Accidentals of their Texts* (Peter Lang Verlag, 2011). He has primarily published on the textual tradition of Geoffrey Chaucer's *Canterbury Tales* and has been editing the "Man of Law's Tale" for electronic publication with Polish Ministry of Education funding. His teaching and research interests focus on written language, especially that of medieval English scribes.

Athanasios Velios is a Research Fellow at the Ligatus Research Unit, University of the Arts, London, where he also supervises several PhD research projects. His research focuses on the digital documentation of binding structures and materials and the classification of bindings. He has developed a methodology for conservation surveys in library collections as part of the book survey at the Library of St. Catherine's Monastery in Sinai, Egypt. He is contributing to the development of the Ligatus glossary of bookbinding terms and investigating its ontological use and visualisation. He is also working in parallel on open source development for Drupal and has proposed new creative archiving techniques online.

Paul Vetch is Research Fellow, Business Innovation Fellow, and Project Manager at the Department of Digital Humanities, King's College London. He is Co-Investigator, Project Manager, or Technical Research Director of a number of major projects with funding from the Andrew W. Mellon Foundation, AHRC, JISC, Leverhulme Trust, British Academy, and UK Heritage Lottery Fund. Paul's research interests lie in web interfaces and UI conventions, particularly within the Digital Humanities and cultural heritage, and his focus is on process, user engagement, and experimental design and development.

Angus Vine is a lecturer in early modern literature at the University of Sussex. He is the author of *In Defiance of Time: Antiquarian Writing in Early Modern England* (Oxford, 2010). He is also one of the editors on *The Oxford Francis Bacon* project; with Dr Richard Serjeantson he is editing *Volume III: Earlier Jacobean Writings, 1603-1613*. He has published a number of articles on early modern manuscript culture. Previously, he was the Senior Research Associate on the *Scriptorium: Medieval and Early Modern Manuscripts Online* project at the University of Cambridge.

Sebastiaan Verweij is the Hardie Postdoctoral Fellow in the Humanities at Lincoln College, Oxford. He is also the Research Associate for The Oxford Edition of the Sermons of John Donne. In collaboration with Peter McCullough he is writing the Textual Companion volume to the edition of Donne's sermons. Verweij has published several articles and book chapters on Older Scottish literature and book history, and is currently at work on his monograph, *Scottish Scribal Culture: Verse Miscellany Manuscripts, 1560-1630*. At Cambridge, he worked on Scriptorium: Medieval and Early Modern Manuscripts Online, a digital edition of twenty miscellany manuscripts and commonplace books.

Paul Werstine is Professor of English at King's University College at The University of Western Ontario. He is co-editor, with Barbara A. Mowat, of the Folger Library Shakespeare edition and co-general editor, with Richard Knowles, of the New Variorum Shakespeare edition. He continues to write extensively about printing, editing, and dramatic manuscripts.

Pip Willcox is a digital editor at the Digital Library of the Bodleian Library at Oxford University, working on encoding projects including the Early English Books Online Text Creation Partnership (EEBO-TCP) and the Shakespeare Quartos Archive (SQA).

Stuart Williams, formerly Assistant Professor of Computer Science at Canadian Mennonite University, is a computer scientist with interests in Computer Ethics and Humanities Computing. He currently works in the financial services industry.

Sebastian Zambanini, MSc., is a research and teaching assistant at the Computer Vision Lab, Institute of Computer Aided Automation, Vienna University of Technology, Austria. He finished his master study 'Computer Graphics & Digital Image Processing' in 2007 and has gained experience in several computer vision research projects. In the field of image-based coin recognition Zambanini participated in the European COINS project and is currently involved in a nationally-funded ILAC project. His research interest focuses on image segmentation, registration, and local image descriptors and he is currently pursuing a PhD in these areas at the Vienna University of Technology.